PHILOSOPHY
AND
PHENOMENOLOGICAL RESEARCH

A Quarterly Journal

Volume XLII

SEPTEMBER 1981 - JUNE 1982

Published for the

INTERNATIONAL PHENOMENOLOGICAL SOCIETY

by

BROWN UNIVERSITY

This journal is the official organ of the International Phenomenological Society. It publishes descriptive, analytical, critical, and historical articles representing the major contemporary trends in philosophy. In addition to the phenomenological research, PPR publishes studies in a wide range of areas including ethics, logic, history of philosophy, metaphysics, and theory of knowledge, as well as applied ethics and the philosophies of art, history, language, mind, religion, and science.

An abstract not exceeding 250 words and two nonreturnable copies of any manuscript submitted for publication are required. The original, ribbon copy will be required if the article is accepted, but it need not be submitted in the first instance. Double spacing should be used throughout, including quotations and footnotes. Footnotes should be numbered consecutively and collected at the end, beginning a new page.

The annual subscription rate for libraries and institutions is $15.00 (foreign $18.00 postpaid); subscriptions for individuals are $12.00 annually (foreign $13.00 postpaid). The rate for single copies of current or available back issues is $3.75 (double issue, $7.50) and $3.00 (double issue, $6.00), respectively. There is an additional charge for postage and handling on all back issues.

Address all communications and payments to *Philosophy and Phenomenological Research*, Box 1947, Brown University, Providence, Rhode Island 02912. The journal office should be notified of any change of address at least six weeks before the next issue is scheduled to appear. A list of the past contents with available back numbers will be sent upon request. For out-of-print volumes write to Kraus-Thompson Organization Ltd., Route 100, Millwood New York 10546. For microfiche copies write to Johnson Associates, P.O. Box 1017, Greenwich, Connecticut 06830; and for microfilm copies write to University Microfilms International, 300 North Zeeb Road, Ann Arbor, Michigan 48106.

Published quarterly by Brown University
Printed by Niagara Printing Corporation, Niagara Falls, New York

TABLE OF CONTENTS, VOLUME XLII (1981-1982)

I. OBITUARY

CHO, KAY KYUNG and ROSE, LYNN E., Marvin Farber 1

II. ARTICLES

ACKERMAN, ROBERT, Context Dependent Knowledge 425

ADAMS, E. M., Persons and Morality 384

AIKEN, HENRY DAVID, The Originality of Hume's Theory of Obligation 374

BIRCHALL, B. C., Frege's 'Objects' and 'Concepts': Revolutionary or Reactionary? 343

BIRCHALL, B. C., The Intentional Project 147

BIEN, JOSEPH, Politics of the Present: Machiavellian Humanism 197

BLOSE, B. L., Materialism and Disembodied Minds 59

BURBIDGE, JOHN, Man, God, and Death in Hegel's *Phenomenology* 183

BURTON, ROBERT G., Choice 581

COOK, DANIEL J., Marx's Critique of Philosophical Language . 530

D'AMICO, ROBERT, Husserl on the Foundational Structures of Natural and Cultural Sciences 5

DUERLINGER, JAMES, Unspoken Connections in the Design Argument 519

HARRIS, N. G. E., Causes and Events 236

HEIL, JOHN, Speechless Brutes 400

HILL, CHRISTOPHER S., Why Cartesian Intuitions Are Compatible with the Identity Thesis 254

HUTCHESON, PETER, Husserl and Private Languages 111

KEMP-PRITCHARD, ILONA, Peirce on Philosophical Hope and Logical Sentiment 75

KÖCHLER, HANS, The Phenomenology of Karol Wojtyła: On the Problem of the Phenomenological Foundation of Anthropology 326

KRELL, DAVID FARRELL, Phenomenology of Memory from Husserl to Merleau-Ponty 492

KUPPERMAN, JOEL J., Value Judgments 506

LACROIX, RICHARD R., Aquinas on God's Omnipresence and Timelessness 391

LAVINE, T. Z., Internalization, Socialization, and Dialectic . . 91

LEVIN, MICHAEL E., Phenomenal Properties 42

LINGIS, ALPHONSO, Sensations 160

MATHUR, DINESH C., Abhinavagupta and Dewey on Art and Its Relation to Morality: Comparisons and Evaluations . . . 224
MORREALL, JOHN, Hume's Missing Shade of Blue 407
NATANSON, MAURICE, Erwin Straus and Alfred Schutz 335
NATHANSON, STEPHEN L., Nonevidential Reasons for Belief: A Jamesian View 572
NIELSEN, KAI, Sociological Knowledge: Winch, Marxism, and *Verstehen* Revisited 465
PARK, YNHUI, The Function of Fiction 416
SOLES, DEBORAH H., Some Ways of Going Wrong: On Mistakes in *On Certainty* 555
STACK, GEORGE J., and PLANT, ROBERT W., The Phenomenon of "the Look" 359
TAYLOR, PAUL, Imagination and Information 205
TESCHNER, GEORGE, Judgment in Perception 119
TYE, MICHAEL, Causal Analysis of Seeing 311
VAN HORNE, WINSTON A., Prolegomenon to a Theory of Deception 171
ZAITCHIK, A., Intentionalism and Physical Reductionism in Computational Psychology 23

III. DISCUSSIONS

ALLEN, JEFFNER, What Is Husserl's First Philosophy? 610
DAUENHAUER, BERNARD P., Schürmann on Political Philosophy 130
DIGBY, TOM F., Kesarcodi-Watson on Atma-Vidya and "Ego" . 123
FODOR, JERRY A., Reply to Professor Zaitchik 292
KESARCODI-WATSON, IAN, Kesarcodi-Watson on Digby on Kesarcodi-Watson 125
KORDIG, CARL R., Evolutionary Epistemology Is Self-Referentially Inconsistent 449
LITTLE, DANIEL, Countervailing Tendencies and Falsifiability in *Capital* 283
MARTIN, R. M., A Memo on Method: Hilary Putnam 587
MORICK, HAROLD, Opacity and Mentality: A Reply to Criticism 128
OAKES, ROBERT, Seeing Our Own Faces: A Paradigm for Indirect Realism 442
PUTNAM, HILARY, Semantical Rules and Misinterpretations: Reply to R. M. Martin 604
SIMON, MICHAEL A., The Primacy of Action 266
STANDLEY, GERALD, The Limitations of Sense Experience 434

Zaitchik, A., Reply to Professor Fodor 294

IV. REVIEWS

Armstrong's *The Nature of Mind and Other Essays* (Conee) . 622
Caputo's *The Mystical Element in Heidegger's Thought* (Bartky) 140
Gustafson and Tapscott's *Body, Mind, and Method, Essays in Honor of Virgil C. Aldrich* (Mahowald) 300
Kalsi's *Alexius Meinong: On Objects of Higher Order and Husserl's Phenomenology* (Smith) 451
Keke's *The Nature of Philosophy* (Hacker) 139
Kneževic's *History, the Anatomy of Time: The Final Phase of Sunlight* (Birx) 137
Machlup's *Methodology of Economics and Other Social Sciences* (Bien) 135
Marti's *The Unconditional in Human Knowledge. Four Early Essays (1794-1796) by F. W. J. Schelling* (Schwarz) 297
Martin's *Semiotics and Linguistic Structure* (Fitch) 453
Mijuskovic's *Loneliness in Philosophy, Psychology and Literature* (Steinkraus) 298
Plantinga's *Does God Have a Nature?* (Mann) 625
Podgórecki and Łoś's *Multi-Dimensional Sociology* (Peterson) 301
Reipe's *Indian Philosophy Since Independence* (Ruben and Rustau) 303
Rickman's *Wilhelm Dilthey: Pioneer of the Human Studies* (Paczkowska-Łagowska) 454
Ricoeur's *Main Trends in Philosophy* (Hunter) 621
Rorty's *Philosophy and the Mirror of Nature* (Ruja) 299
Slaate's *Time and Its End: A Comparative Existential Interpretation of Time and Eschatology* (Munk) 296
Wallack's *The Epochal Nature of Process in Whitehead's Metaphysics* (Ford) 133

This journal is the official organ of the International Phenomenological Society. It publishes descriptive, analytical, critical, and historical articles representing the major contemporary trends in philosophy. In addition to the phenomenological research, PPR publishes studies in a wide range of areas including ethics, logic, history of philosophy, metaphysics, and theory of knowledge, as well as applied ethics and the philosophies of art, history, language, mind, religion, and science.

An abstract not exceeding 250 words and two nonreturnable copies of any manuscript submitted for publication are required. The original, ribbon copy will be required if the article is accepted, but it need not be submitted in the first instance. Double spacing should be used throughout, including quotations and footnotes. Footnotes should be numbered consecutively and collected at the end, beginning a new page.

The annual subscription rate for libraries and institutions is $15.00 (foreign $18.00 postpaid); subscriptions for individuals are $12.00 annually (foreign $13.00 postpaid). The rate for single copies of current or available back issues is $3.75 (double issue, $7.50) and $3.00 (double issue, $6.00), respectively. There is an additional charge for postage and handling on all back issues.

Address all communications and payments to *Philosophy and Phenomenological Research*, Box 1947, Brown University, Providence, Rhode Island 02912. The journal office should be notified of any change of address at least six weeks before the next issue is scheduled to appear. A list of the past contents with available back numbers will be sent upon request. For out-of-print volumes write to Kraus-Thompson Organization Ltd., Route 100, Millwood New York 10546. For microfiche copies write to Johnson Associates, P.O. Box 1017, Greenwich, Connecticut 06830; and for microfilm copies write to University Microfilms International, 300 North Zeeb Road, Ann Arbor, Michigan 48106.

Published quarterly by Brown University
Printed by Niagara Printing Corporation, Niagara Falls, New York

VOL. XLII SEPTEMBER 1981 NO. 1

PHILOSOPHY
AND
PHENOMENOLOGICAL
RESEARCH

A Quarterly Journal

Published for the

INTERNATIONAL PHENOMENOLOGICAL SOCIETY

by

BROWN UNIVERSITY

This journal is the official organ of the International Phenomenological Society. The editors are not necessarily in agreement with the views expressed by the various writers. Papers submitted for publication will not be returned unless accompanied by a self-addressed, stamped envelope, or return postage. The annual subscription rate for libraries and institutions is $15.00 (foreign $18.00 postpaid); subscriptions for individuals are $12.00 annually (foreign $13.00 postpaid). The rate for single copies of current or available back issues is $3.75 (double issue, $7.50) and $3.00 (double issue, $6.00) respectively. There is an additional charge for postage and handling on all back issues. Address all communications and payments to *Philosophy and Phenomenological Research*, Box 1947, Brown University, Providence, Rhode Island 02912. The journal office should be notified of any change of address at least six weeks before the next issue is scheduled to appear. A list of the past contents with available back numbers will be sent upon request. For out of print volumes write to Kraus-Thomson Organization Ltd., Route 100, Millwood, New York 10546. For microfiche copies write to Johnson Associates, P.O. Box 1017, Greenwich, Connecticut 06830; and for microfilm copies University Microfilms International, 300 North Zeeb Road, Ann Arbor, Michigan 48106.

Published quarterly by Brown University
Printed by Niagara Printing Corporation, Niagara Falls, New York

CONTENTS

I. OBITUARY
Marvin Farber, by KAH KYUNG CHO and LYNN E. ROSE.... 1

II. ARTICLES
Husserl on the Foundational Structures of Natural and Cultural Sciences, by ROBERT D'AMICO.... 5
Intentionalism and Physical Reductionism in Computational Psychology, by A. ZAITCHIK.... 23
Phenomenal Properties, by MICHAEL E. LEVIN.... 42
Materialism and Disembodied Minds, by B. L. BLOSE.... 59
Peirce on Philosophical Hope and Logical Sentiment, by ILONA KEMP-PRITCHARD.... 75
Internalization, Socialization, and Dialectic, by T. Z. LAVINE.... 91
Husserl and Private Languages, by PETER HUTCHESON.... 111
The Undifferentiated Conjunction of Sensation and Judgment in Perception, by GEORGE TESCHNER.... 119

III. DISCUSSIONS
Kesarcodi-Watson on Atma-Vidya and "Ego," by TOM F. DIGBY.... 123
Kesarcodi-Watson on Digby on Kesarcodi-Watson, by IAN KESARCODI-WATSON.... 125
Opacity and Mentality: A Reply to Criticism, by HAROLD MORICK.... 128
Schürmann on Political Philosophy, by BERNARD P. DAUENHAUER.... 130

IV. REVIEWS
F. Bradford Wallack's *The Epochal Nature of Process in Whitehead's Metaphysics,* by LEWIS S. FORD.... 133
Fritz Machlup's *Methodology of Economics and Other Social Sciences,* by JOSEPH BIEN.... 135
Božidar Kneževic's *History, the Anatomy of Time: The Final Phase of Sunlight,* by H. JAMES BIRX.... 137
John Kekes's *The Nature of Philosophy,* by EDWARD A. HACKER.... 139
John D. Caputo's *The Mystical Element in Heidegger's Thought,* by SANDRA LEE BARTKY.... 140

V. RECENT PUBLICATIONS.... 143

MARVIN FARBER (1901-1980)

Marvin Farber, known throughout the world as the Editor of the journal, *Philosophy and Phenomenological Research,* died in Minneapolis on November 24, 1980, at the age of 78. His death came as a shock to his many friends and colleagues who had known the extraordinary mental alertness and physical durability of the soon-to-be octogenarian. What the world did not know, if fact, was that Farber was critically ill for many months during the year, though he maintained firm control of the journal from his place of retirement.

The oldest of the fourteen children of Simon and Matilda (Goldstein) Farber, Marvin Farber was born in Buffalo, New York, on December 14, 1901. The Farber family as such was already unusual, with seven of those fourteen earning either M.D. or Ph.D. or law degrees, and others distinguishing themselves in business, in teaching, and in the arts. Marvin Farber took academic training and positions in great strides. He graduated *summa cum laude* from Harvard in 1922, and received his Ph.D. from Harvard three years later, at the age of 24. While in graduate school, he studied for two years in Berlin and Freiburg, and after a one-year stint as Instructor in Philosophy at The Ohio State University, he returned to Germany for another year in Heidelberg. His early acquaintance with Edmund Husserl in Freiburg was to have a profound influence on Farber's subsequent career. He is to be credited with having introduced phenomenology to the United States, and decisively shaped its initial reception in this country.

Farber was appointed Assistant Professor of Philosophy at the University of Buffalo in 1928, and was promoted directly to Professor two years later. In 1954 he was named Distinguished Professor of Philosophy. He served as Chairman of the Department of Philosophy from 1937 to 1961. From 1961 to 1964 he was Chairman of the Department of Philosophy at the University of Pennsylvania. In 1964 he returned to the University of Buffalo (which had become the State University of New York at Buffalo in 1962), as Distinguished Professor of Philosophy. He retired from active teaching in 1974.

Dr. Farber's many honors include his having been awarded the degree of Docteur de l'Université de Lille in 1955, and his having been chosen President of the American Philosophical Association, Eastern Divison, in 1963. He was active in numerous philosophical and professional societies, including the Creighton Philosophical

Club, the Charles Sanders Peirce Society, the Symbolic Logic Association, and the Institute Internationale de Philosophie, Paris. He served as President of the International Phenomenological Society since its founding in 1940. The principal project of the Society has been the publication of *Philosophy and Phenomenological Research,* which Farber edited for the first forty years of its existence.

In his capacity as Editor of the Charles C. Thomas series of American Lectures in Philosophy (since 1951) and of the Warren H. Green series of Modern Concepts of Philosophy (since 1968), Farber was personally responsible for the publication of nearly fifty volumes. He also served as Co-Editor of the *Phenomenologica* series since 1958.

In addition to his own nearly one hundred articles, reviews, and contributions to anthologies, Farber was the author of six highly influential books: besides his earliest work on phenomenology, *Phenomenology as a Method and as a Philosophical Discipline* (1928), and his major contribution to the interpretation of the logical basis of Husserl's philosophy, *The Foundation of Phenomenology* (1943), he also published *Naturalism and Subjectivism* (1959), *The Aims of Phenomenology* (1966), *Phenomenology and Existence* (1967), and *Basic Issues of Philosophy* (1967). Several of these books have already gone through multiple editions. *The Foundation of Phenomenology* has been translated into Spanish, and both *The Aims of Phenomenology* and *Basic Issues of Philosophy* have been translated into Italian. Farber edited and co-authored *Philosophical Essays in Memory of Edmund Husserl* (1940), and *Philosophical Thought in France and the United States* (1950), which was published simultaneously as *L'Activité Philosophique Contemporaine en France et aux Etats-Unis.* His other co-edited or co-authored volumes, *Philosophy for the Future* (1949), *Philosophical Perspectives on Punishment* (1968), and *The Idea of God: Philosophical Perspectives* (1969), indicate the extremely wide range of his interests and concerns.

Farber's philosophy, although issuing forth from Husserlian phenomenology, was chastened with more than a handful of antiseptic to be in line with his own scientific conception of human and social reality. He maintained, to be sure, a deferential attitude toward his former teacher and the values that Husserl's radically reflective thinking stood for, but he himself applied a different standard of rigor, leavened by a more robust sense of reason within nature, to phenomenology, and subsequently moved beyond it. As a brilliant educator on the academic podium, and as a masterly moderator of the open forum that he provided, through his journal, to the international community of philosophical aspirants, Farber realized early enough the barren prospect of carrying on fideistically, as so many others did, the reclusive subjectivism of transcendental phenomenology. Throughout his teaching career, Farber struggled both against those who would make phenomenology the sole key to unlock the treasures of cosmic insights and against those who would graft onto phenomenology other branches of fashionable philosophies. He remained firmly committed to a scientific, socially engaged philosophy. But it is also true that his public image revealed another side of his scholarly personality, namely, that of an extremely open-minded and understanding intellectual leader, with an enviable blend of dignity and warmth, rigor and sense of discretion.

But above all, Marvin Farber had a tremendous capacity for work, and he thouroughly enjoyed it. In addition to all of his administrative and editorial responsibilities, and his own research and writing projects, through all the years at Buffalo he maintained a heavy teaching schedule, and encouraged others to do likewise. Several generations of his students remember Professor Farber as an eminent teacher who opened new vistas for them and encouraged them to explore and to inquire for themselves. He built the Department of Philosophy from a two-man department offering elective courses for a few upperclassmen to a large and diversified department with a substantial freshman and sophomore enrollment as well, with a complete program for undergraduate majors, and eventually with a full graduate program leading to the doctorate.

Farber himself directed numerous doctoral dissertations over the years. He always gave generously of his time, and provided a model of erudition. Behind his erect posture, which was that of a dignitary in the old Continental tradition, there was an air of personal warmth often verging on a fatherly affection. He frequently would say that one of his great satisfactions was the opportunity that his professorial and editorial positions gave him to help deserving younger scholars develop and establish themselves, especially in cases where their articles and books might not easily see print except through his efforts. He not only reaped from the rich soil that he tilled, but he had also generously sown for others to reap.

Marvin Farber is survived by his wife, the former Lorraine F. Walle, whom he married in 1930. There are three children, Lawrence, Roger, and Carol (Reddy), all of whom are medical doctors. He is also survived by eleven grandchildren.

As a towering intellectual leader of our time, Marvin Farber is already greatly missed.

KAH KYUNG CHO.
LYNN E. ROSE.

STATE UNIVERSITY OF NEW YORK
AT BUFFALO.

HUSSERL ON THE FOUNDATIONAL STRUCTURES OF NATURAL AND CULTURAL SCIENCES

Husserl's reflections on culture and history in the *Crisis* volume are part of his philosophic program since he concerns himself with these fields only as possible sciences. Thus the human sciences *(Geisteswissenschaften)* have the possibility of thematizing a certain attitude *(Einstellung),* namely the human attitude, and in that thematization can exhibit the essential process of constitution. It is this process of constitution that allows the natural sciences to be directed at realities existing in themselves. The late writings of Husserl on the human sciences however are related to the inability of the natural sciences to grasp their own foundational structure. Consequently, Husserl suggests that the human sciences can escape the objectivistic fate of the natural sciences.[1]

The crisis in the natural sciences, for Husserl, occurs when Nature comes to be identified with its constituted mathematical, quantifiable object. The foundational acts whereby the object is abstracted from prescientific experience are forgotten. Husserl calls this the objectivistic misconception of the natural sciences and suggests that it is encouraged by the very technical success of science. The broad technical use and operational character of modern science is due precisely to the ability to separate inquiry from these constitutive acts. Therefore, a continual return to self-evidence, for example, is not required for each step in scientific methodology. This shortcut, which allows the sciences technical mastery, also constitutes the objective domain as given, passively there. Two consequences follow for Husserl. First, the giveness of its object leads the sciences to

[1]In the subsequent discussion references will be to E. Husserl. *The Crisis of European Sciences and Transcendental Phenomenology,* trans. David Carr (Evanston: Northwestern University Press, 1970) which will be cited as *Crisis.* This includes both the *Vienna Lecture* and*The Origin of Geometry.* However some of the *Beilagen* of the German edition are not included in the English translation. In those cases reference will be to E. Husserl, *Die Krisis der europäischen Wissenschaften und die transzendentale Phänomenologie: Eine Einleitung in die phänomenologische Philosophie,* ed. Walter Biemel (1954:2d printing, The Hague: Nijhoff, 1962) which will be cited as *Krisis.*

identify nature (in its pretheoretical, preconceptual domain) with the mathematical, quantifiable ideality (the formation of a conceptual structure) and remove subjectivity (specifically the constitutive subject) from the domain of knowledge. Such would account for the success of technique in itself. In the establishment of efficient and mechanical operations for achieving direct results there is no need to keep in mind the original meaning formation or acts constituting the objective domain. But for Husserl constitution and objectivity are inseparable:

> Actually the process whereby material mathematics is put into formal-logical form . . . is perfetly *legitimate,* indeed necessary . . . But all this can and must be a method which is understood and practiced in a fully conscious way. It can be this, however, only if care is taken to avoid dangerous shifts of meaning by keeping always immediately in mind the original bestowal of meaning *(Sinnebung)* upon the method, through which it has the sense of achieving knowledge about the *world.*[2]

Second, having established itself in the natural sciences, objectivism is taken up in the human sciences where a "naturalistic" psychology or sociology tries to transform its data into objectivities conforming to the scientific attitude. It is at this point that Husserl approaches the particular problems of the human sciences.

The crisis in the natural sciences is due to its blindness to the basis for technical success. The natural sciences, according to Husserl, refuse to thematize the constitutive subjectivity underlying their original meaning formation. The act whereby original human intentions (control over natural processes, for example) form the object of science out of pretheoretical experience is continually forgotten. But the realization of a science's project is not impeded by this repression. In fact, as Husserl argues, it facilitates realization of its ends since nature appears to be immediately given as an object for control rather than constituted as such. Objectivism accounts for the remarkable consensus around evidence, truth, and consistency that characterize the modern cumulative and operational sciences.

Husserl is obviously struck by the fact that this unique success is not also found in the human sciences. It is not due, Husserl argues, to a lack of empirical research or even the need for a new method. Rather, the human sciences suffer from a systematic deception revealed precisely in their naturalistic attitude. Husserl asks, "What does in-itself mean in the case of nature of an animal, of a human being, of a human community, or cultural objects and the universal

---

[2] *Crisis,* p. 47.

culture of a human civilization?"[3] We are confronted not with a separate problem for the human sciences but the same problem that was concealed by the technical success of the natural sciences. How is rigorous knowledge constituted and what are the essential characteristics of the acts which constitute a domain of objectivity and evidence? Husserl's analysis of objectivism within the natural sciences concerned the distance between operationalism and the original meaning or intention behind a science's ideal objects. Objectivism treats the ideal object of the science as always, already there but not there because of human intentions:

> . . . a purpose which necessarily lay *in* the prescientific life and was related to its life-world. Man (including the natural scientist), living in the world, could put all his practical and theoretical questions only to *it* — could refer his theories only to it, in its open, endless horizon of things unknown.[4]

Therefore the human scientist, concerned as he is with explaining purpose, motive, intention (what Husserl calls the human attitude), does not require a special or separate "method" due to the unique characteristics of his object. The neo-Kantian distinction between *Erklären* and *Verstehen,* or explanation and comprehension, is totally rejected by Husserl. Dilthey is obviously the object of Husserl's criticism. There is no need for a unique understanding according to Husserl since in the human sciences, from the viewpoint of foundation, all sciences have the same essential structure. An original, meaning-giving act constitutes an objectivity or ideal object from a *Lebenswelt.* Dilthey was led to the division between the natural and human or cultural sciences because he took the objectivism of the natural sciences at face value and without question. Faced with attempts at replicating this naturalistic attitude in the human sciences, as in the case of positivism, Dilthey sought a separate and distinct scheme of theory formation.

Though Husserl had no need of what was called *Verstehentheorie,* he does recognize a significant difference for the human-cultural sciences. Since science and even theory itself are part of culture the human sciences are forced to become self-reflection. As sciences they must also take science itself as their object. In this thematization there is a kind of built-in defense against objectivism. Therefore the human sciences play a major role in Husserl's project of a rigorous philosophy, namely phenomenology.

---

[3] *Ibid.,* pp. 316-17.

[4] *Ibid.,* p. 50.

> Natural science is a culture (and) it belongs only within the culture world of that human civilization which has developed this culture and within which, for the individual, possible ways of understanding this culture are present.[5]

There is a convergence for Husserl, brought out most explicitly in these late writings, between the investigations of original meaning carried out by a systematic phenomenology and the historicity of human culture. Husserl will describe this as the teleology of the theoretical attitude discovered by tracing the given, historical meaning structures to their original self-evidence. It should be emphasized that Husserl is not concerned with factual history or the question of origin as a problem of dating. For Husserl what allows the constitution of factual data and establishing a field for investigation is the thematization of the ideal object for any person or environing world. It is the problem of origin that all sciences share. In constituting ideal objects, so that there is always an identical repetition of concepts and operations, sciences achieve a theoretical attitude which modifies the pregiven world of experience and becomes a tradition, capable of transmitting its knowledge to those beyond its present immediate experience. What Husserl proposes is that we study the origin of the ideal objects characterizing science. By "ideal" he means, in this context at least, not only constitutive but repeatable, reiterable, replicable knowledge that can form a tradition of inquiry. Thus an origin is not a localization of time and place per se but rather the genetic tracing back of an intention which is, of course, still possible for present experience as long as the inquiry is continued and the object is taken as an ideality.

> Let us illuminate first of all the remarkable, peculiar character of philosophy, unfolding in ever new special sciences. Let us contrast it with other cultural forms already present in pre-scientific mankind: artifacts, agriculture, domestic arts, etc. All these signify classes of cultural products with their own methods for *assuring successful production. Otherwise they have a passing existence in the surrounding world.* Scientific acquisitions, on the other hand, after their method of assured successful production has been attained, *have quite another manner of being, quite another temporality.* They are not used up; *they are imperishable; repeated* production creates not something similar, at best equally useful; it produces in any number of acts of production by one person or any number of persons *something identically the same,* identical in sense and validity . . . In a word, what is acquired through scientific activity is not something real but something ideal.[6]

---

[5]*Ibid.*, p. 332.

[6]*Ibid.*, p. 277-78, emphasis added.

The Origin and the Pretheoretical

The Origin of Geometry is Husserl's most developed interpretation of the relation between science and history and returns to the problem of historicism that he had discussed earlier with respect to Dilthey.[7] The title of the work describes it as an "intentional-historical" study to be distinguished from a "philological-historical" approach. Husserl concerns himself not with the location in terms of date or person of the original geometers, but with the "originary insight" or "original sense" which makes it possible to thematize the ideal objects of geometry and the self-evidence underlying all its procedures.

> . . . our interest shall be the inquiry back into the most original sense in which geometry once arose, was present as the tradition of millennia, is still present with us, and is still being worked on in a lively forward development; we inquire into that sense in which it appeared in history for the first time — in which it had to appear, even though we know nothing of the first creators and are not even asking for them.[8]

Geometry is essentially a tradition, that is its character as a cultural object. Also it is able to become a tradition and be handed down for the same reasons that it is a science. Its idealities, in the form of concepts or functions, can be repeated without variation and these ideal objects *(ideale Gegenständlichkeit)* are not, as individualized events or personal psychic experience, restricted to temporal-spatial conditions. Thus Husserl connects the possibility to reproduce the same essential self-evidence (the existence of a tradition) and a science's ideal objectivity.

> Indeed, it has, from its primal establishment, an existence which is peculiarly supertemporal and which — of this we are certain — is accessible to all men, first of all to the actual and possible mathematicians of all peoples, all ages; and this is true of all its particular forms. And all forms newly produced by someone on the basis of pregiven forms immediately take on the same objectivity.[9]

As Husserl notes, however, the condition of ideal objectivity is not restricted to scientific or mathematical constructions but holds, in fact, for all cultural products (music, for example) which though repeated in specific individuated sensible utterances are still identical and unchanged from being grasped in the original. That is, what

---

[7]E. Husserl, "Philosophy as Rigorous Science," in *Phenomenology and the Crisis of Philosophy,* trans. Quentin Lauer (New York: Harper and Row, 1965).

[8]*Op. cit.,* p. 355.

[9]*Ibid.,* p. 356.

characterizes such objectivity in a cultural product is not production at some specific time and place but the possibility for it to be *reproduced* in its original meaning generation after generation.

Let us emphasize some points in this attempt to treat science as a form of cultural tradition. Husserl holds that from the viewpoint of essential structure the natural and human sciences are identical (though this is obscured by objectivism). However the human sciences, by virtue of including the theoretical attitude as an object of study, are immanently self-reflective (and even in a fashion converge with the project of phenomenology itself). Once we inquire into a science or a theoretical attitude as a cultural object (geometry in this case) we see that what characterizes it as a tradition (a culture) is also its condition for ideality, namely reproduction, repeatability and replication for future generations. But if we consider this from the vantage point of any cultural object we must immediately ask if geometry is not a special case. In the cultural traditions of literature, music or religion — the objects of the cultural sciences — there is always the problem of whether a repetition is in fact "authentic" and not in some sense a distortion or loss of the original meaning. The study of the cultural sciences always involves the question of whether tion. In this sense geometry is a "limit case" with regard to the confidence that something is grapsed in its original sense. It is a limit of an object's identity throughout repetition. In Husserl's approach this relation between ideality and the corruption of cultural transmission is central.

Husserl's central point in *The Origin of Geometry* concerns the connection between tradition and ideality. Husserl argues that the basis of continuity through repetition is language. Language is the objective intersubjectivity that allows both the formation of idealities and their reaccomplishments in a tradition. In this context Husserl makes the distinction between the "sensible utterance" or means of expression (signifier) and the meaning of what is asserted or said (signified). The ideal object is at the level of the signified as a thematic assertion or meaning. The signifier would be the historically contingent vehicle for the signified (for example, a certain written or spoken language or set of signs and symbols). The signifier can be replaced with no loss of ideality or meaning since that aspect of the sign is fundamentally *arbitrary*. Ideality means, on the contrary, that the object suffers no loss of original self-evidence. The necessity within geometry would appear to be the limit case of such flawless replication. Science consequently merges with cultural production in general because both are dependent on the ability of any signified ideal meaning (found in concepts and operations) to be continually transmitted and worked over, while remaining invariant throughout these repetitions. Thus Husserl concludes that the spiritual products of the cultural world *(geistegen Erzeugnissen der Kulturwelt),* including science, can be encompassed by the concept of "literature" or transmission of the written sign.

> That is, it belongs to their objective being that they be linguistically expressed and can be expressed again and again; or more precisely, they only have meaning and significance from the speech of objectivity *(Reden die Objektivität),* as they have existence-for-everyone. This is true in a peculiar fashion in the case of the objective sciences; for them the difference between the original language of the work and its translation into other languages does not remove its identical accessibility *or change it into an inauthentic, indirect accessibility.*[10]

The use of "inauthentic" in the above quote suggests the problem raised about the distortion or loss that haunts the replication or transmission of cultural forms. It had seemed originally that some cultural products were more "burdened"' with the materiality of the sign[11] and therefore ran a greater risk of distortion and loss of meaning through replication than geometry did. However Husserl will go on to show that even the purity of geometry is also prey to the effects of repetition and reiteration. Since the written sign cannot convey the original experience of self-evidence that is the foundation of geometry, geometry soon becomes reified into the manipulation of symbols. If even the most ideal object fails to replicate authentically we are lead to wonder if Husserl has failed to see an inseparability between the concept of tradition and the inauthenticity of replication and repetition.

Husserl's account of geometry is meant as an example of how the "crisis" in science demands an intentional-historical analysis that can uncover the original meaning and idealization which is lost and concealed in the conversion of science into technique. The problem of the sign, what Husserl calls its "sedimentation," turns out to be inseparable from the concept of a crisis.[12]

---

[10]*Ibid.*, p. 357, translation modified.

[11]"From the start the 'spirit' is afflicated with the curse of being 'burdened' with matter, which here makes its appearance in the form of agitated layers of air, sounds, in short, of language." Marx and Engels, *The German Ideology* (Moscow, 1968), p. 42.

[12]A much more detailed and intricate account of these philosophical issues in Husserl can be found in the work of Jacques Derrida. See J. Derrida, *Speech and Phenomena.* Trans. David B. Allison (Evanston, 1973) and Derrida's introduction to his French translation of *The Origin of Geometry* in E. Husserl, *L'origine de la géométrie.* (Paris, 1962).

By using the example of geometry Husserl attempts to specify how the written sign established a separation between the operational aspects of a science and its original self-evidence. In its authentic accessibility the meaning of the various operations, transmitted symbolically in a science, has to be made explicitly self-evident by reexperiencing or reactivating the primal establishment *(Urstiftung)* of the science. *The Origin of Geometry* shows how the process of reactivation (as well as "forgetting") is bound up with language and speech.

> Clearly it is only through language and its far-reaching documentation, as possible communications, that the horizon of civilization can be an open and endless one, as it always is for men . . . The objective world is from the start the world for all, the world which 'everyone' has as a world-horizon. Its objective being presupposes men, understood as men with a common language. Language, for its part, as function and exercised capacity, is related correlatively to the world, the universe of objects which is linguistically expressible in its being and its being-such.[13]

Husserl argues that the primal establishment, the original self-evidence, can only achieve ideality and objectivity by being able to be communicated and therefore retained and repeated. In fact, repetition, ideality, and representation (through the sign) form a single whole, for Husserl, as the theoretical attitude. In reawakening or reexpressing the act of meaning-formation we realize that it is identical and that the self-evidence thereby remains unchanged.

But until that reexperience can become an inter-subjective act shared by a community, it remains merely a personal recollection. For geometry to pass beyond the individual act and become a cultural object it requires a linguistic community and a written sign. In a communicative act the object is recognized by another not merely as similar but identical in each reproduction.[14] In such "speaking" of objectivity, in thematizing the signfied as distinct from personal im-

---

[13] *Ibid.*, p. 358.

[14] In *Beilagen XXVII* Husserl writes, "Everyone and every group always lives in certain individual and particular situations—and for everyone there is a situated truth and falsity, that of prescientific everydayness *(Alltäglichkeit)*. Scientific knowledge surveys *(Übersicht)* all situations . . . Its aim is the knowledge of *objective truth* which permeates the relativity of all possible situations, a truth which can be construed by anyone in his own situation . . . Each scientist is as such necessarily conscious of himself researching in an open community of coscientists *(Mitwissenschaftlern)*, and of taking over, situating in himself, their own doings and horizon of activity." *Krisis*, pp. 506-7.

mediacy, it takes on the status of an objectivity for everyone. Its original meaning is grasped by a community. However for there to be a *cultural or historical* tradition the product must also persist beyond these immediate acts of communication, since actual speech is restricted to a single contemporaneous community.

> What is lacking is the *persisting existence* of the 'ideal objects' even during periods in which the inventor and his fellows are no longer wakefully so related or even no longer alive. What is lacking is their continuing-to-be even when no one has (consciously) realized them in self-evidence.
>
> The important function of *written*, documenting linguistic *expression* is that it makes communication possible without immediate or mediate personal address; it is, so to speak, communication made virtual. Through this, the communalization of men is lifted to a new level.[15]

Husserl has argued as follows. The sign is the unity of signifier and signified (the sign vehicle or sensible utterance and the ideality or meaning). In the case of speech communication there is a *transparency* of signifier and signified such that the original self-evidence is immediately reexperienced and thus experienced as repetition without variance for everyone. However this transparency is limited to personal contact and spoken communication. To extend the object as a tradition requires placing a written sign (here standing for *both* the meaning-signified and the reexperiencing of that meaning as self-evident) in substitution for the immediate speech act. The problem is that the written sign is only a *passive* reexperience because the sign can be utilized without a return to its original self-evidence and the sign allows objectivity to appear as given passively in phenomena rather than produced through a constitutive act. By standing between the conceptual structure of a science and its original sense the written sign both advances the sciences toward technical and instrumental success (allowing for complex chains of reasoning without continually returning to original self-evidence) and blinds the science to how the theoretical attitude is formed out of the many human interests found in a pretheoretical world of experience.

> Accordingly, then, the writing-down effects a transformation of the original mode of being of the meaning-structure (e.g.), within the geometrical structure which is put into words. It *becomes sedimented,* so to speak. But the reader can make it self-evident again, can reactivate the self-evidence.[16]

---

[15] *Crisis,* pp. 360-61.

[16] *Ibid.*

Reactivation always means for Husserl a return to the transparency of signifier and signified, a return to the "speech" of objectivity. As has been shown the reproduction of original self-evidence proceeds at first from personal recollection, then to the empathy of communication and objectivity, and finally to the written sign as tradition or history. In each of these cases there is a difference between the passive acceptance of validity and *explication (Verdeutlichung).* It is precisely explication which becomes so difficult in the sedimentation of the written sign and leads science to forget the "source of its meaning." Thus Husserl says, "without the 'what' and the 'how' of its prescientific materials, geometry would be a tradition empty of meaning . . . we could never even know whether geometry had or ever had a genuine meaning . . . Unfortunately, however, this is our situation, and that of the whole modern age." Any cultural structure appears as a tradition claiming an original meaning, which is frequently lost to a present consciousness, and thus the specific crisis in the science with regard to the meaning and purpose of their rationality converges with the question of whether there can be truth within history, within the variation and contingency of a tradition.

> By exhibiting the essential presuppositions upon which rests the historical possibility of a genuine tradition, true to its origins, of sciences like geometry, we can understand how such sciences can vitally develop throughout the centuries and still not be genuine . . . idealities can continue without interruption from one period to the next, while the capacity for reactivating the primal beginnings, i.e., the *sources of meaning* for everything that comes later, has not been handed down with it. What is lacking is precisely what had given and continues to give meaning to all propositions and theories, a meaning arising from the primal sources which can be made self-evident again and again.[17]

The point here is most important. Husserl is again confronting the problem of a tradition which entails in an essential fashion the irreducible loss or distortion of the meaning replicated and passed on. We have already seen that geometry, the apparent limit case of ideality, does not therefore escape this corruption of "inauthenticity" which leads it into objectivism. But now Husserl offers an explanation. The replacement of the written sign for speech, which allows the sign to *persist,* does so only at the cost of introducing an *opacity* with regard to original experience. Such opacity stands in contrast with the immediacy and transparency of the spoken word as the carrier of meaning. The reactivation and replication of meaning is inseparable

[17] *Ibid.*, p. 367.

from the threat of loss and crisis except now this loss is displaced, not onto the distinction between real and ideal (or contingent and necessary) as it was at first, but onto the more fundamental opposition of speech and writing.[18]

The possibility of tradition, of a cultural world, which Husserl reveals as inseparable from the ideality and objectivity characterizing the theoretical attitude in general, is, at the same time, what makes it possible for the original meaning to be forgotten. By establishing the continuity of ready-made, passively accepted methods and practices, these can be handed down "without the ability for original self-evidence." Thus the kind of regressive inquiry Husserl is carrying on with regard to geometry has to be reawakened and the basis of such an inquiry (the possibility of an historical a priori, of a self-evidence extending beyond historical facticity) has to be established. So Husserl makes the claim that:

> Our results based on principle are of a generality that extends overall the so-called deductive sciences and even indicates similar problems and investigations for all sciences. For all of them have the mobility of sedimented traditions that are worked upon, again and again, by an activity of producing new structures of meaning and handing them down. Existing in this way, they extend enduringly through time, since all new acquisitions are in turn sedimented and become working materials. Everywhere the problems, the clarifying investigations, the insights of principle are *historical*. We stand within the horizon of human civilization, the one in which we ourselves now live.[19]

Before briefly discussing what Husserl means by an historical a priori two points made at the conclusion of *Origin* need to be stressed. First, Husserl argues for the continuity between epistemological and genetic inquiry. As has already been shown, Husserl merges the problem of cultural tradition and the truth-meaning of scientific propositions. He argues that tradition does not merely mean a succession of factual situations known by inductive generality, rather it is itelf possible because what is handed down and continuous in the sign or document is an ideal objectivity excluding the contingent and the variable. On the other hand, the explication of a self-evidence is not a passive acceptance but a reflective and genetic inquiry proceeding back through sedimented meaning-formations.

> For a genuine history of philosophy, a genuine history of the particular science, is nothing other than the tracing of the historical meaning-

---

[18]See J. Derrida, *Of Grammatology,* trans. Gayatri Chakravorty Spivak (Baltimore, 1974), for the important role of the division between speech and writing in the history of philosophy. Especially pp. 97-98.

[19]*Ibid.*, pp. 368-69.

> structures given in the present, or their self-evidences, along the documented chain of historical back-references into the hidden dimension of the primal self-evidence which underlies them . . . The problem of genuine historical explanations comes together, in the case of the sciences, with 'epistemological' grounding or clarification.[20]

Second, Husserl argues that "historicism" is a countersensical position, in much the same way that "psychologism" in logic produces a countersensical position. Repeating arguments that Husserl developed in his early essay on Dilthey, he indicates that determining historical conditions for knowledge cannot also entail the relativity of the knowledge produced to those conditions. The ability to determine and establish facts and the background of certainty therein, constitute history as a possible object of knowledge, i.e., replicable and not time-bound. "Accordingly, we need not first enter into some kind of critical discussion of the facts set out by the historian; it is enough that even the claim of the factualness presupposes the historical a priori if this claim is to have a meaning." But Husserl adds a further and more subtle argument when he indicates that only if there is an essential-meaning structure to history would it be possible for there to be a tradition (the extension of meaning beyond the spatial and temporal immediacy of its production) and for a document or sign to be handed down which is capable of repeating, innumerable times, an original insight. Thus only because there is such an essential invariance can one grasp the variability within historical life. Without the always present possibility of *tracing* the meaning-signs back to their primal self-evidence, neither knowledge nor meaning in history would be possible.

> Were the thinking activity of a scientist to introduce something 'time-bound' in his thinking, i.e., something bound to what is merely factual about his present or something valid for him as a merely factual tradition, his construction would likewise have a merely time-bound ontic meaning; this meaning would be understandable only by those men who shared the same merely factual presuppositions of understanding.[21]

Teleology and the Historical A Priori

The priority of thematic elements in Husserl's approach, the priority of the signified, dissolves everything that is extrathematic (the signifier, for example) into contingency. What is invariant is the

[20] *Ibid.*, p. 372.
[21] *Ibid.*, p. 377.

thematic meaning and history is the movement between the original meaning formation and sedimented reformulations. "We can also say now that history is from the start nothing other than the vital movement of the co-existence and the interweaving of original formations and the sedimentations of meaning." In the *Vienna Lecture* (given on May 10, 1935, six months before the Prague lecture on which the *Crisis* volume is based) Husserl gives a familiar periodization of history. He divides history into stages corresponding to the problems of epistemology and identifies the final stage with his own theoretical enterprise. Husserl calls these stages: natural, reflective, and transcendental. The natural stage epistemologically corresponds to the naive immediacy of "naturalism" and is apparently historically identified as kin-organized society. In each stage there is always a relation of human interests *(praxis)* and knowledge. Husserl holds that the formation of a relation between the object as known and the living world of experience must have an essentially invariant form characteristic of human history. In the "natural primordial attitude" what is thematized is the immediate object or direction within the surrounding world-horizon or life-community, taken unreflectively as a given. Practically and theoretically this is thematized as the mythical attitude.

> The mythical-religious attitude exists when the world as a totality becomes thematic, but in a practical way . . . But insofar as the whole world is seen thoroughly dominated by mythical powers, so that man's fate depends mediately or immediately upon the way in which they hold sway, a universal mythical world-view is possibly incited by praxis, and then itself becomes a practically interested world-view.[22]

In the immediate universality of the mytho-practical attitude is also found the "origin of philosophy." Prior to Plato and Aristotle we have the first attempts at a theoretical attitude.

> Man becomes gripped by the possession of a world-view and world-knowledge that turns away from all practical interests and, within the closed sphere of its cognitive activity, in the time devoted to it, strives for and achieves nothing but pure *theoria.*[23]

Husserl defines the tradition of Greek philosophy as the second stage of reflection going beyond the first immediate attempts at knowledge by *critically* relating the theoretical effort to practical concerns of life. Therefore the whole of cultural life becomes subject to the problem of objective truth, and all of experience is subjected to critical reason.

[22] *Ibid.*, p. 284.

[23] *Ibid.*, p. 285.

> Philosophy, spreading in the form of inquiry and education, has a twofold spiritual effect. On the one hand, what is most essential to the theoretical attitude of philosophical man is the peculiar universality of his critical stance, his resolve not to accept unquestioningly any pregiven opinion or tradition so that he can inquire, in respect to the whole traditionally pre-given universe, after what is true in itself, an ideality . . . Thus ideal truth becomes an absolute value which, through the movement of education and its constant effects in the training of children brings with it a universally transformed praxis.[24]

Finally after reflection we have the historical role of transcendental reflection. The transcendental preserves the inner teleology of the theoretical attitude against specialization, one-sidedness and objectivism. These are all part of "the constant threat of succumbing to one-sidedness and to premature satisfaction, which take their revenge in subsequent contradictions." Hence where a one-sided rationality produces obscurities and contradictions the task of "universal reflection" is set for thought. Husserl believes this corresponds to the moment when the European world knows itself as a culture and questions its foundation and meaning.

> Only through this highest form of self-consciousness, which itself becomes one of the branches of the infinite task, can philosophy fulfill its function of putting itself, and thereby a genuine humanity, on the road (to realization). (The awareness) that this is the case itself belongs to the domain of philosophical knowledge at the level of highest self-reflection. Only through this constant reflexivity is a philosophy universal knowledge.[25]

This historical theory in Husserl is wholly formed by the movement of theoretical reflection. The "teleology of European history" is the genesis of ideal objectivities. In addition such teleology includes Husserl's assumption of historical continuity in which history is characterized by cumulative development from lower to higher forms. Husserl even goes to the point of showing that therefore nothing is "lost" because even the "mythical-practical world-view . . . can give rise to much knowledge of the factual world, the world as known through scientific experience, *that can later be used scientifically.*"

These points which bear on conclusions below can be summarized as follows. Husserl's notion of the priority of the signified meaning over the historical signifier is connected to the manner in which he privileges ideality over reality and necessity over contingency. The

---

[24]*Ibid.*, pp. 286-87.
[25]*Ibid.*, p. 291.

concept of teleology then serves to relate the inner criticism of rationality and the history of European society. The return to the "origin" of Western rationality still preserves the continuity of the tradition (and thus the possibility of "telos") *against* any "loss" or "inauthenticity". If *writing* seems to threaten this replication with loss then phenomenology rediscovers the experience connecting constitutive subjectivity and the *continuous* historicity of the thematic, ideal objectivity.

> (Transcendental phenomenology) overcomes naturalistic objectivism and every sort of objectivism in the only possible way, namely, through the fact that he who philosophizes proceeds from his own ego . . . *of which he becomes the purely theoretical spectator.* In this attitude it is possible to construct an absolutely self-sufficient science of the spirit in the form of consistently coming to terms with oneself and with the world as spiritual accomplishment.[26]

Conclusion and Criticism

Husserl has provided in his schematic history several "classical" philosophical themes, specifically the identity between genesis in thought and historical genesis.[27] All the contingencies of actual historical development are submerged by pure theoretical reflection. This confusion is not unknown or unique in philosophies of history. As Marx said of Hegel:

> Hegel fell into the illusion of conceiving the real as the product of thought concentrating itself, probing its own depths, and unflooding itself out of itself, by itself, whereas the method of rising from the abstract to concrete is only the way in which thought appropriates the concrete, reproduces it as the concrete in the mind. But this is by no means the process by which the concrete itself comes into being.[28]

---

[26] *Ibid.*, p. 298.

[27] For example, the clear implication of the following statement as it *inverts* the relation between theoretical attitude and material history. "The historical course of development is prefigured in a determined way by the attitude toward the surrounding world." *Ibid.*, p. 293.

[28] Karl Marx, Grundrisse: *Introduction to the Critique of Political Economy*, trans. Martin Nicolaus (London: Pelican Books, 1973), p. 101. Of course it would be illusory to believe that Husserl possessed even a rudimentary knowledge of historical method or developments within the social sciences sufficient to concretize his general comments. As Marvin Farber says, "While radical in his way, Husserl was himself naive with respect to human society and history. He knew very little about the positive findings of social scientists and objectivistic philosophers, and he was really not very interested in socioeconomic problems. He was interested in a nontemporal ('supertemporal') order which he extolled as being above the lowly

What Marx has argued is that the manner by which we come to know and thus advance from immediate and naive knowledge to that of reflective self-understanding is not identical to the way in which the object (as real object, rather than object of knowledge) came about historically and materially. History does not recapitulate the methodology of knowledge. Philosophy is, however, pushed to this obvious error because any contingency or materiality threatens the supremacy of the ideal.

Husserl's approach to the formation of meaning—the problem of origin as giving of meaning *(Sinngebung)*—leads directly to the illusion of a teleological and continuous history. Over and above cultural diversity is the continuity of the theoretical attitude as an unconditioned teleology of truth and reason. Husserl removes the horizon of all contingency or materiality from the history of science and thus restores the classical conception of theory and truth. As Habermas has said:

> Husserl would like to show that this productive subjectivity disappears under the cover of an objectivistic self-understanding, because the sciences have not radically freed themselves from interests rooted in the primary life-world. Only phenomenology breaks with the naive attitude in favor of a rigorously contemplative one and definitely frees knowledge from interest . . . Husserl identifies transcendental self-reflection, to which he accords the name of phenomenological description, with theory in the traditional sense. The philosopher owes to the theoretical attitude a transposition that liberates him from the fabric of empirical interests . . . He (Husserl) errs because he does not discern the connection of positivism, which he justifiably criticizes, with *the ontology from which he unconsciously borrows the traditional concept of theory.*[29]

Such a sense of "theory" then escapes what Marx called the "burden" of matter and, more than that, it escapes the very problems of inauthenticity and distortion of meaning that Husserl analyzed in

---

mundane order of problems. Even his treatment of intellectual history in one of his most mature writings was detached from the realities of history. Philosophical positions and issues . . . assumed the role of decisive historical forces in the modern period. Apart from that, the concept of essence, to which the pure reflective procedure of phenomenological subjectivism is restricted, serves to remove the subjective realm from the existing world." M. Farber, *Basic Problems of Philosophy: Experience, Reality and Human Values* (New York: Harper & Row, 1968), p. 232.

[29]J. Habermas, *Knowledge and Human Interests,* trans. J. Shapiro (Boston: Beacon Press, 1971), pp. 304-5.

the formation of a cultural tradition. We have already seen that this very "ideality" Husserl struggles to isolate is *inseparable* from the structures of repetition and the signifier or material sign which expose knowledge to contingency, to loss, and to the irreducible impact of historicity.

In other words, in spite of Husserl's claims about the radical and novel character of these foundational studies in phenomenology, his conclusions concerning the history of science are remarkably traditional. Husserl's conception of the theoretical attitude and its history leads him to view science as a continuous enterprise, developing by accumulation and teleologically oriented toward truth. That seems to lend support to a comment by Michel Foucault in *The Birth of the Clinic* that phenomenology and positivism are in fact internally related positions.

One can not fail, in examining Husserl's position, to be struck by the side Husserl would take in the debate that Kuhn helped popularize about the history of science. In opposing the positivist view of science and philosophy of science Kuhn took on what he called the "cumulation model" and the teleologically oriented histories that philosophers of science tried to construct. Kuhn suggested that we approach "the scientific revolution as a displacement of the conceptual network through which scientists view the world." In that case the meaning structures of science do not reveal a continuity of development:

> These characteristic shifts in the scientific community's conception of its legitimate problems and standards would have less significance to this essay's thesis if one could assume that they always occurred from some methodologically lower to some higher type. In that case their effects, too, would seem cumulative . . . Yet the case for cumulative development of science's problems and standards is even harder to make than the case for cumulation of theories . . . What occurred was neither a decline nor a raising of standards, but simply a change demanded by the adoption of a new paradigm.[30]

We have seen in conclusion that Husserl's treatment of the human sciences is really a confrontation with the problem of the inauthentic, with the loss of meaning and ideality in the history of science. Even in the case of geometry we find the acquisition and transmission of knowledge comprised by the need to be converted into a sign and thus a tradition. Husserl struggles to neutralize this loss at every turn, to show that, even though the very concept of ideality is bound together with reiteration, somehow the inevitable distance

[30]T. Kuhn, *The Structure of Scientific Revolutions* (Chicago: University of Chicago Press, 1970), p. 108.

created by this reiteration through the sign can be treated as an accidental or separable moment. The effort to save the theoretical attitude involves Husserl in the perennial oppositions of reality and ideality or necessity and contingency. In each case, while his analysis shows an inseparable connection, Husserl only "values" ideality; and thus the material, the different, and the contingent are denied or removed from the domain of knowledge. His efforts culminate in the concept of teleology which is, in fact, the attempt to represent a "perfected" tradition. However such a tradition must deny the very aspects of the sign which make replication and therefore continuity possible. Husserl's invented tradition prepares the way for phenomenology, which is its basis and explanation. Husserl has shown us the mechanisms whereby the concept of continuity is always linked, in idealism, to the study of science and history. Husserl's attempt at an intentional-history shows how the ideal of continuity and cumulation are rooted in the classical theory of truth.

> Making historical analysis the discourse of the continuous and making human consciousness the original subject of all historical development and all action are two sides of the same system of thought. In this system, time is conceived in terms of totalization and revolutions are never more than moments of consciousness.[31]

ROBERT D'AMICO.

UNIVERSITY OF FLORIDA.

[31]M. Foucault, *The Archaeology of Knowledge*, trans. A. M. Sheridan-Smith (New York, 1972), p. 12.

INTENTIONALISM AND PHYSICAL REDUCTIONISM IN COMPUTATIONAL PSYCHOLOGY[1]

I

Since the demise of behaviorism, many psychologists have adopted research programs that call for the formulation of *computational models* that simulate psychological capacities.[2] But how can a simulation model of this sort, essentially a merely predictive, input-output device, be etiologically explanatory of an organism's exhibitions of a psychological capacity? Or, if the computational model is *not* held to refer to causally efficient factors in perception, cognition, etc., to what extent can an attitude of theoretical realism be maintained in respect of the computational model?

One answer to the first of these questions is that of (as I shall call it) *Intentionalism:* the propositions specified in the model should be taken as the propositional contents of the organism's beliefs, goals, desires, fears, guesses, etc.—in short, let us say, its *Intentions;*[3] the computational rules of the model, in virtue of which some propositions are formally derived from others, are to be taken as the rules by which the organism "is guided" in computing its Intentional contents, i.e., as rules which the organism "applies" or "follows."[4]

If Intentionalism is true then we can understand how a computational model has etiological or causally efficient, explanatory force. For even if the Intentional idiom is not *always* best understood as invoking causally efficient, process notions, as Anscombe and others

[1]I want to thank Y. Lurie, Y. Freundlich, J. Samet, and R. Kaufman for helpful suggestions and comments.

[2]For example, see [1], [19], [23] and discussion in [8] and [12]. Later I shall return to the notion of a computational model. At this point the reader may understand it as a computer program in some formal language.

[3]My use of 'Intention' follows that of Dennet ([9]). I shall use 'Intentional content' to refer to the propositional content of an organism's Intention (in the above sense).

[4]—and to which it does not merely "conform." On the distinction between "being guided by/applying/following" rules and "merely conforming to" rules, see [2], [8], [21], [25], and [12], p. 74, n. 15. See also below, note 7.

have argued, it surely *sometimes* is. To answer "Amy calculated that 20 x 2 = 40 by first multiplying 2 x 2 and then adding a '0'" is to give an etiological, process-invoking reply to the question "How did Amy arrive at her belief that 20 x 2 = 40?" The computation process adduced can take time, can be interrupted, can be done quickly or slowly, etc.[5] So there is no problem in viewing the statement that Amy calculated thus-and-such as one that refers to a process; it also seems unquestionable that in *some* sense such a calculation process might *bring about* knowledge that 20 x 2 = 40. One might insist that this type of "bringing about" is interestingly different from general (Humean) causality, but that would not change the fact that Intentionalism casts computational models as etiologically efficient (in perhaps a distinctive sense of 'efficient'). There is, then, something attractive about the Intentionalist interpretation of computational psychology. For it seems plausible to say that *ceteris paribus* we would *like* our philosophical account of computational models to secure for them etiological, explanatory force.

Trouble is, the *ceteris* are not *paribus;* the price we must pay in conceptual confusion for our Intentionalist interpretation[6] of com-

[5]I am not implying that *all* cases of arithmetical competence should be modelled computationally. On pain of infinite regress a computational psychologist *cannot* hold thus. Moreover, there are no *logical* guarantees that even something as "complex" as the knowledge that 10,564 ÷ 76 = 139 might not be as "perceptually obvious" as 2 ÷ 2 = 1. Whether an arithmetical (or any other sort of) competence should be treated computationally or not is not a matter of *a priori* decision; it depends upon such empirical and contingent questions as: is there a satisfactory S-R explanation available? are there interesting patterns of characteristic errors in the exhibition of the competence in question? to what extent will a computational approach reveal "overlap" between various competences? etc.

[6]In referring to Intentionalism as a type of "interpretation" to be given a computational model, I want to emphasize that Intentionalism is a philosophical or metatheoretical position viv-à-vis computational psychology proper. We must thus beware such comments as those of Apter who, in contrasting *computer simulation* with *computer synthesis,* says that the former (but not the latter) is constrained by the demand that the simulation of behavior must "be produced in the same way . . . as in the system being modelled" ([1], p. 28). Apparently Apter does not mean merely that computer simulation must simulate the organism's behavior *under the finest input-output analysis warranted by experimental results,* including experimentally elicited "intermediate outputs", for then simulation would be no more than *sophisticated synthesis.* We would have a genuine difference in kind between the two fields if we assumed that simulation, unlike synthesis, is committed to the view that "the way" that behavior is "produced in the system being modelled" includes the occurrence of Intentional acts of computation and the existence of Intentional states, on the part of the organism—but this, as I have noted, is an assumption that belongs to what we may call "the philosophy of computer simulation," not to computer simulation itself. So Apter's distinction really can mean no more than the degree of "fine grainedness" of the input-output matching to be modelled.

Similar remarks apply to Meisel's comment that he "does not attempt to exputational models is quite steep. For what, after all, can it mean to say that the average English speaker believes (or "tacitly believes" or "tacitly knows"; [10], [15]) that the deep structure of 'Robert is easy to please' is thus-and-such, or that the average speaker "applies" the rule of Dative Movement, etc.? Or, perhaps worse still, that the fish arrived at its mistaken perception of the Muller-Lyer arrows as a result of its having been "guided" by the rules (or its having "solved" the equations) of constancy scaling (see [16], p. 162)?

Various answers have been suggested to this sort of question (e.g., see [10], [15]), none of them, to my mind, satisfactory ([32]).[7] Here, however, I shall assume the weak claim that Intentionalism suffers from a serious *prima facie* conceptual problem which we would be glad to avoid *if there were an acceptable alternative*. The obvious alternative is that of physicalism (to be explained below). So my working assumption gives us the following weak corollary: if an Intentionalist account unwittingly guarantees that there is a (no less satisfactory) physicalist option available, then that Intentionalist position is self-defeating. I shall be claiming that one of the best known Intentionalist positions, that of Fodor ([12]), is a "suicidal" position of this sort.

II

Fodor sees it as a necessary and sufficient condition for imposing

---

plain or model pattern recognition in humans . . ." ([31], p. xi). Once again this must be understood to refer to the degree of fine-grainedness of the simulation challenge. (I do not mean to imply that Apter or Meisel are necessarily guilty of missing this point, but only that their comments must be understood carefully lest they generate as much confusion as Chomsky's famous "competence/performance" distinction.

[7]Generally these answers are of two sorts. One (e.g., [15]) tries to explain a puzzling introduction of some Intentional concept (e.g., "tacit knowledge") in terms of some other Intentional notion (e.g., "tacit deduction") which turns out to be no less puzzling. Another surreptitiously retreats from Intentionalism by explicating not the Intentional idiom we started with but some *other* concept. For example, Fodor defends the propriety of saying that organisms, but not the heavens, "follow" rules and do not merely act in accordance with them by explicating this apparently Intentional notion as follows: "a representation of the rules they follow constitutes one of the causal determinants of their behavior" ([12], p. 74, n. 15). But suppose we so condition a pigeon that it pecks at a screen only when the rule "Peck here now" is projected on the screen. In this case a "representation" of the rule is one of the causal determinants of the pigeon's behavior, but clearly the pigeon does not "follow" the rule *in the Intentional sense* of 'follows a rule'. For fuller discussion of this example see [29] and [32].

a computational interpretation upon a physical system that ([12], p. 73):

> it is possible to devise some mapping which pairs physical states of the device with formulae in a computing language in such fashion as to preserve desired semantic relations among the formulae. For example, we may assign physical states of the machine to sentences of the language in such a way that if $S_1 \ldots S_n$ are machine states, and if $F_1 \ldots F_{n-1}$, F_n are the sentences paired with $S_1 \ldots S_{n-1}$, S_n, respectively, then the physical constitution of the machine is such that it will actually run through that sequence of states only if $F_1 \ldots F_{n-1}$ constitutes a proof of F_n.

I shall use 'thesis (I)' as short for the claim that the above condition does in fact hold in those cases where psychologists want to provide computational models, i.e., as short for the claim that the F and S systems do in fact dovetail in the way Fodor demands. Also, I shall use 'the computational model F' to refer to $F_1 \ldots F_n$ together with the set of rules in virtue of which $F_1 \ldots F_{n-1}$ (as Fodor puts it) "constitutes a proof of F_n."

Before proceeding with the main argument I want to register a few important caveats regarding thesis (I). First, (I) is clearly not intended to be a sufficient condition for a computational interpretation's being an *interesting* interpretation of a physical system. But more importantly, (I) is also not intended to be a sufficient condition for assigning *Intentional* status to a computational model. (Fodor discusses additional conditions for adopting an Intentional attitude to a computational model on pages 73-76, *ibid;* see also note 7 above.) It will be enough for my present purposes that thesis (I) is put forward as a necessary condition for the possibility of computational psychology itself.

Second, we should not insist that $F_1 \ldots F_{n-1}$ constitute a proof of F_n in the sense of *logical proof.* The rules of the model (by which F_n is formally derivable from F_1 through F_{n-1}) may deviate from the truth-preserving rules of logical inference. Indeed, if there are to be computational simulations of perceptual illusions such an *a priori* exclusion of non-truth-preserving rules may prove quite inconvenient.[8] Also, models for language behavior may turn out to be most naturally formulated with grammatical rules rather than inference rules. The

[8]Even if the model seeks to derive the false F_n 'The arrow with the acute angled head is shorter than the arrow with the obtuse angled head' by applying truth preserving rules to *false* F_i (e.g. 'The acute angled arrow is closer than the obtuse angled arrow', following [16]), at least some of the latter will probably derive from *true* F_1, F_2, . . . through the computational rules; so not all the rules will be truth preserving. (But clearly there is no logical necessity here.)

important thing is that the rules of the model (whatever they are) define some formal condition on "derivational validity." (Of course, *extreme* deviation from truth-preserving rules might result in a situation where the organism modelled does not exhibit sufficient "apparent rationality" to invite Intentional characterization or, perhaps, even warrant a computational stimulation! (Compare Dennett's remarks in [9], pp. 95-96.)

Finally, note that F_n will typically be *non-problematically* ascribable to the organism as an Intentional content. Indeed, the organism's Intention that F_n will generally define the *terminus ad quem* for the simulation problem.[9] The major conceptual difficulties with Intentionalism arise with respect to those F_i which are not simulation termini for the capacity in question or for any other capacity.[10]

[9]—e.g., the speaker's Intention that: 'Toby hates raisins' means that Toby hates raisins. In calling such ascriptions *non-problematic* I have ignored two important sources of difficulties which ought to be mentioned. First there is the issue of the *technical vocabulary* in which an F_n might have to be couched if it is to be formally derivable by the rules of the model. The obvious move is to have the model "translate" a technically formulated, formally derivable F_{n-1} into a nontechnically formulated, formally nonderivable (by the computation rules of the model other than the translation rules) F_n. Thus F_n (in "ordinary language") is a "non-problematic" Intentional content. This move faces many difficulties in its own right, but I shall not consider them here since my purpose is to argue *against* Intentionalism, not in its favor.

Second, we have the problem of identifying Intentional contents that pertain to behavior proper rather than cognition or perception. Some notion of "practical knowledge" or of a "maxim of behavior" is required, but it is unclear that this notion is readily available. (See [26] for an attempt to provide such a notion that would, I believe, be acceptable to computational psychologists as well.)

[10]Mention of 'for any other capacity' is required by the fact that a computational model for one capacity will often be composed of "sub-models" for various "sub-capacities". For example, a model for sentence comprehension will clearly include a model for sentence perception. So some of the F_i that are non-sequence-final in the matrix model will be seqence-final in the embedded model, and hence "non-problematically" billed as Intentional contents of the organism. In fact, we can understand much of the experimental work of psychologists (of a computational persuasion) as an attempt to experimentally elicit such "component simulation termini", to constrain the choice of computational model for the matrix capacity. Compare note 6 above and its mention of "fine grained input-output analysis". A fine grained analysis of the matrix simulation problem is often surprising and nontrivial. For example, psycholinguistic research (summarized and discussed at length in [13]) reveals that an adequate simulation model for the comprehension of such sentences as 'The mayor ordered the police to prevent gambling' and 'The mayor ordered the police to cease gambling' must account for subjects' greater ease in recalling that 'police' and 'gambling' occurred together in some sentence in the stimulus list when the list contains the latter rather than the former of the above two sentences. Many such data taken together would seriously constrain the formulation of a matrix model for sentence comprehension.

Let us now return to thesis (I) and its (alleged) unwitting commitment to a physicalist reduction of Intentionalism. Note that $S_1 \ldots S_n$ are physical state types that recur in regular fashion and fall under causal laws that belong to physical (presumably neurophysiological) theory ([12], p. 74). This must be the case if neurophysiological research is to provide empirical contraints upon computational modelling, for only the assumption of lawlike recurrence relations among the S_i will enable us to, for example, reject a tentative computational model as physically unrealized—if, say, it postulates a computational recurrence of some F_i where we do not find any recurrence of the paired S_i. Now, we could decide to dispense with this source of empirical (dis)confirmation and try to make do with empirical contraints proprietary to psychological experimentation, of the sort mentioned in note 10 above. But there are good grounds for not eschewing neurophsiological data, chief amongst which is the sober realization that psychological techniques of eliciting observable responses intuitively associated with the various F_i are, it seems almost certain, destined to meet with failure, at least with respect to the *full* range of F_i that we would want to build into our computational model on purely computational grounds (to maximize the systematic simplicity of the set of computational models for the various capacities of the organism[s] being modelled).[11]

The question before us, then, is this. Consider any Intentionalist generalization of the sort (1):

(1) Organism O Intends that F_j as a result of its applying rule R to its Intention that F_i.

We are guaranteed that $F_i \vdash F_j$ (where the connective is read as: 'F_j is formally derivable from F_i according to some rule[s] of the model'). Now, under what circumstances would the physicalist, lawlike generalization '$S_i \rightarrow S_j$' (= O's being in S_i causes O to then be in S_j) not be a true, lawlike generalization?

One possibility is where S_i is a state that O is in *after* it is in S_j. Then we could not say that O's being in S_i brought about O's being in S_j. This case is not excluded by thesis (I) alone, nor by the assumption $F_i \rightarrow F_j$, for neither of these claims guarantees that the conditions on derivational validity specified by the rules of the model will not

[11] The possibility of neurophysiological (dis)confirmation of psychological models is a commonly shared assumption even on the part of Intentionalists. Compare Fodor's early [11] and [15], p. 326. Dennett also is committed to it, if I understand him correctly ([9], pp. 89, 96).

sanction "retrospective validation." So even if S_i "occurs" after S_j it could still be true that $F_1 \ldots F_j \ldots F_i \ldots F_n$ is derivationally valid and that $F_i \vdash F_j$. What *does* exclude this case, however, is the Intentionalist's claim that (1). For (1) to be true O must have the Intention that F_i before it has the Intention that F_j. Since S_i and S_j are paired with F_i and F_j, respectively, we need not worry about temporal sequence and reverse causation.

A more difficult objection is the following. '$S_i \rightarrow S_j$' might well fail to describe the organism, even if (1) is true, in case the organism does not *always* end up in S_j after being in S_i. Note that we have assumed the truth of (1) and (I). So on those occasions that O does not end up in S_j it will end up in some other physical state (or states) S_j' (or S_j", S_j''', etc.). F_j will be paired, then, not with S_j alone but rather with a set of physical states S_j, S_j', etc., in one of which the organism will end up after having been in S_i. (Since our only grounds for attributing to O the Intentional state whose content is F_j is precisely an Intentionalist interpretation of a computational interpreation of a regular physical system of states, if (I) is accepted, this could not fail to be the case.)

Is one-many F-S pairing likely? If it is likely, does it foreclose physical reduction of (1)? Can '$S_i \rightarrow .S_j$ v S_j' v S_j" v . . . ' be taken as a reducing law for (1)? These are the questions to be addressed in the following section III.[12]

---

[12]Note that if reductionism is to be blocked by giving up the idea of one-one F-S coordination, then Fodor will have to give up his 1968 claim ([10], p. 627) that what happens when one ties one's shoes is this—

> There is a little man who lives in one's head. The little man keeps a library. When one acts upon the intention to tie one's shoes, the little man fetches down a volume entitled *Tying One's Shoes*. The volume says such things as: "Take the left free end of the shoelace in the left hand. Cross the left free end of the shoelace over the right free end of the shoelace . . ., etc." . . . When the little man reads the instruction 'take the left free end of the shoelace in the left hand', he pushes a button on a control panel. The button is marked 'Take the left free end of the shoelace in the left hand'. When depressed it activates a series of wheels, levers, cogs, and hydraulic mechanisms . . . Similarly, *mutatis mutandis,* for the rest of the instructions. . . . When the little man reads the word 'end', he returns the book of instructions to his library.

Even allowing for metaphor, Fodor thus commits himself to one-one F-S pairing in this passage, for he makes a "one-button-one instruction" assumption. To clinch the reductivist's case we need only replace the little man with a physical device that upon receiving the instruction 'Tie shoes' from the instruction source automatically and sequentially activates the relevant buttons, or their neurophysiological equivalents. (Cummins' argument in [8] is essentially just this.)

III

Fodor's own discussion of the reduction of psychology to physiology (see [12], pp. 9-26; cf. [3]) suggests that he believes that F-S coordination will not turn out to be one-one. For Fodor argues that propositional attitude states are quite differently realized in the physical "hardware" of various species and in the exhibitions of a psychological capacity by a single type of organism in different contexts or settings. There is plainly no reason to expect one-one pairing of physical states and computational states, if we lack it in the case of physical and propositional attitude states.

In the last section we broached the question of the nomological status of such generalizations as '$S_i \rightarrow S_j \vee S_j' \vee S_j'' \vee \ldots$'. But in fact there is no reason to suppose that our problem pertains only to the causal consequent of the physical state (S_i) paired with F_i; the same problem may be expected with respect to the causal antecedent. Instead of S_i we may expect on the left-hand side of the connective '$\rightarrow$' a disjunction such as '$S_i \vee S_i' \vee S_i'' \vee \ldots$'. Which members of the two disjunctions flanking the connective will be realized will depend upon biological species, upon stage of development of the organism, upon setting, etc. So rather than the simple thesis (I), I believe that Fodor wants to hold something like the more complicated thesis (II):

(II) Let $O^1, O^2, \ldots, O^m$ be different types of organisms, or similar types of organisms but in different contexts, settings, stages of development, etc. Let $S_1{}^1, S_2{}^1, \ldots, S_n{}^1$ be a sequence of physical states of O^1; let $S_1{}^2, S_2{}^2, \ldots, S_n{}^2$ be a sequence of physical states of O^2, and so on for all of the O's. The sequence of propositions $F_1, F_2, \ldots, F_n$ is a computational interpretation for each of the S sequences only if, for each O^h, O^h will run through the S^h sequence ($S_1{}^h, S_2{}^h, \ldots, S_n{}^h$) only if $F_1 \ldots F_{n-1} \vdash F_n$, where each F_i is assigned to the set ($S_i{}^1, S_i{}^2, \ldots, S_i{}^m$). Furthermore, it is extremely likely that for many values, i, j, k $S_i{}^j \neq S_i{}^k$.

How does thesis (II) block physical reduction of (1)? We can adapt Fodor's argument from [12] as follows. We cannot not attempt to reduce the Intentionalist's (1) to the simple '$S_i \rightarrow S_j$' since there may be no predicates 'S_i' and 'S_j' that apply to the full range of O's that fall under (1). (This is the import of the last clause in thesis [II] above.) Instead, it seems, the physical reductivist would have to reduce (1) to (2):

(2) $S_i^1 \vee S_i^2 \vee \ldots \vee S_i^m \rightarrow S_j^1 \vee S_j^2 \vee \ldots \vee S_j^m$.

But, argues Fodor, such generalizations as (2) are not *laws,* for what flanks the connective are not *natural kind predicates* but, at best, disjunctions of natural kind predicates. So the Intentionalist's (1) is left unreduced and uneliminated. (See pp. 20-23 in [12].)

There are a number of ways to meet this challenge. One might balk at the hasty dismissal of (2) as unlawlike solely on the grounds that it connects a disjunction of predicates. Moreover, one might seriously query Fodor's pessimism about our finding "super-predicates" 'S_i' and 'S_j' of which the disjunctions are merely "local instantiations" the differences amongst which may be explained away. But here I want to pursue a different line of attack which throws light on an important feature of the Intentionalist-physicalist debate regarding computational psychology.

Briefly, the idea is this. Even if the Intentionalist's (1) is not reducible to any lawlike generalization in physical theory, that does not show that (1) is the *preferred account* we should give of (3):

(3) '$F_i \vdash F_j$' appears in the computational model for all of O^1 through O^m even though their S sequences are different.

There is no reason why the physicalist must take it upon himself to reduce (1) to some lawlike generalization of physical theory. It will suffice if he can give some other, no less satisfactory account of the computational model shared by the O's. If the physicalist can do this he will have shown that the Intentionalist's (1) is not inevitable; he can then dismiss the Intentionalist's postulated Intentional-states-that-F_i as entirely superfluous; a better (albeit, nonreductive) account will have been given for the computational model.[13]

Can the physicalist achieve this nonreductive elimination of Intentionalism? Recall that *ex hypothesi* we have the following set of true, lawlike generalizations:

(4) $(S_i^1 \rightarrow S_j^1, S_i^2 \rightarrow S_j^2, \ldots, S_i^m \rightarrow S_j^m)$.

Each member of (4) describes an organism belonging to $O^1 \ldots O^m$. So with respect to any particular O^h we have, repeating the argument of section II (this time undefeated by reversion to thesis [II]), a physical account that subsumes the various S^h-states of O^h under relevant causal laws. What we do *not* have—and here the Intentionalist

[13] If one chooses to call "global replacement" of one theory by another a "reduction," then in the subsequent paragraphs we shall still be considering physical reductivism. Issues of paradigm shift and incommensurability arise here, of course—see [17] and [22].

will try to bring push to shove—is an explanation of the fact that all the physically heterogeneous S sequences are susceptible to a common computational interpretation. The Intentionalist will now demand a hearing, insisting that the only explanation of this higher-level regularity is that all the organisms Intend the items in the F sequence.

It is worth stating more precisely what the higher-level regularity allegedly unexplained by the physicalist is. Clearly it is not anything like (5):

(5) (1) holds for all the O's in $O^1 \ldots O^m$,

for the physicalist denies that there are any such Intentions-that-F_i and that-F_j, *ergo* that (1) is a true generalization about the O's. Rather, the Intentionalist claims that the physicalist cannot explain (6):

(6) Whenever an organism belonging to $O^1 \ldots O^m$ is in a physical state that can be paired with F_i according to the conditions laid down in thesis (II), the organism will then go into a physical state that can be paired with F_j according to those same conditions.

The Intentionalist argues, then, from the alleged inability of the physicalist to explain (6) and the Intentionalist's own ability to explain (6) in terms of (1)—to the inevitability of adopting Intentionalism as the preferred account.

But why should the physicalist find (6) difficult to explain? The O's are biological organisms that fall in the domain of non-Intentionalist theories of evolution and natural selection, according to the physicalist. It is thus understandable, from the physicalist's point of view, that there should develop biological systems of different physical constitution that all share the same computational model. This is so since on all accounts the computational model F articulates a series of propositions that it *would be* rational and useful to compute. (Recall our assumption that the rules of the model will not deviate *too* much from truth-preserving rules of logical inference.)

We might say that F is a "teleology" for the various S sequences in that it articulates why it would be advantageous from the point of view of natural selection for such S sequences to exist. If anything like current evolutionary theory is even approximately correct[14] the no-

[14] This is not to deny that a fully adequate, non-Intentional account of teleology may be hard to provide. (See, for example, [18], [27], and [28] for recent discussion and proposals.) It is, however, to bet on the exclusion, from theories of evolution, of Divine and organismic purposiveness.

Bennet's interesting account ([30]) will not help us, for his notion of *registra-*

tion of teleology required will not have to be Intentional. So it looks as if apart from the issue of law-by-law reduction of such Intentionalist claims as (1), the physicalist can reasonably hope to present an attractive alternative to Intentionalism.

There are, however, some serious residual difficulties. First, not so much a difficulty as a complication, we now have a sharp dichotomy between that component of our psychological theory which will provide causally efficient explanations, namely the physicalist story of S sequences which replaces computational relations and posits as etiologically explanatory, and that component which addresses phylogenetic issues, namely the computational account. The latter, with its specification of the "apparent reasonableness" of the S sequences, will not attempt to explain a particular organism's actually running through the sequence of S states that it in fact runs through, on those occasions that it runs through them; at best it will explain why such sequences might be expected to develop and sustain themselves. Intentionalism sought to subsume both sets of explananda under a single rubric, the Intentional purposiveness of the organism; our physicalist, teleological account of computational models must sacrifice this homogeneity for its greater conceptual clarity. The trade-off seems, however, to be well worth it, and I am inclined to view our bifurcation of theory as no more than a minor disappointment, rather than as a major setback or problem.

The real problem is whether the physicalist can indeed give a fully satisfying account of computational regularities (such as [6]) in non-Intentional, teleological terms. Recall that *ex hypothesi* we have a very fine-grained dovetailing between each F_i and a set of S_i^h. But this commonality between S^h sequences (viz., the fact that they all share the same computational interpretation) seems, at first sight, to be far too elaborate to exhaust its "explanation providing potential" in none-too-exciting teleological observations. Surely stronger explanations are warranted and possible.

To reply that the F_i-S_i^1-S_i^2- . . . -S_i^m coordination assumed in thesis (II) is an artifact of the theory builder is to move in the direction of nonrealist attitudes towards theories, a direction we have eschewed in this paper. But what realist alternative is there, apart from Intentionalism? (The Intentionalist will explain this multiple isomorphism by claiming that each organism Intends F_1 . . . F_n and

tion would have to be Intentional to apply to computational contexts; the non-Intentional, minimalist type of registration, viz., sensory stimulation, is largely irrelevant to the "intermediate F_i" of computational models. I have discussed this issue at somewhat greater length in [32].

makes use of whatever physical hardware is at its disposal.) Note that a teleological, non-Intentional story seems plausible with respect to the fact that all the various S^h sequences manage to end up in a physical state S_n^h (S_n^1 or S_n^2 or . . . S_n^m) that is paired with F_n, the content of a nonproblematically ascribed Intentional state of the organism; this is because, he noted, the computational rules are generally "logical," and getting into an Intentional state whose content is F_n, in circumstances associated with the initial F_1, is in some sense "useful" and "reasonable," hence, presumably, teleologically explicable.[15] But the teleological account seems inadequate with respect to those intermediate F_i not intuitively ascribable to the organism as Intentional contents, and the computational regularities defined over these F_i.

What is the teleological value in achieving physical states paired with the F_i, unless the S_1-to-S_n nexus has already been established? In part this problem is a common one in biology. What is the teleological value of mutating in the direction of the visual system of the human brain, in the absence of a prior mutation in favor of the human eye, and vice versa? Since simultaneous, fortuitous mutation that secures both structures and their interlocking functions seems entirely too facile a hypothesis, we may wonder why humans didn't remain like the earthworm, with its light-sensitive cells scattered over the surface of its skin.

We can put the present point this way. The dovetailing of the F system and the physically heterogeneous S systems appears to be too excessive, too indicative of apparent purposiveness, to be explained by merely teleological factors. Are we not ignoring too much in consigning computational homogeneities between physically heterogeneous systems, to the realm of teleology?

I believe that our present problem has an interesting analog in the physical sciences, specifically in Geoffrey Chew's "hadronic bootstrap hypothesis" formulated in the context of S matrix theory.[16] There, too, we find what I have been calling "apparent

---

[15] I have here conveniently compressed all circumstantial or stimulus information into "F_1" and have also skipped over the question how the information content of "start conditions" (for the exhibition of a capacity) is to be identified and formulated. A consideration of these problems, by no means trivial, would take us too far afield.

[16] The reader altogether unfamiliar with S matrix theory or the Bootstrap Hypothesis is referred to the Appendix. In the text I shall assume a general familiarity with Chew's theory.

reasonableness" that cannot be blamed on hadronic Intentionality or teleology. I shall conclude this paper by drawing the analogy and its moral.

Chew seeks to explain the physics of hadron scattering by rejecting hadrons as particle-corpuscles and instead reverting to an explanatorily (and ontologically) more basic level at which we find a "strong force" of which hadrons are merely *manifestations*. But the strong force is not arbitrary, as is, say, the gravitational force (as far as we know); if Chew is correct, the strong force is what it is because it is the only *logically possible* strong force compatible with quite general logico-epistemic considerations. (See Appendix for details.)

The hadrons cannot be said to Intend the satisfaction of these logico-epistemic considerations or constraints. (Recall, again, that we have here foresworn nonrealist approaches that pin the nice logical fit of hadron behavior and the logico-epistemic constraints upon the theorist's own theory constructing endeavors.) Nor, quite obviously, are non-Intentional, teleological factors from evolutionary theory relevant to hadron physics. In computational psychology, too, the apparent reasonableness and apparent Intentionality articulated by the logico-semantic character of computational models will not be pinned on the Intentionality of organisms; often it will go far beyond what seems required (and hence explained) by teleological considerations. Unlike hadrons, the S sequences are not *ontologically secondary*. They are, however, for the computational psychologist, *explanatorily secondary* or non-basic, just as "force talk" replaces "particle-corpuscle talk" at what Chew sees as the explanatorily primary level of analysis and explanation in hadronic physics.

At the explanatorily basic level of analysis computational states of the model (the F_i) are sharply distinguished from Intentional states of an organism. The notion of information or propositional content required is that of "ownerless information," reminiscent of Popper's "world three" ([20]). Indeed, just as hadrons are metaphysical-programmatic *reifications,* so too computational states are programmatic *statifications* of ownerless information found in computational, simulation models. In principle one can dispense with hadron "particle" talk and with computational "state" talk, if our goal is merely to predict. Realism, however, leads us to talk of singularities of complex functions as particles; it also leads us to treat the propositions in the computational model as *states of something*. There is only one thing *of which* the latter can be states—the world. We must say that the model's informational contents are "realized in the world."

If thesis (II) is assumed, then all issues of causally efficient etiology will be dumped in the lap of the neuro-physiologist. This leaves the psychologist (the computational psychologist, that is) the task of exhibiting the "logicality" of physical systems belonging to a certain class, the class of psychological organisms. The logicality in question is not the *logicality of organisms* (i.e. the logicality of their Intentions) but rather the *logicality of the world of organisms*. To the extent that the logicality discovered overshoots the requirements of teleology (and I think this extent must be great) there is no further explanation to be given *why* the world of organisms is as logical as it is. Similarly, there may be no further explanation *why* the world of hadron behavior is knowable. In both cases, that of the computational psychologist as well as that of the hadron bootstrapper, the scientist's research goal is to exhibit in full detail the apparent reasonableness and nonarbitrariness of reality.[17]

To sum up, even if thesis (II) rather than thesis (I) (or some other alternative) is correct, we need not adopt Intentionalism just because we fail to get item-by-item physical reduction; we can avoid the problematic ascription to nonverbal organisms of abstract, Intentional states. A deeper understanding of the computational psychologist's autonomous program reveals that he can define and pursue explanatory goals that do not include those of causally efficient explanation. And once computational generalizations about organisms are *not* held to refer to etiologically interesting factors, there is no *need* to interpret computational posits Intentionally and to ground the etiological effectiveness of the computational posits in the Intentional causality of "applying rules" to bring about belief states.

---

[17]A view somewhat similar to mine is advanced by Sanders and Martin in [24]. But they seem to ignore the complicated relationship that will obtain between causal explanations falling under what they call the "classical paradigm" and the non-causal explanations generated by their "grammatical paradigm". They also do not address the issue of realism.

BIBLIOGRAPHY

1. Apter, M. J. *The Computer Simulation of Behaviour*. London: Hutchinson, 1970.
2. Black, M. "Rules and Routines." *The Concept of Education*, R. S. Peters, ed. London: Routledge and Kegan Paul, 1967.
3. Block, N. and J. A. Fodor. "What Psychological States Are Not," *Philosophical Review* 81 (1972): 159-81.
4. Capra, F. *The Tao of Physics*. Boulder, Colo.: Shambhala, 1975.
5. Chew, G. F. "Crisis for the Elementary Particle Concept," *U. of California Lawrence Radiation Laboratory Reprint* #17137 (1966).
6. Chew, G. F. "'Bootstrap': A Scientific Idea?" *Science* 161 (1968): 762-5.
7. Chew, G. F., M. Gell-Mann, and I. Rosenfeld. "Strongly Interacting Particles," *Scientific American* 210 (1964): 74-83.
8. Cummins, R. "Programs in the Explanation of Behaviour," *Philosophy of Science* 44 (1977): 269-87.
9. Dennett, D. C. "Intentional Systems," *Journal of Philosophy* 68 (1971): 87-106.
10. Fodor, J. A. "The Appeal to Tacit Knowledge in Psychological Explanation," *Journal of Philosophy* 65 (1968): 627-40.
11. Fodor, J. A. *Psychological Explanation*. New York: Random House, 1968.
12. Fodor, J. A. *The Language of Thought*. New York: Crowell, 1975.
13. Fodor, J. A., T. Bever, and M. Garrett. *The Psychology of Language*. New York: McGraw-Hill, 1974.
14. Gale, G. "Chew's Monadology," *Journal of the History of Ideas* 35 (1974): 339-48.
15. Graves, C., J. J. Katz, *et al*, "Tacit Knowledge," *Journal of Philosophy* 70 (1973): 318-30.
16. Gregory, R. L. *Eye and Brain*. New York: McGraw-Hill, 1966.
17. Kuhn, T. S. *The Structure of Scientific Revolutions*. Chicago: U. of Chicago Press, 1962.
18. Nagel, E. "Goal-directed Processes in Biology" and "Functional Explanations in Biology," *Journal of Philosophy* 74 (1977): 261-301.
19. Norman, D. A. *Memory and Attention*. New York: Wiley and Sons, 1969.

20. Popper, K. *Objective Knowledge.* Oxford: Oxford U. Press, 1972.
21. Quine, W. V. O. "Methodological Reflections on Current Linguistic Theory," *On Noam Chomsky,* G. Harman, ed. New York: Anchor Books/Doubleday, 1974.
22. Rabb, J. D. "Incommensurable Paradigms," *Inquiry* 21 (1978): 201-12.
23. Sanders, D. A. *Auditory Perception of Speech.* Englewood Cliffs: Prentice-Hall, 1977.
24. Sanders, R. E. and L. W. Martin. "Grammatical Rules and Explanations of Behavior," *Inquiry* 18 (1975): 65-82.
25. Sellars, W. *Science, Perception, and Reality.* London: Routledge and Kegan Paul, 1963.
26. Shwayder, D. S. *The Stratification of Behaviour.* London: Routledge and Kegan Paul, 1965.
27. Woodfield, A. *Teleology.* Cambridge: Cambridge U. Press, 1976.
28. Wright, L. "The Ins and Outs of Teleology," *Inquiry* 21 (1978): 223-37.
29. Zaitchik, A. "Explanations in Psycholinguistics" (in Hebrew), forthcoming.
30. Bennett, J. *Linguistic Behaviour.* Cambridge: Cambridge U. Press, 1976.
31. Meisel, W. L. *Computer-Oriented Approaches to Pattern Recognition.* New York: Academic Press, 1972.
32. Zaitchik, A. "Intentionalism and Computational Psychology." *Grazer Philosophische Studien* = 10 (1980): 149-66.

APPENDIX

The following is a brief and simplified account of the basics of Geoffrey Chew's Bootstrap Hypothesis ("BH"), a knowledge of which is presupposed in the text of this paper. I have run together under the label "BH" ideas that belong both to Chew's hypothesis proper and to S matrix theory (in the context of which the bootstrap hypothesis is formulated).

Hadrons are the "strongly interacting" particles that compose the nuclei of atoms. One possible hadron scattering (or interaction) is depicted in diagram 1. A proton (p) and a negative pion (π^-) combine to form a neutron (n) which then decomposes into another proton-negative-pion pair. If diagram 1 is rotated in the relevant mathematical space, we get diagram 2, a representation of another possible hadron interaction. A convention on the arrow has us read diagram 2 as: an antiproton ($\bar{p}$) and a proton (p) combine into a neutral pion (π°) which then decomposes into a negative pion (π^-) and a positive pion (π^+). (Reversing the direction of an arrow means that we must substitute an antiparticle for a particle; the positive pion is the antiparticle of the negative pion.)

DIAGRAM 1

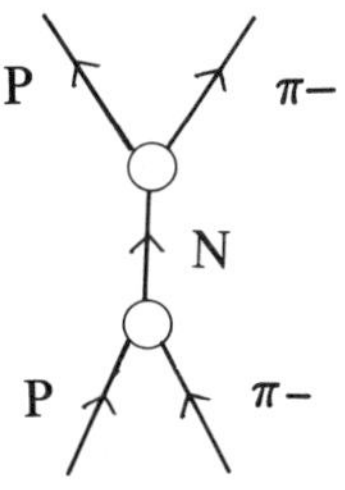

DIAGRAM 2

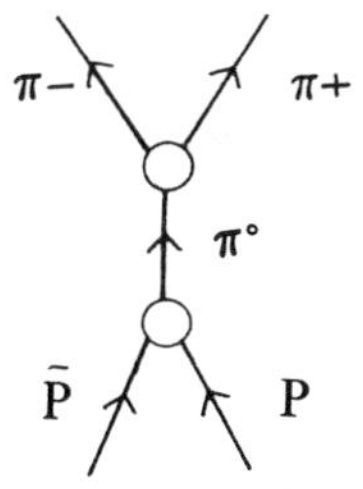

According to BH the interactions in diagrams 1 and 2 (and in still others) are analytic continuations of the same complex function, or "manifestations of the same force." Which manifestation will occur depends upon available energies and momenta. But this is not the "usual" theoretical abstraction from "local particularities" that mask a common, underlying structure or composition, for BH does not view the hadrons as merely different arrangements of more basic constitutents. Nor are the hadrons "elementary" in the sense that they lack internal constitution. Rather, the very notion of a particle is challenged, for BH maintains that we often find a "particle" X composed of particles Y and Z — where Y itself is composed of X and Z! Chew refers to this situation as "circular and violently non-linear" ([7], p. 93); to make sense of it, and of other bootstrap claims (e.g., "every particle consists of all other particles," [4], p. 295) we must reject the notion of a particle as a corpuscle and revert to "force talk." Gale ([14], p. 342; cf. [7], p. 79) says that we must treat a hadron as a *manifestation of the strong force;* corpuscular particles play no role in BH.

But how is particle talk related to force talk? Diagrams 1 and 2 are called, respectively, "direct channel" and "cross channel" views of a type of interaction. Note that the diagrams feature quite different intermediate particles *(n)* and π°, respectively). Capra explains as follows:

> The connection between forces and particles is established through the intermediate states in the two channels. In the direct channel . . . the proton and the π^- can form an intermediate neutron, whereas the cross channel can be made up by an intermediate neutral pion (π°). This pion—the intermediate state in the cross channel—is interpreted as the manifestation of the force which acts in the direct channel binding the proton and the π^- together to form the neutron. . . . (W)hat appears as a force in one channel is manifest as an intermediate particle in the other. ([4], pp. 272-73; cf. [14], p. 343)

I doubt that such explanations as these are metaphysically satisfying, but they serve at least to emphasize that the explanatorily basic (and, albeit somewhat unclearly, ontologically primary) notion is not that of the corpuscle or particle in the traditional sense but rather that of forces.

What makes this view philosophically exciting is Chew's claim that the different manifestations of the forces are *logically required* for there being any hadrons at all. Even if one entry in the S matrix (the table of possible hadron interactions) were changed the rest of the hadron family could not exist.

> The self-consistency hypothesis makes it possible to imagine that for *any* hadrons at all to exist, the entire family must exist in a mutually supporting framework ([5], p. 7).

Or less guardedly,

> nature is as it is because this is the only possible nature consistent with itself ([6], p. 762).

Thus the term 'bootstrap'. The hadron family must, so to speak, "pull itself up by its own bootstraps."

Chew believes that eventually the bootstrap approach will be extended beyond hadron physics. Then even the allegedly "arbitrary" fundamental constants of physical theory will be shown to be logical consequences of more general conditions. (Chew thinks that this idea is so radical a departure from accepted scientific thinking that it may be "unscientific" (see [6]). The reason that it is so extraordinary is that the more general conditions in question are not merely more general laws of nature, themselves arbitrary, but are conditions on the very possibility of scientific knowledge itself, or, more exactly, are mathematically rigorous formulations of such conditions.

Capra interprets these conditions as follows. (i) the Lorentz invariance, intuitively associated with the requirement, refined by relativity theory, that experiments done "here" and "now" must yield the same results as those done "there" and "then." (ii) the Unitarity requirement, viz., that the sum of probabilities of all possible hadronic scatterings equals 1, intuitively associated with the idea that complete (probabilistic) knowledge is in principle attainable. (iii) the Causality thesis, that a particle can be created in one interaction and destroyed in another only if the first occurs before the latter. Mathematically this principle is recast as the demand for "smooth" complex functions except where singularities (particle creations) occur. Intuitively it involves the methodologically necessary axiom that efficient causes are never temporally consequent to their effects. (iv) so-called "Nuclear Democracy," viz., there are no elementary particles. This thesis, too, pertains to the very possibility of scientific knowledge, for, as Chew puts it, "a truly elementary particle—completely devoid of internal structure—could not be subject to any force that would allow us to detect its existence. The mere knowledge of a particle's existence, that is to say, implies that the particle possess internal structure." (quoted in [4], p. 274). (It should perhaps be noted that in presenting (iii) and (iv) above I have not followed Capra's discussion.)

In short, BH eschews the analysis of differential hadronic behavior into the consequences of different arrangements of ultimate, corpuscular constituents, a line of thought that eventuates in ultimately arbitrary facts about the elementary particles postulated. Instead BH attempts to seriously attenuate the notion of a particle, to eliminate the idea of ultimately simple constituents, and to derive the laws of the "strong force" from a set of nonarbitrary, logico-epistemic considerations concerning the very possibility of scientific knowledge (of hadrons).

A. ZAITCHIK.

BEN GURION UNIVERSITY.

PHENOMENAL PROPERTIES

The aim of this paper is to explore one theme that runs through much of the recent literature on the mind-body problem: the issue of phenomenal properties of psychological states. My main interest in raising this issue is that these alleged properties represent the chief intuitive objection to the thoroughgoing materialsim I advocate.[1] But more than this, the issue focusses a variety of problems in the philosophy of language.

Let us start slowly, with this question: why would anyone *not* be a materialist? Why should anyone doubt that mentality is completely explainable by the principles that have proved so eminently successful in explaining all other phenomena? (I cannot digress here to explain what I mean by "completely explain" and "material," among other things; see *MMB*.) Let's sharpen the question just a bit: why should anyone doubt that mental states are physical? If you think that by definition what is mental cannot be physical, let me rephrase the question: why should anyone doubt that what we are accustomed to calling "mental states" will turn out to be physical states? Before addressing that question, let me stress that by putting it as I have I do not mean to endorse states as parts of any reasonable ontology. Quite to the contrary, I concur with Hobbes's somewhat redundant aphorism that every thing is particular. It is, however, obviously convenient to be able to talk of states, instead of having constantly to cash in such talk for talk of predicates and satisfaction. I see states, properties, events, and processes as akin to the totality of sets, the totality of all non-self-membered sets, the totality of ordinals: the proper classes of axiomatic set theory. We can for special purposes talk as if there were a totality of all the ordinals, but when the chips are down the truth-conditions for statements about the totality of ordinals involve no such entity, using as they do only the predicate "x is an ordinal." Following Quine, who calls such proper classes virtual, I think of properties and the rest as virtual entities. It is as virtual en-

[1]See my *Materialism and the Mind-Body Problem* (New York: Oxford University Press, 1979), henceforth *MMB*. The present paper is intended in part to extend some of the lines of argument in *MMB*.

tities that mental states enter this discussion. You may, if you like, chalk up this reluctance to reify states merely to ontological caution. I argue below that the reification of states is part of the process by which we erroneously come to believe in phenomenal properties.

This caveat entered, let us try again: why don't mental states seem physical? A popular answer suggested by Descartes and recently amplified by Kripke[2] is that we can *imagine* a mental state *m* existing apart (or distinct) from any physical state *p*. Since we cannot imagine *m* distinct from *m*, *m* cannot be *p*. I have no general quarrel with the form of this argument; some ascriptions of imaginability are referential at all positions and sustain application of the diversity of discernibles. The real question is: how is it that we can imagine *m* existing without *p*? To put the question in a way that does not beg any questions against the materialists, why do we think we can imagine *m* apart from *p*? And the only answer there can be is that we think of *m* as having peroperties that *p* does not have. Indeed, the only reason we ever have for supposing any two things diverse is that one has properties the other lacks—even if we cannot say precisely what those properties are supposed to be.

What properties of psychological states, then, motivate the intuition of diversity? A brief summary of recent thought about psychological states will be helpful. It has become a commonplace by now that psychological states are identified by the role they play in some larger context, a role specified by some more-or-less complicated theory. Thus, being in pain (or just pain, for the moment) is—following Smart[3]—that state which results from organic damage and causes flight. The role might be more complicated: David Lewis[4] takes pain to be whatever has most of the causes and effects ascribed to pain in that compendium of beliefs that constitutes common-sense pain theory. The role might not even be causal: Putnam[5] takes pain to be whatever satisfies some abstractly described state in a machine program, and Harman and Fodor[6] take it to be whatever plays some

---

[2]See his "Naming and Necessity", in D. Davidson and G. Harman, eds., *Semantics of Natural Language* (Dordrecht: Reidel, 1972).

[3]"Sensations and Brain Processes", in J. O'Connor, ed., *Modern Materialism* (New York: Harcourt, Brace and World, 1969).

[4]"An Argument for the Identity Theory," *Journal of Philosophy* 63, no. 1 (Jan. 6, 1966): 17-25.

[5]H. Putnam, *Mind, Language and Reality* (New York: Cambridge University Press, 1975), Introduction and essays 14-22.

functionally described role in the behavior of organisms. I argue in *MMB* that the last two positions reduce to the first two, but that is a side issue. What is important is the widespread agreement that psychological states are identified in a way which involves no commitment to their inner nature, and in particular, in a way which involves no appeal to any automatically nonphysical traits. In short: if $T(m)$ is the theoretical description by which pain is identified, pain is $(\iota x)T(x)$, where nothing about $T(x)$ prevents m from being a physical state. I have so far used the intentionally vague word "identify": do such topic-neutral descriptions as $(\iota x)T(x)$ *analyze* the terms that denote psychological states, or do the former just fix the reference of the latter? This latter view—that topic-neutral, causal-or-functional-role descriptions are simply how we in fact pick out the referents of psychological terms—seems preferable, for it is intuitively clear that "pain" does not *mean* "what results from skin damage." Skin damage might not hurt if our neural wiring were different.[7] So taking topic-neutral descriptions nonanalytically leaves the meaning of psychological terms an open question—or perhaps closes the question, and assimilates such terms to purely indexical names. I return to this issue below. (The theory of meaning Putnam develops in "The Meaning of 'Meaning'"[8] allows "*A*" to mean "*B*" even if some A's are not B's. As this would sever the intuitively unbreakable link between meaning and necessity, it is best to take Putnam's theory of meaning as an account of what Kripke calls "reference-fixing.")

---

[6]See G. Harman, *Thought* (Princeton: Princeton University Press, 1973), chapter 3; J. Fodor, *Psychological Explanation* (New York: Random House, 1968).

[7]Lewis defends "analytic topic neutralism" against this objection (in "Psychophysical and Theoretical Identifications," *Australasian Journal of Philosophy* 50 (December 1972): 249-58) via the idea of *near-realization*. $T(x)$ is nearly realized if $-(\exists ! x)T(x)$ but $(\exists ! x)T^1(x)$, where $T^1(x)$ differs slightly from $T(x)$. But this doesn't address the possibility that pain might have occupied a very different causal role than it actually does, and hence does not even nearly realize commonsense psychology. Lewis addresses this problem obliquely when he says that even if $-(\exists ! x)T(x)$, "$(\iota x)T(x)$" is meaningful because we know what it would name in any possible world *w* in which $(\exists ! x)T(x)$ were true. But this evidently leaves Lewis saddled with the implausible consequence that if, in *w*, tickles played the causal role pains actually play, tickles would be pain in *w;* hence that tickles might be pains. But surely tickles could *not* be pains.

[8]In K. Gunderson, ed., *Language, Mind and Knowledge* (Minneapolis: University of Minnesota Press, 1975).

What is more immediately important than how psychological states are identified is the following intuition, which seems compelling on whatever account we adopt. Saying that psychological states are the *x*'s that cause and result from certain physicalistically described situations simply omits how such states appear to their subjects. This is the essence of the phenomenal-property objection to materialism. The title of Thomas Nagel's article "What Is it like to Be a Bat?"[9] puts the problem in a nutshell. Even if mental states are first identified by their causal properties, and even if (as the materialsit expects) scientific investigation shows that the states which in fact have these causal properties are physical states, this whole account leaves out the fact that it *feels like* something to be in one of these causally-identified states. Pain is not only a state which makes us flee or fight or a state engendered by tissue lesions: pain is a state it feels like something to be in. The same cannot be said for most states. It does not feel like anything to be an electron with a certain charge; it is not like anything to be an electron. These feeling properties go under many names: phenomenal properties, felt qualia, immediate phenomenological properties, appearance properties, and aspects under which psycho-physical states are apprehended. It is in virtue of these, says the antimaterialist, that materialism cannot be the whole truth about the mind. These phenomenal properties have eluded the materialist's grasp even when his main hypotheses are granted. The antimaterialist can press his point more forcefully, insisting that the materialist has simply pushed the mind-body problem back a step. Even if *pain* is what has certain typical causal relations, the distinctively *mental* aspect of pain is surely what pain, or being in pain, *feels like* to someone in pain. The real mind-body problem becomes not whether pain is a physical state, but whether how pain feels to someone in pain is a physical property of pain. And it is materialism about this feature — how pains feel — that is so implausible; indeed, it is difficult to see how materialists could begin to answer the question of what such properties are, or even frame the question.

Such is the problem of phenomenal properties. Shoemaker, Block and Fodor, Keith Campbell, Kripke, and Mackie all seem to endorse various versions of it; Rosenthal and Armstrong worry about

---

[9] *Philosophical Review* 83 (October 1974): 435-50.

it.[10] To put my rejoinder to this objection most bluntly: I do not think there are any such things as phenomenal properties, at least as I (and their proponents) have characterized them. The standard examples of phenomenal properties of mental states are not properties of mental states at all, and indeed mental states do not appear to those who have them except in ways harmless to materialism. The question of why there seem to be phenomenal properties raises broader and independently interesting questions in the theory of reference, questions I touch on below. And of course any attempt to explain phenomenal properties away should be compatible with the plain facts of introspection.

Let me begin with Mackie: "We could say that pain is just the C-fibre stimulation. But this leaves untouched its phenomenal quality, how it feels to me, in fact its painfulness" (loc. cit., 169). Mackie thus takes the painfulness or hurtfulness of pain as typical of the "phenomenal qualities in experience [that] form an . . . obstacle [for physicalism]" (ibid., 167), and so far as I can tell most proponents of the phenomenal property objection would agree that the hurtfulness of pain is the one thing left unexplained by the physical properties of any process pain is supposed to be. But surely hurtfulness is not a property of pain, or of being in pain, at all. Pains do not hurt, nor do they present a painful experience. Pains *are* hurtings; to say that "*A* is in pain" is just to say that something is hurting *A*. All sorts of things hurt: physical objects, bodily parts, social situations. In one of his movies, Jerry Lewis confesses that "what I don't like about pain is that it hurts." Like all gags, this one works (to the extent it does) because it contains incongruity, the incongruity here being a blend of falsehood and tautologicality. Of course pains hurt in the sense that to be in or experience pain is for there to be something hurting you. In this sense it is analytic that pain involves hurting. It is just here that the reification of pain is so misleading. If pain is turned into an object, the

---

[10]S. Shoemaker, "Functionalism and Qualia", *Philosophical Studies* 27 (1975): 291-315; N. Block and J. Fodor, "What Psychological States are Not", *The Philosophical Reivew* 81 (1972). Keith Campbell, *Body and Mind* (New York: Anchor, 1970); Kripke, *op. cit.*,; J. L. Mackie, *Problems from Locke* (Oxford: Oxford University Press, 1976), pp. 167-69; D. M. Armstrong, "Epistemological Foundations for a Materialist Theory of the Mind," *Philosophy of Science* 40 (June 1973); 189-91; D. Rosenthal, "Mentality and Neutrality," *Journal of Philosophy* 73 (July 15, 1976): 386-415.

analytical connection between pain and hurtfulness irresistibly suggests that the *thing that hurts* is pain, that pain is the bearer of the property of hurtfulness. As is well known, what the materialist identifies with a physical state is the state of being in pain. He takes *A*'s being in pain (say) as having the logical form, roughly, of "*A* is aware of his toe," and he holds further that *A*'s being aware of his toe is a state *p* of *A*'s nervous system. The problem of what to do with *p*'s phenomenal hurtfulness simply does not arise.

But this reply seems like a paltry evasion of the antimaterialist's point. Surely *A* is aware of his being in pain in a way in which no one else is aware of *A*'s being in pain. This "how *A*'s pain appears or makes itself known to *A*" constitutes what is distinctively sentient about *A*'s being in pain, and—even if *A*'s being in pain is a physical state—it has so far eluded the physicalist's net. This reply can be amplified. First, *A* is or can become aware of his pain in a way no one else can; *A*'s awareness is noninferential and unerring. Second, not every awareness of a bodily part is a hurting. *A*'s having a pain in his leg cannot be parsed simply as "*A* is aware of his leg," for *A* may be aware of his leg even if his leg is tickling him, or not bothering him at all. There must be something about how *A* is aware of his leg that makes his awareness of the painful sort. And not only must his awareness of his leg have some trait which makes it pain-awareness rather than, say, tickle-awareness; *A* must be aware of this difference, for, as was noted, *A* has no peer in telling when he is in pain. And, it seems, the only way *A* can discriminate his being in pain from his being tickled is by noticing some trait that distinguishes pain-awareness from tickle-awareness. Yet materialism is mum about this trait. Even if pain-awareness is itself a physical state, it does not follow that the trait that distinguishes pain-awareness is itself a physical trait. The immediate access we have to our pains now appears to be immediate access to that trait which makes them pains and by which we identify them. Since we apparently have no comparable access to any physical state or physical traits or physical states, these second-order traits of psychological states give every promise of eluding materialism and establishing property dualism at the second level. Perhaps, indeed, painfulness is not an example of a phenomenal trait; perhaps we have no words that clearly and unambiguously refer to such phenomenal traits. Nonetheless they exist. This attack seems to reinforce the deliverances of common sense.

The materialist might charge in return that the argument just adumbrated proves too much by working against every scientific identity. Every interesting scientific identity $a = b$ requires that $a(= b)$ have been noticed in two different ways, that "a" be introduced into language as the name of the object exhibiting one trait, and that "b" be introduced as the name of the object exhibiting some other, independent trait. "Lightning = electrical discharge" is informative because "lightning" was introduced as denoting those flashes in the sky, while "electrical discharge" was introduced to denote what had some other trait. But then, even if $a = b$, a dualism remains between the "a"-introducing and "b"-introducing *properties*. Even if lighning is electrical discharge, the one phenomenon is not completely reducible to the other, since the trait that makes (some) electrical discharge lightning, or by which we identify it as lightning, remains distinct from the trait by which we identify electrical discharges in general. But this result, says the materialist, is a reductio. Any argument which refutes the complete lightning-electrical discharge identification along with mind-body identification is valueless.

The phenomenal property dualist will reply that scientific identities usually rely on a dualism between the intrinsic nature of some phenomenon, and how that phenomenon appears to us. (Lightning's intrinsic nature is electrical, but it appears to us as flashes in the sky.) The properties by which we initially identify the subjects of scientific reduction are, to a scientist, merely apparent, and he can simply hand over to the philosopher the question of what to make of the fact that some physical phenomena create sensory states in observers. But the materialist cannot do this; he cannot say that science has penetrated behind the sensory state pain induces in us, into pain's intrinsic nature. What his theory is about, after all, is pain, and pain is a sensory state. He abandons his position if he appeals to the sensory states certain physical states give rise to, for it was sensory states he was out to identify in the first place.

If this asymmetry can be sustained, the materialist cannot use the proves-too-much argument. He will have to pay closer attention to the claim that each of us is aware of his psychological states. It is indeed a fact that we are aware of our inner states and that we can discriminate, identify, and reidentify them. Some philosophers have, perhaps, denied this; if so, they have denied the obvious. It should also be obvious how the materialist will want to characterize introspective awareness. I am aware of my pain just when I am aware of one of my awarenesses; when (say) I am aware of my awareness of my leg—or, perhaps, when I am aware that I am aware of my leg. My second-order awareness is a physical state, having my awareness of my leg as its object, just as my primary awareness has my leg as its object. Since the materialist takes my awareness of my leg to be a physical state, he finds no anomaly in classing both conditions of legs and awarenesses as suitable objects of awareness. Both are physical states of physical objects. Nor need he decide which — awarenesses or legs—are *the* objects of awareness. He sees no incoherence in the common sense idea that both can be objects of awareness, although of course no *single* awareness can have both a leg and an awareness of a leg as its object. The materialist's job is to show that this conception of introspective awareness is compatible with the facts about introspection lately canvassed and to show, in particular, that these facts do not require the introduction of appearance-properties.

A Closer Look at Inner Sense

It would embarrass the materialist if we were always and necessarily—infallibly—aware of our inner states, for there are no logically self-revealing physical states. Not only is it unclear how a physical state could necessarily reveal itself, but it also is unclear why there should always be some large system present for that state to reveal itself to. So if we were logically or metaphysically necessarily aware of our inner states, materialism would be wrong. But we are not thus necessarily aware of our inner states. I try below to characterize "privileged access" positively; for now, let me suggest that the very idea of infallible awareness wars with Hume's ban on necessary connections between distinct existences. My awareness of my foot is one thing, and my awareness of that awareness is another. If, as seems likely, Hume is right, the first cannot entail the second. But surely, you will protest, it is inconceivable that I experience searing pain without being aware of it. (I omit here the question of unconscious pain, to give the antimaterialist his best case.) Now the slogan underlying this protest—"you can't be in pain without being aware of it'"—plays on the ambiguity of "of" in "awareness of pain". "Of" here can be the "of" of identity, as in "a meal of meat and potatoes." So taken, there indeed cannot be a pain without an awareness of pain, precisely because the awareness *is* the pain. But so taken, it does not yield a case in which one awareness implies the existence of another. If, on the other hand, the "of" in "awareness of pain" is understood as the object-taking "of," any suggestion that the existence of a pain necessitates awareness of it vanishes. You have to be aware to be in pain; this is all the slogan supports. Consider this analogy. I hold object *o* up to mirror *m: m* reflects *o,* and I refer to "the image of the reflection of *o* by *m.*" Since a reflection is an image, it is logically necessary that when there is a reflection there is an image of the reflection. But suppose another mirror m^1 reflects *o* being reflected by *m.* We might also call what m^1 shows "an image of the reflection of *o* by *m.*" This second "image of" does not involve the "of" of identity, and it is in this sense merely contingent that there is both a reflection and an image of the reflection. Conflating these two senses of "image of" might suggest that reflections violate Hume's law by being logically connected to images they are distinct from.

I find this rejection of infallibility to cohere with my experience of what it is like to be a conscious being. Most of the time I am aware of the world, including that especially prized part called my body. Ocassionally, I notice facets of this ongoing awareness; that, for example, the pain in my ankle is distracting me from some philosophical argument. But most of my time is taken up with unselfconscious monitoring of my ankle and things beyond. Indeed, the notion of awareness covers a rather wide area. It ranges in meaning all the way from such paradigms of confrontation as being aware of a bull charging at you, to the mere being apprised of some state of affairs. My second order awarenesses need not be of precisely the same sort as my primary awarenesses. There are pains I take no reflective note of; when I broke my ankle, I was aware of my ankle to the extent that my attention was consumed by it. And, as I noted, there are times when I take note of the fact that I am aware of my leg. So the materialst's account of introspection need not multiply identical awareness.

Let me sketch briefly what I take to be the correct positive characterization of our knowledge of our inner states. It is, first, *incorrigible;* by this I mean that it is causally impossible for someone to be wrong in thinking that he is in a certain mental state, if he so thinks. Second, one is *directly aware* of his inner states, where this means that, if *A* believes he is in inner state *b,* this belief is noninferential. The materialist sees you as so hooked up to your own nervous system that, if your nervous system is in state *b* and you decide to determine what state your nervous system is in, your nervous system must, of causal necessity, lapse into state *b',* awareness of *b.* The move to *b'* involves no inference. Both incorrigibility and direct awareness are weaker than infallibility. It may be causally impossible for me to go wrong about something, and I may come to believe it without inference, even if it is logically possible for me to be mistaken. Directness and incorrigibility are, moreover, independent. I might form spontaneous, noninferential beliefs that were usually wrong—about the surface of Alpha Centauri, say. It is also possible (indeed probable) that some of my inferential beliefs approach incorrigibility. The causal structure of the world evidently insures that beliefs acquired from the *Guiness Book of World Records* are true.

I will say more about this view of introspection below; I want now to trace the issue of introspection back to that of phenomenal properties. The antimaterialist is prone to object at this point that even if everything I have said about introspection is correct, I have quietly ignored how one learns to refer to and discriminate inner states. Is it not obvious that we master these skills by noticing some property that pain-awarenesses have but tickle-awarenesses (say) lack? And if so, are we not once again left with appearance-properties of inner states? But we need not follow this appealing line. It is in fact perfectly possible to account for recognition of and reference to inner states without mention of any properties of inner states that we use to discriminate one from another. (I argue below that the foregoing argument derives its appeal from the Frege-Russell theory of reference, which has in recent years been discredited on grounds independent of present concerns.[11]) The account I favor centers on the topic-neutral approach to psychological terms, some version of which is clearly supported by common-sense reflection on how children learn to use words like pain.[12] A child first encounters the word "pain" when his parents notice that he has sustained some bodily damage. He impales himself on a splinter, and his mother commiserates, "Oh, how that must hurt." A child learns "pain" in terms of events involving bodily injury; the referential force of "pain" is closely tied initially to "what goes on when *e*," where *e* is some description of a public event. The tie is reference-fixing, not synonymy. Such a view concedes that pains could exist in the absence of *e,* and could have existed even if they did not occur when *e* did. It also accommodates the intuition that there is "more to" pain than its causal role. These are facts that "analytic" topic-neutralism has dif-

[11]Kripke, *op. cit.,* K. Donnellan, "Reference and Definite Descriptions," *Philosophical Review* 75 (1966): 281-304.

[12]The reader might compare the remarks that follow with A. E. Falk's "Learning to Report One's Introspections," *Philosophy of Science* 42 (September 1975): 223-41, a paper which, unfortunately, came to my attention only after completion of *MMB* and the present paper. Despite some difficulties in detail, Falk's approach is quite similar to mine.

ficulty with. Thus, the reference-fixing account of how a child learns to name his experiences is compatible with the child noticing what he experiences when its public occasion is absent. The child, then, will usually come to notice that what goes on when he stabs himself may happen in the absence of points and blades, and that this is, more precisely, what his linguistic community calls "being in pain". In Skinnerese, the nonpublic stimulus gains control over the response "yes" to the question "Are you in pain?" This is how the child eventually distinguishes the states from the circumstances which accompany them. I suspect that children acquire the *general* ability to identify psychological states by extending this process. This would explain the semiautonomy of the introspective reports of adult speakers. However, even an adult can tell others what is going on in his mind only via descriptions that depend in complex ways on descriptions of public circumstances. In any case, if the materialist is right, the stimulus that eventually suffices to elicit "yes" to "pain?" is a state of the nervous system.

Fall in with me in ignoring the complaint that an account of word-learning is not necessarily an account of word meaning. I cannot see that there is any more to understanding the meaning of introspective language than the sort of genetic account of it I have sketched. Still, have I not persisted in avoiding the issue of how the child *tells* when the state first identified as "pain" has recurred? Surely, one supposes, it must be by noticing some property that distinguishes pain from other inner states. But this supposition is mistaken. A subject can be conditioned to respond to a certain feature of situations even if he does not explicitly notice it or is unable to describe it. This general fact about conditioning holds in particular about the conditioning of verbal responses. We can all tell an ironic remark from a sarcastic one, but most of us cannot say right off what distinguishes irony from sarcasm. Most of us can tell a Rembrandt portrait from a Hals or Rabelais's ribaldry from Groucho's, although it takes an art critic to articulate *what* differentiates a Hals from a Rembrandt, what features cue our classificatory responses. It is for *us,* the outsiders commenting on a subject and his conditioning, to describe what he has been conditioned to respond to, and how he has been conditioned to respond. The subject himself need not use this description as his reason, ground, or criterion for his verbal or nonverbal responses; nor need he know that his cue fits this description. Thus, not only can *A* use "pain" to refer to what goes on when . . . without realizing what he is referring to; he need not use any property of his pain at all to guide his saying that he is in pain. We are all trained to assent to "I am in pain" when a certain event occurs; it may take detailed scientific investigation to delineate what prompts this response. There is, then, no pressure to say that one must notice some property of pain in order to talk about it—although of course there are *causal* questions about just what events prompt just what introspective reports. One must of course be able to "notice pain" in order to talk about it, if "notice" just means "be able to respond differentially to". But this weak sense of "notice" is useless to the phenomenal-property theorist, since the whole issue is what endows an introspector with the ability to respond differentially to his inner states. Unless it is the detection of properties that distinguish pains from other internal states, the phenomenal-property objector has gotten nowhere.[13]

I note in passing that this external approach to reference suggests a shift from an object-linguistic to a metalinguistic perspective in other areas of philosophy of language. Thus, I think, the best way to reckon a speaker's ontological commitment is to formulate, in the language of our own best scientific theory, the truth-conditions of his utterances, and reckon him ontologically committed to the values of the variables of our scientific metalanguage. Similarly, we can take two of a speaker's predicates to "express the same property" if our scientific metalanguage assigns them the same satisfaction-condition. (Properties remain virtual.) By divorcing our description of the reality a speaker is addressing from what he thinks about it, the present proposal permits nontrivial attributions of property-identities to speakers.[14] If we follow what Bennett calls the "meaning-nominalist's strategy"[15]—and construe absolute semantic notions as reducible to their person-relativized counterparts—an "absolute" account of nontrivial property identities emerges.

---

[13]Smart falters slightly when he writes that his topic-neutral analysis "depends on the possibility of our being able to report that one thing is like another without being able to state the respect in which it is like" (loc. cit., 42). Smart may be conceeding, unnecessarily, that when I say "I see a lemon-colored after-image", I do at least have to recognize that what is now going on is like what goes on when . . . Even this is not so. I can be trained to treat two things similarly even without forming the propositional belief that they are similar.

[14]I discuss these proposals at greater length in *MMB,* Chapter 1.

[15]See J. Bennett, "The Meaning-Nominalist's Strategy," *Foundations of Language* 10 (1973): 141-68; see also his *Linguistic Behavior* (New York: Cambridge University Press, 1976), passim.

Let us return to the main issue. If the present account of reference to inner states is correct and—as I think it is—intuitively satisfying, why is it so natural to suppose that we identify inner states by phenomenal properties? Part of the answer, we saw, is the reification of inner states. Another part is the description theory of reference, which holds that you refer to and reidentify *x* by using some description *F* which you know or believe *x* uniquely satisfies. Since we refer to pain, there must be some description (or, in the material mode, property) that pains satisfy and by which we refer to them. The conditioning view of reference, which lets *us* attribute unique properties to referents but does not have to endow referrers with knowledge of these properties, renders gratuitous the appeal to phenomenal, or any other, pain-properties. But this does not go far enough toward explaining the intuition that we identify inner states phenomenologically, by how they appear to us. *Why* does the description theory seem so natural for "pain"? Because, I think, names and other purely indexical expressions are easily transmuted into predicates, which predicates appear to express a distinctive property of the named item, that *in virtue of which* the name applies where it does. We think of this property as explaining how we reidentify the named object, or classify together the members of the named class or natural kind. A well-known *New Yorker* cartoon shows several 16th-century Frenchmen seated around one paricularly hearty-looking fellow. One of his companions is saying to him, "Ah, M. Rabelais, there is simply so word for your earthy sense of humor." We chuckle, for we have just the word for that purpose: "rabelaisian." But just having this word does not mean that we can do what Rabelais's companions could not: say what it is that makes an anecdote of the sort Rabelais recounted. It still takes an external observer to articulate the cues of our intuitive judgment that "The Miller's Tale" and *Animal House* are rabelaisian while "The Importance of Being Earnest" and "The School for Scandal" are not. "Rabelaisian" is simply a name for whatever it is that a certain group of jokes and stories have in common.[16] Trouble starts when we think "rabelaisian" tells us what the members of this group have in common, that ingredient which Rabelais's contemporaries found ineffable. We then erroneously suppose we have filled the explanatory blank that Rabelais's contemporaries could not. Strawson notes that descriptions like "The Round Table" can "grow capital letters" and turn into names.[17] Conversely,

[16]Putnam has emphasized the indexical character of many seemingly descriptive words; see his "The Meaning of 'Meaning.'"

[17]See P. F. Strawson, "On Referring", *Mind* 59 (1950): 320-44.

names can become predicates and have their indexicality eclipsed.

So it is, I think, with pain. "Pain" begins life as an indexical expression, naming that *x*, whatever it is, that goes on when my skin is damaged. The name "pain" is then transformed into the adjective "painful." It applies to occurrences similar to my first pain, but we lose sight of the fact that (roughly speaking) it means "what is similar to that initial *x*" and take it to express what that similarity is, what it is that is cuing our classificatory response. In the material mode: painfulness comes to be viewed as a determinate observable property of pain. Add to this the phenomenon of privileged access, and it is only a small step to the view that painfulness is a property of pain that only the sufferer notices, an appearance-property of pain.

Let me stress that in repudiating appearance-properties, I am not denying that primary awarenesses, like (being in) pain, have some properties. The pain in my ankle, for example, is an awareness I would rather be without. But "being wished absent by me" is certainly no phenomenal property; it it shared by my pain and my more tiresome students. Nor is it difficult to explain why pains have such properties. Evolution has shaped me to be concerned to eliminate what co-occurs with damage to my skin, precisely because, on the whole, my skin is being damaged when what usually happens when my skin is damaged occurs. If my ancestors had any competitors who didn't mind the inner state damaged skin causes, these competitors were eliminated in short order. That is why I have a spontaneous tendency to try to alleviate pain—although, to be sure, there is more that needs saying about the causal mechanisms linking pain and the motor centers. You may complain that evolution has confused cause and effect here; but how better is nature to help her creatures avoid damage than by building in a dislike of what damage is a sufficient condition for?

This account of inner awareness leaves other questions open. When I am aware of my awareness of my foot, what is the "I" that has this second-order awareness? I can see no reason why it cannot be the same "I" that is its object—the central nervous system, or whatever persons turn out actually to be. In *MMB* (chapter 5) I describe a sealed machine *M* containing two lightbulbs hooked up in series and so connected to a bulb on *M*'s surface that the brightness of the external bulb directly and incorrigibly registers which internal bulb is on. It will not do to say that it is the outside bulb that monitors *M*'s internal state; it is how the outside bulb is connected to the interior bulbs, and so on. Now I take "*M* is a self-monitoring system" as just a summary of all the facts I am supposing to obtain. Of course, *M* cannot monitor how *M* is monitoring *M*'s inner states—only a larger system M^1, containing *M*, could do that. But if M^1 did keep an eye on how its part *M* monitored itself, M^1 would also be a self-monitoring system. To be sure, to every self-monitoring system there corresponds a point beyond which it cannot monitor its own self-monitoring; but since the same is true of ourselves, this is no objection to a physicalistic model of the supposedly transcendental self. Such models also clarify the idea of Ryle and Quine[18] that our knowledge of our inner states is the same in principle as the knowledge others have of them. This is false so far as directness goes; your knowledge of my inner states is always inferential. But incorrigibility does come out a matter of degree. If I know how *M* is built, I can infer *M*'s inner state from the condition of its outer bulb almost as reliably as the outer bulb itself reacts to *M*'s inner state. Certainly the subject of my beliefs about my inner states has turned out to be rather pedestrian. There is no significant difference between "Am I now in the state I was in when last I banged my elbow?" and "Am I now wearing what I wore when I last banged my elbow?"[19]

A quite different objection is this: since language teacher *B* has no direct control over learner *A*'s inner states, how does *B* know that what *A* finds similar to what goes on when *A* is jabbed by a pin, is what *B* finds similar to what goes on when *B* is jabbed by a pin? If *B* has to trust that *A*'s sense of similarity is sufficiently like his own, has not the present account foundered on the problem of other minds? No—all language-learning and all conditioning whatever presuppose this preestablished harmony. Wittgenstein and the Intuitionists have made it clear that mathematics would be impossible as a human activity if children had no innate tendency to apply general rules the same way in new situations. Language is possible because evolution has shaped us to agree on what is similar to what. *B*'s assumption that *A* spontaneously generalizes *A*'s conditioning stimuli as *B* does is a special case of an assumption that must be made by any teacher of a word, and by any account of human linguistic competence.

---

[18]This view is a steady theme in Ryle's *The Concept of Mind;* see also Quine's "Mental Entities" in *The Ways of Paradox,* 2nd ed. (Cambridge: Harvard University Press, 1976).

[19]This physical model can be extended to cover optional activation of the exterior light, and "training" the machine to shift its attention from the external events that turn on its interior lightbulbs to the state of the lightbulbs themselves.

But this assumption, when made for the teaching of words for public objects, is confirmed by the observed agreement in usage among trainees; there can be no such direct verification when it comes to teaching words like "pain." True, but as Falk (loc. cit.) argues, there can be indirect verification that (all) our trainee(s) use "pain" to refer to the same thing. We might discover that people in our linguistic community respond affirmatively to "pain?" just when their central nervous system is in a certain state. In fact, the only grounds for supposing that our trainees are not responding to this CNS state itself is the idea that what is really controlling their affirmative response is how this CNS state appears to them. But we have seen that there is no positive support for such a view, and considerations of simplicity militate against it. We've got the CNS state for them to be responding to uniformly; why haul in anything else?

It is obvious that I am presupposing a broadly behavioristic conception of language: we are conditioned to respond verbally to certain stimuli, and the objects of reference are, roughly speaking, the causes of these stimuli (or, in certain cases, the stimuli themselves). I will end by defending this presupposition against the widely-held view that Chomsky has undermined any possible behavioristic approach to language. This supposition is groundless; Chomsky has shown at most that no stimulus-response theory can adequately account for the acquisition of *syntax*. I have elsewhere criticized Chomsky's arguments to the effect that the grammar of natural languages is too complicated to be learned by induction on the acoustical properties of sentences that children are told are acceptable.[20] But even if these arguments are sound, they are not to the present point. They concern syntax and its acquisition, and have no tendency to impugn a purely behavioristic account of semantics. For all that we may or must be born with the active-passive transformation, or the idea of all possible grammars, we may still learn to associate word and object as Quine has supposed.

I might be reminded that some followers of Chomsky, Katz, Vendler, and Fodor, for example,[21] have attempted to carry Chom-

---

[20]See my "On Explanation and Prediction in Grammar (and Semantics)", *Midwest Studies in Philosophy* 2 (1977): 128-37; see also *MMB*, Chapter 6.

[21]J. Fodor, *The Language of Thought* (New York: Crowell, 1975); J. Katz, *The Philosophy of Language* (New York: Harper & Row, 1966), pp. 244-82; see also Z. Vendler, *Res Cogitans* (Ithaca: Cornell University Press, 1972), esp. p. 141.

sky's apriorism into the realms of semantics. I find the considerations these writers have so far presented to lack force. If I understand him correctly, Katz holds that, because a systematic semantic classification of the expressions of English uses certain maximally general categories, the ideas corresponding to these categories must be innate. But surely more needs to be done in a way of justifying the "psychological reality" of what may prove to be an artifact of Katz's semantic theory. The point is a familiar one, but one that has never been adequately answered. Moreover, even if certain concepts are intrinsically maximally general, it is not clear why they, and the words learned for them, could not be learned by the same techniques involved in the mastery of lower-level concepts and their associated words.

Part of the obscurity of Katz's semantic apriorism is its conception of communication as the encoding and decoding of sentences into messages composed of "ideas."[22] Fodor carries this line of thought further; since all communication is the translation of what we hear or read into the language of thought, we must already have the language of thought before we understand anything said to us; we must, that is, have been born with translations of every possible English sentence. But this means that even such ideas as 'inaccessible cardinal' and 'the average rainfall in Borneo' are innate. Let us take this as a reductio of the idea that understanding the spoken word consists in mapping it to an unheard, unspoken word, or that everything that happens when we understand the spoken word is something we *do*. Finally: even if some more moderate version of semantic apriorism is correct, it would not follow that we learn to associate the names for psychological states with psychological states themselves in any other way than purely inductive conditioning.

MICHAEL E. LEVIN.

THE CITY COLLEGE, CUNY.

---

[22]See Harman, "Language, Thought and Communication," in Gunderson, ed. Harman correctly diagnoses Katz's mistake as a mistake about how language is used to communicate, but he goes wrong in opposing to Katz's view of language the view, attributed to Quine, that language is primarily used for thinking. Quine also sees the use of language for communication as at least as important as its use in cogitation; Quine simple has a different, less intellectualistic, view of *how* language is used in communication.

MATERIALISM AND DISEMBODIED MINDS

I.

"If you say: 'I can imagine myself being a disembodied spirit. Wittgenstein, can you imagine yourself as a disembodied spirit?'—I'd say: 'I'm sorry. I [so far] connect nothing with these words.' "—Ludwig Wittgenstein, *Lectures and Conversations on Aesthetics, Psychology and Religious Belief,* ed. Cyril Barrett (Oxford: Basil Blackwell, 1966), p. 65 *(Lectures on Religious Belief,* III).

Many, of whom I am one, would say that if this incomprehension is where one is led by Wittgenstein's conception of our mental life, that is so much the worse for his conception of our mental life. Whatever the empirical facts about our futures, it certainly seems that there is a *sense* attached to the phrase 'disembodied existence'. The hypothesis that I shall survive as a disembodied mind, though it is supported by meager evidence and that from the most disreputable of sources, seems a hypothesis that is empirically testable, at least in principle (albeit asymmetrically, allowing its truth, should it be true, but not its falsity, should it be false, to be learnt). For, as P. F. Strawson says, it seems that the effort needed for imagining one's own disembodied existence "is not even great. One has simply to think of oneself as having thoughts and memories as at present, visual and auditory experiences largely as at present, even, perhaps—though this involves certain complications—some quasi-tactual and organic sensations as at present, whilst (a) having no perceptions of a body related to one's experiences as one's own body is, and (b) having no power of initiating changes in the physical condition of the world, such as one at present does with one's hands, shoulders, feet and vocal chords [*sic*]. Condition (a) must be expanded by adding that no one else exhibits reactions indicating that he perceives a body at the point which one's body would be occupying if one were seeing and hearing in an embodied state from the point from which one is seeing and hearing in a disembodied state" *(Individuals* [London: Methuen, 1959], p. 115). And so the hypothesis of one's own eventual disembodied existence will be tested, it seems, by a procedure no more taxing than that of waiting to see whether this easily imagined state of affairs ever occurs.

The suspicion, consequently, gnaws that Wittgenstein's failure to connect anything with the words 'disembodied existence' and 'disembodied spirit' comes not at all from the phrases' intrinsic unintelligibility but wholly from the logical tensions he feels between the disembodied-existence hypothesis and the particular conception of mind he wishes to uphold. Whatever the doubts, and they are legion, that Wittgenstein is an analytic behaviorist—whatever the doubts, that is, that he wishes in some sense to "reduce" mental states to behavior or dispositions to behave (say, by making mental states logical constructions out of the behavior and behavioral dispositions)—there is not the slightest doubt that he does accept a *behavioral-criterion* conception of mind states. Maybe Wittgenstein accedes to the view that the mind and its phenomena are something over and above behavior and behavioral dispositions (over and above in the same sense in which the antiphenomenalist asserts that physical things are something over and above sense data and appearances). But even if there is this accession, Wittgenstein will not abandon his insistence that inner processes stand in need of outward criteria. There must be, at least in principle, some way of checking the correctness of our use of the vocabulary for talking about the mental, and this check would, according to him, be impossible, even in principle, unless there were a necessary criteriological tie between external happenings and mental—that is, unless whenever there were a mental happening there were also necessarily the logical possibility of discovering in external events, bodily and behavioral, whatever is needed for warranting the assertion that there has been the mental happening. But in the case of disembodied existence, it seems plain that there are *ex hypothesi,* and so necessarily, no external happenings to be tied in this way with the disembodied existent's mental life: it seems that the disembodied person's mental life cannot, even as a logical possibility, be manifested in bodily behavior, for the simple reason that necessarily and *ex hypothesi* the person has no body to do the behaving.

If Wittgenstein was led to his inability to conceive disembodied existence because he judged all conceptions of it logically incoherent on his behavioral-criterion view of mind, he traveled a road that has since become a highway. There is among philosophers today virtually complete unanimity that behaviorism (by which I shall mean both analytic behaviorism and the behavioral-criterion view) renders disembodied existence a logical impossibility. D. M. Armstrong, for instance, in *A Materialist Theory of the Mind* (London: Routledge and Kegal Paul, 1968) devotes time and ingenuity to determining whether what he calls " 'Bundle' Dualists" and "Attribute theorists" can consistently admit the logical possibility of disembodied existence. But when he turns to behaviorism, he writes simply "It is clear that a Behaviourist cannot allow the logical possibility of the disembodied existence of a mind. Yet we saw that this seemed to be a meaningful conception" *(A Materialist Theory of the Mind,* p. 56). He neither amplifies nor explains, the assumption apparently being that anyone too thick to see the incompatibility right off is also too thick to benefit from philosophical argument on the point. It is taken to be just obvious that, if mental states are necessarily connected with behavioral and other bodily criteria, as they are for both analytic behaviorist and behavioral-criterion theorist, then denying the body necessarily denies also the mental states connected with it.

It is Armstrong's position, like mine, however, that if a theory of mind rules out the logical possibility of disembodied existence, this is a mark of the inadequacy of the theory. A materialist himself, Armstrong disbelieves that there is any disembodied existence, but he just as firmly, for reasons much the same as Strawson's, believes that we can understand the disembodied-existence hypothesis. He believes that disembodied minds, like purple cows, are a logical possibility, and just as he would be prepared to reject a theory of mind that entailed that purple cows are not logically possible, he is also prepared to reject any theory of mind that entails the logical impossibility of disembodied minds. Armstrong, hence, satisfied on this account as well as on a number of others that behaviorism fails, replaces it with a different materialist theory that he thinks fares better, the central-state theory of mind. Since for central-state materialism, it is a merely contingent fact that the mind is identical with something bodily—the brain and central nervous system—there is not, as there is for behaviorism, a necessary connection between the mind and body. It is not that, whenever there is a mental happening, there is necessarily the logical possibility of detecting the happening by examining bodily and behavioral events, but that there is, merely as an empirical matter of fact, some bodily—brain or nervous-system—event identical with the mental happening. If the central-state theory is true, the disembodied-existence hypothesis is, of course, false: states of a disembodied mind cannot be identical with states of the brain or central nervous system, and so, if all mental states are nervous-system states, there are no states of disembodied minds. But still the central-state theory, in entailing that the disembodied-existence hypothesis is mistaken, entails this only as a matter of fact, not as a logical truth. It does not say that disembodied existence is a logical impossibility: it is rather that the disembodied-existence hypothesis, as a rival hypothesis, could be true, but that the hard fact is that it is not.

Now, when the central-state theory acknowledges the logical possibility of disembodied existence, it is acknowledging (and acknowledges that it is acknowledging) that mental states could, as a logical possibility, be states of a Cartesian spiritual substance *(A Materialist Theory of the Mind,* p. 91). This I find exceedingly troubling. For though, as I have already said, I believe myself capable of conceiving existence in a disembodied state, I am not at all sure that I can conceive of a Cartesian spiritual substance. Hence, I am not at all ready to agree with Armstrong that the Cartesian dualist or the central-state theorist offers me the conception of disembodiment that is mine. In fact, what I wish to argue in this paper is that, paradoxically, the behaviorist in the last analysis has the best resources for providing an adequate conception of disembodied existence. Armstrong is taken from behaviorism to the central-state theory because (among other considerations) the central-state theory seems to him the only kind of materialism that lets him conceive what he is certain he can conceive. I am taken back from the central-state theory to behaviorism because I too want a theory of mind that explains the possibility of conceiving what I conceive. Once I see the disembodied mind that Armstrong's central-state theory grants to be intelligible, I realize that this is not what I am so sure *I* find intelligible: I must look elsewhere. When I reexamine behaviorism, I find that the reasoning, such as it is, that conduces to the conclusion that a behaviorist must deny the logical possibility of disembodied existence is flawed. Even though there is a necessary tie between, on the one hand, mental states, and on the other, bodies and behavior, it is evident to me that this necessary tie is not exactly as it has usually been understood and that, once it is properly understood, it no longer excludes what I find thinkable.

II.

But before trying to lay all this out, I should like to consider an argument that purports to prove that *no* theory of mind will ever elucidate our conception of disembodied existence. For, it is claimed, the unvarnished truth is that we have no such conception: it is only by taking conceptions of *other* states of affairs falling far short of really disembodied existence, and by putting, with no right and only because of confusion, the face of disembodied existence on these, that we so much as dream that we find disembodied existence conceivable. Max Hocutt ("Armstrong and Strawson on 'Disembodied Existence' " in this journal, XXXV, 1974-75) calls to our attention that Strawson, in drawing up a recipe for imagining oneself disembodied, makes it sound as if all we must do is imagine ourselves having experiences without experiencing our bodies. But, as Hocutt notices, even if we can imagine this, the conclusion that disembodied existence is imaginable is a *non sequitur.* For disembodied existence, we should have to imagine having experiences without *having* our bodies. That we can imagine having experiences without *experiencing* our bodies is insufficient for demonstrating this. As Hocutt says, "I think it is clear that we can imagine seeing while being unconscious of our eyes. Indeed, we do not need to imagine it. We often do it. We are seldom conscious of our eyes. Something must go wrong with vision for us to remember that it requires eyes in good working order. But what is needed to prove the possibility of disembodied existence is having experiences without having bodies. We must be able to see though dispossessed of eyes" (p. 53). According to Hocutt, as soon as we ask the correct question, whether we can imagine having experiences without *having* a body, the further question arises "by what mechanisms, if dispossessed of eyes and ears and nose and palate and skin and muscles, [I should] manage all this" (p. 54). He asks "What nonphysical processes of stimulation will replace [the normal] physical processes, and what organs will receive stimulation?" Again, "*How* will I be caused to perceive what I perceive, or will I perceive absolutely everything there is without cause?" And he believes that "unless we have *some* idea, no matter how vague, of the mechanisms by which we would perceive which goings-on in the world, then we do not have *any* idea of what it will mean to perceive those goings-on. The rule is that the better an understanding we have of *how* and *why* something takes place, the better an understanding we have of *what* takes place; and the less, the less" (p. 54).

Because we have absolutely no idea of the mechanisms by which a disembodied mind would experience his world, we have, Hocutt tells us, absolutely no idea of what it would be to be a disembodied mind experiencing a world. "I do not know what it would mean, and I doubt that it would mean anything, to say 'X sees without eyes.' It does sound suspiciously like 'Sam is an unmarried husband' " (p. 54). This is not to say that Hocutt takes 'One sees with one's eyes' to be *a priori* analytic: he himself resists drawing the analytic-synthetic distinction, but if it is drawn, he suggests that possibly one would want to consider the proposition *a posteriori* analytic.

Now, Hocutt is undoubtedly right in his claim that, if Strawson is saying what it sounds as if he is saying, then he has given us an irrelevant recipe. Nor is the recipe repaired by Strawson's proviso that it must be imagined that no one else shows signs of perceiving one's body: what must be imagined is not that no one shows such signs but that, signs shown or not, there is no body there. But Hocutt's further claim that being able to imagine or to understand what something is requires us to imagine or to understand the process by which it takes place is, it seems to me, preposterous. An acceptance of this principle would mean that, though I have *seen* how one of two apparently identical knives I own takes a sharper edge than the other, I should have to say that I do not understand *at all,* I cannot *begin* to imagine, what it is for one of the knives to take a sharper edge. For I have no idea *why* this occurs: to the best I can see, both knives were made of exactly the same materials on exactly the same automated machinery. No doubt there is an explanation, but I cannot begin to guess what it could be. At first I suspected that the steel used in the two knives was different, but there is expert assurance that this is not so. And in fact the serial numbers prove that the two were made from the same batch of steel within minutes of each other.

To say in this case that I have no understanding *at all* of what it is for one knife to take a sharper edge would be to accept an absurd "high redefinition" of 'understand'. Of course, I understand this: I can explain the different results I get on putting the two knives to a sharpening steel. I shall also act differently depending on which of the two knives I have within my grasp. And if doing and being able to do the like of this is not to understand *at all,* I do not know what understanding is. The language we use contains both the phrase 'understand what it is for one knife to take a sharper edge' and the phrase 'understand why one knife takes a sharper edge'. To claim with Hocutt that the two phrases draw no distinction is to be deaf to more that nuance.

The knife example is, I think, about as unfavorable to Hocutt as any example one will find. There are other examples that would be much more favorable. If I were to watch my skis disappear into thin air, it seems to me I might, without taking any literary license, very easily say that I just cannot understand at all what a disappearance into thin air is. I might even say that I cannot *begin to imagine* what such a disappearance is. And I cannot begin to imagine it even though I have seen it happen. This is, I think, an established use for 'I cannot understand at all . . . ' and 'I cannot begin to imagine . . . ' in connection with marvels. (The knife case, though it perplexes me, is not a marvel.) To say of a marvel that one cannot understand at all or begin to imagine what it is, is probably more often than not to say that one cannot understand how or why the marvel occurred. But though this example is somewhat more favorable to Hocutt, it is still not favorable enough. For suppose that disembodied existence, if it occurred, would be a marvel. And suppose also that to understand it would be to understand how it occurs, what its mechanisms are. This would require us to understand the processes involved in seeing without eyes, hearing without ears, tasting without palates. And so it follows that Hocutt would be right in holding that, to understand what a marvel like disembodied existence is, one would have to understand perceptual processes that he and we, anyway at the moment, do not understand. But this would be merely a technical victory for him. For even though it would not be a misuse of language to say that we are completely unable to understand what disembodied existence is, in the sense that we do not understand the perceptual mechanics involved, it still remains true that in another sense, the sense in which we were able to understand what it is for one knife to take a sharper edge, we may still understand what disembodied existence (or, for that matter, disappearance into thin air) is. We would understand disembodied existence in this sense, just provided that we knew what evidence would count in favor of the disembodied-existence hypothesis. If there is imaginable evidence we would be prepared to take as showing the truth of the hypothesis, we understand the hypothesis *in the only sense in which it must be understood for it to be a genuine hypothesis.* For it to be genuine, it is not needed that we be able to conceive what the mechanisms are that are involved in everything hypothesized; it is sufficient that we conceive what would show that the hypothesis is correct. Hocutt may say that, because 'One sees with one's eyes' is a queer kind of analytic truth, nothing can count in favor of the disembodied-existence hypothesis, if disembodied existence involves sight. But the fact that I can imagine (know what would count as) a freak with no eyes who nonetheless finds his way around as competently as I do—exhibits all the kinds of behavior I do—tells me that this is not analytic. Hocutt might, of course, say that this freak must have eyes at that part of his head to which, his behavior being like mine, he moves the book closer in order to read it better, even if his eyes are altogether unlike my eyes. But this is an evasion that does not aid Hocutt: the very criterion now for having eyes has become seeing, and so a disembodied mind will have eyes just provided he sees. Hocutt cannot go on to maintain that it is also analytic that eyes are *physical organs,* for our freak has eyes, where seeing is the criterion, but his eyes are, investigation discloses, not physical organs. Or if one wants to say they are physical organs, they are at least physical organs of a kind that cannot have their mechanics unfolded by the physical scientist and that, inasmuch as the organs are simply regions of physical space, a disembodied mind, seeing first from this perspective and then from that, might itself borrow.

Now, Hocutt could take a last stand on the contention that, unless we can conceive the mechanisms by which a marvel occurs, we shall never be prepared to accept anything as evidence that it has occurred. There is, however, nothing to recommend the acceptance of this contention. Both the freak example and the ski example should be enough to persuade us of this. There is much that I would be willing to accept as evidence for the skis' disappearance into thin air: my perceptions, your perceptions, and everyone else's perceptions, not to mention that it happens during every full moon. The point can be put generally, in a *reductio* argument. The principle that, unless we can conceive the mechanisms by which a marvel occurs, we shall never be prepared to accept anything as evidence that it has occurred leads directly to the conclusion that the word 'marvel' is, as a matter of logical necessity, a word we can never apply. For before we will be prepared to admit that something has occurred, we, according to the principle, must be knowledgeable about its mechanisms, and it will thus have ceased to be a marvel. But I take it that we all know that, whether there are marvels or not, there might be, and these marvels might be recognized as marvels by us: this is not a logical impossibility. Marvels, after all, are not miracles: there is nothing said about their being outside the causal economy. All that is said is that we have not yet discovered the causes of such striking anomalies. Consequently, I take it also that we all can see that the principle leading to the idea that recognizing marvels as marvels is a logical impossibility is to be spurned.

III.

The job remains to show how the behaviorist can make sense of the hypothesis of disembodied existence, how he can find, in bodily and behavioral phenomena, criteria for nonbodily existence. Most philosophers who try to bring out what would count in favor of the hypothesis concentrate exclusively on the first-person singular. Each, like Strawson or Armstrong, thinks he can understand what it would be for *him* to survive unembodied. Armstrong never asks whether anything would, for him, count in favor of *Strawson's* disembodied survival. But the behaviorist is not allowed similarly to shackle himself to the first-person singular. If there were bodily and behavioral criteria by which I told that I am a disembodied mind, the criteria, since bodily and behavioral, would at least in principle be as accessible to others as to me. And this is to say that, for others besides myself, there would be something that could count in favor of the claim that I have survived in a disembodied state. But, of course, there are no bodily and behavioral criteria for my recognizing my own existence as a disembodied mind. There may be criteria by which I recognize that my body no longer exists. But there are none by which I recognize that I have a mental life: I just, purely and simply, recognize this. But it does not suffice, for purposes of showing that the behaviorist can supply an intelligible conception of disembodied existence, to produce the criteria by which I could tell that my body no longer exists and to retail the recognition, unaided by criteria, that I have a mental life, and then to make an end of it. For, though I do not use criteria for determining that I have a mental life or for discovering what my mental life is like, every event and state constitutive of my mental life is, according to the behaviorist, one for which there are bodily and behavioral criteria by which it is logically possible for others to inform themselves about my mental condition. Hence, if the hypothesis of my disembodied existence makes sense to the behaviorist, there must be bodily and behavioral criteria by which others can, in principle, detect my mental life—and this even though I do not ever resort to these criteria myself. Thus, if the hypothesis of my disembodied existence makes behavioristic sense, there must also be something bodily and behavioral that could, as a matter of logical possiblity, count, for me, as evidence that Strawson is or has become a disembodied mind.

As a first step toward surveying the behaviorist's possible maneuvers here, let us look at other conceivable futures the philosophically uninitiated might think could be in store for Strawson. If he is not after death to return to dust and nothing more, and if he is not to survive in disembodied form, then, they might say, it must be that he is going to survive in a body that begins at the instant his original body is departed, and this body may be similar to or dissimilar from his original body (the body he now has will be called his original body); or he may cease to exist when he dies and then after a time be restored to life in the same body or in another body, again either similar to or dissimilar from the one he has at present. When he is introduced into a body, but a dissimilar one, the new body may be either an altogether new body or the old body of someone else either living or dead: he may inherit someone else's body, or he may chase someone out of that person's original body, or he may reside (amicably or not) in someone else's body at the very same time that that person continues to reside in it too.

Now, those unencumbered by philosophical preconceptions think this is the range of possible futures for Strawson. They think they can understand (i.e., know what would count as but not what would cause) Strawson's appearing at a later time in some world, this or another, as a very Strawsonian logician with views slightly more mature than those held by the Strawson we know or as a maiden who develops into a flautist the like of which the world has never experienced or as a person inhabiting Millicent Fenwick's body, whether a co-tenant with Millicent Fenwick or not. They think they know what it would mean to say that, despite the recent *photographies épatantes,* it is not really Miss Fenwick who smokes that pipe but Strawson in her body.

Moreover, the behaviorist is capable of understanding all this too. He can make sense of every one of these kinds of survival without abandoning his linchpin tenet that a mind and person's existence and survival must be understood by reference to bodily and behavioral criteria. He can besides argue that even the Cartesian dualist will understand each kind of survival by reference to these very same criteria. The Cartesian will as much as anyone else have to paint the cases so that the new Strawsonian logician, the developing flautist, and the ostensible Millicent Fenwick behave or might behave, given the right inducement, in particular ways—ways that show ostensible memories of living the old-Strawson life, perhaps even of living aspects of it that no one else knew about until the new-Strawson brought them up and his (or her) hearers checked out what he said; ways that are in character for Strawson; ways that exhibit the distinctively Strawsonian mind set.

That bodily and behavioral criteria are used for identifying a person does not entail that a person must, on pain of ceasing to be that person, continue always in the same body. Even in the case of the wildest bodily transfers, there will remain the possibility of bodily comportment criterial for the continuity of a single person. I am indeed aware that some, like Bernard Williams in "Personal Identity and Individuation" *(Proceedings of the Aristotelian Society,* LVII, 1956-57), would dissent from this. But I take it that Williams's objection that we have no criteria for distinguishing the cases of (a) the same person reembodied, and (b) a mere duplicate of the same person, is not ruinous. For if, as he thinks, the possibility of there appearing two ostensible Strawsons after Strawson's death shows the want of these criteria, the possibility of the living Strawson's splitting into two instantaneously before our eyes, each "Strawson" equally displacing the other, shows that there is a comparable want of criteria for distinguishing (a') a particular living person, and (b') a mere duplicate of him. Hence, the possibility of duplication is as much a problem for the identity criteria of living beings as of those reembodied. And hence, too, since we are prepared to accept bodily comportment as criterial for the identity of the living person in cases where we have only one body on our hands, and not two similar and similarly behaving bodies (two "Strawsons"), we should be ready to accept it also for the identity of the reembodied person in like circumstances. True, Williams argues that speaking of this reembodiment is vacuous, since there is no conceptual difference here between identity of character and exact similarity. But I think if what Williams is supposing is that with living beings, as against those undergoing reembodiment, there is always the logical possibility of monitoring their spatiotemporal movements, I shall have shown, by the time I finish, that even persons in transit from body to body admit of the *logical possibility* of such monitoring.

Now, if the reembodied person can show continuity with his former self, the question will at once be raised why a disembodied mind cannot just as easily behave in a continuity-betokening way.

The short answer is that, if it does so behave, or if it behaves in any way at all, it is simply not disembodied. It will be recalled that the second condition imposed by Strawson for the realization of disembodiment is that the disembodied mind have "no power of initiating changes in the physical condition of the world, such as one at present does with one's hands, shoulders, feet and vocal c...ords." Strawson allows how one could imagine a form of (he would say nonstrict) disembodiment where this second condition is not satisfied. But he calls this "a rather vulgar fancy, in the class of the table-tapping spirits with familiar voices" (p. 115). Strawson is apparently himself interested only in disembodiment of a more satisfyingly empty-blooded sort.

Even if one is not this abrupt with the sort of disembodiment that allows for physical behaving, one would be unwilling, I think, to take disembodiment of this stripe to be the full disembodied-existence story. To show me that the behaviorist can allow for the logical possibility of disembodied existence in *this* sense is as unappeasing as to show me that the central-state materialist can allow for the logical possibility of disembodied Cartesian spirits. I am sure that I am conceiving something less than Cartesian spirits when I think of the possibility of Strawson's being disembodied, but I am also sure I am thinking of something less (less in a different way) than the disembodiment that necessarily carries with it the power of the disembodied being to insinuate itself contemporaneously into the affairs of the bodily world. And so, even if this kind of disembodiment is to be considered an interesting variety, it is not the only variety I think I can understand.

What may seem worse, it is not even clear that this kind of "disembodiment" is disembodiment at all, strict or nonstrict. What one has here is something like a poltergeist who does things (in character, and all the rest, for Strawson), thereby manifesting Strawson's presence. But suppose he slams a door (let us suppose in Strawsonian wont), breaks three drinking glasses by tossing them into the fireplace, and rumples the rug to trip a Mr. Quine. By what right does one say that one disembodied person has performed all three of the acts? Could they not just as well have been done by three different agents? And furthermore, by what right does one say that all this was done by *any* person or persons? Why is it not that the door, drinking glasses, and rug have simply themselves behaved in irregular ways? Well, there is an order to the events. In life Strawson (let us pretend) habitually slammed doors, threw glasses, and set traps for Quine after

Strawson-Quine symposia. But this does not seem to be enough. Let us suppose, though, that somehow we warrant the claim that *one person* is responsible for all three acts. Why, even so, should we say that this is a *disembodied* person? Why not say that it was a person who, for a time, was embodied in the door, then later found embodiment in the glasses, and still later in the rug? Why should we say that what we are considering is disembodied rather than reembodied existence? (That this question must be asked was first drawn to my attention by Mary Mountford, in the spring of 1972. I have since noticed that the same point is made by Terence Penelhum in *Survival and Disembodied Existence* [London: Routledge and Kegan Paul, 1970], p. 42.)

Now so far, our hypothetically disembodied but behaving Strawson has been uncharacteristically voiceless. What would be gained by making him a speaking, as well as otherwise behaving, mind? In the first place, this could very well provide what is needed for saying that the three phenomena—slamming of door, shattering of glass, and rumpling of rug—are person-originated and, indeed, authored by a single person. For we can now imagine the imprecations that occur during the door banging and glass breaking to turn, but in the same distinctive voice, to chuckles and grunts and a self-satisfied "Aha: the carpet—I must do it" just before the crease is folded into the rug. We can hear the voice travel the room from door to cabinet to fireplace to floor level.

Would this be sufficient for saying also that the single agent involved is disembodied rather than possessed only of an existence through reembodiment in the door, glasses, rug, and such? The voice, after all, speaks as if it is outside the goods it acts on. Not only does it continue across the room when the glasses are not in motion, but the very comments it makes show that it views itself as external to the furniture. But now notice that the voice itself is a physical phenomenon, and the disembodiment hypothesis cannot be shown preferable to that of reembodiment (or perhaps it should here be called just physical realization) so long as there is a chance of identifying the person with the vocalizings. (This has long left Malcolm's idea that a person must have a face, but who cares?) It is only natural that a person whose existence was in these vocalizings would think of itself as external to the furniture, for it would *be* external. Nor would the fact that the voice speaks as if there is a person beyond the vocalizing—in saying things like "I should have kept silent" and "Oh dear, why did I say that?"—show that there is something disembodied that is speaking through the sounds: for the very speakings as if there is a person beyond the vocalizings can be construed as the person-realizations from which perspective there is regret about other realizations.

But by now the next step in unfleshing our conception of disembodied existence is clear. We must imagine our disembodied Strawson to utter not only rueful verdicts on what he should and should not have said, but also "reports" of how things went with him *between* the times when he spoke or otherwise behaved. Even if every time he speaks, he is reembodied or physically realized, the fact that he tells us of an active life of thought, perception, and feeling between the speakings, and that we can see both in his words and in his other behavior advances in his intellectual and emotional life such as, were Strawson embodied as we are, we should attribute to exposure to experiences of a wide-ranging assortment and to deep cogitation, can be taken as criteriological for saying that Strawson exists disembodied between his overt sayings and doings. Here, I think, we have some bodily and behavioral criteria—in Strawson's nonverbal behavior and his utterings—for saying that there is a truly disembodied person and not just a reembodiment. For, it seems to me, those utterings and doings can without implausibility be taken to be exactly what it would be for a disembodied person to manifest to us his existence. If anything counts as disembodied existence, it is something like this, the behaviorist might tell us; and when you think you can understand the notion of disembodiment, it is this you understand.

Still, the disembodiment here limned is the disembodiment of a person who *ex hypothesi* acts on or in the world of bodily existence, at least sometimes. But as I have already stressed, it seems to me that I am capable also of understanding a disembodied-existence hypothesis where there is no suggestion of such action. That Strawson will survive as a disembodied mind is, I am convinced, a hypothesis I understand, even if we suppose that he will have no power to act in the world of bodily existence or to speak in it either. But are there bodily and behavioral criteria for this more attenuated version of disembodied existence? Or am I deluding myself in thinking I both understand this and do not understand the Cartesian hypothesis?

From here on, the tale spins out so predictably that there is little profit in belaboring it. The tale is finished as soon as it is recalled that the behaviorist is requesting nothing more of the criteria offered for disembodied existence than that there be a logical possibility of discovering that they are fulfilled. And this means that the behaviorist can allow disembodied existence to be understood in terms of criteria described in the subjunctive mood, in counterfactuals. Even that disembodied existence which includes no conception of any actual impingement on the world of bodily existence can be understood counterfactually in terms of just such impingements. If Strawson will be out of touch with the bodily world so far as without power of acting on it, to say that he will nonetheless survive as a disembodied mind is still to say something about which there is a logical possibility of ascertaining the truth or falsity: for if he *were* to acquire the power of acting in the world, or of being reembodied or physically realized, the kind of power that on the other disembodiment hypothesis he was said to have, then it *would be* possible to see from his actions, just as one did in the other case, that Strawson had not indeed been insentient when he was overtly inactive. To the degree that it is intelligible that Strawson might acquire the power of acting in the world, and to the degree that it is intelligible that he might be tested for the experiences he had prior to the acquisition, it is also intelligible that he might have experiences as a disembodied person lacking the power of acting in the world. All this would parallel the behaviorist's understanding of the mental life of the totally mute and paralyzed: just as there is a logical possibility of finding the mental life of these poor souls reflected in their behavior, insofar as there is the logical possibility of their shedding their disabilities, so there is the logical possibility of finding a disembodied Strawson's mental life reflected in the behavior of a Strawson who has shed his inability to act on the world or to be reembodied. For the analytic behaviorist, though not necessarily for the behavioral-criterion theorist, it would thus be that all one asserts in asserting the disembodied existence of Strawson is the possibility, if Strawson were to acquire the ability to act in the world or were to be reembodied, of eliciting certain responses, behavioral, including vocal. This conception of disembodied existence would also in many respects bear a likeness to Malcolm's conception of dreams.

IV.

I have taken to task what I think to be a belief almost universally held by philosophers: that the behaviorist cannot understand, cannot allow for the logical possibility of, disembodied existence. I hope to have exhibited two sorts of disembodied existence that he can understand—one that involves the power of acting on the bodily world or of being reembodied or realized in it, and the other that is understood in terms of the logical possibility of acquiring this power. I myself am convinced that I can understand both sorts and that I cannot understand the Cartesian sort. I am forced to conclude, therefore, that of the two prevailing materialisms—behaviorism and the central-state theory—behaviorism, at least with respect to the understanding of disembodied existence, more adequately conforms to my intuitions than does any central-state theory that fails to incorporate a behaviorism. For the only conception of disembodied existence that this manner of central-state theory can afford us is the Cartesian. Beyond this, behaviorism possesses the altogether tidy advantage over its competitor (and even if the competitor incorporates behaviorism) of being consistent not only with the logical possibility of disembodied existence but (should it, surprise of surprises, be the case) with its actuality.

B. L. BLOSE.

UNIVERSIDADE FEDERAL DA PARAÍBA.

PEIRCE ON PHILOSOPHICAL HOPE AND LOGICAL SENTIMENT

One of the most confusing themes in Peirce's thought is his position on philosophical hope and the social sentiments necessary for reasoning. One might expect a philosopher to discuss hope, fair-mindedness, and the social principle when examining theological questions; it is usual for a philosopher to consider virtuous emotions and attitudes when exploring existential issues, or various positions in the domain of value theory. But for a logician-mathematician-scientist like Peirce to be so preoccupied with hope and selflessness is remarkable, and it deserves more attention than it has received.

What seems startling, in particular, is that a rather rigorous logician should sometimes speak as if logic were founded upon emotion. In one passage (1877), he explicitly states that " . . . logic depends on a mere struggle to escape doubt, which as it terminates in action, must begin in emotion . . ." (2.655)[1] He discusses the three social sentiments which are "presupposed in reasoning" as:

> . . . interest in an indefinite community, recognition of the possibility of this interest being made supreme, and hope in the unlimited continuance of intellectual activity . . .

A foundational connection between virtuous emotions and correct reasoning is very evident here. There are three sentiments required for the grounding or founding of logic. The connections are more difficult to characterize in Peirce's later writings. While he does not continue to specify the relationship as foundational, he does continue strongly to associate moral sentiments and attitudes with good logic, fruitful science, and adequate metaphysics.

For example, when classifying the sciences, Peirce is quite emphatic about the dependence of logic upon esthetics and ethics

---

[1]Throughout the article, I will follow the standard scholarly practice of citing volume and paragraph numbers when referring to the Collected Papers; thus 7.457 means volume 7 paragraph 457.
The Collected Papers of Charles Sanders Peirce, Volumes I-VI, eds. Charles Hartshorne and Paul Weiss, Cambridge, Belknap Press (Harvard University Press) 1931-1935; Volumes VII-VIII, ed. Arthur Burks, Cambridge, Belknap Press (Harvard University Press)1958.

(1.573-1.615). His post 1900 investigations of the architectonic clearly separate off the normative sciences as a distinctive domain of philosophy, and just as clearly point toward esthetics as the first normative science. While Peirce admits that he is no expert in esthetics, and does in fact write comparatively little about either esthetics or ethics, he is convinced that these two heuretic sciences are necessary for the founding of logic.

Since esthetics relates to feeling, ethics to action, and logic to thought (1.573-4), it is evident that Peirce does continue to speak as if there is a link between right feeling, right conduct, and correct reasoning. In these passages, he specifically describes self-controlled thought as a species of self-controlled action (1.606-607, 1.609-610), and talks about the correspondence between logical norms and moral laws. He declares that both ethics and logic are dependent upon esthetics because both the science of right action and the science of that species of right action which is right thought require that the science of ideals have already determined the ultimate aim.

Peirce views actions as serving ideals. The most moral actions are those which serve the "broadest, highest and most general possible" ideal (1.611). It is the task of esthetics, as the theory of the admirable in itself, to find that purpose behind all purposes. The normative sciences of ethics and logic are thus dependent upon esthetics.

Another example is Peirce's doctrine of agapasm. While he is not clear about the precise relationship, agapasm is a derivate of three components: 1) evolutionary doctrines 2) synechism (the principle of continuity) and 3) the Christian conception of love (6.287-289). The Darwinian model is rejected because of its alleged support for individualism and the Gospel of Greed (6.293-295, 297). Peirce views Darwin's explanatory scheme as an unintentional, but nonetheless forceful support for political and economic self-interest. In contrast to Darwin and his tychasm, he proposes a model of universal evolution which embodies creative love. He proposes to synthesize Christianity and evolutionary theory, to substitute a model which posits development as a loving process whereby the novel or irregularly deviant is brought into "harmony" with the already established (6.288).

As Darwin's views are said to support individualism, Peirce considers agapasm to be supportive of community, and in particular of the ever enlarging community in the long run. Agapasm has the advantage of recognizing positive sympathy among the peoples of an age. (6.304, 6.307, 6.315). It leaves room for the notion of communal or collective development of an idea. It recognizes that a worthy idea will not become dominant "needlessly," due to chance, but rather will increase its governing power through its own attraction for minds who encounter it. Peirce is a firm believer that an idea's value — its esthetic, moral, and cognitive significance — will lure the minds of each age to nurture it.

He prefers agapasm to anancasm because the former respectfully incorporates the notion of purpose. The idea which grows in the minds of a historical period, which is cultivated and developed by its participants, functions as the final cause or purpose of that age. A people are "welded," they are rendered homogenous or continuous, through their universal involvement with this aim. The purpose of an age calls out its members to participate in something which is beyond their individual capacities.

What should be clear from this brief description, is that Peirce's predilection for agapasm is not value-neutral. He has included theoretical considerations of a biological sort in his judgment. He has tried to reconcile his evolutionary views with his metaphysical commitments, i.e., with his commitment to synechism or the principle of continuity. However, the sum of his special scientific knowledge and his metaphysical commitments does not add up to his conclusion. There is clearly a valuative stance at stake here. He is decidedly in favor of that model which serves or does at the very least support the Gospel of Love. He is advocating a doctrine of evolution which encourages devotion to the highest purposes of another, and in general to the highest purposes of the continuing human community.

The two models already outlined i.e., 1) the dependence of logic upon esthetics and ethics, and 2) the value-laden character of Peirce's advocacy of agapasm — are supplemented by other, more scattered instances.

There is, for example, Peirce's position on the virtuous character of the scientist and the scientific philosopher. He firmly believes that philosophy ought to take on the scientific attitude, that it ought to adopt the habits of the laboratory and not the seminary. (1.44, 1.126-129). He lauds philosophers who focus upon ongoing inquiry and persistent observation, and not upon the dissemination of already organized knowledge. The scientific attitude involves several major moral virtues. The scientist is an exemplary person — (s)he is dedicated to truth for truth's sake (1.45), or has what is otherwise described as a "passion to learn" (1.47) or "intense desire to find things out" (1.14). As opposed to those who pursue learning for the sake of some "ulterior purpose," (1.45) the scientist qua scientist has one and only one aim in mind, i.e., the gaining of truth.

This characteristic "joy in learning" (1.127) brings other virtues along with it. Peirce holds that unless a scientist or scientific philosopher is single-minded and sincere with (her)himself, the "love of truth," will "melt away" (1.49). Honesty, fair-mindedness, and devotion to the life of inquiry, are necessary accompaniments to the desire to learn, if that desire is to function effectively. Probity and industry (1.576) are required to cultivate the life of investigation. Cognitive flexibility and intellectual humility are needed to fortify the scientific spirit (1.13-14, 1.55).

Peirce goes so far as to say that there are no criminals among those who have greatly contributed to the growth of knowledge (1.576). He talks about "true" inquirers as having a "lofty character" and suggests that there is a correlation between minor "obliquities" and lack of scientific success. In sum, he may be held to believe that ". . . on the whole, scientific men have been the best of men" (1.49).

II

Clearly Peirce does not abandon the connection between philosophy and the special sciences on the one hand, and right emotions, attitudes, and values on the other. His later writings manifest a strong, even if not a clearly demarcated relationship, between purely theoretical parameters and emotional and/or value-laden characteristics.

This finding is significant for several reasons. To begin, we need only recall our opening remarks about the unusual relationship between a logician-mathematician-scientist, and his preoccupation with values and moral emotions. Like Plato, Peirce seems to have a marked tendency to connect the true with good. Then there are the internal inconsistencies. At the same time that he talks about scientists and scientific philosophers as the best of persons, he also makes a clear distinction between heuristic sciences and practical sciences, between sciences whose task it is to analyze and pursue truth, and sciences (or arts) which aim to guide conduct, or promote the useful (1.45, 1.50, 1.55-7, 1.76).

In an uncharacteristic vein, Peirce is quite emphatic about the clear-cut nature (1.618) of this distinction. The sciences of discovery, the speculative or heuretic sciences, are not meant to guide behavior. He distinguishes between ethics and morals (1.577, 1.573, 1.667), and only allows the latter to regulate practice. This is because it is not a heuristic science, and is therefore properly independent of theoretical reflection.

In a doctrine which Peirce labels as "philosophical sentimentalism," (1.632) he makes explicit his firm belief that conduct must be governed by sentiment and instinct. These subconscious roots of cognition form the basic substance of the person. They are sufficient to guide everyday affairs and all "matters of vital importance." In point of fact, they are more masterly than reason when the task at issue is practical. As the scientist is corrupted if (s)he pays attention to an "ulterior purpose" or considerations of utility, so everyday affairs are practically and morally endangered by a theoretical approach to their management (1.666, 1.655, 1.633-4).

In viewing philosophical sentimentalism as a kind of conservatism, Peirce emphasizes the notion of conservation. The moral rules which a culture teaches to its young are the product of tradition. They are a repository of the wisdom which experience has taught humankind over the ages. They contain a residual lesson which has been modified and corrected through cumulative experience. Situated in common sense, instinct, and the sentiments, they rule human conduct with a wisdom that no individual intellect can match.

If one places Peirce's views on the architectonic and on philosophical sentimentalism side by side with the connections between theory and virtuous emotions and attitudes that we have already discussed, then problems of internal inconsistency emerge clearly. Peirce seems to want to have it both ways. Heuretic sciences must be disconnected from the regulation of conduct, at the same time that ideals, virtuous emotions, and attitudes are made a significant component in the formulation of theories. Sentiment and instinct are said to have no weight in theoretical matters (1.634); they are also said to support, or at the very least to accompany good science and scientific philosophy. A sharp distinction between the heart and the head, between the requirements of theory and those of practice, exists side by side with the claim that there are social sentiments necessary for right reasoning, and that self-controlled thought is a species of self-controlled action.[2]

[2]The connection between this set of ambiguities and pragmatism is an interesting question to explore. It is not, however, one which is relevant to the aims of this article. I am concerned with the evaluation of consequences, and not merely with the consideration of those effects which thought has or could have upon action.

This confusion in Peirce's thought is heightened when the principles of synechism and fallibilism are introduced. These highly valued principles forbid the founding of rationality upon the irrational (1.139, 7.170). They do not permit the inquirer to rest explanation upon the inexplicable. Appeals to intuition, revelation, feeling, and a priori considerations are ruled out as inadmissable ways to verify claims (1.143-146, 1.162-163, 2.170-171). Their presumed self-evidence or self-warranting character makes these modes of evidence suspect.

Peirce is specifically critical of what he describes as the German penchant for the subjective (2.170-171, 2.173). Logic, he holds, defending the so-called English view, would be on very shaky footing if it relied upon feelings of rationality to substantiate arguments. Not only are these feelings (of rationality) confused and indistinct versions of what could be clarified by self-controlled thought, but they are also not rationally functional. The task of logic is to reason correctly, to reason in a way which fits the facts, to be able to capture semiotically and predict the course of experience — its task is not to provide agreeable sensations or to satisfy "intellectual impulses" (2.173-4). The latter Peirce claims are irrelevant to logic's proper aim.

Clearly then Peirce has many inconsistencies to explain. His synechism and fallibilism do not cohere with his various appeals to the virtuous feelings and attitudes that are associated with "true" science and scientific philosophy.

Several writers on Peirce have remarked upon these problems. Manley Thompson, Murray Murphey, and Thomas Goudge have all taken Peirce to task for appealing to inexplicables. They each claim that Peirce founds logic and inquiry in general upon inexplicable assumptions.[3] More specifically, both Murphey and Goudge believe that Peirce rests a great deal upon appeals to sentiment. In a trend which Goudge denominates as transcendentalism, he accuses Peirce of often making simple appeals to feeling. Murphey is particularly critical of Peirce's regular arational appeals to hope.

---

[3]Thompson, Manley, *The Pragmatic Philosophy of C. S. Peirce,* University of Chicago Press, 1953, pp. 128, 144; "The Paradox of Peirce's Realism," *Studies in the Philosophy of Charles Sanders Peirce,* first series, eds. Philip Wiener and Frederick Young, Harvard University Press, 1952, p. 138.
Murphey, Murray, *The Development of Peirce's Philosophy,* Cambridge, Harvard University Press, 1961, pp. 170-1, 302.
Goudge, Thomas, "The Conflict of Naturalism and Transcendentalism in Peirce," *Journal of Philosophy,* Vol XLIV #14, July 3, 1947.

III

We have explored the problems. Now the question is — is there a way to save Peirce from attack? Is there a way of interpreting his often conflicting statements in such a manner that we may capture his insights? Can we rework and seek to systematize fragments which are clearly important and intentional, but also difficult to reconcile?

I submit that we can. I would like to propose a reading of Peirce that does justice to the complicated nature of his insights. I would like to suggest an interpretation that explains textual inconsistencies as different but complementary partial statements of a complex and sophisticated truth.

The best way to begin is by emphasizing the hypothetical or retroductive character of Peirce's philosophy. Peirce is quite proud of the third branch of reasoning that he has discovered and developed in his theory of logic (2.102). In addition to deductive and inductive reasoning, he has focused upon retroductive or abductive reasoning, the kind of reasoning which is involved in hypothesis-formation.

An extended study of hypothesis making as what takes place in the special sciences, allows Peirce, the philosopher, to recognize the pivotal significance of retroduction in all cognitive pursuits. Whether one is discussing a perceptual judgment, an analytic or heuristic model, a theory or a metaphysical claim, in each case Peirce is quite emphatic about the abductive character which belongs to each.

All cognitive claims are retroductive in the sense that they are conclusions based on the evidence accumulated thus far. Regardless of the quality and quantity of evidence that has been gathered, any truth claim is always subject to further verification. Peirce's synechism and fallibilism require that the road of inquiry be left open, that cognitive stances be subject to continued testing and continual modification and correction.

This is certainly one meaning which the concept of hope has in Peirce's system. When Peirce claims that " . . . all that logic warrants is a hope and not a belief" (2.113), this is at least part of what he means. The employment of "hope language" is not meant to signal that emotions are necessary to ground logic or inquiry in general. Rather it is used to signify that adequate reasoning should always be conscious of its fallibility.

It is important to notice that Peirce employs this signal in his later writings. Although he has (by 1902) recognized that logic is a normative as well as a constitutive science, he does not discontinue his association of hopes with fruitful philosophy (2.113-118, [1902], 1.81 [1896], 1.121 [1896]).[4] He has changed his mind about the foundational nature of emotion, but he had not ceased to link theoretical reflection with emotional humility and optimism. He is just as liberal in his utilization of the language of feeling and sentiment. This later tendency has a particular significance. In addition to signalling that all claims function for the inquirer as hypotheses, Peirce is also specifying a series of emotional and behavioral norms. These are the attitudinal norms which ought to accompany good reasoning.

Synechism and fallibilism have their human correlate in a particular type of habit. If one were a believer in absolute universality, certainty, and exactitude, then the habits of "cocksureness" and dogmatism would be appropriate. If one were a committed skeptic, then pessimism would be the proper habit of sentiment. As a synechist, the inquirer must be suitably tentative and hopeful. This is the regularity of emotion which nurtures ever corrigible investigation.

A similar case could be made for a variety of other attitudes and emotions. In particular, Peirce defends the following as being necessary to inquiry: the passion to learn, fair-mindedness, devotion, honesty, probity, industry, and cognitive flexibility. These are the attitudinal norms worth cultivating whether one be a scientist, a philosopher, or a theorist of any kind. They are the human correlates of cognitive development and advance.

While these may not be the character traits which inquirers do have, Peirce's point is that they are the habits which investigators should cultivate. Truth will be pursued in the most effective and unblemished fashion, if inquirers take on these attitudes toward inquiry. Behaviorally then, in terms of what Aristotle would call the dispositions of human character, these norms parallel the regulative claims of esthetics, ethics, and logic.

---

[4]There are several passages in the Peirce manuscripts which reinforce this point: MS 24, p.2 (1903) In this passage, he discusses the "hope" that the world is intelligible. MS 290 p. CP 31 (1905) In this manuscript he describes the "need" to think of the universe as intelligible as a "postulate." MS 339, 293 r (August 28, 1908), Here he talks about logic as requiring the thinker to postulate that any given phenomenon is capable of rational explanation.
Peirce, Charles Sanders, Manuscripts, 33 reels, 35 mm, Microfilm, Harvard University Library.

IV

Hope does have another meaning. In addition to signalling that a fallible claim is at stake, in addition to being a proper behavioral accompaniment to inquiry, Peirce also utilizes the concept of hope in a very special sense, when he is talking about regulative principles and prenormative indubitables. There are a number of methodological principles which Peirce advocates — these are the leading principles ". . . generally conducive to the ascertainment of truth . . ." (2.588). They are general habits or methods for the conduct of reasoning, habits which are broad guidelines for the progress of inquiry.

Examples of such normative principles are: 1) pragmatism or pragmaticism, 2) "Do not block the road of inquiry!" i.e., the ordering principle of synechism, 3) "Let us not pretend to doubt in philosophy what we do not doubt in our hearts" (5.265), 4) "Let us not precide our conclusions beyond what our premisses definitely warrant" (8.244), and 5) when there is a choice between calculational and experimental methods, and the former are easily pursued, the former should be developed as far as possible before turning to the latter (4.69).

Prenormative indubitables are a special class of general facts. They are the general facts which are needed to ground to normative sciences of esthetics, ethics, and logic. They are the metaphysical claims which allow normative inquiry to go forward. They are facts which are so general in nature that cognition often fails to notice them, even though they are continually confirmed by experience and are therefore not doubted.

Peirce mentions the following as examples: 1) that truth is real (2.205, 2.135-139), 2) "that there is knowledge embodied in some form and that there is influence in the sense that one embodiment of knowledge affects another" (2.66), 3) that "there are such states of mind as doubt and belief — that a passage from one to the other is possible, the object of thought remaining the same, and that this transition is subject to some rules by which all minds are alike bound" (5.369), 4) that there is good as well as bad reasoning (2.128, 2.151), and 5) that there is some connection between the "reasoner's mind and nature's," a connection which makes any process of verification both possible and legitimate (1.121).

There are other general facts which function in the same way, i.e., as indubitables needed to found normative inquiry. Peirce does not explicitly identify them as such, but they can be discriminated through their use. The reality of community, and of the cumulative community of humankind are examples. The constitution of the General or Reason as that which governs individual events, and which grows through embodiment is another (1.615).

What regulative principles and prenormative indubitables have in common, is that they are adopted for reasons which augment their analytic and empirical warrant. As Peirce is careful to note, they are not cognitively important simply because they are needed. He chides Kant and the trancendentalists for their " 'indispensable presuppositions,' " and indicates that his philosophical claims require evidence which is "more substantial" (2.113). In a seeming response to those who would charge him with injecting inexplicables into his system (e.g., several commentators on Peirce, see pages 80 and 81), he states quite definitively that indispensability is not a sufficient ground for cognitive authority.

In the case of both regulative principles and prenormative indubitables, there are ideal and/or empirical reasons for their adoption. Peirce is far from arbitrary in his acceptance of any truth claim. He does, for example, *argue* that the growth of Reasonableness should be chosen as the summum bonum (1.611-615). He relies upon the meaning of terms like "higher," "lower," "love," and "reason" to work through his position. Another example is his treatment of the reality of truth. Empirical evidence of a pervasive sort is spotlighted when establishing the status of truth — he substantiates his position through a focus upon secondness, or the element of brute force in experience (1.137-139).

Regulative principles and prenormative indubitables are then rooted in evidence; there is a varying degree of analysis and empirical warrant accompanying their assertion. However, in Peirce's view, such evidence is not sufficient. When dealing with normative or regulative claims, when considering general facts whose function is to found normative inquiry — in more general terms, to ground the very pursuit of truth — there is an additional kind of evidence which is required.

Peirce's employment of "hope language" in *this* case is an indication that the evaluation of consequences has been operative. As opposed to the more conceptual or value-neutral concerns of pragmatism, the concerns are in this case value-laden. Peirce is interested in norms, rules, or principles, he is interested in general facts, which, when adopted, have *positive* consequences. He is desirous of taking normative and prenormative stands which promote valuable effects that would not have been possible without their adoption.

To put the point in Peirce's language, there is one passage particularly revealing of his intention. In trying to decide whether to posit generality as a third mode of being, Peirce makes the following comment:

> Our sole guide must be the consideration of the use to which the answer is to be put — not necessarily the practical application, but in what way it is to subserve the *summum bonum* (2.116).

As he indicates here, purpose is an important variable in determining a commitment to a hypothesis, but he is not discussing a limited or narrow conception of purpose. The usefulness in question is being judged relative to the growth of concrete reasonableness. A hypothesis is chosen if it promotes universally worthy results.

Without being specific, Peirce makes the same general appeal when examining any regulative principle or prenormative indubitable. His primary focus is upon hypotheses whose acceptance promotes the developmental growth of inquiry. He favors hypotheses which encourage inquirers to take seriously the results of experience, which stimulate the development of logic (1.611), which open new areas of explanation, which provide "pigeonholes" for already observed facts (1.153), which promote continued testing and modification of established conclusions, which catalyze humankind to fully utilize their reasoning powers.

It is from this consequential approach or "hopeful" perspective that Peirce argues for treating humankind as a indefinite community, and inquiry as nonterminating. Murphey is incorrect when he asserts that Peirce views the former as a fact (see pages 80 and 81). Thompson is incorrect when he asserts that Peirce views the latter as a fact. Both of these otherwise insightful commentators mistake a normative claim for a fact. In opting for either of these two closely related theses, Peirce is adopting a position which has strongly positive consequences for the pursuit of Truth.

V

The relationship between esthetics, ethics, and logic is still in need of examination. While we may be right in holding that Peirce meant the hopeful attitude to be a signal of abductive status, and a proper emotional accompaniment to synechism and fallibilism; while his many references to moral emotions, logically necessary social sentiments, and virtuous attitudes may be interpreted as a designation of human character as it ought to be shaped by human inquirers; while he may be using the habit of hope to indicate that a normative or prenormative stance is at stake, none of these positions explains the unusual and ambiguous relationship between the three normative sciences.

I must admit that this is a most troublesome intellectual knot to untangle. Peirce has provided a nexus of inconsistent statements which is difficult to make sense of, never mind to reconcile.

I will begin by more closely examining the reasons why he has set up the architectonic in this way. He has, in my view, mistaken a specific dependence of logic upon ethics and esthetics, for the general exclusively one way dependence of these three sciences. More particularly, Peirce has focused upon the notion of self-controlled action as what can serve an ideal, in making the connection between ethics and logic. He has linked ethics and esthetics through a concentration upon the concept of final cause as a purpose behind all purposes.

While these two connections are interesting and suggestive, they are far from being all encompassing. Surely good reasoning is needed to discriminate, examine, and select ideals. And again, valid processes of arguementation are a definite requirement for the development of an ethical standpoint. While logical action may be a species of action, esthetic and ethical thought are also species of thought.

An analogous point can be made about the relationship between disciplined action and the ideals which it serves. While a science of disciplined efforts must presuppose that aims have been selected, a science of aims or purposes must rely upon a knowledge of how means accomplish ends. It must rely upon an understanding of workable means and achievable ends. In Aristotle's terms, such a discipline will presuppose that the relationship between efficient causation and final causation has been comprehended.

Though Peirce never admits it, I believe that he was looking for a normative scheme which would adequately establish logic. So few of his comments are about either ethics or esthetics. In contrast, he writes extensively about logic. I believe that the other two normative sciences were introduced into the architectonic, when their use relative to logic's function became apparent.

It is quite clear that Peirce's summom bonum is a reasoner's ideal. Those devoted to theoretical investigation would be likely to choose the same. However, persons of other vocations, other lifestyles, more varied commitments, would be likely to demand an aim of wider scope. The ultimate aim which Peirce chooses is not one which would include the other two "classes of men" that he himself discusses. Persons of feeling and persons of action (1.43) can only shine forth as underdeveloped or degenerate forms of the highest purpose.

My basic contention is that Peirce developed a network of esthetic and ethical considerations which are specific to the domain of logic. He then mistakenly supposed the network to be generally applicable. When he discovered that these conclusions were inconsistent with his "philosophical sentimentalism," he decided to take refuge in a clear-cut distinction between heuretic and practical pursuits.

This distinction does reinforce my position that Peirce's ethics is an ethics for theoretical investigators. It reinforces my position that Peirce's esthetics, paltry as it is in terms of development, is an investigation of the inquirer's ideals. The logician's ethics and the logician's esthetics are separated from the more encompassing practical sciences which are their counterparts.

Peirce does not have very much that is important to say about these more encompassing practical sciences. His sentimentalism or conservatism seems to me to be nothing more than a warning that moral change must come slowly. In recognizing the importance of human instinct and sentiment as a repository of cultural tradition and natural necessity, Peirce is not, I believe, denying that long run processes of deliberation are necessary for moral purposes. What he is denying, is that short run, more impulsive, rational experiments should be trusted in periods of crisis and situations of immediacy.

His emphasis upon "matters of vital importance" is a focus upon the local and the narrow — it is a spotlighting of the individuality of situations and generations. In such crises, Peirce advises humankind to utilize the wisdom of the ages. Sentiment and instinct, as the deepest pathways within the person, as the very substance of the individual, are the reliable sources of advice (1.661).

In my judgment, Peirce is not making a sharp distinction between the heart and the head, either in the domain of theory or in the domain of practice. Heuretically, his critical common-sensism is meant to be a synthesis of two important sources of cognitive evidence. He is seeking to adjudicate the demands of biology, culture, and critical inquiry. In addition, there are, as we have already discussed, virtuous emotions and attitudes which Peirce acknowledges ought to accompany true science and scientific philosophy.

In the domain of practice, there is a difference of emphasis, but not a radical, dichotomous shift. Since Peirce approaches the domain of practice as everyday affairs, considerations of immediate utility, and "matters of vital importance," critical inquiry is not an appropriate method of management. The individual and immediate are not meant to be handled in the same way as the general and long run.

However, it should be remembered that instinct and sentiment are formed by unconscious mental processes which parallel their more voluntary and disciplined counterparts. Unconscious mental development is thus neither unlike nor disconnected from deliberate reasoning. It should also be remembered that Peirce expects radical changes in morality in the long run (1.648, 2.198). As theoretical change is imbedded in the roots and substance of the person, moral changes will follow.

VI

Returning to the theory of agapasm, we find a metaphysical hypothesis which has been adapted because of its positive consequences. Peirce does not select agapasm as the preferred theory of evolution simply because of heuretic considerations. He is, as we have already discussed, convinced that the theory of creative love will both discriminate and nurture communal sentiments of the best kind. He is equally convinced that negative consequences, i.e., the promotion of greed, are fostered by one competing theory, tychasm, and that neutral and therefore nonpositive consequences are fostered by the other, anancasm.

One major problem with Peirce's evaluative approach is significant here. In considering the worth of predictable results, Peirce must be careful that he does not impose a valuational structure upon a resistant world.

Peirce's commitment to synechism is a notable case in point. The methodological assumption that the pursuit of knowledge is possible, and that it will eventually lead to the truth, is a hypothesis without negative consequences. Either the truth will be approximated, or humankind will discover its own folly. In either case, the actual state of affairs will become apparent; reality's intelligibility and unintelligibility will be made manifest.

The retroduction of agapasm is not in the same situation. Like Peirce's cosmology, his theory of evolution tends to assume that reason will conquer all — that the impulsive, deviant, chaotic, and erroneous will be eliminated from the nature of things. A benevolent thirdness will rule.

It is not at all clear that this is a fruitful or even an innocent hypothesis. While it tends to encourage human participation in inquiry and community, it tends to ignore: 1) the different senses in which complex forms of rationality will evolve or be accompanied by complex forms of irrationality, and 2) the possibility that increased lawfulness may have destructive or evil effects upon the universe.

Again the parallel with synechism is helpful (see page 88). Peirce claims that infallibilists have blinders which do not permit them to discriminate the continuity, uncertainty, and intellectual life and freedom which pervade the universe (1.153). The hypothesis of infallibilism is said to limit the scope of perception. In a precisely analogous vein, I think Peirce ought to have reflected on the perceptual effects of agapasm. His commitment to Agapé seems to have rendered him unable to recognize the more complicated forms that irrationality may take. As the deviant and erroneous may be harmonized, so the organized and lawful may grow rigid, turbulent, and cancerous. Agapasm makes him blind to the possibility that increased lawfulness may not mean increased morality or loveliness. It blocks his ability to discern moral retrogession, and/or aesthetic sterility and regimentation.

Further, and perhaps most interestingly, Peirce's commitment to Agapé seems to have blocked his ability to consider diverse alternatives. In a puzzling collapse of his usual triadic scheme, Peirce posits a universe with unidirectionality. He does not consider the possiblity of multiple trends and directions, each course being the fulfillment of a specific purpose. In effect, he does not allow for the continuing secondness of historical movement. A model which does actually follow from his characteristic reliance upon triadicity, would have "pigeonholes" for both negative and positive movements. It would adequately take account of particular changes from period to period, and individuated fluctuations over the course of history.

Peirce has in this case, and in the case of his cosmology, overstated the significance of valuative parameters. He has allowed various moral and religious allegiances to influence the exercise of his critical acumen.

VII

In conclusion, I hope that I have unravelled some of the mysteries involved in Peirce's position. As in other areas, Peirce's stance toward the philosophical value of virtuous emotions and attitudes is not an easy one to systematize. He was indeed committed to the idea of system, but did not discern the systematic connections and problems evident in his own display of scattered insights.

ILONA KEMP-PRITCHARD.*

C. W. POST COLLEGE.

*Professor Ilona Kemp-Pritchard died in October 1979.

INTERNALIZATION, SOCIALIZATION, AND DIALECTIC*

This paper will offer three contributions to the theory of internalization: (1) It will seek to distinguish Freud's concept of Oedipal internalization from current usage of internalization in the social sciences in the sense of socialization. The revisions of Freud's concept of internalization which are the result of the taking over of this concept by sociology and ego psychology will be examined and their implications discussed. As a cultural and historical product, Freudian internalization can only with caution be generalized as an abstract sociological mechanism; the deeply rooted cultural significance of Oedipal internalization suffers neutralizing distortion insofar as it is put to use in sociology primarily as a stabilizing agency for a social system or in ego psychology as a generalized concept of internalizing external regulations. (2) The theoretical model for internalization which Freud reaches will be shown to be a conflict model of reappropriation as may be found in Fichte and as developed by Hegel. Application of this model to Freud's theory of internalization and superego formation makes it possible to identify and to explain some long-standing difficulties on the part of Freud and many Freudians with regard to the relationships among object loss, identification, internalization, and superego formation. (3) Lastly, in order of archaeological descent, it will be seen that Freud's account of internalization is mediated by a network of subtheoretical religious, cultural, and historical significance which brings it under the "canopy" of Western culture and certain persistent themes in the complex Western tapestry of Hellenic, Judaic, Christian, Enlightenment, and Romantic strands. But since Freud's subtle yet powerful cultural thematics was given no theoretical significance in his own systematic formulations, it remains subtheoretical and fails to survive when Freudian theory is abstracted, generalized, and transferred to other disciplines.

---

*Presented to the American Philosophical Association, 73rd annual meeting, December, 1976, Society for the Study of the Unconscious.

I

Internalization and Socialization

Recent social scientific and psychoanalytical discussions have centered upon Freud's concept of internalization. Sociologists and social psychologists have increasingly taken over the concept of internalization and accommodated it to the purposes of their disciplines with the result that internalization has entered into the common language of these sciences. In current usage in contemporary social science to internalize a normative element of one's society is to render it a (relatively) stable and enduring structure within the inner life of the individual. The significance of the internalization of social norms is frequently linked in recent sociological literature with its consequences, in the form of the habituation and conformity which internalization brings about; specifically, the internalization of social norms is regarded as a necessary condition of social order and stability.

Talcott Parsons is without doubt the sociological theorist who has been most influential in the interdisciplinary effort to utilize the psychoanalytic concept of internalization as a link between personality and society, and between the conceptualizations and explanatory laws of sociology and those of psychoanalysis. In the essays gathered together in the volume *Social Structure and Personality,* Parsons claims that "Freud's discovery of the internalization of moral values as an essential part of the structure of the personality itself" constitutes a "crucial landmark in the development of the sciences of human behavior" and is "dramatically convergent with . . . that of the social role of moral norms made by the French sociologist Emile Durkheim." Parsons emphasizes the significance of what he has discerned:

> (It is) the massive phenomenon of the convergence of the fundamental insights of Freud and Durkheim, insights not only as to the fundamental importance of moral values in human behavior, but of the internalization of these values. This convergence, from two quite distinct and independent starting points, deserves to be ranked as one of the truly fundamental landmarks of the development of modern social science.[1]

In the interests of maximizing the general implications of this convergence of Freud and Durkheim on the role of moral norms, Parsons

[1]Talcott Parsons, *Social Structure and Personality* (Free Press, 1968), pp. 18-19.

arrives at the "inescapable conclusion that not only moral standards, but *all the components of the common culture* are internalized as part of the personality structure."[2] Internalizing the interrelated cognitive, affective, and moral components of culture turns out to be "a process of social learning" motivated by rewards and punishments and having the function of integrating the personality in a social system. With his recognized mastery of conceptual analysis and integration Parsons transforms Freud's concept of Oedipal internalization into the generalized concept of socialization, the process by which individuals learn, in types of social situations which provide appropriate rewards and punishments, the network of patterns of meaning, value, and affect of their culture.

This transformation by Parsons of Freud's Oedipal concept of internalization into a generalized concept of socialization or social learning is made at the expense of major surgery on the Freudian concept. Excised wholly or partially are the following components of Freud's theory of internalization: the theory of the instinctual source of motivation; the necessary conflict relationship between the individual and society; the conflict relationship between the id and social and cultural reality; the intrapsychic conflict relationship between the id on the one hand and ego and superego on the other; the intrapsychic conflict relationship between libidinal and aggressive impulses; the theory of the prefigurative influence of infantile attachments and anxieties; the centering of internalization upon the Oedipal phase of the life cycle and upon the formation and destruction of the Oedipus complex. With the removal or reduction of these sources of conflict, ambivalence and agression, the internalization of the common culture becomes a predominantly non-conflictual learning process at once stabilizing and harmonizing personality structure and social order. Parsons has successfully rendered internalization theory functional as a well-articulated theory of the multiform integration of the personality into the social system.[3]

---

[2] *Ibid.*, p. 23.

[3] In a now celebrated acrimonious exchange with Parsons, the sociologist Dennis H. Wrong argues that sociologists have come to equate internalization with learning, or even with habit-formation, and consequent conformity; with the result that tension between impulses and superego controls "drops out of the picture," and so also does the tension between "conformity and rebellion, social norms and their violation, man and social order." The outcome of the view of conflict-free socialization, says Wrong, has been an *over-socialized view of man* and its social counter part: an *over-integrated view of society*. *Psychoanalysis and the Psychoanalytic Review*, vol. 49, No. 2, Summer 1962, pp. 553-79. See also Dennis H. Wrong, *Skeptical Sociology* (New York: Columbia Univ. Press, 1976).

Freud's concept of internalization received comparably serious modifications at the hands of recent ego psychology, which has shifted the psychoanalytic center of interest from the id to the ego and its intrapsychic defensive and adaptive functions and its "object-relations" with the external world. Ego psychologists are interested in de-emphasizing the id-focus (upon aggression and libido) of Freud's concept of Oedipal internalization and its motivational and dynamic viewpoint in favor of a functional and adaptive conception of internalization. Where Freud has spoken of internalization as a kind of "mourning" for an "object loss" and of a "cannibalism" by which the object is retained, ego psychologists wish to expand the variety of types of internalization in coordination with the expanding functional and adaptive roles given to the ego in ego psychology.

To accommodate these revisions a redefinition of internalization by ego psychology was required. As in the case of Parsons' reconstruction of the Freudian concept of internalization into the unconflicted, adaptive, functional, and generalized concept of socialization, so ego psychology revises the Freudian dynamic concept of internalization into the structural, adaptive, functional, and generalized concept of replacing external regulations with internal regulations. Two outstanding exponents of ego psychology, Heinz Hartmann and R.M. Loewenstein, provide a generalized version of internalization: "We would speak of *internalization* when regulations that have taken place in interaction with the outside world are replaced by inner regulations."[4] In *Aspects of Internalization,* Roy Schafer offers a broader general formulation of internalization, holding that it

> refers to all those processes by which the subject transforms real or imagined regulatory interaction with his environment, and real or imagined characteristics of his environment, into inner regulations and characteristics.[5]

Schafer provides exquisitely formulated distinctions among incorporation, introjection, and identification as processes contributing to internalization. For Schafer these processes both precede and follow the Oedipal occurrence of identification and internalization, which is thus stripped of its decisive, axial role in personality development.

---

[4]H. Hartmann, E. Kris, R. M. Loewenstein, "Papers on Psychoanalytic Psychology," *Psychological Issues,* Monograph 14 (International Universities Press, 1964), p. 150.

[5]Roy Schafer, *Aspects of Internalization* (International Universities Press, 1968), p. 9.

Identification with parents and others as models is for Schafer the key process in personality formation; it functions within all systems of the personality, id, ego, and superego, as a socializing influence. The importance which Schafer gives to the benign, socially integrative influence of the parental models with whom the child identifies permits Schafer to de-emphasize the importance of conflict between the child's id or ego and the external (parental, social) world. Most notably, Schafer attempts a specific de-emphasis of the Freudian Oedipal conflict relationship itself. Where Freud spoke of the boy's representation of the parents' strictness and severity, their prohibiting and punitive function,[6] Schafer pointedly calls attention to a "benign parental agency to be internalized."[7] Where Freud spoke of the "harshness and cruelty" of the superego—"its dictatorial 'Thou Shalt',"[8] Schafer wrote significantly under the title "The Loving and Beloved Superego . . . "[9]

The convergence on the role of moral norms between Durkheim and Freud, which Talcott Parsons identified and hailed as "a landmark in the development of the science of human behavior," may be seen to have reappeared in a new convergence between contemporary sociology and ego psychology. These disciplines converge in their revision of Freudian internalization into a generalized concept of various modes of relatively conflict-free adaption on the part of the individual to the regulating structures of the social system. There is a temptation to say that Parsons and the ego psychologists have brought about an Americanization[10] of psychoanalytic internalization by their repression of conflict, aggression and ambivalence, elements suggestive of the tragic sense of life and offensive to American innocence.

---

[6]*New Introductory Lectures on Psycho-analysis,* "Dissection of the Personality," 1933, XXII, 62, *Standard Edition of the Complete Psychological Works of Sigmund Freud,* ed. James Strachey (London: Hogarth Press, 1953-74). All references in this paper to the published works of Freud are to the Standard Edition and follow its conventions of identification. The translation by Joan Riviere, *Collected Papers,* v. I-V (New York: Basic Books, 1959) has been used where preferable.

[7]Schaefer, p. 226.

[8]*The Ego and the Id* (W. W. Norton), SE 1923b, XIX, p. 55.

[9]Roy Schafer, "The Loving and Beloved Superego in Freud's Structural Theory," *The Psychoanalytic Study of the Child,* v. 15, 1960. For a contrasting view, see Hans W. Loewald, "Internalization, Separation, Mourning and the Superego," *Psychoanalytic Quarterly,* 31 (1962), pp. 483-504.

[10]This suggestion of Americanization was made by Prof. Clark Butler, in his commentary on this paper, American Philosophical Association, Eastern Division, December 1976.

II

Freud's Early Internalization Theory

Freud wrote of internalization only in respect to the Oedipus complex. For Freud, the incestuous love for the mother and the parricidal hatred of the father are the principal components of the Oedipus complex. Freud claims that the impulses for incest and parricide are overcome and replaced by the father's rules which prohibit them, and with the superego as a new internal self-monitoring agency which administers the rules. This remarkable turnabout is achieved according to Freud, by the processes of internalizing the father's rules and identifying with the father. How can this be understood?

As early as 1912 with *Totem and Taboo,*[11] Freud had begun to explore the idea of a self-reproaching internal agency whose formation was linked with loss. Here in *Totem and Taboo* the origin of "conscience" as an internal self-criticizing agency is tied to the loss of the primal father by parricide for his cruel suppression of the libido of his sons, a loss which was actively inflicted, rather than a loss suffered (as in bereavement or in the withdrawal of love by a loved one). It is significant that in pursuing at a later time the linkage of an internal critical agency and loss, Freud does not draw upon *Totem and Taboo,* where the oppressive and hated father is "lost" by being murdered, but upon the paper "Mourning and Melancholia" (1917) and the earlier paper on Leonardo (1910) where loss is presented as a loss suffered, the emotional loss or the loss by death of a loved one.[12] Both of these cases are referred to in *Group Psychology and the Analysis of the Ego* (1921)[13] where Freud presents his first detailed discussion of the process of identification in its relation to internalization. Identification is here presented as the process of substituting, or compensating for a lost "libidinal object-tie" by "assuming the characteristics of the object," and in this sense internalizing the object ("as it were by means of introjection of the object into the ego.")

---

[11]Sigmund Freud, *Totem and Taboo,* SE 1912x, XIII, ix.

[12]Sigmund Freud, "Mourning and Melancholia," SE 1917e, XIV, 239; "Leonardo da Vinci and a Memory of His Childhood," SE 1910c, XI, 59.

[13]Sigmund Freud, *Group Psychology and the Analysis of the Ego,* SE 1921c, XVIII, 67.

Two problems were created at this point for Freud in his pursuit of a theory of the formation in the self of a self-critical internal agency perceived as linked with loss. The overwhelming loss, in the early childhood Oedipal phase is the loss of the mother as libidinal object, a loss which is suffered by the boy through his defeat in the conflict with the father. The logic of identification as restitution or compensation for a lost love-object would require that the boy identify with the mother's characteristics, thus introjecting her and, in a sense, preserving her despite the loss of her as a love-object, by making her an internal part of himself. But the identification of the boy with the mother as a model cannot, on Freud's view, be normative for his development; for the psychosexual development of the male, his identification must be with the father, i.e., he must assume the characteristics of the father. How can this difficulty be overcome? In the speculative anthropology of *Totem and Taboo* the identification of the remorseful sons with the lost-by-murder father had been a cornerstone of the argument upon which the self-critical agency ("conscience") had been built, as well as law, morality, justice, and civilization itself. But how can this speculative myth of group psychology be made to appear as individual psychology using Freud's conceptual device of internalization as a function of identification with a lost love-object? This road leads to the mother.

The second and related difficulty in establishing in individual psychology the boy's identification with the father as lost loved one is the role of the father in the Oedipal conflict, in which he is not the object of libidinal cathexis but is hated and feared, the object of aggression and the powerful source of dreaded counter-aggression.

It is in *The Ego and the Id* (1923) that Freud at last believes himself to be in possession of a theory of the formation of the self-critical agency, described in the now familiar phrases as "a grade in the ego, a differentiation within the ego, which may be called the 'ego-ideal' or 'super-ego' . . . "[14] Again, at the beginning of the discussion the mourning and melancholia arguments are invoked, but are now simplified to a formula for superego formation: "an object which

---

[14]Sigmund Freud, *The Ego and the Id,* ibid., p. 28. See also earlier in *Group Psychology and the Analysis of the Ego:* "The assumption of this kind of differentiating grade in the ego as a first step in the analysis of the ego . . . " SE 1921c, XVIII, 130.

was lost has been set up again inside the ego—that is, that an object-cathexis has been replaced with an identification." He presents phenomenologically the introjection of a lost sexual object as "a kind of regression to the mechanism of the oral phase" of earliest childhood, and further suggests the analogy with primitive cannibalism, the totem meal, and Holy Communion. Incorporating the object "makes it easier for the object to be given up . . . It may be that this identification is the sole condition under which the id can give up its objects." But the tormenting question is what does this have to do with the role of the father, who is not the boy's love object, and with the father's connection with the formation of the critical agency, the superego, this differentiating grade in the ego? How can the formula for superego formation: *an object-cathexis has been replaced by an identification,* be applied to the father?

Suddenly, Freud gives up and decides that it cannot. The identification with the father is not "the consequence or outcome of an object-cathexis; it is a direct and immediate identification."[15] Furthermore, Freud protests in discomfort, "behind the origin of the superego . . . there lies hidden an individual's first and most important identification, his identification with the father." Now, presumably, the path is cleared to superego formation which is linked to the father. Freud moves ahead.

> . . . the boy's sexual wishes in regard to the mother become more intense and his father is perceived as an obstacle to him; from this the Oedipus complex originates.

It is at this point that the boy's early "identification with his father takes on a hostile coloration" and changes into a wish to get rid of the father in order to take his place with the mother. But the Oedipus complex must undergo "demolition" and when, "along with it," the object-cathexis of the mother is given up, its place will be taken by "an intensification of the identification with his father."

At this point Freud perceives and acknowledges what he himself has just given up. "These identification are not what we should have expected, since they do not introduce the abandoned object into the ego." Immediately, however, he tries to salvage the formula by invoking the theory of bisexuality, which he believes will help with the application of the formula to the father: since the father is a libidinal object for the bisexual boy, this object-cathexis is replaced by an identification.

---

[15] *Ego and Id,* Part III, SE 1923c, XIX, 31.

Unfortunately for this last effort to show the self-critical agency as linked to the father and yet as a replacement for an object-cathexis, Freud's own formulation of the normative Oedipus complex concentrates on the incestuous love for the *mother* as the object-cathexis to be surrendered and replaced by the stern rules of the father.

Yet Freud purports to have safely traversed the tortuous path from *Totem and Taboo* to *The Ego and the Id.* The formula for identification in individual psychology has been bent in an attempt to show that here in individual psychology, as in the anthropological origins of the human race, it is identification with the father and the internalization of the father's restrictions which make law, morality, society, and civilization possible. Since we have in this paper traversed Freud's tortuous path and have observed his stumblings and bold plunges ahead, we should not be surprised that by the end of this remarkable Chapter III of *The Ego and the Id* he has achieved closure on this problem ("has got it all together" as we say) and is invoking "the hypothesis I put forward in *Totem and Taboo,* that religion, morality, and a social sense . . . were acquired phylogenetically out of the father-complex." As for the formation of the superego, he insists that is it a perfect fit with the formula: it is an identification with the father as a substitute for an object-cathexis upon the father: *"the longing for the father."*

Finally, the significance of Freud's theoretical end-in-view in the course of the difficulties he encountered can be stated. His theoretical goal from 1912 until its consummation in 1924 was the development of a theory of the formation of the critical internal agency, the superego, as the link between personality and culture, which he understood as the link between the boy and the world of the father.

Within his own thought-structures, Freud had two available explanatory models for superego-formation, for the formation of a "critical internal agency." (1) The older one is the *Totem and Taboo* conflict model, in which the genesis of the superego and the root of morality and civilization is in the negation of desire (for incest and parricide). And it is the conflict with the hated and feared father which frustrates desire and provides the negation of desire. It is the father who defeats the boy and commands the fear which is the necessary condition of internalizing the father's rules against such desires. It is this coerced and fearful internalization of the father's rules which is the crucial preparation for the boy's "becoming like" (identifying with) the father. (2) Competing with this *Totem and*

Taboo conflict model, in which the relation to the father is one of aggression and fear, there is a lost-love model available to Freud, its source in "Leonardo" and "Mourning and Melancholia," in which superego-formation can be seen as the preservation by identification of a lost-love object, a lost-love cathexis.

In turning away from the conflict model, as we have seen him do, Freud is seeking to represent the link to the father as one of love, so that the relation to the father is idealized on both sides, with the father inspiring, and the boy returning, love. On this model the link between the boy and the father's world and thus the link between personality and culture, would be the positive and unifying cathexis of love rather than the negative relation of reaction formation against parricide, the hatred of the father. But this second model fails for the following reasons: First, it is the mother who is the object loved and lost; second, the element of conflict with the father remains unaccounted for, is dissociated, "drops out of the picture"; and third, the coercive power of the superego and its negative rules is unaccounted for.

(3) Briefly, he tries another model: Identification and bisexuality. Identification with the father is the boy's first identification. It is not a substitute for a lost object-cathexis, but it is immediate, primitive and pre-Oedipal. When the Oedipus complex is destroyed and the object-cathexis upon the mother is surrendered, hositility to the father is overcome and the boy's love of the father leads to an intensificaion of the original pre-Oedipal identification with the father and to the formation of a superego. But this third venture fails for the following reasons: First, countering a lesser quantum of love for the father to the powerful love of the mother leaves unexplained why the mother is not the lost love-object which is preserved by identification; second, this model fails to explain the intensity of the boy's hostility to the father; and third, it remains unclear why identification with the father's rules is an intensification of the original identification.

We have seen Freud end Chapter III of *The Ego and the Id* with a wavering attempt at conflating his two principal models, with a reference to the "hypothesis" in *Totem and Taboo* that "religion, morality and a social sense" are acquired out of the father-complex"; and with a rcaffirmation of his second model and its formula for the boy's relation to the father: from object-cathexis to identification. But by 1924, in "The Dissolution of the Oedipus Complex" Freud has reverted to the conflict model. In this essay and in the "closely related" "Some Psychological Consequences of the Anatomical Distinction between the Sexes" (1925), both of them focussed upon the differences between the psychological development of the boy and the girl, the conflict model (for the boy) is not only reaffirmed but achieves its most complete conceptual and philosophical formulation. By 1931 in "Feminine Sexuality" he announces that the crucial determinant of superego formation is fear of the castrating father.

III

Internalization Theory and Dialectic

Thomas Mann sadly rebuked Freud for having too little love for philosophy. The philosophical problems concerning the internalization of objects were largely ignored by Freud and account for some of the confusions we have observed. An epistemology of the ego and its "object-relations" must be inferred from Freud's arguments and supplied for him. For the purposes of the present paper, we shall confine ourselves to the key concepts which we have seen that Freud employs: object-cathexis, object loss, substitution by identification and internalization. These concepts locate his theory of knowledge for us. Contrary to the frequent labelling of Freud as a positivist, mechanist, or materialist, his theory of knowledge is subsumable as a variant under the dialectical concept of knowledge (first formulated by Fichte and developed by Hegel) as entailing three "moments" or components: *a first moment of affirmation of the ego* (Freud: the ego's primary narcissism, and subsequent libidinal-cathexis of the mother); *a second moment of opposition to the first, as a negation or cancellation of it* (Freud: oppressive opposition by father, retaliatory aggression by son, and surrender following castration fear); *a third moment in which the ego reaffirms itself by negating the second moment, and reappropriating to itself and preserving by sublimation (Aufhebung) what is significant for it in the other two moments* (Freud: demolition, repression, object-loss; internalization, incorporation, and identification with a desexualized object, the setting up of the desexualized object inside the ego; sublation as sublimation or reaction-formation).

The reappropriation model of knowledge is a conflict model, for Freud as much as for Fichte. For Fichte the external object is a *Widerstand,* something that stands in opposition to me, and which must be overcome "as an alien element";[16] for Freud, "hate originally betokens the relation of the ego to the alien external world."[17] Hegel articulated the multiform modes that negation, overcoming, cancelling and annulling the object may take, as well as the interdependency of negation and reappropriation. So also Freud, in *The Ego and the Id,* explicitly designated the superego as "an energetic reaction formation," that is, in the relation of negation, opposition, conflict to the Oedipus complex which "the ego ideal (superego) had the task of repressing." With these words Freud undermined his two nonconflictual models of superego formation as a product of identification with the father. The superego, he adds, more cautiously, has a "double aspect." "Its relation to the ego is not exhausted by the precept: 'You *ought to be* like this (like your father).' It also comprises the prohibition: 'You *may not be* like this (like your father)—that is, you may not do all that he does; some things are his prerogative."[18] What explains this double aspect, specifically the prohibition? This is the superego's task, says Freud in a turnabout, to repress the Oedipus complex; "indeed, it is to that revolutionary event that it owes its existence." He has here conceded that the function of superego-formation is not adequately grasped as linkage with the father in loving identification, but as counterrevolutionary, the repression of the Oedipal revolt against the father. The superego as a reaction formation negates the Oedipal desires by internalizing the father's specific rules against them. These desires are transformed by the negation of reaction formation into the superego rules which repress them.

We are now in a position to formulate Freud's theory of Oedipal internalization and superego formation in terms of the Fichtean-Hegelian reappropriation-through-conflict model of knowledge. The world of the boy's primal "happy love . . . in which object-libido and (narcissistic) ego-libido cannot be distinguished,"[19] giving way to a

[16] J. Fichte, *Science of Knowledge* (1797), ed., P. Heath and J. Lachs (New York: Appleton-Century-Crofts, 1970), p. 233. On the relation of Hegel to Fichte's theory of dialectic, see Hans-Georg Gadamer, *Hegel's Dialectic* (Yale University Press, 1976), pp. 6, 26ff.

[17] "Instincts and their Vicissitudes" SE 1915c, XIV, p. 111; see also "On Narcissism," SE 1914c, XIV, 67.

[18] *Ego and Id,* Ch. III, p. 34.

[19] "On Narcissism," p. 98.

libidinal cathexis of the loving mother represents the moment of affirmation. This world is invaded, negated, threatened with loss and destruction by the father, whose earlier strength as benevolent protector is now the strength of an obstacle, a *Widerstand* to the small boy's intensifying sexual wishes, incurring the boy's aggressive, parricidal impulses, and responding to these with what the boy perceives as castration threats. This is the second moment, the world of the Oedipus complex, harboring the libidinal, positive cathexis to the mother and the primarily aggressive, negative relation to the father. In the third moment both the desired and the hated objects must be abandoned, "lost," and the libidinal and aggressive cathexes to them must be negated, annulled, repressed, demolished, and sublated in de-libidinized and de-aggressivatized forms. These are the objects lost, the desires and aggressions which are replaced, compensated for, restituted or restored in the third moment by the boy's internalization of the father's restricting rules and identification with him. In the Oedipal world these rules had been external. Internalized, these are the rules which negate, by reaction formation, the Oedipus complex of the second moment, the libidinal impulse toward the mother and parricidal hatred of the father. The self-critical agency which, as it were, administers these restrictions against incest and parricide, "retains the character of the father":

> The child's parents, and especially the father, were perceived as the obstacle to a realization of his Oedipal wishes; so his infantile ego fortified itself for the carrying out of the repression by erecting this same obstacle within itself.[20]

The "longing for the father" may now be understood. It is not, as Freud tried to argue, a longing for a lost love-object, but a longing, appropriately, for the *strength* of the father as parenting figure to overcome the libidinal and aggressive impulses he forbids, as when we say, "Lord, give me strength to resist."

Two remaining aspects of the third moment may now be understood: first, that the superego is a self-parenting agency as well as a self-critical agency. It is the boy's early, primitive, immediate identification with the strong protecting father in the first, pre-Oedipal moment which now, in the third moment, is "longed for," restored, preserved and sublimated into the strong self-parenting

---

[20] *The Ego and the Id,* p. 34.

function of the superego, as the evocative language of Freud clearly announces:

> The superego fulfills the same function of protecting and saving that was fulfilled in earlier days by the father and later by Providence or destiny.[21]

Secondly, with the superego having been shown to be the outcome of a process of sublimation as well as of reaction formation, we may now perceive the third moment, Freud's moment of superego formation, as having the characteristic dialectical function of synthesis, sublating through sublimation elements of the first moment and sublating through reaction formation, elements of the second, Oedipal moment.

Why did Freud not explicitly follow this dialectical model of reappropriation-through-conflict in his account of Oedipal internalization and superego formation? That this model is not only recognized but employed by him is clear from innumerable passages in which identification and internalization are interpreted as third moment resolutions (sublimations) of the conflict between libidinal desire for the mother and fear of the father's prohibition against this:

> The object cathexes are given up and replaced by identification . . . The libidinal trends belonging to the Oedipus complex are in part desexualized and sublimated, which probably happens with every transformation into identification; in part they are inhibited in their aim and changed into affectionate feelings.[22]

But Freud encountered two stumbling blocks in the way of his following the dialectical model presented here, in which in the antithesis or second moment the mother as love-object and the father as aggression-or-hate-object constitute the Oedipal objects to be negated and sublimated. The two stumbling blocks relate to the father: Freud wished, as we have seen, to present the father as the love-object to be lost and restored; secondly, he did not wish to represent the father as hated aggressor. The result is a distortion of the dialectical model in which libidinal cathexis alone is what must be overcome, desexualized, repressed, and sublimated, lost and restored by identification.

It is interesting to observe that Freud is under the constraints of his dualistic instinct theory. Freud as a dualist viewed "cathexis" as an affirmative (libidinal) relation to the object, and hate as its instinc-

---

[21] *The Ego and the Id,* p. 58.

[22] "The Dissolution of the Oedipus Complex," SE 1924d, XIX, 176-77.

tual dualistic opposite, a repelling (aggressive) relation to the object. Freud was determined to present the Oedipal father as the libidinal object lost,to be restored by identification rather than as the object of the boy's aggression. Ironically, it is his own dualism which he is desparately seeking to turn around in order to demonstrate the Oedipal father as the love-object lost. It is his own dualism which requires that libidinal-object is the Oedipal role in which the mother is cast, and that the Oedipal role of the father springs from the dualistically opposing instinct of aggression. The boy's relationship to the father is indeed characterized by ambivalence, owing to the boy's bisexuality and to the father's protective parenting, but this quantum of love for the father does not alter the impossibility of demonstrating the Oedipal father as the love-object lost. Yet Freud persisted in his long-standing effort to show that the superego (the third moment) is formed by the internalization of the loved father rather than by the internalization of the primarily feared and hated father in relation to the primarily desired and loved mother, as in the model presented above.

But one may pursue this problem and ask why, then, did Freud not avail himself of aggression as an alternative route to identification, arguing that the boy defends against the threatening father by identification with him (Anna Freud's "identification with the aggressor")? The critical consideration for Freud's failing to make use of counter-aggression against a threatening father, sublated into identification, was Freud's determined effort to idealize the father. *The formula for superego formation—from libidinal cathexis to identification—was designed to fit the father.* For Freud it is the father, not the mother, who is loved and lost, mourned and internalized. The relation to the father is presented as consistently positive: from love-object to admired internalized source of authority, and provider of protection and entry into civilized society. With rare exceptions, Freud's followers and interpreters have contrived, like him, to present the father as the cathected love-object who is replaced by superego identification. The most common rhetorical device for doing so is to include the father in the libidinal cathexis by pluralizing references to "oedipal love objects" or "love of parents," thus blurring the actual oedipal relations of predominant love for the mother and predominant hate for the father.[23]

---

[23]Also, see, e.g., Freud's own pluralizing references cited above to "parental obstacles" to Oedipal wishes.

We have so far been occupied in *The Ego and the Id* with the structural aspects of the superego formation, "the differentiation of a grade in the ego." But the probing of the significance of internalization requires an understanding of its motivational or "dynamic" aspects as well. Freud moved on to the motivational problem in the following year, 1924, in the paper "The Dissolution (Passing) of the Oedipus-Complex."[24] What motivates the repression and dissolution of the Oedipus complex? Up to this point psychoanalytic theory had not adequately addressed this problem. Here, in "The Dissolution of the Oedipus Complex," in providing a theory for the motivation to give up the Oedipus complex, Freud decisively reverts to his conflict model for explaining superego formation. And in the two later papers focussing upon differences between the psychology of the male and female, "Some Psychological Consequences of the Anatomical Distinction Between the Sexes" (1925) and "Female Sexuality" (1931) Freud boldly leaps to an embrace of the dialectical model of conflict and reappropriation. Freud now provides the theory that the motivation for giving up the Oedipus complex is fear of castration, which is repeatedly threatened by the hated and feared father as the boy's "interest turns to his genital organ." However, this is a necessary but not yet a sufficient condition for the abandonment of the Oedipus complex. "The observation that finally breaks down the child's unbelief in the possibility of being castrated is the sight of the female genitalia . . . He must then become convinced of the absence of a penis in a creature so like himself. With this, however, the loss of his own penis becomes imaginable, and the threat of castration achieves its delayed effect."[25]

The phenomenological cogency of Freud's newly revived and conceptually clarified conflict theory is immediately apparent here. It may be seen that the "boy now strongly motivated" to dissolve (negate, repress, annul) the Oedipus complex is himself the destructive agent, "borrowing from the father" the strength to kill the defiant rebel and the incestuous lover in himself and to destroy the world in which he related to the parents through these roles. It is, however, a creative destruction. The substitution for the destroyed Oedipus complex is the boy's formation within himself of a father-like self-critical agency which promotes and strengthens earlier identification with the father. Identification with the castrating father gives en-

[24]"The Dissolution of the Oedipus Complex," SE 1924d, XIX, 173.
[25]*Ibid.*, p. 176.

try to the world of the benign father, to the macro-world of morality, law, social order, civilization, etc.[26] Freud acknowledges the creative destruction which is entailed in superego formation in the 1931 paper on "Female Sexuality":

> It is thereupon the discovery of the possibility of castration as evidenced by the sight of the female genital which necessitates the transformation of the boy's Oedipus complex, leads to the creation of the superego and thus *initiates all the processes that culminate in enrolling the individual in civilized society.*[27]

Freud's perception of the dialectical character of his theory of internalization became sharper the more he turned to the problems of female psychology, which he had in the past dismissed as "analogous" to male psychology. In the essay "Some Psychological Consequences of the Anatomical Distinctions Between the Sexes" he presents the three moments of the dialectic of internalization, in what is perhaps his most complete articulation of the reappropriation-through-conflict model.

> In boys, the complex is not simply repressed, it is literally smashed to pieces by the shock of threatened castration. Its libidinal cathexes are abandoned, desexualized and in part sublimated; its objects are incorporated into the ego, where they form the neculeus of the super-ego and give that structure its characteristic qualities. In normal, or rather in ideal cases, the Oedipus complex exists no longer, even in the unconscious; the superego has become its heir . . . The catastrophe of the Oedipus complex (the abandonment of incest and the institution of conscience and morality) may be regarded as a victory of the race over the individual . . . In girls the motive for the destruction of the Oedipus complex is lacking. Castration has already had its effect . . . [28]

The girl of necessity lacks the boy's apocalyptic prototypal experiences of the Oedipus complex and its destruction and replacement by identification with the father by that "energetic reaction formation," which culminates in the superego. There is no Electra complex. "It is only in male children that there occurs the fateful simultaneous conjunction of love for one parent and hatred of the other as rival . . . which . . . leads to the creation of the superego and thus initiates all the processes that culminate in enrolling the individual in civilized society."[29] Therefore, no entry into the world of

---

[26]Schafer's treatment of the "benign" parents emphasizes this phenomenon.

[27]"Female Sexuality," SE 1931b, XXI, 229.

[28]"Some Psychological Consequences of the Anatomical Distinctions Between the Sexes," SE 1925j, XIX, 257.

[29]"Female Sexuality," SE 1931b, XXI, 229.

the father is available to the girl (she does not experience the processes that culminate in enrolling her in civilized society); her superego formation being weak (presumably its development is by Parsonsian socialization), she has a lesser sense of justice; never having experienced the boy's fearful lesson of sublimation under threat of castration, she has a lesser capacity for sublimation and therefore for intellectual work, for the important cultural tasks of civilization; never having destroyed an old self and its world, and created a new self and world, the girl lacks the prototypal experience of creativity. In Freud's mature internalization theory, conflict is a necessary condition of the "catastrophic" defeat which yields the great victories of prototypal self-overcoming by creative destruction and of a father-and-power-linked superego, by reaction formation. These heroic sufferings and achievements are available only to the male.

It should not pass unnoticed that the female loses out whether Freud pursues the conflict model or the internalized lost love-object model. As mother, she is denied what theory entitles her to, to be the love object lost and internalized; as daughter, she is represented as lacking the Oedipal experience of conflict and catastrophe which provides intitiation into all the goods and work of the civilized world.

Contrary to the common charge that Freud was overly-focussed upon id-psychology, from the time of *Totem and Taboo* his persistent concern, as we have seen, was the ego's object-relations, and primarily to discover the structure and dynamics of the tie between the boy and patriarchal society. The tie is by the process of internalization; its occurrence as finally perceived by his dialectical conflict theory is so devastating a reputiation of the previous desires of the boy as to suggest that Freudian internalization is more aptly seen as a conversion than as one type of generalized socialization (Parsons) or as one type of generalized internalization of external regulations (Hartmann, *et al.)*.

IV

Freud's Cultural Thematics

There exists a rich, evocative sub-theoretical layer of significance in the writings of Freud which appears to be both independent of, yet intimately connected with, his explicit conceptualization and argumentation. In this respect Freud is like Hegel. Their writings are sub-theoretically evocative of the history of Western culture, perhaps in both cases from a sense of having achieved intellectual closure with regard to it, and from a sense of its ending. Through analogy, metaphor, allusion, symbolism, myth, and fantasy both writers, in differing ways, reveal their ties to Romanticism and to older Hellenic, Judaic, Christian and Enlightenment sources and they sensitize us to the "canopy"[30] of culture which defines our world.

In Freud's studies on internalization and superego formation, myths, fantasies and metaphors mediate the concepts and expositions. The "objects" which are identified with and internalized are persons, their passions and powers, as well as the worlds which they and their historic and mythic prototypes have left to our time to inherit. The primal crime of *Totem and Taboo* has the appearence of myth mid-way in construction out of primary process fantasy. The primal father appearing at the dawn of history calls to Freud's mind an image of Nietzsche's Superman of the future. The primal-crime myth is the phylogenetic counterpart of the boy's fantasy of parricide as a way of banishing the hateful sovereign father, and instituting a social contract on behalf of the siblings. Long past lies the fantasy of libidinal merging with the loving and beloved mother, a Jocasta fantasy of a Hellenic golden age in a cosmos of Fate governed by Empedoclean forces of Love and Hate in endless cyclical conflict.

Freud's most powerful and pervasive subtheoretical references in the context of internalization are to Judaism and Christianity. The Paradise of Eden (the "happy love" of self and mother fused and unified) is the eternal lost object. To protect the Eden world against the rival for the mother, it was fated that one undertake a Risk, an ordeal, but this was doomed and fated to fail, since the other was the Father and the desire for the Mother who is his wife is sinful. Hence the sense of crisis and catastrophe, the kairos time, the axial time after which all is changed; the fantasy of the End-of-the-World. It is the tormented Eden-parricidal world that must be destroyed like Carthage, demolished and buried like Sodom and Gomorrah; yet there is an apocalyptic promise of deferred wonders to come in the world of the Father; and there is the loss (by sacrifice) and internalization of

[30]Cf. Peter Berger, *The Sacred Canopy* (New York: Doubleday, 1967). Also, Peter Berger and Luckmann, Th., *The Social Construction of Reality* (New York: Doubleday, 1966).

His Son. The Fall has been a Fortunate Fall; the boy is the Prodigal Son; he is the Holy Sinner who achieves virtue through sinning. But since there has been a fall, a restitution or ransom must be paid. Thus intitiation into the world of the father is by submission, by symbolic emotional castration, by circumcision, by internalizing a conscience whose stern voice is that of the castrator-father, whose "Thou shalt" is the commandment of Jehovah. Here we have come upon the Freudian myth of The Yoke of the Law.

Renunciation symbols and allusions in the Oedipal context relate to the female as mother and seducer, with echoes of Saints Paul and Augustine. But he who gives up his libidinal life with the mother gladly, will find it again at a future adult time when he is safely initiated into the father-world. Novalis's Romantic dictum of Magical Idealism holds good: If you cannot make external objects of your throughts, then make thoughts of external objects. The passage is from object-cathexis (loving) to internalization and identification (being like); from object-cathexis to narcissistic cathexis; from alloplastic to autoplastic.

Ahead lies the long vista of the world of work and sublimated libidinal passion. The defeated small boy will, in the latency period, relate to objects in a neutral way, continuing to internalize the father's discipline and learning various skills by reward and punishment. After the risk and life-and-death struggle, like Hegel's slave, through work he will objectify himself and to some degree liberate himself as an independent person from the Father-Lord-Master. The future is with him, but preserved within him are the libidinal, nurturing mother; his moment of rebellion and his murderous defeat by the protecting father; the model of the Father-God and His suffering Son; and various newer significant others, most notably the woman he marries, but who loves not him as his mother had loved him, but their son; and finally the Earth Mother who waits to receive him. No voice is wholly lost. Internal objects are eternal.

T. Z. LAVINE.

THE GEORGE WASHINGTON UNIVERSITY.

HUSSERL AND PRIVATE LANGUAGES

1. Some philosophers believe that Husserl is committed to a private language; accordingly, they think that Husserl's position is subject to Wittgenstein's objections in *Philosophical Investigations.* It seems that phenomenological reduction — the methodological device with which Husserl begins philosophical analysis — requires some sort of private language; and if the notion of a private language is incoherent, then Husserl's position is likewise. Unfortunately, this thesis has rarely been examined.

Recently, however, Suzanne Cunningham[1] uses arguments inspired by Wittgenstein in order to argue that Husserl's position is unintelligible. I intend to show that her arguments presuppose an erroneous interpretation of the reduction.

2. Cunningham's interpretation of the phenomenological reduction sets the stage for the arguments against Husserl's "private" language. She believes that the phenomenological reduction has two characteristics: (a) the reduction of real transcendent objects to immanent objects, and (b) the refusal to accept anything as true unless it is "immediately self-evident" (LPR, p. 7). We shall disregard (b), as only (a) is relevant to the argument. A few pages later she identified immanent objects with *private* objects (LPR, p. 16). In what sense of 'private' are the objects of phenomenological discourse purportedly private? They are private in that they are inaccessible; and 'inaccessible' means 'not capable of being known, understood, or used by other persons' (LPR, p. 18). Something can be either contingently or logically inaccessible. 'Contingently inaccessible p' means 'p happens to be inaccessible to all but one person, but can be made accessible to others', whereas 'logically inaccessible p' means 'the very concept of p requries that it remain inaccessible to all but one person'.

---

[1]Suzanne Cunningham, *Language and the Phenomenological Reductions of Edmund Husserl,* The Hague: Martinus Nijhoff, 1976. Hereafter, I shall refer to this work in the text as LPR.

Since language is a means for referring to objects rather than an object itself, it is necessary to classify private languages in terms of the inaccessibility of both their referents and the words that are used *to* refer. The relevant questions are "Who has (or can have) experience of the *referents* of the language?" and "Who understands (or can understand) the language?", yielding a fourfold classification of private languages:

(1) a language that refers to contingently private objects,

(2) a language that refers to logically private objects,

(3) a contingently private language, or a language that only one person understands, but which could be understood by others, and

(4) a logically private language, or a language that only one person *can* understand (LPR, p. 19).

Private languages (1) and (2) have been described imprecisely. A *language* does not refer; rather, terms *in* that language refer. So, private languages (1) and (2) should be described as follows: (1) a language, all of whose referring terms refer to contingently private objects, and (2) a language, all of whose referring terms refer to logically private objects. This is no trifling distinction, since it is the key to the refutation of one of Cunningham's arguments. She thinks that Husserl's post-reduction language is a private language (1) and (3).

3. Cunningham raises the following objection to private language (1):

(a) Every language requires logical connective terms.

(b) But logical connective terms do not refer to private objects.

(c) Thus, private language (1) is parasitic on a public language, which requires commitment to the existence of other speakers. (LPR, p. 27).

Let us assume that it is correct to say that every language must have logical connective terms.

4. Although Cunningham believes that the preceding objection militates against private language (1), her argument actually has nothing to do with a language that is called "private" solely in terms of its referents. Her own premises imply that this is so, since she says that logical connective terms do not refer (LPR, p. 22). If so, then the necessity of terms for connectives *cannot* constitute an objection to a language that is private only because its referring terms refer to private objects. If the necessity of such terms *were* an objection to a private language (1), then logical connective terms would have to

refer to nonprivate objects. But Cunningham denies that they refer at all. Thus, there is a confusion between meaning and reference here, the argument being nothing but an objection to a private language (4). Since she grants that Husserl's language is not private in that sense, the argument is not an objection to Husserl's post-reduction language *at all.*

There is, however, a way of construing the argument as an objection to languages that are called "private" solely in virtue of (nonpublic) referents. One may respond to my criticism of the argument as follows: By calling our attention to logical connective terms, Cunningham is pointing out that not all terms refer to objects. So, her criticism *is* a legitimate attack on a language that has *only* terms that refer.

But this is no objection to private language (1). In the first place, the argument is not an objection to private languages *per se.* It is an objection to *any* language, public or private, that consists solely of referring terms. Secondly, is a language that consists solely of terms that refer to nonpublic objects a private language (1)? No. There is nothing in the description of a private language (1) that requires that all of its terms refer to objects. The sole description of that language is that none of its terms refer to contingently public objects, which does not imply that all of its terms refer to (contingently) private objects, since the following two propositions are consistent: (a) None of the terms of L refer to contingently public objects, and (b) Some of the terms of L do not refer at all. So even if we interpret the argument in this charitable way, it is still irrelevant to the point at issue. A language does not refer; terms *in* a language refer.

5. We have seen that Cunningham's objections to private language (1) do not work. But she contends that Husserl's language is also a private language (3). What are her objections to that kind of private language?

Her argument can be summarized as follows:

(a) Any language is bound by rules for the proper use of words.

(b) The only way to check to see if one is following rules is to appeal to (actually existing) other speakers of that language.

(c) Such appeals cannot be made if one's language is a private language (3). Thus, Husserl has no way of checking for consistency in the use of his words. So either the reduction cannot be performed successfully, or one has a language that cannot be used to describe (LPR, pp. 27-29).

I think that the thesis that Husserl's post-reduction language is a private language (1) or (3) requires an erroneous interpretation of the phenomenological reduction. Let me show why.

6. The claim that phenomenological reduction includes the reduction of all transcendent (real) objects to private objects would be true only if intentional objects and transcendent objects were two mutually exclusive classes. However, Husserl argues against that thesis. In the case of perception, the intentional and real (transcendent) objects are *identical.* To assert the opposite is to be involved in an infinite regress, to substitute consciousness of an image of x for perception of x.[2] Husserl, then, believed that he could talk about transcendent realities post-reduction; and he did not think that intentional and transcendent objects (even real ones) form mutually exclusive classes.

There is a misunderstanding of the meaning of 'bracketing out transcendent reality', as this passage illustrates: "The reduction brackets out all transcendent reality, and it would be important to have a language which reflects this. *Thus, the referents of the language must be exclusively immanent*" (LPR, p. 28, emphasis mine).

Husserl explains the meaning of 'bracketing real objects'. Briefly, it means that although one continues to undergo perceptions, *one makes no use of the judgments that are based on them.* That is, as a phenomenologist who is describing and analyzing perception (say), one makes no judgment that entails the existence (or nonexistence) of the thing perceived.

> As *phenomenologists* we avoid all such affirmations. But if we 'do not place ourselves on their ground', do not 'co-operate with them' we do not for that reason cast them away. They are there still, and belong essentially to the phenomenon as a very part of it. Rather, we contemplate them ourselves . . . and we *take the thesis of perception and its components as constituent portions of the phenomenon* (Ideas, p. 244, last emphasis mine).

The phrase 'the *thesis* of perception' is important. Part of the thesis of perception is that (generally) the perceived thing exists. Post-reduction, however, one treats the thesis of perception as a thesis, rather than making use of it. To a perceiving subject in the natural attitude, the thesis of perception does not appear as a thesis; rather, perception reveals the way things *are* to one in the natural standpoint. If one asserted the thesis of perception, existential propositions would be involved. Accordingly, one makes no such assertions after

[2] Edmund Husserl, *Ideas,* Trans. W. R. Boyce Gibson, London: Collier Books, 1969, pp. 242-43. Hereafter: Ideas.

the reduction. But that does not prevent one, *qua* phenomenologist, from talking *about* what is "there for him" from the natural standpoint.

> To speak in an image: The 'bracketing' which perception has undergone prevents any judgement being passed on the perceived reality (i.e., any judgement that has it ground in the *unmodified* perception, and therefore accepts its thesis as its own). But it does *not* hinder any judgement to the effect that perception is the consciousness *of* a real world (provided the thesis thereof is not set in action) . . . (Ideas, p. 244, first two emphases mine).

To talk about perception as the consciousness of the real world is only to say that we *take* ourselves to perceive the real world (usually), which is part of the thesis of perception. Such observations do not imply commitment to the existence of the real world.

When Husserl discusses the phenomenological reduction in chapter 3 of *Ideas,* characterizing it as the suspension of the thesis of the natural standpoint, his detailed description of what is there for any subject from that standpoint is itself a phenomenological description (Ideas, p. 95). Such a description would be impossible if Cunningham's interpretation were correct, since therein Husserl refers to transcendent realities or, more precisely, transcendent realities *for a subject*.

So, the suggestion that phenomenological reduction would lead to phenomenal*ism* if it were not for the eidetic reduction is simply not true (LPR, p. 10). It presupposes (falsely) that the reduction involves a form of reduction*ism*, whereby physical objects are reduced to appearances of them or possibilities of appearances. Such reductionism could take place only if one systematically confused the appearance of a physical object with the thing itself. Husserl *never* confused the two. For similar reasons the contention that "In consequence of its metaphysical neutrality, Husserl's inquiry was to be about *consciousness* and not about the nature of the objects of consciousness" (LPR, p. 7) is mistaken, too. As we have seen, it *is* about the objects *of consciousness*, or the relationships that necessarily obtain between consciousness and any given kind of intentional object. Husserl's works are filled with such analyses. It is a mistake to think that phenomenological reduction yields what is "inner" as its object of inquiry, setting aside what is "outer." The reduction has nothing to do with this inner/outer picture; it requires only that all objects be *intentional,* some of which are transcendent.

Surprisingly, there is a passage in which Cunningham says something true about the reduction and the referents of phenomenological discourse.

> By the first [the phenomenological] reduction Husserl merges both physical and psychic phenomena into the group known as 'intentional objects', suspending consideration of their existence in any natural-scientific or psychological sense. For an object to be 'intentional' the *only* thing that need be said about its status is that it is *intended* by consciousness. Whether that object could, under other circumstances, be classified as physical or psychical, immanent or transcendent, is *irrelevant*. All that has been said by calling it 'intentional' is that the object is *meant* or intended by an act of consciousness. *Its status as intentional does not emanate from any of its own qualities, but rather from its relationship to an intending act* (LPR, p. 38, first, third, and last emphases mine).

I agree wholeheartedly. But this is inconsistent with the thesis that no intentional objects can be transcendent.

7. We are now in a position to respond to the suggestion that Husserl's post-reduction language is a private language (3). Is Husserl's post-reduction language a language that is (in fact, not logically) understood by only one speaker? I believe that this question cannot be answered on the basis of Husserl's philosophical position. Let us see why.

After the reduction, one is not permitted to *assert* that others exist or anything that entails the existence of others. Nor can one say that others do not exist or anything that implies it. If so, then Husserl is not committed to the thesis that his post-reduction language is understood by only one speaker. Since Husserl is neutral regarding the existence of others, he is philosophically neutral with respect to the question "Do other speakers of phenomenological langage exist?".

The only question that is relevant to the successful performance of the reduction is whether Husserl's philosophical statements imply the existence (or nonexistence) of things or other subjects. If those statements do not have such implications, and the statements consist of only analyses of the relationships that necessarily obtain between consciousness and a given kind of intentional object, then phenomenological reduction has been performed successfully.

A comparison can be made with the status of intentional objects. We have already seen that an object is intentional irrespective of its own qualities. An intentional object can be the same object that, under *other* circumstances, (i.e., when we are no longer adopting the phenomenological attitude), can be classified as existing, not existing, etc. It is simply that we are precluded from *saying* that it exists (or does not exist), once we have adopted Husserl's standpoint.

Similarly, the status of phenomenological language is not a function of its own qualities. If the statements constitute analyses of the relationships that necessarily obtain between consciousness and a given kind of intentional object, and none of the statements have existential implications, then the discourse is phenomenological. Solely the use of language to do phenomenological analyses makes it phenomenological. Thus,it is (numerically) the *same* language that, under other circumstances, could be said to be understood by others. Someone who has adopted the phenomenological standpoint is simply not permitted to *say* that it is understood by others, which clearly does not imply that his language is not public. Therefore, our question ("Is Husserl's post-reduction language understood by only one speaker?") is unanswered and unanswerable. Both possibilities (a public language and a language that happens to be understood by only one speaker) are consistent with the phenomenological standpoint. Consequently, the view that Husserl's post-reduction language is understood by only one speaker is unfounded.

8. Heretofore I have been entertaining the hypothesis that Husserl's post-reduction language is a language whose referring terms refer to contingently private objects. Now I wish to argue that one is never entitled to say that Husserl is philosophically committed to a private language (1).[3]

My argument is of the same kind that I just used. Husserl is not entitled to say that the intentional object being analyzed is actually intended by a number of subjects, since if he said that, he would be philosophically committed to the existence of others. But that restriction does not imply that it is *not* intended by many subjects.

As we have seen, the status of objects as intentional is not a function of any of their own qualities. This means that when we are no longer adopting the phenomenological attitude, we could truthfully say that the object is actually intended by a plurality of subjects, provided only that that is the case. Therefore, it does not follow from the characterization of the reduction that all the referents of phenomenological discourse are contingently accessible to only one subject. If one *takes no stand* with regard to the actually public qualities of any given intentional object, then it is an open question whether the intentional object is public or private.

---

[3]Robert Solomon misinterprets Husserl's post-reduction language just as Cunningham does, in an otherwise fine article. "Similarly, Husserl's language, insofar as it is a 'private' language, is what Castañeda has called *strictly* private language, a language *all* of whose terms (i.e., all of whose referring terms) refer to private objects." Robert Solomon, "Husserl's Private Language," *Southwestern Journal of Philosophy* 5, #3 (Fall, 1974), p. 215. But cf. p. 226.

Suppose that someone is reading a phenomenological paper at a philosophical meeting. Suppose that the reader used a table at the front of the room as an example, in order to analyze our concept 'physical object'. Now is our imaginary reader precluded from using that table as an example simply because it is actually intended by a number of subjects? Hardly. The only question that we need to ask is "Does the reader make any philosophical statements that imply commitment to the existence (or nonexistence) of others or the table?" If not, then his analysis is within the restrictions imposed by the phenomenological attitude, so long as he is analyzing the relationships that obtain between consciousness and a given kind of intentional object. Of course, our reader may make *incidental* remarks that betray the fact that he believes that the table exists and others see it. In Husserl's writings, too, one will find the pronoun 'we' and similar locutions. But Husserl recognizes that such locutions are for the sake of ease in making philosophical points only, and are avoidable. Accordingly, the presence of such locutions in Husserl's writings does not constitute an objection to Husserl's post-reduction language. So the view that all of the referents of phenomenological referring terms are private is unfounded, too.

9. Thus, only a misunderstanding of the phenomenological reduction prompts the charge that Husserl's philosophical language is (as a matter of contingent fact) private. Cunningham's objections are unusual, since most commentators on Wittgenstein take him to be attacking only the notion of a *logically* private language. I think that I can show that Husserl's post-reduction language is not logically private, either. But that is outside the scope of this discussion paper.

PETER HUTCHESON.

SOUTHWEST TEXAS STATE UNIVERSITY.

THE UNDIFFERENTIATED CONJUNCTION OF SENSATION AND JUDGMENT IN PERCEPTION

In the psychology of perception, the explanation of spatial illusion takes the form of showing how cognition alters the perception of an object. In the moon illusion, the apparent distance theory argues that cognition represents the sensation of the moon according to the principles governing the spatial relationships between size and distance. This is also true of the Müller-Lyer illusion and the Ponzo illusion. In each case, the explanation takes the form of showing how cognition produces alteration in the perception of the sensation. Based on certain schemata that define objective spatial relationships, what is assumed, with justification, is that cognition combines directly with sensation to alter the way the sensation is perceived. The perceptual judgment does not stand outside the sensation as an interpretation or concept, but instead seems to enter into a homogeneous union with it. In the moon illusion, the observer actually *sees* the moon as larger. In all perception, there is this complete fusion between the sensation and judgment. The question which this paper asks is, what is the nature of sensation and cognition that such an undifferentiated union is possible?

There is no sense in perceptual consciousness that judgment is present. For the perceiver, the experience seems to be wholly a sensory phenomenon. Furthermore, not only is there no indication to consciousness that judgment is present, but there is no indication what part of the sensation is actually due to judgment and what part is not. The sensation of the larger moon seen on the horizon when compared with the moon seen at the zenith is a result not of extra visual material being added to the image of the moon, as would be the case if a line was extended before the observer. The act of addition which judgment makes goes unnoticed.

If a physiological model is adopted, the problem does not arise, since both the sensory and cognitive elements of the perception are both viewed as neurological. Because of this monistic view, there is no difficulty in principle in understanding how sensation and judgment, reduced to the same kind of substance are combined. However, if we remain on the level of describing sensation and judgment as they are given to consciousness, they appear different in kind and the task becomes, from a phenomenological point of view, understanding the nature of sensation and judgment in such a way that their undifferentiated unity is a logical possibility.

Why it would be thought that sensation and cognition could not unite is that, like Descartes' distinction between mind and matter, one is conceived as extended, the other, not. Vision comes easily to mind, but it applies to the other senses as well. The visual sensation that I am having of an object is extended in space, whereas the thought that the sensory object is at a certain distance is an idea in the mind possessing neither size nor shape. How can the visual impression of size be enlarged by the addition of what is nonextended? The temptation to which physiological explanations willingly yield is to leave the field of consciousness and argue that such a union takes place in the head, thereby locating the union in space, describing it as an unseen physical process. But we must recall that we have adopted a phenomenological attitude and are committed to regarding such explanations as making presuppositions about what lies outside the realm of consciousness. We instead seek to understand by essential insights what it is that is taking place before consciousness.

A union between sensation and thought would seem differentiated not only because of the character of extension but also because of the distinction between particular and universal. In the case of taste, reaching for the glass of lemonade, thinking it is milk can produce the perception of sour milk. It is not hard to imagine a similar experience for olfactory and tactile sensations as well. Expectation can alter the perception of a sensation. Now, what the understanding brings to the sensation can be stated in the form of a universal judgment, as for instance in the present example, "milk is not tart," or "sour milk tastes tart." This judgment combined with the taste of the lemonade produces the peculiar perception of sour milk. How can the idea of milk, generalized from tasting skim milk, buttermilk, etc., which is a universal, combine with the sensation of lemonade, which is a particular, to produce the sensation of sour milk? The question then becomes, how can what is spatial and particular combine with what is nonspatial and universal to form a homogeneous sensory perception?

Historically, thinkers have resolved the dilemma by reducing sensation to thought, or thought to sensation. Hegel denied the sensory particular and analyzed perception entirely into universals. Hume, on the other hand, denied universals, treating ideas as copies of sense impressions. For both, how thought interacts with sensation was not a problem, for in the case of Hegel, sensation was the specificity of thought and for Hume, thought was faint sensations. Physiology reduces both to physical particulars. The logic is clear; to combine thought and sensation, it is necessary to reduce one to the other,or perhaps reduce both to a third thing, but, if both are kept distinct, then it is impossible to explain how they unite. We could think of Hegel's analysis as a cognitive reduction and Hume's as a phenomenalistic reduction. The explanation which this paper proposes might also be thought of as cognitive, but differing from Hegel's in that the anoetic sensation is retained.

I want to employ first a distinction which Leibniz uses in describing the monad. For Leibniz, the monad is a simple substance without parts. It is a unitary being which is nonextended that he identifies with perception. Although it does not consist of a discrete multiplicity, it contains a plurality in a unity which he calls a manifold. For Leibniz, a multiplicity would consist of an aggregation of simple substances, whereas manifold describes the structure of one simple substance. The monad, as a manifold, refers to the unity of the present moment of consciousness. In any perception, for instance, a plurality of mental events is given instantaneously in the form of sensations, images, judgments, etc. At the given moment, when I look out my window at the landscape, what is given to the unity of the instant of consciousness is singular and simple. However, that I am conscious, at that moment, of distinct objects distributed in space is a result of the mind representing the simple plurality as a discrete multiplicity. Even though a simplicity that contains a plurality may characterize the sensation, this is unthinkable for the understanding, and only representable as distinct objects extended in space. The sensation, however, that is given to the moment of consciousness, insofar as it is simple, is not spatially extended, for anything spatial must consist of a left side and a right side, an inside and an outside; that is, it must consist of discrete parts. The perception of space arises when the understanding represents the sensation as a discrete multiplicity. Therefore, spatiality which distinguishes sensation from judgment is no longer a characteristic of sensations as they are in themselves, and that which gave to sensation the character of physical reality in contrast to what is cognitive or intellectual itself becomes a product of cognition.

In the case of distinguishing sensation from thought according to particular and universal, it is possible to regard the sensation as a limiting concept that is forever escaping specification. Whenever a sensation is attended to, a judgment is made about it, and with the judgment an application of concepts. To be conscious of the landscape beyond the window as a landscape involves the universal concept landscape, a category that has been applied to experiences that have had something in common with the scene that I now see. If I wish to avoid the use of the concept landscape, then I can focus upon a portion of the scene, such as a patch of grass, consciously trying to avoid categorization, but I find no matter how successful I am in making my awareness of the object indeterminate, I am still conscious of it through the mediation of some concept. Despite the way in which I attend to the sensory experience, I am always aware of its being something, or having some meaning, defined by a universal. In other words, there seems to be no consciousness of a sensation that is not a consciousness of a universal. In this sense, it could be thought that instead of making a judgment about a sensation, the mind is making a judgment about a judgment. I am making a judgment about a judgment when I assert or am aware of this green patch as being part of a landscape. It would appear then that a line of demarcation cannot be drawn between sensation and judgment in experience. What always occurs is a judgment about judgment. The moon on the horizon is judged to be at a greater distance than the moon at the zenith and consequently is perceived as larger. But the perception of the moon in either case already contains judgments. To try to disregard the judgments of its size and distance nevertheless, leaves a bright area of a certain shape which is itself still an object of judgment.

The union of sensation and judgment is not the differentiated union of the spatial and the nonspatial, or of the universal and the particular. The sensation, in itself, is a simple plurality that appears spatially extended when represented as a discrete multiplicity by the understanding. It is, as a particular, a limiting concept that always escapes in the direction of specificity with each attempt at distinguishing it from a universal. Therefore, the fusion of sensation with judgment is not the combining of what is different in kind. This is why, even though perception consists of both sensation and judgment, there is no clear demarcation between them in perception and why, whether in illusion or in an objectively valid perception, sensation and judgment combine to form an experience which for consciousness appears wholly sensory.

GEORGE TESCHNER.

CHRISTOPHER NEWPORT COLLEGE.

DISCUSSION

KESARCODI-WATSON ON ATMA-VIDYA AND "EGO"

As a sympathizer with his conclusions, I found Professor Kesarcodi-Watson's discussion of the superiority of the concept of *atma-vidya* over the concept of "ego-sense" (*Philosophy and Phenomenological Research,* September 1979, pp. 130-134) interesting, and illuminating in a sort of negative sense. For his argument seems as good as one could expect, yet it fails to establish any such superiority. What he does do is to bring to our attention once again the deficiencies of the Western approach to the problem of self-knowledge.

Certainly those who have experienced *atma-vidya* are convinced by Professor Kesarcodi-Watson's argument, but only because they have had the experience and thereby know that it is possible and real. The skeptic will say to Professor Kesarcodi-Watson: "There is no doubt that this *atma-vidya* you describe would be a conception of self-knowledge superior to the Western one, which makes the self as object into a thing distinct from the self as knower, if only it referred to something real in human experience. But, alas, we know that the structure of knowledge (or perception) is such that I can know myself only in an objective sense, i.e., as aspects of an accumulation of states, properties, and tendencies. As far as a self that I can know is concerned, there is *nothing* else. So you see, this *atma-vidya* is just another quaint Hindu fantasy." Never mind the neatness or possible explanatory power of the concept of *atma-vidya;* if the skeptic cannot relate it to his own experience, he is not the least bit interested. Thus any "argument" that *atma-vidya* is "more correct" or that it bespeaks "what I really am" is bound to fail, for there is no way for it to convince the skeptic that *atma-vidya* is even possible in the first place.

Another flaw in Professor Kesarcodi-Watson's discussion arises from his attempt to explain *atma-vidya* in terms of the Western idea of the subject-object dichotomy. He first introduces a structure of the "experience-situation" consisting of "three at least apparently disparate things:

(i) a subject experiencing;
(ii) an object experienced;
(iii) an operation of experiencing."

He then tells us that the *atma-vidya* kind of self-knowledge involves all three, but as the "*same* thing," not as "*distinct* things." What is happening here, he explains, is that there are "three distinct terms, used distinctively to convey in each case a *different* conceptual nexus, or 'understanding,' which nonetheless refer at once to quite the same 'thing,' or to be more exact, enjoy quite the same *referring value.*" He confesses this to be a "puzzle," and indeed it is.

The solution to the puzzle lies in the nature of the *atma-vidya* experience. It is not an experience of things (in any sense) or properties or relations. It can only be described as *pure awareness* or *pure consciousness.* Being without boundaries, this experience is unitary, and essentially so. To talk about subject and object in the context of this experience is to import alien concepts that simply do not fit. And to expect any skeptic to accept *atma-vidya* as a valid kind of knowledge, prior to his having had the experience of *pure consciousness* is to ask him to accept as knowledge something which he considers to be altogether impossible. He will fail to see that Professor Kesarcodi-Watson's argument is "embarrassing in its conclusiveness," not because he is incapable of following the "rigors of *argument*," but because of the gap of experience which leads him to reject the empirical presuppositions of this *particular* argument.

One further point made by Professor Kesarcodi-Watson, in his last paragraph, deserves a reply. He says,

> Nothing is incidental, or by accident, in spiritual matters. Nor is anything ever one jot more — or less — than it ought to be. Everything is exact: and this includes the techniqums I have mentioned here merely in brief.

This is a very surprising statement, considering the obviously varying degrees of efficacy among the hundreds of spiritual techniques which are available from the East. Some very few of these techniques have been scientifically confirmed to have apparently beneficial physiological and psychological effects on their practitioners. As for the techniques' relative successes in producing *atma-vidya*, this is a much more difficult matter to assess, but surely it would be quite gullible to accept all claims as equally valid. In fact, if the inadequate experience of most Western philosophers continues to close their minds to the concept of *atma-vidya*, one reason may be their frustration with the *inexactitude* of some Eastern spiritual approaches and with the ineptitude of some well-intentioned but misguided spiritual teachers. Of course, the more important and usual reason will be philosophical and cultural conceit.

TOM F. DIGBY.

UNIVERSITY OF COLORADO AT BOULDER.

DISCUSSION

KESARCODI-WATSON ON DIGBY ON KESARCODI-WATSON

I note with delight Tom F. Digby's serious appraisal of my recent piece on "ATMA-VIDYA AND 'EGO'" (*Philosophy and Phenomenological Research;* Sept. 1979). I trust he will not mind if I put right some less than careful errors. Nor are these errors minor, but in one or two cases, a misconstrual of the most central thing I have argued.

Firstly, the suggestion that my discussion is of "the superiority of the concept of *atma-vidya* over the concept of 'ego-sense,'" is wrong in three ways. In the first place, *my* term was "ego"-sense, not "ego-sense." Misquotation must always cast shades of doubt. In the second, "superiority" is Digby's word, not mine. I do not like terms like this; for whether one understanding or achievement is "superior" to another will in much, and always, rest with what you on any occasion want. My piece makes no claims about what people want, or should want. And in the third place, and most importantly, I certainly was in no way arguing a case for "the superiority of the *concept* of *atma-vidya* over the *concept* of 'ego-sense.'" I have spent most of my career resisting the suggestion that philosophy has centrally to do with analyzing, or even merely with understanding, *concepts.* This piece is no exception: it is *atma-vidya* and "ego"-sense I am talking of, not anyone's concept of them.

Secondly, that "the skeptic" should not be "the least bit interested" in my suggestion, *because* he can in no way relate them to "his own experience," naturally in no way interests me. For I have in the first place roundly denied the self-knowing I advert to in talking of *atma-vidya* to be *any kind* of "experience"; and, in the second, told him, though briefly, where to go to effect this self-knowing. Whether "the skeptic" then goes there is up to him, not me. As is whether he then effects this nonexperiential manner of knowing. I can assure him that an open mind will likely bring him success. As a "philosopher," I can do no other. And that there are "hundreds of spiritual techniques . . . available from the East" (Digby; p. 124) is quite as irrelevant as it sounds. The only way to *test* techniques is *to* test them, personally; and that there are "hundreds" — a misleading suggestion, as most are *essentially* similar — may prove a wretched nuisance, or it may merely witness to richness. I suspect the latter. I also suspect that Digby is wedded to one, or some particular set, of such techniques, and derogates others. There are very few I would derogate, though there are some. The very many not relevant to me in no way incline me to feel them not useful in some measure to at least some others.

Thirdly, it is wrong to say I "attempt to *explain atma-vidya in terms of* the Western idea of the subject-object dichotomy" (italics, mine); quite as it is wrong to suggest there is anything specially *Western* about this dichotomy. A mere glance at the *sad-darśana* material of Hinduism, or the *Madhyamika* material of Buddhism, would if anything evidence a far greater concern with this dichotomy, its status and understanding, than found almost anywhere in Western thought. But this aside, it is anyway wrong to say I "explain" *atma-vidya* "in terms of" this dichotomy; unless "in terms of" means, as it surely rarely does, "by contrast with." After suggesting experience in our world to take a threefold structure — that of a (i) subject, (ii) object, and (iii) experience linking the two —, far from then explaining *atma-vidya* by imputing this structure to it, I comment, "Self-knowing can take two forms — one that involves the '(i) to (iii)' structure above, and one that does not." *Atma-vidya* is the one that does not. Anything *subsequently* said must be taken in that light first. I might note that what I *do* then say is not confessed by me "to be a 'puzzle' " (Digby, p. 124); but, *"on its face* a puzzle" (Kesarcodi-Watson, p. 131). In fact, I don't think it is, as I have tried to explain at length elsewhere ("Can I Die?: An Essay In Religious Philosophy," *Religious Studies;* 1980).

Finally, he mentions my words: "Nothing is incidental, or by accident, in spiritual matters. Nor is anything ever one jot more — or less — than it ought to be. Everything is exact: and this includes the techniques I have mentioned here merely in brief." To these words, he comments: "This is a very surprising statement, considering the obviously varying degrees of efficacy among the hundreds of spiritual techniques which are available from the East." I confess any link between my words here and his to escape me; since I am not talking of "hundreds of spiritual techniques," still less merely of ones "available from the East." I speak only of "what is suggested by those sages who claim this clarity" (p. 133), that is, *atma-vidya*. And by "sages" I *mean* "sages," not hranks.

I might by the by note another hunch: that many of the "hundreds" Digby talks of as "from the East" are in fact from the West.

There are in truth very few authentically traditional Eastern techniques in this area; and the welter now confronting "Western philosophers" (Digby, p. 124) stems mainly from Western bastardizations, not from anything authentically Eastern. It matters not at all that sometimes these bogus misconstruals have flourished in the West in the guise of Eastern ones, nor that they often are put abroad there by persons from India (etc.). There are Indian cranks as well as non-Indian ones; for Eastern and Western are not ethnic terms, but refer to predominant spiritual orientations. But that is another story.

IAN KESARCODI-WATSON.

LA TROBE UNIVERSITY.

DISCUSSION

OPACITY AND MENTALITY: A REPLY TO CRITICISM

In a previous note I argued that referential opacity is a mark of the mental; modality notwithstanding, every opaque sentence has a mentalistic subject matter.[1] I want here to provide a simpler argument for this conclusion, using the usual idea of opacity as the occurrence of a term that cannot in general be supplanted by another term referring to the same thing without altering the truth or falsity of the containing sentence. There are two views about modal claims.

The first is that such claims are

> based on the putative notion of *analyticity* as follows: a statement of the form 'Necessarily . . . ' is true if and only if the component statement which 'necessarily' governs is analytic.[2]

Given this view,

(1) The number of planets is necessarily less than eleven, can be paraphrased as

(2) 'The number of planets is less than eleven' is analytic.

The second view is the denial of the first: It is mistaken and dangerous to assume that claims of the form 'X is necessarily Y' are the same as claims of the form '"X is Y" is analytic'.

> This conclusion is dangerous because is involves us in such obviously fallacious paradoxes as the view that, if the number of planets is necessarily less than eleven—which it is because the number of the planets is nine and nine is less that eleven—therefore, the proposition that the number of planets is less than eleven is [analytic]; which it is not.[3]

---

[1]Harold Morick, "Extensionalizing the Nonpsychological," *Philosophy and Phenomenological Research* (1976), pp. 551-53. This paper has been criticized by Herbert Heidelberger, "Transparency and Modality" and James A. Thomas, "Morick on Extensionality for *De Re* Sentences," *Philosophy and Phenomenological Research* (1978), p. 549 and p. 544.

[2]Willard Van Orman Quine, "Reference and Modality," in his *From a Logical Point of View,* 2nd ed., New York (1961), p. 143.

[3]Alan R. White, *Modal Thinking,* Oxford (1975), p. 170.

The first view, then, it that

> it's only a *statement* . . . which can be either necessary or contingent. Whether a *particular* necessarily or contingently has a certain property depends on the way it's described.[4]

It is not unreasonable to say that the subject of a *de dicto* modal claim is always either a statement, sentence, or Fregean thought. It is, I believe, uncontroversial that statements are the products of embodied thinkers. Next, as yet nobody has demonstrated false the commonsense intuition that talk about the meaning of sentences is always elliptical for talk about what thinkers mean. Finally, nobody has demonstrated that Fregean thoughts can be defined without reference to mental acts, nor, more specifically, that Frege and Chisholm misdefine thoughts.

> A state of affairs is whatever may be considered or entertained . . . Frege used the term 'thought' (*Gedanke*) as we are using 'state of affairs' and observed, 'The being of a thought may also be taken to lie in the possibility of different thinkers' grasping the thought as one and the same thought'.[5]

So it is hardly unreasonable to draw the following tentative conclusions. Given the first view of modal logic, modal logic has a mentalistic subject matter—statements, sentences, and Fregean thoughts are mental entities—which makes it come as no surprise that modal claims, e.g., (1) are referentially opaque. The other view of modal logic agrees that modal claims are opaque to the extent that they are *de dicto* modal claims, but denies that all modal claims are *de dicto*. So given either view, if there is such a thing as modal logic at all, its opaque portion is part of the study of Mind. It is reasonable to venture that opacity is a sufficient condition for mentality.

HAROLD MORICK.

STATE UNIVERSITY OF NEW YORK
AT ALBANY.

---

[4] Saul Kripke, "Naming and Necessity," in (eds.) D. Davidson and G. Harman, *Semantics of Natural Language*, Boston (1972).

[5] R. M. Chisholm, *Person and Object*, LaSalle, Ill. (1976), pp. 117-18.

DISCUSSION

SCHÜRMANN ON POLITICAL PHILOSOPHY

Reiner Schürmann's essay, "The Ontological Difference and Political Philosophy," *(Philosophy and Phenomenological Research,* Vol. XL, No. 1, 1979, pp. 99-122) substantially clarifies the results of the line of inquiry he had proposed, among other places, in "Political Thinking in Heidegger," *Social Research,* Vol. 45, No. 1 (Spring 1978), pp. 191-221 and "Questioning the Foundation of Practical Philosophy," *Human Studies,* I, 1978, pp. 357-68. This new clarity allows one to probe Schürmann's position more precisely than I was able to do in my "Does Anarchy Make Political Sense? A Response to Schürmann," *Human Studies,* I, 1978, pp. 369-75.

My discussion here will be confined to only one point. But that point, I think, is crucial. Schürmann tells us that "Heidegger's insistence on releasement and 'life without why' as the practical a priori for the thought of Being opens an alternative way to think of life in society. The symbolic difference allows for the elaboration of an alternative type of political philosophy. *This is not a theory of organization of man into collectivities.*" (p. 122. My emphasis). Earlier in this essay, Schürmann had noted that Heidegger is indebted to a tradition which scarcely encounters "the Aristotelian and Anglo-Saxon interest in the organization and well-being of the polity." (p. 101).

It is now clear that Schürmann's alternative proposal for political philosophy is one which explicitly dispenses with questions concerning political organization. But can such a political philosophy be considered complete? Indeed, is it political philosophy or only propadeutic to political philosophy?

As Merleau-Ponty said, a political philosophy must be attentive to political men. Consider just one concrete matter, the matter of coercion. The organization of men into political entities always involves coercion, even if it is the coercion that one imposes upon himself as it would be in Sartre's pledged group, a group constituted by the vows of its members. How does one get from Heideggerian releasement and "life without why" to exercises of coercion? Obviously the tyranny of "coercion without why" is not acceptable. But whence the appropriate measure of coercion?

In the absence of such a measure, there remains a substantial gap between Heidegger's thought of the ontological difference, even when supplemented with Schürmann's symbolic difference, and a political philosophy which seriously attends to political men. Perhaps, as Robert Sokolowski suggests in *Husserlian Meditations,* p. 212-13n, what Heidegger cum Schürmann provide is a political philosophy for the village but not for the city or the nation. Or perhaps, applying a criticism made by Werner Marx in *Heidegger and the Tradition,* Heidegger cum Schürmann present a politics for poets and thinkers but not yet one which heeds the whole range of political men.

This gap notwithstanding, this essay of Schürmann's, with its companion pieces, makes an important contribution to political thought. His work shows how Heidegger's thought can account for fact that no form of political organization, neither democracy, nor oligarchy, nor monarchy or nor any other form, is the ideal form toward which all men should aspire. This fact, noted among others by Aristotle and Montesquieu, is no mere contingency. On Heidegger's account, things could not be otherwise. The epochal characer of Being precludes any unequivocally preeminent form.

But if there is no preeminent political form, are there forms which are intrinsically deviant, e.g., tyranny? On Schürmann's version of what can be educed from Heidegger, and here I am not yet convinced that Schürmann has not distorted Heidegger somewhat, one would apparently have to say no. Thus, while there is no mandate in favor of coercion of any sort, if there is coercion, then it, like everything, is without measure. Schürmann does not even have available the Hobbesian basis for restraint, for in his politics there is "a certain disinterest in the future of mankind due to a shift in the understanding of destiny. . . ." (p. 122).

Finally, Schürmann's essay has the merit of requiring the following question. If "life without why" and releasement function as the practical a priori for the thought of Being, why is regulated and limited political coercion so generally experienced as a practical necessity for human well-being? The pervasiveness of this view is not attenuated by the mystical tradition to which Schürmann refers. The mystical tradition, while eschewing coercion, is hardly the tradition of a substantial range of political men. If the putative practical necessity for restricted political coercion is indeed an illusion, then on Heideggerian grounds both the illusion and its pervasiveness must be accounted for. But if, as I think is the case, it is no illusion, then the Heideggerian doctrine of releasement must either be able to be amplified so as to provide a basis for restricted political coercion or it must be judged to be radically defective. Schürmann's work, happily, has brought this issue into clear focus.

BERNARD P. DAUENHAUER.

UNIVERSITY OF GEORGIA.

REVIEWS

The Epochal Nature of Process in Whitehead's Metaphysics. F. BRADFORD WALLACK. Albany: State University of New York Press, 1980. Pp. 369.

Wallack proposes that Whitehead's actual occasions need not be small, short, or impalpable, but can be of any size whatever. Moreover, she holds this to be Whitehead's own intention, arguing that the association of atomicity with microscopicity is a feature of the scientific materialism Whitehead was combating to overcome. Actual occasions, according to his own account, include such things as: a bird, a tree, the sun, Socrates, the Castle Rock at Edinburgh, ancient imperial Rome, the solar system, a nebula, a system of nebulae (pp. 28f).

All previous commentators who have investigated this issue have held actual occasions to be spatiotemporally quite small. No matter; they must all be wrong. The list of those Wallack charges as misinterpreting Whitehead, on this and other points, includes: Pols, Palter, Fitch, Shimony, Leclerc, Rorty, Emmet, Jordan, Christian, Griffin, Chappell, Lango, Overman, Sherburne, Das, Ford, Brennan, Reeves, Cobb, and Capek.

In part Wallack seeks to establish her case by pointing to the many macroscopic examples Whitehead uses when he can afford to neglect the microscopic nature of the actual occasions as irrelevant to the particular point he is making. But there is also a theoretical justification: (a) She emphasizes the extremely important insight that the epochal nature of becoming, by itself, entails no particular size for individual occasions; (b) she sees every actual occasion as spatiotemporally including a subordinate nexus or grouping of smaller occasions within itself, ad infinitum. (This also means that every occasion is included within one or more larger occasions as well.) Here she does not make the mistake of simply identifying events with occasions, for she does not treat phases of concrescence as if they were tinier occasions. The subordinate occasions to be included constitute the many to be unified by that occasion, not stages in the process of that unification. The argument for this sort of spatiotemporal inclusion can cite Whitehead's authority on many points, but only by systematically neglecting the specific context of his remarks. Whitehead is almost always analyzing the way in which present experience can include past data, never how the present can include the present within itself.

Judged in terms of its own central claim, the book is quite unconvincing, and might simply be relegated to one of the curios of Whiteheadian scholarship. Aside from the first chapter, however, the book is quite sober and sound, showing to what great extent Whitehead's theory can be applied to occasions of any size whatever. It is rigorous and well-argued throughout, and exhibits an impressive knowledge of the secondary literature. That Whitehead took occasions to be microscopic is clear (her arguments to the contrary notwithstanding), but that Whitehead *should have* so regarded them is much less clear. Wallack's book is, despite itself, an impressive contribution to the revision of Whitehead on this point.

Wallack's main difficulty appears to be excessive piety toward Whitehead's genius. Convinced that many macroscopic realities are individually actual, she cannot bring herself to believe that Whitehead himself did not concur. Since Whitehead *must have* held such macroscopic realities to be actual, all contrary readings of the text *must be* wrong. By so generalizing Whitehead's discussions to fit occasions of any size, she has cut herself off from the possibility of limiting them at all. Actuality now means everything and nothing. The sunrise is an actual occasion; so is laughter at dinner. Moreover, now we have pansubjectivity with a vengeance, since every occasion enjoys its own subjective immediacy. The American nation, so long as it lasts, must on this account be accorded its very own subjective feelings.

Had she directed her efforts towards revision instead of interpretation, Wallack could have devised an adequate limiting criterion eliminating such absurdities, and perhaps given us an adequate theory for such inclusive occasions. The reasons Whitehead required very small occasions need not have entailed that all occasions be small. *Some* occasions must be small, in order to account for change, since he interpreted change as the difference between successive occasions. If, however, smaller occasions could be included within (temporally) larger ones, then there could be occasions of any size. Whitehead, we may suppose, saw this. Why did not he, with Wallack, adopt some theory of inclusive occasions?

The problem, as I see it, primarily concerns causal interaction. If the relation of spatiotemporal inclusion is to be effective, there must be some way for the included occasion to causally affect the more inclusive occasion, and vice versa. But if these two occasions were equally present to one another, they would be contemporaries, which by definition cannot causally influence each other. By Whitehead's principles, only past occasions can causally affect present ones. This means that the way included occasions interact with inclusive occasions could only be in the same way that past occasions affect present ones. Thus Whitehead lacks any means whereby he could distinguish included occasions from past ones.

We might argue that an included occasion, since its becoming terminates before the completion of the inclusive occasion, lies in the past of that concrescence, yet because the concrescence of the included occasion began after the initiation of the inclusive concrescence, that it was somehow affected by that concrescence as lying in its future. Such included occasions would thus be different from merely past occasions, since the causal interaction, though different, would be mutual between included and inclusive occasions. Since no one has proposed such a theory of interaction between inclusive and included occasions, however, and Whitehead clearly had none to offer, we must conclude that this—or something quite similar—prevented Whitehead from adopting a view of occasions of variable sizes, leaving him with the microscopic actualities we are familiar with.

LEWIS S. FORD.

OLD DOMINION UNIVERSITY.

Methodology of Economics and Other Social Sciences. FRITZ MACHLUP. New York: Academic Press, 1978. Pp. xiv, 567.

As the title indicates, this collection by the well-known economist deals primarily with questions of methodology and theory in the social sciences. While such a printing of essays is always welcome, it should be noted that one-fifth of them have appeared twice before. This is possibly countered by the fact that the three new essays for this volume make up approximately one-third of its length. The author also supplies us with helpful introductions to each section. With a total of twenty-six essays it is difficult to do more than merely give the broadest outlines of the work.

The first section entitled "On the Nature and Significance of Methodology" includes a long essay dealing with such a wide range of philosophical thinkers as Kant, Royce, Croce, Whitehead, Schutz, Carnap, Popper, and Hempel. This is used as a general introduction to a variety of methodological approaches while insisting on the importance of philosophy in discussing the grounding of much of social science. Also included in this section is a discussion of 'if-then' statements and their varying degrees of validity. "On Facts, Models, and Theories in Economics" is most interesting for its now somewhat dated but still important reminder of the varying applicability of the use of models to different economic instances, the author's examination of indeterminancy in reference to the theory of oligopoly, and his qualified attack on hidden value judgments and the problems this presents for economic measurement. In "On Verification and Operationalism" such issues as verification, confirmation, and falsification of general and special hypotheses are discussed as well as a number of illustrations concerning operationalism in economics. Section four entitled "On Ideal Types and the Interpretations of Reality" contains some of the more immediately interesting materials for a philosopher, relating various notions of ideal types with the false understanding of economic man when separated from his class. "On Comparisons Between Natural and Social Sciences" contains rather impassioned pleas for social scientists not to see their work as inferior to 'hard' science but rather to understand that the difficulty in carefully interpreting their conclusions points up differences between the two endeavors but the differences found in the social sciences are significant in their own right. "Some Aspects and Applications of Economic Methodology" contains three essays that are more directly related to economics. The first gives us four major areas of economic disagreement: semantics, logic, factual assumptions, and value judgments. According to the author the first two are easily resolved while with the latter two it is almost impossible to find agreement. The result is that economics often appears to have more disagreements than other social sciences. The second essay is a review of the Lester-Machlup controversy of the 1950's with a review of what developments took place in the succeeding twenty years and Machlup's continued conviction that the marginal-productivity theory of demand for factors of production remains valid. The third essay is an analysis of positive and normative economics and examination of the nature of the welfare state. The final section of the book entitled "On Various Methodological Positions" for the most part consists of old book reviews or short critiques of the work of leading economists. Two essays stand out. His piece on Schumpeter traces his entire opus giving special attention to his realization that although economics is highly quantifiable, this does not allow for it to be a basis of induction nor to verify or refute economic theories and second to his relatively early emphasis on methodological individualism. The essay on Samuelson is an attack on dismissal of the view that economic theories can be wider than their consequences. Through Samuelson's theorem on international equalization of the prices of equal productive factors Machlup shows that Samuelson's own theorem must do the very thing that he is attacking.

JOSEPH BIEN.

UNIVERSITY OF MISSOURI – COLUMBIA.

History, the Anatomy of Time: The Final Phase of Sunlight. BOŽIDAR KNEŽEVIĆ. Translated by George Vid Tomashevich in collaboration with Sherwood A. Wakeman. New York: Philosophical Library, 1980. Pp. xvii, 258.

This important volume is a clear and comprehensive introduction to the fascinating mind and provocative thoughts of Božidar Knežević (1862-1905). It is primarily a translation from Serbo-Croatian into English of Knežević's own abridgement of his two major works, *Succession in History* (1898) and *Proportion in History* (1901). The philosopher presented an original world-view that ingeniously synthesizes both historicism and positivism with a cosmic scheme of things. The result is a vast, dynamic, and unique vision of mankind's place and destiny within the determining laws of an evolving then devoluting universe.

In his brief but authoritative preface, W. Warren Wagar places Knežević's thought-world in its proper intellectual context and correct historical perspective. Wagar acknowledges the philosopher's indebtedness to Comte and Hegel as well as Darwin, Marx, and Spencer. He emphasizes the modern relevance of Knežević, who envisioned a worldwide sociocultural system as the outgrowth of human progress grounded in science and historical understanding.

In the excellent introductory essay by translator George Vid Tomashevich, one is presented with not only biographical insights but also the major concepts of this great social scientist and bold speculative thinker: the cosmic perspective, a wholistic/organismic orientation, universal history as evolutionary teleology and determinism, human history as sociocultural convergence, and the increasing freedom and growing consciousness within a developing mankind.

Knežević's encyclopedic interests ranged from astronomy and geology to biology and anthropology. His thoughts are remarkably free from religious bias, ethnic partiality, and academic dogmatism. He was committed to science, reason, and the brotherhood of mankind.

The Serbian philosopher recognized three major stages of universal history: inorganic, organic, and psychic levels of development. The planet earth is not the center of the cosmos, nor is the human animal a divinely chosen creature. Mankind is a recent product of and totally within natural history; its destiny is bound to the general life of the universe itself.

Concerning cosmic process and progress, Knežević wrote: "Now that astronomy has bound the earth to the cosmos, and biology the animals to the earth, and man to the animals, and psychology the soul of man to the soul of the animal, it remains for scientific history to bind man to man; history is to bind all peoples and all times, to bring them closer to one another and to reconcile them." He saw planetary history as a single semicircle: an evolutionary ascent from unconscious chaos to the moral/intellectual convergence and global unification of a free mankind, followed by a reverse process of disintegrating descent back into the disproportion and necessity of primordial chaos.

Unlike Nietzsche's eternal recurrence, Knežević's semicircular interpretation of earth history has only one beginning and only one end. Although he anticipated Teilhard's noosphere, there is no mystical omega point to save mankind from universal entropy. An untimely death prevented him from writing his contemplations on the probability of future evolutive cycles (yet he apparently never envisioned life or intelligent beings elsewhere among the other cosmic worlds).

Knežević held the universe to be absolutely indifferent to the fleeting incident of man. Since all things born must die, the human species with its society and civilization is merely a luxury of nature that will inevitably disappear within the flux of reality (as will the organic and inorganic realms). Only God/Nature is the necessary and essential eternal Being, as in Spinoza's system.

Predicting our energy crisis due to the earth's finite and therefore exhaustible resources, Knežević claimed that a cult of the sun as the final religion of nature will mark the end of conscious science just as it marked the beginning of unconscious religion.

Fifty selected aphorisms (1902) are included and an extensive bibliography is provided.

H. JAMES BIRX.

CANISIUS COLLEGE.

The Nature of Philosophy. JOHN KEKES. Totowa, New Jersey: Rowman and Littlefield, 1980. Pp. xiv, 226.

A timely and provocative book whose thesis is "that it is the task of philosophy to show how to live well by the construction and rational justification of worldviews" (p. xii). A worldview, Kekes says, must have "the following five components: a theory of the nature of reality or a *metaphysics;* an account of the human significance of the nautre of reality or an *anthropology;* a system of ideals or a *culture;* an explanation of the discrepancy between the ideal and the actual state of affairs or a *diagnosis;* and a program for overcoming or minimizing the discrepancy or a *policy*" (p. 59).

In my opinion the most interesting idea in Kekes's book is his account of philosophical justification of worldviews. He argues that there are two contexts of justification: the context of introduction and the context of acceptance. He states that the "considerations that justify the introduction of a theory are different from the considerations that justify its acceptance. For what could make it reasonable to suppose that a theory *may* be successful is different from what could make it reasonable to suppose that it *is* successful" (p. 100).

The standard of justification in the context of introduction is *problem-solving;* in the context of acceptance, *truth-directedness.* Kekes says "a theory is justified [in the context of introduction] if it is a possible solution of an enduring problem in accordance with an ideal and [it is justified in the context of acceptance] if it is the best available solution; where the best is the closest approximation of the truth" (p. 101).

By recognizing these two levels of justification "both the selection of possible solutions and the selection of the best available solution are brought under rational control" (p. 101). Also this distinction recognizes the influence of culture in philosophical justification: "In the context of introduction cultural influences are essential to justification" (p. 102), and in the context of acceptance "cultural influences have a lesser role" (p. 102).

In the context of introduction the justification of a worldview "depends on it being able to cope with those enduring problems its predecessors could, and, in addition, also with those which its predecessors could not handle. The standard of justification being appealed to in this context is problem-solving" (p. 194). In the context of acceptance the question to be answered is "which of the theories whose introduction has been justified has the best chance of being true?" (p. 195). the standard of justification being appealed to in this context is truth-directedness.

Kekes says that "the truth-directedness of a theory is determined by comparing it to its rivals on the basis of their logical consistency, adequacy of interpretation, and capacity to withstand criticism" (p. 195).

Kekes also discusses the relation of common sense, science, and history to philosophy. Concerning common sense he argues that "there are some facts that no philosopher can dismiss or dispute" (p. 145) and that "there is a common starting point for all philosophical theories about reality" (p. 145). Concerning science he argues that "philosophy, and not science, is a stronger candidate for being the paradigm of rationality" (p. 158). And concerning history he argues "for the relevance of historical consideration to three different matters: to philosophical justification, to the improvement of worldviews, and to the formation of sensibility" (p. 165).

Kekes's book does not present a worldview, but it does clearly present a *rational* methodology for the construction of such views. Given the present state of the world such a methodology is needed.

EDWARD A. HACKER.

NORTHEASTERN UNIVERSITY.

The Mystical Element in Heidegger's Thought. JOHN D. CAPUTO. Athens: Ohio University Press, 1978. Pp. 292.

While there is a decided "mystical element" in Heidegger's thought, Heidegger himself is no mystic. This Prof. Caputo concludes on the basis of an exhaustive comparison between Meister Eckhart, a 13th century mystic who stands at the beginning of the German speculative tradition and Heidegger, who claims to have surpassed it. Heidegger's admiration for Eckhart is apparent, not least in the freedom with which he appropriates the mystic's vocabulary: a verse from a follower of Eckhart, Angelus Silesius ("The rose is without why; it blooms because it blooms . . . ") runs like a leitmotif throughout *Der Satz vom Grund* where it is meant to suggest the possibility of a disclosure of Being wholly other than the technological world-epoch, that bad destiny of Western metaphysics, which now holds sway.

Caputo finds an "analogy of proportionality" between the two thinkers: Being is to Dasein as God is to the soul. For neither thinker is human reality a set of species-specific properties, but rather a *relation* to what transcends it, albeit a relation in danger of "fallenness" away from its "ownmost" potentialities. In the event *(Ereignis)* of its advent, Being "comes to word" in Dasein, a happening Heidegger often describes in the language of grace; this Caputo likens to Eckhart's doctrine of the birth of the Son in the soul. Surrender to a loving God as well as release into the "play of Being" require *Gelassenheit* (a term Heidegger takes directly from Eckhart), a "letting-be" from which every trace of willing has been extinguished, including the will to demand of things their reasons ("The rose is without why.")

But these analogies, however striking they may seem, are overpowered in the end by disanalogies. Eckhart's mystical communion can never by expressed in words, while for Heidegger, it is only through the creation of a transformed language that there can come to pass a new dispensation of Being at all. Being "needs" Dasein, but God needs no one. Heidegger's Being is thoroughly temporal and historical while for Eckhart, God is timeless and eternal, an *ens separatissimum*. Such a conception of God, however, depends upon a hypostatized conception of time as 'permanent presence' *(Anwesen)* and reveals the extent of Eckhart's debt to Augustine and Plotinus. Caputo regards Heidegger as the more radical thinker by far, who, by laying bare its limitations and distortions, has surpassed the entire metaphysical tradition in which Eckhart's mysticism is still confined.

There are disturbing dimensions to Heidegger's thought that Caputo finds entirely lacking in Eckhart. The mystical union occurs as the crown of an ethical life, whereas Heidegger has "thoroughly purged his thought of any ethical or moral dimension" (236)—a judgment in my view difficult to maintain in the face of the elitism and quietism of the later philosophy. For Eckhart, God is a plenum of perfection and intelligibility while Heidegger's "play of Being" is finally unintelligible, a disclosure which is also a concealment and which has cast us not into the goodness of creation but into a technological *Weltnacht* which threatens the "human essence" itself. Eckhart can give himself to a loving God with perfect confidence, while Dasein can merely wait, in anxiety and unease, without final assurance that "the 'danger' will yield to the 'saving element' within it" (248), preparing itself for an event which may never occur.

While Caputo's final assessment of Heidegger is not one with which I agree ("Heidegger is the great thinker of this century and this philosophical age will likely bear his name" [262]), I consider this to be one of the best Heidegger commentaries to have come along in recent years. The use of an Eckhart-comparison as key to unlock the later Heidegger is successful. Prof. Caputo's prose is extraordinarily lucid and direct, his expositions of specific texts exemplary. The whole question of Heidegger's "mysticism" has been so vexing for students of his thought that it is no small relief to see it dealt with at last in such an authoritative fashion.

SANDRA LEE BARTKY.
UNIVERSITY OF ILLINOIS AT CHICAGO CIRCLE.

RECENT PUBLICATIONS

Landgrebe, Ludwig, *The Phenomenology of Edmund Husserl, Six Essays*. Edited by Donn Welton. Ithaca: Cornell University Press, 1981. Pp. 205. $19.50.

Ruthrof, Horst, *The Reader's Construction of Narrative*. Boston: Routledge & Kegan Paul, 1981. Pp. xiv, 231. $27.50.

Waterhouse, Roger, *A Heidegger Critique: A Critical Examination of the Existential Phenomenology of Martin Heidegger*. Harvester Philosophy Now, No. 15. Atlantic Highlands: Humanities Press, 1981. Pp. xi, 239. $49.00.

Wallace, William A., *Prelude to Galileo: Essays on Medieval and Sixteenth-Century Sources of Galileo's Thought*. Boston Studies in the Philosophy of Science, Vol. 62. Dordrecht: D. Reidell Publishing Co., 1981. Pp. xvi, 369. Dfl. 95,--. $49.95, cloth; Dfl. 45,--. $23.50, paper.

Kruks, Sonia, *The Political Philosophy of Merleau-Ponty*. Harvester Philosophy Now, No. 13. Atlantic Highlands: Humanities Press, 1981. Pp. xiv, 152. $41.00.

Elrod, John W., *Kierkegaard and Christendom*. Princeton: Princeton University Press, 1981. Pp. xxiv, 320. $22.50.

Dallmayr, Fred R., *Twilight of Subjectivity: Contributions to a Post-Individualist Theory of Politics*. Amherst: University of Massachusetts Press, 1981. Pp. xi, 360. $20.00, cloth; $10.00, paper.

Kaufmann, Walter, *Discovering the Mind*. Vol. 3: *Freud verses Adler and Jung*. New York: McGraw-Hill, 1981. Pp. xviii, 494. $17.95.

Swain, Marshall, *Reasons and Knowledge*. Ithaca: Cornell University Press, 1981. Pp. 243. $22.50.

Zaner, Richard M., *The Context of Self: A Phenomenological Inquiry Using Medicine as a Clue*. Series in Continental Thought. Athens: Ohio University Press, 1981. Pp. xiii, 282. $18.95, cloth; $8.95, paper.

Lukas, Mary and Lukas, Ellen, *Teilhard*. New York: McGraw-Hill, 1981. Pp. 376. $6.95, paper.

Webb, Eugene, *Eric Voegelin: Philosopher of History*. Seattle: University of Washington Press, 1981. Pp. ix, 320. $20.00.

One Hundred Years of Thomism: Aeterni Patris and Afterwards: A Symposium. Edited by Victor B. Brezik. Contributions by: L. E. Boyle, R. McInerny, L. Sweeney, and others. Houston: Center for Thomistic Studies, 1981. Pp. 210. $7.00, paper.

Levi, Albert William, *Nature and Art.* New Orleans: Tulane University, 1980. Pp. 36.

Thought Probes: Philosophy through Science Fiction. Edited by Fred D. Miller, Jr. and Nicholas D. Smith. Contributions by: R. G. Smith, A. C. Clarke, R. A. Heinlein, and others. Englewood Cliffs: Prentice-Hall, 1981. Pp. vi, 362. $11.95, paper.

Crosby, Donald A., *Interpretive Theories of Religion.* Religion and Reason, 20. The Hague: Mouton Publishers, 1981. Pp. xi, 335. DM 65,--. $38.25.

Longley, Peter, *Contemporary Logic.* Washington: University Press of America, 1981. Pp. vi, 172.

Mullen, John Douglas, *Kierkegaard's Philosophy: Self-Deception and Cowardice in the Present Age.* Bergenfield: New American Library, 1981. Pp. 176. $2.95, paper.

Hodges, Donald C., *The Bureaucratization of Socialism.* Amherst: University of Massachusetts Press, 1981. Pp. xiii, 210. $15.00.

Beauchamp, Tom L., and Rosenberg, Alexander, *Hume and the Problem of Causation.* New York: Oxford University Press, 1981. Pp. xxiv, 340. $23.50.

Fortin, E. L., *Dissidence et philosophie au moyen age: Dante et ses antecedents.* Cahier d'Etudes Medievales, 6. Montreal: Editions Bellarmin, 1981. Pp. 201. $12.00, paper.

Justice, Social and Global. Papers presented at the Stockholm International Symposium on Justice, September 1978. Edited by Lars O. Ericsson, Harald Ofstad, Guiliano Pontara. Contributions by: B. Barry, W. K. Frankena, J. Galtung, and others. Stockholm: Akademilitteratur, 1981. Pp. 111.

J. Biard, D. Buvat, J.-F. Kervegan, et. al., *Introduction a la lecture de la Science de la logique de Hegel.* Vol. I: L'etre. Collection Philosophie de l'esprit. Paris: Editions Aubier-Montaigne, 1981. Pp. 302.

Hegel, G.W.F., *Les ecrits de Hamann.* Translated by Jacques Colette. Bibliotheque philosophique. Paris: Editions Aubier-Montaigne, 1981. Pp. 142.

Mora, Jose Ferrater, *De la materia a la razon.* Madrid: Alianza Editorial, 1979. Pp. 217.

Chisholm, Roderick M., *The First Person: An Essay on Reference and Intentionality.* Minneapolis: University of Minnesota Press, 1981. Pp. 135.

Verene, Donald Phillip, *Vico's Science of Imagination*. New York: Cornell University Press, 1981. Pp. 227. $19.50.

The Great Chain of Being and Italian Phenomenology. Edited by Angela Ales Bello. Contributions by: J. De Finance, Y. Belaval, W. H. Werkmeister, and others. *Analecta Husserliana,* Volume 11. Dordrecht: D. Reidel Publishing Company, 1981. Pp. xix, 347. Dfl. 110,-- / $58.00.

Findlay, J. N., *Kant and the Transcendental Object: A Hermeneutic Study*. New York: The Clarendon Press; Oxford University Press, 1981. Pp. xxiv, 392. $24.00.

Flew, Antony, *The Politics of Procrustes: Contradictions of Enforced Equality*. Buffalo: Prometheus Books, 1981. Pp. 216. $16.95.

Stojanovic, Svetozar, *In Search of Democracy in Socialism*. Buffalo: Prometheus Books, 1981. Pp. 145. $16.95.

Srinivasan, G., *The Phenomenological Approach to Philosophy: Indian and Western*. Delhi: Caravan Publishing Company, 1980. Pp. 80. Rs 35.00

Anton, John P., *Critical Humanism as a Philosophy of Culture: The Case of E. P. Papanoutsos*. North Central Publishing Company, 1981. Pp. 44.

Berndtson, Arthur, *Power, Form, and Mind*. New Jersey: Associated University Presses, 1981. Pp. 296. $24.50.

The Foundations of Analytic Philosophy. Edited by Peter A. French, Theodore E. Uehling, Jr., and Howard K. Wettstein. Contributions by: R. M. Chisholm, P. Benacerraf, T. D. Parsons, and others. Midwest Studies in Philosophy. Volume VI. Minneapolis: University of Minnesota Press, 1981. Pp. 524.

Berenson, Frances M., *Understanding Persons: Personal and Impersonal Relationships*. New York: St. Martin's Press, 1981. Pp. xiv, 198. $19.95.

Brentano, Franz, *Sensory and Noetic Consciousness*. Edited by Oskar Kraus; English edition edited by Linda L. McAlister. Atlantic Highlands: Humanities Press, 1981. Pp. xxv, 139. $20.75.

VOL. XLII DECEMBER 1981 NO. 2

PHILOSOPHY AND PHENOMENOLOGICAL RESEARCH

A Quarterly Journal

Published for the

INTERNATIONAL PHENOMENOLOGICAL SOCIETY

by

BROWN UNIVERSITY

This journal is the official organ of the International Phenomenological Society. The editors are not necessarily in agreement with the views expressed by the various writers. Papers submitted for publication will not be returned unless accompanied by a self-addressed, stamped envelope, or return postage. The annual subscription rate for libraries and institutions is $15.00 (foreign $18.00 postpaid); subscriptions for individuals are $12.00 annually (foreign $13.00 postpaid). The rate for single copies of current or available back issues is $3.75 (double issue, $7.50) and $3.00 (double issue, $6.00) respectively. There is an additional charge for postage and handling on all back issues. Address all communications and payments to *Philosophy and Phenomenological Research*, Box 1947, Brown University, Providence, Rhode Island 02912. The journal office should be notified of any change of address at least six weeks before the next issue is scheduled to appear. A list of the past contents with available back numbers will be sent upon request. For out of print volumes write to Kraus-Thomson Organization Ltd., Route 100, Millwood, New York 10546. For microfiche copies write to Johnson Associates, P.O. Box 1017, Greenwich, Connecticut 06830; and for microfilm copies University Microfilms International, 300 North Zeeb Road, Ann Arbor, Michigan 48106.

Published quarterly by Brown University
Printed by Niagara Printing Corporation, Niagara Falls, New York

CONTENTS

I. ARTICLES

The Intentional Project by B. C. BIRCHALL 147

Sensations by ALPHONSO LINGIS 160

Prolegomenon to a Theory of Deception by WINSTON A. VAN HORNE 171

Man, God, and Death in Hegel's *Phenomenology* by JOHN BURBIDGE 183

Politics of the Present: Machiavellian Humanism by JOSEPH BIEN 197

Imagination and Information by PAUL TAYLOR 205

Abhinavagupta and Dewey on Art and Its Relation to Morality: Comparisons and Evaluations by DINESH C. MATHUR 224

Causes and Events by N. G. E. HARRIS 236

Why Cartesian Intuitions Are Compatible with the Identity Thesis by CHRISTOPHER S. HILL 254

II. DISCUSSIONS

The Primacy of Action by MICHAEL A. SIMON 266

Countervailing Tendencies and Falsifiability in *Capital* by DANIEL LITTLE 283

Reply to Professor Zaitchik by JERRY A. FODOR 292

Reply to Professor Fodor by ALAN ZAITCHIK 294

III. REVIEWS

Howard A. Slaatte's *Time and Its End: A Comparative Existential Interpretation of Time and Eschatology* by ARTHUR W. MUNK 296

Fritz Marti's *The Unconditional in Human Knowledge. Four Early Essays (1794-1796) by F. W. J. Schelling* by WOLFGANG SCHWARZ 297

Ben Lazare Mijuskovic's *Loneliness in Philosophy, Psychology & Literature* by WARREN E. STEINKRAUS 298

Richard Rorty's *Philosophy and the Mirror of Nature* by HARRY RUJA 299

D. F. Gustafson and B. L. Tapscott's *Body, Mind, and Method, Essays in Honor of Virgil C. Aldrich* by MARY B. MAHOWALD 300

Adam Podgórecki and Maria Łoś's *Multi-Dimensional Sociology* by RICHARD T. PETERSON 301

Dale Reipe's *Indian Philosophy Since Independence* by WALTER RUBEN and HILTRUD RÜSTAU 303

IV. RECENT PUBLICATIONS 306

THE INTENTIONAL PROJECT

Problem of the Intentional Nexus

For Brentano, what is characteristic of every mental activity is 'the reference to something as an object'.[1] Whenever we have a mental act, whether it is presentation, judgment, love, hate, or desire, there is always *something* that is the 'object' of that act. But what is it for a mental act to have an object, and what sort of object might it be? The second part of the question is concerned with the ontology of objects (what sorts of 'entities' can *be* objects?) whereas the first part of the question is concerned with what might be termed the epistemology of the intentional nexus — with the way in which mental acts can be 'involved with' or 'connected to' their objects. Some mental acts, like knowing and finding, for example, appear to pose no peculiar problems. In knowing, it might be said, we are simply related to the actual state of affairs which is known. In finding, it might be said, we are simply related to the actual state of affairs which is found. But what of mental acts like believing and seeking? They also have objects, but in this case, objects which may not exist. No similar straightforward answer to the questions: what is the *object* of these acts? and what is it for these acts to *have* objects? seems possible.

The Classical Dilemma

The classical dilemma is based on the assumption that for a mental act to have an object, the mental act must be in some way *related to that object.* In knowing or true belief, as suggested above, we have a relationship between two existing entities, the mental act and the object. For false belief, then, we must be related to something other than the state of affairs which would make the belief true. But this is no solution. Either what we *are* related to in false belief is the object of that belief or it is not. If it is the object of belief, then we are

---

[1]Brentano, F. *Psychology from an Empirical Standpoint,* p. 271.

related, not to something other than what would make the belief true, but to what *would* make the belief true, in which case the belief would be true not false. On the other hand, if it is not the object of belief, then no account has been given of the object of belief. It might be contended that the surrogate entity (idea, etc.) to which we are related is supposed to 'stand for', 'refer to' or simply 'intend' the real object of belief. On the account offered of what it is for a false belief to have an object, viz., to be related to something other than what would make the belief true, no account could be given of the intentional nexus now said to hold between some 'intermediate entity' and the real object of belief. If such an account could be given, then there was no reason for introducing 'intermediate entities' in the first place.[2]

The apparent failure of the relational interpretation of the intentional nexus or 'having an object' has led some philosophers[3] to reject the relational interpretation. But because they accept the assumption on which the classical dilemma is based, viz., that for a mental act to have an object, the mental act must be related to that object, they have no alternative but to reject the very notion of 'having an object', or reinterpret it along what Armstrong, for example, calls 'adverbial' lines.[4] Just as dancing is not a relation which holds between the person and the dance he dances, believing is not a relation between the person or his belief and some 'object of belief'. So to believe that p is not to be related to some object or proposition p, but is to believe in a p-ish way.

It may well be true that when someone believes that p, that person does believe in what might be described as a p-ish way. But if beliefs are not to be totally disconnected from the occurrences in the world which make them true, the person's belief state must still 'involve' or 'intend' those occurrences. Indeed, if the statement 'Tom believes that the sun is shining' is to be reinterpreted so that we lose all reference to what would make the belief true, then we find ourselves in the illogical position of not being able to believe anything *about the world,* not even the view that Armstrong espouses. On the other hand, if the belief is not totally disconnected from what would make it true, the problem of the intentional nexus remains. Merely to say

---

[2]This ambivalence is typical of correspondence theories.

[3]Notably, Brentano (with difficulty), Quine, and Armstrong.

[4]Armstrong, D.M. *Belief, Truth and Knowledge,* p. 45.

that whenever one believes that p, one believes in a p-ish way, does not provide an account of how believing in a p-ish way can 'intend' or 'refer to' something independent of that believing.

The classical dilemma seems unavoidable. Once 'having an object' is understood as a relation holding between a mental act and its object, the postulation of 'peculiar entities', at least in the case of false belief, seems inevitable. To reject the view of mental acts as relations, however, seems to have an equally unacceptable implication. As Grossmann puts it: 'If acts are not relations, no connection is left between a self and the rest of the world'.[5] Grossmann thinks a solution can be found by rejecting the traditional view of relations which assumes that for a relation to hold between two entities, *both entities must exist*.

> It is sometimes said that the intentional relation could not possibly hold between an existent and a non-existent, because this would mean that it would have to be a relation with only one term and a one term relation is simply an absurdity. An entity with just one term, in the sense in question, would have to be a property, if anything at all, but could not possibly be a relation. In short, it is said that the very notion of a relation requires it to have more than one existent term. But this argument seems to rest on an equivocation. The notion of a relation with just one term is absurd; a relation with just one term would be an ontological absurdity. But when we assert that the intentional relation can connect an idea with a non-existent object, we do not imply that it is such a one term relation, and hence, an absurdity. The intentional nexus is a two term relationship. But, and this is the crux of the matter, the entities which stand in this two term relation need not exist. We must distinguish between the terms of a relation, the number of terms which a relation has, on the one hand, and the entities which stand in this relation on the other.[6]

For Grossmann, then, false belief, for example, poses a problem only if we assume, mistakenly, that for a relation to exist between the mental act of believing and the object of belief, *both* 'entities' must exist. Such an assumption leads, understandably, to the postulation of 'peculiar entities'. In their place, Grossmann proposes a way of being related to ordinary things in the world, which, in the case of false belief, do not exist. In the place of an ordinary relationship said to hold between a mental act and a 'peculiar entity' ('peculiar' because it

---

[5]Grossmann, R. 'Acts and Relations in Brentano', *Analysis,* 21.1, October, 1960, p. 2.

[6]Grossmann, R. 'An Introduction to Kasimir Twardowski's *On the Content and Object of Presentations*' (mimeographed copy), pp. 17-18.

has to function both as an object of belief and not as an object of belief), Grossmann proposes a 'peculiar relationship' said to hold between a mental act and an ordinary entity ('peculiar' because the ordinary entity, in the case of false belief, does not exist). In this way, he attempts to avoid the dilemma whilst retaining a realistic sense of the object of belief.

Grossmann either says or implies that for there to *be* a relation, there must *be* more than one term, that is to say,more than one term must exist. At the same time he says that the *entities* which stand in a two-termed relation need not exist! In other words, Grossmann is separating *terms* from *entities*. This being so, the fact that in false belief we have a relationship holding between two existing *terms* does not in any way explain how this relationship is to be construed as one involving a nonexistent object or entity. Grossmann could argue that the existing term somehow 'stands for' or 'intends' the nonexisting entity. This reply would be inadequate, however, since he would be faced, once again, with the problem of the intentional nexus, which has been moved from the context of *belief* ⟶ *nonexisting entity*, to the context of *term* ⟶ *nonexisting entity*. An explanation, then, is given of how we can have a relationship between two existing terms, but given Grossmann's separation of existing terms from nonexisting entities, no explanation is given of how we can have a relationship between an existing term and a nonexisting entity — between an existing mental act and an object which does not exist.[7]

What explanation *could* Grossmann give of his 'intentional relation'? So much depends on how we are to understand the ontology of his 'nonexisting entity'. In the case of Tom's believing that there is a golden mountain, the intentional nexus is to be explained as a 'relation' holding between an 'idea' (of the golden mountain?) and the 'nonexisting golden mountain'. But what does it mean to say that there *is* a 'nonexisting golden mountain'? What is the ontological status, in other words, of 'the golden mountain which does not exist'? On the face of it, there are two possible answers to this question. In the first place, we might be related to a 'false proposition' or some entity with the 'attribute of nonexistence' (understood positively as 'sub-

---

[7]Grossmann tries to support his division between terms and entities by appealing to the 'identity relation'. But even if we accepted the division in this case it does nothing to explain how an *existing term can be related to a nonexisting entity*. See p. 18 of the above 'Introduction'.

sistence'?). The problem with this interpretation is to explain why being related to a 'false proposition' or entity with the 'attribute of nonexistence' is to be taken as a belief that there *is* (exists) a golden mountain. In other words, the object to which one is related in false belief would be categorically different from the object to which one is related in true belief (see my comments on this point in second paragraph of page 147). In the second place, we are not related to a 'false proposition' or some entity with the 'attribute of nonexistence', i.e., some entity ontologically distinct from true propositions or existing entities, since a 'false proposition' or 'nonexistent entity' is no more than the truth of the contradictory. That is to say, we are related to the contradictory of the proposition *some mountains are golden,* viz., the true proposition or fact that *no mountains are golden.* But in this case we would be related to an *existent,* not a 'nonexistent', entity. And being related, intentionally or otherwise, to the true proposition or fact that no mountains are golden could not be construed as *believing that there is a golden mountain.*

The more one examines the possible ontology of Grossmann's 'nonexisting entity', the more one is inclined to the view that he avoids postulating 'subsisting entities' only by postulating 'ontologically peculiar relations', which, interestingly, turn out to be 'ontologically peculiar' precisely because of the assumed 'ontological peculiarity' of the 'nonexisting entity' to which the believer is supposedly related in false belief. Once the ontological status of 'nonexisting entity' is cleared up, it appears that Grossmann has not found a way out of the classical dilemma. Grossmann's analysis of the intentional nexus as being a relation between an 'idea' and a 'nonexistent entity' is little more than an attempt, in the context of the classical dilemma, to have it both ways: to say that we *are* related to an existent entity but, at the same time, that we *are not* related to an existent entity.

The Intentional Project

Earlier in the paper I distinguished between two questions: what is it for a mental act to *have* an object? and what sort of *object* might it be? Logically it can be argued that the object of false belief must be the same as the object of true belief.[8] If it were different, false belief

---

[8]I am talking here about the *ontological status* of the object of belief. Obviously, I am not wanting to identify the belief that the *earth is flat* with the belief that the *earth is round.*

could not logically be true belief, but it is false belief precisely because the object it *intends as true* is not true. The same point can be made with respect to the mental act of seeking. If the object of seeking were not the same as the object of finding, what we were looking for could never, in principle, be found, and what was found could never, in principle, have been sought. But the object of true belief and the object of finding is an actual occurrence or state of affairs.[9] On the argument advanced so far, this means that the object of false belief and the object of seeking is also an actual occurrence or state of affairs. But how can this be, given the fact of *false* belief and the possibility that what we are seeking does not exist? This question reintroduces the problem of what it is for a mental act to have an object.

The classical dilemma seems to force a choice between being related to the object or not being related to the object. Being related seems necessary if the mental act is to have any connection with the external world. On the other hand, not being related seems necessary if we are to explain the possibility of there being objects that do not exist. So we appear to be left with the paradox of the intentional nexus having to be both a relation and not a relation. To say, however, that believing, for example, is both a relation and not a relation might be incomplete, but it is not paradoxical. Remember that the classical dilemma was based on the assumption not that 'having an object' *is a relation* but that 'having an object' is a relation *between the mental act and the object.* In rejecting this assumption, we can still argue that 'having an object' is a relation, but not one holding between the mental act and its object. In so far as we concentrate on the *act* we can say, for example, that believing is a relation. In so far as we concentrate on the *object* we can say that believing is not a relation — not a relation between the act and the object.

If believing is a relation but not one holding between the mental act and the object of belief, what are its terms? Russell's 'multiple relation' theory of believing[10] goes some of the way towards providing an answer. In believing that X is Y, we are not related to the complex occurrence X being Y, but are multiply related to the relevant components of that complex, viz., X and Y. While this account does not assume that we are related to the object of belief, viz., X being Y, and thus avoids the difficulties of the classical dilemma already canvassed,

---

[9] I leave an examination of the metaphysics of states of affairs for another paper.

[10] Russell, B. *The Problems of Philosophy,* Ch. 12.

it presents new difficulties. Russell does not explain why being multiply related to the components of the complex X is Y is to be taken as a *belief* that X is Y. For this to be explained, we need to move from the simple cognitionalism of Russell to the conationalism of Alexander.[11]

Cognitionalism, in its characterization of mind as a passive cogniser, is unable, according to Alexander, to give an account of mental *activity* — of mental *acts* such as knowing, believing, remembering, and expecting. Indeed, it is the failure of cognitionalism to answer such fundamental epistemological questions as 'why do we know one thing rather than another?' and 'why do we know some determinate features of one thing rather than other equally determinate features of that same thing?' that has given support to idealism and has led to the 'gradual demise of the independence of the object'.

For Alexander, however, it is not realism that is in question here, but the doctrine of cognitionalism (which has, in fact, more affinities with idealism). To solve the problem of knowledge from the point of view of the knower, in a way consistent with realism, and to get a general theory of mental activity, we need to introduce the notion of *conation or willing* — to move from the standpoint of *passive receptivity* to that of *active initiation/reciprocity*. Anderson comments, 'Taking conation as striving, however, we find in the first instance that the conational theory of mind — exemplified in Alexander's "Foundations and Sketch-Plan of a Conational Psychology" and again in Freud's recognition of the characteristic mental process as a *wish* — suggested also in the general position of the pragmatists — certainly marks an advance on the cognitional theory. This is particularly so in respect of the theory of knowledge itself (including the theory of error).'[12]

How does this work in the case of knowledge or cognition itself? The point stressed by Alexander is that we do not, contrary to much of cognitionalist theory, *first* cognize an object and *then* act accordingly. 'It is never true that we have first an object cognized and that the cognition of the object determines the appropriate conative response.'[13] Such a cognitionalist approach would be unable to

[11]Alexander, S. 'Foundations and Sketch-Plan of a Conational Psychology', *British Journal of Psychology,* December, 1911.

[12]Anderson, J. 'Mind as Feeling', *Studies in Empirical Philosophy,* p. 70.

[13]Alexander, S. *Ibid.,* p. 250.

answer either of the fundamental epistemological questions raised above. 'On the contrary, according to the character of the conative act, however brought about, *the object is revealed under a certain aspect.*'[14] (my emphasis). Illustrations of this general thesis could be multiplied, but two examples should suffice for the purposes of this paper. We do not first cognize an apple as having certain features, a cognition which then brings into operation the desire to eat it, rather 'we are aware of it as edible in and by the act in which we seek to eat it.'[15] Similarly, we do not first cognize the direction in which a cricket ball is coming to us and then adjust our actions to catch it, rather 'in performing the mental act which ends in holding our hands so as to catch the cricket ball which is coming to us in a certain direction, we are conscious of the direction in which it is coming to us.'[16] *In wanting* to eat the apple we are conscious of certain features of the apple just as *in wanting* to catch the cricket ball we are conscious of the direction in which it is coming to us. Had we different conations operative in those circumstances, then we would have cognized — been conscious of — *other* features of the objects or situations in question. So 'the selection which we call "knowing" is made more precise if we can say that we *pursue* states of the things that surround us and they *satisfy* processes in our minds.'[17] In other words, knowing, on a conationalist theory of mind, is not a passive reflection or representation of what is known, but is a determinate activity coming to terms with or in interaction with certain equally determinate features of the environment in which the knowing takes place.

Earlier I said that Russell does not explain why being multiply related to the components of the complex X is Y is to be taken as a *belief* that X is Y. The problem seems to be that of wanting to combine X and Y, in some sense, in order to explain the belief that X is Y, yet in order to accommodate the possibility of false belief, recognizing that they cannot be combined in fact, hence the 'multiple relations'. It might be thought that we can combine the 'ideas' of X and Y. But a combination of the 'idea' of X and the 'idea' of Y which may resemble or fail to resemble something which is not itself an 'idea', could not constitute a *belief* that X is Y.[18] By incorporating the general cona-

[14] *Ibid.*

[15] Alexander, S. *Space, Time and Deity,* Vol. II, p. 119.

[16] *Ibid.*

[17] Anderson, J. 'The Knower and the Known', *Studies in Empirical Philosophy,* p. 40.

[18] See Anderson, J. 'Empiricism and Logic', *Studies in Empirical Philosophy,* pp. 168-69.

tionalist approach to the understanding of mental activity in his epistemology, Anderson comes up with a *conational* interpretation of believing as *acting upon X as if it were Y* or simply *taking X to be Y.*[19] In acting upon X as if it were Y or in taking X to be Y, the believer is *acting as if X and Y were combined in fact,* i.e., he treats an apple as if it were edible (picks it up, bites it, tastes it, etc.). So it is conation or mental activity, not 'ideas', which provides the necessary link, as it were, between the distinguishable components of the complex X is Y to which the believer is said to be multiply related. It is this 'conative link' between X and Y which cognitionalists, like Russell, ignore, and which leaves Russell's 'multiple relation theory of belief' incomplete.

Of course, in taking X to be Y, the believer is involved in a relationship with the components X and Y but not one that requires that X *be* Y. Taking X to be Y, then, is not a relationship between a mental act and the object of belief, viz., X being Y, but it does not preclude there being a relationship between the mental act and the object of belief, namely, in those cases where the belief is true. The relationship in this case is not believing but, rather, *finding* the object of belief. In cases of false belief the believer may still take X to be Y even though X is not Y, and it is precisely this notion of *taking*-something to be what it is not that enables us to explain error or false belief.

> The doctrine of striving permits us to distinguish cases where we are mistaken from cases where we are not. We are right, it may be said, when we get what we strive for and wrong when we do not. Error, at least, is comparable to missing one's mark (mis-taking); and here the Freudian theory of errors as satisfactions of (unacknowledged) wishes is important. We are in error when we treat A, which is not B, as if it were B; when we mistakenly *use* it as a B — e.g., when we treat a red danger signal as if it were a green safety signal, or treat as a friend a man who will actually deceive us.[20]

Through conationalism, we can be related to the external world and avoid postulating such peculiar entities as 'nonexistent objects' or 'false propositions' to which we are supposed, by some, to be related in false belief.

At the beginning of this section I said that the object of belief, whether true or false, is a state of affairs. It remains to explain in what way a state of affairs can be said to be the object of false belief. To believe that X is Y is to treat X as if it were Y. In the case of false

[19] Anderson, J., particularly 'Empiricism and Logic', p. 170.

[20] Anderson, J. 'Mind as Feeling', *Studies in Empirical Philosophy,* pp. 71-72.

belief we are entitled to say two things at least: (i) X is not Y, hence the belief is false, and (ii) the object of the belief, even though false, is X is Y. To say what the object of a false belief is, or for that matter, what the object of a belief is, is to do no more than *specify* what state of affairs would make the belief true, or in conational terms, what state of affairs would satisfy the believing. But the specification of the state of affairs that would satisfy or is necessary to the satisfaction of the believing is not a specification of a peculiar relationship holding between the belief and the object of belief, nor is it a specification of some peculiar entity to which the believer is supposed to be related. To reiterate, it is a specification of the state of affairs that would complete or is necessary to the completion of a particular intentional project, whether that project be one of believing, seeking, expecting, or whatever. The concrete case of Tom believing there is a golden mountain presents, on the account outlined above, no insuperable problems. Admittedly there is no golden mountain, and this is why his belief is false; but we can still say that the object of his belief is a real golden mountain, meaning by this that it is a real golden mountain that *would* make the belief true, or in general terms, is *necessary* to completing the intentional project in question.

> It is clear now what the object of volition is, which is thus entertained in the initial stage of willing and realized in the completed will. It is some matter of fact in the most general sense of that phrase, some connexion within the real world, which real world includes our self. This reality of the object is the cognitum which is the object of the *fiat* or *consent* of the will. In other words, it is in willing, that objects . . . become known *as* real, where, once more, "real" means non-mental reality and does not imply contrast to the illusory. Such a matter of fact is stated in a proposition. This proposition states the so-called end of the volition and states that end as attained.[21]

In this way we dispense with the need for 'subsisting golden mountains' to which the believer is supposed to be related in false belief and retain *in fact* Russell's often-acclaimed 'robust sense of reality'.

---

[21] Alexander, S. 'Foundations and Sketch-Plan of a Conational Psychology', pp. 265-66. The same idea is present in Freud: 'the object (Objekt) of an instinct is the thing in regard to which or through which the instinct is able to achieve its aim'. (Freud, S. 'Instincts and their Vicissitudes', Papers on Metapsychology, in *The Complete Psychological Works of Sigmund Freud,* ed. James Strachey, Vol. XIV, p. 122.) None of this implies that the volition or instinct is *already* related to what can satisfy it, or, in my terms, complete the project.

Conclusion

The classical dilemma cannot avoid the unacceptable implications of its basic assumption that for a mental act to have an object, the mental act must be related to that object. Rejecting this assumption, however, does not mean a loss of relation between the mental act and the world, nor a loss of the object. Understood conationally, believing that X is Y, for example, is acting upon X as if it were Y, this being one example of an intentional project which would be satisfied or completed by the occurrence of Y in X. 'Having an object', then, *is* a relation, but not one holding between the mental act and its object. Rather, it is a specific causal relation holding between a mental striving (whatever its distinctive character) and the terms involved in the object of belief whether they are in fact combined or not. The object of belief is a state of affairs, meaning by this no more than that it is a state of affairs, in this case X being Y, that would complete the intentional project. But whereas *completing* the intentional project is a relation between the mental act and its object (knowing, finding, etc.), the specification of what *would* complete the intentional project is not a specification of any such relation, nor does it involve any such relation. Possibly, believing, seeking, etc., could be described with respect to the object of belief or the object of search, as 'anticipated relations'.[22] 'Anticipated relations', however, are not themselves relations, even though the anticipation will involve relations, but not to the object anticipated. So intentionality *may* be a mark of the mental in so far as mental acts are the sorts of activities, like interests, wishes, desires, etc., that can be satisfied under certain conditions. But if this is so, this is no more than a *qualitative* peculiarity of mind, not a relational or logical peculiarity.[23] The rela-

[22]Cf. unpublished Doctoral thesis, *The Identity Theory of the Proposition,* submitted by the author to Sydney University in February 1972.

[23]While it is true that the recognition of mind as active as found, for example, in Alexander's 'Foundations and Sketch-Plan of a Conational Psychology', is an advance upon cognitionalism, the *description* of mental acts as interests, wishes, desires or beliefs, is liable to misunderstanding. Mental acts are not interests, wishes, or desires, or beliefs *in and for themselves,* but are the sorts of *qualities* (Anderson suggests in 'Mind as Feeling', emotions or passions) that are able, under certain conditions, to take up relations of being interested in, wishing for, desiring, and believing in. And it is only in taking up these relations, but not relations to the objects of the acts, that mental acts can be said to 'have objects'. To describe a mental act or quality in terms of its relations, as a belief, for example, is to suggest, mistakenly, that mental acts or qualities *always* 'have objects', even in those cases when they are not actively related to the surrounding world in which they exist. Possibly this is one reason why Brentano and others thought that mind had to be *defined* in terms of 'intentionality' or 'having an object'.

tions involved in acting upon X as if it were Y or finding the object of belief, for example, are straightforward causal relations, not relations of a peculiar sort, nor relations holding between peculiar sorts of entities.

B. C. BIRCHALL.

UNIVERSITY OF NEW ENGLAND,
N.S.W., AUSTRALIA.

BIBLIOGRAPHY

Alexander, S. 'Foundations and Sketch-Plan of a Conational Psychology', *British Journal of Psychology,* December 1911.

Alexander, S. *Space, Time and Deity,* Vols. I & II, foreword by D. Emmet, Macmillan & Co., London, reprint, 1966.

Anderson, J. *Studies in Empirical Philosophy,* Angus & Robertson, Sydney, 1962.

Armstrong, D. M. *Belief, Truth and Knowledge,* Cambridge at the University Press, 1973.

Arnaud, R. B. 'Brentanist Relations', in Analysis and Metaphysics, (Essays in Honour of R. M. Chisholm), ed. K. Lehrer, D. Reidel, Dordrecht-Holland, 1975.

Bergmann, G. *Logic and Reality,* The University of Wisconsin Press, Madison, 1964.

Brentano, F. *Psychology from an Empirical Standpoint,* Routledge & Kegan Paul, London, 1973 edition.

Freud, S. 'Instincts and their Vicissitudes', Papers on Metapsychology, *The Complete Psychological Works of Sigmund Freud,* ed. J. Strachey, Vol. XIV. The Hogarth Press and the Institute of Psycho-analysis, London, 1971 edition.

Grossmann, R. 'Acts and Relations in Brentano', *Analysis,* 21.1 October, 1960.

Grossmann, R. 'An Introduction to Kasimir Twardowski's *On the Content and Object of Presentations*' (mimeographed copy).

Grossmann, R. *Reflections on Frege's Philosophy,* Northwestern University Press, Evanston, 1969.

Prior, A.N. *Objects of Thought,* ed. P.T. Geach and A.J.P. Kenny, Oxford at the Clarendon Press, London, 1971.

Quine, W. V. *Word and Object,* The M.I.T. Press, Cambridge, Massachusetts, 1960.

Russell, B. *The Problems of Philosophy,* Home University Library, 1912.

SENSATIONS

1. The Repudiation of Analysis into Sensations

The term sensation is ambiguous: on the one hand, to sense something is to catch on to the sense of something, its direction, orientation, or meaning. On the other hand, to sense something is to be sensitive to something, to feel a contact with it, to be affected by it.

The level of sensation would be the original locus of openness upon things, or contact with them. But in classical epistemology, this layer also came to have the function of the simples, into which the complex acts of cognition could be etiologically decomposed. Sensation would be the stratum of here-and-now givens, facts, as opposed to the relations and references in which they could function as terms. It would consist in a multiplicity of impressions, points of impact or of contact. It would consist in moments of intensity, or qualities, taken without their quantitative extensions and relationships and their referential meanings.

For Merleau-Ponty the cause of phenomenology requires a resolute rejection of any notion of analysis into sensations. One cannot decompose the primary experience into meanings and impressions, structures and elements, relations and terms, complexes and simples. The concept of Gestalt expresses this indecomposability, where, although the whole and its properties are indeed seated in the parts and on the same level as they (not an ideal form imposed from without), the parts themselves derive their properties as parts and their very partitioning to the sites and roles they receive from the whole. A figure against a ground is already such a Gestalt—and it is the most elementary experience; to experience *is* to discern a figure against a background. What there is is not sensations which are then patterned or interpreted, but perceptions, perceptions of things, and not of qualities or impressions. And the background that regulates the position and contours of the things is not a psychic space or empty field; it is the world-horizon, system of planes, levels, ordered gradation. The apparent sizes and shapes of fragmentary percepts, the sensory constants, the regulation of degree of illumination and tonal density—all this reveals, Merleau-Ponty set out to show in detail, a telos of perceiving things in our perceptual life, and an imperative of compossibility and concordance of things. From its most rudimentary experience, our sensitivity per-ceives—goes out to, captures—things, and is open to *the world*. The perceiving subject has to be desubstantialized, and conceived as an intentionality, a self-transcending movement of ex-istence, and no longer as the place of inscription of impressions. The repudiation of all etiological analysis into sensations opens the field for a descriptive inventory of phenomenal structures—for phenomenology.

But Merleau-Ponty came to present the perception of a thing not so much as a grasp of its form, contours or configuration, as a capture of its inner axes, the inner pulse with which it actively occupies its zone of space-time. The Gestaltist notion of structure is already, in the *Phenomenology of Perception*, being supplanted by a more phenomenological notion of essence—but essence as sensuous sense, described sometimes as a matrix or pregnancy, sometimes as an utterance. The water of the pool is present across the garden; "this red" is in fact a "punctuation" in the phrasing of a field, already an element of the *logos endiathetos*. In *The Visible and the Invisible* the Saussurian notion of structure brings about a mutation in terminology with which Merleau-Ponty now describes the sensorial field; it is articulated not so much into terms, as into differences between terms. With its oppositional contrasts, its synchronic reliefs and diachronic recurrences, the conjunctive tissue of the sensible field is described as a text incarnating a wild, preconventionalized logos; the operational language, the speaking word, *la parole parlante*, is but the utterance of what the things silently mean—mean to say. The silent world is already structured like a language.

2. The Motile Nature of Sensorial Intentionality

It seems to us that this phenomenology, making perception primary, veers toward a certain idealism. Is not something lost, in the measure that sensation becomes the perception of a sense—that by which sensation is sensuous? The exposure to the field of the sensuous is not only a capture of messages, things tapped out on our receptors; it is contact with them in their resistance and materiality, being sensitive to them, susceptible to being sustained and wounded by them. Sensation also means feeling pleased, exhilarated, or being pained by the sensible. A sentient subject does not innocently poise objects about itself as its decor, it is not only oriented by their sense; it is subject to them, to their brutality and their sustentation.

Heidegger had used the idea of a projective prehension to circumvent both the idea of the primacy of sensations and that of the primacy of perception. The first contact with the world is in teleological and motile dealings with the instrumentalities at hand, and the comprehension it involves is not a subsumption under ideal identities of signification, but a power to take hold of possibilities with what is at hand. However, Heidegger had thematized the subjection to the world, the being oriented, affected, attuned, disposed by it, the finding oneself in it and the being cast in it even as one distances oneself with regard to it and projects oneself into it, in the thematics of *Befindlichkeit, Geworfenheit* and *Stimmung*. It is true that there was still something ethereal in this sensitivity, for the Heideggerian affectivity is more a matter of being disposed by the layout of the world-clearing than a susceptibility to being gratified, exalted, or pained by things. Heidegger seats our vulnerability and mortality in our self-transcending and self-projective spontaneity, rather than in subjection to the contingencies and brutalities of matter. This sensitivity or susceptibility is conjoined with the comprehensive or comprehending thrust of the practical prehension of instrumentalities when Heidegger interprets them as dimensions of one temporal thrust. The being subjected to and affected by what has come to pass and the efficacious projecting oneself out to what is possible and to come are the two temporal dimensions in which presence to the real world is realized.

In *Phenomenology of Perception* Merleau-Ponty sought to avoid the idealist character of the Husserlian, sense-ascribing intentionality by appealing to the Heideggerian concept of prehension. Things are com-prehended not when an identifying intentionality has supplied an identity with which to interpret their sensuous aspects, but when there is a "*prise*," a hold on them. Not only vectors of transmission of instrumental force, but the very sensuous materiality of things is given in a motor apprehension. The sensorial *quale* itself, the blue or the red, occupies its space with a certain condensing, radiant, recessive or rhythmic schema; and it is this inner movement or extensive essence which is captured by the abductive, adductive, or recessive motility of the sensitive organism.

The inner micromovement with which each sensorial consistency occupies its space is caught up in the motility of the exploring eye or hand, and communicated across the sensibility through the transversal unity of the corporeal schema. Thus the synthesizing agency is not the spontaneity of the mind, but the corporeal schema, which does not engender or posit the ideal term of their unity, but focuses upon a thing as upon a transversal unity of the different sensorial tones and textures concording, fitting together, expressing one another. The model is the way the monocular images are assembled into one visual objective: the agency that synthesizes the images on the two eyes into one transcendent object is a corporeal synergy which coordinates all the receptor surfaces of the body into one organ axed on the exterior pole. *The Visible and the Invisible* and *Eye and Mind* maintain this motor character of the intentionality in perception; the sense or essence of the water of the pool is sensed as the eye follows the way it holds and lets play the streaks of sunlight, the way it contrasts with the repose of the garden, the way its liquid undulations organize shifts of light and tonal contrasts across the field. This sirupy and aqueous essence speaks to the motility of our sensibility. The impressional side to sensation is in fact this *being moved*. The grasp of the sense or essence involved is a capture of a schema of movement.

In *The Visible and the Invisible* the Saussurian way of describing the vectors of signification in the field of language supplies Merleau-Ponty with new terms and a new model for describing the sensible field. *Phenomenology of Perception* showed everywhere that the perception of things is not an interpretation of signs, an ascribing meanings to terms. But de Saussure's structuralism convinced Merleau-Ponty that speaking is not either—that the meanings are not deposited in terms, but lie between them, in their oppositions, and that the making of the verbal material significant is not a connecting it up term by term with an order of ideal essences, but an operating with these internal differences, a "gesturing" with them. The way such a differential linguistic meaning is captured and conveyed in a speech act, or gesture, will serve as the model for the way a sense is captured in the motor intentionality of perception. No doubt this kind of "*prise*"—"hold" on to a difference—is going to be very difficult to describe; it is indeed inevitably going to be a different notion from that of the "*prise*"—hold that measures the sizes and orientation of things, hold that feels the throbbing or the rest in their colors—which the *Phenomenology of Perception* found in all kinds of sentience.

And Merleau-Ponty sought to restore its carnal and sensuous character, its sensitivity, to sensibility by a description of subjectivity as the locus where there is an overlapping or folding over of being upon itself. The sensible flesh can be a locus where all schemes and movements of things can be captured, not because it is a blank slate or hollow of nothingness and thus a pure receptivity, but because it already contains all that the visible, the tangible, the audible is capable of, being visible, tangible, and audible itself. Itself a field where the sensible radiates and schematizes itself, it captures the patterns the exterior things emit on the variations or frequency modulations of its own body schema.

3. Subjectivity as Subjection

And yet how much still there is lacking in this account of the carnal contact with the world! Merleau-Ponty's carnal subjectivity figures as a measurant for the gradations and reliefs of a field, as the locus where the most remote radiations of the sensible are captured. But there is utterly missing that character of anxious and solicitous care for the world with which the Heideggerian *Dasein* was absorbed in its clearing. There is complete silence about what the late Heidegger felt compelled to thematize as the divine—that promise of sustenance and wholesomeness, that remoteness or sacredness that draws as it withdraws, and which is not a "value" which our own appraisal assigns to things, but the goodness of things by which they assemble us and are attractions—*Dingen*. There is lacking, we can say, a substantial sense of things. To conceive of things as substances was not only to conceive them as substrates the understanding posits to support the attributes it predicates of them. It is also to sense what is supporting and sustaining in them, the sensible layout as a ground that supports our movements and our aspirations, and as a nourishing medium for life. And there is lacking a sense of the capacity to gratify us, to please us, to delight us and not only illuminate our understanding, and to pain us, which is involved in the sense of things as nodes of pregnancy and resistance. For to be sentient means that, too: not only to catch on to their sense, but to be susceptible and vulnerable with regard to them, sensitive and subject to them. It is even in the midst of things—and not only in the projection into nothingness—that we are mortal. It is in our sensuality, our gratification and our pain, that we sense that we are mortal.

What is lacking in the phenomenology of perception is—sensation.

4. The *Apeiron*

The sensible field does not consist only of configurations against a background of potential things, or instrumental connections, or paths and planes. There is also an unformed prime matter. Sensibility occurs in a medium which is pure depth, but not empty space; filled with qualitative opacity. It has no contours, does not present itself through profiles, does not have sides, is depth without surfaces. It is neither delimited, nor positively without limit: it is indefinite, *apeiron*. It presents itself through pure qualities, which do not qualify any substrate. Pure chaos, pure flux, it is present through incessant oncoming. It fills out a space-time presence, marks a presence with its density, through condensation and rarefaction, blotting out the wake of the passed through, obscuring the horizons of the future. In it all directions are equivalent and neutralize; the present does not adumbrate the absent, the absent does not promise the present. It extends a sphere of presence, within which one can move indefinitely without diminution or loss. It has no orientation—no sense. It is not going anywhere. But it is immediately there.

Things take form neither in the emptiness of space, nor out of a field of potential things. Colors concretize in a chromatic medium, solids and vapors form in the density, sounds emerge in the sonorous element. "This red," Merleau-Ponty wrote, "emerges from the less precise, more general redness, in which my gaze was caught, into which it sank, before—as we put it so aptly—*fixing* it." (*V.I.*, p. 131) There was first this sensuous element, formless as a sea, dense as a sea, into which the gaze sank. The things do not crystallize along the axes of a space-time framework, or at the intersections of instrumental pathways; they solidify in a depth—in the day, in the atmosphere, in the density and din of the world.

The light is such a medium; it envelops us, and extends neither infinitely nor unto frontiers—nor does it have horizons. It dilates, fills a clearing, dikes off the darkness, which it hides with the incessance of its presence. The light is without parts, without sides, without contours, without profiles, without referentiality, without substance. It is like an adjective predicated of nothing. The night, opaque and full of the dark, is such an element, general thing that fills space, that draws one's gaze, one's hearing into its somber spaciousness without sites or axes. The ground is also such an adjective, a supporting without substrate, a depth beneath all things, sustaining every scene and every upright or unstable object, a presence everywhere felt, which one neither approaches nor withdraws from, since one needs its support in order to approach or pull back. Merleau-Ponty has himself said that the silence between particular sounds is not an auditory zero, like the soundlessness between colors; it is positive as the ground out of which or upon which the sounds come to posit themselves. But this stillness is not a field or a dimension; it is a pure element, pure sensuous matter without form. The heat, the monsoon, is neither a thing nor a field for things; it is a qualitative intensity without structure, a clarity without distinctness, tropical element.

In *The Visible and the Invisible* Merleau-Ponty had learned, from Schoenberg, that all sensuous particulars of their own force of presence schematize themselves. Ex-istence, that is, transcending one's here-now, becoming general, becoming a level or a schema or a dimension, is not only the property of the mind—or it is the property of the mind because the sensitive mind is sensible, and this schematizing oneself, this veering into generality, is the nature of all that is sensible. Points become pivots, lines become levels, planes become horizons. But in addition, things grasped, when let go, revert to the elemental. The red of the blood, out of the excess of its redness, does not only become the level against which the other colors situate themselves; it becomes the element in which crimes, lust, landscapes, wars, revolutions swim and are caught sight of. The solidity of the ground, paced off after the sea voyage, a crust, remains as the element in which solid things are posited. The savor of the wine turns into an element in which vitality surges. The sparkle of the day turns into a medium in which the look is buoyed up, borne from plane to plane, from visible to visible. In the core of the things one senses the element. One sinks one's teeth into the fruit, and discovers the nutritive element; one samples the liquid and joins the flux of the alimentary, general and undivided, a depth sounding into the sensuous.

5. The Involution of Sensation

How diagram the inner movement of the sensing of this sensuous element? The core idea in intentionality hardly suits it. There is not a positing of an ideal identity-term, maintained selfsame, to unify a multiplicity of sensuous givens. The solidity of the ground, the airiness of the atmosphere, the luminosity of the light, are not invariants, matrices of a system of profiles, or schemas elaborated in the reciprocal referentiality of sensuous aspects. There is not the tension of intentionality, not orientation, attention, focus. One finds oneself within the sensuous element; one does not have to aim at it or orient oneself toward it. Here one does not see why the essential would be in our motility; sensing the element is not a "*prise,*" a taking hold of it; it would rather be a being taken, being held, or being taken in by it.

Here to sense is to sense the substantial—not the substrate that supports the qualitative properties, but rather the qualitative properties found supporting oneself. The force of things is not only experienced as resistance, as exclusion, by which the thing is *partes extra partes*, and excludes us from its place and time. The forces with which we hold ourselves in our posture and exert our motility have incorporated the supporting force of the ground. This incorporation senses the ground. The look does not only probe with its own forces in a space emptied out by the light; in fact is not the space rather filled with the light, and the gaze buoyed up by this radiance and activated by it? Is not the chromatic field, intense or vague, more than an opaqueness that stops the ray of sight and encases in themselves the things it identifies; is it not also sustenance for sight? It is the richly colored zones, and not only the spaces between them, that elicit the look, that concentrate, fortify and uphold it.

Not all the force prehended is formed in the synthetic unity of a posture or a gesture; there is a surplus—sensation glows in the surplus. This surplus vibrancy is affective in character; it is a feeling gratified, contented with a content. It was not preceded by a lack. The sensation of light was not preceded by a longing for light, did not come to answer a question or a quest. The flux of the sensuous element piles up in pleasure, in the reflux of the first ipseity.

Husserl thinks that the nascence of subjectivity in sensation has to be conceived as intentionality, because he conceives of the sensuous impression as passing, already passing as soon as it comes, a point of plenitude (*Randpunkt*) already sinking away into emptiness; the subject that receives it is already straining to retain it. The subject of the impression, then, the sensibility for it, is already retentional, retroactive, intentional. But the sensuous element—the light, the color, the tone of the world—is not a tide already passing, but an oncoming abundance. The relationship with the sensuous element is from within, and the ipseity in sensation should be diagrammed as an involution.

The pleasure of sensation is not identifying, neither in the sense of positing an ideal ego identity-pole to which to ascribe its differentiated temporal phases, nor even in the sense of directing itself back to itself as to one focus. To feel oneself sensuously contented is not to posit oneself, objectify oneself or identify oneself; it is not even to take up a stand, to stand in oneself. It seems to us striking that no one has noted that the pleasure of sensation, in its reflexivity or its ipseity, refracts each time, disperses, spreads, such that the one that is contented with the sensuous content is a labile identity. Merleau-Ponty emphasized that the apprehension of the color is immediately transferred across the whole body sensibility; the subject in Goldstein's and Rosenthal's laboratory who senses the blue before it become a visual when it is the blue itself, when the visual sensation is there, there is a feeling for the blue that closes in upon itself in this zone—and this moment, The moments of sensuous content—and the ipseity in them—form moments of surplus—of pleasure—each a surplus over and beyond the forces comprehended in the stance of the organism, each a surplus beyond the others.

Against the empiricist conception of sensation, which conceives of the sensuous as a multiplicity of impressional points collected in the undifferentiated unity of a passively one psychic sphere, and against the intellectualist conception, which conceives of the sensuous as a manifold of givens synthesized by the original and originating identity of one ego, it seems to us that sentience is a manifold of points of ipseity contained in the undifferentiated unity of the sensuous element.

6. The Mortal Taste of Sensuality

If sensation is the original subjectivity, it is because there is effected in it our original subjection to beings. *The Visible and the Invisible* conceptualized this by speaking of the sensitive being as the locus where there is a folding back of the world upon itself. This inscription of the world upon the subject is the very carnality of existence, the structure of flesh. Merleau-Ponty always sought to explicate it by looking at the overlapping of the visible and motor; the look that palpates the visible has already been imprinted with the pacing, speed, and direction of its movement by the things it will see. That is only possible because it is itself something visible, and it is its own visible being that extends outward in the field of movement, or the visible being of the field of movement that extends inward. In fact this continuity is realized by the movement and by this imprinting.

But this imprinting of the movement by the moved cannot be conceived objectively, as a transmission of force in the continuity of a field already objectified. The continuity of the visible field of the world and the visible flesh is not itself something perceived or effected through perception, if it is what makes perception possible.

If this subjection to the world before it is objectified, this folding back of the world upon the subject before the subject unfolds the world about itself, is not of the order of perception, is it not rather, as Heidegger thinks, of the order of affectivity? Is it not felt in feeling oneself born, that is, given one's being, laden with it, afflicted with it, subjected to it? There is something vertiginous in the weight of this being, fully, definitively, effected, which one can never get to the bottom of, or put oneself at the beginning of. This weight is felt in the effort to assume one's existence, to take it on or take it up, to appropriate it, and in the irrecuperable lag of this appropriation, always come too late, unable to exist the instant of one's birth. Across this feeling of the weight of one's own being, one feels the weight of the world in which it is deposited and feels the weight of its beings.

But this lag is also what makes it possible for this being to be definitive. The imposition of being could be sensed only in a movement impotent in its regard, a movement that produces impotence. Such are the movements of a subject that exists only in engendering potentialities for existence, potentialities which are potential only by being possibly impotent—movements by which a subject casts itself into a field of possibilities which are possible only because they are possibly impossible. Indeed all of our movements produce anxiety, the sense of casting oneself into the emptiness, the anticipation of dying. It is by making itself a pool of anxiety that our existence makes itself subject to being, and the beings not only signal to us with their orientations, but weigh on us with their being, which is definitiveness and subjection itself.

In this analysis our feeling of having been born and our mortality enter into our sensibility as a subjection to the world. Our feeling for things is made of our stupor over finding ourselves born, and our anxiety over finding ourselves dying.

It does not seem to us, however, that anxiety—the being exposed to nothingness—itself elucidates the subjection being can be. In order to understand sensation as susceptibility, to be affected by beings, and by one's own being, is it not the capacity of being pained by things that should be explicated? Sensibility, as the capacity to capture the sense or orientation of beings, is also susceptibility to being afflicted by their force, sensitivity for them, capacity to be pained by them.

Pain seems to be completely immanence: pain is the experience of the contexture of consciousness by itself, according to the Sartrean definition. Pain is wholly within the vibrancy of consciousness; an unconscious pain does not pain at all. The suffering of pain is a being passive with regard to oneself. To suffer the pain is to be unable to flee and to be unable to retreat, to know this impotence in a vain struggle to get out of oneself, to open wide upon the world, or to get back from oneself. One flees the pain by losing oneself in the spectacle outside, or, failing that, in making it a spectacle, retreating behind it to objectify it. To suffer is to find oneself mired in oneself.

Pain then is the inner experience of one's own being as a weight, an affliction. The subjectivity that is susceptible of being pained is not one that stands in its own potentialities, in an ecstatic projection into distance, futurity, nothingness, but one that turns in being, in the definitive, the irrevocable. Pain is the inner sense of this irremissible bond sealed within the very capacity of subjectivity for its own being.

But pain is at the same time a strange evidence of the continuity of one's own being with that of the world. The plenitude, presence and force of being, with which a thing so securely is, within its own frontiers, is for subjectivity an excess—and strangely, one with the excess it own being is for itself. Mired in oneself one is also wracked to the world. But is it the world as such? That which afflicts and oppresses beyond one's own being is not the cosmos, the framework or the field, the universal and the necessary—nor the vectors of instrumental referentiality—nor the style or styles, horizon of all horizons. What wounds may be the instrument, but what pains is the sensuous element. In pain what oppresses is the light, the heat, the din, the density, the depth as such. In pain the sensuous is an oppression before it is a sense impression, impression of a sense. In this oppression being is not an instrumentality that imposes his stance and his posture on the user, or a content held that imposes its pacing, speed and direction on the movement that takes hold, but a materiality without form that wounds without informing, an opacity without sense, ends or end. And even the sensuous that contents pains. In all sensation our being exposed and vulnerable to, our being subject to, the sensuous element is felt.

At the limit of pain there would be the prostration and agony in which dying is at work. Dying is anticipated in our existance not only in the anxiety which feels itself being cast adrift in the emptiness as it casts itself into the world; it is also anticipated in the agony which feels itself being crushed, prostrate, in a being turning more and more into weight and stupor. That being is one's own; pain is the inner travail of materialization. But the sense of mortality is not only the sense of being cast adrift in the emptiness, when the world withdraws. It is, in pain, the sense of being cast into the world, into the utter materiality of the sensuous element.

ALPHONSO LINGIS.

PROLEGOMENON TO A THEORY OF DECEPTION*

And the Lord God said unto the woman, What is this that thou hast done? And the woman said, The serpent beguiled me, and I did eat.
Genesis, 3:13

The serpent deceived the woman. Wives and husbands deceive one another; doctors deceive their patients; college professors deceive their students; military strategists deceive the enemy; businessmen deceive one another; and politicians deceive the people. Deception is as commonplace as laughter and sorrow; its historical ubiquity is unquestionable; yet the details of its anatomy remain obscure. In an era marked by astounding scientific and technologic advances that have made possible the rapid and widespread dissemination of conflicting, and sometimes contradictory, bits of information simultaneously, there has been a corresponding increase in the methods and techniques of deception. It is thus useful to expose the details of the anatomy of deception in order to make known more fully the possibilities and limits of its use.

At the outset, it is important to draw a distinction between an act of deception and deception itself. An act of deception is designed to exploit the relevant ignorance of an individual, or set of individuals, and is the efficient cause of the individual's belief concerning a given event, thing, object, or state of affairs for the sake of a reason, or set of reasons, and a purpose, or set of purposes, known to its artificer(s) but unknown to its sufferer(s). Deception itself occurs in

*A decade has passed since I first began my work on deception. Over the years many of those who understood what I was doing were not interested, and many of those who were interested did not understand. Of those who understood and were interested I should like to thank O.R. Dathorne, Lawrence Herson, and Giacomo Sani, former colleagues, as well as Robert Baskin, Philip Code, and Richard Medley, Jr., former students, all of The Ohio State University. I should like to reserve a special word of thanks for Jack Schoemperlen, my Graduate Research Assistant here at The University of Wisconsin-Milwaukee, for the superior quality of his work for me over the past academic year, and for the rigorous discussions, that proved to be of no little value in the preparation of this version of an earlier manuscript, in which he engaged me. Finally, I should like to thank my wife Mary Ann for listening patiently to my incessant mumblings about deception.

a given instance if, and only if, (i) there is an individual, or set of individuals, whose intentional, deliberate, and purposeful assertions/statements are believed to be true by another though he himself knows that they are true, but believes correctly that they will be believed to be false; (iii) there is an individual, or set of individuals, statements are believed to be false by another though he himself knows that they are true, but correctly believes that they will be believed to be false; (iii) there is an individual, or set of individuals, whose intentional, deliberate, and purposeful assertions/statements, though true, are made in such a way that they constitute the efficient cause of another (others) believing that a certain state of affairs will be actualized, though he himself knows that such cannot obtain; (iv) there is an individual, or set of individuals, whose actions are designed to, and do in fact, conceal their intended purpose(s) from the one(s) who suffer them, thereby occasioning in the sufferer(s) an error, or set of errors, of belief concerning the actions' purpose(s). These together constitute the defining attributes of deception itself. Each is necessary though not sufficient to the idea of deception, yet sufficient though not necessary to particular instances of deception.

Observing (i) — (iv) closely, one is struck by an underlying uniformity, the absence of prior notification concerning the intended purpose of the act of deception that the deceived suffers. The intention and purpose of the deceiver is always, and without exception, concealed from the deceived, thus deception[1] is marked by the absence or prior notification of the deceived in relation to the deceiver's true aim. When we speak of, say, X's deception of Y, we imply that X intentionally, deliberately, and purposefully engaged in conduct that deceived Y, who was ignorant of its intended purpose. X's ability to withhold from Y notification of the intended purpose of his act of deception increases his chances of deceiving Y. It is, of course, possible that Y, unbeknownst to X, may receive prior notification concerning the intended purpose of X's act of deception and act to shield himself from being deceived, even as he in turn deceives X by pretending to be deceived. This possibility is exposed by the Anatomical Tree of Deception, which is presented later.

Every act of deception is grounded simultaneously in intention, deliberation, and purpose, which demarcate it from two other types

---

[1]In this essay I am concerned with deception involving two or more individuals, and not with what is commonly termed self-deception.

of conduct frequently, though incorrectly, conflated with it, namely, lying and misleading. It may thus be well at this juncture to clarify the differences between three terms that are oftentimes used synonymously in ordinary discourse: deceive, lie, and mislead. Central to these differences are the ideas of intention, purpose, and deliberation, thus I shall begin by drawing distinctions between these three ideas.

By intention I mean a fixed direction of the mind "to do . . . ;" by purpose, a fixed direction of the mind "to do . . ." in order for a desired end, or set of ends, to obtain; and by deliberation, the sizing up, or weighing, of alternatives pertaining to that which is to be done. Intention does not imply either deliberation or purpose logically necessarily, despite the fact that empirically it is usually accompanied by purpose and sometimes deliberation. Purpose, on the other hand, implies intention logically necessarily, though not deliberation, which is often essential to its empirical actualization. And deliberation implies neither intention nor purpose logically necessarily, though they often accompany it empirically. How are these ideas helpful in the clarification of the differences between deceive, lie, and mislead? Consider now the following examples.

1) L & M & N & O are thieves acting in concert to rob a gasoline station located on a lonely strip of road. Each thief has a walkie-talkie. L & M have the task of robbing the station, while N & O, the sentinels, are stationed a quarter of a mile due east and due west of the station respectively. A car travelling due west approaches N and stops. Its driver, P, inquires of N concerning the nearest station where gasoline can be purchased. N informs him that there is a station five miles due north of their present location, which is a crossroads, where gasoline can be bought. But N knows that the station is closed, and has been closed for the past two weeks. He also knows that if L & M were not in the process of robbing the station a quarter of a mile due west of their present location, P could purchase gasoline there. P thanks N and proceeds due north. On arriving at the station to which he had been directed, P observes that it is boarded shut.

P has been deceived by N. He believed to be true, and acted upon, statements made intentionally, deliberately, and purposefully by N, who knew that they were false. N's purpose was to direct P away from the gasoline station that his cohorts were in the process of robbing, and sizing up the situation at hand, he intentionally made false statements which P believed to be true. N deceived P, but was P deceived by Q from whom he had received directions ten minutes prior to coming upon N?

2) Suppose Q has an instinctive dislike of strangers. Also suppose that Q experiences a particular kind of physiological pleasure on each occasion that he lies. On the impulse of the moment he informs P, who has stopped to ask him for directions to the nearest station where gasoline can be bought, that petrol can be purchased at the station two miles due west of their present location. Q knows that there is no such station. He also knows that there is a station approximately twelve miles due north, but he does not know that it has been boarded shut. P thanks Q and proceeds according to his instructions. After travelling at forty-five miles per hour for more than five minutes, P observes only cornfields on both sides of the road. He assumes that Q must have erred in estimating the distance of the station. He continues due west and eventually comes upon N. Following N's directions, he arrives at the station of which Q knew, but towards which he had not been directed by Q. P, a priest, is upset, for very little gasoline remains in his tank, but does not believe that either Q or N lied to him. He belives instead that Q simply erred in his estimate of the station's location and distance, and N did not know that it was boarded shut.

P is obviously wrong in his belief. He was deceived by N, but was he also deceived by Q? Q's false statements were made purposefully and intentionally, but without deliberation. There was no weighing of alternative courses of conduct, no sizing up of the situation at hand. Rather, Q acted impulsively for the sake of an intended purpose, which was actualized when he observed that P had acted in conformity with his false statements. Q lied to P, who was, for want of a better term, lieled[2] by conduct that resembles an act of deception but is nonetheless qualitatively different. It is therefore not the case that each instance of the successful use of a lie is an instance of deception itself, nor is it the case that each act of lying is an act of deception.

3) Suppose that at the spot where P met N he had met R—who had stopped to fix his right rear tire—instead, and had never encountered Q. Now suppose that R abhors lying, and is known in his community for his truthfulness. P asks R where is the nearest station at

[2]I was forced to coin the term *lieled.* This was not done from a desire to claim esoteric terminology, but from the rather surprising realization that there was no word, which, by itself, described accurately the object of a successful lie, that is, one that is believed, acted upon, and yields the liar's desired outcome(s). My aversion to coining a new term impelled me to seek the assistance of linguists. They all suggested that I call the object of a successful lie "the lied-to," but this term applies equally to one who believes a given lie as well as one who does not.

which gasoline can be bought. R knows that there is a station a quarter of a mile due west. He also knows that the station where he purchases gasoline regularly is located five miles due north, but, having been out of the country on a business trip for the past three weeks, does not know that is it closed. Believing that this station is open, R informs P of both stations, and mentions that the station where he usually buys petrol not only gives very courteous service, but also sells premium gasoline for five cents per gallon less than the closer station. P, being a thrifty individual, proceeds towards the station due north. On arriving, P observes that the station is boarded shut.

P wonders whether R lied to him or was simply unaware that the station was closed. But R did not lie to P. R, being in his right mind, and without ulterior motives, believed to be true the statements he made in good faith to P concerning the station located due north, and that it was open. Having no ulterior motives, R simply sought to direct P towards the better of the two stations, from his perspective. His intention and purpose was to do P a favor, hence his conduct did not exploit P's relevant ignorance in order to actualize an intended purpose concealed from P. Thus P was not lieled by R, neither was he deceived by him, since none of the defining attributes of deception presented earlier is satisfied. P was, however, misled. Opting to proceed to the station preferred by R, P obtained an unsatisfactory outcome in consequence of R's error—made intentionally and in good faith, but out of ignorance of a substantively relevant state of affairs.

It is, then, neither logically nor empirically true that an individual is always, and without exception, deceived whenever he believes to be true the false statements of another. And one is not necessarily a deceiver if his false statements are believed to be true, or his true statements are believed to be false. To determine whether one is a deceiver, liar, or misleader, the intentionality, purposefulness, and deliberateness of his conduct must first be ascertained.

Whenever one lies deliberately one attempts to deceive another. The phrase 'lied deliberately' implies the phrase 'sought to deceive' in virtue of the deliberateness of the lie. Thus if one says that X lied deliberately to Y one implies that X sought to deceive Y, and that X deceived Y if Y believes the lie. Of course, X, lacking grounds for either knowing or believing that Y believes his lie, may be unaware that he has actually deceived Y.

In contrast to a deceiver who sets out to deceive, and a liar who sets out to lie, a misleader never sets out to mislead. Though one may mislead another intentionally, and perhaps even after careful deliberation, one never misleads another *on purpose.* Moreover, one may deceive or lielead another *for a purpose,* but one never misleads another *for a purpose.* Given the ideas I have been developing, it does not make conceptual sense to say that one's purpose was to mislead another. One may actualize a given purpose in consequence of having misled another, but such actualization is always *independent* of the purpose of the conscious design by which the other was misled. This stands in sharp contrast to deception, in which the conscious design, or plan, has as its purpose the actualization of a particular outcome, or set of outcomes. This brings us to the matter of a plan in relation to deception.

A plan is the purposeful ordering of means designed consciously to secure the actualization of a given end, or set of ends. Whenever one formulates a plan one engages in a process of articulating an intended purpose, sizing up the alternative means for its actualization, and choosing among them. Deliberation, intention, and purpose are thus entailed by a plan, but they are also entailed by deception, which is conceptually and empirically distinguishable from a plan. What, then, is the relation between a plan, an act of deception, and deception itself?

A plan is a necessary constituent of an act of deception—and deception itself if the one(s) who suffers/suffer the act is/are actually deceived by it—if, and only if, (i) it presents false statements in such a manner that they appear to be true; (ii) it presents true statements in such a manner that they are believed to be false; (iii) it either explicitly or implicitly requires forms of conduct that conceal their intended purpose from the one who suffers them; (iv) it states explicitly, or indicates implicitly, a given desired outcome, or set of outcomes; (v) it contains logical and/or probable connections between the desired outcome(s) and its statements, as well as the form(s) of conduct it requires and/or recommends. In cases where a plan consists of the foregoing elements, and the one who formulated and/or executed it either has knowledge of these elements, or good reason to believe that it consists of them, we are entitled to call one a deceiver if another is deceived in consequence of one's conduct, and a would-be deceiver if none is deceived. An act of deception, as well as deception itself, is thus *distinguishable* from a plan, but each is *inseparable* from it.

Now, a knowledge of what may be termed the resultant complex of possibilities of an act of deception is of no little value to a student of deception—as well as a deceiver or would-be deceiver. And it is to this matter that I now turn my attention.

From an original diagram that included three individuals, an act of deception, and two possible results of the act—the act's object could either be deceived or not deceived—a tree has been constructed which covers any number of individuals from two to infinity, and consists of eighty-three resultant possibilities for one individual and forty-three for another. It exposes the *significant* anatomical details of deception, and provides the foundation of a theory of deception that I shall develop in another work.

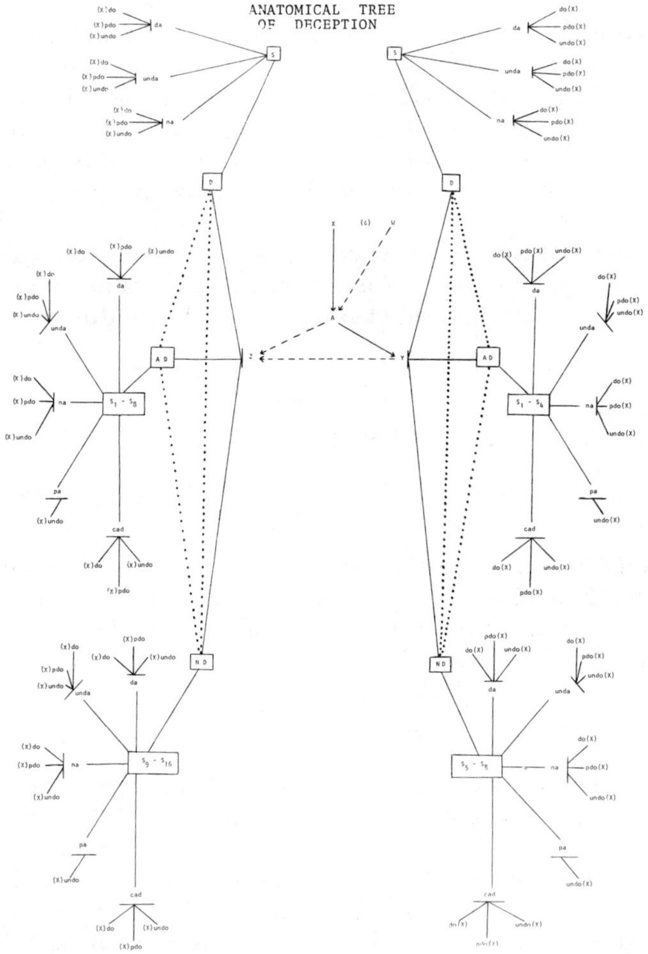

X is either a deceiver or a would-be deceiver.
A is X's act of deception.
Y is the intended direct object of the act of deception.
Z is either the intended indirect object, the unintended indirect object, or the unintended direct object of the act of deception.
W is an individual who is not, in fact, involved in the act of deception, but is believed to have participated by Y and/or Z.

D (deceived) is the case when Y and/or Z incorrectly believes X's statements/assertions to be true or false when the obverse obtains, and/or is fooled about the purpose of X's conduct.
AD (adeceived) is the case when Y and/or Z is in a state of perplexity or uncertainty concerning the truth of X's statements/assertions, and/or the intended purpose of X's conduct.
ND (not deceived) is the case when Y and/or Z rejects completely X's statements/assertions, and/or is not fooled about the intended purpose of X's conduct.

S . . . S_{16} symbolize states of belief.

When it is the case that Y and/or Z are/is deceived, S means that each incorrectly believes X's statements/assertions to be true or false when the obverse obtains empirically, and/or is fooled about the intended purpose of X's conduct.

When it is the case that Y is adeceived, in state S_1 Y holds no belief about the identity of his would-be deceiver(s);
S_2 Y is inclined to believe that X is his would-be deceiver;
S_3 Y is inclined to believe that X and W are his would-be deceivers;
S_4 Y is inclined to believe that W, alone, is his would-be deceiver.

When it is the case that Y is not deceived, in state S_5 Y holds no belief about the identity of his would-be deceiver;

S_6 Y knows/believes that X is his would-be deceiver;
S_7 Y believes that X and W are his would-be deceivers;
S_8 Y believes that W, alone, is his would-be deceiver.

When it is the case that Z is adeceived, in state S_1 Z holds no belief about the identity of his would-be deceiver(s);
S_2 Z is inclined to believe that X is his would-be deceiver;
S_3 Z is inclined to believe that X and W are his would-be deceivers;
S_4 Z is inclined to believe that W, alone, is his would-be deceiver;
S_5 Z is inclined to believe that Y, alone, is his would-be deceiver;
S_6 Z is inclined to believe that X and Y are his would-be deceivers;
S_7 Z is inclined to believe that W and Y are his would-be deceivers;
S_8 Z is inclined to believe that X, W, and Y are his would-be deceivers.

When it is the case that Z is not deceived, in state S_9 Z holds no belief about the identity of his would-be deceivers;
S_{10} Z knows/believes that X is his would-be deceiver;
S_{11} Z believes that X and W are his would-be deceivers;
S_{12} Z believes that W, alone, is his would-be deceiver;
S_{13} Z believes that Y, alone, is his would-be deceiver;
S_{14} Z believes that X and Y are his would-be deceivers;
S_{15} Z believes that W and Y are his would-be deceivers;
S_{16} Z believes that X, W and Y are his would-be deceivers.

---

da (desired action) is the case when Y and/or Z being deceived, adeceived, or not deceived behaves in a manner consistent with the desire(s) of X.
unda (undesired action) is the case when Y and/or Z being deceived, adeceived, or not deceived behaves in a manner that is inconsistent with the desire(s) of X.
na (no action) is the case when Y and/or Z being deceived, adeceived, or not deceived take(s) no action relevant to X, which may either be consistent or inconsistent with X's desire(s).
pa[3] (punitive action) is the case when Y and/or Z being either ade-

[3]Punitive action is not meant to cover only a narrow range of options, but is designed to take in a broad spectrum of actions, ranging from a situation where Z, overhearing the falsehood told to Y by X in their conversation, interrupts and informs Y that X's statements are false, to one which finds Y so outraged by X's violation of his trust that he picks up a gun and shoots him.

ceived or not deceived take(s) some form of punitive action against X and/or W (including Y in Z's case), exclusive of engaging in an act, or acts, of deception.

cad (counter-act of deception) is the case when Y and/or Z being either adeceived or not deceived engage(s) in an act, or acts, of deception directed towards X and/or W (including Y in Z's case).

---

do (desired outcome) is the case when the behavior of Y and/or Z being deceived, adeceived, or not deceived enable(s) the desired outcome(s) of X to obtain.

pdo (partial desired outcome) is the case when Y and/or Z being deceived, adeceived, or not deceived behave(s) in a manner that yield(s) a partially desired outcome, or set of outcomes, for X.

undo (undesired outcome) is the case when the behavior of Y and/or Z being deceived, adeceived, or not deceived yield(s) an outcome, or set of outcomes, undesired by X.

Scrutinizing the anatomical tree of deception, one observes a variety of lines. Those lines that end in arrows show temporal and contingent relations between the deceiver, or would-be deceiver, his act of deception, and the intended direct or indirect object, or the unintended direct or indirect object, of that act. Thus, for example, X⟶A⟶Y shows that X, the deceiver or would-be deceiver, is prior to A, the act of deception, which must be executed before it, itself, can have an effect on Y.

There are two different types of lines ending in arrows. Relationships indicated by the solid lines from X to A to Y (X⟶A⟶Y) obtain for every act of deception, A, where there is an *intended direct object,* Y, and an individual, or set of individuals, X, who perform the act. The relationship indicated by the broken line from A to Z (A····→Z) may or may not obtain. X⟶A····→Z shows an individual, or set of individuals, Z, who may or may not become an object of X's act of deception, A. If Z were to become the unintended direct object of X's act of deception, the line connecting A to Z would become solid. The relationship indicated by the broken line from Y to Z (Y···→Z) may or may not obtain. X→A→Y···→Z shows an individual, or set of individuals, Z, who may or may not be an object of X's act of deception, A, in virtue of Y being an object of that act. The broken line connecting W to A never becomes solid, for W performs no act of deception, though Y and/or Z may, mistakenly, believe that he did so.

The solid lines from Y and Z to D, AD, and ND indicate sets of states of belief of Y and Z in relation to A. The solid lines from D, AD, and ND to S . . . S_n indicates various elements of the sets of Y's and Z's belief states pertaining to the initiator of A. The solid lines from S . . . S_n to da, unda, na, pa, and cad indicate possible courses of action by Y and/or Z grounded in the belief/knowledge of each concerning A and its initiator. The solid lines from da, unda, na, pa, and cad to do(X), pdo(X), and undo(X) indicate the range of possible outcomes of Y's and/or Z's action(s) for X. The X's in parentheses are designed to show the dynamics of an act of deception in relation to its initiator.

The dotted lines between D and ND, D and AD, and AD and ND indicate possible shifts over time in Y's and/or Z's states of belief pertaining to A and its initiator.

The Anatomical Tree of Deceptions shows the complexity of the resultant possibilities of an act of deception. It exposes a variety of possibilities, but does not specify which one will obtain if there is an act of deception. The possibility, or set of possibilities, that is most probable in a given instance of an act of deception is best computed from a consideration of the relevant contextual contingents[4] impinging upon the one who performs, as well as the one who suffers, the act, and the logic of the situation at hand.

Having presented the key elements of deception, and exposed the significant resultant possibilities of an act of deception, I should like to end by presenting four lawlike statements, intuited from reflection upon the ideas that have been presented, concerning the probability of deception.

[4]By relevant contextual contingents I mean the pertinent elements of the context in which the act occurs that structure its form and content.

(1) The probability of deception decreases as the quotient

$$\frac{\text{knowledge/belief of X}}{\text{knowledge/belief of Y and/or Z}}$$

approaches 1.0, and increases as the quotient approaches 0 or ∞.

(2) The probability of deception decreases as the quotient

$$\frac{\text{trust of X by Y and/or Z}}{\text{distrust of X by Y and/or Z}}$$

approaches 1.0, and increases as the quotient approaches 0 or ∞.

(3) The probability of deception decreases as the quotient

$$\frac{\text{obedience of Y and/or Z to X}}{\text{disobedience of Y and/or Z to X}}$$

approaches 1.0, and increases as the quotient approaches 0 or ∞.

(4) The probability of deception decreases as the quotient

$$\frac{\text{conformity of Y and/or Z to established norms of conduct familiar to X}}{\text{nonconformity of Y and/or Z to established norms of conduct familiar to X}}$$

approaches 1.0, and increases as the quotient approaches 0 or ∞.

These four statements are grounded in the posit that the probability of deception is a function of the symmetry and asymmetry of relations relevant to an act of deception. As the symmetry in the relations increases the probability of deception decreases; as the symmetry in the relations decreases the probability of deception increases. There is thus a correspondence between the increased probability of deception and greater asymmetrical relations, and the decreased probability of deception and greater symmetrical relations. The empirical soundness of these ideas will be tested in a subsequent work.

The purpose of this essay was to present the conceptual foundation upon which a theory of deception can be built. Its capacity to withstand the pressure of rigorous and dispassionate critical scrutiny will surely be the measure of whether it is really a prolegomenon to a theory of deception.

WINSTON A. VAN HORNE.

UNIVERSITY OF WISCONSIN – MILWAUKEE.

MAN, GOD, AND DEATH IN HEGEL'S *PHENOMENOLOGY*

In an appendix to his *Introduction à la lecture de Hegel* Kojève contrasts the Christian religion to Hegel's historical humanism as positive to negative:

> In the final analysis, the God of Christian theology (of ancient or pagan inspiration) is given-Being [*Sein*], eternally identical to itself and revealing itself in and through a natural world, which only manifests the essence and the power of existing of a Being that *is*. The Man of Hegel, on the contrary, is the *Nothingness* [*Nichts*] that annihilates given—Being existing as World, and that annihilates itself (as real historical time or History) in and through that annihilation of the given.[1]

As Kojève realized, man's negativity is most critically present in death. For death is not only the ultimate limit of natural life; but man can consciously anticipate, and indeed may freely choose death. But Kojève's wide-ranging exposition of this thesis is limited in its reference to some passages in the preface to the *Phenomenology*. Only in conclusion does he illustrate his point with reference to earlier writings from the Jena period, and from the life-and-death struggle.

For Hegel, however, the substance of his philosophical position is not to be found in the more relaxed discussion of the preface. It is the text of the *Phenomenology* itself that carries the weight of his argument. There one indeed finds death playing a crucial role in the development. Not only the life-and-death struggle and the slave are marked by the stark evidence of mortality, however, but also unhappy consciousness, the ethical order, absolute freedom and terror, and revealed religion.

By looking at each of these sections in turn, we can begin to articulate the ways in which death and negativity serve as necessary conditions for knowledge. Such a discussion will not only add substantial support for Kojève's thesis regarding the essential negativity of man's historical existence, but will invert his conclusion by showing that, far from alienating man from God, the centrality of death is the necessary condition for a complete reconciliation.

---

[1](Paris: Gallimard, 1947) p. 574; ET "The Idea of Death in the Philosophy of Hegel" (J.J. Carpino) in *Interpretation*, III (1973) p. 155. Portions of this paper were first prepared as a response to "Death and Politics in Hegel's *Phenomenology of Spirit*" by Leah Bradshaw, and read at the annual meeting of the Canadian Political Science Association at London, Ontario, May, 1978.

I

In the most primitive form of self-consciousness that Hegel isolates, the individual is not yet aware of his own mortality.[2] His environment presents no insurpassable limit to his dynamic activity, but is rather the object of desire—raw material to be appropriated into his indeterminate and all-inclusive living reality.

This expansive totality meets its limit in another self who has the same view of the world.[3] Since neither will allow the other to appropriate himself, a struggle results—a struggle whose inherent motivation will be satisfied only where one or both of the combatants dies.

In Hegel's analytical reconstruction of experience, this moment of death marks the first point at which an individual consciousness becomes aware of its finitude and of its limitations. What was taken to be limitless is discovered to have inescapable boundaries. For it matters not what one intends to achieve if one dies. Therefore death can here be called the first negation that becomes present in the experience of self-consciousness.

Self-consciousness, however, does not simply come to an end. Because its basic desire extends beyond what it is already, it can anticipate what is to come. When it knows that death is possible—that a limitation can in fact be imposed—it can seek to cancel that inevitability. Since such a move endeavours to negate finitude, it can be called the second negation—or the negation of negation. In its most primitive form this transition takes place when a combatant realizes his vulnerability, and instead of continuing to the bitter end, surrenders and becomes a slave of the other.[4]

This is not the last word, however, for the consciousness of death on the part of the slave transforms the second negation into something positive. For in having his self-certainty shaken to the core, he becomes aware of himself as living process, not as enduring essence, and discovers that the products of his labour embody the dynamic activity that constitutes his life.[5] The finitude that was first

---

[2]PhG 139f; PhM 225ff; PhS 109ff. [PhG = *Phänomenologie des Geistes*, ed. Hoffmeister, Hamburg: Meiner, 1952; PhM = *Hegel's Phenomenology of Mind*, tr. Baillie, London: Allen & Unwin and New York: Macmillan, 1955; PhS = *Hegel's Phenomenology of Spirit*, tr. Miller, Oxford: Clarendon, 1977.]

[3]PhG 143ff; PhM 231ff; PhS 113ff.

[4]PhG 145f; PhM 234; PhS 115.

[5]PhG 148ff; PhM 237ff; PhS 117ff.

acknowledged only through the threat of death is no longer known as a bare limitation, but rather as a positive and determinate character. This third negation cancels the negativity of the previous two moments and allows their positive import to become evident. The fear of death, the sovereign master, is the beginning of wisdom.

Throughout this development, death is present as something that happens to the self—a threat produced by another self-consciousness. It is, to that extent, conditioned and cannot generate pure self-knowledge. On the other hand, as the slave realized, to die, even at one's own hand, is to cancel all possibilities. This results in a double tension in self-consciousness. To achieve pure knowledge one must pass beyond one's limitations; but one cannot end one's life. Therefore one has to overcome those elements of life that manifest finitude.

This happens in the stage of unhappy consciousness, where the self knows itself as changing, and attempts to cancel this changing character so that it can be reconciled with the unchanging.[6] This involves self-mortification. While there is here no physical death, the self consciously attempts to exterminate its individuality. In this process the first negation is the finitude of change and decay which is not consciously produced but is consciously acknowledged. The second negation is the process of self-mortification; but the third negation is the awareness that the mediated process of self-mortification is the concrete dynamic of unchanging reality itself. This opens up the perspective of reason.[7]

II

The section of the *Phenomenology* that discusses the master-slave relationship and the unhappy conscioueness focuses on the individual self, abstracted from its social context. But men are social beings, and they come of age, not as individuals in an indifferent world, but as integrated members of a mature society. The social and historical dimension of man's maturity is explored by Hegel in his

---

[6]PhG 158ff; PhM 251ff; PhS 126ff.

[7]In the discussion of "Pleasure and Necessity" (PhG 265; PhM 387f; PhS 220) death reappears as the impersonal, indifferent necessity that the individual consciousness experiences when it affirms its life by seeking only its own pleasure. This experience of lifelessness marks the finitude of pleasure's abstraction from the total dynamic of life, and is therefore the first negation; but as *experienced* it has already been transcended. Therefore it becomes the second negation, which will lead on to the subsequent stage of "The Law of the Heart."

discussion of spirit, where he talks not about individuals conscious of themselves, but about the characteristic ethos of a people.[8] At this stage death reappears as a significant theme.

In the immediacy of its primitive cultural ethos, a people finds that there is a tension between the divine law inherent in the family or clan, and the human law of social organization.[9] On both sides of the tension, death has a role to play. On the one hand, the divinity inherent in family bonds achieves universality only when, through death, the finitude of relatives and ancestors has been dissolved. Here death is not the first negation. That is rather the particularity of diverse, living individuals. By cancelling individuality, death negates that negation, allowing the inherent divine law to become self-contained as a universally significant (but dark and shadowy) force in human society.[10]

On the other hand, the contrary human law maintains its authority by threatening death and by reminding citizens of their inherent limitations. "In order not to let them get rooted and settled in their isolation and thus break up the whole into fragments and let the common spirit evaporate, government has from time to time to shake them to the very centre in war."[11] By forcing individuals to feel the power of their lord and master, the government uses death as a first negation, reminding them of their finitude so that they will transcend its limitations by participating in the life of the community.

In Hegel's discussion, the archetype of the conflict between the two laws is found in Sophocles' *Antigone*.[12] When Oedipus, the king of Thebes, dies, he leaves behind two sons who, as brothers, are bound by the divine law of the family. Since they cannot both share in the

---

[8]"Der Geist ist das *sittliche Leben* eines *Volks*. . ." PhG 315. (Compare PhM 460; PhS 265). In the 20th century, *Volk* is better translated as "people" than as "nation." Until the 18th century "sittliche" meant the characteristic ethos of a community or people. It would appear that this sense is in Hegel's mind more than the now current sense of "ethical" or "moral."

[9]PhG 318ff; PhM466ff; PhS 267ff.

[10]It may be misleading to see this as applying only to the Greek city state. After citing examples of belief in life after death and of belief in communication between mankind and the spirits of the dead from Australia, Egypt, China, Rome, and America, Cassirer concludes: "All this shows in a clear and unmistakable manner that we have here come to a really universal, an irreducible and essential characteristic of primitive religion." *An Essay on Man* (New Haven: Yale, 1944), 85.

[11]PhG 324; PhM 474; PhS 272.

[12]PhG 337ff; PhM 493ff; PhS 284ff.

royal power they agree to take turns. When, at the end of his term, the elder refuses to transfer authority because of his seniority, the other, grounding his claim on the original agreement, initiates a struggle. No longer a personal dispute, it becomes a war, for the rebel enlists the support of neighbouring states. After both brothers die in personal combat, the new monarch, as punishment, refuses to grant the rebel the proper rite of burial. In the person of Antigone, the divine law of the family unsuccessfully challenges this decree of human law. But her protest awakens the consciousness that it is the divine law that sanctions oaths and establishes the positive unity of the community. At first bloodless and ineffectual, it opens up the possibility of the civil order dissolving and of justified retribution by other communities; and the government has to surrender. In this denouement, human law is weakened by its lack of independent authority; while divine law is shown to be impotent in having its universal bond adequately translated into the discrete decisions of civil society.

The two roles that death plays here intersect and interact. The punishment of the criminal's corpse both defines his finitude and translates his cause into a bloodless universality. The resulting struggle that threatens to become a war both redefines the authority of the civil government, and marks its demise. The conflict, thus archetypically represented, results in the inexorable dissolution of the power of both divine and human law, replacing them with the abstract individualism of legal personality. The fateful movement of destiny through the medium of death dissolves the contradiction between the two laws into an abstract unity—a result that only formally embodies the third logical moment, in which a second negation is cancelled so that a positive may emerge.

Hegel's subsequent discussion of spirit estranged from itself takes place in the abstracted realm of culture. As such it is not concerned with the immediate reality of death. Hegel signals this loss by noting that the counsellor, who serves culture's "realm of actuality," would give sound, or universally valid advice were he prepared to surrender his particular interests to the point of death.[13] When he pulls back, however, he falls into the attitude of flattery in which he only reaffirms his changing, contingent, and finite individuality.

In the unreal world of pure speech that results, the debate between pure insight and faith, between enlightenment and superstition, takes place.[14] Faith represents in its objective doctrine the death of a

[13]PhG 361; PhM 528; PhS 307.
[14]PhG 385ff; PhM 561ff; PhS 329ff.

finite individual who also is God. But its subjective response is a positive trust or acceptance of that dogma. In contrast the enlightenment subjectively actualizes the negative dynamic through constant criticism; and it destroys all reference to a beyond by showing the inherent finitude and limitation of the faith that is supposed to be universal. Yet death itself is not objectively affirmed, only the positive reality of the present. Ironically each embodies subjectively what the other affirms objectively.

The negative practice of the enlightenment, however, is not limited to the cut and thrust of debate. It challenges individual finitude in order to show that what is important is the universal. When it turns to nature and the social order, anything that is determinate and particular is shown to be simply useful. Its value is derived not from its positive reality, but from its negative role as passing over to something more comprehensive. In the last analysis only the negatively active subject who is the "enlightened" agent is inherently valuable in its own right.

This is the structure of absolute freedom. When all independent ideas have been demolished, the enlightenment continues to actualize itself only by venturing into overt action. Nothing is conceded that would limit the negative capacity to use. Everything is simply grist for its mill, lacking independent reality.

Absolute freedom only knows how to say: NO! But now the only thing that continues to resist its universal ability to use things for its own purpose is the negative activity of other individuals. To say: NO! to such action is to send the agent to his death.[15]

Once again, then, death becomes an important condition for the advance to absolute knowledge—death that is chosen in absolute freedom. And once again it performs three different functions, all negative, but ordered in sequence.

The first negation is the individual willed decision to condemn to death. For the exercise of freedom, as a specific act, is finite and particular.

The purpose of absolute freedom, however, is to dissolve just such resistant finitude. For it is the positive determination of individual activity that is to be destroyed. Therefore the reign of terror develops as one after another, ignoring the finitude of his own decision, condemns it in others.

If the *decision* to condemn to death is the first negation, its execution is the second, for finitude and particularity are thereby

[15]PhG 414ff; PhM 599ff; PhS 355ff.

cancelled. However, a significant third moment is introduced: the absolute character of the free act. Since freedom's purpose is to exterminate *all* recalcitrant individuality, it is its own free act that it wills to destroy. The self-confidence of pure freedom dissipates into absolute fear. No longer is this the slave's fear of that which is alien, unknown, or independent; it is terror before the fact that, in absolute freedom, one is choosing one's own death. And in contrast to the universality of the divine law, there is here no beyond into which one's individuality can disappear. For it was destroyed by enlightenment's victory over faith.

This moment of pure self-knowledge generates the third negation. Not only is man's finitude actualized; not only is that finitude cancelled; but by bringing the two together so that pure self-knowledge knows that it wills its own death through its own inherent activity, the terror of absolute annihilation opens up. Shaken to its roots, the bacchanalian revel of purely negative activity collapses into a transparent and simple calm.[16] For at this point man becomes aware of the positive fact he is free to create *ex nihilo,* and the prospect of genuinely moral action opens up.

By consciously dwelling with the negativity of the terror, spirit knows itself as it is, not only as able to use everything in self-contained freedom, but also as the inherently negative power of destruction, and therefore of genuine creativity. Implicit in the divine law of the family and in the willed decision of human government, present in the irony of enlightenment's struggle against superstition, this its own inherent reality now becomes explicitly acknowledged and comprehended. Apart from this self-knowledge, political man appeals either to the irony of history, or to the inexorable laws of the social order to explain what happens, and in either case he denies his responsibility. With it, a political organization of rationally free people becomes possible.

Through the demise of the city state in which the contradictory roles of death dissolve the social order, through the superficiality of a culture that endeavours to ignore death, and through the trauma of the reign of terror, then, men and women come to the level of self-awareness that recognizes how they as individuals come of age are integrated with a society that has come of age.

III

As Kojève suggests, then, death is a necessary condition for

[16]See the Preface: PhG 39; PhM 105; PhS 27.

mankind reaching maturity. The contradictory trauma of the reign of terror turns upside down to ground the coming of age of modern man. But does this also mean that man becomes alienated from God—that the simple positivity of religious belief is simply left behind? For when enlightened man has become fully confident in his own powers and has accepted the radical creativity that lies within his own freedom, he would seem to have no further need of transcendent and supernatural powers.

Even were we simply to reflect on the passages already discussed, we would soon realize that, for Hegel, religion is not a matter of simple positive dogma and faith. For in the discussion of master and slave, where Hegel talks of death as the sovereign master, he evokes themes from the Old Testament with its assertion that the fear of the Lord is the beginning of wisdom. Indeed in his lectures on history and religion Hegel refers to this relationship when talking of Judaism or of the claim to divinity in oriental and Roman despotism.[17] Similarly, in a primitive cultural ethos, the law of the family immortalized in the dead is called the divine law and is indeed contrasted with the positivity of the human law. Finally, the dogmatic content of faith pictures the death of God even though it asserts it positively.

Even so it is possible that those more primitive levels of superstition could be dissolved with the arrival of modern man, were it not for the fundamental tension inherent in the latter achievement. For the moral autonomy of radical creativity, which generates its own laws, is bivalenced. On the one hand it asserts man's self-sufficient independence as being solely responsible for what he has become. On the other it discovers that man is still a conditioned product of his environment, of the location in time and space where he is thrown into existence. The universe itself is seen as indifferent to his moral courage, such that his efforts to do good turn out to generate evil—so much so that he cannot forgive himself. Therefore he has attained neither absolute freedom nor comprehensive knowledge. Instead he is either presumptuous in asserting his ultimate dignity even as his insignificant existence is being bypassed by an indifferent and impersonal world, or deluded into taking his partial perspective as the key to all truth.

It is this experience of the very one who has achieved historical maturity that requires Hegel's transition from the heights of moral responsibility to the perspective of religion. For religion is that sphere

[17]See *On Art, Religion and Philosophy* (New York: Harper, 1970), 299f; and *Lectures on the Philosophy of Religion* (London: Kegan Paul, 1895) II, 206ff.

of human life in which man acknowledges the essential limitations of mankind as a whole, and opens himself to the beyond that transcends such limitations. The self-surrender of devotion, however, would leave man's finitude unresolved were the divine simply to introduce a positive counterpoint to man's negativity. The ultimate reconciliation of man with his cosmic limitations would be achieved only if both sides — God and man — embody the same dynamic structure. The central significance of Christianity for Hegel lies in the fact that, long before the traumatic achievements of modern autonomy, its dogma reported that God himself had in fact become a finite man and had died. In other words, the radical negativity of self-chosen death is also affirmed to be a central constituent of the divine life.[18]

The central Christian doctrine of the incarnation presents the divine initiative as passing through three stages that reproduce the first, the second, and the third negation. In the first, God limits himself and becomes finite — an individual man specifically located in space and time. In the second, this individual dies; his finitude is cancelled. In the third, the negative force of his death is dissolved, and he becomes univerally present as the resurrected Christ.

In this deposit of faith, the Christian is told that the negativity of death is an integral part of divinity — that the universe itself embodies the structure of triple negation. But the information thus communicated is not appropriated in a way that comprehends the significance of what is involved. At one time, the response is that of unhappy consciousness, which believes that the history of salvation introduces no change or process in God himself and which tries only to overcome its own changing impermanence through self-mortification. There is here no recognition of how essential is the negativity of change and transformation to a complete reconciliation. At another time the Christian response is faith, the object of enlightenment's derision. It accepts the doctrine as given, simply asserting it to be true on the basis of positive authority, whether scripture, miracles, or church. In both unhappy consciousness and faith there is no ultimate reconciliation between man and God, because man's subjective response embodies characteristics contrary to those presented in the divine history.

Following Luther, and in German pietism, however, a third response develops, which recognizes that the appropriation of divine reality comes by way of an existential dynamic involving the Christian community. This dynamic, however, does not happen simply in the

---

[18]PhG 531; PhM 762f; PhS 462.

self-consciousness of the Christian believer. It requires as its necessary condition the dogmatic representation of the history of salvation. This happens in three stages.[19]

First, Christian theology says that God created the world out of nothing and in this world created man in his own image. Since God was not limited by an alien matter, there is nothing inherent that would absolutely frustrate a reconciliation. Man and God, however, are not identical; for men and women are finite, whereas he is thought to be infinite and complete. When finite men and women seek to become self-contained and independent as God is thought to be, they break apart the homogeneous fabric of the universe and introduce the difference between good and evil. For evil is the self-contained refusal to allow oneself to be incorporated into the larger totality.

Man, as self-contained finitude, is inherently evil. But when this story is appropriated in the Christian community, the self-conscious believer becomes aware of himself as evil, and his agony and despair increase.[20] For he knows himself as that which is absolutely other than divine reality.

In this first stage, death is simply the evidence of man's finitude, the "wages of sin." When, in the doctrinal story of the fall, self-centred and independent man isolates himself and thus transforms his limits into an absolute limitation or barrier, he renders himself radically finite; death, as the first negation, actualizes that finitude. However, the Christian community's self-conscious awareness of its own inherent sin focusses on this first negation as its object, and in so doing takes its distance, implicitly introducing the second negation. As yet, however, this is only inherent, not fully developed in consciousness.

In the second stage, Christian doctrine represents the self-emptying initiative of divine reality in becoming a man and in dying so that mankind and its evil might be reconciled with God.[21] His death is, as we have seen, confirmation of the radical finitude of the incarnate one. But in the context of the Christian community it is given a contrary sense. Rather than being the first negation of limitation, it is the second; it cancels particularity and finitude so that the incarnate one continues to live universally. Not limited by space and time, he dies and is raised again daily in the worship and devotion of the Christian community.

[19] PhG 534ff; PhM 766ff; PhS 464ff.
[20] PhG 537ff; PhM 771ff; PhS 467ff.
[21] PhG 540ff; PhM 774ff; PhS 470ff.

The Christian believer thus becomes conscious of the fact that the reconciliation is already achieved. The second negation that was only implicit in the consciousness of evil here becomes explicitly acknowledged and affirmed. For this story of salvation lets him know that, through the divine initiative, the confession of sin has become a necessary condition for atonement, making it possible. However complete reconciliation, which would transform the cancelling of sin's limitation into a dynamic positive community of spiritual life, is only present in principle. It has not yet become explicit in believing consciousness. That is achieved only in the third stage of revealed religion.

The final integration of man with God comes about because the religious consciousness acknowledges that the total dynamic of the reconciling events takes place in the living consciousness of the Christian community.[22] It is universally present only because it is thought and appropriated by the believing self. But as this becomes self-consciously articulated, new levels of awareness appear. In the first place, as we have seen, the self-contained independence of the mediator's objective life is dissolved into the universal dynamic of Christian self-consciousness. In the second place, it is through this self-consciousness that the promise of the spirit to the Christian community, contained in Christian doctrine, leaves the abstract world of thought objectivity and becomes actual. However, in the third place, the believer realizes that there no longer remains a transcendent divine reality that is independent and self-contained, above and beyond human existence. For that has been dissolved in the incarnation and death of the mediator. And when the believer opens himself totally in worship and devotion, he does not encounter a God out there, but only himself. He is overwhelmed by the dark night of the soul, in which he as conscious ego encounters only himself. He realizes that *God himself has died*. While radically conscious of his own evil, the believer finds no beyond to provide a remedy. This trauma marks his spiritual death, for his particularity expires into the abyss of meaninglessness, and there remains no solid substantial foundation on which he can trust.

At first this is the second negation, for it cancels the positive universality of the hoped-for reconciliation and transforms it into the negative subjectivity of an intensely personal dynamic. It runs through the moments from hope to despair as it appropriates existentially the content of what is presented dogmatically and transcends its

[22]PhG 545ff; PhM 780ff; PhS 475ff.

positive form. But in fact it is the third negation. For this dynamic, which both reaches out to what is independent, incorporating it into one's life, and surrenders one's own independence, has become identical in finite man and God. The painful awareness of the death of God allows the spiritual integration of the human with the divine not only in dogmatic theory but in actual fact. In other words, in the revealed religion of Christianity God is negatively defined as dying, not only in the objective content of its positive doctrine, but in the subjective, existential consciousness of the believer. And when this takes place death not only defines the limits of man's finitude, nor cancels the mediator's particularity, but reveals the fundamental identity of God and man. Both become actual by negatively dissolving the negativity through which their negatively determined isolation (whether abstract beyond or self-contained evil) is cancelled.

When one lives in a reconciled relation with God, then, God ceases to be wholly other and is present in the spiritual community that incorporates both God and man. Since such a community requires the active participation of both the divine and the human partners, the negative death of God as abstract other has converted into the positive presence of God as Spirit.

Until this final move is acknowledged and articulated through the self-conscious comprehension of thought, man has not achieved absolute knowledge.[23] Only when he recognizes that the negative dynamic that has radically defined man come of age is identical with the negative dynamic of manifest religion is he able to know that his secular experience is not a misleading delusion, but the achievement of maturity.

But does this mean that once such knowledge is achieved, modern man can dispense with religion? If this were the case, Kojève's thesis would have some plausibility: not that man's negativity dissolves God's positivity, but that God's negativity dissolves itself. Thus man come of age embodies in his own humanity the truth of religion. There are reasons, however, why such a conclusion is not convincing. After all, Hegel consistently states that the result abstracted from the process that leads to it, is false and misleading. The integration of God and man can only be maintained if it continually incorporates within itself the total dynamic through which God dies and is yet affirmed to be present in the life of man. Once Feuerbach and others divorce man's maturity from that which constitutes it,

---

[23]See PhG 549ff; PhM 789ff; PhS 479ff.

their assertions become finite and positivistic claims, not negatively comprehensive self-knowledge. For indeed Hegel is recapitulating in philosophical terms what Christians of profound faith have articulated throughout the ages; that the experience of personal reconciliation with God is the inversion of the experience of the death of God.[24]

Because Kojève does not acknowledge this, he is left with an unresolved historicism. For the ultimate question that needs to be answered if one is to distinguish between truth and historically conditioned opinion concerns the criterion that establishes one method or one way of self-definition as being the essential characteristic of the world as such. This, suggests Hegel, is only achieved in religious consciousness where the assertions of doctrine are not only accepted as true, but are appropriated through the dark night of the soul into the subjectivity of pure self-consciousness.

The preceding discussion of death throws light on negation in the Hegelian method.[25] For death is the most radical phenomenological evidence of negativity. In the first place a simple positive is negatively defined as something finite and limited. In this way it is rendered clear, precise and determinate. In the second place, that limitation marks its own demise. Dialectic shows that the result is contradictory and must disappear. Its finitude is dissolved. In the third place, this negative conclusion is cancelled, because when the contradiction is pushed to its most radical limits, its mediating ground is made evident, not as something static and independently determinate, but as dynamic and self-defining. No longer isolated from others, it is constantly interacting with them. This movement of three negations transforms the simple and immediate into a self-mediating process. Barely has the result appeared, however, than the negative process continues, defining, isolating and rendering precise the result that has been achieved, taking it as an immediate to be rendered determinate. Thus no conclusion is final. It only opens up a new set of transitions.

[24]Two examples will suffice: "Although during the time of privation it seemed to me that I had utterly lost thee," wrote the mystic, Madame Guyon, "a certain deep support remained, though the soul knew it not: and she only became aware of that support by her subsequent total deprivation thereof." [Cited in E. Underhill, *Mysticism* (New York: Meridian, 1957), 384]. And Luther wrote in his *95 Theses,* "God works by contraries so that man feels himself to be lost in the very moment when he is on the point of being saved." [Cited in R. Bainton, *Here I Stand, a Life of Martin Luther* (New York: Merton, 1959), 63]. Luther, unlike the mystics, stops at a negative definition of Christian doctrine without progressing to a positive comprehension of the dynamic negativity.

[25]Compare the final chapter of the Larger Logic on "The Absolute Idea."

Showing how this methodological principle is but the distilled essence of the total dynamic of human experience is the task of Hegel's *Phenomenology*. This is why death plays such an important role in its development.

JOHN BURBIDGE.

TRENT UNIVERSITY.

POLITICS OF THE PRESENT: MACHIAVELLIAN HUMANISM

Machiavelli has often been described as at least a precursor of humanism inasmuch as he accurately described the political structures of reality on which a humanism might be built and eliminated the ethical in his attempt to found the state on a permanent basis. To the extent that he was successful in this, it is claimed, he reduced the destructive force of fortune and allowed a new discussion of human relationships to begin, thus permitting the founding of a humanism.

It is the contention of this paper, however, that Machiavelli's conception of politics and political action ignores the realm of the individual through its stress on that of the general and therefore excludes the possibility of an enduring humanism and indeed even the possibility of a philosophical discussion of political reality. After examining two views that depict Machiavelli as a humanist, I will briefly examine the uses he gives to fortune and necessity and then turn to his use of virtue. It is in this last case, I believe, that Machiavelli fails as a humanist. Finally, I will contend that because of his denial of the role of the individual in the founding of the state, the very solidity that many commentators applaud renders the political realm static and denies it other than stipulative justification. We are in effect left with Book I of the *Republic*.

Both Merleau-Ponty's discussion in *Signs*[1] of a world of violence and Gramsci's treatment of historical myth in *The Modern Prince and Other Essays*[2] lay stress on Machiavelli's idea of fortune. Let us consider Merleau-Ponty first. To acknowledge the role of fortune is not, according to Merleau-Ponty, to end discourse, but rather to see the need for a greater understanding of the present historical situation. If fortune seems at one time to aid man and at another to ruin him, this is not strictly to equate fortune with chance, because man at one time understands his historical situation and at another does not,

---

[1]Trans. Richard C. McCleary (Evanston, 1964), pp. 211-23. See also his larger treatment of violence with occasional references to Machiavelli in *Humanism and Terror,* trans. John O'Neill (Boston, 1969).

[2]Trans. Louis Marks (New York, 1957), pp. 133-88.

and hence can partially determine his fortune, whereas he can never affect sheer chance.[3] What is called for is knowledge, which in turn will lead to political power. In the past Christianity had seen fortune as chance and thought it knowable only through an abstract principle of divinity. What Machiavelli is said to have called for is a turning from God to man (an anthropological move *à la Feuerbach*) in order to understand that, while chance exists, fortune can better be understood as the constructions or omissions of men themselves. In other words, the task is one of making sense out of man's relations with his fellow men. Machiavelli must therefore show both what factors are operative within man, i.e., what is his nature, and also what factors are operative between men, i.e., what is social activity. These are best seen in history, the study of which can lead us to the nature of social and political configurations. Values are a necessary but not sufficient condition for a well-formed society, since one must know not only who to choose for this mission, but also how it is to be carried out.[4] Anyone can fight in the name of justice and liberty, but the question remains as to how to best realize these values in particular historical instances.

It is here that Merleau-Ponty qualifies his evaluation of Machiavelli's humanism. While it may be true that "the idea of a fortuitous humanity which has no cause already won is what gives absolute value to our virtue," and that "when we have understood what is humanly valuable within the possibilities of the moment, signs and portents never lack,"[5] nonetheless the understanding of virtue itself is not resolved, and we are left within the realm of stipulative justification in choosing a direction and the means to attaining it. Merleau-Ponty thus saw Machiavelli as a precursor of humanism, inasmuch as Machiavelli rejects absolute values and admits of the historical situation of man, but not as a true humanist. The problem remains as to just what, beyond mere description, political reality is in a given moment.

Gramsci in his essay on the "Modern Prince" takes up where Merleau-Ponty left off. For Gramsci,

> Machiavelli wanted to persuade these forces (the people) of the necessity for a 'leader', who would know what he wanted and how to obtain it and to accept him even if his actions might be or appear to be contrary to the widely held ideology of the time, religion.[6]

---

[3] Merleau-Ponty, *op. cit.*, p. 218.

[4] *Ibid.*, p. 221.

[5] *Ibid.*, p. 219.

[6] Gramsci, *op. cit.*, p. 142.

At first the prince is seen in opposition to the people, but later he merges with them—not with some general idea of mankind, but with the very men that he has convinced of his leadership.[7] The prince appears to be some form of abstract embodiment of the general will of a given people. Gramsci even goes so far as to suggest that *The Prince* is not a treatise written for those in power but for those who do not yet know how to rule; in Machiavelli's time this would have been the revolutionaries who were to lead Italy to unification. Gramsci lays particular stress on Machiavelli's concluding exhortation for the liberation of Italy. For Gramsci the epilogue is to be read " . . . as a necessary part of the work . . . which sheds a true light over the whole work and makes it seem like a 'political manifesto'.[8] Without getting into textual disputes as to the relative importance of the concluding epilogue, it must be noted that while historically speaking the Italian people needed to be mobilized to bring about Machiavelli's dream of a unified Italy no longer under the control of a feudal 'internationalism', Machiavelli's aim was the seizure of power by the prince to bring about the modern national state strong enough to withstand external attacks.

Both interpretations of *The Prince* claim that Machiavelli was a humanist insofar as he was concerned with the state as well as the ruler and with the latter becoming an expression of the general will of the citizens. What is interesting to note, however, is that the way in which Machiavelli recommended this be done could not be in greater dispute. While both commentators agree on a changing nature of man and compliment Machiavelli for his distinction between ethics and political theory, their views of the Machiavellian state are in opposition. On the one hand, Merleau-Ponty emphasizes that consolidation of political power at whatever cost is necessary to bring about a stable state wherein the interests of the people may best be served; Gramsci, on the other hand, through his Marxist interpretation attempts to find already in 16th century Italy a proletarian leader who urges the masses to seize state power for their higher interests. Both commentators look for a leader who will realize these humanist ends, and both leave us without a means of identifying that leader, and even without any knowledge of what this political power, once attained, will lead to, except perpetuation of itself as political

[7] *Ibid.*, p. 136.
[8] *Ibid.*

power. If ethical values and religion are found wanting, then the historical situation itself is all that remains to determine the course of man's political decisions. History is movement revealing itself through the workings of fortune. It is to be understood through the causal factors operative in political life, which in turn can best be seen by an examination of past history.

****

In the introduction to the second book of the *Discourses on the First Ten Books of Titus Livius,* Machiavelli tells us why and how he is to proceed with his instruction:

> I shall boldly and openly say what I think of the former times and of the present, so as to excite in the minds of the young men who may read my writings, the desire to avoid the evils of the latter and to prepare themselves to imitate the virtues of the former, whenever fortune presents them the occasion. For it is the duty of an honest man to teach others that good which the malignity of the times and of fortune has prevented his doing himself; so that amongst the many capable ones whom he has instructed, some one perhaps, more favored by Heaven, may perform it.[9]

He is appalled by the almost total lack of historical knowledge in his day[10] and points to Rome and Greece as historical moments wherein the public good was realized within secure states. That the examples he gives us are, for the most part, varying forms of republicanism might lend credence to the claim that he is primarily concerned with the well-being of the citizens. Even his description of a sagacious republican legislator appears to confirm this, for he says that a man

> . . . whose object is to promote the public good, and his private interests, and who prefers his country to his own successors should concentrate all authority in himself, and a wise mind will never censure any one for having employed any extraordinary means for the purpose of establishing a kingdom or constituting a republic.[11]

While 'public good' and 'public liberty' are often used in the *Discourses,* the two expressions are never really defined. The contexts in which the terms occur sometimes seem to support the identification of public good with the continuance of public liberty, which in turn rests on civic independence of the sovereign of the state. In other

---

[9] Trans. Christian E. Detmold (New York, 1940), II, 1, pp. 274-75.

[10] *Ibid.*, I, Introduction, pp. 103-105.

[11] *Ibid.*, I, 9, pp. 138-39.

words, the end of the state (public good) is the sovereignty of the state. We are back, then, to Merleau-Ponty—the enduring state is to be established at whatever historical cost proves necessary, but there is not further reason for its being established. This can also be seen when Machiavelli compares the constitutions of Sparta and Athens and prefers Sparta's, because its government proved to be the more durable of the two.[12] In short, while Machiavelli may well be interpreted as having professed humanitarian ends, his writings will not allow us to get beyond the formula that the end of the state is its own self-perpetuation.

While claims for Machiavelli's humanism suppose a theory that ascribes value to the individual, it is difficult to say just what role the individual really plays in his political theory. A key term of Machiavelli, both for the individual and for the prince, is virtue. Virtue for the individual citizen involves civic duties which maintain a stable order; it involves a readiness to devote oneself to the 'common good', that is, to the continuance of the state. While he suggests that the citizen's virtue allows for private morality, he reminds us that such a morality can flourish only in a state where the citizens see their first duty in conforming with a stable sovereignty. By contrast the ruler's virtue is of a higher order, for it is he who is ultimately charged with preserving the state's security. His furtherance of the common good requires the preservation of power. One way in which this can be seen is by observing how the ruler is to be instrumental in instilling civic virtue in his citizens. The ruler is to use whatever means are necessary to do this, for the citizens themselves may not recognize this common good of the state. A virtuous ruler will then see the necessity for his action and by so acting will have furthered the common good of ruled and ruler. Chaos will have been avoided and stability achieved, and the state will endure. Fortune will no longer be seen as mere chance, but will instead be understood to be caused by men knowledgeable of their own interrelationships. This for Machiavelli supposedly means that men must be able to understand and participate in the political process.[13] The individual citizen participates through his recognition for the need of stable government, while the ruler participates by making the citizens aware of this common good and by securing the state at any cost that the political process may dictate.[14]

[12] *Ibid.*, I, 2, p. 115.

[13] *The Prince*, trans. Luigi Ricci and E. R. P. Vincent (New York, 1940), pp. 91-93.

[14] *Ibid.*, p. 64; *Discourses*, I, 33, pp. 198-99 and III, 49, p. 540.

Machiavelli's claim to being a humanist thus ultimately rests on his having freed mankind from the dictates of fortune and having shown men how to realize themselves through the political process. Violence as a continual world situation can now somehow be overcome by further violence, but violence now understood as an almost therapeutic means to ending the continual state of immediate conflict. Humanity's proper justification is defined in terms of political process. The end of man is to further this process, the means to achieving this end is the understanding of the process, and the goodness or badness of the players, the rulers and the citizens (both men) – is seen in their attempts to advance or thwart its continuance. Both ruler and individual citizen are sublimated into the process, and one ends with a picture, not of man's concern with his fellow men – in other words, not with a humanism – but rather with a picture of persons bound together and defined by a process of government that is itself not only impersonal but self-justifying. Machiavelli's attempt to overcome fortune understood as chance, to go beyond some divine but unknowable abstract principle, has failed by presenting us with another abstract principle, political process, which itself is not understood in terms of mankind, but only in terms of individual repetitive instances of negating the worth of man in the particular for its own perpetuation.

In moments of crisis it is the universal interest, the political process, that must be adhered to, for men can best be served by the continuation of the process. If Merleau-Ponty's interpretation of Machiavelli's picture of the human condition as one of immediate conflict is accepted, then the question of deciding whether at any given time the majority (here understood as those somehow representing the common good of preserving the state) has rights over an individual's actions cannot even be posed in ethical terms. Rather the individual is lost in his participation in the common good of the process. To attempt to question this on ethical grounds is to oppose individual rights to majority rights, but individual interests are meaningful only insofar as they conform to the common good. In short, such questions cannot be decided at the level of human personality, but only in the course of political action. This is another way of saying that politics can justify itself independently of human concerns.

****

One can see that the opposition of chaos to social stability is so strongly put by Machiavelli, and right is so strongly identified with the side of social unity, that the very persistence of social unity is enough to justify a society. Just how he arrived at this conclusion might best be seen in a brief reconstruction of his argument. Machiavelli explains that:

> If all men were good, this precept [of denying moral principles whenever necessary] would not be a good one; but as they are bad, and would not observe their faith with you, so you are not bound to keep faith with them.[15]

Machiavelli calls on the prince to abandon what ought to be done in favor of what is done whenever it is necessary; his justification for doing so is simply that it is done.[16] Such stipulative justification is of value only when one has already decided that what is done should on occasion supersede what ought to be done. The reason given for doing so is that otherwise one will soon have no possibility of acting at all, for the ruler will be superseded by someone else who is aware both of the 'reality' of the political process[17] and of the manner of continuing it—namely, by divorcing morality or individual interests from political decisions.

This all rests on the claim that power is the only realm of activity that makes a difference for man[18] and that power in turn must be secured. Hence the need for a stability of the state, for the civic virtues among subjects, for the nefarious actions of the rulers—all go to the consolidation of power through the perpetuation of the political process. This has the result of denying an ontological status to powerless things, and, inasmuch as some men may be outside a powerful state, they lose this status. Men cannot be praised or blamed as persons, but only as the foci of power within a given state. The individual person is lost and with him any discussion of his humanness; all that is left is the role of slot-filler within the self-perpetuating political process.

The commentators originally praised Machiavelli for allowing a humanism wherein man could recongize himself in his fellow men. But as a result of the unmediated character of the opposition of human personality to political process, the category of the political is in fact jeopardized. The theory uses its own failure to explain the political as a reason in its argumentative array. The claim that men are always on the edge of slipping into chaos is considered a satisfac-

[15]*The Prince,* p. 64.

[16]*Ibid.*

[17]*Ibid.,* p. 56.

[18]*Ibid.,* pp. 38-44, 77-85.

tory justification of the political. If the claim were true, it might serve as a justification, but in what way the claim can be demonstrated to be true is not evident. Normally one would ask for reasons for making such a claim. But reason has already been denied: in the previous discussion, the only justification for men's actions was held to be a descriptive one — this is the way it is actually done. If one were now to ask why this new claim is true, more stipulative justifications would be given and no reasons. If reason is denied, all that remains as an answer is intuition: the Machiavellian way of seeing reality is universally available to all men. Again reasons would have to be given to prove this claim, and Machiavellianism stops short of such reasons. It may well be that many things can be sacrificed in maintaining a rigorously realistic stance, but reason cannot be one of them, for reason is active in defining what reality is. If such a situation exists, it may well be the case that power (in the form of the most powerful men) will in effect impose a political process but this would bring us no closer to realizing human values than we were at the outset of our discussion of Machiavellian humanism.

In closing, it is worth noting that if Machiavelli's claim — that chaos is the alternative to political process and thus that political process is justified — is accepted, this is in itself an admission that men are unchanged by being made political, and that the sphere of the political remains external to the real sphere of human concern. What such a sphere of human concern might be is never answered, and we at best are left in the descriptive existence of political sociology which has no way of justifying itself other than by stipulation in terms of reference to its perpetual state of presentness. From the human perspective, then, the political would be static, or at best a repetitive mode of existence. In drawing such a conclusion I am not attempting to deny the political an essential role in defining man's existence in the world, but only, hopefully to look elsewhere than to interpretations of Machiavelli's supposed humanism for an answer.[19]

JOSEPH BIEN.

UNIVERSITY OF MISSOURI – COLUMBIA.

[19] I wish to thank Robert Audi, Charles Nauert, and Mark Stevens for their remarks on earlier versions of this paper. Several of Claude Lefort's suggestions in reference to his *Le travail de l'oeuvre Machiavel* (Paris, 1972) were especially helpful.

IMAGINATION AND INFORMATION[1]

I. *The Informativeness of Mental Images*

It is a common sentiment among philosophers that we can learn little or nothing from voluntarily conjured mental images. In *The Psychology of Imagination*[2] Sartre writes: "The image teaches us nothing . . ." and explains that this is because "no matter how long I look at an image, I shall never find anything in it but what I put there" (p. 7). He says that this, in turn, is always something I already know. Thus the image "suffers from a sort of essential poverty" (p. 8).[3] Wittgenstein, in *Zettel,*[4] is no less emphatic on this matter and writes: "Images tell us nothing, either right or wrong, about the external world" (par. 621). This, for him, as with Sartre, follows from the nature of their origin, there being nothing more to the image than what is put there by the one who forms it: "It is just because forming images is a voluntary activity that it does not instruct us about the external world" (par. 627).

In what follows, I wish to defend the view that we can arrive at information about ourselves, each other, and certain features of objects through the exercise of the imagination. This statement of my intention clearly needs expansion.

On at least one interpretation, the claim that imagination can give us knowledge is uninterestingly true. There is a sense in which to do something with imagination is to do it with a special originality or freshness, and if I am investigating some or other question and suc-

---

[1]My thanks to Richard Wollheim, Malcolm Budd, Tom Baldwin and David Brooks, whose comments helped me to improve an earlier version of this paper.

[2]Anonymous English translation (Methuen, London, 1972). In referring to Sartre's writings in what follows, I will confine myself to this work.

[3]It would not be entirely fair, in spite of these quotations, to say that Sartre always denies that images can provide knowledge of any kind. For instance, he says at one point: "It can, of course, happen that a memory image presents itself unexpectedly, and presents some new aspects" (p. 8). But Sartre does not elaborate on this remark. Elsewhere he concedes that mental images can assist the memory, but does not consider this to conflict with his negative thesis. On the image as a memory-jog, see below.

[4]English translation by G. E. M. Anscombe (Blackwell, Oxford, 1967).

ceed in giving my effort these desirable qualities, then, it seems, I am more likely to produce a solution or make some relevant discovery. Who would deny that, other things being equal, it is the imaginative person who is more likely to advance our knowledge in this or that area of investigation?

But Sartre (about whom I will be saying more in what follows) is clearly not talking about imagina*tiveness,* with its connotations of creativity and originality, when he speaks of the poverty of the image. There is a different concept of the imagination, where the idea is not that of a special quality with which any number of different activities can be endowed. To exercise *the* imagination is, in this second sense, to engage a particular mental skill or "faculty." In the quoted remarks, Wittgenstein and Sartre are talking about the forming of mental images (or imaging). A related activity would be to entertain, in the mind, some make-believe series of events, or to think of possibilities—possible creatures, episodes, or the like—which are not part of the actual world. (Within the group of such activities, one might wish to distinguish imaging from imagining, but this distinction is largely artificial and not to be pressed hard. The term "imaging," significantly, is not in common usage, and the notion of imagining is generic and includes image conjuring.)

Now when someone is imagining this or that in the sense described, the kind of activity we refer to here need not be (and indeed usually is not) practised with any special degree of originality. Nothing is implied about imaginativeness. (Again, the distinction between imagining and imaginativeness is not straightforward, nor is it lacking in philosophical interest. But it is not central to my concerns here, and given that the intuitive distinctness of the notions has been indicated, I will not discuss it further.)

In general, we can regard imaging and imagining as a particular subspecies of thinking—a subspecies which can be characterized, roughly, as an inward process of representation whereby the things, situations, and trains of events represented are not necessarily meant to portray the world as it actually is. My project is a defence of the informativeness of agreed examples of the sort of activity here at issue.

A clearer statement of the sort of information gain I am concerned with can be achieved by distinguishing my thesis from a number of others. Among the ways in which imagination has been thought to contribute to our knowledge are (i) as a part of the process of ordinary perception, where, as in the philosophies of Hume and Kant, the imagination may be thought to supplement our sense-impressions in such a way as to give us a fuller sense of the objects around us as solid and persisting entities in their own right, and (ii) as a faculty, much prized in Romantic aesthetics, for giving us an awareness of the universal significance to be found in that which is particular and finite. In what follows I will not concern myself with either of these conceptions of the epistemological role of the imagination.

There are two further ways in which information gains are associated with the function of the imagination which are more important for me to distinguish from my own thesis, since confusions here would lead (as with the point alluded to earlier concerning inventiveness) to the trivialization of the thesis. For again, there are those who would say that imaging and imagining can, of course, lead to gains in information, but not in an interesting way, and not in a way that generates any counter-examples to the denials of Sartre and Wittgenstein. Firstly, it is unlikely that Sartre and Wittgenstein would have been impressed by the undoubted fact that (iii) the conjuring of images can serve as a jog to the memory. My forming an image of something might refresh memories I have about that thing. If such an exercise leads me to decisive conclusions, it is because I had the information all along. The imaging is merely a recall device. What Sartre and Wittgenstein are denying is the possibility of gaining *fresh* knowledge by this means. And again, they would, I think, be justifiably unmoved by the consideration (iv) that imaging and imagining can be of use in constructing hypotheses. By imagining various possible ways in which something might work, I may produce a series of possible explanations for subsequent testing. But here the role of imagination in any resulting discovery would be, at best, indirect. The conjuring of images cannot *test* hypotheses of this sort.

Most important about (iii) and (iv) is that in neither of these cases can the imagination be regarded as having an essential part in the process of discovery, since any act of recollection and any piece of hypothesis formation which occurred with the help of imagination might have occurred in the absence of any such heuristic process. An interesting defence of the informative value of imagination must, I believe, be one which claimed to find substance in the tempting, but also philosophically much maligned, view that imagining can perform something *like* the function of the sense organs, in furnishing us with new empirical knowledge about the way things are in the world, and doing so, furthermore, in such a way that its role cannot be regarded as being of merely accidental assistance in the epistemological process.

I will argue (section III below) that there are important connections and points of analogy between imagining and certain forms of direct experience (perception being a central example of the latter), and connections such that certain acts of imagination can be regarded as voluntarily induced "trial experiences" which have a genuine role to play in our assessment of the way things are in the world. Given that certain things can only be known through experience, my claim (in section IV) will be that imagination can, and often does, function as a much needed substitute for direct experience, as a source of "knowledge by experience."[5] I will argue that imagination, in its epistemological role, goes beyond memory recollection, and I will sketch (in section V) how this can be so. My initial examples (introduced in section II) will concern the epistemological function of imagination in making aesthetic assessments. In the concluding sections of the paper I will broaden the discussion to include questions of affective knowledge.

II. A Range of Related Cases.

Let us consider what lies at the crux of Sartre's argument against the possibility of imaging producing knowledge. There is an assumption running through his discussion to the effect that imaging must be uninformative *because* "I shall never find anything in [the image] but what I put there." Now a central idea behind the argument might be this: that I cannot *gain* knowledge about something through a *purely* mental activity—i.e., without taking in something "from outside" or, more specifically, without perceiving something about it.

Any such claim, as it stands, is clearly wrong. It is worth noting that, for Sartre, imaging is a subspecies of thinking (p. 140); and considered in relation to this more generally specified activity, the assumption that fresh knowledge must come through perception is manifestly false. A mathematical calculation can clearly extend one's knowledge without any information inflow through perception. Philosophical reflection (on the question: What is knowledge? for example) can lead to new conceptual knowledge. If it is countered that

[5]The meaning I attach to the phrase "knowledge by experience" will become clearer in what follows. I have in mind such things as the following: a sense of the pleasure taken in contemplating this or that object of beauty, an appreciation of what it is like enduring a certain trying emotional experience, and so on. This concerns knowledge of the *quality* of experiences.

there is no "genuine" knowledge gain in such activities but only the unravelling of what is already known implicitly (because, for example, the knowledge is implied by already learned principles, rules or concepts) then this must be considered a harsh claim to make against a logician or philosopher who believes his work to have advanced the boundaries of human knowledge by the discovery of an important new proof or conceptual insight.

But even more to the point in the present context is the fact that thinking, by itself, can produce new knowledge of an empirical kind. The clearest examples are acts of simple synthesis. For example, if I know the starting date and length of duration of a tennis tournament, and happen to be able to recall the dates when it rained during the month of the tournament, I can now work out whether it rained during the tournament's final day. Far more striking examples of empirical discoveries can be found in the theory-building activities of scientists working with facts they already know.

What light do these examples throw on the possibility of making empirical discoveries through acts of imagination? A sympathetic reader of Sartre will point out that, irrespective of Sartre's own claims about the close relation between imagining and other forms of thought, there is little analogy to be found between the kinds of thinking involved in a calculation or a piece of theoretical reflection on the one hand, and any straightforward act of the imagination, on the other. The weather calculation mentioned above was, indeed, a simple *calculation,* and scientific theory-building involves calculations of a more complex sort; there is deductive activity involved, concerning the consequences of hypotheses, and so on. No such thing is involved in image-formation, and the same applies to other acts of imagination of the relevant sort. If there is a possible analogy to be found between such acts and a process which undoubtedly leads to an increase in empirical knowledge, the analogy must be with perception.

Conjuring mental images may indeed involve a visual aspect, or be related to some other sense modality. It is this, a supporter of Sartre might argue, which encourages the view that imagination leads to knowledge; the sensory aspect of imagery can mislead one into thinking of imaging as the perception of some kind of inner analogue of what exists in the world.

Now this way of thinking about imagery certainly does seem to be mistaken. If I cannot recall the colour of a friend's eyes, I may conjure up an image of her face, and then it comes to me: grey eyes beneath fair hair. But the description of this case has already given away its claim to be a genuine case of knowledge gained. Without attempting to make a clear distinction between relearning and recollecting, it seems correct to say that this is a case of recollection. Sartre would surely be right to point out that the image would not correctly and nonaccidentally have portrayed my friend as having grey eyes had I not already known their colour. The initial failure to remember simply called for a jogging of my memory, and the act of forming the image did precisely this.

Now we can be certain that this was no case of relearning through observation; any such analogy with perceiving must be disallowed. For first, what we perceive are public items, allowing the possibility for our checking our observations for accuracy: looking again, using a different sense organ, asking someone what they see, and so on. We are, in contrast, only subjectively aware of our mental images. But second, and more important with regard to Sartre's views, when I have a mental image of my friend, the content of the image comes from my past experience and what I already know. My mind is unaffected by any present external factors. By contrast, a condition of perceiving is that a cause-effect relation holds between the subject's experience and the perceived object.

Because of these contrasts with perception, there is no question of my coming to know the colour of my friend's eyes by conjuring up an image of her face. The image, if it is to be correct in respect of any detail, must, in respect of that detail, be constructed from what I already know. If the detail is not already, so to speak, on the horizon of my memory, the image will not help me to arrive at it.

But we cannot, on these grounds alone, rule out the possibility of imagination being a source of empirical knowledge. As I have pointed out, it is clearly false to regard the information inflow involved in perception as the only source of such knowledge, since calculations upon and syntheses of what has been already learned can lead to further knowledge. Although imaging is not a form of calculation (at least in any ordinary sense), nor of perception, it can involve spontaneous acts of synthesis, and in this way, I will argue, it can lead to certain kinds of knowledge about the world.

Consider the following case. A friend writes to tell me she has recently been advised to wear spectacles, and has bought a pair with hornrims. Wondering whether she will still look pretty wearing them, or now look bossy, or perhaps funny, I picture her to myself in her new spectacles, and form a fair idea.

Here is a similar example: I come across an antique cupboard in a shop, and although I like it and consider it cheap at the price, I hesitate before buying it since I am uncertain whether it will go well with the rest of my furniture. I picture it in a certain corner of my house and am enough pleased by the result to make the purchase.

These two cases are representative of a procedure of assessment which is undeniably used, possibly by everyone. While such a procedure may only be a rough substitute for actual perceptions, it can result sometimes in confident assessments (I am confident enough to buy the cupboard). But a number of pertinent questions now arise. For example: In what way can imagination be a *substitute* for perception? Is it a special kind of knowledge which is obtained in this way? Is imagination a crucial means to such knowledge? If imagination involves no "calculation" and no direct causal contact with the world, then how does it produce knowledge? I will try to answer these questions by means of a series of related theses about imagination.

III. Imagination as Quasiobservation.

The best way of finding out how my friend's new pair of spectacles suit her is to *observe* her wearing them. The question concerns how she will *strike* people—whether, for example, they will find her looks pleasing when they see her wearing the spectacles. It is a question concerning the quality of the experience evoked. And so the question demands to be answered through experience.

In answering a question of this sort, imaging and imagining can be a substitute source of reference precisely because they have a qualitative dimension which is analogous to that of related direct experiences. In this section of my paper I wish to explore this analogy.

Sartre has claimed that imaging is a form of quasiobservation. He contrasts thought with observation (or perception), and claims that imaging falls somewhere between the two. I have said that for Sartre imaging is a subspecies of thinking. Thinking, in general, and so also imaging, are subject to the will. As Sartre sometimes puts it, our thoughts, like our conjured images, are, at least typically, "spontaneous." Along with this "spontaneity" goes their alleged "essential poverty" or lack of informativeness. These features set thinking (and thus also imaging) apart from perception.

But Sartre also points out a feature common between imaging and perceiving and which makes imaging a *special* kind of thinking.

He notes that when we perceive an object, it necessarily presents itself to us "in profile" (p. 6); that is to say, our awareness of it is always limited to a particular point of view which excludes an infinite number of alternative ones, so that there is always scope for advancing our knowledge of the object through a further perception. In this, Sartre goes on to claim, perceiving an object contrasts with thinking of it (in the usual sense of "thinking"), because to think of something (in this sense) is to have immediately before one's mind all one's conceptual knowledge of that object; when I think of a cube, "I think of its its six sides and its eight angles all at once" (p. 6). Here there is only "knowledge which is conscious of itself" (p. 7). Now in this respect, Sartre notes, imaging is closer to perceiving. When I have an image of an object I am always aware of it in profile; if the image is visual, for example, then the imaged object appears to me from a particular point in space. In presenting its object as if from a particular point of view, this mode of awareness is like observation, but on the thesis presented we can learn nothing through it, so it is merely "quasiobservation."

In pointing out that the content of an act of imaging, or of a perception, is always presented "in profile," Sartre is drawing attention to a qualitative feature common to imaging and perceving. What, more precisely, is this feature?

To say that visual perception is always from a point of view is to allude to the fact that this sense modality involves an essential dimension of spatiality; to see is (among other things) to be aware of objects within a unified set of spatial relations, including, importantly, relations to the perceiver himself. All sense modalities involve a spatial aspect. And besides this "spatiality," perceptions are also essentially temporal; they are dateable occurrences carrying immediate information about the perceptual field.

Conjured mental images ape actual perceptions. To visualize, for example, is to seem to *see*. Thus a famous psychological experiment has shown that a test subject can be led to mistake, for his own mental imagery, real images projected onto a screen before him.[6] The features of spatiality and temporality characteristic of perceptions are carried over to mental imagery as well. In general, to have a mental image is to have (perhaps in an attenuated form) a kind of experience which is primarily associated with some form of direct causal

[6] C. W. Perky, "An Experimental Study of Imagination," *American Journal of Psychology* (Vol. 21, 1910).

contact with the world (a paradigm is visual perception) and which, in the act of imaging, can be *voluntarily* evoked in a way which reproduces to a greater or lesser degree the *quality* of such primary experience. To conjure an image is to evoke a *quasi*experience.

We can view imagining, in general, as the evocation of quasiexperiences. But this view is not obviously correct; certainly, we cannot infer from the nature of imagery to the nature of imagination in general, as if all imaginings implied the evocation of imagery. I need not, in making up a story to myself, have any mental images of things relevant to the story (though such imagery would be a natural accompaniment to my activity). Still, there are reasons for expecting imaging and imagining to be analogous activities. I remarked earlier that ordinary language marks no distinction between imaging and imagining; and the root of the word "imagination" seems to justify the expectation of at least one feature which would make the two activities closely alike.

Significantly, the content of an act of imagination always incorporates a spatiotemporal setting, and it is this which makes it correct to say that imagination and imaging both involve the evocation of quasiexperiences. Thus, to begin with, there seems to be a significant difference between my merely entertaining the thought that a certain possible state of affairs pertained, and my imagining that state of affairs. The mere consideration of a possibility—a mere supposition—is not an act of imagination. There is a minimal sense of supposing where, were I to suppose, say, that I had the body of an insect, I shall not have imagined that I had such a body. One might muse as follows: "Suppose that my body belonged to the same category as that of cockroaches, beetles, crickets, etc." No imagining need take place here.

In what way does imagining, in the required sense, differ—involve more than—the sparser mode of thinking? I believe the answer is this: that the mere supposition specifies nothing about the circumstances, sketched in at least broadly spatiotemporal terms, in which I might find myself with the body of an insect. Were someone to claim that he had imagined himself to have the body of an insect, we would have the right to expect of him that he be able to fill in at least some details not essential to the pure supposition. Specifically, we could demand details concerning events and states of affairs which placed the supposition in a spatiotemporal context. We could demand from him something like a narrative, as if his claim had been to have experienced something that had happened. Thus, in imagining, the purity of a supposition is lost; it becomes, to use an image of Sartre's, "debased";[7] it takes on a relatively specific form in time and space, and an infinity of alternative possibilities are excluded. The matter is best put by saying that the imagination presents a supposition about a possible state of affairs as a *quasiexperience.* A pure supposition leaves all inessential spatiotemporal possibilities open. The imagination fills some of these in, as if to furnish us, from experience, with a concrete example of what is born in mind. This is no real experience, but rather what can be called a trial one, since experiences are typically based not merely on supposition but on belief; the experience of visually perceiving something, for example, is (at least normally) accompanied by a belief that there is something before me.

Acts of imagination, by contrast, remain a subspecies of supposition. But in virtue of their capacity to give us an impression of the quality of direct experience, they have an important epistemological function. The imagination can function in this way: faced with the need to acquaint myself with a certain situation, but where direct experience is unavailable, I summon a kind of *trial*-experience as a substitute. Clearly, if certain questions cannot be answered except by recourse to experience, then the skill of evoking substitute experiences can have an important role.

IV. When Does Imagination Have an Epistemological Role?

The two examples I gave earlier of cases where knowledge is obtained by acts of imagination were both cases of aesthetic appraisal. I do not believe that the epistemological role of imagination is limited to such cases, but they are a good starting point for investigating the informativeness of imagery. In both the example concerning the new pair of spectacles and the one concerning the antique cupboard, we have to do with appearances, and specifically, with the impression a certain situation could be expected to make on me, as a possible observer. In each case I supposed myself resorting to acts of imaging in order to assess appearances which were not available for direct scrutiny. And I claimed that in both these cases, unlike the one where the image acted as a memory-jog assisting me to a recollection of the colour of my friend's eyes, the act of imagination was somehow essential to my arriving at my conclusion.

---

[7]Sartre's account (see pp. 63-75) corroborates the point that imagination locates its objects spatially.

But in what way essential? Let me elaborate briefly. A memory-jog is never an intrinsic part of any act of recollection; the information to be recalled can always be brought forth directly. Contrast, for example, the role of imaging, on the one hand, when this functions as a memory-jog, and perceiving, when the latter is the means whereby I come to know something about my surroundings. The memory-jog can drop out of the former process in a way which does not necessitate any substitute. It is merely heuristic. Now when I discover something by means of perceiving, it is also true that I could make the discovery by some other means—by reading someone else's verbal report, for example. But here the direct perceiving has to be substituted with something else; it does not occupy a place in the process which could fall out altogether, as it were, but one which must be filled by a suitable alternative, otherwise the information will not be forthcoming. It is in this way that, as I wish to maintain, imaging is *sometimes essential* to a process of information gathering. It sometimes functions as more than a heuristic device. In the examples concerning my friend's spectacles and the antique cupboard, I could have arrived at my conclusions by means other than imaging, but then the role of imaging would have been, and would have to have been, replaced by an alternative means to information. (I will say more about such alternatives below).

Now in these examples there was no question of my *calculating* my reponses to the aesthetic situations in question. In the absence of the possibility of actual observation, I resorted to a form of quasiexperience or "inner observation." Why was this necessary?

An explanation lies in a thesis that has been argued for and much discussed; the thesis, namely, that it is not possible to lay down in advance the conditions for the application of aesthetic concepts.[8] Without such rules of application each new aesthetic situation calls for a fresh appraisal; its quality cannot be calculated in advance, and so it must be experienced for itself. Now all I wish to extract from this (after all debatable) view is the point that the aesthetic appraisal of a situation requires, ideally, that I experience that situation at first hand.

I say ideally, for I do not wish to imply that we are left with no idea at all of what our response would be if we did not experience an aesthetic situation directly. At least three alternatives, while falling short of the ideal, can lead to an appraisal which amounts to more

[8]See F. N. Sibley, "Aesthetic Concepts," *Philosophical Review*, 1959.

than guesswork. First, while I may not have experienced the situation itself, I may have experienced something very like it. For example, confronted with a question like the one concerning the antique cabinet, I may decide to buy the cabinet on the following grounds: I see that the cabinet is very similar in appearance and size to one in my neighbour's sitting room, and I know that my neighbour's sitting room, except for the presence of a cabinet in the corner, is arranged similarly to my own, and that I like the appearance of that corner of his room. A second alternative way of coming to an appraisal is this: I may know someone whose taste is very similar to my own, so that when he likes the look of something I have not seen, I can make a reasonable estimate of my own likely response based on what he has said.

But far more important than these two responses to the ideal — the direct experience of aesthetic situations — is a third one: we can conjure up an image of the situation. In the given example I visualize a certain state of affairs, because this trial-experience is the most readily available alternative to that direct experience which is the best, indeed the only foolproof, means to a correct aesthetic evaluation of the considered situation. Certainly, my living through the situation in my mind's eye does not usually offer an altogether accurate estimate of what my response will be to the actual situation, but people commonly do have sufficiently reliable visualization to make reasonable decisions by this means, and such decisions are not just guesses.

Two factors give imaging a special importance among alternatives to direct experience: the *scope* of situations open to scrutiny by the mind's eye, and the more or less immediate *accessibility* of mental imagery. Furthermore, it would be a mistake to think of the decision-making role of imagery as being limited to rare or unusual questions. Take the following case. Suppose that my two favourite ice cream flavours are vanilla and peppermint. One day I pass an ice cream stall and realize I want an ice cream. But I must decide between my two favourite flavours; sometimes I much prefer the one, sometimes the other — I do not know why. Almost automatically, I conjure up the image of the one taste, then the other, and realize that today I would enjoy the peppermint more.

Now one could point out in connection with this case that it would appear to involve a question which is decidable without resort either to direct experience or to imaging or to one of the other forms of indirect experience I mentioned earlier. I could, for example, conclude that I prefer peppermint today on the grounds that I generally prefer it on a hot day. We are not limited to decision-making via direct experience or some mode of indirect experience such as one of the three I mentioned on p. 216. I do not want to argue for this even with regard to typical questions of aesthetic evaluation, where it would be a more plausible view. My point is simply that imaging *may* sometimes be the best means, and perhaps the only one, for my arriving at a good decision about questions which frequently arise, particularly concerning my personal reactions to situations.

It is worth noting that I am likely to have been unable to analyse my reactions to ice cream into a manageable set of probabilities according to which I could have predicted my preferences on particular occasions. The variables of the situation are likely simply to have been too complicated. (Consider the possibly relevant factors: advertisements seen, meals recently taken, and so on.) And the fact that most perceptual and affective reactions involve this kind of complexity underlies the importance of imaging. For is it feasible that someone should come to know—in general terms—his probable reactions to any substantial proportion of the possible situations which could occur in his experience, so that these became a possible subject of prediction and calculation? Yet imaging seems able to give us an idea of experiences which go beyond those we have actually lived through. In this it appears mysterious—literally, a conjuring process. Let us now consider how this process might work.

V. How Does Imagination Go beyond Remembered Experiences?

In setting about answering this question I begin by underlining what is, I think, a familiar fact: that imaging and imagining are parasitic activities; they are parasitic on the experiences in relation to which they can be described, in the way I have done, as *quasi*experiences. If I visualize X, it is a matter of logic that I have the quasiexperience of seeing X, and I cannot set out to visualize X if I do not know what it is to see X. To some degree, I will maintain, imagining incorporates what we have learned and not forgotten about our direct experiences. In what follows, I will try to make clearer how it is always, to an extent, a manifestation of remembered experiences.

Once we have seen the relation of imagining to memory, a simple answer will offer itself to the question of how imagination can enlighten us about what it is like to experience events without our ever having been physically present as spectators. Memories have various kinds of content; we can remember things (last Christmas, for example), facts (that it rained on Christmas day), particular experiences (my embarrassment at having to act as Father Christmas), and kinds of experiences (what it is like being the centre of a group of children's attention). The last two sorts of cases, comprising remembered *experiences,* are, I contend, the elements out of which every imagined scene is constructed. This is so no matter how farfetched, unique, or alien to one's actual past experience is the situation imagined.

Thus consider the described case where I conjure up an image of my friend wearing spectacles. Here visualization can give me a good idea of how she would look, but only if I can remember how some related things look—for example, how spectacles look, and how she looks without them. If I had no past experience of spectacles it is difficult to see how I could visualize anyone wearing them. Perhaps I could build up a picture of spectacles by having them described to me in terms of elements of which I did have experience. Someone could say: visualize two roundish glass discs connected by wire in this and that way . . . and so on. But here I am simply falling back on still smaller elements of remembered experience. The underlying process remains the same: what I do is synthesize elements from past experience into a quite new quasiexperience.

At this point the progress of my argument may seem open to an objection. In the considered example—so it may be claimed—I do not gain knowledge of how my friend looks in spectacles by means of a synthesis of past experiences, since I do not *gain* knowledge here at all. The criteria for knowing how something looks—the objection continues—show that in this case I had that knowledge before I conjured up the image of my friend in spectacles, since this very ability to picture her thus is a criterion of knowing how she looks in them. And, supposedly, another criterion of knowing the looks of something is the ability to recognize that thing when I see it, and surely I would instantly have recognized my friend in a pair of spectacles on the first occasion I had seen her wearing them.

Now this objection cannot be allowed to stand without inviting the emergence of a serious paradox. For it is surely possible that I might conjure up a picture of my friend in spectacles and then be struck by how strange she now appears in my mind's eye. I have become aware, perhaps, of some unsuspected incongruity. Alternatively, I may be surprised by the transformation in my friend's appearance when I next meet her wearing her new spectacles. I had never before realized how she would look—how they would transform her appearance. But it is almost certain that I would still have recognized her in them. We must conclude that the objection went wrong in its stipulation of the criteria for knowing the looks of something. The ability to form images and to recognize cannot, in themselves, constitute the required criteria; these need something more written into them. They must incorporate something concerning our reaction to the imaging or perceptual recognition—namely, that we are not surprised by the looks of something if we already know how it looks; its appearance ought to contain little that we could not have anticipated.

But there is another possible objection to the present view of imagination which must be considered briefly. This concerns a problem which Hume raised concerning the sort of account of imagination which I have given. My account has a clearly Humean ring. In the *Treatise,*[9] Hume claims that "we cannot form to ourselves a just idea of the taste of a pineapple, without having actually tasted it" (p. 5). Further, though he sees that "I can imagine to myself such a city as the *New Jerusalem,* whose pavement is gold and walls are rubies, tho' I never saw any such" (p. 3), he nevertheless also states that "neither the ideas of the memory nor imagination . . . can make their appearance in the mind, unless their correspondent impressions have gone before to prepare the way for them" (p. 9). Imagination, he holds, is able to produce images which do not correspond to any from direct experience, because, unlike memory, it "is not restrained to the same order and form with the original impressions" (p. 9).

Hume produced a famous possible counter-example to his account, and this is clearly relevant to my own thesis. He conceded that it would be possible for someone to visualize a particular shade of blue the likes of which he had never seen before (pp. 5-6). Hume considered this case "so particular and singular, that [it was] scarce worth our observing" (p. 6). This is too brief a dismissal of the case, but Hume is correct to point out that it is a special one. A correct response to it is, I think, to point to an analogy with the case of mixing shades of paint. Some elementary colours are clearly required, and also a knowledge of certain likely results of combining them. Similarly, a new colour which I visualize may be a simple combination of colours with which I am familiar. Alternatively, my ability to visualize such a colour could, it seems, depend on my familiarity with the way in which colours can shade gradually from dark to light—as a

[9] I will quote from the Selby-Bigge edition.

blue sky may grow paler towards the horizon. This could enable me to imagine such a shading process occurring with a colour whose shadings I have not seen before. What is significant about these cases is that it does not seem possible that I should be able to imagine a quite new colour *except* when it is a simple combination of colours with which I am familiar, or simply a new shade of one of them.

VI. *Affective Knowledge*

Questions concerning our reactions to experienced situations—that is, the whole class of questions which have knowledge by experience as their object—range over matters which include our emotional responses. So far, I have argued that imagination can be used to assess certain sensory properties of absent objects and situations, or our likely sensory responses to them. In this function it is a source of what can be called *phenomenal* knowledge. (I have emphasized certain cases of aesthetic appraisal, where the categories of aesthetic and phenomenal overlap.) *Affective* knowledge—that is, knowledge of our personal emotional states and dispositions, as well as those of others—can also be gained through imagination, insofar as the latter is a means whereby we can assess our likely emotional responses to absent situations, and whereby we gauge the feelings of others who are in situations we have not experienced.

Here, then, are two further cases where an effort of imagination could lead to knowledge.

a) I reflect on what it would have been like to be present during a violent period preceding the emergence of a certain tyrannical political regime.
b) I wonder at the behaviour of a friend who was present during the turbulent events referred to in (a), and consider, specifically, whether his actions condemn him as a coward, or whether, alternatively, it would be unduly harsh to expect more of a man in such a situation.

In attempting to decide the question posed in (a), I might imagine myself in a certain situation minimally involving the existence around me of a certain political state of affairs. I tell myself a certain story in which I am, at least, one of the main characters. The story proceeds in the unfolding of a series of events which I believe are possible or likely, given the general facts I know about the situation in question (say, as reported in the newspapers), and given, also, my own experience of other situations with various points of similarity. By thus localizing myself in a complex set of political events I am likely to find myself reacting, in my imagination at least, in some possibly surprising ways. Perhaps, as I describe the situation to myself, the unfolding picture first of all reminds me of a number of relevant details which I had not taken into account on first estimating my likely response. The imaginative act has, in this respect, the function of a memory-jog. But there is a more essential revelatory or informative function which the whole exercise has. As I remarked earlier, I usually simply cannot tell, by detached calculation, what my personal reacton would be in a supposed situation which I have not experienced before. Through imagination I can put myself through a trial-experience of the event, and thereby discover perhaps unexpected feeling stirring in me.[10] The surprise with which we can discover unsuspected emotional dispositions within ourselves is likely to be familiar to devotees of serious films, novels, and other forms of fiction. And we can make these discoveries by fictions of our own devising.

The connection between the questions raised in (a) and (b) shows the importance of imagination as a means to *moral* understanding. We share with others a great many of our affective reactions and we *assume* such sharing. Thus a knowledge of our own emotional dispositions leads to an understanding of other people—an understanding which is essential to a certain order of moral insight. While the factors which may *justify* an inference or assumption I make about the feelings of another (given my knowledge of the way I would feel in his situation) are not easy to spell out, this should not obscure the importance in our daily lives of the kinds of inference and assumption in question.

VII. Final Remarks

Two of my claims in the foregoing might be said to have been insufficiently defended: (i) that the exercise of imagination can give us

[10]These feelings are "defused" and not felt in their fullness. (See also my remarks about quasiexperiences on p. 214). Just as a stage presentation of a scene does not delude us, but evokes, nevertheless, a *tendency* to believe in the portrayed scene, so the imagination can produce in us a tendency towards a certain identifiable feeling—where this tendency is rooted in make-believe rather than (as with "fully" experienced emotions) in real belief. Discussions relevant to this distinction are R. Wollheim, *Art and Its Objects* (New York, 1968), Section 43; R. Scruton, *Art and Imagination* (London, 1974), Chap. 9; R. K. Elliott, "Aesthetic Theory and the Experience of Art" in H. Osborne (ed.) *Aesthetics* (Oxford, 1972).

knowledge of *objective* features of the world, and not just of our own mental dispositions, and (ii) that assessments we arrive at through imagination can properly be called *knowledge*. I conclude with brief remarks on each of these points.

One could justifiably reply to (i) by saying that my knowledge of a mental disposition, whether my own or that of someone else, *is* knowledge of an objective feature of the world, if it is knowledge at all. But perhaps the real worry here is whether *nonmental* features of objects can be discovered in the ways I have described; for someone might hold that a claim (to take an example upon which I have placed some weight) about whether such and such an arrangement of furniture is an elegant arrangement or not is simply an expression of a personal preference—a "subjective" matter. Now it is not my present task to settle what is, in fact, a general issue of aesthetics. I will simply remark that it would be a mistake to conclude that the ascription of some property, F, is no more than the expression of a personal preference, just because the discernment of F might depend on the perceptual response of the one who ascribes it. A simple example which shows the shortcoming in such a piece of reasoning is the case of colour perception, which is arguably a good analogy through which to view aesthetic appraisals. It does, in any case, seem wrong to construe aesthetic assessments as mere matters of personal taste (like my preference for chocolate ice cream) since if they were, they would not give rise to the sorts of reasoned debate to which they are undoubtedly subject.

The objection raised by (ii) is that imagination, while it can lead to very rough assessments of the kind I have described, cannot lead to anything approaching *justified* beliefs. I have conceded that the mind's eye is a far from ideal organ of perception—or rather, that it is not an organ of perception at all, but a faculty of quasiperception. I further concede that, typically, it gives us only an estimate of the real situation, and that this is often an inaccurate assessment, and always one which is overridden when in conflict with firsthand experience. Now I do not wish to quibble about the use of a word. What we call "knowledge" is commonly open to *some* doubt. On the other hand, I take my examples to have shown that imagination can lead to what are assessments rather than mere guesses, and this implies that some pointer towards the truth has been consulted. Once this is granted, then it must further be granted that, conceptually, there is nothing absurd in supposing that a particular case could result in sufficient certainty to warrant an attribution of knowledge. Hence, the matter at issue becomes an empirical one. Assessments via the imagination involve a skill, and I can improve upon my performance through practice. (Why should I not measure my progress inductively, according to the number of subsequently confirmed assessments?)

Through a combination of natural ability and practice, an impressive degree of reliability has been known to be achieved. Anyone who doubts this should observe artists, architects, or interior designers at work. Commonly, they will be able to study an empty space, see what is not there, and know what to do next.

PAUL TAYLOR.

UNIVERSITY OF CAPE TOWN.

ABHINAVAGUPTA[1] AND DEWEY ON ART AND ITS RELATION TO MORALITY: COMPARISONS AND EVALUATIONS

It may seem preposterous to juxtapose and compare the aesthetic theories of the metaphysical idealist Abhinavagupta (ca. 1000) with that of the naturalist *par excellence* John Dewey. The former lived and developed his aesthetic theory in a cultural climate which was radically different from that of Dewey, whose life spanned almost a century from the mid-nineteenth to the mid-twentieth. The one belonged to the alleged "spiritual" East whereas the other to the "materialist" West. The metaphysical idealism (Kashmir Śaivism) and mysticism of Abhinava was completely foreign to the naturalism and the experimental temper of Dewey. And yet it is astonishing to find that despite their divergent philosophical positions there is a remarkable similarity between the theory of *rasa* as developed by Abhinava following Bharata's *Natya-Śāstra* and Dewey's key aesthetic concept of "consummatory experience." It is the intention of this paper to analyze, compare and evaluate the aesthetic theories of these two seminal aestheticians and explore their bearing on the relation of art to morality. Incidentally, it will also show how a sound philosophy of art and aesthetic experience need not be tied down to any preconceived "metaphysical" or "subjectivistic" assumptions.

Whereas Abhinava derived his theory from a close study of the forms, techniques, and values of drama, poetry, music, and other related arts of the theatre, Dewey's studies in aesthetics were based mostly on the arts of painting and literature. Dewey's classic *Art as Experience*, published in 1934, suprised both his followers and critics alike who were skeptical about the relevance of Dewey's naturalism to an adequate understanding of art both in its creative and appreciative aspects. If we could set aside metaphysical overtones in Abhinavagupta's aesthetics we would be suprised to find that both he

[1]My understanding of Bharata's *Nātya-Śāstra* and Abhinavagupta's aesthetic theory is based on the well-known series of volumes on *Comparative Aesthetics* by Professor K.C. Pandey published by Chowkhamba Sanskrit Series Office, 1956-59. References in this paper are to the second edition of his *Comparative Aesthetics*, Vol. I (Indian Aesthetics), 1959 as well as to his later book *Abhinavagupta, An Historical and Philosophical Study* (Varanasi - I, India, Chowkhamba Sanskrit Series Office, 1963).

and Dewey employed a common methodology and appealed to a phenomenological analysis of what was actually *presented* in a work of art whether it was a drama, novel, poem, or painting. The same method was adopted for analyzing aesthetic experience from the point of view of the spectator or of the appreciator. No wonder there is a marked resemblance between Abhinava's theory of *rasa* and Dewey's concept of "consummatory experience." Both of them analyzed the aesthetic object or work of art in terms of the total pervasive quality of the aesthetic situation which is neither purely objective nor purely subjective but is a dynamic union of various constituents. For both, a work of art clarifies, heightens, and accentuates the quality of experience by a proper use of sense, emotion, and imagination. And lastly, both of them gave a prominent place to the factor of conflict and its resolution in artistic creation. They realized that life is not all milk and honey, and therefore a creative artist makes proper use of the factors of resistance and tension in carrying forward the work to its fulfilling consummation, giving rise to an intensified and heightened experience. And yet, despite these common aesthetic insights Abhinava and Dewey differed on the final import of art, its ultimate meaning, as well as its relation to ordinary experience. These various points of resemblance and contrast will become clear as we proceed to understand the meaning of *rasa* in Abhinava's aesthetics and that of "consummatory experience" in Dewey's theory of art.

When then is *rasa*? In ordinary language the word *"rasa"* is used both for the quality of taste or relish as experienced, as well as for the object of relish. In the context of art it stands for the aesthetic object as *presented* by the dramatic artist through various techniques. It is the whole aesthetic situation unified by a pervasive emotional quality. Dr. Pandey speaking of *rasa,* puts it this way:

> It is not pure unity, but unity in multiplicity. The unifying factor in the multiplicity is a basic state of mind *(sthāyibhāva)* which binds together in an organic whole (1) the emotive situation in human setting, consisting of the physical cause of the basic mental state (*vibhava*), (2) the mimetic changes, which are inspired by the aroused basic mental state and as such are indicative of the internal state (*anubhāva*) and (3) the transient emotions (*vyabhichāribhāva*).[2]

He goes on to emphasize that for Abhinavagupta "aesthetic experience is not the experience of basic emotion (*sthāyin*) in isolation from situation, mimetic changes and transient emotions, but in union with them."[3] Thus *rasa*, while retaining its link with ordinary sen-

[2] *Comparative Aesthetics*, Vol. I, p. 22.

[3] *Ibid.*, p. 183.

suous experience, is transmuted through the creative genius of the dramatist into an aesthetic category having a double connotation as that which a dramatist presents and also as the unique qualitative experience of the spectator as a result of his rapt participation in the aesthetic situation. Aesthetic experience of *rasa* is a state of pure joy which depends on our intuitive capacity to perceive the dominant emotional quality of the total situation presented by the dramatist. In such an experience private personal feelings are suspended and detached from the particular time and place of actual occurrences and are elevated to the plane of universalized human emotions. Purity of the joy experienced is a consequence of the intuitive insight gained into the basic structure and essence of human emotions as they occur in characteristic situations. However, such a capacity for *rasa* experience is not entirely cut off from its empirical and natural moorings. The usual eight kinds of *rasa* mentioned by Bharata such as the erotic, the comic, the pathetic, the furious, the heroic, the terrible, the odious, and the marvellous are transformations of our natural human feelings of love, laughter, sorrow, anger, effort, fear, disgust, and surprise brought about by dramatic art. The question whether there is a ninth *śānta rasa* apart from these eight has been a moot point among medieval Indian aestheticians. Abhinavagupta, however, holds that there are several levels of aesthetic experience such as sense, imagination, emotion, catharsis, and transcendence. At the highest level of transcendence *rasa* experience is one of perfect repose and serenity (*śānta)* no matter what the emotion involved is. Therefore, at the transcendental level there is only one type of *rasa* which is one of unmixed bliss where the duality of subject and object disappears and the self is merged in the Absolute giving rise to pure spiritual rapture. Such an experience is supposed to be out of this world. At the same time, says Dr. Pandey, Abhinavagupta "denies antagonism between sensuous joy and spiritual bliss *(Ānanda),* recognizes the former to be a means to the latter, and asserts that it is meant for the few."[4] Despite such an apologetic statement it remains true that *rasa* at its highest level was regarded by Abhinava as extraordinary, otherworldly and mystical. Such an idealistic and absolutistic interpretation of *rasa* could have been obviated if Abhinavagupta had adhered simply to a descriptive analysis of the experience without regarding it as a symbolic adumbration of a Reality beyond our world of natural existence. In other words, instead of regarding aesthetic experience (*rasa*) as one *instance* among

[4] *Abhinavagupta*, 2nd ed., p. vii.

others through which human beings manifest their spiritual quality, he almost subordinated it to the position of a *means* for the realization of one's identity with the Absolute. And yet Abhinavagupta kept close enough to the actual process of dramatic presentation when he emphasized the role of *reversal* in the fortunes of the hero or heroine in bringing out the quality of *rasa* in a heightened and intensified manner. Kalidāsa's *Abhijñanā Śākuntalam* as well as the epics, the *Rāmāyana* and the *Māhābhārata* illustrate the incidence of conflict, strife, separation, and frustration in human affairs and bring home to us in a vivid manner the tragic quality and poignancy of the human situation. Speaking from the point of view of the cathartic level, he admitted nine *rasas* of which four were regarded as the principal ones and the rest subordinate. These four principal *rasas* were the erotic (*śrngāra*), the furious (*rāudra*), the heroic (*vīra*), and the serene (*śānta*). And aesthetic experience at the cathartic level was described as one of self-forgetfulness and empathetic identification with the psychophysical condition of the hero.[5] Keeping in view the above account of *rasa* in Abhinavagupta's aesthetics, let us consider its implications for morality.

The problem of the relation of art to morality was handled by Abhinava as well as Bharata in a sensitive manner. They rightly held that the primary aim of artistic creation was to provide aesthetic enjoyment to the spectator. Dramatic presentation was not subservient to any narrowly conceived code of moral rules in the form of "Do's and Don't's." It was not meant for sectarian propaganda either. But that did not mean that dramatic art had no moral implications. It did bring out the moral improvement of the spectator more effectively than would have been possible through didactic moralizing and sermonizing. It appealed to their imagination and made them perceive in a vivid manner, through a process of identification with the hero in his varied situations, the relation between his actions and their consequences. The climactic experience of the basic emotion (*rasa*) chastened the spectator and brought about his moral edification as a result of a greater understanding of life and its problems. However, despite its basic soundness the theory of a fixed number of aesthetic qualities (*rasas*) as well as their role in promoting the four traditional values of *Dharma, Artha, Kāma* and *Moksha,* appears to be rigid and a bit oversimplified. But this only shows that no creative artist, however great, could ignore the cultural climate of his period.

[5]*Comparative Aesthetics,* Vol. I, p. 20?.

Making a transition from Abhinavagupta's aesthetics to that of Dewey and discovering their common insights is nothing less than having the exhilaration of bridging the alleged gulf between the "mystic" East and the "scientific" West. As far as I know, Dewey had no acquaintance with Oriental aesthetics at all. And yet, his philosophy of art shares some essential characteristics with that of Abhinavagupta. Dewey, in contradistinction to Abhinavagupta, was a thoroughgoing naturalist, and as such emphasized the continuity between nature, experience, and art. His view of nature was not one of "reductive" materialism but an imaginative one which included the inorganic, the organic, and the human in active interrelation. He endeavored to break down the alleged unbridgeable "dualisms" between the natural and the supernatural, mind and body, the spiritual and the material. His key aesthetic concept, "consummatory experience" or "*an experience,*" was an elaboration and enrichment of his general concept of experience developed in his *Experience and Nature* (1929). Not only his aesthetics but his entire philosophy is dominated by the basic concept of "pervasive quality" which he elaborated in that illuminating essay, "Qualitative Thought," published in the volume *Philosophy and Civilization* (1931). Dewey wrote his essay under the influence of William James' famous piece, "The Place of Affectional Facts in a World of Pure Experience." He, following James, repudiated Humean "atomistic" and "psychologistic" theory of experience and put forward in its place an interactional and a contextual one. Experience for him is not a series of disjointed particulars but is a product of a dynamic transaction between a live organism and a changing natural and social environment. It is constituted by "doing-and-undergoing," and is always situational. It occurs in specific situations, each of which is unified by its own pervasive quality. It is an ongoing process of *continuous change* as the organism responds to one situation after another. It is not a passive reception of external sensations, nor it is merely a "subjective" something occurring exclusively "inside" a mind. He replaced the "spectator" concept of an aloof self by the dynamic concept of a live organism who, in its encounter with objects and events, brings to bear upon the environment its entire past experience in the form of habits, attitudes, and funded meanings. Dewey is here giving a phenomenological account of what he designates as "immediate experience." He says:

> The organism acts in accordance with its own structure, simple or complex, upon its surroundings. As a consequence the changes produced in the environment react upon the organism and its activities. The

> living creature undergoes, suffers, the consequences of his own behavior. *This close connection between doing and suffering or undergoing forms what we call experience. Disconnected doing and disconnected suffering are neither of them experiences*[6] (emphasis added).

Speaking about the situational nature of immediate experience, he points out the distinction between a situation and an object thus:

> By the term situation in this connection is signified the fact that the subject-matter ultimately referred to in existential propositions is a complex existence that is held together, in spite of its internal complexity, by the fact that it is dominated and characterized throughout by a *single quality*. By "object" is meant that some element in the complex whole that is defined in abstraction from the whole of which it is a distinction.[7]

A crucial point relevant to the understanding of Dewey's philosophy is that for him there is no gap between nature, experience, and thinking, and that "experience is *of* as well as *in* nature . . . . Experience thus reaches down into nature; it has depth."[8] There is thus a continuity between nature, experience, and the various products of human thinking such as the scientific, moral, aesthetic, and the religious. The basic rhythm of experience for Dewey is (i) immediate qualitative experience of doing and undergoing in specific situations giving rise to (ii) reflective experience under problematic conditions in which the organism not only "has" the experience but understands its meaning by perceiving the relation between his "doing" and "undergoing." And (iii) as a result the final phase of experience incorporates the significance and meaning of the reflective phase and is thereby rendered more rich and deepened in its immediacy. It is a *consummatory experience* or *an* experience.

Dewey, therefore, does not regard aesthetic experience as peculiar or isolated from our ordinary experiences. Patrick Romanell wrongly accused Dewey of confusing art as a special type of experience and as a special phase of it.[9] Dewey's reply to him clarified his position.[10] For Dewey every normal experience has an aesthetic

---

[6]John Dewey, *Reconstruction in Philosophy* (New York: The New American Library, 1951), p. 86.

[7]John Dewey, *Philosophy and Civilization* (New York: Minton, Balch and Co., 1931), p. 97.

[8]John Dewey, *Experience and Nature* (New York: Dover Publications, Inc., 1958), pp. 4a-1.

[9]Patrick Romanell, "A Comment on Croce's and Dewey's Aesthetics," *The Journal of Aesthetics and Art Criticism*, 8, 2, (December 1949) pp. 125-29.

[10]John Dewey, "Aesthetic Experience as a Primary Phase and as an Artistic Development," *The Journal of Aesthetics and Art Criticism*, 9, 1, (September 1950), p. 56.

phase, and the so-called aesthetic experience in the arts is only a conscious and deliberate development of that phase of ordinary experience. He emphasized the fact that every type of experience, however far back we push our analysis, has that ever-receding horizon encompassing it, that fringe, that aura of something beyond ourselves, that feel of the More which we call the Universe. To acentuate this feeling of belonging to the whole, to arouse this sense of unity through shared experience is the great function of art. As he puts it:

> But however broad the field, it is still felt as not the whole; the margins shade into that indefinite expanse beyond which imagination calls the Universe. This sense of the including whole implicit in ordinary experience is rendered intense within the frame of a painting or a poem. It, rather than any special purgation, is that which reconciles us to the events of tragedy.[11]

Again:

> A work of art elicits and accentuates this quality of being a whole and of belonging to the larger, all inclusive whole which is the universe in which we live.[12]

He believed that in two kinds of worlds there would be no aesthetic experience: a world of mere change or disjointed particulars would be a madhouse; a world of no change and movement would be dead, mechanical, and lifeless. It is change and order, movement and stability, contingency and regularity that constitute the fabric of life and experience as we know them. For him all genuine art both in its creative and appreciative aspects has what he called this "consummatory quality." It is *an* experience. And since artistic experience is not cut off from our ordinary experiences, the latter, too, can have this artistic quality. Here a possible misunderstanding of Dewey's position should be avoided. In these concepts of "*an* experience" and "consummatory experience" Dewey has inadvertently mixed their descriptive and prescriptive meanings giving rise to some misinterpretations. For example, Marshall Cohen accused Dewey of regarding "consummatory quality" as *the* common essence of *all* aesthetic experience when in much of what goes by the name of modern art or "anti-art" "various artistic techniques are often exploited to create just that gappy, breathless, or discontinuous quality that Dewey assigns to practical experience."[13] Such a charge would undermine

[11]John Dewey, *Art as Experience* (New York: Minton, Balch and Co., 1934), p. 194.

[12]*Ibid*, p. 195.

[13]See Max Black, ed., *Philosophy in America* (Ithaca, N.Y.: Cornell, 1965), p. 119.

Dewey's theory only if he had maintained that *all* art and *all* ordinary experience actually had this common quality. But he was not so naive as to fail to notice that most of our experience under the contemporary industrial age of mass production and mass consumption is either a routine drudgery or a disjointed pursuit of momentary sensations. In both cases it is divorced from meaning and significance. It is, in short, not *an* experience. Dewey was aware that much of our contemporary art does not possess this consummatory quality and is not expressive of *an* experience. It reflects a restless desire for sheer change, newness, and unpredictability. In its self-conscious and deliberate effort at being "modern" contemporary art is caught up in the paradoxical situation of becoming old-fashioned at the very moment of its birth. Obsolescence is built in the very concept of modernity which glorifies the fleeting moment and is restlessly opposed to the past. It has no concept of the future either. It has no unifying principle whatever and no cumulative continuity. It certainly reflects our contemporary life of anxiety, drift, and meaninglessness. But Dewey points out that if much of our ordinary experience, as well as much of contemporary art, lacks this consummatory quality and is not *an* experience in its most significant and pregnant sense, it is due to special causes which lie in our cultural conditions, and therefore it need not be so in the nature of the case.

What then does Dewey mean by "consummatory experience?" And how does it compare with Abhinavagupta's concept of *rasa*? According to Dewey every significant experience in its situational context has a dynamic pervasive quality that is immediately felt. It is a whole of parts which moves through conflict and resistance. When the organism becomes conscious of the process and perceives the relation between what he does to the final phase of his experience, the whole experience becomes meaningful, significant, and valuable. The final situation arrived at has its own unifying pervasive quality which has been enriched, deepened, and intensified by the consciousness of the intermediate process. It is a *consummatory* experience. Dewey's point is that such a thorough interpenetration of means and ends, the process and the product makes the entire experience *artistic* whose final phase may be characterized as genuinely aesthetic. The difference between ordinary experience having such an artistic quality and the creative experience of a consummate artist lies in the greater expressive skill of the latter. But there is no essential break between the two. In his book *Art as Experience* Dewey develops this thesis with great sensitivity. A genuine artist begins with an artistic "idea," a vague something which is *felt* in its immediacy as the initial subject matter. It has its own pervasive unifying quality. It is a dynamic quality which inspires the artist to work it out and express it progressively through a medium whether in colors, lines, volumes, masses, sounds, or words. The artist does not know the outcome as he proceeds and manipulates his materials, But the process is not blind. At each stage of development there is a perception of relations between what the artist has done and what he is going to do. In other words, doing and undergoing, activity and enjoyment of meanings go side by side in the artistic process. The whole creative process is controlled and guided by the initial pervasive quality—supplemented, modified, and enriched by the perception of qualities of the intermediate stages. Creative artists like Picasso and Henry James confirm Dewey's view on the role of the pervasive individualizing quality in the creative process.[14]

It should be clear from the above argument that both Dewey and Abhinavagupta agreed on the role of the pervasive unifying quality in the artistic process. The latter, as has been pointed out above, had emphasized the role Sthāyibhāva—the basic emotion in unifying the various factors of dramatic presentation leading to the final consummatory phase designated as *rasa*. The final phase whether designated as *rasa* or "consummatory experience" comes as a culmination of the whole process of artistic presentation or appreciation. The intuitive and imaginative quality of such an experience had been emphasized equally by Abhinava and Dewey. But their interpretations of such an experience differed because of the wide gap between their metaphysical standpoints. Dewey, while recognizing the "revelatory" quality of aesthetic experience refused to mystify it by giving a "transcendental" explanation of it as was done by Abhinavagupta. For the latter *rasa* was entirely different in kind from any natural experience, and at its highest level it symbolized the union of the self with the Absolute leading to pure spiritual ecstasy (*śānta rasa*). Dewey did not think that such a speculative explanation of aesthetic experience was needed to render it intelligible. It could be fully understood in naturalistic terms. It is because aesthetic experience breaks our habitual and stereotyped ways of looking at things and enables us to get out of the rut and "see" things in a fresh and imaginative manner that it is deemed to have a "spiritual" quality. But for him the "spiritual" is not an ontological *realm* apart from and

[14]See Brewster Ghiselin, ed., *The Creative Process* (New York: The New American Library, 1955), pp. 55-60, and 147-56.

above the natural. Spirituality is a quality of human experience when the latter is freed from private, selfish, and narrow considerations. Phenomenologically speaking, therefore, both Abhinava and Dewey would agree in describing the aesthetic experience as "spiritual" because it lifted the person out of himself and transported him to a level where he gained an insight into the universal structure of human experience. *Abhijñāna-Shākuntalam* of Kālidasa, *Othello* and *King Lear* of Shakespeare, to take a few examples, are great works of art precisely because they lead to such an insight into basic human emotions. Another common point worth noting is that both Abhinava and Dewey gave a prominent place to "reversal" or conflict in the creative process. It was this factor of resistance and tension and its proper use in artistic creation that accounted for the intensified and heightened experience of the qualities of things and events. And yet unlike Abhinavagupta, Dewey did not regard aesthetic experience as completely sundered from ordinary experience because, as shown above, he rightly held that even ordinary experience could have "consummatory quality" which is found in a heightened form in a work of art.

We now pass on to the problem of the relation of art to morality as viewed by these thinkers. Here again there is a close resemblance between their positions. We have already seen that for Abhinavagupta the immediate aim of dramatic presentation was enjoyment of *rasa* but its ultimate goal was to promote the four traditional values of *Dharma* (Virtue), *artha* (economic prosperity), *kāma* (pleasure) and *moksha* (liberation) in their proper relationship. Abhinava did not regard sensuous joy and spiritual bliss to be mutually incompatible. And yet one has the feeling that in the final analysis, while maintaining the autonomy of the aesthetic category of *rasa*, he maintained the supremacy of the moral and religious over the purely aesthetic. This is evidenced by the fact that the Indian Dramatist did not present "an ordinary daily experience of the common run of men, but that of an ideal man in an ideal situation."[15] But such a rigid view of art belongs to medieval Indian culture. The problem of the relation of art to morality in our own times is a more complicated affair. Dewey addressed himself to this problem in a broad manner in the context of his pervasive naturalism. For him art is a quality of experience. In so far as ordinary experience shares this "consummatory quality" with the creative arts it becomes truly artistic. The so-called fine arts therefore are not isolated from the natural and the socio-

[15] *Comparative Aesthetics*, Vol. I, p. 180.

historical milieu of the artists. They could express and communicate in an artistic form values of any kind—moral, religious, or scientific. The subject matter of art by itself is not aesthetic. It is the mode of apprehension and its imaginative expression in an appropriate medium that convert the initial subject matter into the substance of a work of art. And the form of a work of art is not opposed to its substance. Form is not mere abstract design. It is the integration of all the constituents in such an imaginative and expressive manner as to give rise to an internally coherent product. The function of such a work of art, according to Dewey, is to clarify, intensify, and deepen our experience of the qualities of things and events. He thinks that the problem of whether art is subservient or indifferent to morality can be solved satisfactorily only when these concepts are understood in a proper manner. He did not identify morality with an unthinking adherence to rigid rules based on custom, habit, or prejudice. On the contrary he pointed out that the basic moral failure of our times, despite the advance in scientific knowledge, is moral isolation, self-centeredness, and an unfeeling hardheartedness of a large number of contemporary men and women. This situation of moral callousness becomes worse when it manifests itself at the level of narrow "group-centeredness" in the form of collective bias of race, religion, caste and creed. It is precisely here that art, with its appeal to imagination and emotion, enlarges our sympathies, breaks down the various barriers which separate men from their fellow beings, and brings about through artistic communication that sharing of values which is the quintessence of morality.[16] Dewey refers to the social and moral effects of the novels of Dickens and Sinclair Lewis. One could add, among others, Mark Twain's *Huckleberry Finn* and John Steinbeck's *Grapes of Wrath*. Quoting Matthew Arnold's dictum "poetry is criticism of life" he explains that poetry performs that function, "not directly, but by disclosure, through imaginative vision addressed to imaginative experience (not to set judgment) of possibilities that contrast with actual conditions."[17] He agreed with Shelley's statement that "the imagination is the great instrument of moral good, and poetry administers to the effect by acting on the causes."[18] Dewey sums up his view on this problem thus:

---

[16]See *Art as Experience,* pp. 344-49, *passim.*

[17]*Ibid,* p. 346.

[18]*Ibid,* p. 347.

> Were art an acknowledged power in human association and not treated as the pleasuring of an idle moment or as a means of ostentatious display, and were morals understood to be identical with every aspect of value that is shared in experience, the "problem" of the relation of art and morals would not exist.[19]

Let us now ask a specific question. Should we allow works of art which are manifestly obscene and pornographic? Should certain novels and works of art be banned because they are offensive to cultivated moral taste? The obvious examples which come to mind are surrealistic paintings, Dada-ism or the works of writers like Marquis de Sade which gave artistic expression to the grossest kinds of sexual perversions. Such works may play havoc with the imagination and ruin the lives of the young and old alike. Could such works of art be justified on the grounds of aesthetic autonomy or on the theory of "art for art's sake"? There is no simple answer. On the one hand, one of the important concerns of morality is that we should face facts as they really are; on the other, moral wisdom requires that our aesthetic satisfactions should be regulated by well-informed judgment and critical insight. Therefore if we take a broad, imaginative view of morality as that which is concerned with the whole range of human values, then it may be said that such a morality would give *due* place to aesthetic satisfaction without letting it run riot to the detriment of the total human personality. Of course, it would be prudish to subordinate the aesthetic to any narrow and rigid view of morality. In any case, a critical judgment on a work of art ought to be based on its aesthetic value as well as its implications for morals as conceived by Dewey in the above quote. Such a balanced judgment is more a matter of informed sensitivity rather than of following ready-made rules. This conclusion, I believe, is supported by the views of both Abhinavagupta and Dewey as presented above despite their metaphysical differences.

DINESH C. MATHUR.
STATE UNIVERSITY COLLEGE AT BROCKPORT.

---

[19] *Ibid*, p. 348.

CAUSES AND EVENTS

The aim of this paper is to offer an account of causation. I believe that the theories of causation which have been put forward by Western philosophers in the last three centuries, including the "constant conjunction" theory, are fundamentally mistaken. I shall, however, neither reiterate the well-known objections to these theories, nor present new arguments specifically aimed to knock them down. Rather, I shall indicate how we have mistakenly assumed that the sensible world can be described in only one kind of way, and that if we drop this assumption it is possible to offer a quite different account of causation from those given hitherto.

Unfortunately, the word 'account' even when used of philosophical projects can refer to enterprises of many varied kinds; thus in order to avoid misunderstanding it is, I think, necessary that I should make some prefatory remarks on just what kind of task I see myself as attempting in this paper.

My main aim will not be to produce an example of what might be called descriptive linguistics, that is, I shall not be concerned primarily with elucidating the conditions under which we do in actual practice use certain words, in this case the words 'cause' and 'event'. This is not to say that I shall not indulge in descriptive linguistics in the course of this paper: I shall indeed do so, but only as a means to a further end. Nor is my main aim to produce an example of prescriptive linguistics, that is, I shall not be concerned primarily with proposing new rules which we should follow when we come to use the words 'cause' and 'event' in our discourse. Some minor modifications to our usage of these terms may seem to be demanded as a corollary to the main theses of this paper, but I shall certainly give no grounds for supposing that there is anything radically defective in the way we now use them in common speech. Indeed the current usage of the words 'cause' and 'event' will be part of the data on which I shall base my claims.

The nature of my enquiry may be described as conceptual, as concerned with the concepts which, to use common (but potentially misleading) expressions, might be said to "lie behind" the words 'cause' and 'event', to be that to which we refer when we use those words. Apart from some brief remarks below, I shall not take up the question of the nature of concepts in general. In particular, nothing I say should be taken as committing me to the view that it is impossible to exclude all talk of concepts from our discourse (by "translating out"), or, on the other hand, to the view that it is possible so to do. The kind of conceptual undertaking I shall attempt in this paper has to do with relations between concepts.

Which concepts any individual person happens to use will depend in part on the circumstances in which his society is placed, on his own circumstances within that society, and on the circumstances in which those who moulded his language existed. The average Frenchman will use fewer concepts for types of ice and snow than the average Eskimo, for his needs for such concepts are less, as too were the needs of those who helped to form the French language; yet a Chamonix mountain guide will use many more concepts of this kind than his average compatriot. This dependence on personal circumstances which affects the usage of concepts does not, however, carry over in any way to the relations between concepts. For instance, the quite simple relationship between the concepts 'cow' and 'heifer' will be quite unaffected by the details of when and by whom these concepts are used. The link between relations between concepts and relations between their extensions is not always a straightforward one. Thus, for example, the concepts 'event' and 'effect' might have the same extension (if every event is caused), but even if they have this would not make the two *concepts* identical; or again, the concept 'centaur' is closely related to the concepts of 'man' and 'horse' though it has no extension at all.

What relations hold between given concepts is a question to which we can (if we are clever enough) give a correct answer, and hence it is a question to which we may give mistaken ones. The negative thesis of this paper will be that philosophers have hitherto given mistaken answers to the question of how the concept 'cause' is related to the concept 'event'; the positive thesis will be an attempt to give a correct one.

The arguments will be set out in the following way. After giving grounds for restricting attention to certain types of causation (in Section I), I shall then argue (in Section II) that we have mistakenly taken the concepts of 'physical object' and 'event' as being more alike than we were justified in doing. Following this I shall discuss the extremely varied ways in which we use the word 'event', and try to isolate a "core" concept of 'event' (Section III). In Section IV I shall attempt to state how the "core" concept of 'cause' is related to the "core" concept of 'event' by giving a series of definitions, and then in Section V I shall attempt to extend this analysis to other cases. I shall answer possible objections in Sections VI and VII, and will conclude, in Section VIII, by drawing some general conclusions about my project as a whole.

I

Consider an example of causation. Say that a stone is cast against a window, and the window shatters. We should (normally) want to say that the throwing of the stone was the cause of the breaking of the window. There may, of course, be special conditions obtaining which make this a misdescription, but I shall not be concerned with this sort of case; I am interested in the case where we should be most happy about saying that the throwing of the stone caused the breaking of the window. In this typical example of causation, the two things we are saying are causally related are events. We are saying that one event caused another: the event described as 'the throwing of the stone' caused the event described as 'the breaking of the window'.

It is not always events which are described as causally related. Sometimes an event is described as the cause of some quality in an object (e.g., the stain in the carpet was caused by Smith's spilling ink on it), or as the cause of some state of affairs (e.g., the state of tension was caused by the assassination of the president). Sometimes, again, an object or state of affairs is described as the cause of a quality in an object, or as the cause of a state of affairs, or as the cause of some event; and there are perhaps other sorts of causally related pairs. Although any adequate treatment of causation must be capable of accounting for all such cases, I shall for simplicity of exposition deal in detail only with cases of causally related pairs of events. This seems justifiable since (i) there is no dispute that very many causally related pairs are pairs of events, and (ii) all the accounts I am rejecting are, or can be, expressed in terms of, or can be taken to apply to, causally related pairs of events. Furthermore, in at least some cases where one or both members of a causally related pair are not events, the situation might be redescribed in such a way that the causal relation is expressed as holding between two events. Thus, for cases of an event causing some quality in an object, the situation might be described as that event causing the event of the object being given that quality. If the stain in the carpet was caused by Smith's spilling ink on it, then Smith's spilling ink on the carpet was the cause of its becoming stained. There are, however, cases where there appears to be no possibility of such redescription. For example, the situation described by the statement "The green colour of the water is caused by the presence of algae" is one for which no description in terms of causally related events seems possible. For although it may be perfectly true that the water's becoming green was caused by the algae becoming present in it, the statement describes a situation entirely in the present and does not refer to how that situation came about; indeed, the water might have been green before the algae became present in it through the presence in it of something else subsequently destroyed by the arrival of algae. In Section V I shall indicate briefly how examples of this kind might be treated.

Even the examples of causation which consist of causally related pairs of events are of considerable variety, and I shall commence by discussing only a limited class of them. (1) I shall say nothing at first about causally related pairs of events where one or both of the events is a mental event, but will confine my attention to events occurring (wholly) within the physical world. I make this restriction entirely for reasons of clarity. The nature of mental events is far more obscure than that of physical events, and they generally occur in far simplest cases first. Nevertheless, I believe that the account of causation I shall offer can cope with mental events equally as well as with physical events, and this is something I shall discuss further in Section V. (2) I shall also defer until Section V consideration of what I shall call "instantaneous events." The word event is commonly used to refer both to changes which occupy a finite duration, and to those which do not. Most events to which we make everyday reference, such as an object travelling from one point to another, have temporal extension, even though this extension may be very small (e.g., an explosion). I shall call these *temporally extended events.* There are, however, some changes which are described as events where the change is instantaneous, and it is these that I shall refer to as instantaneous events. An example would be of a sprinter in a race reaching the tape: there is no finite period during which the reaching of the tape is occuring. The account I shall give of instantaneous events will be dependent on my treatment of temporally extended events, and I shall therefore refrain from further discussion of the former until I have dealt with the latter.

II

I have suggested that the theories of causation put forward to date, including the "constant conjunction" theory, are all erroneous. If this is so, then why have philosophers been misled for so long? The reason is, at least in part, that they have wrongly assumed that events are entities as discrete as physical objects. If one assumes this, then theories like the "constant conjunction" theory appear to be the only ones possible. The assumption has remained unquestioned largely, it would seem, because the Indo-European languages in which philosophers have thought and written give a peculiarly central status to concepts concerned with objects. Thus, for instance, in English the most general referring word, 'thing', which in this paper I use to refer to events, has a connotation such that it is used most appropriately when used to refer to objects. But this peculiarity of our language need not be a true reflection of the nature of the spatiotemporal world. Indeed, it seems significant that there are languages such as that of the Hopi[1] in which reference is made far more to events than to objects; whereas objects play the central role in our conceptual scheme, events play the central role in that of the Hopi. Now the fact that it is possible to have a language in which objects do not have a central status shows, I think, that there are quite different ways in which we may choose to split up the spatiotemporal world of sense into identifiable units.

There is a tendency amongst Western philosophers to consider the sensible world as a succession (possibly compact) of spatial manifolds—the spatial manifolds being capable of division into discrete objects and, perhaps, voids. Were this taken as the sole way of considering the sensible world, changes could be thought of only as being a succession of segments of the spatial manifolds. But the sensible world may equally well be considered as a single spatiotemporal manifold which can be cut up into events and segments embracing only temporal change. I do not want to suggest that we should replace the former kind of division by the latter. What I want to suggest is that (1) we should treat the two ways of dividing up the sensible world as complementary, and (2) we should look for an account of causation in terms of events rather than in terms of spatial manifolds or the objects and voids which form them.

The sensible world considered as a spatiotemporal manifold does not divide up into events in as obvious a manner as spatial manifolds divide up into objects. The divisions between events are not marked by the same discontinuities as those between objects. All spatial manifolds will split up into objects in a largely unambiguous manner. (I am here considering only a division where the segments involved are generally such as are observable by the unaided human eye.

---

[1]See B.L. Whorf, "The Relation of Habitual Thought and Behavior to Language," in *Language, Culture, and Personality: Essay in Memory of Edward Sapir*, ed. L. Spier (Menasha, Wis., 1941), pp. 75-93. Reprinted in *Language, Thought and Reality*, ed. J.B. Carroll (Cambridge, Mass, 1962), pp. 134-59.

Quite different divisions will occur with microscopic or macroscopic segments.) Within a given spatial manifold there will be a small proportion of segments which on different occasions one may consider either as consisting of one object, or of more than one. Thus, on different occasions one might treat a jigsaw puzzle as one object, or as a thousand objects. Watches, aircraft, and many other kinds of machines provide further examples. Such cases are, however, relatively rare (although the increasing production of complex apparatus is making them less of a rarity).

Between events there are far less obvious breaks in continuity. The way we divide up the spatiotemporal manifold into events is far more a matter of our choice. Of course, there are some limited forms of discontinuity which we follow in making our division, but the discontinuity is seldom, if ever, as complete as that which divides physical objects. Consider, for instance, the event consisting of a rail journey from London to Edinburgh. The termination of this event, say, the alighting at Edinburgh Waverley Station, marks a break in continuity in at least one respect (up to this point in time there is occupation of a railway carriage, after it there is not), but the break in continuity is far from being complete. Suppose that the passenger concerned, after alighting, walks to a taxi-rank, and travels by cab to a house in Leith. Then although the alighting at Edinburgh Station involves a break in continuity in one respect, in another respect at least there is no break in continuity—the movement of the passenger relative to the surface of the earth continues. Because of this continuity we may very well take the complete journey from London to the house in Leith as a single event. On the other hand we should not take a table, and a vase standing on the table, as a single object. This is because between the table and the vase there is a break in continuity in respect of a far wider range of features than normally occurs with the breaks between events.

This lack of discontinuity between contiguous events has been overlooked by those who have confined their attention to considering the sensible world as consisting of successive spatial manifolds divisible into objects. This oversight has been made so generally that mistaken views, such as the "constant conjunction" theory, have gained root. For if one looks upon contiguous events as being as discrete as, say, a table and the vase upon it, then one is puzzled as to what sort of connexion there can be between two events which are causally related.

If one takes events, not as things which are to be fitted into the picture of the sensible world as a succession of spatial manifolds, but as the units of one other of the possible analyses of the sensible world, then an account of causation can easily be given; but in order to give such an account we need to isolate a central use of the word 'event' from other more peripheral uses.

III

Just as the word 'thing' is more typically used to refer to a physical object, so the word 'event' likewise has a paradigmatic use; yet both words are also similar in commonly being used much more widely. In the case of the word 'thing' we can usually avoid misunderstandings about how wide a scope is being given to it by using some other expressions, e.g., 'material object', 'concept', 'claim', etc.; but because in English the vocabulary used to refer to events is so sparse, such paraphrasing of event statements is seldom possible, and this raises special dangers. Imagine what it would be like if we had the word 'thing', but not the word 'object' or any expression synonymous with 'object'. This would create difficulties for the person who tried to give a philosophical analysis of the concept 'object', for if he used the word 'thing' to refer to this concept and then claimed, e.g., that all things had spatial extension, he would be "refuted" by those who pointed out that we use the word 'thing' for, e.g., thoughts, which do not have spatial extension. To avoid this danger such a person might introduce a technical term to pick out the narrow range of "things" with which he is concerned. Unfortunately, it is a rather similar difficulty with which I am faced in the case of the word 'event', for when I use the word 'event' in my account of causation I do not want this word to be taken to apply to just any of the wide variety of things to which it is from time to time taken to refer. This is not because I wish to restrict my account only to certain kinds of causally related pairs of events, but because there are certain kinds of events, pairs of which would satisfy the conditions I state in Section IV for being causally related, but of which, for reasons connected with their being events of that particular kind, there is no question of the one causing the other.

I shall therefore introduce 'primitive event' as the technical term which will pick out a paradigmatic use of the word 'event'. This should not be looked upon as an *ad hoc* device for ruling out counterexamples, for the sorts of reasons for denying that certain events are primitive events are very similar to the sorts of reason we have for denying that certain *things* are *objects*.

I shall now give two instances of what I should exclude from the category of 'primitive event'. There might well be other kinds of event, not listed here, which should be excluded as well.

(1) What one might call *purely institutional* events. These are such as can be regarded as a unity only insofar as they are seen in insitutional terms. Examples would be a performance of a symphony, a round of golf, or a rubber of bridge. The numerous events consisting of movement of cards, vocal utterances, etc., which make up a rubber of bridge can be seen as making up one event only be seeing such constituent events as having an institutional role: unless a person watching bridge-players is acquainted with the institution of bridge-playing, or similar institutions, he will not be able to pick out the rubber of bridge as something which has a unity unshared by the other conglomerations of events consisting of movements of cards, vocal utterances, etc., which he will observe. I use the word 'purely' because I do not want to exclude those events which can be described in institutional terms, but which can be otherwise identified. Thus I should not wish to exclude, say, a conversion kick in rugby football, if this can be seen as just consisting of running up to a stationary ball, kicking it, and the movement of the ball through a trajectory subsequent to this; someone who knew nothing about rugby football could pick out a conversion kick as an event, though he would be quite unaware of its significance within the game, or of the criteria which distinguish a conversion kick from others.

(2) What one might call *collective* events. Sometimes it happens that a number of very similar events occur in close proximity over a short period of time, and if such collections of events of a particular kind are not uncommon, we may use a collective term to refer to them. An example would be the collective term 'meteor shower' which would be used of a collection of events, each of which consists of the burning up of a meteor on entering the earth's atmosphere. We may refer to a meteor shower as an event, but this is a little like calling a flock of sheep "an object": in both cases the unity referred to by the collective term comes *only* from the collection being one of proximate like things.

IV

In this section I shall give a series of definitions relating the concept 'cause' to the concept 'temporally extended primitive event occurring wholly within the physical world'. Throughout *this section* I shall use the word 'event' as an abbreviation for 'temporally extended primitive event occuring wholly within the physical world'.

(D1) The *amalgam* (signified by AB) of two events A and B is that part or parts of the spatiotemporal manifold including all of A and all of B, but nothing else.

The notion of the 'amalgam' of two events resembles the set-theoretical notion of the 'union' of two sets. For most arbitrary pairs of events no part of one event is a part of the other. In this case the amalgam of the two events just consists of the two events considered collectively. Some pairs of events, however, are such that the two events have a part in common. Such events will be said to *overlap*, and the common part will be referred to as the *overlap* of the two events. In this case the amalgam will consist of the overlap plus the part of each event not occurring in common with the other.

(D2) Two events *A* and *B* are *directly related causally* if the amalgam *AB* is an event, not identical with *A* or with *B*.

This is the most important of the definitions. It links the concept of 'causal relation' to that of 'event'. The implications of such a linking will be considered further below. The last clause in the definition is inserted merely to exclude describing an event as being a cause of itself, or part of itself, or of an event as being caused by part of itself.

In the case of the next definition, I shall first give a simple provisional definition (D3′) and discuss it, before showing how this definition needs amending in order to deal with a prolematic kind of example.

(D3′) An event *A* is a *direct cause* of an event *B* if *A* and *B* are directly related causally, and if no part of *B* is temporally prior to every part of *A*.

This definition excludes a number of cases of events *A* and *B* that are directly related causally, from being cases of *A* being a direct cause of *B*. These can be represented by diagrams as follows, where the lines represent temporal duration, and the passage of time is taken from left to right:

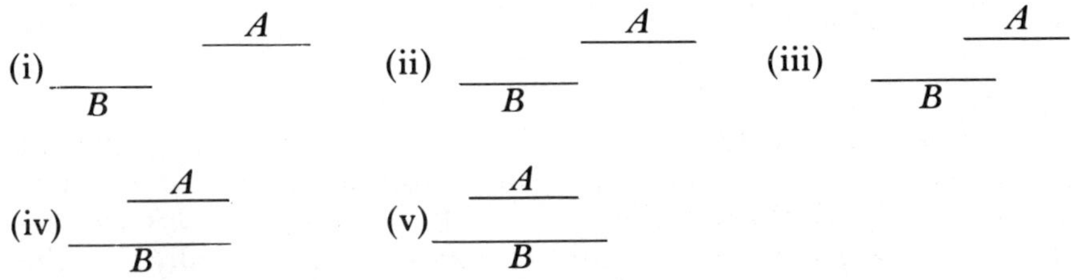

In all of these cases it would be correct to describe *B* as being a direct cause of *A*.

It might be thought that the condition " . . . and no part of *A* is temporally posterior to every part of *B*" should be suffixed to (D3′), in order to exclude the following cases:

(vi)

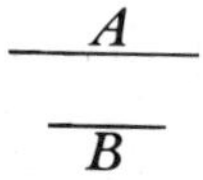

(vii)

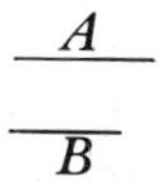

Thus it might be claimed that it is a misdescription to call an event *A* which extends later than an event *B*, a direct cause of *B*; for is it not just the part of *A* which occurs prior to some point at which *B* is occurring which is correctly described as a direct cause of *B*? Thus, if we were to say that the movement of ice-sheets southwards at the onset of the last Ice Age directly caused the extinction of certain plants in the Shetland Isles, this should be considered as a loose way of talking; for the southward movement of the ice-sheets continued after the extinction of the plants, and this continued movement could in no way be responsible for the extinction of the plants. What we should say is that the part of the southward movement of the ice-sheets up to the extinction of the plants was a direct cause of their extinction. However, I see no good reason for reforming our normal manner of speaking in this way. There is no doubt that we do speak perfectly intelligibly of events which endure later than other events as being a direct cause of those other events. What we might very well want to say is that it is correct to talk of *A* being a direct cause of *B* in cases of types (vi) and (vii) only if it would be correct to talk of the part of *A* which occurs prior to some point at which *B* is occurring as a direct cause of *B*.

Both cases (vii) and the following cases:

(viii)

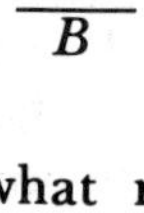

(ix)

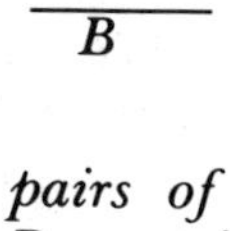

are examples of what may be termed *pairs of events of initial simultaneity*. According to (D3′), if *A* and *B* are pairs of events of initial simultaneity such that *A* and *B* are directly related causally, then not only will *A* be a direct cause of *B*, but in addition *B* will be a direct cause of *A*. Thus, for instance, if the emission of an electron occurs simultaneously with the decaying of an atom of Helium[6], into

Lithium^6, and these two events are directly related causally, then it will be just as correct to say that the emission of the electron is a direct cause of the decaying of the atom of He^6, as it will be to say that the decaying of the atom of He^6 is a direct cause of the emission of the electron.

There are, however, example of pairs of events of initial simultaneity of which it would seem very odd to say that each event is the cause of the other. A good example[2] is that of a locomotive and a caboose which are so firmly linked together that they commence moving together. In this case we should want to say that the movement of the locomotive is a direct cause of the movement of the caboose, but not that the movement of the caboose is a direct cause of the movement of the locomotive. In order to cope with this sort of case we need to amend (D3′) to obtain the following definition:

(D3) An event *A* is a *direct cause* of an event *B* if *A* and *B* are directly related causally, and either (a) some part of *A* is temporally prior to every part of *B*, or (b) *A* and *B* commence simultaneously and there is no event *B′* such that part of *B′* is temporally prior to *B*, *BB′* is identical with *B′*, and *A* and *B′* are directly related causally.

This definition treats pairs of events other than ones of initial simultaneity, exactly as (D3′). It will, however, give a different treatment in the case of some, though not necessarily all, cases of pairs of events of initial simultaneity. Thus, in the example of the locomotive and the caboose it will lead us to say that the movement of the locomotive is a direct cause of the movement of the caboose, but not that the movement of the caboose is a direct cause of the movement of the locomotive. For we can identify an event consisting of the amalgam of the locomotive being fired (or switched on, or otherwise started) and moving which satisfies the conditions for *B′* of (D3)(b) when the movement of the locomotive is taken as *B*, and that of the caboose as *A*. This amalgam must be an event, for we can clearly say that the firing of the locomotive is a direct cause of its moving. (cf. (D3)(a) and (D2)). We cannot, however, identify an event which satisfies the conditions of *B′* of (D3)(b) when the movement of the locomotive is taken as *A*, and that of the caboose as *B*.

But suppose the caboose has a brake, and it is this alone that is preventing the locomotive and caboose from moving; and suppose

[2]This example is discussed by Richard Taylor in "Causation," *The Encyclopedia of Philosophy*, ed. P. Edwards (New York, 1967), Vol. 2, p. 65.

that the brake is let off and the locomotive and caboose together begin to move. Then would we not have an example of an event satisfying the conditions for *B'* when the movement of the locomotive is taken as *A*, and that of the caboose as *B*? If so, then the movement of the locomotive could not be a direct cause of the movement of the caboose. The answer is that the release of the brake on the caboose will not be a *direct* cause of the movement of the caboose (it will satisfy the conditions, by (D5) below, for an indirect cause), the amalgam of the release of the brake and the movement of the caboose not being an event. The release of the brake will however be a direct cause of the combined movement of the locomotive and the caboose.

(D4) An event *B* is a *direct effect* of an event *A*, if *A* is a direct cause of *B*.

(D5) An event *A* is an *indirect cause* of an event *B* if there are events C_1, C_2, . . ., C_n, $n \geq 1$, such that *A* is a direct cause of C_1, C_i is a direct cause of C_{i+1} for all i, $1 \leq i \leq n\text{-}1$, and C_n is a direct cause of *B*.

(D6) An event *B* is an *indirect effect* of an event *A*, if *A* is an indirect cause of *B*.

It may be noted that according to the above definitions a *part* of an event *A* that is a direct cause of an event *B* may be only an *indirect* cause of *B*, and that a *part* of an event *B* that is a direct effect of an event *A* may be only an *indirect* effect of *A*. Thus, to take an example of the former kind, although the collapse of the Tay Bridge in 1879 was a direct cause of a passenger train falling into the River Tay, the snapping of the first bolt of the bridge that occurred as part of the collapse was an indirect cause of the falling of the train. This may at first sight seem an odd way of speaking, but on reflection one can see that it fits very closely with the way we are accustomed to talk; the apparent oddness is probably due only to the fact that we seldom talk at the same time about an event and a part of that event as causes of another event. Whereas a great deal more had to happen besides the first bolt snapping before the train plunged into the Tay, the collapse of the bridge was quite enough to send the train into the river.

(D7) Two events *A* and *B* are *indirectly related causally* if *A* is an indirect cause of *B*, or *B* is an indirect cause of *A*. We cannot define two events *A* and *B*

We cannot define two events *A* and *B* as being 'indirectly related causally' on condition that there are events C_1, C_2, . . . C_n such that the amalgams AC_1, C_1C_2, . . . C_nB are all events, for this would mean that two events *A* and *B* would be indirectly related causally if they were different direct effects of an event C_1, or even if they were respective direct effects of events C_1 and C_3 where in addition C_1 and C_3 were both direct causes of an event C_2.

(D8) An event A is a *cause* of an event B, if A is either a direct or an indirect cause of B.

(D9) Two event B is and *effect* of an event A, if A is a cause of B.

(D10) Two events A and B are *causally related, if* A is a cause of B or if B is a cause of A.

These definitions will allow not only that an event may be an effect of many causes and be a cause of many effects, but that it may be an effect of many *direct* causes and a cause of many *direct* effects. Furthermore, some of the causes of an event may not overlap one another at all, whilst some may be merely proper parts of others. The storm of 28th December, 1879, and the travelling of the 4:15 p.m. mail train from Edinburgh to the Tay Bridge on the same day were both causes of the train plunging into the Tay that evening, although the two events did not overlap. On the other hand, although the snapping of the first bolt of the bridge on that night was only a part of the collapse of the bridge, both the snapping of that bolt and the collapse of the bridge were causes of the train falling into the river. Even more importantly, my definitions allow that there may be an overlap between a cause and one or more of its effects. When we say that the heating of a piece of butter was a cause of its melting, the event consisting of the heating of a piece of butter and the event consisting of its melting overlap, for part of its melting will occur within the same spatial region during the same period of time as part of its being heated.

It may also be noted that my definitions do not decide on the question of whether every event has a cause. This question is, in my view, another way of asking whether for every event there is some other event which commences not later than the event in question, and such that the two events together form an event.

V

I want now to show how my analysis of causation can be extended from the case of causally related pairs of temporally extended events occurring wholly within the physical world, to deal with the other kinds of cases of causation I mentioned in Section I.

1. Consider first the case of instantaneous events, such as the event of a sprinter reaching the tape in a race. Such an event may be viewed as a spatial section through a segment of the spatiotemporal manifold. The event of the sprinter reaching the tape is a section

through, amongst others, that temporally extended event which consists of the race as performed by the sprinter in question. I say "amongst others," for there are many temporally extended events of which any given instantaneous event will be a section, and when we talk of an instantaneous event we need not have any particular one of these temporally extended events in mind. It seems that we cannot use my definitions (D1)—(D10) to identify causes, etc., in the case of instantaneous events, for by (D2) no instantaneous event can be directly related causally with any temporally extended event of which it is a section. This follows because given an instantaneous event *X* and a temporally extended event *A* of which it is a section, the amalgam *AX* will be identical with *A*.

It might be thought that the last clause of (D2) should be dropped in order to accommodate examples of instantaneous events. But I do not think this would be a satisfactory solution. We do not normally talk of the temporally extended events of which a given instantaneous event is a section as being the causes of the instantaneous event. We do not talk of the journey of a moon probe from the earth to the moon as being the cause of its reaching a point at which the gravitational pull of the earth and moon cancel out. We do, however, talk of any cause of a temporally extended event of which a given instantaneous event is a section as being a cause of that instantaneous event. Thus, any cause of a moon probe's journey to the moon will be a cause of that probe's reaching a point at which the gravitational pull of the earth and moon cancel out.

Thus we should define the 'cause' of an instantaneous event as follows:

(D11) An event *A* will be a *cause* of an instantaneous event *X*, if there is a temporally extended event *B* of which *X* is a section such that *A* is a cause of *B*.

It may be noted that this gives a definition of a 'cause' of an instantaneous event, not of a 'direct cause' or an 'indirect cause' of such an event. I think it is our normal practice not to make a distinction between direct and indirect causes in the case of instantaneous events, and there is no good reason to give (purely stipulative) definitions of these two notions.

Given (D11) we can make the following definition:

(D12) An instantaneous event *X* will be an *effect* of an event *A*, if *A* is a cause of *X*.

Besides cases in which we talk of instantaneous events being caused by temporally extended events, there are cases in which we talk of temporally extended events being caused by instantaneous events. Thus, for instance, we talk of two copper wires reaching a point at which an electric spark will jump from one to the other as being, say, a cause of a fire. Such cases can be dealt with by definitions similar to (D11) and (D12):

(D13) An instantaneous event X will be a *cause* of an event A, if there is a temporally extended event B of which X is a section such that B is a cause of A.

(D14) An event A will be an *effect* of an instantaneous event X, if X is a cause of A.

It should be noted that in definitions (D11)—(D14) I have talked of "an event A," not of "a temporally extended event A." This was done so that the definitions will apply equally as well to cases in which we want to say that one instantaneous event caused another instantaneous event. Thus the events referred to as "A" in each of the four definitions can be either instantaneous events or temporally extended events.

2. Consider next the case of mental events. I want to hold that the kind of analysis I have given by definitions (D1)—(D14) applies just as much to events which in whole or in part occur within the mind (or minds) of some person (or persons) as to events which occur wholly within the physical world. Anyone who accepts my analysis in the case of pairs of primitive events occurring wholly within the physical world will, I think, have no difficulty in also accepting a similar analysis in the case of pairs of primitive events occurring wholly within the mind. To say, for instance, that a man's dreaming of a tombstone caused him to think of his dead wife would be to say that the thinking of the tombstone and the thinking of the dead wife together form an event.

Cases of purely mental events causing or being caused by purely physical events, and cases of causation in which one or both events are partly mental and partly physical, can also be subjected to the same kind of analysis. Thus, for instance, to say that someone's thinking of doing a certain action was a cause of the action being done by that person will be to say that the thinking of doing the action and the action being done together form an event. However, in this sort of case the analysis may appear to have practically no explanatory value. The reason for this is that we know so much less about the nature of events which are partly mental and partly physical than we do about the nature of purely mental or purely physical ones.

3. I want to say something briefly about situations such as that described by the statement "The green colour of the water is caused by the presence of algae." It appears that this sort of situation cannot

be redescribed in terms of events, and hence that my analysis in Section IV will not be applicable.

Consider the situation which could lead to a statement of this kind being made. What must be observable on the level of everyday experience is a liquid; the statement says that a property of that liquid (namely, being green) is due to its being water with algae in it. The linking of a cause and its effect here is merely the linking of a microcondition with a macrocondition. Why this has been seen as related to the more central notion of 'cause' is probably because the introduction of the microcondition results in the macrocondition, but not vice versa. If you place algae of a certain kind in sufficient quantities in reasonably pure water then the result will be a green coloured liquid; but one could, of course, make the water turn green by other means such a dissolving a powdered dye in it. The use of the word 'cause' in this kind of context is, however, generalized to cases where there seems no possibility of our introducing the microconditions, e.g., we might explain the shape of crystals of a certain substance by saying that the shape is caused by particular features of the molecular structure of the substance.

VI

In order to make my view a little clearer, I want in this section to consider the attack made by A.J. Ayer in *The Foundations of Empirical Knowledge* on a position which is similar in some respects, to mine. I shall distinguish my own view from the one that Ayer criticizes, and show that, whether or not his objection has any weight against the view he attacks, it carries no weight against mine. Ayer says:

> . . . it is often urged as an objection to Hume that he misconceived the initial situation by treating a cause and its effect as two distinct events. What we observe, it is said, in the case of a particular causal sequence, is not just two separate events in a relation of spatiotemporal contiguity, but a unified complex; we observe that one event is, as it were, "glued" to the other; and it is suggested that this gives us reason to believe that the connexion is necessary and universal. Now, for my part, I have never observed this peculiar linking of events, and I am disposed to doubt whether anyone else has ever, in fact, succeeded in observing it.[3]

The position Ayer is attacking is not, of course, quite the same as mine, for from my claim that pairs of events are causally related if they form a single event, I neither wish to conclude, nor think one

[3]A.J. Ayer, *The Foundations of Empirical Knowledge* (London, 1940), p. 192.

could have grounds for concluding, that the connexion is somehow necessary and universal. Furthermore, to describe my view as saying that with causally related pairs of events "one event is, as it were, 'glued' to the other" would be highly misleading. Indeed, this use of a spatial metaphor implying that events are as discrete as objects, provides an excellent example of an application of the assumption I criticised in Section II. The kind of unification of the two events which I want to claim is involved in their being causally related is no more odd than the unification involved in *any* temporally extended event, for any such event (other than perhaps some at a microscopic level) will consist of parts which are themselves events. If we are able to see the sequence of events which make up the throwing of a stone as a single event, then there is no reason why we should not see the throwing of the stone and the breaking of the window together as one event. Ayer appears to have no difficulty at all in observing many everyday events; but since these events *are themselves* "unified complexes" of pairs of causally related events, Ayer cannot but observe a "linking of events" of a sort whose existence he would appear so strenuously to deny.

VII

Day and night are sometimes referred to as events, and it might seem that because of this we can construct a counter-example to the definitions I gave in Section IV. For if a day (i.e., the complement of night) is an event, and a night is an event, then since these two together form a day they would appear to form an amalgam which is an event and hence be causally related. Yet we surely do not want to say that day causes night.

Such a purported counter-example relies on an ambiguity in the words 'day' and 'night'. 'Day' (as the complement of night) and 'night' can be interpreted in three ways, (1) as referring merely to the presence and absence of sunlight (direct or diffused) (cf. "It is the bright day that brings forth the adder" [Shakespeare]), (2) as referring merely to periods of time (cf. "For a day and a night Love sang to us" [Swinburne]), or (3) as referring to the presence of sunlight for the whole period of its presence, and to the absence of sunlight for the whole period of its absence (cf. "The night is long that never finds the day" [Shakespeare]). Only the last of these can be considered as events; the first can be considered as causes or effects of some kind, but the second can neither be considered as events or as any of the other kinds of things which enter into causal relationships. Yet it is only in the second sense, the sense of just periods of time, that we see the combination of day and night as a unity; it is only in this sense that we use the word 'day' of a day and a night together; there is no unified happening consisting of the presence of sunlight and then its absence (or vice versa) for a period totalling approximately 24 hours. Thus the amalgam of day (as an event) and night (as an event) is not itself an event, and so there is no counter-example here.

VIII

What I have attempted to do in this paper is to throw new light on the way that the concepts 'cause' and 'event' are related; and that is all. Such concepts as these are related closely, not just to *one* but to a *number* of other concepts. Both 'cause' and 'event' are, for instance, closely related to the concept 'change' about which I have said nothing; further elucidation of the concept 'cause' would undoubtedly come from analysing its links with that concept. And it may be that one could obtain further understanding of causation by investigating the links between the concept 'cause' and yet other concepts. From this it should be clear that I think any attempt somehow to "reduce" the concept 'cause' to some other concept, so that we could if we chose get along without it, is misguided, and that what I have done in this paper is not to be seen as such an attempt.

N. G. E. HARRIS.

UNIVERSITY OF DUNDEE.

WHY CARTESIAN INTUITIONS ARE COMPATIBLE WITH THE IDENTITY THESIS

I

In "Naming and Necessity,"[1] Saul Kripke claims that the relationship between sensations and brain processes "seems to have a certain obvious element of contingency" (p. 341). This view is surely correct, and it can be seen to be correct in two different though closely related ways.

For one thing, the view is supported by certain of our intuitions concerning unactualized possibilia. It is easy to imagine situations in which unactualized human brains pass through all of the states that actual brains pass through, but in which none of the states is accompanied by sensations. It is also easy to imagine unactualized sequences of experiences that are not accompanied by brain states. Moreover, it is entirely natural to feel that unactualized entities of these two kinds are objectively possible, that they might well have been fully actual.

Second, Kripke's view is supported by modal intuitions concerning actual sensations and actual brain processes. Thus, when we consider the basic characteristics of brain processes and focus on sensations that we have actually experienced, it is entirely natural to feel that the sensations could have existed without being accompanied by the brain processes that actually did accompany them, and natural also to feel that the sensations could have existed without being accompanied by any brain processes whatsoever. Equally, it is entirely natural to feel that any given event in the brain could have existed without being accompanied by a sensation.

These intuitions seem to pose serious problems for certain forms of the psychophysical identity thesis. Thus, some versions of the thesis imply (1):

(1) It is necessarily the case that every sensation of a human being is necessarily identical with some brain process.

Moreover, there are versions which fall short of implying (1) itself, but which do imply the following consequence of (1):

---

[1]S. Kripke, "Naming and Necessity," in D. Davidson and G. Harman, *Semantics of Natural Language* (Dordrecht, D. Reidel, 1972), 253-355. All parenthetical page references in the text are to this essay.

(2) Every sensation of a human being is necessarily identical with some brain process.

(2) is a *de re* modal statement about all actual human sensations: it asserts that each such sensation is identical with a brain process in the actual world, and also that identities of this sort are necessary. (1) makes a similar claim about the relationship between human sensations and brain processes, but it differs from (2) in that its subject matter includes unactualized sensations. The forementioned intuitions call both of these doctrines into question: (2) is contradicted by intuitions of the second kind, and intuitions of both kinds are in conflict with (1).

I am a fan of the psychophysical identity thesis, I prefer versions of the thesis that imply (2) to versions that do not. Moreover, I accept the unpopular view that every phenomenal property of a conscious mental event is identical with some neurophysiological property. This view implies (1). Thus, I have an obligation to show that the forementioned intuitions can be explained away. In the present paper I take some steps toward discharging this obligation.

It will be useful to have a couple of technical terms in hand. Henceforth I will use the term 'Cartesian intuitions' in referring to intuitions of either of the forementioned kinds, and I will use 'strong versions' in referring to versions of the psychophysical identity thesis that imply (1). Moreover, it will simplify the discussion if we assume that pain is invariably accompanied in the actual world by a particular pattern of brain activity, and that this pattern of activity is invariably accompanied in the actual world by pain. 'Brain activity of type Φ' will be used as though it were the standard neurophysiological term for the type of brain activity that satisfies this assumption. Finally, definiteness, I will henceforth focus on pain. No other sensations will be mentioned. However, all sensations fall within the intended scope of the discussion: what I have to say about pain seems to me to be true, or at least to be approximately true, of the other sensations as well.

II

What goal should one aim at when he is trying to explain an intuition away? What is a reasonable criterion of adequacy? Well, suppose that it seems to be the case that p, where p is a nonmodal proposition. To explain this intuition away, it would clearly be sufficient to show that there is a theory T that satisfies the following conditions: (i) T implies that p is false; (ii) apart from the fact that it seems to be the case that p, there is every reason to believe that T is true; and (iii) either *T* itself affords an adequate basis for explaining *why* it seems to be the case that *p,* or *T* is compatible with an acceptable theory that provides such a basis. It is much the same, I suggest, in the case of modal intuitions. Thus, if one wishes to explain away the intuition that it is possible that *p,* he can achieve his goal by showing that there exists a theory *T'* that satisfies (iv)-(vi): (iv) *T'* implies that it isn't possible that *p*; (v) apart from the fact that it seems to be possible that *p*, there is every reason to believe that *T'* is true; and (vi) either *T'* affords an adequate basis for explaining *why* it seems possible that *p,* or *T'* is compatible with an acceptable theory that affords such a basis.

I will not attempt to prove that (iv)-(vi) constitute a trustworthy criterion of success, for it seems that proof is unnecessary. It is obvious, I think, that (iv)-(vi) are sufficiently stringent. (If a theory satisfies each of the three conditions, what more can one ask of it?)

Now in order to show that the criterion is satisfied by a strong version of the identity thesis, it would be necessary to establish that a special case of (v) is true. That is to say, it would be necessary to show that at least one strong version is immune to every objection that is not based on Cartesian intuitions. But this is beyond the scope of any one paper. Accordingly, instead of showing that Cartesian intuitions can be explained away, I must settle for a weaker conclusion.

I will try to establish the following claim: every strong version of the identity thesis provides an adequate basis for explaining why Cartesian intuitions occur. This claim implies that strong versions of the identity thesis tend to satisfy the appropriate special cases of condition (vi). For this reason, the claim shows that the following conditional is true: if one holds that it is possible to defend a strong version of the identity thesis against all other objections, then he should also hold that it can be defended against objections that are based on Cartesian intuitions. It is obvious that this conditional is an important asset. It shows that advocates of strong versions of the identity thesis can afford to focus on the nonmodal objections to their views. And by the same token, it reduces the number of objections that demand separate attention. Thus, even though my conclusion falls short of the claim that Cartesian intuitions can be explained away, it promises to be quite valuable.

Perhaps the activity of explaining intuitions away can take more than one form, and perhaps each form has a different criterion of adequacy. Perhaps there is a criterion which requires only that one establish a comparatively weak conclusion like mine. However, as long as it is agreed that my conclusion reduces the number of objections to the identity thesis that demand separate attention, it is of little importance whether we say that the conclusion partially satisfies a strong criterion, or say instead that it fully satisfies a weaker one.

III

My conclusion is warranted by (3), (4), (5), and (6):

(3) One does not have a basis for thinking that an event is a case of ϕ-activity simply in virtue of being aware that it is a pain. That is to say, insofar as one is in a position to claim that he is aware of a pain, it does not *seem* to him that he is thereby aware of ϕ-activity.

(4) One does not have a basis for thinking that an event is a pain simply in virtue of being aware that it is a case of ϕ-activity. That is to say, insofar as one is in a position to claim that he is aware of a case of ϕ-activity, it does not *seem* to him that he is thereby aware of pain.

(5) Every strong version of the identity thesis provides an adequate basis for explaining the facts mentioned in (3) and (4).

(6) The facts mentioned in (3) and (4) provide an adequate basis for explaining why Cartisian intuitions occur.

In the present section I comment briefly on (3), (4), and (6), and in the next section I attempt to establish (5).

As is customary in discussions of Cartesian intuitions, I am prescinding from the fact that one can be said to be aware of pain in virtue of being aware of pain behavior. By awareness of pain I mean awareness of the sort that occurs when someone is aware of a pain that he himself *has*. Accordingly, (3) has the following significance: when one is *directly* aware of a pain, it does not seem to him that the object of his awareness has the properties that are possessed by cases of ϕ-activity.

I am also prescinding from the fact that someone who is aware of pain behavior can be said to be aware of ϕ-activity. By awareness of ϕ-activity I mean awareness of the sort that occurs when one views ϕ-activity through a cerebroscope, or when one observes that a brain process is affecting a ϕ-meter in a certain way. (Please join me in pretending that the cerebroscope and the ϕ-meter have already been invented.) Given this stipulation, (4) is equivalent to the following statement: when one subjects a case of ϕ-activity to scrutiny in the laboratory, it does not seem to him that the object of his awareness is a pain.

(6) rests on several laws of conceivability. First, where α and β are any two concepts, if it doesn't seem to one that he is aware of an instance of β when he is justified in claiming to be aware of an instance of α, then he is able to conceive of an instance of α without conceiving of it as something that seems to be an instance of β. Second, if one is able to conceive of an instance of α without conceiving of it as something that seems to be an instance of β, then he is able to conceive of an instance of α without conceiving of it as something that *is* an instance of β. Third, if one is able to conceive of an instance of α without conceiving of it as an instance of β, then he is able to conceive of an instance of α while conceiving of it as something that *fails* to be an instance of β. And fourth, if it is conceivable that p, then it seems to us that it could be the case that p. That is, conceivability is a sufficient condition of the appearance of possibility.

These laws imply the following generalization: if it doesn't seem to one that he is aware of an instance of β when he is justified in claiming to be aware of an instance of α, then it seems possible for instances of α to exist without being accompanied by instances of β. This generalization is lawlike. Moreover, it shows that the fact mentioned in (3) is a sufficient condition of the fact that it seems possible for there to be pains that are not accompanied by ϕ-activity. It also shows that the fact mentioned in (4) is a sufficient condition of the fact that it seems possible for there to be cases of ϕ-activity that are not accompanied by pain. In view of these considerations, it is clear that the facts mentioned in (3) and (4) provide an adequate basis for explaining Cartesian intuitions about unactualized entities.

In order to show that the facts cited in (3) and (4) provide an adequate basis for explaining Cartesian intuitions about actual entities, it is necessary to appeal to a second generalization. Here it is: if it doesn't seem to one that he is aware of an instance of β when he is justified in claiming to be aware of a *particular* instance of α, then it seems possible for that particular instance of α to exist without being accompanied by any instance of β. Fortunately, it is no more difficult to defend this generalization than to defend its predecessor. To obtain a full defense, we need only make a few obvious changes in the first, second, and third of the foregoing laws of conceivability and combine the resulting principles with the fourth law.

IV

One *never* has a basis for thinking that a particular is a case of ϕ-activity simply in virtue of being aware that it is a pain. Equally, one *never* has a basis for thinking that a particular is a pain simply in virtue of having determined that it is a case of brain activity of type ϕ. Insofar as one is justified in claiming to be aware of a pain, it seems that he has ceased to be in touch with the distinctive nature of ϕ-activity; and insofar as one is justified in claiming to be aware of a case of ϕ-activity, it seems that he has ceased to focus on the distinctive nature of pain. Thus, if the psychophysical identity thesis is true, then the real nature of the relationship between pain and ϕ-activity is separated from the relationship as it is revealed at the level of awareness by an enormous gap.

According to one line of thought, which is suggested by certain passages in "Naming and Necessity", the psychophysical identity thesis does not provide an adequate basis for explaining this gap. Here is one of the relevant passages:

> In the case of molecular motion and heat there is something, namely, the sensation of heat, which is an intermediary between the external phenomenon and the observer. In the mental-physical case no such intermediary is possible, since here the physical phenonmenon is supposed to be identical with the internal phenomenon itself. Someone can be in the same epistemic situation as he would be if there were heat, even in the absence of heat, simply by feeling the sensation of heat; and even in the presence of heat, he can have the same evidence as he would have in the absence of heat simply by lacking the sensation *S*. No such possibility exists in the case of pain or in [the case of] other mental phenomena. To be in the same epistemic situation that would obtain if one had a pain *is* to have a pain; to be in the same epistemic situation that would obtain in the absence of a pain *is* not to have a pain (p. 339).

The facts mentioned here show that there is no difference between pain itself and that which justifies us in claiming to be aware of pain. This suggests, in turn, that there is no difference between pain itself and the appearance of pain. But if there is no difference between pain and the appearance of pain, then it might seem that it is impossible to use the distinction between appearance and reality in explaining why awarness of pain and awarness of ϕ-activity fail to attest to the truth of the identity thesis. Moreover, it might be felt that if an explanation cannot be obtained from the distinction between appearance and reality, then an explanation does not exist.

It seems to me that this worry rests on a false presupposition. According to the presupposition, if the psychophysical identity thesis was true, then the thesis would be supported by awareness of pain or by scrutiny of the brain. But in fact, there is no reason whatsoever for thinking that it should be possible to find evidence for the thesis at the level of awareness.

Here is an argument that calls the presupposition into question. First of all, it is conceptually true that a person's being aware of a pain is the very same state of affairs as his being *in* pain. (In view of the foregoing quotation, it seems fair to say that this point is acknowledged and even insisted upon by Kripke himself.) Further, according to strong versions of the psychophysical identity thesis, a person's being in pain is the same state of affairs as his undergoing brain activity of type ϕ. If any strong version is true, therefore, one's being aware of a pain is the same state of affairs as one's being in a brain state that involves ϕ-activity. Moreover, it is conceptually true that to be aware of brain activity of type ϕ is to *observe* brain activity of type ϕ, where 'observe' is used to stand for any way of studying a phenomenon that involves the use of the senses. Accordingly, awareness of pain can be said to differ from awareness of ϕ-activity in the way that being *in* a brain state that involves ϕ-activity differs from using the senses to *observe* a brain state that involves ϕ-activity. It would be amazing if states of awareness of these two kinds provided any basis for thinking that pains are identical with cases of ϕ-activity.

The ideas of the preceding paragraph provide an adequate basis for explaining the forementioned gap. Thus, it is possible to explain the gap by appealing to the following facts: first, a person's being aware of a pain is the same state of affairs as his being in pain; second, a person's being in pain is the same state of affairs as his being in a brain state that involves ϕ-activity; third, a person's being aware of ϕ-activity is the same state of affairs as his observing ϕ-activity; fourth, one can observe ϕ-activity in someone else's brain without thereby being in a brain state that involves ϕ-activity; and fifth, one can be in a brain state that involves ϕ-activity without being in a position to observe ϕ-activity. The first, second, third, and fourth of these facts explain why one can be completely justified in claiming to be aware of brain activity of type ϕ without being in a position to claim that he is aware of pain. And the first, second, third, and fifth of the five facts explain why one can be completely justified in claiming to be aware of pain without being in a position to claim that he is aware of brain activity of type ϕ.

A qualification is in order. If the identity thesis is true, then one is in some sense aware of pain when he observes a case of ϕ-activity, and is in some sense aware of ϕ-activity when he feels a pain. As a fan of the identity thesis, therefore, it seems to me that there is more than one way of being aware of a pain, and by the same token, it seems that there is more than one way of being aware of a case of ϕ-activity. Thus, I do not wish to maintain, *without qualification,* that one's being aware of a pain is the same state of affairs as his being in pain, or that one's being aware of a case of ϕ-activity is the same state of affairs as his observing a case of ϕ-activity. I wish to maintain only that there is at least one form of awareness of pain which satisfies the first of these two theses, that there is at least one form of awareness of ϕ-activity which satisfies the second, and that the forms of awareness which satisfy the two theses are the only ones which are of importance in discussions of Cartesian intuitions.

The forementioned gap is similar to a number of other gaps, and I would like to call attention to some of the main features of the reasoning we use in coping with the others. I believe that when one considers the differences between the line of thought I have just recommended and the standard ways of handling gaps with a similar form, it becomes somewhat easier to see why philosophers have sometimes held that the task of explaining Cartesian intuitions away is either extremely difficult or impossible.

Although heat and molecular motion (of a certain kind) are the same phenomenon, one can be completely justified in claiming to be aware of heat without being in a position to claim to be aware of molecular motion. If someone were to find this puzzling, we would try to dispel his puzzlement by appealing to the distinction between appearance and reality. Thus, we could remind him that it is not heat itself but only the appearance of heat which justifies him in claiming to be aware of heat, and that the appearance of heat does not always carry information about the features of heat in virtue of which it is true to say that heat is molecular motion. To express the point in Kripkean terms, we could remind the puzzled individual of three facts. First, there is always an "intermediary" between heat and the observer. Second, when the observer encounters heat in an ordinary setting, using only the modes of cognitive access that are normally available, the "intermediary" between himself and heat is the familiar sensation that Kripke calls 'S'. And third, *S* does not reflect the features of heat in virtue of which the scientific theory of heat is true. There is no reason to doubt that we would be able to reassure the puzzled individual by referring to these facts.

It is also true that one can be completely justified in claiming to be aware of molecular motion without thereby being in a position to claim to be aware of heat. If this were to lead to puzzlement, we would again appeal to the distinction between appearance and reality. Our response would take the form of an observation about the difference between the criteria associated with the concept of heat and the criteria associated with the concept of molecular motion. We would point out that although the criteria associated with the first concept stipulate that the sensation *S* is to bear the primary burden of justifying claims to be aware of heat, the criteria associated with the second concept stiuplate that certain different sensations are to bear the primary burden of justifying claims to be aware of molecular motion. Thus, our answer would reflect the fact that there is a difference between heat itself and the experiences which justify us in claiming to be aware of heat.

In the passage quoted above, Kripke calls attention to facts which show that there can be no hope of using lines of thought like those sketched in the previous two paragraphs to dispel puzzlement about the claim to be aware of pain and the claim to be aware of ϕ-activity. There is no difference between pain itself and the experiences which justify us in claiming to be aware of pain; and for this reason lines of thought of the standard types are not available. Accordingly it might seem that advocates of the identity thesis are in an extremely difficult position. I have tried to show, however, that this pessimistic view is wrong. *Although advocates of the identity thesis cannot deploy the distinction between appearance and reality in the standard ways, they are entitled to make full use of the distinction between being in a brain state and observing a brain state, and this second distinction is entirely adequate for their purposes.*

V

After reminding us of the existence of Cartesian intuitions and showing that they call certain versions of the psychophysical identity thesis into question, Kripke argues that they cannot be explained away.[2] I wish to conclude by stating an objection to his argument.

When Kripke tries to explain unwelcome modal intuitions away, his reasoning appears to rest on two theses. In the first place, he seems to use the view that we have a deep-seated tendency to conceive of things in terms of the properties by which they are identified in the

[2] Kripke smiles on certain attempts to explain modal intuitions away, and he frowns on others. However, he does not state the criteria of adequacy that he uses in evaluating such attempts. It may or may not be the case that he would accept the criteria that are stated in II.

Accordingly, in discussing Kripke's position, I will not assume that attempts to actual world—even when we are dealing with questions about the properties they exhibit in other possible worlds. Thus, according to Kripke, if one wishes to determine whether a given actual entity could have had a certain property, one finds it natural to try to answer the question by attempting to conceive of something which possesses the property and which also possesses a property by which the given entity is normally identified. Second, Kripke seems to rely on the thesis that the properties by which we identify actual entities are typically contingent properties. This thesis implies that when someone conceives of a situation in which there is something with a property by which an entity is normally identified, he may not be conceiving of a situation in which the given entity exists.

Once one has accepted the theses, he is in a position to explain away almost all of the modal intuitions that are either problematic or definitely false. Take, for example, the intuition that it is possible for heat to exist without being accompanied by molecular motion. It can be explained away as follows. When we try to determine whether heat is necessarily accompanied by molecular motion, we check to see whether we can conceive of a situation which lacks molecular motion but which contains something that produces the forementioned sensation *S*. (According to Kripke, we identify heat by the fact that it causes observers to experience *S*.) Finding that it is easy to conceive of such a situation, we conclude that the connection between heat and molecular motion is contingent. But this is a mistake, for in conceiving of a situation which contains something that produces *S* we are not necessarily conceiving of a situation which contains heat. It is only a contingent feature of heat that it produces *S*.

Kripke maintains, however, that it is impossible to explain Cartesian intuitions away by a similar line of thought. When we try to determine whether it is possible for pain to exist without being accompanied by ϕ-activity, we check to see whether we can conceive of something which has the property by which pain is identified and which fails to be a case of ϕ-activity. And we find that we can do so. However, this case differs from all others in that the property by which we identify pain is not contingent. Pain "is picked out by the property of being pain itself, by its immediate phenomenological quality" (p. 340). Thus, when we conceive of a situation in which

explain modal intuitions away must satisfy the criteria of II. I will assume instead that an attempt is successful just in case it can appropriately be seen as similar (in all relevant respects) to the attempts that draw smiles from Kripke. (My main objection to Kripke can be stated in this way: although he does not think so, certain attempts to explain Cartesian intuitions *are* similar to attempts on which he smiles.)

there is something with the property by which pain is identified, we are conceiving of a situation in which pain itself is present. And by the same token, since we can conceive of a situation which lacks ϕ-activity but which contains something with the property by which pain is normally identified, it is genuinely possible for pain to exist without being accompanied by ϕ-activity.

I believe that this line of thought is wrong. As we have just noticed, Kripke holds the following view: when we wish to determine whether it is possible for heat to exist without being accompanied by molecular motion, we check to see whether we can conceive of a situation which lacks molecular motion but which contains something that has the property by which heat is identified. But if this claim is granted, then two others should be granted as well. Here is one: when we wish to determine whether it is possible for ϕ-activity to exist without being accompanied by pain, we check to see whether we can conceive of a situation which lacks pain but which contains something that has the property (or properties) by which ϕ-activity is identified. And here is the second claim: when we wish to determine whether it is possible for pain to exist without being accompanied by ϕ-activity, we check to see whether we can conceive of a situation which contains pain but which does not contain anything that has the property (or properties) by which ϕ-activity is identified. It is clear that Kripke's view about heat stands or falls with these two claims about pain. Moreover, if the two claims are granted, then it is possible to explain Cartesian intuitions by a line of thought that is quite similar to the foregoing explanation of why is seems possible for heat to exist without molecular motion. Accordingly, one should not accept Kripke's explanation of modal intuitions about heat unless he is prepared to accept a similar explanation of Cartesian intuitions.[3]

[3]It may be that Kripke does not hold the view I have attributed to him. He may hold instead that when we wish to determine whether it is possible for heat to exist without being accompanied by molecular motion, we check to see whether we can conceive of a situation which satisfies these two conditions: it contains something that has the property by which heat is identified; and it does not contain anything with the property by which molecular motion is identified. If so, then the two claims about pain should be replaced by others. (For example, the first one should be replaced by the claim that when we wish to determine whether it is possible for ϕ-activity to exist without being accompanied by pain, we check to see whether we can conceive of a situation which satisfies these two conditions: it contains something that has the property (or properties) by which ϕ-activity is identified; and it does not contain anything with the property by which pain is identified.) However, the force of my objection is not affected by this qualification. Even if the second view is the one that Kripke actually holds, it remains true that Kripke's view stands or falls with the two claims about pain that are cited in the text. (Since pain is identical with the property by which pain is identified, the two claims cited in the text are equivalent to their longer replacements.)

It may be useful to express this point in terms of Kripke's technical vocabulary. Suppose that α and β are two rigid designators, that we have modal intuitions which count against the claim that [$\alpha = \beta$] is necessarily true, and that we also have good reasons for wanting to explain these intuitions away. According to Kripke, if the reference of α has been fixed by a contingent designator and the same is true of the reference of β, then it is possible to explain the intuitions away by reasoning like that given above. (See the explanation of why it seems possible for heat to exist without being accompanied by molecular motion.) However, he appears to think it is impossible to give an explanation of the preferred type if the reference of only one of the terms has been fixed by a contingent designator. For when he tries to show that it is impossible to use reasoning of the preferred type in explaining Cartesian intuitions away, he focuses on a single issue—the question of whether we use contingent designators in fixing the reference of 'pain'. But Kripke provides no justification for his negative view (i.e., for the view that it is impossible to give an explanation of the preferred type when the reference of only one of a pair of terms is fixed by a contingent designator). Moreover, it is clear that no justification can be given, for as can be seen by reflecting on the two claims about pain that are cited in the previous paragraph, it is possible to give a fully Kripkean account of the modal intuitions that count against 'pain = ϕ-activity' despite the fact that the reference of 'pain' is not fixed by a contingent designator.

The line of thought we have been considering in the present section is quite similar to a line of thought that we considered in IV. Kripke argues that it is impossible for advocates of the identity thesis to explain Cartesian intuitions away, and in doing so, he relies heavily on the premise that pain is not picked out or identified by a contingent property. The line of thought of IV opens with the premise that there is no difference between pain itself and the appearance of pain, and ends with the conclusion that it is impossible to explain why neither awareness of pain nor scrutiny of the brain attests to the truth of the identity thesis. The two premises are best seen as sides of a single coin. Moreover, the conclusions of the arguments are closely related. Finally, each of the arguments fails to establish its conclusion, and they fail for reasons that are much the same.[4]

CHRISTOPHER HILL.

UNIVERSITY OF ARKANSAS.

---

[4]I would like to thank Ivan Fox for many profitable conversations about the mind-body problem, and also for his valuable criticisms of two earlier versions of this paper.

DISCUSSION

THE PRIMACY OF ACTION

According to the naturalistic conception of social science—the view that human social phenomena can best be explained using the methods and concepts of natural science—we should be able to understand humans in the way we understand tin, tornadoes, and termites. If a science of human action modelled on the natural sciences is possible, it is because there is nothing intrinsic to the behavior of humans that prevents its being given the same kind of treatment as is appropriate for the movements of the heavens or the growth of a forest. The aim of such a science will be the identification, classification, and systematic ordering of all social phenomena.

Social science is the study of human action and its effects. Its aim is to provide an understanding of human social phenomena, to discover what people do and how they come to do the things they do. The notion of human action or agency that lies at the core of all social phenomena, I shall argue, must be conceived as a logical primitive, as something whose concept is irreducible to any other set of concepts that do not themselves presuppose the concept of action or agency. I shall also attempt to show that there is no proper study of human social behavior that does not so regard action, that there is no analysis of action or agency in terms of other concepts that does not abstract from those features of social phenomena that give them their peculiarly human character.

What sort of phenomena are actions? From a naturalistic perspective, they are most straightforwardly regarded as a species of bodily movements. Not all bodily movements are actions, of course; we should not count involuntary movements such as tics and sneezes as actions, nor should we include internal processes such as acid secretion and blood circulation. The movements we call actions must be limited to voluntary behavior, or at least behavior that is *sometimes* voluntary. Actions are not predicable of persons as things that happen to them; they are things that people do.

Let us suppose that every action is a bodily movement. A science of action would then have to pick out this class of movements, specify them in neutral observation language, and order them in accordance with principles that would have to be discovered as a result of empirical investigation. A difficulty arises, however, with respect to how these movements are to be specified, for a given action-type may be associated with bodily movements of quite disparate types. An action such as paying a bill or combing one's hair can be performed in any of a number of different ways, using different sequences of bodily movements. There is more than one way to skin a cat, but a proper bodily-movement description must pick out all the possible cat-skinning specifications if the equivalence of action description and bodily-movement description is to be sustained. Since action descriptions ordinarily pick out rather loosely-defined classes of bodily movements, it will be impossible to know on the basis of an action description alone what bodily movements are supposed to occur, or even what all the possible movements are that will satisfy the description. If actions are a species of bodily movements, bodily-movement descriptions cannot be restricted to specific lists of arm and leg motions.

The fact that a given action description does not entail any *particular* movement description does not rule out the possibility that *some* bodily-movement description *or other* is implied whenever any action description is employed. Stating that a person has secured a door does not reveal what moves he has made, but it does imply that systematic account of actions is possible, actions will have to be systematic account of actions is possible, actions will have to be specified using a vocabulary that is not so rudimentary as what we would use for "mere" (i.e., ordinary) bodily movements. Even if actions are no more than bodily movements, the observation language of a science of action need not be translatable into the more fundamental vocabulary of bodily movements.

It is worth noting that this feature of action description, that it warrants its own terminology, is by no means unique to that domain but is a feature of scientific description generally. The biologist does not identify what he seeks to explain simply as a change in color, shape, or position; he describes it rather as a change in neuromuscular structure or in the chemical composition of the blood, or as an instance of an organism going to sleep or becoming rigid. Nor does the meteorologist have to describe what he sees as clouds and columns of mercury and movements of pointers; the things he deals with are more likely to be described as storm centers and cold fronts. Even in chemistry and in the several areas of physics, wherein what one "observes" may be specified as crystallization or adsorption or superconductivity, concepts enjoy descriptive autonomy, in the sense that translatability into a "more basic" terminology is neither demanded nor assumed.

It is therefore not an objection to the identification of actions with bodily movements that one cannot plausibly substitute movement descriptions for action descriptions. Another possible objection is one that arises from noticing that a particular bodily movement may, in different surroundings, count as an instance of two or more quite different actions. The hand movement that in one context is an act of hailing a taxicab could in another set of circumstances be an act of volunteering to answer a question. Removing one's eyeglasses in one situation may be getting ready to fight, whereas in another it could be making a bid in an auction. This objection is the converse of the previous one: it points out that not only is there no unique movement that corresponds to a given action description, but there need be no unique action that corresponds to a particular movement.

What makes a bodily movement an action of a given type is often not revealed in the description of the movement alone. All that this shows, however, is that a movement may have to be properly connected in order for it to count as an instance of a particular type of action. Movements become actions only when they are executed in appropriate contexts. Pulling down a lever counts as casting a vote only when certain conditions are fulfilled: the lever must be part of a voting machine, there must be an election actually being held, and the machine must be hooked into the electoral process in such a way as to give its operation a definite connection with the outcome. The fact that turning a key in a lock may either turn on a light or open a door does not contravene the thesis that actions are a species of bodily movements, any more than the fact that the spontaneous snapping of a cable may amount either to the collapse of a bridge support or to the cutting off of a town's electricity supply falsifies the claim that both of these events are cases of a mechanical breakdown. Action descriptions, it should be noted, are typically relational—but then, so are most movement descriptions.

The distinction between an action and a bodily movement cannot, therefore, be made on the basis of the impossibility of obtaining translations between action descriptions and movement descriptions. If there is a distinction to be made, it must depend on something that an action is and a movement is not. It is a distinction that resides in the fact that an action involves somebody *doing* something, whereas a bodily movement connotes merely a *happening*. To say that there is a difference between an action and a bodily movement is to say that there is a difference between Jack closing his fist and Jack's fist closing. Whether or not every action entails some bodily movement or other, it is clear that the converse does not hold, even in the case of a movement that carries the same description as one that *is* an action. Not every movement of my arm or leg is an action that I perform. My actions are comprised only of those movements that I *make* happen.

Actions cannot therefore be *simply* bodily movements. How shall we delimit the sphere of actions? One suggestion is to suppose that only persons and other creatures that can move their bodily parts intentionally can properly be said to perform actions. To adopt such a suggestion, however, would amount to legislating the usage of a term whose range of ordinary application is in fact much broader. It would make it incorrect, for example, or at least suspect, to speak of the action of the wind on the sand or that of a dye on a piece of fabric, or of the action of a padlock or heart valve. A more general definition of action appears to be needed, one that allows for a category of inanimate action. One such definition has been offered by D.G. Brown: action is the producing of effects in other things.[1] By this definition, actions are distinguished from movements in that they presuppose agents; they are movements that are attributable to things that produce them.

If action can be adequately characterized in such a general and nonanthropocentric manner, then a science of human action would amount to a systematic means of accounting for those effects which happen to be produced by humans. Persons, however, produce their effects in ways that are quite different from the ways inanimate objects do.[2] When a person performs an action, he does what he does at will. He sets something in motion, and it is *he* who sets it in motion. When the sun melts a piece of ice, on the other hand, or an injection slows a patient's heartbeat, the change that is effected is one that is understood as a causal consequence of something else that happens. It is not simply the sun that melts the ice, but the event of the sun shining on it. But when I move my finger in the act of pushing a button, the "I" that performs the action is not similarly understandable as an incomplete specification of an event. This point is revealed by the fact that we do not ordinarily say that one causes one's finger to move; rather we say that one moves it. A human agent, unlike a non-

[1] D.G. Brown, *Action* (Toronto: University of Toronto Press, 1968), p. 35.
[2] Even Brown (*op. cit.*), who insists on the primacy of inanimate action, considers human and inanimate action to be of two *kinds* of action.

conscious one, stands outside the causal processes whereby its actions are mediated.[3]

What is peculiar to human action, then, is a special kind of agency. Actions are events for which it is always appropriate to ask who (or what) performed them. When we inquire as to *how* someone or something performed a given action, we ultimately expect different kinds of answers, depending on whether we are dealing with a human or an inanimate agent. In the latter case, such as that of sunlight or a spot remover, the inquiry terminates with a statement of causal law or natural necessity: sunlight produces growth in green plants because it delivers photons which provide energy that splits water molecules, thereby triggering the synthesis of carbohydrates from carbon dioxide; a spot remover works because it contains an organic solvent that dissolves the chemicals that make up a greasy stain. With respect to human agency, on the other hand, the interrogation comes to an end upon reaching a basic action, an action that one performs directly and not by doing something else. Human actions, unlike the actions of chemicals, are not explainable as law-governed sequences of change, as movement or change in one set of objects caused by movement or change in another set.

Actions, as performed by humans, have a very special status as a kind of event: that is the upshot of our discussion of attempts to assimilate them to bodily movements. The disposition to participate in such events, furthermore, can be taken as the thing that distinguishes humans from other beings. To be human, as Marx saw, is to be a potential agent, a doer and a maker. How then shall we make out the distinction between human events that are actions and human events that are not, between events such as pulling off one's gloves and digesting one's lunch? An appropriate response, I believe, is suggested by Aristotle when he says of the voluntary that it is "that of which the moving principle is in the agent himself."[4] Voluntary

[3]Chisholm has re-introduced the medieval distinction between *transeunt* and *immanent* causation as a means of distinguishing the causation of events by events from the causation of events by agents; see his "Freedom and Action," in Keith Lehrer (ed.), *Freedom and Determinism* (New York: Random House, 1966), p. 17. G.H. von Wright makes the same distinction, but what Chisholm calls "immanent causation," he calls "action," preferring to opt for a single kind of causation. See his *Explanation and Understanding* (Ithaca, N.Y.: Cornell University Press, 1971), pp. 64-69, 191-92. Though I tend to agree with von Wright that agency is less confusingly conceived as not requiring a special notion of causation, it does not matter for my purposes, which of these positions is adopted, so long as the distinction between actions and other kinds of events is maintained.
[4]*Nicomachean Ethics,* 1111a22.

acts are distinguished from compulsory acts, he says, by the fact that in the case of the latter, "the moving principle is outside, the person compelled contributing nothing."[5] Actions are events that are *originated* by a human agent: "Man is a moving principle or begetter of his actions."[6]

Since it is unclear just how and in what sense agents are supposed to initiate or contribute to the movements that comprise their actions, the suggestion is unfortunately a rather crude one. Nevertheless, it does succeed in capturing an important part of what we mean when we describe something that occurs as an act that someone performed: that what we do when we act freely we do on our own, of our own accord. Saying of action that it "originates" with the person who performs it also delivers the implication that it is an occurrence that might not have occurred, even if everything else had been the same. Or as Aristotle puts it, "the things of which the moving principle is in a man himself are in his power to do or not to do."[7] Of course, we do not *know* that the event that we have designated as an action could have been forborne even if all the antecedent conditions had been the same. The point is rather a conceptual one: when we identify an event as a free action, we *presume* that the agent could have done otherwise,that he did not *have* to do as he did.

The aim of this paper is to show that the Aristotelian conception of human action is correct, that action must be conceived as a logical primitive and hence as not capable of analysis in terms of other types of occurrences. In order to make this claim more plausible, I shall try to show that the leading alternative modes of conceiving human action either fail to capture what is distinctive and epistemologically relevant about human action or else are reducible to the account I shall be defending. I shall be concerned to reply both to accounts that seek to deny special or irreducible status to action as a subject for inquiry, and to attempts to analyze human action in terms of alleged fundamental features other than voluntary action itself. The human being is *sui generis,* I want to argue, because action is.

The most prominent alternative to this position, at least in the English-speaking countries, is the form of materialism known as behaviorism. When presented as a philosophical and not merely a methodological thesis, behaviorism holds that whatever human be-

---

[5]*Ibid.*, 1110b15-16.
[6]*Ibid.*, 1113b17-18.
[7]*Ibid.*, 1110a16-17.

ings do can be analyzed in terms of overt behavior and dispositions to behavior. What this amounts to is a denial of the importance of the distinction I have been urging between actions and other forms of behavior. Behavioral science is supposed not to need to pay attention to the distinction between human actions and bodily events that are not actions. The behaviorist cannot, of course, deny that there is a difference between what a person does and the physical changes his body undergoes—e.g., between his act of biting down hard and the event of his jaw snapping shut. His position must be either that the distinction is an irrevelant one, or else that it is capable of being characterized and elucidated in terms that do not presuppose the very difference that is to be illuminated. What he must reject is the view that action is something that is somehow irreducibly different from other sorts of events and must be for its explication be set outside the framework of events in inanimate nature.

I have suggested that what precludes assimilating actions to bodily movements is the special character of human agency. The behaviorist who denies that the distinction between these two classes of events is a meaningful one may insist that his project does not require separating out and marking off for special treatment those items of human behavior that we have identified as voluntary actions. He may argue that the distinction is not a tenable one from the point of view of behavioral science, because there are in fact no clear dividing lines by which we can separate what people do consciously and deliberately from what they do unconsciously or unwittingly or from what they do unintentionally or automatically. He may also note that behavior includes a range of bodily responses that are not actions at all, such as blushing, bleeding, and shivering. So long as the event can readily be identified at the level of overt behavior, it might be maintained, there is no need to pay serious attention to the distinction between actions and other kinds of behavior and bodily changes.

The lack of a clear line of demarcation between actions and non-actions cannot be used to show that there is no distinction to be made, however. It certainly does not damage the claim that there is a difference between red and orange to point out that there is no natural way of separating shades of red from shades of orange. If there are reasons for wanting to study actions apart from other human events, such a program does not automatically become groundless upon discovering that actions apparently grade into nonactions, any more that biology must be supposed to lack a proper domain once it is pointed out that organisms can be seen to grade into actual or possible artifacts.

The behaviorist who finds it acceptable to ignore the peculiar facts of agency does so because he believes nothing turns on it. He is, after all, concerned only with how people behave and what makes them do so. He may very well acknowledge that the events we call actions are brought about by different sorts of events and circumstances from those that produce (mere) bodily movements. The difference between actions and nonactions will be presumed to depend entirely on a difference in causal histories. A shaking of the head that signifies a negative reply will simply have different causal antecedents from one that occurs as the result of a tic. So far as behaviorism embraces the causal analysis of all kinds of behavior, and actions can be construed as events having certain kinds of causes, the behaviorist does not have to set up a special class of events that pick out actions specifically.

According to the behaviorist thesis, all moral behavior can be represented as a function of prior behavior and external events. The program can be seen to run into trouble with regard to actions, however, once it is noticed that is is not external events and circumstances that explain a person's actions but rather his beliefs about them. Someone may lock his doors not because there have been thefts recently but because he *believes* that there have been, or that he believes that locking the doors may in fact prevent a theft. A particular set of circumstances will trigger off different kinds of behavior depending on the beliefs and desires of the individuals acting. The behaviorist, however, must avoid mentioning such unobservables. What the behaviorist program requires is not merely that behavioral patterns and dispositions determine the knowledge conditions for the correct ascription of beliefs and desires, but also that there be no need to acknowledge the existence of intermediaries, whether these be thought of as mental states or as internal physical ones. If there are such things as beliefs and intentions, and it is their presence that, at least in some cases, is what makes a piece of behavior an action, then no behavioristic account will be able to show that actions do not deserve to be regarded differently from other kinds of events.

Rather than simply ignore the distinction between actions and movements, the behaviorist may try to resist the view that action deserves separate explanatory treatment: he may insist that actions are not irreducible. Action statements are translatable, so it may be claimed, into statements in which the notion of agency has been eliminated. We should then be able to replace a statement such as

"Harry pulled his hat down over his ears" with an event-description in which there is no ascription of agency except in the sense that inanimate things such as chemicals are said to be agents. If what Harry did can be reduced or assimilated to something that happened, then actions should be treatable as entirely on a par with other events in the world.

A way that has been suggested of assimilating human agency to ordinary causal processes has already been alluded to above: introducing the notion of agent causation. According to this idea, *Harry* is the cause of his hat being pulled over his ears. Just as the sun may be the cause of ice melting and digitalis may be the cause of an increase in rate of heartbeat, so a person is the cause of whatever he does, the actions he performs. Agents may themselves be caused to act by prior events, so it is supposed, allowing us to conceive what the agent does as part of a causal chain, the elucidation of which may be taken to fall within the purview of behavioral science. What I do, the changes I bring about in the world, are caused by me, and I may be caused to do these things by other things that happen to me.

This is not the only interpretation of agent causation that has been offered, but I believe it is the only one that seeks to reconcile agency with behaviorism. Appealing to agent causation will not help the behaviorist, however, because it involves an entirely different conception of causality from that used in event causation. Harry is not a cause in the sense that the sun or digitalis is, for what is designated in the latter two cases is really an event, the shining of the sun or the taking of digitalis. In Harry's case there in no event, at least of a behavioral sort, other than the event of Harry pulling down his hat. If causes are always events—which is what they would have to be in a behavioristic causal explanation—then agents are never causes but rather substitutes for causes.

It may be concluded then, that the notion of human agency cannot be eliminated by analysis on a behavioral level. If there is a theory of action that is capable of representing actions as a species of bodily movements, it will have to consider events below the level of the whole organism. Such a move is made by the materialist who argues that the way to resist the idea that agency is irreducible is to regard human actions as causal consequences of certain kinds of internal bodily processes. Actions can be identified with bodily movements, on this view, provided that the latter are understood to include those neural events that can be identified with the mental events that are the concomitants of actions. Thus to say that a person P performed action A is taken to be equivalent to saying that events in P's brain caused a bodily movement or series of movements that constituted the performance of A. Actions are interpreted as bodily movements that result from certain sorts of brain processes. The difference between bodily events that are actions and ones that are not is preserved, on this analysis, by identifying actions with just those bodily movements that are mediated by brain states that are associated with the agent's intentions in performing the actions he does.

An account of this sort, in order to be plausible, must be capable of showing that the concept of agency or of agent causation is eliminable, that the facts that is has been introduced to explain are analyzable in terms of ordinary event-causation. A method that would achieve this result is one that would enable us to *subtract* the movement from the action and to obtain as remainder only elements that are linked to the movement in the same way the physiological events are linked. An action would have to be regarded as a compound event consisting of the event whose occurrence is what happens as a result of someone's performing the action and whatever remains after that event has been subtracted. (Cf. Wittgenstein: "What is left over if I subtract the fact that my arm goes up from the fact that I raise my arm?"[8] If what is left over is another event, then actions will have been analyzed in terms of event-causation. And if all of the constituent events are physical or physiological events, then actions must be identical with a subclass of bodily processes.

There are at least two major difficulties with this suggestion. The first is that it is not clear that it even makes sense to speak of subtracting movements from actions.[9] The fact that an action involves some physical movement does not imply that that movement is a part or element of the action. Every act of visual perception requires the reflection of light by an external object, but the reflecting of light by that object is not a part of the perceptual act. Nor are inscriptions, which are presupposed by reading, elements of the act of reading that can properly be subtracted from it. Movements certainly do not *have* to be related to actions as parts to wholes, and if they are not, then subtraction must be construed as merely a metaphor for what occurs in a certain kind of thought-experiment.

---

[8]Ludwig Wittgenstein, *Philosophical Investigations*, translated by G.E.M. Anscombe (London: Macmillan, 1953), Part I, §621.

[9]See Robert A. Jaeger, "Action and Subtraction," *Philosophical Review*, LXXXII(1973), 320-29.

The second difficulty associated with attempting to analyze actions as compounds of physical events is that, even if subtraction is conceptually possible, it may be a mistake to assume that what is left over is an event.[10] If an action is an event that includes an overt bodily movement that is its culmination, what is obtained upon removing that bodily event may be an unrepresentable conceptual fragment, like a voice without sound. Only if we insist that what makes a bodily movement happen *must* be another event do we need to believe that what is left over after the movement from an action is an event.

There is a further argument that may help to show why the materialist analysis of actions into bodily processes does not enable him to dispense with agency. Suppose it is possible to subtract movements from actions, and that what is left over are events that are causally linked to the movements. Consider, for example, Danto's suggestion, that 'm does b' can be resolved into two events, m does-b and b, where the former involves an *intentionalistic* sense of doing, according to which 'm does-b' could be true without b occurring; one could be said to do-something without that thing actually happening, just as one can (intentionalistically) see a dagger without there in fact being a dagger that one sees.[11] The problem that besets an analysis of this kind is that it leaves us with an anterior event that still involves someone doing something. Agency is not eliminated; it is merely detached from the successful outcome of the action. If we try to analyze this event still further, we will still generate an event in which an agent (or protoagent) occurs. Continuing the analysis leads to an infinite regress. So the idea of agency is not capable of being eliminated through any procedure of analyzing actions into constituent parts.

Many of the arguments that have been adduced for denying the materialist thesis that actions are reducible to physical events also apply to dualistic attempts to account for the facts of human agency. Like the materialist, the psychophysical dualist also wants to show that actions can be resolved into components that are causally connected. Actions differ from bodily movements, according to the dualist, in that they include mental states or processes such as voli-

---

[10]This, ultimately, is what Danto argues, after considering and rejecting the possibility that an action is a compound event all of whose elements are also events. See his *Analytical Philosophy of Action* (Cambridge: Cambridge University Press, 1973), chap. 3.

[11]*Loc. cit.*

tions and intentions: the difference between my leg swinging and my swinging my leg is that in the latter case the bodily happening is driven by a mental concomitant, which is what gives it its character as an action.[12] What I do when I perform an action is what happens to my body as the result of the occasion of my willing that my body should so move.

To regard volitions as essential ingredients of action is to view actions as bodily events with mental causal antecedents. Actions are held to be events that occur at the interface of the mental and the physical; volitions are the way the soul or self gets things to happen in the physical world. Volitions may be taken to be caused by prior mental or physical events or, conceivably, by nothing at all. A volition, in any case, is what is supposed to be left upon subtracting the bodily movement from an action.

The attempt to account for agency by analyzing it in terms of volitions and bodily movements is no less problematic than the attempt to reduce agency to brain processes and bodily movements. For how is this volition that is supposed to be obtained by subtracting the bodily movement from an action related to the person whose volition it is? If volitions are the causal antecedents of actions and are what make bodily movements voluntary, then either they are actions themselves, in which case nothing is explained, or else they are things that happen to people such that their occurrence is sufficient to trigger off behavior that we identify as actions. But as Ryle has argued, absurdities result from both suppositions.[13] Volitions cannot be actions, for that would involve an infinite regress, since every volition would itself need to be caused by a action. But if volitions are events that are not actions, then it is hard to see how we can plausibly call the bodily movements that result from them voluntary.

The idea that every voluntary act is accompanied by a volition or act of willing is attended by other problems as well. There is a question as to what grounds we have for supposing that there are such occurrences. We are, after all, rarely if ever aware of a separate experience of willing as distinct from acting, even though we do know which pieces of our behavior are voluntary. Ultimately, the only basis we have for ascribing volitions or acts of will is the performance of the movements that they are supposed to cause.

---

[12]For a clear statement and defense of this view, see, e.g., Jerome A. Shaffer, *Philosophy of Mind* (Englewood Cliffs, N.J.: Prentice Hall, 1968), chap. 5.

[13]Gilbert Ryle, *The Concept of Mind* (London: Hutchinson, 1949), pp. 67-69.

Then there is the problem of how volitions are supposed to be connected with actions. The concept of willing seems to imply that it is logically impossible for someone to will something without doing that thing unless he is specifically thwarted or dissuaded subsequent to the act of willing. To say that a person willed to move his fingers but they failed to move makes no sense in the absence of explicit or implicit reference to circumstances that could be cited to explain the nonoccurrence of what was willed. Willing *must* lead to acting, or at least to an attempt at acting, if it is willing that occurs. If the occurrence of a volition is logically sufficient for the occurrence of the movement it precedes, it cannot be the cause of movement.

If volitions were logically independent of the voluntary acts with which they are associated, on the other hand, then they could not serve as part of the analysis of action. For if volitions can occur as discrete events, then there could be cases of bodily movements preceded by volitions that would not deserve to be counted as actions. If a pistol in my hand fires as the result of a sudden seizure, the firing of the gun would not be a voluntary action, even if it were preceded by my thinking that I wanted to shoot. In order for a mental occurrence to make a bodily movement a voluntary action, it must be connected with the movement in a more intimate fashion. A mental occurrence that gets me to *do* something must get *me* to do it; it must work through *my* agency. If actions are movements produced by volitions, the volitions cannot be separable from the actions. In other words, if actions presuppose volitions, they cannot be *analyzed* in terms of them. A volitional account cannot reduce agency.

An agent is someone who is able to bring about states of affairs; he is able to change the world. I want to say that an action is an event of which it can be said categorically that the agent *could have done otherwise.* A person can be said to have acted when and only when it can also be said that he could have acted differently, not merely under different circumstances, but that he could have acted differently right there and then.[14] To ascribe agency to a person is to say of him that there is something X that he has brought about such that he could also have brought about not-X; where he could have failed to bring about X only if certain conditions were present, the bringing about of X was not an action.

Whether or not there are such happenings as actions (in this

[14]Or as Austin has put it, 'could have if I had chosen' is not a causal conditional; see J.L. Austin," 'Ifs' and 'Cans'," in *Philosophical Papers* (London: Oxford University Press, 1961), pp. 153-80.

sense) depends on whether or not persons may properly be conceived as executors of events for which there are alternate possiblities. When we say that someone has performed a free action, we are saying that he did not *have* to do as he did, that he could have refrained from doing it. But what about the situation in which a person does something, not knowing that, were he to attempt to do anything else, he would be prevented and forced to do just that thing?[15] In such a case, it might be argued, a person could be said to act freely despite the fact that it is false that he could do otherwise.

One way of responding to this objection would be to deny that the behavior in question deserves to be counted as free action. To give this reply would imply that agents and others who claim to recognize a piece of behavior as an action may very well not be in a position to know whether it is an action or not. It would imply that actions are not always identifiable as such on the level at which we conceive them as actions. Knowing whether an event is an action, on this interpretation, could depend on knowledge that is not available to those present.

But there is no reason why there has to be an incompatibility between acting freely and unknowingly acting in circumstances that would have precluded any alternative. The phrase 'could not have done otherwise', so far as it is analytical of the concept of a free action, does not have to be interpreted as having a reach beyond what the agent is in a position to know. A person who jumps from a diving board does so freely even if he would have been blown off by a sudden gust of wind had he not jumped, just so long as he does not know that he could not have prevented himself from going off the board. Furthermore, the fact that a person would have been knocked off the diving board had he not jumped does not show that it is false that he could have done otherwise. Falling off a board is not the same as jumping off, so we can still maintain that if he performed the act of jumping he *could* have done otherwise, viz., not jumped off. In fact, any story we tell about what will happen if a person does not act in a certain way presupposes the possibility of his not acting that way, and thus that he *can* do otherwise.

What the case of overdetermination shows is not that actions do not have to be conceived as avoidable, but rather that identification of a piece of behavior *as* an action depends on the describer's concep-

---

[15]Such a situation is described by Harry G. Frankfurt in "Alternative Possibilities and Moral Responsibility," *Journal of Philosophy*, LXVIII(1971), 829-39.

tual point of view. Whether or not one construes his own behavior as free action clearly is connected with whether or not one conceives it as allowing for the possibility of choice. Similarly, the identification of another's behavior as action, as opposed to bodily response, presupposes that the person could have refrained from making it; certainly this much is implicit in regarding someone as a free agent. The conceptual necessity that attaches to the connection between action and alternate possibilities can thus be represented as follows: behavior that one takes to be action cannot at the same time from that point of view be conceived as constrained in such a way as to make no other behavior possible.

Action statements have a peculiar logical status, which can be seen by considering the role they play in explanations of things that happen in the world. Chains of explanation, like chains of movers, can in principle go on forever. When we seek an explanation of why a bridge collapsed, we may be given an account in terms of the structural features and forces that led to its collapse. If we pursue the matter further and ask how the bridge came to be built in the way it was, we may find that the explanation is made to rest on someone's action (or inaction). In many cases, that is where the explanation ends; attributions of agency often serve as terminators of explanatory series. By identifying an event as the result of someone's action, as something he had the power to do or not do, we are designating that event as a starter-event in a causal series. The agent is what gets the casual process going.

It is true that we can continue the search for explanation by asking what caused the agent to act as he did. To do so, however, if it does not involve reverting to a behaviorist conception of action, embodies a shift to a different mode of explanation, one that relies on the agent's reasons for acting as he has done. An action that is free cannot be compelled, nor can it be causally necessitated. So far as action-ascriptions provide causal explanations with pragmatic termini, no further causes are demanded, regardless of whether the act that begins the causal sequence is supposed to have been done for reasons or for no reason. A person who acts for a reason acts freely; he is free to act or not act on that reason.

In arguing that there is no way of analyzing human action that satisfactorily eliminates the notion of agency, I am not saying that the human organism is an entity that fails to behave in accordance with the laws governing the behavior of matter in other animate and inanimate bodies. Neither am I saying that it is impossible to look upon humans as complex systems whose behavior can be treated merely as the effects of interactions between external stimuli and internal configurations. We do not *have* to characterize as agents those entities that ordinarily get classified as human beings. The question is not whether a science of human beings *qua* objects or *qua* organisms is possible, but rather whether a science of that kind is capable of telling us what we want to know about people and society.

No account of human behavior that ignores or tries to reduce action and its related concepts can capture those features or aspects of behavior that will be counted as distinctively human. So far as a social science is concerned, the question is not whether we *can* dispense with talk about actions—talk, I have argued, that commits us to treating action as a category that is not reducible to other concepts of scientific description—but whether we can do so and still have an account of behavior that is adequate to persons. The reason action descriptions are employed is that they are useful; they provide means of organizing our experience with respect to those things we call persons. An approach to human behavior that treats as unimportant the difference between behavior that is action and behavior that is not action assumes a different standard of cognitive usefulness from the standard that is implicit in an approach that takes action as fundamental.

The kinds of features that are missing from a reductionist or materialist account of action are precisely those that are important from the point of view of anyone who coexists in the society of human subjects whose behavior is being studied. For the notion of action is bound up with a whole cluster of concepts that are constitutive of the human condition—ideas of freedom, morality, and responsibility. Actions, as distinguished from movements, play a special role in human societies, and it often matters a great deal whether an event that occurs is someone's action or not. The distinction between what a person does and what merely happens is one that is at the core of all ethical and legal systems, and is relevant for every society that employs any sort of concept of individual or collective responsibility. Whoever tries to fashion a natural science of human behavior, a science that seeks to treat actions as on all fours with other kinds of observable events, allows no place for such concepts.

It is a contingent fact that the world allows for the possible use of action concepts, that there exist creatures that can be characterized as agents. It is another contingent fact that these concepts are in fact deployed. That they are deployed reveals something about the nature of human existence, given that the notion of agency is tied to a whole network of concepts that are constitutive of persons' being-in-the-world—concepts that include those of ethics, law, politics, religion, and human relationships in general. Part of being human is being a responsible agent and recognizing other responsible agents. Action concepts have sustained their place in language because of the continued relevance of moral and legal ideas to human life and to the dependency of such notions upon them. Action is not a strictly behavioral notion, nor is it behavior alone that prompts us to use the language of action. The study of action is *essentially* anthropocentric: in order for action terminology to be employed, the subjects of action—agents, in other words—must already be identified, if not as persons directly, at least as things that are to be conceived on the model of persons. The distinction between what happens and what is done by agents is one that both presupposes and conditions a human social life that treats it as a distinction that matters.

If the concept of action is both primitive and indissolubly linked to that of a person, and persons are essentially doers, then a science of human beings will have to be intrinsically anthropocentric and hence separate from a science of nature. Human events cannot be construed merely as happenings or occurrences, for that is precluded by our interest in their rationale, their morality and legality, and their social significance in general. The content of a human science must be what people do—how they live, what they make, what they do to each other, for each other, and with each other. That humans are agents as well as patients is what makes them unique as a subject for science, and it also is what makes the idea of a human science different from the start.

MICHAEL A. SIMON.
THE STATE UNIVERSITY OF NEW YORK
AT STONY BROOK.

DISCUSSION

COUNTERVAILING TENDENCIES AND FALSIFIABILITY IN *CAPITAL*

One of Marx's distinctive contributions to social philosophy is his claim to have based his radical critique of modern society on a scientific analysis of capitalism. He advances *Capital* as a scientific and objective account of the fundamental properties of capitalism. This account is intended to have the status of science and to enjoy the rational force which accrues to well-confirmed scientific theories. Moreover, the theory of capitalism constitutes the heart of Marx's critique of modern society; for he believes that *Capital* demonstrates that the inadequacies of modern society are essential and ineliminable from the capitalist mode of production.

Central to Marx's mature social theory, therefore, is his claim of scientific objectivity for the analysis advanced in *Capital.* This claim is controversial, however; for Popper and others argue that Marx's theory of capitalism is devoid of empirical content and therefore not genuinely scientific. Popper's central idea is the 'falsifiability criterion', which maintains that a theory is scientific in proportion to the degree to which it is in principle falsifiable. Popper argues that Marxism fails the falsifiability test, in that it is an endlessly flexible instrument which can be brought to 'account' for every imaginable social state of affairs. Since Marx does not specify conditions which would irreversibly refute the theory, Popper contends that the theory is unscientific.[1]

Popper's criticisms of Marx are often based on an incomplete reading of Marx's economic writings. However, one argument in particular warrants discussion. This is his thesis that Marx's frequent appeal to 'countervailing tendencies' serves to make the system as a whole unfalsifiable. A countervailing tendency is a previously unknown factor which is hypothesized in order to account for discrepancies between theoretical expectations and observed fact.

[1]The falsifiability thesis is developed throughout Popper's works. For a simple statement see *Conjectures and Refutations* (Harper, 1968), pp. 36-37, and *The Logic of Scientific Discovery* (Harper, 1968) pp. 78-92. For Popper's application of falsifiability to Marx, see *Conjectures and Refutations,* p. 37, and *The Open Society and its Enemies,* v. 2 (Princeton, 1971), pp. 187-89.

Marx frequently appeals to such factors in order to make his analysis consistent with the observed facts of capitalism; and Popper maintains that such appeals are inherently ad hoc and incompatible with science.

In this paper I will analyze the claim that appeal to countervailing tendencies serves to reduce the empirical content of Marx's analysis, on the basis of central insights from the 'new' philosophy of science.[2] I will argue that the falsifiability thesis is an unreasonable restriction on theory formation, and that the relevant concern is not to avoid 'auxiliary hypotheses' at all costs, but rather to advance restrictions on their use. Appeal to countervailing tendencies is in fact a necessary and progressive part of scientific method. Finally, I will argue that Marx's research program satisfies the standards of theory change which emerge from this recent work in the philosophy of science. In consequence, the strongest leg of Popper's case against Marx as a scientist is shown to be shaky.

1. Marx's use of countervailing tendencies.

We may begin our analysis with an example. In Vol. III of *Capital* Marx confronts an important theoretical problem in political economy: how to explain the falling rate of profit in British industries at mid-19th century. Marx provides an explanation of this tendency on the basis of his theory of surplus value. Profits are equal to surplus labor, and therefore proportional to the amount of labor employed. As capitalists introduce more productive techniques in order to improve profitability, they normally cause the capital-labor ratio to rise. The rate of profit, however, is equal to the ratio of the surplus to total capital employed (wages and machinery); and as wages come to be a smaller share of the total capital, the rate of profit tends to decline. Consequently, Marx's theory of surplus value entails the law of the

---

[2]By the 'new' philosophy of science is meant the anti-positivist philosophy of science which originated with Thomas Kuhn, Stephen Toulmin, and Norwood Hanson, and includes the work of Imre Lakatos, Paul Feyerabend, Hilary Putnam, and Rom Harre. This approach to the philosophy of science is characterized by a rejection of the logical positivist model of scientific theory and by an increased attention to the actual conduct of science. See Harold Brown's *Perception, Theory and Commitment* (University of Chicago, 1977) for a summary treatment of the differences between the old and new philosophy of science; and see Frederick Suppe's long essay in *The Structure of Scientific Theories* (University of Illinois, 1977) for a detailed discussion of the development of recent philosophy of science.

falling rate of profit.[3] Given the details of the theoretical argument, however, one would expect the rate of profit to fall much more rapidly and constantly than it is observed to do. Whereas orthodox political economy is embarrassed by the mere fact of the fall in the rate of profit, Marx is embarrassed by its relatively slow rate of fall.[4]

Marx's response to this anomaly is to maintain that only a 'law of tendency' has been discovered, which may be offset by other factors not yet represented; he then tries to discover the factors which might interfere with the mechanisms specified by the theory of surplus value. The factors which he cites as countervailing tendencies are unobjectionable: he observes that employers are under a constant incentive to increase the intensity of the labor process, thereby offsetting the decline in the rate of profit; similarly, capitalists are induced to depress the wage below the value of labor power; thirdly, the capitalist can offset the decline by finding foreign markets on which commodities may be sold above their value (and labor employed below its value); and so forth.[5] All these factors have obvious effects on the fundamental mechanisms of the labor theory of value; and they plainly serve to offset the tendency created by the theoretical mechanisms Marx cites. We may readily see, moreover, the social mechanisms by which they emerge: capitalists, as they are caught in a situation of generally falling profits, will do what they can to minimize their costs and increase productivity. Introducing these factors into the analysis at a higher level, moreover, seems to be unobjectionable, and not to be a way of reducing the empirical content of the theory, since the end result is an increase in the realism of the theory.

Popper's attack on countervailing tendencies, however, derives from the following consideration: given that it is always possible to save a theory from false consequences by referring to interfering factors which are not accounted for in the theory, doesn't the appeal to such factors reduce the empirical commitment of the theory? And if a

---

[3]*Captial III,* pp. 211-31.

[4]"If we consider the enormous development of the productive forces of social labour in the last thirty years alone as compared with all preceding periods . . . then the difficulty which has hitherto troubled the economist, namely to explain the falling rate of profit, gives place to its opposite, namely to explain why this fall is not greater and more rapid. There must be some counteracting influences at work, which cross and annul the effect of the general law, and which give it merely the characteristic of a tendency, for which reason we have referred to the fall of the general rate of profit as a tendency to fall." *Captial III,* p. 232.

[5]*Capital III,* pp. 232-40.

scientist is prepared to make some such appeal in every anomalous case, doesn't he relinquish claim to having provided an empirically significant hypothesis? Isn't it reasonable in such a case to conclude that the theory is unfalsifiable by stipulation, and therefore devoid of empirical content? In other words, isn't Popper right in describing recourse to countervailing tendencies as the 'conventionalist twist', which establishes the truth of the theory by stipulation?

This conclusion would be justified only if it were impossible to impose limits on the appeal to countervailing tendencies—only, that is, if it were impossible to give any way of distinguishing between ad hoc and progressive modifications of the theory. And it presupposes that the criteria of scientific rationality attach to formal theories rather than to programs of research. But a good deal of recent philosophy of science has undermined both of those assumptions.

2. Anomaly and theory change.

Popper's falsifiability thesis arises in response to the general problem of anomaly in science. Anomalies—facts or discoveries which appear inconsistent with accepted theory—arise everywhere in the history of science, since scientific inquiry is inherently fallible. If a theory implies some sentence P, and P is false, then it follows that the theory must be false as well. Prima facie, the scientist is faced with a range of choices. He may reject the theory as a whole; he may reject some portion of the theory in order to avoid the conclusion P; he may modify the theory so as to avoid the conclusion P; or he may introduce some additional assumption in order to show how the theory is consistent with 'not P'. A strict falsificationist would presumably require that we disavow the theory; but this response is both insensitive to actual scientific practice and implausible as a principle of methodology.

Post-positivist philosophy of science has directed much of its effort to formulating more adequate standards for modifying theory in the light of anomaly. Its chief insights have resulted from a shift of attention from the level of finished theories to the level of the research program: that is, from the formal laws and principles of a theory to the more encompassing set of presuppositions, methodological commitments, and research interests which guide the scientist in the conduct of research and theory formation. The central focus of neopositivist theory of science was the scientific theory, conceived ideally as a formal system of axioms and deductive consequences. Neopositivists distinguished between the context of discovery and the context of justification; and they argued that only the latter fell within the scope of rational control. This meant that only finished theories could be rationally evaluated; whereas the conduct of research was conceived of as an exercise of pure, unregulated imagination.[6] From this judgment followed falsificationism, verificationism, and various forms of confirmation theory.

The 'new' philosophy of science focuses rather on the 'context of discovery'—the assumptions and research goals which guide the scientist in his research. Philosophers of science in this area reject the idea that the conduct of research is an unstructured, nonrational process; and they have tried to formulate a theory of the rules which serve to distinguish good scientific research from bad. From this starting point, the 'research program'—the broad set of assumptions which serve to direct research—becomes the central interest.[7]

What is a research program? It is the framework of assumptions, experimental procedures, explanatory paradigms, and theoretical principles which serve to guide the conduct of research. Lakatos[8] has provided an especially clear formulation of the concept. First, he argues that any research program possesses a 'hard core' of theoretical principles which constitute its central insight into its subject matter. This core of theoretical principles is taken as fixed; the 'negative heuristic' of the program forbids the scientist from interpreting anomalous results as falsifying this core. Instead, the scientist is directed to construct a 'protective belt' of auxiliary assumptions intended to secure the correctness of the theoretical principles at the core; and scientific research takes the form of an effort to modify or replace the assumptions included in the 'belt' so as to make the core

---

[6]"The initial stage, the act of conceiving or inventing a theory, seems to me neither to call for logical analysis nor to be susceptible to it. The question how it happens that a new idea occurs to a man . . . may be of great interest to empirical psychology; but it is irrelevent to the logical analysis of scientific knowledge . . . Accordingly I shall distinguish sharply between the process of conceiving a new idea, and the methods and results of examining it logically." *The Logic of Scientific Discovery,* p. 31.

[7]Larry Laudan's *Progress and Its Problems* (University of California, 1977) provides a good discussion of the concept of a research program in the new philosophy of science (pp. 70-120).

[8]Imre Lakatos, "Methodology of Scientific Research Progammes" in *Criticism and the Growth of Knowledge* (Cambridge, 1970), pp. 132-38. While I believe that Lakatos's criterion of progressiveness shows Marx's social theory to be genuinely scientific, it must be noted that Lakatos does not ("Methodology," p. 92 and elsewhere).

consistent with experimental results. Finally, the RP includes what Lakatos calls a 'positive heuristic': a set of principles and assumptions which provide guidance in extending and developing the 'belt'. This conception of scientific inquiry could be summarized in the form of a slogan: Defend and extend! Built into the view is a rejection of falsificationism; for far from seeking to refute the central theoretical principles, the scientist is directed to defend and extend them as forcefully as possible.

With this fundamentally different starting point, the new philosophers of science have posed a different question for themselves from that of the positivists. Rather than the positivist's question—What is the criterion of an empirically adequate theory?—they have asked, what are the features which distinguish a rational and progressive program of research from its contrary? The problem of theory adequacy does not disappear; but it becomes a subordinate concern. This broader approach to the problem of empirical rationality lays the emphasis upon the degree to which the commitments of the research program successfully serve to direct research productively, and to suggest empirically adequate theories—rather than upon the narrower question of the criterion of empirical adequacy of theories. On this view, empirical rationality is a feature of the program of research rather than the finished theory; theories are tools for understanding empirical phenomena which are created by the scientist within the context of a framework of methodological and substantive assumptions.

From this research-oriented point of view, falsificationism is an unsound principle of theory choice, since it is an extreme principle which requires the rejection of any theory with false consequences. A more conservative strategy is required, one which allows the scientist to preserve the old theory at minimum cost. On this view, it is generally a reasonable methodological principle to try to formulate a hypothesis which would account for the truth of a theory and the falsehood of P—either by supposing P is really true (i.e., experimental error), or by modifying the theory, or by positing some unobserved factor which, together with the theory, predicts 'not P'. (Consider, for example, the anomalies arising in the Newtonian description of the planetary orbits which lead to the subsequent positing of Uranus.) It is reasonable, that is, to take as a research strategy the maxim of least harm: try to produce a reconciliation of theory and observation which requires the least change in the theory. And the general success of scientific theory formation guided by this maxim vindicates the strategy.

The problem with this sort of methodological principle of least harm is that it allows us to stave off rejection of the theory indefinitely; it potentially makes the theory irrefutable. Once we widen our vision from theories to research programs, however, we find that the key problem is not how to keep a theory falsifiable, but rather how to impose a set of rational constraints on the principle of least harm: how to avoid ad hoc modifications of theory which fail to advance the empirical power and explanatory adequacy of the theory.

This is a question which Lakatos has discussed in detail. His account is not altogether adequate; but it gives an indication of the sort of criterion of adequacy which seems to have some promise of success. On his view, the problem is how to define the notion of a 'progressive problem shift'—that is, a modification of theory in light of conflicting experience which improves the empirical adequacy of the theory. Lakatos gives a twofold criterion of 'progressiveness'. A modification of theory is theoretically progressive if the modification has some excess empirical content over its predecessor; and it is empirically progressive if some of this content is corroborated. If the theory change is not progressive in these senses, then the research tradition is in a state of degeneration, and ought to be replaced.[9]

This conception of a progressive research tradition can be amplified into a more specific criterion of rational adherence to an empirical theory in the face of anomaly. First, the theory in question must have achieved some empirical success. That is, it must produce empirically adequate explanations of phenomena in areas other than those affected by anomaly; otherwise it would be irrational to remain committed to the theory. And secondly, the modifications of the theory must themselves be, at least potentially, empirically significant. (a) They must give rise to other consequences besides the range of phenomena they were introduced to explain; and (b) they must be amenable to further investigation. If these conditions obtain, and if independent justification is produced for the new factors, then both they and the earlier theory are vindicated.

3. Application of these results to Marx's research program.

Does Marx's research program satisfy these standards of progressiveness? I believe that it does, and therefore constitutes an empirically defensible effort in social science. First, the program defines a 'hard core' of theoretical principles which appear to constitute an

[9]Lakatos, pp. 116-22.

important insight into the workings of the capitalist economy, and constitutes a fairly precise tool for further investigation. This core includes the theory of the class nature of capitalism; the theory of the organization and dynamic of the capitalist economy; and the theory of the superstructure (the theory of the relationships between economic structure and ideology and politics). Furthermore, this core has some notable empirical successes, in the areas of macroeconomics and the theory of politics. So the research program possesses the basic empirical credentials which we found to be necessary above.[10]

Secondly, the program has been fertile in directing research. Within the area of social science loosely inspired by the Marxian theory of capitalism are to be found indisputably fruitful examples of social scientific research. Marxist economic theory has included the contributions of Paul Sweezy, Maurice Dobb, Ernst Mandel, and Michio Morishima; Marxist historiography has produced Eugene Genovese, E.P. Thompson, Albert Soboul, and others; the Marxist theory of politics has given rise to Ralph Miliband, Nico Poulantzas, and Theda Skocpol; and Marxist sociology has inspired Tom Bottomore, Anthony Giddens, Robert Blauner, and others. This variety of productive efforts indicates that the program has provided the sort of heuristic value which research programs are expected to provide.

And finally, the modifications of the theory, and the appeals to countervailing tendencies (the development of the 'protective belt'), which subsequent Marxist social science has witnessed seem by and large to have the progressive properties which Lakatos requires. They have served to enhance the empirical power and scope of the theory; and they have been amenable (by and large) to further empirical research (contrary to Popper's assertion that they are merely conventionalist strategies). They have led to a more precise formulation of the economic model; a more detailed model of class stratification; a more finely drawn analysis of the influence of the financial system on the dynamic of capitalist accumulation; a more precise analysis of the influence of economic structure on the system of education; and so forth.[11] So Marx's program gives every appearance of having been

[10]Ernst Mandel marshals some of the empirical support available for Marx's economic analysis in his introduction to *Capital I* (Penguin, 1976), pp. 22-24 and 80-86. His treatment is of special interest because it directly responds to Popper's charge of unfalsifiability.

[11]Consider Michio Morishima's *Marx's Economics* (Cambridge, 1973), J.H. Westergaard's *Class in A Capitalist Society* (Basic, 1976), James O'Connor's *The Fiscal Crisis of the State* (St. Martins, 1973), and Bowles' and Gintis' *Schooling in Capitalist America* (Basic, 1976).

both theoretically and empirically progressive, in Lakatos's terms; and it seems to have been fruitful in just the way a successful program of research ought to be.

Conclusion

On the interpretation of theory change in science sketched above, then, the appeal to countervailing tendencies is neither irrational nor uncontrollable; it is rational to try to save the theory, and we can specify relatively clear criteria of success and failure in the attempt. Appeal to such factors can in principle constitute a progressive research strategy, and does not prima facie affect the empirical content of the theory. It may well transpire that the theory is not progressing; and if this is the case, it must ultimately be rejected. But merely to look for ways of accomodating recalcitrant data is not by itself irrational. This is all we need in order to conclude that the appeal to countervailing tendencies does not by itself reduce the empirical content of the theory. Popper's charge that Marxist social theory is devoid of empirical content is therefore unsupported.

DANIEL LITTLE.

COLGATE UNIVERSITY.

DISCUSSION

REPLY TO PROFESSOR ZAITCHIK

Professor Zaitchik's "defense" of physicalism would have gladdened the heart of Mr. Pickwick, but it gladdens not mine. My point was that, on what seem plausible assumptions about the non-coextensivity of physical and psychological kinds, we must give up either (1) the reduction of intensional to physical explanation, or (2) the construal of intensional theories as enunciating true causal explanations. What Zaitchik has done is simply to opt for (2), accepting the consequence that there may be *no* science in which we can articulate such causal explanations as our linguistics, our decision theory, our psychology of perception, our learning theory, etc., now appear to provide. There *will* be no such science if, as could well turn out, our neurology (or our physics) provides no projectable predicates coextensive with those that our intensional sciences deploy. In that case, on Zaitchik's view, there will be an explanation of the fact that certain formulae occur in all optimal computational models of the organism, but those formulae will be—as it were—mentioned rather than used. The success of the computational models will therefore *not* be explained in the way that we explain the successes of other highly valued scientific theories: viz., by the assumption that they are true. We will be able to say—to put it vulgarly—that and why "if you itch you want to scratch" occurs in all optimal models, but we will not be able to say that it is because if you itch you want to scratch. Indeed, we will not, ex hypothesi, be able to say that if you itch you want to scratch *at all*, no projectable predicates coextensive with 'itch', 'want' and 'scratch' having been provided. That is what it is like to give up your psychology on grounds of physicalist prejudice. But now: if it is *not* an objection to the physicalist methodology that it rules out on a priori ground what appear to be scientific explanations in good standing, what *would* be an objection to that methodology?

By the way, the putative counterexample in footnote 7 cuts no ice since, in the circumstances imagined, the token of "peck here now" is not functioning as a representation of a rule (or of anything else) in the etiology of the pigeon's behavior; it is just functioning as a discriminative stimulus. What this shows is only what is obvious on independent grounds: that to flesh out the intensionalist story we need an account of what it is for a token to represent—and, more generally, for something to be a token of a formula in a system of representations. I see no reason to doubt that this can be done; certainly Zaitchik has given no argument for doubting that it can. *If* it can, then the idea that intensionally characterizable behavior is behavior in which mental representations are causally implicated will be *just* what we need to explain why the postman is—and the planets are not—following rules in the execution of their appointed routes.

JERRY A. FODOR.
MASSACHUSETTS INSTITUTE OF TECHNOLOGY.

DISCUSSION

REPLY TO PROFESSOR FODOR

The problem is not whether such lawlike generalizations as "If you itch you want to scratch" or "In a Muller-Lyer Arrows situation you see the figure with the outgoing fins as having a longer shaft than the figure with the ingoing fins" are *true*. Of course they are true. (And their Intentional character is no problem, for the standard criteria for applying their Intentional components are satisfied.) The question is, rather, whether such generalizations are *explanatorily adequate*. Computational psychologists answer "no" and seek to explain these generalizations by reference to theoretically posited computational states and processes. It is when *these* lawlike generalizations are read Intentionally (in the spirit of Realism) that problems begin, for we face criteria failure. That is where Physicalism comes in; it seeks to eliminate Intentionalism not at the superficial level of our initial generalizations but at the deeper level of the computational accounts of those initial generalizations. On everyone's account you want to scratch when you itch.

As for the counterexample in note 7, I quite agree that *if* we had "an account of what it is for a token to represent" we might be able to exclude the screen projection of "Peck here now" as other than a representation (in the proprietary sense). But that is precisely the point: not only have we so far been given no such account, there seems to be no way of coming up with one without begging the very question at issue, viz., the propriety of a full-fledged Intentional characterization of the organism according to which the organism *intends* that some token inscription represent something. As I noted in the text I believe such intentions lead us through an infinte regress of interpreters, as Dennett argued. Systematic pairings between formulae and behavior/physical states cannot secure an Intentional significance for the Intentional idiom; neither can systematic pairings between inscriptions of formulae and behavior/physical states. The postman *understands* his duties, while the heavens do not. Our problem is the relationship between an organism in general and the computational states and processes postulated in a predictively adequate model of the organism's behavior. Let the neurological inscriptions of the model's rules be as causally implicated as you like; they are not understood by the organism nor intended to represent information. Unlike the postman, but like the heavens, the organism "follows" these rules only in the sense that it "conforms" to them in its behavior.

ALAN ZAITCHIK.

BEN-GURION UNIVERSITY OF THE NEGEV.

REVIEWS

Time and Its End: A Comparative Existential Interpretation of Time and Eschatology. HOWARD A. SLAATE. Washington, D.C.: University Press of America, 1980. Pp. 279. $11.75.

This book was written by the chairman of the Department of Philosophy at Marshall University. It was the paper that Slaatte read at the recent meeting of the Institute for Advanced Philosophic Research that caused this reviewer to become interested in his book. His paper, "The Existential Creativity of Consciousness," was certainly *outstanding*.

As the title and subtitle indicate, the book itself consists of an exploration of the *perplexing* problem of time. As over against literalistic, fundamentalistic approaches to eschatology, Slaatte's approach is profoundly philosophical. While, in terms of his existentialistic point of view, the author makes special use of the thought of the Russian philosopher Nicholas Berdyaev (1874-1948), his synoptic, comprehensive method involves due consideration of the views of thinkers from the Greeks to the present day. At the same time, however, he constantly refers to Berdyaev because he believes that the latter actually presents the *most balanced* view of the relations of time and eternity.

Following Berdyaev and others like him, this philosopher really considers the appearance of Christ as the greatest single creative factor in history. For he maintains that here, as nowhere else, God, as the Eternal, enters history—and, by His entrance, transforms it. Like some extentialists, however, the author is at times inclined to overemphasize faith at the expense of reason. Nevertheless, this book is certainly very significant. As such, it would serve well as the basis of discussions in which both professors and students might take part.

ARTHUR W. MUNK.

ALBION COLLEGE.

The Unconditional in Human Knowledge. Four Early Essays (1794-1796) by F. W. J. Schelling. Translation and Commentary by FRITZ MARTI. Lewisburg: Bucknell University Press; London: Associated University Presses, 1980. Pp. 271.

These four essays are entitled: "On the Possibility of a Form of All Philosophy"; "Of the I as the Principle of Philosophy or on the Unconditional in Human Knowledge"; "Philosophical Letters on Dogmatism and Criticism"; "New Deduction of Natural Right." Each is preceded by a translator's introduction and followed by commentary in colpious notes which show the author's didactic talent. Is there, however, as much harmony between Kant, Fichte, Schelling, Spinoza, and even Augustine as the commentaries propose?

In Schelling's words, Kant established, "though nowhere immediately," the absolute I as "the ultimate substrate of all being" (146). Assuredly, not even by implication. The proposition, I exist thinking, as Kant writes, determines "the subject (which then is at the same time object) in respect of existence" (B 429). This empirical truth neither identifies subject with object nor asserts anything like Schelling's I which, along Fichtean lines, "produces itself by its own thinking—out of absolute *causality*" (75). The translator's introduction maintains that we owe to Kant the undeniable knowledge "that ratiocination is concerned with the conditional and reason with the unconditional" (21). "Ratiocination," however, is Kant's term for reason's syllogistic acts (*ratiocinatio* [B 387, 368]), not for obtaining conditional knowledge through the understanding. There is no deriving of "the unconditional from the conditional" in Kant, as Schelling would have it (23). The English translation "the unconditional" for *das Unbedingte,* incidentally, may serve to indicate a postcritical outlook as distinguished from theologically precise term "the unconditioned" (which appears several times in the notes in the context of quotations).

When Kant calls the existence of God a *bestimmte Bedingung,* a determinate or definite condition of the binding power of the moral law (B 662), he does not "obviously mean," according to the author's commentary, *bestimmende,* determining condition (206). Within ten lines, Kant says *twice* determinate, *bestimmte,* condition: the moral law, of course, is itself determining, not determined by any outside condition (B 661, 662); similarly, Kant does not "obviously" mean "transcendent" when saying (B 404). *transzendental* (25).

Any attempt to hoist Kant onto the bandwagon of the German

idealists must fail. Their ready abandonment of Kantian mental discipline can be witnessed in the notes of this volume in a wealth of philosophic-historical data. Had the author taken Kant's vehement dissociation from Fichte's system ("completely untenable") seriously and not tried to erase the great divide between Kant and this philosophical aftermath, his book would provide us with a revealing account of a sudden historical disintegration. The historian Tennemann reported that among Schelling's adherents a certain *Schwindelgeist* developed. Kant called it *Schwarmerei* ("visionariness"). In the end, the translator suggests that any uninitiated reader still frustrated by the Fichte/Schelling claim of a self-positing I even after studying ten of his relevant notes "is not yet ready for philosophy" (36). Or has he perhaps started on a critical road?

WOLFGANG SCHWARZ.

VANCOUVER, CANADA.

Loneliness in Philosophy, Psychology & Literature. BEN LAZARE MIJUSKOVIC. Assen: Van Gorcum & Company, 1979. Pp. 100.

Leibniz argued, with good reason, that the monads have no windows, but he also held that monads mirror each other and operate in harmony with each other and with God. The author of this book proposes that a view like Leibniz's as well as the epistemological solipsism of Descartes somehow support his highly interesting theme that "loneliness" is the universal principle through which human nature, motivation and meaning may be understood. He claims that loneliness is engrained in the conscious structure of Western man. "Enforced loneliness is the dominant theme of Western Civilization" (68). He has thought long and interestingly about this stimulating view in previous articles and in this book offers support for his thesis from philosophical, literary, and psychological perspectives. Moreover, he reveals a sensitive appreciation of phenomenological insights (Chapters III and VI) and makes pointed criticisms of others like Nicholas Berdyaev and Rubin Gotesky who regard loneliness as only a recent concern of humans (Chapter V).

But can one move so readily from epistemic and ontological analyses to conclusions about psychological and cultural states? The word "lonely" is freighted with meanings not intended by the purely methodological solipsism of Descartes or Berkeley's tentative "solitary man." If, as the author says, "we are sentenced to loneliness" (100) it cannot be because it is an "undeniable fact that all men are separately, monadically lonely" (99). Indeed, Vedantist thinkers hold that our loneliness is a product of karmic ignorance for we are, they maintain, foundationally one with the Absolute and our lives should be spent trying to come to the realizaton of that "undeniable fact." Royce and Hocking maintained that the basal fact is social reality; we find our unique identities by means of the "given" community. Theravadin Buddhists, on the other hand, prize loneliness initially. "Make yourself an island" says the Buddha, and thereby seeks to achieve "extinction without remainder." For others, loneliness is a deserved mental state resulting from sheer ethical solipsism.

The author's claims are appealing and suggestive but they are also extravagant. That extravagance is based on some categorial confusions. It does not appear that one can establish the nature of personality by an examination of epistemology nor by selected literary insights. Being "trapped within our own sphere of awareness" (38) epistemically does not imply that our primary psychological state is necessarily loneliness. Even if we are monads ontologically, we do by nature mirror each other. The fact of self-transcendence is as fundamental a fact as the fact of privacy.

There is a deal of interesting scholarship in the book. It would have been better appreciated had there been an index.

WARREN E. STEINKRAUS.
STATE UNIVERSITY OF NEW YORK,
COLLEGE AT OSWEGO.

Philosophy and the Mirror of Nature. RICHARD RORTY. Princeton, N.J.: Princeton University Press, 1979. Pp. 401. $20.00.

The central contention of this book is that the time has come to abandon the concept of mind as mirror and its accompanying epistemological doctrine that truth consists of correspondence with reality, and to replace that doctrine not with another doctrine but with an activity, viz., conversation. The philosopher has claimed to know things about knowing which no one else knows as well and has viewed himself in consequence as a proper critic of science, morality, and religion, but neither claim is warranted.

The three most important philosophers of our century, in Rorty's opinion, viz., Wittgenstein, Heidegger, and Dewey, traveled the Cartesian route early in their careers and, disappointed in their efforts within the traditional boundaries of "philosophy of mind," concluded that the conception of knowledge as accurate representation made possible by special mental processes and intelligible through a general theory of representation must be abandoned. Rather than thinking of "truth" as accurate representation, we should think of it as what it is better for us to believe. The notion of "accurate representation" is simply an empty compliment for those beliefs which help us do what we want to do. It is time to discard the Greek contrast between contemplation and action, between representing the world and coping with it.

We have here, as should already be clear, a restatement of the pragmatic point of view. Rorty indeed in his 1979 presidential address to the Eastern division of the American Philosophical Association characterized pragmatism as "the chief glory of our country's intellectual tradition." James' "definition" of "the true" as that which is "good in the way of belief" is a proper "definition" just because it does not "define" in the Aristotelian sense. It does not identify an "essence"—but then "truth" does not *have* an essence.

This book is long on claims and polemic but short on argument. One argument which does appear comes from Sartre: if mind is an unclouded mirror, it would be indistinguishable from what it mirrored. Is this not an example of the fallacy logicians call "extension": assuming that what is untrue in the maximum degree is also untrue in moderate degrees? Maps are certainly useful and accurate "mirrors" though they do not duplicate in full and identical detail what they represent.

The paucity of rigorous argumentation in this book will not be judged a flaw by those already sympathetic to its pragmatic orientation, for after all the point is to keep the conversation going (but what shall we talk about?), not to seek, in vain, for "objective truth." For the unregenerate rationalists among us, the abandonment of the search after truth will be viewed as an irremediable loss if not a manifestation of disloyalty to the philosophic enterprise.

HARRY RUJA.

SAN DIEGO STATE UNIVERSITY.

Body, Mind, and Method, Essays in Honor of Virgil C. Aldrich, edited by D. F. GUSTAFSON and B. L. TAPSCOTT. Synthese Library/Volume 138. Dordrecht, Holland: D. Reidel Publishing Company, 1979.

This book is a fitting tribute to the man in whose honor it was compiled. Virgil Aldrich has pursued a variety of philosophical interests—epistemology, philosophy of science, aesthetics, metaphysics, logic. His diverse concerns have not produced a heterogeny, however; instead they have lent considerable dimensionality and depth to his "doing" of philosophy. The essays here assembled exemplify similar diversity in content, as well as in the perspectives they represent. Aldrich is a common denominator only by reason of the articles addressing his favorite themes. Although Aldrich himself would delight in such conflicting viewpoints analytically developed, substantive coherence is lost in a work of this type.

Still the essays are strongly written by strong philosophers; in fact each is worthy of its own critical review or at least an abstract. Unfortunately all I can do here is list the authors and titles so as to cue the reader to the topics covered. Two are by the editors: " 'Pain', Grammar, and Physicalism" (Gustafson) and "Deterministic Predictions" (Tapscott). Other authors are Fred Dretske ("Simple Seeing"), Alastair Hannay ("The 'What' and the 'How' "). T.M. Reed ("Dreams, Scepticism, and Waking Life"), Kai Nielsen ("Reasonable Belief Without Justification"), Richard Rorty ("The Unnaturalness of Epistemology"), Daniel Dennett ("On the Absence of Phenomenology"), Douglas Long ("Agents, Mechanisms, and Other Minds"), Stanley Munsat ("Memory and Causality"), John Canfield ("Calculations, Reasons and Causes"), Keith Gunderson ("Purposes and Poetry"), Guy Sircello ("Beauty and Sex") and Robert Howell ("Fictional Objects: How They Are and How They Aren't").

All of the pieces are solid, written in the Aldrichian tradition of workers rather than funsters of philosophy. By that I mean that the authors uniformly avoid appealing to ridiculous or "far out" examples, and tend to use, whether for support or refutation, the more "canonical" sources, especially Wittgenstein and Norman Malcolm. Once in a while some even refer to Aldrich.

A brief biographical sketch of Aldrich and a useful bibliography of his published works is appended to the collection.

MARY B. MAHOWALD.
INDIANA UNIVERSITY AT INDIANAPOLIS.

Multi-Dimensional Sociology. ADAM PODGÓRECKI and MARIA ŁOŚ. London, Boston, and Henley: Routledge and Kegan Paul, 1979.

This is a rather loose collection of pieces (each authored separately) by two émigré Polish sociologists who advocate a pluralistic approach to social study. The book falls into three parts. A series of chapters on major sociological schools is followed by a number of brief studies on aspects of 'Social structure and consciousness'. Lastly, the problem of the relation between social theory and practice is treated in terms of 'sociotechnics', a kind of social engineering.

The authors draw on a broad knowledge of the sociological literature while making frequent references to both research and social conditions in Poland. This national emphasis is to be welcomed, given the unavailability in English of much of the Polish literature and the importance of ongoing political developments in that country. But the present work contrasts notably with recent immanent critiques of Eastern European socialism (e.g., Bahro in East Germany and Konrad and Szelenyi in Hungary). While Podgórecki and Łoś have been deeply influenced by the Marxist tradition, they do not attempt to revitalize it or to draw from it for a systematic critique of Eastern socialism.

Their accounts of sociological schools cover functionalism, systems theory, and a variety of Marxisms, along with phenomenologically oriented approaches and symbolic interactionism. Studies of the formation of individual identity and attitudes in various kinds of group contexts allow them to pursue their interest in the interrelations of social structure and individual experience. Discussions of class and national ethos in particular offer evidence for the fruitfulness of their pluralism, even if this means an occasional uneasy juxtaposition of concepts from incompatible kinds of analysis (for example, the uneasy co-existence of functionalist and class analysis ideas).

Questions about the coherence of a 'multi-dimensional' approach are less easily set aside when it comes to practical uses of sociological knowledge. Given their adherence to a variety of social engineering, one might hope for some reflection on the social character of the knowledge so used, or on the nature and impact of the interests of the engineers themselves. Such issues are not really considered in this book, though we are given the sketch of a 'global ethics' which is to help unite intellectuals of all countries as well as to promote universalistic content for social programs. Since the authors pay little attention to conflicts within and between societies, their ethic seems premature, however laudable its aim. Perhaps a certain skepticism bred of experience prevents them from confronting their technocratic inclinations with Marx's programmatic critique of the division of labor. On the other hand, their own position is not markedly different from an enlightened version of bureacratic rule.

In general, the importance of the issues the authors raise makes one wish they had engaged in a more searching reflection on their theoretical and political commitments. Nevertheless, for its reading of the sociological tradition, its various instructive analyses, and its muted political statement, this must be counted a provocative and useful collection.

RICHARD T. PETERSON.
MICHIGAN STATE UNIVERSITY.

Indian Philosophy Since Independence. DALE RIEPE. Calcutta: Research India Publications, 1979. Pp. 360.

Riepe's book gives evidence of the immense variety of Indian philosophical thought since independence as well as of the author's profound philosophical knowledge and his ability for creative and critical thinking. Professor of Philosophy at the State University of New York at Buffalo, Riepe is one of the very few who not only have a deep knowledge of the history of Indian philosophy, especially of its development in modern times, but are also familiar with the main content of modern European and North American thought, and last but not least, are capable of comprehensive and critical analysis on the basis of a keen intellect and politically oriented, well-founded, and clear-cut philosophical standpoint of their own. In many ways this book is a review of world philosophy and can give impetus to further studies of scholars whose field of research is not only Indian philosophy but modern philosophy in a broader sense.

The author has used a tremendous amount of source material in writing this first comprehensive analysis of what has actually been going on in Indian philosophy since independence. He visited India four times, lectured at many universities, studied in libraries and archives, and interviewed hundreds of scholars. Thirty philosophers are dealt with extensively, and the bibliography mentions the names of 140 Indian philosophers, apart from the numerous articles in periodicals, etc., referred to in the text.

Riepe's analysis mainly deals with the Indian philosophy that is influenced by Western European and North American philosophy, respectively. He shows the general trends of this philosophy as tending to subjectivism, irrationalism, and fatalism and its tendency to avoid the burning social question with which mankind in our days is faced. He shows the social connections of these philosophical phenomena and offers an example of militant and sometimes polemical disputation, a compassionate outlook, common sense, and wit.

Riepe draws the conclusion that the younger generation of Indian philosophers in its majority imitates the predominant philosophical models of Western European and North American countries. It needs to be stressed that he offers a very careful analysis in criticizing the different Indian philosophers. He shows all the elements of realistic, rationalistic thinking which are able to lead to a scientifically based philosophy.

The contents of the book can be described as follows: Chapters 1-5 contain the introduction and deal with Indian philosophy immediately before and since independence, social factors in estimating Indian philosophy today, foreign influences on India, Indian philosophy since independence, and social obstacles to the development of objective and scientific philosophy in India. He stresses the subtlety of Indian philosophy and its achievements in the field of ontology, epistemology, logic, ethics, and aesthetics.

In Chapters 6-8 several Indian philosophers are analyzed from the point of view of three main branches of philosophy: metaphysics, epistemology, and dialectics. Chapter 7 deals with the development of Indian logic since independence and Chapter 8 shows that modern Indian gnoseology is overshadowed by traditional Indian thinking as shaped by philosophers like Shankara and Nagarjuna.

Riepe thinks that "philosophy will be the last to change in India because is has been farthest removed from reality— from the productive world." But he leaves no doubt that the scientific world outlook will eventually be victorious in Indian philosophy.

As Riepe has shown, the different schools of Western European and North American idealistic philosophy are not able to contribute to the improvement of social conditions in India, and the question whether this philosophy should be preferred to the traditional idealistic philosophy of India cannot be simply answered with a "yes" or "no." In the final analysis, both are not able to solve the burning philosophical problems. Therefore there should be no nostalgic mourning if traditional Indian philosophy is vanishing.

But can the endeavor of Indian philosophers during the struggle for independence be called chauvinistic simply because they were trying to prove to the world that Indian philosophy was not only not inferior to the Western, but that it was essentially the correct view in the contemporary world? It cannot be denied that the feeling of national unity in the anticolonial struggle was strengthened by it. We cannot agree when Riepe writes: "contemplative and conservative outlook streamed through pre-Independence philosophy" (p. 28). We think therefore that Riepe's evaluation has to be reexamined.

The book discussed here is the first volume; another volume will contain chapters on contemporary subjectivism in the philosophy of science as a background to Indian philosophy of science, ethics and social philosophy today, Indian aesthetics, and philosophy of art. We look forward to it.

WALTER RUBEN AND HILTRUD RÜSTAU.
HUMBOLDT UNIVERSITY OF BERLIN.

RECENT PUBLICATIONS

Rapp, Friedrich, *Analytical Philosophy of Technology.* Boston Studies in the Philosophy of Science, Volume 63. Dordrecht: D. Reidel Publishing Company, 1981. Pp. xiv, 199. Dfl. 65,--. $34.00, cloth; Dfl. 30,--. $14.95, paper.

Hegel, G. W. F., *The Berlin Phenomenology.* Edited by M. J. Petry. Dordrecht: D. Reidel Publishing Company, 1981. Pp. cx, 210. Dfl. 90,--. $47.50, cloth; Dfl. 32,50. $15.00, paper.

Gier, Nicholas F., *Wittgenstein and Phenomenology: A Comparative Study of the Later Wittgenstein, Husserl, Heidegger, and Merleau-Ponty.* Albany: State University of New York Press, 1981. Pp. xix, 268. $34.00, cloth; $9.95, paper.

Angeles, Peter A., *Dictionary of Philosophy.* New York: Harper & Row, 1981. Pp. ix, 326. $5.95, paper.

Boehm, Rudolf., *Vom Gesichtspunkt der Phänomenologie.* The Hague: Martinus Nijhoff Publishers, 1981. Pp. 262. Dfl. 120.00. $63.00.

Brentano, Franz., *The Theory of Categories.* Melbourne International Philosophy Series 8. The Hague: Martinus Nijhoff Publishers, 1981. Pp. ix, 275. Dfl. 85,--. $45.00.

Buroker, Jill V., *Space and Incongruence: The Origin of Kant's Idealism.* Synthese Historical Library 21. Dordrecht: D. Reidel Publishing Company, 1981. Pp. 143. Dfl. 60,--. $31.50.

Dretske, Fred I., *Knowledge and the Flow of Information.* Cambridge, Mass.: The MIT Press, 1981. Pp. xi, 273. $18.50.

Fodor, Jerry A., *Representations: Philosophical Essays on the Foundations of Cognitive Science.* Cambridge, Mass.: The MIT Press, 1981. Pp. vii, 343. $20.00.

Loeb, Louis E., *From Descartes to Hume: Continental Metaphysics and the Development of Modern Philosophy.* Ithaca: Cornell University Press, 1981. Pp. 382. $24.50.

Mensch, James R., *The Question of Being in Husserl's "Logical Investigations."* The Hague: Martinus Nijhoff Publishers, 1981. Pp. ix, 211. Dfl. 78,--. $39.00.

Kraft, Victor., *Foundations for a Scientific Analysis of Value.* Edited by Henk L. Mulder, translated by Elizabeth Hughes Schneewind, with an introduction by Ernst Topitsch. Vienna Circle Collection 15. Dordrecht: D. Reidel Publishing Company, 1981. Pp. xvi, 195. Dfl. 95,--. $49.95, cloth; Dfl. 45,--. $23.50, paper.

Capaldi, Nicholas; Navia, Luis E.; and Kelly, Eugene, *An Invitation to Philosophy.* Buffalo: Prometheus Books, 1981. Pp. x, 295. $11.95, paper.

Rescher, Nicholas, *Leibniz's Metaphysics of Nature.* Western Ontario Series 18. Dordrecht: D. Reidel Publishing Company, 1981. Pp. ix, 126. Dfl. 60.--. $31.50, cloth; Dfl. 27.50. $14.50, paper.

White, Morton, *What Is and What Ought to Be Done: An Essay on Ethics and Essay on Ethics and Epistemology.* New York: Oxford University Press, 1981. Pp. x, 131. $12.95.

Wittgenstein—Aesthetics and Transcendental Philosophy. Proceedings of an International Symposium held at Bergen (Norway), April, 1980. Edited by Kjell S. Johannessen and Tore Nordenstam; contributions by V. Rossvaer, R. Haller, W. Röd, and others. Dordrecht: D. Reidel Publishing Company, 1981. Pp. 193. Dfl. 62.--. $29.50, paper.

Katz, Jerrold J., *Language and Other Abstract Objects.* Totowa, N.J.: Rowman and Littlefield, 1981. Pp. viii, 251. $25.00, cloth; $9.95, paper.

Mueller, J. J., *Faith and Appreciative Awareness: The Culture Theology of Bernard E. Meland.* Washington, D.C.: University Press of America, Pp. xx, 146. $17.75, cloth; $8.75, paper.

Steigerwald, Robert, *Marxism and Late Bourgeois Ideology.* Praxis: Philosophical and Scientific Reprints, Volume 5. Amsterdam: B. R. Gruner Publishing Co., 1981. Pp. 95. Dfl. 25.--. $12.50.

Science and the Sciences in Plato. Edited, with an introduction by John P. Anton; contributions by G. Vlastos, A. P. D. Mourelatos, R. G. Turnbull, and I. Mueller. Delmar, N.Y.: Caravan Books, 1981. Pp. xvi, 127.

Chennakesavan, Sarasvati., *Concept of Mind in Indian Philosophy.* Delhi-Varanasi-Patna: Motilal Banarsidass, 2nd ed. 1980; 1st ed. 1960. Pp. xvi, 177. Rs.55.

Chennakesavan, Sarasvati., *A Critical Study of Hinduism.* Delhi-Varanasi-Patna: Motilal Banarsidass, 2nd ed. 1980; 1st ed. 1974. Pp. xvi, 159. Rs. 40.

Dallmayr, Fred R., *Beyond Dogma and Despair; Toward a Critical Phenomenology of Politics.* Notre Dame and London: University of Notre Dame Press, 1981. Pp. x, 358. $19.95.

Garfinkel, A., *Forms of Explanation: Rethinking the Questions in Social Theory.* New Haven and London: Yale University Press, 1981. Pp. xi, 186. $16.00.

Lafrancé, Yvon., *La Théorie Platonicienne de la Doxa.* Montreal and Paris: Bellarmin-Les Belles Lettres, 1981. Pp. 475.

Lebeuf, Roger J. A., *Cosmic Presence: A Dynamic Vision of Life.* Montreal: Les Editions Bellarmin, 1980. Pp. 557.

Mishra, Sabhajit, *The Anwished Freedom: A Study in Sartre's Philosophy of Subjectivity and Human Freedom.* Delhi: GDK Publications, 1979. Pp. xviii, 184. Rs.45.

Sexist Language: A Modern Philosophical Analysis. Edited by Mary Vetterling-Braggin. Totowa, N.J.: Littlefield, Adams & Co., 1981. Pp. 329. $15.00, cloth; $7.95, paper.

Michaels, Claire F. and Claudia Carello, *Direct Perception.* Englewood Cliffs, N.J.: Prentice-Hall, Inc., 1981. Pp. viii, 200. $18.00.

Christensen, Ronald, *Entropy Minimax Sourcebook. Vol. I: General Description.* Lincoln, Mass.: Entropy, Ltd., 1981. Pp. xx, 692. $39.50.

Delius, Harold, *Self-Awareness: A Semantical Inquiry.* Munich: C. H. Beck, 1981. Pp. xii, 276. D.M. 148.--.

Friedman, James Michael, *Dancer and Other Aesthetic Objects.* San Francisco: Balletmonographs, 1980. Pp. xii, 144.

Kamm, Peter, *Paul Häberlin: Leben und Werk.* Band II Die Meisterzeit (1922-1960). Zürich: Ott Verlag AG, 1981. Pp. 720. D.M. 68.--.

Levinson, Henry Samuel, *The Religious Investigations of William James.* Studies in Religion Series. Chapel Hill, N.C.: University of North Carolina Press, 1981. Pp. xii, 312. $24.00.

Loscerbo, John, *Being and Technology: A Study in the Philosophy of Martin Heidegger.* Phaenomenologica Series. The Hague, Boston, London: Martinus Nijhoff Publishers, 1981. Pp. xii, 286. Dfl. 95.00. $47.50.

Nalimov, V. V., *Faces of Science.* Edited by Robert G. Colodny. Philadelphia: Isi Press, 1981. Pp. xvi, 298. $22.50.

Nebreda, Jesús J., *La fenomenología del lenguaje de Maurice Merleau-Ponty: Prolegómenos para una ontología diacrítica.* Serie I: Estudios. Madrid: Universidad Pontificia Comillas, 1981. Pp. 254. Ptas. 600.

Neville, Robert C., *Reconsruction of Thinking.* Axiology of Thinking Series. Albany, N.Y.: State of New York Press, 1981. Pp. xii, 350. $23.50.

Porter, Dale H., *The Emergence of the Past: A Theory of Historical Explanation.* Chicago and London: University of Chicago Press, 1981. Pp. x, 206. $19.00, paper.

Quine, W. V., *Theories and Things.* Cambridge, Mass., and London: Harvard University Press, 1981. Pp. viii, 220. $12.50.

Schleiermacher, Friedrich D. E., *On the Glaubenslehre: Two Letters to Dr. Lucke.* Trans. by James Duke and Francis Fiorenza. American Academy of Religion Text and Translations Series, Chico, California: Scholars Press, 1981. Pp. x, 136.

Scruton, Roger, *From Descartes to Wittgenstein: A Short History of Modern Philosophy.* London, Boston, and Henley: Routledge & Kegan Paul, 1981. Pp. vi, 298. $18.50.

Van de Vate, Dwight, Jr., *Romantic Love: A Philosophical Inquiry.* University Park and London: Penn State Press, 1981. Pp. vi, 150. $15.75.

Wolz, Henry G., *Plato and Heidegger: In Search of Selfhood.* London and Toronto: Bucknell University Press, 1981. Pp. 312. $24.50.

Philosophical Problems in Psychology. Edited by Neil Boulton. Contributions by: M. A. Boden, N. Bolton, J. M. Heaton, and others. Psychology in Progress Series. New York: Methuen, Inc., 1979. Pp. xiv, 207. $22.00, cloth; $11.95, paper.

Wittgenstein: To Follow a Rule. Edited by Steven H. Holtzman and Christopher M. Leich. Contributions by: G. Baker, S. Blackburn, G. Evans, and others. International Library of Philosophy Series. London, Boston, and Henley: Routledge & Kegan Paul, 1981. Pp. xiii, 250. $25.00.

Encyclopedia of Indian Philosophies: Advaita Vedanta up to Samkara and His Pupils. Edited by Karl H. Potter. Princeton: Princeton University Press, 1981. Pp. x, 635. $45.00.

Business in the New South: A Historical Perspective. Edited by Fred Bateman; contributions by S. L. Engerman, T. Weiss, G. Wright, and others. Sewanee, Tenn.: The University of the South, 1981. Pp. vi, 158.

Elder, Crawford, *Appropriating Hegel.* Scots Philosophical Monographs Number Three. Aberdeen: Aberdeen University Press, 1981. Pp. xx, 65. £5.00.

Tiles, J. E., *Things that Happen.* Scots Philosophical Monographs Number One. Aberdeen: Aberdeen University Press, 1981. Pp. xv, 116. £5.00.

Rescher, Nicholas, *Induction: An Essay on the Justification of Inductive Reasoning.* Pittsburgh: University of Pittsburgh Press, 1981. Pp. 225. $34.95.

Odobleja Between Ampère and Wiener. Bucharest: Editura Academiei Republicii Socialiste Romania, 1981. Pp. 204.

VOL. XLII MARCH 1982 NO. 3

PHILOSOPHY
AND
PHENOMENOLOGICAL
RESEARCH

A Quarterly Journal

Published for the

INTERNATIONAL PHENOMENOLOGICAL SOCIETY

by

BROWN UNIVERSITY

This journal is the official organ of the International Phenomenological Society. It publishes descriptive, analytical, critical, and historical articles representing the major contemporary trends in philosophy. In addition to the phenomenological research, PPR publishes studies in a wide range of areas including ethics, logic, history of philosophy, metaphysics, and theory of knowledge, as well as applied ethics and the philosophies of art, history, language, mind, religion, and science.

An abstract not exceeding 250 words and two nonreturnable copies of any manuscript submitted for publication are required. The original, ribbon copy will be required if the article is accepted, but it need not be submitted in the first instance. Double spacing should be used throughout, including quotations and footnotes. Footnotes should be numbered consecutively and collected at the end, beginning a new page.

The annual subscription rate for libraries and institutions is $15.00 (foreign $18.00 postpaid); subscriptions for individuals are $12.00 annually (foreign $13.00 postpaid). The rate for single copies of current or available back issues is $3.75 (double issue, $7.50) and $3.00 (double issue, $6.00), respectively. There is an additional charge for postage and handling on all back issues.

Address all communications and payments to *Philosophy and Phenomenological Research*, Box 1947, Brown University, Providence, Rhode Island 02912. The journal office should be notified of any change of address at least six weeks before the next issue is scheduled to appear. A list of the past contents with available back numbers will be sent upon request. For out-of-print volumes write to Kraus-Thomson Organization Ltd., Route 100, Millwood, New York 10546. For microfiche copies write to Johnson Associates, P.O. Box 1017, Greenwich, Connecticut 06830; and for microfilm copies write to University Microfilms International, 300 North Zeeb Road, Ann Arbor, Michigan 48106.

Published quarterly by Brown University
Printed by Niagara Printing Corporation, Niagara Falls, New York

CONTENTS

I. ARTICLES
A Causal Analysis of Seeing by MICHAEL TYE 311
The Phenomenology of Karol Wojtyła: On the Problem of the Phenomenological Foundation of Anthropology by HANS KÖCHLER 326
Erwin Straus and Alfred Schutz by MAURICE NATANSON .. 335
Frege's 'Objects' and 'Concepts': Revolutionary or Reactionary? by B. C. BIRCHALL 343
The Phenomenon of "the Look" by GEORGE J. STACK and ROBERT W. PLANT 359
The Originality of Hume's Theory of Obligation by HENRY DAVID AIKEN 374
Persons and Morality by E. M. ADAMS 384
Aquinas on God's Omnipresence and Timelessness by RICHARD R. LACROIX 391
Speechless Brutes by JOHN HEIL 400
Hume's Missing Shade of Blue by JOHN MORREALL 407
The Function of Fiction by YNHUI PARK 416
Context Dependent Knowledge by ROBERT ACKERMANN .. 425

II. DISCUSSIONS
The Limitations of Sense Experience by GERALD STANDLEY 434
Seeing Our Own Faces: A Paradigm for Indirect Realism by ROBERT OAKES 442
Evolutionary Epistemology Is Self-Referentially Inconsistent by CARL R. KORDIG 449

III. REVIEWS
Marie-Luise Schubert Kalsi's *Alexius Meinong: On Objects of Higher Order and Husserl's Phenomenology* by QUENTIN SMITH 451
R. M. Martin's *Semiotics and Linguistic Structure* by FREDERIC B. FITCH 453
H. P. Rickman's *Wilhelm Dilthey: Pioneer of the Human Studies* by ELŻBIETA PACZKOWSKA-ŁAGOWSKA 454

IV. RECENT PUBLICATIONS 459

A CAUSAL ANALYSIS OF SEEING*

Causal theorists have advanced a number of plausible arguments in support of the view that a person cannot see a material object unless there is a causal connection linking the object to his sensory state.[1] My purpose here is not to review or to defend directly these arguments but rather to produce an acceptable analysis of statements of the form 'Person *P* sees material object *x*' which is consistent with the causal view. In section I, I discuss some of the problems which are faced by the more obvious versions of such an analysis. Then, in section II, I propose a version which seems to me to cover the cases we want it to cover while excluding the cases which should be excluded.

I

The simplest causal analysis of '*P* sees *x*' is one which makes the causal connection between *x* and *P*'s visual experience not only necessary but also sufficient for *P* to see *x*. Initially, then, we might offer the following definition:

(D1) *P* sees *x* = df *x* causes P to have some visual experience.

So stated, (D1) is not wedded to any particular analysis of the concept of visual experience: whether a sense-datum analysis should be preferred to, say, the adverbial theory of Sellars and others is left open.[2] Later in the paper I shall have something to say about this matter. For now let us ignore it.

There are two obvious problems with (D1). First, it overlooks the fact that events and not material objects stand in causal relations.

---

* I am grateful to Harold Brown for his comments on an earlier version of this paper.

[1] See e.g., H. P. Grice, "The Causal Theory of Perception," *Proc. Aristotelian Society*, supp. vol. 35 (1961), pp. 121-68; also Frank Jackson, *Perception* (Cambridge: Cambridge University Press, 1977), pp. 97-99; Richard J. Hall, "Seeing and Naming," *Syntheses*, 35 (1977), pp. 381-93.

[2] For an account of the sense-datum analysis, see, e.g., H. H. Price, *Perception* (London: Metheun, 1954); also Frank Jackson, ibid. The adverbial theory is developed by Wilfrid Sellars in, e.g., "Empiricism and the Philosophy of Mind," in *Science, Perception, and Reality* (London: Routledge and Kegan Paul, 1963), pp. 127-96; see also R. M. Chisholm, *Perceiving: A Philosophical Study* (Ithaca, N.Y.: Cornell University Press, 1957).

Secondly, it lets in a number of unwanted material objects as objects of seeing. For example, it has the consequence that the source of illumination, the eyes, and the optic nerve are all typically seen in ordinary cases of visual perception, since these objects are all normally included in the causal processes by which persons see.

The first problem is a minor one. It can be overcome simply by replacing 'x' in the *definiens* by 'some event involving x'. The second problem is not so easy to deal with. H. H. Price has argued that a distinction between standing and differential causal conditions is relevant here.[3] Let us see whether this is so. According to Price, a standing condition is any material object in the absence of which none of the sense-data (of a given sense) can come into being. A differential condition, however, is any material object, the existence of which is necessary for some but not all the sense data (of a given sense).[4] Applying this distinction (and extrapolating away from Price's sense-datum analysis of visual experience), we can revise (D1) so it becomes:

(D2) P sees x = df (i) x is a differential condition, and (ii) some event involving x causes P to have a visual experience.

(D2) succeeds in excluding some of the material objects we want it to exclude. Take, for example, the optic nerve. This object is a standing condition. Hence, it cannot fit (D2)'s *definiens*. Unfortunately, this conclusion goes too far. For what we want is a definition which conforms to the fact that persons do not normally see their own optic nerves, and not a definition which entails that persons could not conceivably see them. Autocerebroscopes may be things of the future, but they are not impossible.[5]

Another objection to (D2) is that it is still much too broad. If, for example, a faulty bomb falls off a moving lorry, and I later see the bomb lying on the ground, (D2) has the consequence that I thereby see the lorry, since this object is a differential condition which plays a causal role in the production of my visual experience of a bomb.

How, then, is the causal theorist to get rid of the unwanted objects of seeing? One way of proceeding is to introduce some of the

[3] H. H. Price, ibid., p. 70.

[4] I assume here for ease of exposition that standing and differential conditions are always material objects. This may be a little oversimplified, since Price seems to imply that events are sometimes standing or differential conditions too (see ibid., p. 70). Nothing much hinges on this however: the criticisms which follow can easily be extended to attempts to revise (D1) using the broader account of Price's conditions.

[5] Frank Jackson makes this objection, op. cit., p. 168.

well-established physical and physiological facts of vision into the analysis of '*P* sees *x*'. Taking this approach, we might revise (D1) along the following lines:

(D3) *P* sees *x* = df *x* reflects light rays into *P*'s visual receptors, thereby stimulating *P*'s optic nerve and producing in *P* some visual experience.[6]

Clearly (D3) excludes the problem cases which undermine (D1) and (D2). But it is, I think, too strong. For it entails that there *could* not be persons who see material objects at times at which the objects are not reflecting light rays into their eyes. Perhaps there are no such persons; perhaps there never will be.[7] Still, it seems to me, there is no logical contradiction in supposing there *could* be. Fred Dretske has illustrated this point by the following case:

> A person, standing behind a massive wall, claims to be able to see everything on the far side. He dutifully recites the appearance and behaviour of every item; he never fails . . . despite our manipulation and alteration of the objects he purports to see. He does not detect anything which depends on his ability to hear, feel, or smell. When he turns away, or closes his eyes, he ceases to 'see'. Elaborate checks reveal no transmission of light from the objects to him. Does he see what he claims to see? How could one deny it? By insisting that he is imagining or somehow being supplied with images which accurately represent the appearance and behaviour of the objects on the other side of the wall? But why does this cease when he turns away or closes his eyes? Is it some miraculous sixth sense? But he only detects those things whose detectability is associated with our sense of sight. He cannot 'read other people's minds' or 'see into the future' . . . I find nothing logically incoherent about saying that the man somehow sees the objects on the far side of the wall, but that our investigations have so far not revealed how he sees them.[8]

As Dretske later notes, although this case is incompatible with the specific causal analysis expressed in the definition (D3), it certainly is not incompatible with every causal analysis. For without *some* causal connection between the objects on the far side of the wall and the man's eyes, the man's phenomenal accuracy in describing the objects

---

[6]R. M. Chisholm takes this line, op. cit., pp. 142-51. Although Chisholm's final definition is much more complicated than (D3), it is still vulnerable to the objection which ensues.

[7]There is room for argument even here. Consider the case of a man who is viewing a perfectly black disc against a white background. The disc reflects no light rays. Does the man see it? Intuitively, I think he does.

[8]Fred Dretske, *Seeing and Knowing* (London: Routledge and Kegan Paul, 1966), pp. 50-51.

would be entirely inexplicable.[9]

I want now to examine two further analyses which attempt to remedy the deficiencies of (D1) and (D2) without introducing scientific facts. Both of the analyses supplement the basic causal condition with another noncausal requirement.

Adding the condition that the visual experience must closely resemble the seen object is perhaps the most obvious way to try to correct (D1) or (D2). On this analysis, we have some such definition as

(D4) *P* sees *x* = df Some event involving *x* causes *P* to have a visual experience which closely resembles *x*.

However, (D4) is too restrictive. There are plenty of cases of seeing in which there is little or no resemblance between the seen object and the visual experience it gives rise to. Take, for example, seeing a ship on the horizon or seeing a painting through thick irregular glass. (D4) is also not restrictive enough. If I have two identical telephones in my home on separate lines, and the sound of one of them ringing causes me to mistakenly pick up the other then, according to (D4), in seeing the telephone I answer, I am also seeing the one which is ringing (even if it happens to be in another room).

An alternative way of supplementing the causal condition is by adding a 'satisfaction' requirement. Let us say that an object *x* *satisfies* a definite description 'the *F*' if, and only if, *x* is the one and only *F*. This permits us to frame the following definition:

(D5) *P* sees *x* = df Some event involving *x* causes *P* to have a visual experience which, in turn, causes *P* to believe that the so-and-so has some property, where *x* satisfies 'the so-and-so'.

But (D5) is too weak. To see this, suppose that I am standing some way from a robot called 'Tim'. Suppose further that I am looking in Tim's direction, and that I have a visual experience which causes me to believe that the robot located in front of me is stationary. If, unknown to me, a mirror located between myself and Tim is reflecting Tim's fellow robot, Tom, who is positioned some way to my right, it seems clear that I see Tom and *not* Tim. Unfortunately, if Tim caused Tom to take up his position facing the mirror by emitting some sort of signal which Tom followed, then (D5) has the consequence that I see Tim despite the fact that he is concealed by the mirror. For Tim is a causal factor in the production of my visual ex-

[9] For some comments on the nature of causation which may be applied to this case (and which also permit the causal theory of seeing to handle the sort of case described in footnote 7), see below, p. 324.

perience, and Tim satisfies the definite description 'the robot located in front of me'.[10]

The sorts of problems which confront (D5) and the other analyses outlined above have led a number of philosophers to deny that causality has any place at all in our understanding of the ordinary concept of seeing a material object.[11] I reject this response for three reasons. First, it is extremely difficult to construct a satisfactory theory which eschews talk of causal connections. Secondly, as I remarked earlier, the view that causality is an essential component in seeing a material object has the support of a number of plausible arguments. Finally, it seems to me that an adequate causal analysis *can* be constructed. In the next section, I defend this last comment by setting out a causal theory which is, I believe, consistent with a very broad spectrum of examples.

II

I want to begin by returning to the question: How is the concept of visual experience which causal theorists appeal to in their definitions of seeing to be analyzed? My reason for taking up this question will surface shortly.

Traditionally, the most popular analysis of visual experience has been the sense-datum theory. According to this theory, having a visual experience amounts to standing in a relation of direct visual awareness to a special immaterial entity called a "sense-datum." Then sense-datum is required, so it is argued, in order to explain the facts of hallucination and illusion: since a person can have a visual sensation of an *F, G* object even when there is no real *F, G* object in his general vicinity, it is inferred that he is related, through his experience, to an *F, G* sense-datum.

The most developed alternative to the sense-datum theory is the adverbial analysis. According to this view, having a visual experience involves undergoing an act of sensing for which there is *no* object, either sensory or material. This position is arrived at by the following

[10] It might be argued that we can overcome this difficulty by replacing the description 'the so-and-so' in both its occurrences in (D5)'s *definiens* by the description 'the object which looks so-and-so to *P*'. But this does not help. If I am facing a long line of pine trees then I may very well see the twenth-fourth tree from the right, say, notwithstanding the fact that that particular tree does not uniquely fit any definite description of the form 'the object which looks so-and-so to me'.

[11] See e.g., Fred Dretske, op. cit.; see also Jaegwon Kim, "Perception and Reference without Causality," *Journal of Philosophy* 74 (1977), pp. 606-20.

grammatical transformations:

(1) *P* has a sensation of an *F, G* object

becomes

(2) *P* has an *F, G* sensation.

In (2) the terms 'F' and 'G' are held to be adjectives which modify the verbal noun 'sensation'. Upon conversion of the verbal noun into a verb, the adjectives become adverbs. Consequently, (2) can be rewritten as

(3) *P* senses *F*-ly and *G*-ly,

or, as it is sometimes put,

(4) *P* senses in an *F, G* manner.[12]

The appeals to grammatical analogies which support each of the above steps are, I assume, familiar. What is striking here is that the sense-datum has disappeared from the analysis. All that is left is an act of sensing with the modes *F*-ly and *G*-ly. It should be obvious that this view can account for the facts of hallucination and illusion. If, for example, I am correctly described as having a visual sensation of a brown, treelike object, then 'brown' and 'treelike' in this description are taken to function as adverbs which express modes of my sensing and not as adjectives which express properties of any object. Hence, my having the sensation does not require that there be a brown tree (or anything else for that matter) in my general vicinity. Since both the adverbial analysis and the sense-datum theory have been elaborated at length elsewhere, I shall not spell out the details any further. I mention the two positions now in order to be able to say something in response to the objection that even if some version of the causal analysis can be made to work for seeing *material* objects, still there are cases of seeing objects for which *no* version of the causal analysis can succeed, namely, cases in which the seen entities are after-images and the like, that is, objects which are components rather than causes of visual experiences.

Clearly, *if* a causal theorist accepts a sense-datum analysis of visual experience, he must grant this objection (assuming he is

[12]Sellars's version of the analysis involves some qualifications which I ignore here. The complexities which Sellars introduces are, I believe, necessary if the adverbial theory is to be able to deal with what has been called 'the many-property problem'. This problem arises in the context of sensations of two or more objects. For details of the problem, see Frank Jackson, "On the Adverbial Analysis of Visual Experience," *Metaphilosophy*, 6 (1975), pp. 127-35; For a Sellarsian response, see my "The Adverbial Theory: A Defense of Sellars against Jackson," *Metaphilosophy*, 6 (1975), pp. 136-43; also Wilfrid Sellars, "The Adverbial Theory of the Objects of Sensation," *Metaphilosophy*, 6 (1975), pp. 144-60.

prepared to accept that our awareness of after-images and suchlike is a kind of seeing). Given an adverbial analysis, however, no such concession is necessary, since after-images, star-like sense-data and other entities of their type simply do not exist. It seems to me, then, that there is some advantage to be gained in underpinning the causal theory with an adverbial approach to visual experience. There are, I might add, other advantages, too, ones which are independent of the causal theory. For example, on an adverbial analysis, puzzles about unsensed sense-data dissolve as do questions about whether two or more persons can experience numerically identical sense-data. In addition, there is, of course, the reward of ontological economy. For these reasons I find the adverbial analysis preferable to the sense-datum theory. However, in what follows, to simplify my presentation of a complex analysis, I shall speak *as if* there are sensa. Let me stress that this is merely a *façon de parler:* everything that I say *could* be said (at greater length) with the use of adverbial instead of sense-datum terminology.[13]

The major difficulty which we face in trying to produce a satisfactory causal definition is one of specifying the position in the causal chain which the *seen* object can occupy. Unless we are able to describe this position without resorting to scientific details of the sort which are used in (D3), the task of constructing such a definition is a hopeless one. Let us begin, then, by considering the following preliminary account:

(D6) P sees x = df (i) There is a causal chain of events C which ends with P's having an experience of a visual sensum S; (ii) within C some event involving P's eyes causally intervenes between some event involving x and P's experiencing S.[14]

[13] The terminology I adopt conforms as much as possible to our everyday talk of visual experiences. So, for example, I should rewrite the ordinary sentence 'Jones has a visual sensation of a red, round object to the left of a green, square one' as 'Jones visually experiences a red, round sensum to the left of a green, square one'; similarly, I should rewrite the sentence 'It looks to Jones as if there is a red, round object which is closer than any other object' as 'Of the sensa which Jones experiences, the red, round one is closest'. The term 'sensum' then, *as I use it,* is merely an abbreviation for the phrase 'object of visual sensation'. And just as our ordinary talk of the objects of sensation includes terms for distance away and relative position so my talk of sensa does likewise. (Incidentally, the occurrence of terms for spatial relations in sensory contexts presents difficulties for the adverbial analysis. For one way of handling these difficulties see Wilfrid Sellars, *Science and Metaphysics* (London: Routledge and Kegan Paul, 1968), pp. 1-30.

[14] I assume that an event e causally intervenes between events f and g if, and only if, f causes e and e causes g.

(D6) places some very general and *prima facie* reasonable constraints on the nature of the causal chain of events *C* and also derivately on the parts of *C* which are available to the seen object *x*. In consequence, (D6) provides us with a foundation upon which we can build, and furthermore it eliminates from normal everyday situations at least one of the unwanted objects of seeing which caused trouble earlier, namely *P*'s optic nerve. However, (D6) does not entail that *P* can *never* see his optic nerve. If, for example, at some future date autocerebroscopes are developed and I examine the appropriate region on my brain through one of these devices, then my optic nerve will transmit light rays to my eyes via the mirrors in the machine. Here, then, events involving my eyes will causally intervene between events involving my optic nerve and my visual experience. So, according to (D6), my optic nerve will be seen.

The immediate problem with (D6), of course, it that it is much too broad. What we need is some way of restricting its *definiens*, some way of narrowing further the portion of the causal chain which the seen object can enter. The intuition I propose to use in formulating the needed restriction may be brought out as follows. Typically, if the shape of the facing surface of a material object *x* is varied while *x* is seen, then the shape of the sensum which is visually experienced varies too, assuming everything else in the situation is left alone. Similarly, if the size of the facing surface of *x* is varied, then, in typical cases, there is a systematic variation in the size of the sensum, again assuming other factors remain untouched. The same comments apply *mutatis mutandis* to the distance away of *x*'s facing surface and also to its relative position. Sometimes the variations in the sensum's properties are of exactly the same type as the variations in the corresponding properties of the material surface. Suppose, for example, that I am seeing a statue in good light without there being anything interposed. If the facing surface of the statue is increased in size, the 'statuelike' sensum I experience becomes larger; if the facing surface of the statue diminishes in size, the sensum I experience becomes smaller. Similarly, if the whole statue is moved to the left, my sensum moves to the left; if the whole statue is moved to the right, my sensum does likewise. And, of course, matching changes also occur in the sensum's shape and distance as the shape and distance of the facing surface of the statue change.

In some cases, however, the situation is not so straightforward. If, for example, I am seeing a statue through distorting glass then although variations in the spatial properties of my sensum are systematically connected with variations in the corresponding properties of the facing surface of the statue, some of the former variations are not going to exactly match some of the latter.

It is also worth noticing that not all of the four spatial properties of sensa which normally enter into the above systematic variations need be exemplified by every sensum which is experienced in seeing. If, for example, a man is viewing a distant star in the night sky then, it seems to me, the tiny bright sensum he experiences has no shape. Thus here changes in the shape of the star do *not* result in changes in the shape of the sensum.

These reflections lead to the addition of a third clause to the *definiens* in (D6). To simplify the statement of this new clause, let us say that in any given case of seeing the *M*-properties of a material object *x* are those spatial properties of *x* which have counterparts in the spatial properties of the experienced visual sensum. So, for example, in the case of the man viewing a distant star, shape is *not* one of the star's *M*-properties. We can now frame the following definition:

(D7) *P* sees *x* = df (i) There is a causal chain of events *C* which ends with *P*'s having an experience of a visual sensum *S;* (ii) within *C* some event involving *P*'s eyes causally intervenes between some event involving *x* and *P*'s experiencing S; (iii) x's position in C is such that it is in principle possible to vary each *M*-property of *x* or some surface of *x* and thereby produce a systematic variation in the corresponding spatial property of *S* assuming other factors are left alone.[15]

Certain features of (D7) require brief comment: (1) The expression 'some surface of *x*' is used in the clause (iii) instead of 'the facing surface of *x*' in order to handle cases of seeing objects via mirrors. (2) On those occasions where the seen object is the surface of a material object, it is not true that the seen object has any surfaces.[16] Hence in these cases it is not true that the spatial properties of the experienced

---

[15] This definition is, in some respects, similar to one which Frank Jackson offers in *Perception,* p. 171. It also has points of contact with one of the definitions which R. M. Chisholm considers in *Perceiving: A Philosophical Study,* pp. 147-48. There are links, too, with certain aspects of the analysis of seeing which Alvin Goldman develops in his interesting paper "Perceptual Objects," *Synthese,* 35 (1977), pp. 257-84.

[16] I assume that the surface of a material object may itself be classified as a material object.

sensum vary with variations in the corresponding *M*-properties of some surface of the seen object (facing or otherwise). Rather what happens here is that the properties of the sensum vary with variations in the *M*-properties of the seen object itself. Clause (iii) is sensitive to this difficulty: it solves the problem by means of the disjunctive expression '*x* or some surface of *x*'. (3) Among the material properties which play a role in (iii) are distance away and relative position. I define the distance away of *x* to be *x*'s distance either from *P*'s eyes or from some mirrorlike surface involved in *C* which faces *P*'s eyes and produces *x*'s image. And I define *x*'s relative position in a similar manner. These disjunctive definitions are introduced so that the distance away and relative position of the seen object can *in principle* always be varied (even when the object is, for example, one of *P*'s eyes seen by *P* via a mirror). (4) I exclude color from the systematic variations referred to in (iii) primarily because I wish to sidestep the disagreement between those causal theorists who maintain that material objects lack color and those who are color objectivists.

It seems to me that (D7) accomodates the various cases of seeing we want it to accomodate. What of the cases which should be excluded?

Consider again the case of the faulty bomb. According to (D7), in seeing the bomb on the ground I do not thereby see the lorry from which it fell, since the spatial properties of the sensum I experience in the presence of the bomb do not systematically vary with variations in the corresponding *M*-properties of the lorry. Similar remarks apply to the case of the two identical telephones. Furthermore, it should be clear that (D7) yields the right result in normal perceptual situations for the source of illumination and the eyes. With respect to the former, the conditions laid down in the second part of clause (iii) are not met, since, for example, varying the distance away of the source of illumination and leaving other factors alone does not normally result in systematic changes in the distance away of the experienced sensum (unless the source itself is the seen object). Wtth respect to the latter, if cases involving mirror reflections of the viewer's eyes are put aside, the distance away and position *cannot* be varied, since for the remaining situations these *M*-properties are measured relative to the eyes themselves. Hence, this time, the conditions in the first part of the clause (iii) are not satisfied.

I come next to the case of the robots, Tim and Tom. A moment's reflection shows that (D7) covers this case, as it stands. But let us complicate the situation somewhat. As before, Tim is hidden behind the mirror and Tom is facing it so that I see Tom but not Tim. Also, as before, Tim is emitting a signal which has caused Tom to take up his position in front of the mirror. The difference between the new situation and the old is that Tom has now been programmed to do two things. First, he is to change his position relative to the mirror as Tim changes his position relative to me. Secondly, he is to exactly copy changes in Tim's shape, size, and distance from me. Thus, if Tim moves to my left, Tom moves to the mirror's left; if Tim doubles in size, Tom doubles in size; and so on. In this situation, I am caused to have an experience of a 'robotlike' sensum by events involving Tim and Tom. Moreover, the spatial properties of the sensum systematically vary with variations in the *M*-properties of either twin. If, for example, Tom's height is increased while Tim's height is left alone, my robotlike sensum becomes taller. And if Tim's height is increased, Tom's automatically follows suit. So again I have an experience of a taller sensum. Applying (D7), then, it follows that I not only see Tom but also Tim.

Other similar difficulties are not hard to construct. Take, for example, this case. Suppose that the robot Tim has been destroyed, and that I am seeing Tom through a plain sheet of glass without there being any intervening mirrors. Suppose moreover that Tom has now been programmed to systematically change his *M*-properties as the corresponding *M*-properties of the glass change. Then the spatial properties of my robotlike sensum systematically vary with the variations in the *M*-properties of both the glass and Tom. Hence, according to (D7), in addition to seeing Tom I also see the sheet of glass. And this, of course, will be false, if the glass is perfectly transparent.

If we are to overcome these difficulties we must find some way of restricting (D7) still further. It seems to me that problems of the above sort arise because the final clause in (D7) ends with the phrase 'assuming other factors are left alone'. As a result, (D7) has to count as seen *all* objects (outside the viewer's body) which, when varied with respect to their *M*-properties but otherwise left alone, give rise to systematic variations in the spatial properties of the experienced sensum, *whether or not* these objects, in varying their *M*-properties, play causal roles which differ significantly from their original roles in producing the sensum.[17] The approach I favor, then, is to modify clause (iii) of (D7) in such a way that certain factors are held fixed. Here is

[17]This (and subsequent) talk of the causal roles of material objects is adopted for reasons of convenience. Of course, I do not mean to suggest that material objects directly stand in causal relations.

my proposal:

(D8) *P* sees *x* = df (i) There is a causal chain of events *C* which ends with *P*'s having an experience of a visual sensum *S*; (ii) within *C* some event involving *P*'s eyes causally intervenes between some event involving *x* and *P*'s experiencing *S*; (iii) *x*'s position in *C* is such that it is in principle possible to vary each *M*-property of *x* or some surface of *x* and thereby produce a systematic variation in the corresponding spatial property of *S*, assuming all other factors are either (a) held fixed, if leaving them alone would result in there being significant differences between the way in which *x* brings about *S* in *C* originally and the way in which *x* brings about *S* as the *M*-properties of *x* or some surface of *x* are varied, or (b) left alone, if leaving them alone would not have that result.[18]

With respect to the final Tim and Tom case, (D8) gives us the desired results. Let me explain. Originally, Tim's role in producing my experience is merely one of causing Tom to take up his position in front of the mirror. But as Tim's *M*-properties are systematically varied, Tim's causal role becomes much more complicated in virtue of his relationship to Tom taking on the new programmed connections which transmit changes in *M*-properties from the former robot to the latter. Now clearly if we were to *hold fixed* the various programmed factors which are responsible for Tim's changing his causal relationship to Tom in this way (while leaving other factors alone), the spatial properties of my robotlike sensum would not systematically vary as Tim's *M*-properties are varied. Hence, (D8) entails that I do not see Tim. But I do see Tom, since the manner in which Tom brings about my visual experience remains substantially the same whether or not his *M*-properties are varied. With respect to the second case involving Tom and the sheet of glass, (D8) entails that I see the former but not the latter (assuming it is perfectly transparent) for similar reasons.

It seems to me that (D8) fits a very wide variety of cases. There are, however, two remaining problems which I wish to discuss. First, consider this apparent counterexample to (D8). A man, upon waking one morning, believes that he has been endowed overnight with the ability to see certain objects which are located in a house some hundreds of miles away. Later that day, he decides to test his belief, and

[18] There may be practical problems involved in holding fixed some factors. These need not bother us, however, so long as this procedure is in principle possible.

he determines (with the help of some assistants) that when he closes his eyes and clears his mind of extraneous thoughts, he undergoes visual experiences which systematically vary in their properties as the corresponding properties of the relevant objects are varied. Since the man's eyes are closed, it seems *extremely* unlikely that they play any role in the production of his experiences. So, assuming the case is logically coherent, (D8) entails via clause (ii) that the man does not really see the objects he believes he sees.

It is possible to defend (D8) here by arguing that this conclusion should be accepted. Adopting such a defense, we could concede that cases of clairvoyance are no doubt very *like* cases of seeing, but we could insist that if the man's eyes are not causal factors in bringing about his experiences then there is in fact no *genuine* seeing going on.[19]

Those who find this line of argument counter-intuitive (and, I confess, it leaves me with some qualms) may simply delete clause (ii) from (D8). Admittedly that clause places a *prima facie* plausible constraint upon seeing. But we are not compelled to retain it in our definition. Indeed, what the above case shows, it might be suggested, is that certain conditions involving the eyes which accompany all normal everyday cases of seeing have been mistaken in the second clause of (D8) for conditions which are essential to all *possible* cases of seeing. (Incidentally, the removal of the clause does not weaken (D8) elsewhere. For example, without (ii), (D8) still eliminates the viewer's optic nerve as an object of seeing in ordinary circumstances via clause (iii).[20]).

[19] According to this view, then, the salient difference between the above case and the one mentioned earlier of the man who is able to see objects on the far side of an enormous wall is that in the latter the man's eyes are open and causally connected with the appropriate objects.

[20] It is perhaps worth noting that the following addition to the above case of clairvoyance does not present any difficulty for (D8), once clause (ii) is removed; suppose the man we have described later loses his eyes through some accident. Still he may retain his ability to see certain distant objects. Is the modified (D8)—specifically the first part of clause (iii)—consistent with this possibility? Yes. The earlier definitions of distance away and relative position entail that the seen objects cannot exemplify these spatial properties unless the viewer has eyes. So, in the case of the clairvoyant who *lacks* eyes, distance away and relative position are *not* M-properties *of* the objects he sees. Consequently, clause (iii) in (D8) does not demand that it is possible to vary these properties. (Another way of handling the case is to broaden the definitions of distance away and relative position by adding further disjuncts which apply only to viewers who lack eyes and which use the viewers' eye-sockets, say, as reference-points. Now distance away and relative position are reinstated as properties of the seen objects.)

The final problem I want to look at is due to Jaegwon Kim.[21] It appears to threaten not just the analysis expressed in (D8) but also *any* causal analysis of seeing. The problem goes as follows. Suppose an astronomer is viewing the night sky through a telescope, and he comes across an area of complete darkness surrounded by scattered light. Later he finds out that the dark patch he had been viewing was really a black hole. It seems plausible to say that he *saw* the black hole. Yet there was no transmission of light or anything else for that matter from the black hole to his eyes.

This difficulty is not peculiar to astronomical contexts. It seems to me that perfectly black objects which are not too small or too distant may be seen with the *naked* eye provided that they are located against light backgrounds.

The obvious response to the problem is to challenge the underlying assumption, namely that causal sequences require the transmission of some energy or force of one sort or another from cause events to effects. It seems to me that this mechanistic claim need not be accepted. Instead it can be argued that causal sequences are to analyzed in some other way, for example, counterfactually, so that the fact that nothing is physically transmitted from the perfectly black object to the viewer does not preclude the object's being causally involved in bringing about the viewer's experience.[22]

The conclusion I draw, then, is that the causal theorist can give a satisfactory account of the concept of seeing a material object despite the difficulties which plague the more straighforward causal analyses.[23]

MICHAEL TYE.

NORTHERN ILLINOIS UNIVERSITY.

[21] Alvin Goldman attributes this problem to Kim in his "Perceptual Objects," op. cit., p. 281.

[22] For a counterfactual analysis of causation, see D. Lewis, "Causation," *Journal of Philosophy,* 70 (1973), pp. 556-67; see also J. L. Mackie, *The Cement of the Universe* (Oxford: The Claredon Press, 1974), pp. 29-58. I might add that Goldman in his discussion of the problem, op. cit., pp. 281-83, rejects an exclusively counterfactual approach to the causal component in seeing in favor of an approach which is partially mechanistic. According to Goldman, since the black hole is responsible (in a counterfactual sense) for a *contrast* between the light transmitted from it (none) and the light transmitted from the surrounding regions (some), it may be said to cause the astronomer's experience. However this constrastive account, once it is coupled with the view that seeing necessarily has a causal component, is incompatible with Fred Dreske's case of the man who sees objects on the far side of a huge wall. Here the seen objects are not responsible for any *contrast* in

light transmission since neither they nor their immediate environment transmit any light at all to the man's eyes. So if Dretske's case is coherent, then it appears that Goldman's alternative is open to objection.

[23] In closing, I want to add two further points. The first of these pertains to the status of my final definition. I hold that the *definiens* provides an analysis of the *definiendum* in the sense of analysis which would be at play were I to claim that 'justified true belief' provides an analysis of 'knowledge'. That is to say, I take it to be *necessary* and knowable *a priori* that something is an instance of seeing a material object if, and only if, it meets the conditions laid out in the final *definiens*. I do not hold that the *definiendum* and the *definiens* are exactly synonymous *if* substitutability *salva veritate* in all belief contexts is used as the criterion of exact synonymity, since I deny that terms expressing philosophical analyses are substitutable in this manner for the terms which they analyze. After all, even if 'justified true belief' *did* give a satisfactory analysis of 'knowledge', surely some people could still believe that knowledge is knowledge without believing that knowledge is justified true belief.

Secondly, it may be objected that the project of this paper is misconceived, since the Kripke-Putnam account of natural kind terms shows that the expression 'seeing' has no *a priori* definition. My response here, in a few words, is that 'seeing' is *not* a natural kind term but rather a nominal kind one. Hence, it should be possible to construct by *a priori* reflection an adequate definition. For arguments which may be applied to the defense of this position as well as an elucidation of the difference between natural kind and nominal kind terms, see Colin McGinn, "Philosophical Materialism," *Synthese*, 44 (1980), pp. 175-82.

THE PHENOMENOLOGY OF KAROL WOJTYŁA: ON THE PROBLEM OF THE PHENOMENOLOGICAL FOUNDATION OF ANTHROPOLOGY

Human sciences have become the most promising field of application for the phenomenological method. In the sciences concerned with the nature of man, the phenomenological method was able—being the articulation of immediate experience—to contribute substantially to the development of the hermeneutical instrumentarium necessary in order to give a sound methodical basis to a theory of mental contexts and structures that does not solely depend on the paradigm of "objectivistic" natural sciences. The necessity of such an instrument becomes, above all, apparent in a (philosophical) *anthropology* concentrated on evolving the specific human nature as distinct from other modes of being.

Wojtyła's anthropological point of departure[1] is founded—in line with a nonobjectivistic, genuine description of the nature of man—on the "experience lived through" *('Erlebnis')*, meaning the immediate experience of man, anteceding any—secondary—distinction between what man "does" and what "occurs" within man (the distinction between the categories of *agere* and *pati*).[2] "Experience lived through" as such constitutes the irreducible premise for human self-comprehension. Referring to it enables us to reach, according to Wojtyła, full comprehension of human subjectivity and human personality that may not, under any conditions, be objectified.[3] This virtually empirical-phenomenological basis, on which Wojtyła grounds his anthropology—in some distance from a "metaphysical"-objectivistic viewpoint—should help to articulate more adequately the nature of the acting man than it has been possible for the traditional nonphenomenological anthropology. Wojtyła distinguishes between a

---

[1] Our interpretation is based mainly on the English translation of Wojtyła's book *Osoba i czyn (Polskie Towarzystwo Teologiczne.* Kraków, 1969), now published under the title *The Acting Person* (Analecta Husserliana, vol. X, Dordrecht-Boston, 1979), as well as on the papers "Subjectivity and the Irreducible in Man" (Analecta Husserliana, vol. VII, 1978, pp. 107-14) and "Participation or Alienation?" (Analecta Husserliana, vol. VI, 1977, pp. 61-73).

[2] "Subjectivity and the Irreducible in Man," p. 110.

[3] Cp. op. cit., p. 112.

comprehension of man in the cosmological sense and an anthropological conception, understanding man primarily as subject. The first (traditional) conception would understand man as object in a (surrounding) world and thereby reduce, principally, the specific human nature to the level of the world; the second conception—as represented by Wojtyła himself—is understood as being an articulation of the principal irreducibility of human nature that, being "subjectivity," cannot be reduced to the level of mere objects of the surrounding world.[4] Thereby Wojtyła formulates a contradiction to the traditional Aristotelian definition of the nature of man as being a ζῷον νοητικον. For Wojtyła the aspect of consciousness and of its specific subjectivity—that cannot be reduced to empirical objects—constitutes the essential property of man.

In this sense we may understand Wojtyła's conception as being phenomenologically founded in its general structure: immediate experience, as it manifests itself, is taken as the only basis (and point of departure) of any reflexion on the genuine nature of man. "Experience lived through" is the phenomenal basis, so to speak, for any description of the human being. The fact that "experience," in its immediateness, cannot be traced back to something outside the subjective, does not, according to Wojtyła, imply that experience would be inaccessible to cognition in the formal-theoretical sense.[5] The adequate form of cognition, therefore, is based on the *phenomenological method* that must not remain on the level of mere description, but should advance to the comprehension of the fundamental structure of the contents of experience. The phenomenological method, therefore (according to Wojtyła), serves the philosophical aim of "trans-phenomenological cognition,"[6] as this method reveals the essential structures of the subjectivity of man.

This implies, according to Wojtyła, that the ultimate truth about man cannot be found when remaining within the limits of the (objectivistic) metaphysical level.[7] A personalistic conception, emphasizing the aspect of consciousness, does not—in this context—constitute any contradiction to the cosmological conception of man but, on the contrary, is complementary to it.[8] With this position of

[4] Op. cit., pp. 108-109.
[5] Op. cit., p. 113.
[6] Ibid.
[7] Op. cit., p. 114.
[8] Op. cit., p. 111.

"complementarity" the seeming antinomy between subjectivism and objectivism may be overcome in a sense, as Wojtyła thinks.[9] He holds that it was precisely the approach of phenomenology that has overcome this antinomy by performing an analysis of consciousness after the act of the εποχή.[10]

This methodical examination of consciousness as such ("experience lived through") does not, however, lead to an ontological scheme according to which consciousness alone would be said to own the quality of real being, and any "validity as such" would have to be ascribed to this "pure consciousness."[11] Wojtyła's examination of consciousness—being not "reducible" in its specific quality—is determined by the methodical necessity of a genuine access to the nature of man; it does not, however, lead towards an "idealism" in the ontological sense. This again means that Wojtyła, in his theory of the human being—that may be understood as phenomenology of the relation between consciousness and the dynamism of the acting person[12]—departs from a conception of consciousness that is essentially different from, for example, Husserl's phenomenology. Whereas Husserl founded "empirical" consciousness on a "pure" consciousness that, in the end, would constitute the dimension of being-real as such[13] (thus also constituting the reality of the world of objects), Wojtyła arrives, by modification of the concept of *intentionality,*[14] at a rather "realistic" position: he holds that consciousness be not of an intentional nature, but that it rather consists of a mirroring of the processes occurring within the acting person.[15] An act of consciousness therefore may not be characterized by an "active" directedness towards a realm of objects. Intentionality rather, in its strict sense, appears to be, as to his view, characteristic of the acts of *"knowledge"*—knowledge understood hereby as an active com-

---

[9]Cp. op. cit., pp. 107-108.

[10]Ibid.

[11]Compare the description of this problem by the author: *Die Subjekt-Objekt-Dialektik in der transzendentalen Phänomenologie.* Meisenheim a.G. 1974.

[12]This corresponds to the conception of his work "The Acting Person".

[13]Cp. especially *Husserliana,* vol. VIII (The Hague, 1959), pp. 281ff, pp. 480ff.

[14]Regarding Wojtyła's conception of the intentional act, cp. his paper: "The Intentional Act and the Human Act, that is, Act and Experience," (Analecta Husserliana, vol. V, pp. 269ff), and the paper of the author: "The Dialectical Conception of Self-Determination," (Analecta Husserliana, vol. VI, 1977, pp. 75-80).

[15]Cp. *The Acting Person,* pp. 31-32.

prehension of objective reality and in this sense also of a more genuine character than consciousness. Knowledge, being directed towards an object, is performing a process of "objectivation" as it would not be possible in (passive) *"consciousness"*. As distinct from the "intentional" function of knowledge Wojtyła ascribes to consciousness a reflexive function. The mirroring by the consciousness will in a sense "subjectivate" the world of the acting man.[16] Turning back towards his own self in this way, the subject only constitutes itself *as* subject. Self-reflexion thus is the fundamental condition for the self-realization of the human being also on the ethical level.[17] According to Wojtyła, however, consciousness must not be taken as something absolute, for it does not own—as merely being for itself—the character of reality. In this regard Wojtyła seems to follow the tradition of "realistic" phenomenology as it has been conceived, for example, by Roman Ingarden and Max Scheler.[18] (Transcendental phenomenology as it has been developed by Edmund Husserl since his 'Ideen' may scarcely be seen as being compatible with Wojtyła's conception emphasizing the passivity of consciousness.) Also the concept of "knowledge" that Wojtyła comprehends as being distinct from "consciousness," is to be understood—because it includes the notion of a dynamic intentionality directed towards the object—as following the tradition of a realistic (though not objectistivic) phenomenology which, in turn, is not compatible with the concept of "transcendentality," expressing the process of creating the object of perception, and relating its character of reality to the "pure" subject. Reflexion essentially determines, according to Wojtyła, the relation between person and action, reflexion understood as the one quality of consciousness that accompanies the intentional act directed towards the object, but that remains unintentional in its nature and is only represented indirectly ('ἐν παρέργῳ') in the act of thinking (here we may see an affinity to Franz Brentano's conception of "secondary consciousness").

In his phenomenological description Wojtyła differentiates, however, between *"action"* and *"activation"* (processes related to the

[16]Cp. op. cit., pp. 42-43.

[17]Cp. op. cit., pp. 48-49.

[18]Regarding Wojtyła's interpretation of Scheler—within the framework of Christian ethics—compare his book: *Ocena możliwości zbudowania etyki chrześijanskiej przy założeniach systemu Maksa Schelera* ('On the Possibility of Creating a Christian Ethics Based on the Assumptions of the System of Max Scheler'). Towarzystwo Naukowe KUL, Lublin, 1959.

"somatovegetative" level, that cannot become accessible to introspection.) This distinction corresponds to the differentiation between (reflexive) *subjectivity* and (pre-reflexive) *"subjectiveness."* Conscious acting of man (connected with an experience of "effecting" something) implies, according to Wojtyła, a free act of decision. Antecedent to the conscious act is, however, the *"potentiality"* of the human being. In this "potentiality" he differentiates between a "psychoemotive" and a "somatovegetative" level.[19] The pre-reflexive unity of "life" on the somatic level is the fundamental condition for the possibility of any kind of consciousness. The variety of potentialities of the individual human being is determined by this pre-reflexive dimension, and not by "consciousness" that is characterized by its dimension of passivity and thus is only originated at a later stage of the process of human self-realization: "Consciousness does not constitute the inner structure of the human dynamism itself."[20] This leads Wojtyła to the formulation of the concept of the *"unconscious"* ("subconsciousness") in his system of a personalistic anthropology. The unconscious, according to Wojtyła, establishes the inner continuity of the subject's flux of experiences (that is: its identity) and, at the same time, determines the subject's internal experience of time. The objectivation of this unconscious realm—which, though being prior to consciousness, does not represent, however, a higher level of values—is, as Wojtyła states, the main task of ethics. (The "somatovegetative" level Wojtyła asserts, nevertheless, to be principally inacessible to consciousness and thus inaccessible to objectivation, which means that this realm may not be subjected to ethical evaluation).

In his "phenomenology of action," as Wojtyła's personalistic conception has been characterized also,[21] the point of departure is the (immediate) phenomenal "situatedness" of man as it manifests itself in the context of the acting in the world. The experience of the real, i.e., effective character of the action represents for Wojtyła such a phenomenal datum. At the same time Wojtyła realizes that the integration of the person into the contextual framework of its acts may be possible only if the "objectivation" of one's own self (qua *"self-knowledge"*) is based on the "potentiality" of the human existence

---

[19] Cp. *The Acting Person,* pp. 90-91.

[20] Cp. op. cit., p. 93.

[21] Andrzej Półtwaski, *Ethical Action and Consciousness.* Philosophical and Psychiatric Perspectives (Analecta Husserliana, vol. VII, 1978, p. 142).

that antecedes any reflexive act. The coherence of *self-knowledge* and *consciousness* is, as to Wojtyła's view, the condition for *the equilibrium* of the "inner" life of the person.[22] (This corresponds to Wojtyła's general phenomenological differentiation between knowledge and consciousness.) This implies that self-reflexion cannot be a formal representation of the acts of consciousness in their specific structure, but must be viewed within the global context of the active self-realization of the person.

Against this background the general traits of a "phenomenological anthropology" may be defined as Wojtyła has worked them out in his philosophical writings.[23] The phenomenological method demands a rather "empirical" proceeding oriented on the facts of the concrete self-realization of the acting person. The "experience lived through" thus is to be accepted (as we have indicated already) as the point of departure for a genuine theory of the human being.[24] As the "given" in the sense of the φαινόμενον it is prior to the "metaphysical" distinction between subject and object (those categories being the modes of existence of the concrete world). The specific character of man as manifested in his personality becomes apparent by precisely this methodical procedure: the methodical emphasis on the "experience lived through" will not permit to comprehend man simply as an object among other objects of the empirical world. An analysis of the structures of this "experience" will lead rather to a comprehension of the human personality as a subjectivity that cannot be reduced to mere objects (i.e., objects of the empirically experienced world). "Personalism," in this context, means that it is not possible to define the fundamental structures of the human being by subsuming man under a universal "nature" in the cosmological sense. This nonobjectivistic approach implies, at the same time, that man, in his genuine mode of being, may not be reduced to the level of the "world." Thus the classical metaphysical systems characterizing the human being mainly as an animal endowed with some "additional" qualities (in line with the Aristotelian

---

[22] *The Acting Person*, p. 37.

[23] In addition to the works mentioned above we refer in our interpretation also to Wojtyła's paper, "The Personal Structure of Self-Determination" (Tommaso d'Aquino nel suo VII centenario—Congresso Internazionale, Roma—Napoli, 17-24 Aprile 1974). A further exposition of his anthropological system was announced by him under the title "Person-Subject and Community" (unpublished manuscript).

[24] Cp. "Subjectivity and the Irreducible in Man," pp. 110-11.

definition of the human being as *animal rationale)* have to be questioned. This understanding of the "irreducibility" of the human nature leads to an original comprehension of "subjectivity" as a mode of being which is based upon itself and thus guarantees freedom understood as personal self-determination.

All the same, Wojtyła's conception does not allow us (as we have been trying to demonstrate) to visualize consciousness as something absolute in the ontological sense. This means a continuation of the realistic tradition of phenomenology and, at the same time, renouncing the reification of an empirical and finite consciousness by hypostatizing it to a so-called "pure" consciousness which is understood then as fundamental dimension of reality (of being "real") (as it is expressed in Husserl's transcendental phenomenology). Transcendentality as the ontological focus of the "world-constitution" of the subject cannot be justified on the basis of a realistic point of departure from which Wojtyła starts out himself. The systematic relevance of the transcendental unity of the subject is replaced in his phenomenological system rather by the "potentiality" of the human being[25] that is prior—in the two dimensions described above—to the acts of consciousness (as their fundamental precondition). This means a substantial limitation of a purely "formal" rationality, which is not apt—because of its contingency as something that is coming into existence only after the original factors of acting have emerged from the core of the personality—to determine the inner structure of the various potentialities of the individual human being. As much as reflexion may be necessary to add an ethical dimension to the process of human self-realization, reflexion does not constitute the quality of being "real." Therefore Wojtyła holds the view that consciousness is of a merely passive character (following thereby the tradition of "classical" descriptive phenomenology, but contradicting, however, the phenomenology of "transcendental constitution"). Consciousness is, according to Wojtyła, a merely concomitant phenomenon, a "mirroring" of the intentional act which directs itself actively towards the object. Therefore—as we have elaborated above—the mode of intentionality may not be ascribed to consciousness itself; for intentionality is only the specific mode of immediate, object-directed "knowledge." This implies that a "transcendental reduction," restricting phenomenological description to phenomena of a "pure consciousness," is not introduced into

[25]Cp. *The Acting Person,* p. 91

the phenomenological system. For this would lead to a circle of self-reflexion, i.e., to consciousness as a self-contained unit (as it may be found in Husserl's idealism). The concept of intentionality thus would get the character of constituting "reality." With this emphasis on the "passivity" of consciousness (of reflexion) Wojtyła's phenomenology remains *method,* it does not constitute an ontological system. The reference to the "experience lived through" is, in this context, distinctly not an indication of a "subjectivistic" tendency; it only has to be understood as a methodical-empirical necessity. The "realistic" dimension of intentionality that becomes apparent in this phenomenological framework, guarantees for a "direction" towards and a perception of real objects that reaches beyond the immanency of the flux of our experiences—as intentionality is not understood anymore as constitution of a general system of ontological reference by constituting any mode of real being. Grounding subjectivity on the "pre-reflexive," on "potentiality," as Wojtyła terms it, means transcending a merely formal phenomenology of consciousness or reflexion. Wojtyła's "material" phenomenology does not accept a transcendental subjectivity as *ens a se* (in the sense of ontological idealism, i.e., as being isolated from the actual world). Human subjectivity is—regardless of its "irreducibility" to the realm of objects of the actual world (i.e., in the cosmological sense)—embedded in a concrete world by the dynamism of its "potentialities." Those "potential" structures exist not only in relation to a consciousness reflecting this dynamism—as was pretended to demonstrate by the idealistic trend of phenomenology because of its hypostatization of the concept of the "phenomenon."

The "irreducibility" of the subject (the person) may—if we accept the fact of this concrete relatedness to the world as explained above—be elucidated yet more clearly: it means the essential irreducibility of personal self-realization to constant factors of the world of objects, i.e., the world as described by the natural sciences. For Wojtyła the specific mode of hermeneutical comprehending of this "irreducible" aspect of man (as required therefore according to the methodology of the human sciences) is the phenomenological method. It is applied to the description of the specific structures of human subjectivity by analyzing human acting and the relation between person and action. In his anthropology based on the phenomenological method Wojtyła solely describes how man "appears," manifests himself in his actions. Subjectivity as it manifests itself in the acting of man, constitutes for Wojtyła a "definite reality."[26] (The special emphasis on this reality may, from a traditional "metaphysical" viewpoint, bear no relevance for anthropology, as Wojtyła explains.)[27] This reality is also characterized, according to Wojtyła, by the social dimension of the human existence, i.e., by the interhuman relations[28] that determine one's own personal self-realization.

As Wojtyła goes beyond the Aristotelian-scholastic conception of man—by emphasizing the "irreducibility" of the subject—and, at the same time, broadens it by his phenomenological method based on the "experience" *('Erlebnis')*—so he tries also—when claiming to formulate phenomenologically founded "transphenomenological cognition"[29]—to transcend phenomenology understood as a system of immanent structures of experience. His phenomenology arises from his effort to elucidate the real nature of man as a person, and he tries to describe the self-awareness and self-comprehension of the person in the process of concrete acting, keeping critical distance in the same time to the "metaphysical" tradition[30] and to an idealistic (subjectivistic) reification of consciousness as something absolute as well. Phenomenology, understood in this sense, is a philosophical method, determined in its structure by the specific realm it is dealing with (i.e., by the task of analyzing consciousness and concrete acting), it is not a metaphysical-transcendental system of "pure" consciousness.

HANS KÖCHLER.

UNIVERSITÄT INNSBRUCK.

---

[26] "Subjectivity and the Irreducible in Man," p. 113.

[27] Op. cit., p. 110.

[28] Cp. Wojtyła's paper "Participation or Alienation?", and the paper of the author "The Dialectical Conception of Self-Determination."

[29] "Subjectivity and the Irreducible in Man," p. 113.

[30] Cp. op. cit., pp. 114-15, where Wojtyła says that "the thinker who by philosophical methods seeks the ultimate truth about man does not limit himself to 'purely metaphysical ground' ".

ERWIN STRAUS AND ALFRED SCHUTZ*

Inside of every long paper is a little paper trying to escape. Liberated, the miniscule version looks homeward toward its full expression. I begin in an alternative way: here are a few pages in search of a larger statement.

The comparison of Straus with Schutz is a natural one and, in my judgment, a productive one. A quick resumé should bring the relationship between the two men into focus.

1. Both were essentially European men of the same period. Straus was German; Schutz was Austrian. Both attended classical gymnasia. Both were highly musical. Both shared in the major events of their time: they served their respective countries in the First World War; they came to the United States in later years as refugees. Both were men of unusual intellectual quickness, wit, and human discernment.

2. Neither Straus nor Schutz took his degree in philosophy. The first was a doctor of medicine; the second was a doctor of law. Both were philosophers; both were intensively trained in domains other than philosophy: Straus in medical science and Schutz in social science. Both were at home in classical and European literature. One could safely have staked his life on expecting to find in their homes a complete set of the works of Goethe.

3. Schutz's central philosophical indebtedness was to Husserl. Max Weber dominated in the realm of social science. Bergson was an early and lasting influence. Among modern philosophers in the broad tradition, Leibniz was—as he was for some other phenomenologists—of special significance. Schutz recognized Heidegger's importance but remained essentially suspicious of his work. Straus, on the other hand, was much more involved in Heidegger's thought, though he was clearly not a disciple. Scheler rather than the early Husserl was more interesting to Straus. The later Husserl he found more appealing. But modern philosophy, whose problems are very much the focus of Straus's writings, was not the fundamental medium of his thought. Rather, it was in classical Greek philosophy that Straus found his home. I will return to that point later.

---

*This paper was first presented at a meeting of the Society for Phenomenology and Existential Philosophy at Evanston, Illinois, on October 6, 1976.

4. The two men knew of each other but never met. Schutz greatly admired Straus's *Vom Sinn der Sinne*. It was only in the late fifties or in the sixties, I would guess, that Straus read anything by Schutz. I doubt that Straus ever read very much by Schutz. From the few pages he may have looked into and from what he read and heard about Schutz, Straus quickly recognized that his poetry was too close to that of Schutz to risk infiltration. In any case, Straus was a highly idiosyncratic reader.

5. Both men were, for most of their lives, part-time teachers but full-time professionals, in the worlds of psychiatry and business respectively. Like the two men, the two worlds are not all that far apart. When I warned Straus about petting a treacherous cat of mine who was, I told him, paranoid, he replied, as his continued stroking brought forth a profound purr, "but that's my business." And it was. Schutz was equally at home with philosophers and businessmen. His presence was contentment-making. It was said of him by his academic colleagues that he was the only one who could really speak to the trustees.

6. Both Straus and Schutz were impressed by Freud and quite critical of psychoanalysis.

Against this background of intellectual and personal attitudes we may now view the more distinctively philosophical interests of the two thinkers. Their similarities are not difficult to locate. For Straus as well as for Schutz, the methodological stratum of Husserl's work which proved to be of decisive importance was phenomenological psychology rather than transcendental phenomenology. It is man in the natural attitude, in the midst of mundane activities, who is the starting point for philosophical inquiry. Whether one speaks of the "axioms of daily life," as Straus does, or refers to the "typifications of common sense," as Schutz does, the rootage of man remains in the taken for granted structures of everyday life. It is the task of phenomenological psychology to present an anatomy of those structures. Certain paradigm examples in the writings of the two men offer a way of approaching the sense of mundanity which they locate and express.

Perhaps the dominant illustration of placement in the natural attitude which Straus relies on, in variant ways, is that of the perception of identity and sameness of the object intended in experience despite the multitude of different observers and discrete perceptual experiences. Straus writes:

> Say that I am in a museum, lost in the contemplation of a painting.

> Another visitor comes up from behind me, at first unnoticed. His mere presence doesn't affect my view of the picture; it neither adds nor takes anything away. Now that he has moved forward several steps, I notice his presence; even so my view of the painting remains as it was before. Looking straight ahead I face the picture; twisting around I see the other visitor and understand him as someone inspecting the same object. While the rays reflected from the picture plane, the stimuli, diverge in separate bundles to his eye and to mine, our gazes converge on the same object. If he should open a conversation and point something out to me that had previously escaped my notice, then I discover something in the see-able that he has already seen for himself. I cannot participate in his seeing; it is forever inaccessible to me. But I can, through his guidance, make actually accessible to my own view something that in principle is visible to both of us.[1]

The commonality of the "see-able" presupposes the actuality of communication in the world of daily life. More specifically, though, communication between fellow human beings is centered in shared space and time. The "see-able" is part of *The* world, not *my* world. Similar paradigm illustrations can be found in Schutz, but the dominant motif is not perception but action. Even further, action as distinctively social involves distance as much as immediacy. Thus, the kind of illustration one finds stressed in the writings of Schutz refers to a domain of largely anonymous activity. "Putting a letter in the mailbox," Schutz writes, "I expect that unknown people, called postmen, will act in a typical way, not quite intelligible to me, with the result that my letter will reach the addressee within typically reasonable time."[2] Here, communication is seen as socialized through the constructs which the individual utilizes of those fellow human beings who are *not* present, with whom we do *not*, at the moment, share space and time. In formulating his illustration of the museum goer, Straus typifies his anonymous reader, surrenders his manuscript to postal officials, gets back galleys prepared by printers who are unknown to him, and receives royalties on a book bought by anonymous others. Yet just as communication with another person at the museum is possible, so understanding others with whom no personal contact ever takes place is also possible.

Communication for both Straus and Schutz is marked by the character of the "wide-awake" man. "All work done by man," Straus

---

[1] Erwin W. Straus, "Psychiatry and Philosophy," in *Psychiatry and Philosophy* (ed. by Maurice Natanson), New York: Springer-Verlag, 1969, pp. 23-24.

[2] Alfred Schutz, *Collected Papers,* Vol. I: *The Problem of Social Reality* (ed. by Maurice Natanson), The Hague: Martinus Nijhoff, 1962, p. 17.

writes, "is accomplished in a state of awakeness."[3] And Schutz writes, "Only the performing and especially the working self is fully interested in life and, hence, wide-awake."[4] These are not random quotations. On the contrary, Straus devotes one of his most penetrating essays to "Awakeness" and Schutz introduces his analysis of the individual's common-sense knowledge of the world by characterizing "the way in which the wide-awake grown-up man looks at the intersubjective world of daily life . . ."[5] Within the naive orientation of the natural attitude, awakeness is simply taken for granted by actors in the everyday world. The reality grasped by mundane man is taken simpliciter. Schutz remarks:

> No motive exists for the naive person to raise the transcendental question concerning the actuality of the world or concerning the reality of the *alter ego,* or to make the jump into the reduced sphere. Rather, he posits this world in a *general thesis* as meaningfully valid for him, with all that he finds in it, with all natural things, with all living beings (especially with human beings), and with meaningful products of all sorts (tools, symbols, language systems, works of art, etc.). Hence the naively living person (we are speaking of healthy, grown-up, and wide-awake human beings) automatically has in hand, so to speak, the meaningful complexes which are valid for him.[6]

Everydayness, in these terms, is a field of action predicated tacitly on the acceptance of ordinary experience as intersubjectively reliable and shareable. Transcendental questions about such reliability and shareability are immanently bracketed. More fundamentally, philosophical questioning about the nature of mundane experience is successfully resisted and, more or less, overcome by the force of a different order of questioning: the pragmatic interest which common sense takes in seeing its projects through to efficacious conclusions. Accordingly, communication between fellowmen arises as a problem within daily life only when the breakdown of the ordinary occurs. And even then, breakdown is viewed as an "in-between" state, one which will eventually return the pathological to the normalcy of everydayness.

For Straus, communication is the certitude of the mundane. He writes: "We view communication as a fact and as beyond any doubt; only the what and how require discussion."[7] Viewing communication

---

[3] Erwin W. Straus, *Phenomenological Psychology,* New York: Basic Books, 1966, p. 101.

[4] Schutz, *Collected Papers,* Vol. I, p. 213.

[5] *Ibid.*, p. 7

[6] *Ibid.*, pp. 135-36.

[7] Straus, "Psychiatry and Philosophy," p. 24.

as a fact means, for Straus, that ego and alter ego share a common world. The commonality of that world is the condition for the possibility of raising serious questions about communication. Thus, ego and alter ego may be opposed to each other at times, but that opposition presupposes partnership. In Straus's words, "Communication is im-part-ing; I meet the other one as a part-ner."[8] Prior to confrontation between individuals, there is a sharing of what is "ours": "We meet one another," Straus says, "in the one world common to us both."[9] As long as one remains in the natural attitude, the "world common to us" is simply lived and appreciated; the "what and how" of the constitution of that world become problematic only with the relinquishment of the natural attitude. It is at this point that we begin to see a difference between the phenomenologies of Straus and Schutz. Both agree in the initial characterization of the man in the natural attitude, but each thinker goes on to a distinct way of interpreting the task of philosophical analysis. For Straus, it is the private rather than the social world which calls for philosophical scrutiny—a claim which brings us back to an earlier suggestion that Straus's intellectual base was classical Greek philosophy. Straus writes:

> In antiquity one's own world, the *idios kosmos,* was considered a private, and that meant a deficient, world. Awakeness was deemed superior to sleep and dreaming. It was not so much communication that called for an explanation as its suspension. In the modern concept of the world as external, constituted in and by the subject's 'mind,' the problem is reversed. Communication thereby becomes a well-nigh insoluble riddle. It seems to me that our account of comportment towards the Allon and the heteros, in their mundane orientation, coincides in many respects with the ancient view.[10]

Here there is an implied distinction between the "having" of experience and the reflective examination of that "having." It would seem that the latter is an answer in search of a question. The "what and how" of communication may need clarification, but the activity of clarifying appears to be supernumerary in some respects—the illumination of that which is already light-saturated. In other terms, the deprivation characteristic of privacy makes philosophy possible.

At the level of the natural attitude, Schutz is largely in agreement with Straus's insistence on the primacy of communication. Schutz writes:

> . . . it is characteristic of the natural attitude that it takes the world and

[8] *Ibid.*

[9] *Ibid.*, p. 53.

[10] *Ibid.*, p. 57.

> its objects for granted until counterproof imposes itself. As long as the once established scheme of reference, the system of our and other people's warranted experiences works, as long as the actions and operations performed under its guidance yield the desired results, we trust these experiences. We are not interested in finding out whether this world really does exist or whether it is merely a coherent system of consistent appearances. We have no reason to cast any doubt upon our warranted experiences which, so we believe, give us things as they really are.[11]

But the intersubjective world of taken for granted experience rests, according to Schutz, on a tacit *epoché* which places primordial doubt in brackets. Philosophical reflection is held at bay by our complicity with everydayness, and our departure from the natural attitude is not the result of privacy displacing commonality but the recognition that commonality conceals its own origin and rationale. But even within the general thesis of the natural attitude, a return to sources is within the purview of phenomenology. Schutz maintains that:

> . . . a special motiviation is needed in order to induce the naive person even to pose the question concerning the meaningful structure of his life-world, even *within the general thesis.* This motivation can be very heterogeneous; for example, a newly appearing phenomenon of meaning resists being organized within the store of experience, or a special condition of interest demands a transition from a naive attitude to a reflection of a higher order . . . If such a motivation for leaving the natural attitude is given, then by a process of reflection the question concerning the structure of meaning can always be raised. One can always reactivate the process which has built up the sediments of meaning, and one can explain the intentionalities of the perspectives of relevance and the horizons of interest. Then all these phenomena of meaning, which obtain quite simply for the naive person, might be in principle exactly described and analyzed even *within the general thesis.* To accomplish this on the level of mundane intersubjectivity is the task of the mundane cultural sciences, and to clarify their specific methods is precisely a part of that constitutive phenomenology of the natural attitude of which we have been speaking.[12]

The closeness of the views of the two men certainly overshadows their differences: both are saying that mundane reality may be illuminated from within, that is, that phenomenological psychology can be pursued without invoking the transcendental reduction. Yet the difference between them to which I am pointing remains: for Straus, mundane existence, the intersubjective domain of the one common world all of us share as common-sense individuals, is essentially luminous and philosophyless. For Schutz, the mundane rests on

[11] Schutz, *Collected Papers,* Vol. I, p. 228.

[12] *Ibid.*, pp. 136-37.

transcendental grounds which common sense masks and, in a pragmatic way, overcomes. The luminosity of daily life, for Straus, is assured by the omnipresence of the sensory order. "Communication," he writes, "is mediated in the last analysis by the sensible."[13] Schutz, on the other hand, considers action to be the fundamental clue to the meaning-structure of the mundane. Communication involves a far wider spectrum than face to face encounter suggests. In turn, phantasy rather than the sensible proves to be the mediator of communication. Schutz writes:

> All projecting consists in anticipation of future conduct by way of phantasying, yet it is not the ongoing process of action but the phantasied act as having been accomplished which is the starting point of all projecting. I have to visualize the state of affairs to be brought about by my future action before I can draft the single steps of such future acting from which this state of affairs will result. Metaphorically speaking, I must have some idea of the structure to be erected before I can draft the blueprints.[14]

The distinction between the sensible and phantasy leads back to significant differences in the ways in which Straus and Schutz support their views of the life-world. In Strausian terms, the sensible is approached by way of Man as part of Nature; in Schutzian terms, phantasy is interpreted as the activity of Man as part of Sociality. Yet, these important distinctions are not indicative of any profound antagonism between Nature and Sociality. For Straus, Man's taking the upright posture brings him face to face with the traffic of the social world. The sensible, though it is rooted in Nature, mediates the sociality of communication. For Schutz, Nature and Society are transcendences which constitute the conditions of human action and of human freedom. As he says, ". . . the order of Nature and of Society is common to all mankind."[15] It is clear in Schutz's view of transcendence that Nature and Society are representative in common-sense thinking of "some kind of order; yet the essence of this order as such is unknowable to us."[16] For Straus, the sensory world gives us unmediated presence. As he writes:

> When I open my eyes the bright sunlight impinges upon me. I am forced to see, to hear, to smell this and that. I am beset, threatened, or protected in my existence between life and death, being and not-being. I do not act as a detached, impartial observer who merely takes cognizance of the occurrence of things, I feel their power. They are real to me, I am

[13] Straus, "Psychiatry and Philosophy", p. 24.

[14] Schutz, *Collected Papers,* Vol. I, p. 20.

[15] *Ibid.*, p. 330.

[16] *Ibid.*, p. 331.

in the game myself, seized by the events in divers *modi.*[17]

Thus, Strausian Man remains at home in the immanence of the sensory; Schutzian Man must come to terms with the transcendences of both Nature and Society.

MAURICE NATANSON.

YALE UNIVERSITY.

[17] Erwin W. Straus, "Aesthesiology and Hallucinations," in *Existence* (ed. by Rollo May, Ernest Angel, and Henri F. Ellenberger), New York: Basic Books, 1958, p. 155.

FREGE'S 'OBJECTS' AND 'CONCEPTS': REVOLUTIONARY OR REACTIONARY?

I

The *form* of the proposition admits of a distinction between subject and predicate[1] but is in contradiction with any transformation of this distinction into a *division* between 'types of entities'. Once a division is drawn between 'subject-entities', on the one hand, and 'predicate-entities', on the other hand, no account can be given of their 'combination' or unity as expressed in the traditional propositional form S *is* P. In such a case, the category of unity disappears into that of 'difference'. But this is a 'difference' that cannot, in lacking unity, find expression in the proposition. One common example of the bifurcation of the proposition is that of the 'pure particular', estranged from, yet somehow to be combined with, the 'pure universal'. This is an estrangement, however, that admits of no genuine reconciliation. The 'pure particular', in lacking the category of universality, cannot *be* 'universalised', i.e., characterised, while the 'pure universal', in lacking the category of particularity, cannot *be* 'particularised', i.e., instantiated. Subject and predicate, as it were, pass each other by.

It might be thought that the 'pure particular' can be combined with the 'pure universal' through the interposition of some such relation as that of 'participation'. A moment's consideration is enough to dispose of this contention. If the interposing relation is itself an instance of 'pure particularity', then it lacks the categorial complexity necessary to combine particular and universal in the proposition. On the other hand, if the interposing relation is itself an instance of 'pure universality', then again it lacks the categorial complexity necessary to combine particular and universal in the proposition. Indeed, if the 'pure particular' is unable to combine with the 'pure universal', then no 'relationship' that is *purely* particular or universal can be of any assistance. There is the possibility, of course, that the interposing

[1] The distinction between subject and predicate *in a proposition* is not to be confused with the distinction between subject and predicate *in a sentence*. We might use sentences to convey propositions, but what we convey is not itself a sentence.

relation is neither a 'pure particular' nor a 'pure universal' but is an 'ontological entity' of a kind quite different to that of subject and predicate. This alternative is in a worse ontological position than the ones already considered. The relation in this case has *none* of the categorial complexity necessary to combine particular and universal in the proposition. 'Falling between' the two extremes of the proposition is in no sense combining them. The final alternative in which the interposing relation is neither a 'pure particular' nor a 'pure universal' but is *both* particular and universal, is hardly a genuine alternative since the problem of combining the 'pure particular' and the 'pure universal' by means of the interposing relation arises only on the assumption that terms[2] of the proposition *cannot* be both particular and universal.

Taking place is the attempt to explain the categorial complexity of the propositional form (unity and difference, for example) in terms of 'entities' that do not themselves exhibit this categorial complexity. This means that any theory of a 'subject-entity' being combined with a 'predicate-entity' to 'make-up' the proposition is one that cannot itself find expression in the proposition. And it is the function of criticism to elicit its contradiction with the basic form of the proposition in which it is attempting to find expression.

II

The refutation of this rationalist division between 'subject-entities' and 'predicate-entities' by absolute idealists and realists[3] alike is no guarantee against reaction. Indeed, we find its recrudescence, albeit in slightly different appearance, in the work of Gottlob Frege.

---

[2]The convention that a theory of *terms* is to be worked out along linguistic lines is based on the false belief that a theory of the proposition is also to be worked out along linguistic lines. Just as there is nothing in the notion of a *subject* or *predicate* to imply a linguistic analysis, there is nothing in the notion of a *term* to imply a linguistic analysis. The conventional meaning given to these words is a classical example of 'facts' (what are taken to be facts) being theory-laden.

[3]Cf. the absolute idealists Hegel, Bradley, Bosanquet, and the realists Alexander and Anderson. Whatever their differences, their concern for 'logical stability' or the unity of existence (unambiguousness of the copula) brought them together in their criticism of such rationalist divisions as that between the 'pure particular' and the 'pure universal'.

He draws an absolute distinction (which amounts to a division) between *objects,* which are the referents of proper names, and *concepts,* which are the senses of grammatical predicates.[4] Corresponding to the two types of grammatical expression, in other words, Frege has two types of 'ontological entity'—a 'proper name-entity' or *object* and a 'predicate-entity' or *concept.* That this is intended as a division between different 'ontological entities' is underlined by Frege's insistence that what is an object cannot be a concept, and what is a concept cannot be an object. Objects and concepts are as logically irreversible as proper names and predicate words. Admittedly, the *distinction* between subject and predicate implies that the subject-distinction is not the predicate-distinction, but it does not imply that *what* is subject in one proposition cannot be predicate in another proposition. Only if there were 'entities' whose *nature* it is to be distinguished as subject and as predicate would it follow that what is subject, or in Frege's words, 'object', in one proposition, could not be predicate, or in Frege's words, 'concept', in another proposition.

Frege's division between objects and concepts is little more than another instance of the division between the 'pure particular' and the 'pure universal'. 'When we have thus admitted objects without restriction as arguments and values of functions the question arises what it is we are here calling an object. I regard a regular definition as impossible since we have here something too simple to admit of logical complexity. It is only possible to indicate what is meant. Here I can only say briefly: An object is anything that is not a function, so that an expression for it does not contain any empty place.'[5] Of *concepts,* Frege describes them variously as being 'unsaturated', 'incomplete', and importantly, as having a 'predicative nature.'[6] To be consistent with his claim that the object does not admit of logical complexity, Frege cannot include the concept as part of its ontological constitution. We seem to have no option but to agree with Grossmann that 'Being simple, Fregean objects have no natures or rather, are no natures. Nor do they contain properties of any kind. Hence they are what other philosophers call bare particulars and what I call individual things.'[7] On the other hand, the concept, being predicative in nature, is what other philosophers would call the 'pure property' or 'pure universal'. Terminologically, then, we have the opposition between the object and the concept, but philosophically it turns out to be one more ex-

[4]Frege, G., 'On Concept and Object', in *Translations from the Philosophical Writings of Gottlob Frege,* ed. P. Geach and M. Black.

[5]Frege, G., 'What is a Function?' ibid., p. 32.

[6]Frege, G., 'On Concept and Object', ibid., p. 46.

[7]Grossmann, R., *Reflections on Frege's Philosophy,* p. 107.

ample of the rationalist division between the 'pure particular' and the 'pure universal'. So Frege's 'great philosophical achievement'[8] and that to which modern logicians owe such universal debt,[9] is neither new nor, as I will argue, in line with previous criticism, correct.

Frege says that objects are not concepts, yet in a typical proposition like *Hegel is wise* we are asserting, in the terms of his theory, that what is an object, viz., *Hegel, is* also what is a concept, viz., *wise*. It is the same insoluble problem of bringing together in the one proposition what has been separated into different 'ontological compartments'.

> . . . it is false to speak of notions differing in kind. The notion, although concrete, is still as a notion essentially one, and the functions which it contains are not different kinds of it. It is equally false to speak of a combination of the two sides in the judgment, if we understand the term 'combination' to imply the independent existence of the combining members apart from the combination. The same external view of their nature is more forcibly apparent when judgments are described as produced by the ascription of a predicate to the subject. Language like this looks upon the subject as self-subsistent outside, and the predicate as found somewhere in our head. Such a conception of the relation between subject and predicate however is at once contradicted by the copula 'is'. By saying 'this rose is red' or 'this picture is beautiful', we declare, that it is not we who from outside attach the beauty to the picture or the redness to the rose, but that these are the characteristics proper to these objects.[10]

Taking the object as that whose nature it is to be particular and the concept as that whose nature it is to be universal, no account of the functions of the object and the concept in the proposition, consistent with these 'ontologically divisive natures', can be given. Characterisation of the object by the concept must always 'fall outside' the object, which is to say, contrary to requirements of propositional form, that the object (subject) cannot *be* characterised by the concept (predicate). At the same time, particularisation of the concept by the object must also 'fall outside' the concept, which is to say, contrary to requirements of propositional form, that the concept (predicate) cannot *be* particularised by the object (subject). And no appeal to mediating relations like that of 'falling under' can, for reasons presented earlier, combine what has been 'ontologically divided'. Frege says that the concept is incomplete without the object,

---

[8]Ibid., p. 83.

[9]Geach, P. *Logic Matters,* p. 59.

[10]Hegel, G. W. F., *Logic: Part I of the Encyclopaedia of the Philosophical Sciences,* (n) pp. 231-32.

i.e., must be combined with the object to form a 'complete thought'.[11] Literally this means that the concept cannot be thought independently of the object. But if it cannot be thought independently of the object, then the view in which there *is* a 'concept-entity' to be combined with an 'object-entity' to form a 'complete thought', is itself unthinkable.

III

The failure to sustain a division between subject and predicate means simply that unity cannot be subordinated to difference, i.e., distinction is not division. To recognise a distinction between subject and predicate is to recognise that the subject-distinction or function is not the predicate-distinction or function. But this distinction is perfectly consistent with the logical reversibility of subject *terms* and predicate *terms*. We do not have 'entities' corresponding to the respective distinctions or functions within the proposition. What we have is the categorial complexity of terms such that the one term is *both* particular and universal, i.e., can stand in either subject or predicate position in the proposition.

> There is admittedly a distinction between subject and predicate but this is a distinction of function and not of kind; and granted that the function of the predicate is to characterise or describe, the very same term can also have the function of indicating, i.e., can be the subject of another proposition. Thus, every term, as a possible description of something else, has universality or characterises, and, as a possible indication of something else, has particularity or locates.[12]

Unity and difference, as part of the one propositional form, can be explained only on the assumption that terms are categorially complex—that the one term exemplifies, for example, both particularity and universality. The fact that the subject-function (indication) is not the same as the predicate-function (characterisation) does not mean that *what* indicates cannot characterise. In such a case, the insoluble problem of how to combine the 'pure particular' with the 'pure universal' does not arise. It is no longer a question of how *can* the elements of the proposition be combined, but rather a question of how *are* they combined. And the answer to this question would be worked out along the lines of space-time and the categories,[13] not, as

---

[11] Frege, G., 'On Concept and Object', ibid., pp. 54-55.

[12] Anderson, J., 'Universals and Occurrences', *Studies in Empirical Philosophy*, p. 117.

[13] Cf. work of Kant, Alexander, and Anderson on problems of the proposition or judgment (predicaments) in respect of space-time and the categories.

Frege presents it, in terms of 'different ontological *entities*'. In so far as place is not the same category as that of character, we have the distinction between subject and predicate, while in so far as character is what has place, we have the combination or unity required to make sense of the propositional form S *is* P.

The conundrum of 'the concept *horse*' can now be solved without the postulation of either 'concept-correlatives' or 'material modes of speech'. In criticism of Kerry's proposal that the distinction between object and concept is merely relative, Frege remarks:

> (Kerry) gives the following example: 'the concept "horse" is a concept easily attained', and thinks that the concept 'horse' is an object, in fact one of the objects that fall under the concept 'concept easily attained'. Quite so: the three words 'the concept "horse" ' do designate an object, but on that very account they do not designate a concept, as I am using the word . . . In logical discussions one quite often needs to assert something about a concept, and to express this in the form usual for such assertions, viz., to make what is asserted of the concept into the content of the grammatical predicate. Consequently one would expect that the reference of the grammatical subject would be the concept; but the concept as such cannot play this part, in view of its predicative nature; it must first be converted into an object, or, speaking more precisely, represented by an object.[14]

The conundrum here is not surprising. It is a consequence of Frege's *division* between objects and concepts that a concept must become what it is not by nature, namely an object, if it is to be spoken of in subject position! Frege's 'solution' in terms of 'conversion' or 'representation' is a mere evasion of the ontological difficulties that his initial division between objects and concepts involves. How some 'entity' whose 'nature it is to be predicative' can be converted into or represented by some 'entity' whose 'nature it is to be particular' is a question that Frege does not, and indeed, could not, answer. Having placed objects and concepts into two different 'ontological compartments', there is no escaping the conclusion that 'the concept *horse*', in subject position, refers to a fundamentally different 'entity' to that when it occurs in predicate position, i.e., we are no longer talking about the same thing. But this means that Frege could not claim, as he does, that *concepts are by their very nature predicative,*[15] for in this case 'concepts' refers to *objects,* and they are not, by their very nature, predicative. For the contemporary linguisticist, however, this is no real problem. By invoking 'the material mode of speech', Frege

---

[14] Frege, G., 'On Concept and Object', ibid., pp. 45-46.

[15] Ibid., p. 46.

could avoid such an apparently paradoxical remark by rephrasing it as (something like) 'concept *words* always stand in predicate position or are true of objects'. This attempt to avoid the problem is naive. It invites the question: are *what* concept words refer to or stand for, predicative by nature? An answer yes *or* no has the problematic implications that 'modes of speech' were introduced to avoid, while to deny that this sort of question can be raised is to be committed to the obviously absurd position of reducing *concepts* (properties) to *concept words* (predicate words). Obviously absurd because a proposition like *the sky is blue* is not attributing the *word* blue to the sky, but a colour or what the word stands for or refers to.

The problem of 'the concept *horse*' can be solved simply by taking the distinction between subject and predicate to be precisely that—a distinction of functions within the proposition—not a division between different types of 'functional entities'. In subject position 'the concept *horse*' refers to or stands for the same complex thing as it does in predicate position. The difference is that in subject position its function of particularising or indicating is being emphasised (what is true of it?) whereas in predicate position its function of universalising or characterising is being emphasised (what is it true of?) And it is because the one term has both place and character that 'the concept *horse*' can function in either position. Of course when it is functioning in subject position (indicating) it is not functioning in predicate position (characterising). But this difference of function would imply that we were talking about different sorts of 'entities' only if difference of *function* were reified into difference of *entity*.

Frege is quite correct in wanting to maintain a distinction between subject and predicate within the proposition, but falls into error in attempting to transform this distinction into a *divison* between objects and concepts. In conflating *what is distinguished* as subject and predicate with *its being distinguished* as subject and predicate, Frege finishes up with 'simple natures' or 'ontological entities': that whose nature it is to stand in subject position (the object) and that whose nature it is to stand in predicate position (the concept). (And we find in such cases of conflating distinctions with what is distinguished, the wish to have it both ways. On the one hand Frege insists on an *absolute* distinction between object and concept [a division], while on the other hand, particularly with reference to the 'incomplete nature' of the concept, he is suggesting, at least, that the distinction is *not* an absolute one [not a division].)

IV

So far I have argued that there cannot be a division between 'subject-entities' (objects) and 'predicate-entities' (concepts) and have outlined what I take to be the correct way of understanding the *distinction* between subject and predicate. But what of the arguments that are used by Frege and others to support a division between 'subject-entities' and 'predicate-entities'? One such argument can be found in Frege's reply to Kerry in 'On Concept and Object'. Here Frege argues that to make sense of a 'complete thought', a distinction must be drawn between the 'saturated' or 'complete' part of the thought and the 'unsaturated' or 'incomplete' part of the thought. The first part of the thought is the object while the second part of the thought is the concept.

> Somebody may think that this is an artificially created difficulty; that there is no need at all to take account of such an unmanageable thing as what I call a concept; that one might like Kerry, regard an object's falling under a concept as a relation, in which the same thing could occur now as object now as concept. The words 'object' and 'concept' would then serve only to indicate the different positions in the relation. This may be done; but anybody who thinks the difficulty is avoided this way is very much mistaken; it is only shifted. For not all parts of a thought can be complete; at least one must be 'unsaturated' or predicative; otherwise they would not hold together. For example, the sense of the phrase 'the number 2' does not hold together with that of the expression 'the concept *prime number*' without a link. We apply such a link in the sentence 'the number 2 falls under the concept *prime number'*; it is contained in the words 'falls under' which need to be completed in two ways—by a subject and an accusative; and only because their sense is thus 'unsaturated' are they capable of serving as a link. Only when they have been supplemented in this two-fold respect do we get a complete sense, a thought. I say that such words or phrases stand for a relation. We now get the same difficulty for the relation that we were trying to avoid for the concept. For the words 'the relation of an object to the concept it falls under' designate not a relation but an object; and the three proper names 'the number 2', 'the concept *prime number*', 'the relation of an object to a concept it falls under' hold aloof from one another just as much as the first two do by themselves; however we put them together, we get no sentence. It is thus easy to see that the difficulty arising from the 'unsaturatedness' of one part of the thought can indeed be shifted but not avoided.[16]

No juxtaposition of 'pure particulars' (objects) will give us a 'complete thought', that is to say, a proposition. In this respect Frege is quite correct. To propose, however, a division between that part of

---

[16] Ibid., pp. 54-55.

a thought whose *nature* it is to be 'saturated' or 'complete' and that part of a thought whose *nature* it is to be 'unsaturated' or 'incomplete', is not to advance beyond mere juxtaposition. If the 'nature' of the concept is to be incomplete, then it *cannot* be completed, (and this is quite independent of its being completed by something whose 'nature' it is to be complete). Marshall comments that 'what is here called completing the function is more appropriately described as converting the function into an object. If a function is completed in Frege's sense, it becomes not a completed function—for that, like the round square, is a logical absurdity—but an object. Ordinary people complete a house and the result is a house. Frege completes a house and finds he has constructed the moon.'[17] I find Marshall's initial account of Frege 'completing a function' almost impossible to follow. He says 'if a function is completed . . . it becomes not a completed function for that . . . is a logical absurdity.' So a function can *be* completed, according to Frege/Marshall without it being a logical absurdity, but if we call it a 'completed function', then suddenly, and without any explanation, it becomes, according to Marshall, a logical absurdity! We can say, then, that when 'a round thing is squared, it becomes not a round square—for that is a logical absurdity—but something quite different!' This is not to take ontology seriously. In insisting that what is an object cannot be a concept and that what is a concept cannot be an object, Frege is insisting on an ontological division between objects and concepts. To say this and then to proceed to 'convert concepts into objects' and to have 'objects representing concepts' is to fail to follow through the ontological implications of this division. On the assumption that the *nature* of the concept is to be 'incomplete' then no coherent account can be given of *its* completion. Talk of 'completing houses' and turning 'houses into the moon' is just that—talk. It does nothing to illuminate the problem of how that whose *nature* it is to be incomplete can be completed.

Frege's distinction/division between the 'saturated' and the 'unsaturated' parts of the thought is a good example of him wanting it both ways. On the one hand, in drawing attention to the fact that the *predicate-function* is incomplete and needs to be 'attached to' a subject to form a 'complete thought', Frege is arguing *against* the reification of the predicate-function into some different ontological 'nature' or 'entity'. On the other hand, in treating the 'incomplete' as some

[17]Marshall, W., 'Frege's Theory of Functions and Objects', in *Essays on Frege*, ed. E. D. Klemke, p. 253.

thing or *entity* whose 'nature' it is to be 'incomplete' (predicative) he is saying 'really it is complete, but in an incomplete sense!' That the predicate-function is 'incomplete' means simply that *it cannot be thought* outside of or apart from the proposition or 'complete thought' in which it is a function.[18] To then assume that its *nature* is to be 'incomplete' or predicative, is to assume that it *can* be thought outside of or apart from the proposition or 'complete thought' in which it is a function, but only in some 'peculiar incomplete sense'. The problem, an insoluble one, is that of combining two essentially different 'natures' or 'entities' in the one proposition or 'thought'. Had Frege not attempted to transform a distinction of functions within the proposition into a division of different ontological 'entities', he would not have been faced with this insoluble problem of '*re*unification'.[19] As it stands, Frege's argument for the postulation of objects and concepts as necessary condition of explaining what it is to be a complete thought, does not work.[20] Indeed, there is much in this argument that can be taken as an argument *against* such an ontological reification/division.

For many, a powerful argument in support of the division be-

---

[18] That the predicate-function cannot be thought outside of or apart from the proposition does not mean that it cannot be *distinguished* from the subject-function *within* the proposition.

[19] There is also the problem of understanding the two different senses of 'complete' that Frege uses. To have a 'complete thought', we need to have an 'incomplete function' *plus* a 'complete object'. In what way are we to take the completeness of the object? Not in the same way as we are to take the completeness of the thought otherwise we would have to treat it as 'incomplete' without the concept or function to complete it. And it cannot be that the object can *exist* without the concept. To say this we have to *think* of it as existing without the concept, but this we cannot do since we need concept *plus* object to get a complete thought. So the idea that 'pure particulars' or objects can exist in their own right without 'supplementation' by concepts turns out to be inconsistent with Frege's own views on what it is to be a 'complete thought'. Moreover, inconsistency aside, the very notion of a 'pure particular' existing in its own right independently of concepts is contradictory. Unless it were the *only* 'pure particular', in which case it would be pointless talking of particularity at all, it would *share particularity with other 'pure particulars'*. If it did not, then we could not talk of pure particulars, while if it did, then the very notion of the 'pure particular' is already charged with the notion of the concept. (Hegel's work on 'Sense-Certainty' in his *Phenomenology of Mind* is important in this respect.)

[20] Frege would have benefited from a close study of Plato's *Parmenides!* See also how easily Grossmann slides from talk about *categories* to talk about *entities*. 'It shows that the Bradley regress cannot arise if one acknowledges the existence of at least two ontological categories—entities that require a connector in order to be connected with other entities and entities that do not.' (ibid., p. 81.)

tween objects and concepts is that which takes its departure from the distinction between proper names and predicate words within the sentence. According to Dummett: 'for Frege the application of the ontological category-term "object" is dependent upon the application of the linguistic category-term "proper name" and not conversely.'[21] Frege does say ' . . . what is here asserted about a concept can never be asserted about an object, for (sic) a proper name can never be a predicative expression, though it can be part of one. I do not want to say it is false to assert about an object what is here asserted about a concept; I want to say it is impossible, senseless to do so.'[22] There is a *non sequitur* in this argument. Just as you cannot treat a term in subject position as if it were a term in predicate position, you cannot treat a proper name as if it were a predicate expression, i.e., not a proper name. But the recognition of this distinction within the proposition on the one hand and the sentence on the other hand, does not license the conclusion that there are 'entities' whose 'nature' it is to be in subject position or named, as opposed to 'entities' whose 'nature' it is to be in predicate position or predicated. This is an *extra*-linguistic conclusion in no way proved by the distinction between proper names and predicate expressions. The position I have outlined in criticism of Frege in no way denies a *distinction* between subject position and predicate position within the proposition nor a *distinction* between proper names and predicate expressions within the sentence. But it is opposed to any attempt to transform these distinctions of function into divisions of 'ontological natures'.

Frege's division between objects and concepts gives rise to equally insoluble problems on the level of language. One such problem is that of explaining the everyday phenomenon of proper names becoming common nouns.

> If proper names as actually understood did not connote many attributes we should be at a loss to understand or explain the everyday phenomenon of a proper name becoming a common noun. A young Danish girl was asked by a Frenchman what her father was, and in her ignorance of the French word for 'sculptor' got out of the difficulty by saying 'Il est Thorvaldsen en miniature'. Oscar Wilde writes: 'Every great man nowadays has his disciples, and it is always *Judas* who writes the biography.' (*Intentions* 81) a transition to *a Judas*. Walter Pater says that France was about to become *an Italy* more Italian than Italy itself. *(Renaissance,* 133). In this way, Caesar became the general name for Roman emperors, German Kaisers, Russian Tsars (in Shakespeare's

---

[21] Dummett, M., *Philosophy of Language,* p. 69.

[22] Frege, G., 'On Concept and Object', ibid., p. 50.

> tragedy III, 2.55, the rabble shouts 'Liue Brutus, liue, liue . . . Let him be Caesar')—to mention only a few examples. Logicians, of course, see this, but they dismiss it with some remark like this (Keynes *Formal Logic* 45) 'Proper names, of course, become connotative when they are used to designate a certain type of person; a diogenes, a Thomas, a Don Quixote, a Paul Pry, a Benedict, a Socrates. But when so used, such names have really ceased to be proper names at all; they have come to possess all the characteristics of general names.' The logician as such with his predilection for water-tight compartments in the realm of ideas, is not concerned with what to me as a linguist seems a most important question, viz., how is it to be explained that a sequence of sounds with no meaning at all suddenly from non-connotative becomes connotative, and this new full meaning is at once accepted by the whole speaking community?[23]

Jespersen's question here is a very important one. To take the Fregean view that proper names designate 'entities' ontologically different to those designated by predicate expressions would thereby preclude any account of how the proper name *Hegel* can be *generalised* into the common noun *Hegelian*. What is 'purely particular' cannot be generalised, or what is an object cannot be 'converted' into a concept. In other words, if having a character or characters were not *part* of the categorial constitution of the so-called 'pure particular' or object *Hegel,* then there could be no ontological or linguistic justification for using the word *Hegel* in any grammatical shape to stand for a certain character or characters, i.e., in predicate position. And if having a character or characters is part of the categorial constitution of the so-called 'pure particular' or object *Hegel,* then (1) *Hegel* is not a 'pure particular' after all, and (2) the proper name *Hegel* does not designate a 'pure particular'. Of course, when words are being used as names, i.e., to indicate or particularise, they are not being used as predicate expressions, i.e., to characterise. This can be accepted (for the sake of argument) without being committed to the conclusion that there are entities whose 'nature' it is to be named or entities whose 'nature' it is to be predicative. Geach says it is clearly nonsense to ask *which* cat 'cat' names in 'Jemima is a cat'.[24] Agreed, but this would be an objection only to those who wanted to deny that there is a *distinction* between proper names and predicate expressions. It is no objection to those, like myself, who accept the distinction but deny that it indicates a division of ontological 'natures'. Indeed, if it did, then Jemima could not *be* a cat!

There is nothing, then, in the grammatical distinction between

[23]Jespersen, O., *The Philosophy of Grammar,* pp. 66-67.

[24]Geach, P., *Reference and Generality,* p. 35.

proper names and predicate expressions to support an ontological division between objects and concepts. On the assumption that there is such a division, there would be much on both the ontological and linguistic levels that would be inexplicable.[25] The error seems to be the common one (already commented upon) of confusing between the term that is distinguished and its being distinguished—of assuming, for example, that because there is something to be named or indicated, then its 'nature' is to be named or indicated. This sort of confusion is facilitated by the fact that many words, like proper names, appear to have their function in the proposition or sentence 'built into' their grammatical shape. But this is no more than an *indicator* of what function they are to have in the proposition or sentence. It is not to be taken as representative of what sorts of 'entities' there are in the ontological inventory.

> Now it would certainly seem that expressions like 'this' are commonly applied only to subjects. But that is because they contain, besides a certain term, the sign of quantity which goes with the subject; the same term could be predicate, but it would not take the sign of quantity with it . . . Briefly, then, 'this' means 'the thing indicated', 'thing indicated' can be a predicate, and 'the' is the sign of quantity like 'all' and 'some', and is in fact equivalent to 'all'. It is from the confusion between the function a term has in a proposition (there being various signs of what that function may be) and the term itself that the doctrine of 'universals' (and of 'particulars' conceived in opposition to 'universals') arises.[26]

A change of function in the proposition will necessitate in many cases a corresponding change of function-indicator qualifications on the grammatical level, but it does not imply, and indeed could not imply, that we are now dealing with a different sort of 'entity'—a 'predicate-entity', for example, rather than a 'subject-entity'. To go from the fact that we cannot reverse *the functions* in the proposition to the conclusion that we cannot reverse *the terms* having those functions, is to assume *that the terms are defined as having those functions.* But this assumption, as pointed out before, is contrary to the form of the proposition in which it has to find expression. Once the

---

[25] Frege rejects the view that proper names can *be* predicates, but admits that they can be *part of* predicate expressions. On the ontological level, how can something whose 'nature' it is to be named or indicated be part of something whose 'nature' it is to be predicative? The simple answer is that it cannot. But if an object cannot be part of a concept (object and concept belonging to two different ontological 'compartments') then it follows that a proper name (whose referent is an object) cannot be part of a predicate expression (whose referent or sense is a concept).

[26] Anderson, J., ibid., p. 119.

term is distinguished from its having a subject or predicate function in the proposition, then it becomes clear that the one term can have either function. It is not, as Frege suggests, logically simple, but is, on the contrary, categorially complex. There is no reason, then, to believe that *ontologically* some terms are 'more' particular or 'more' universal than others. That a term X (for example, a person) can come to occupy subject position more frequently than predicate position can be explained by reference to the sort of interest there is, in those circumstances, in that term. It can be expected that in periods of individualism there would be more of an interest in the person as an individual (as having a subject-function in the proposition) than as the bearer of characteristics in common with other persons and other things (as having a predicate-function in the proposition). This has obvious implications for the doctrine of proper names.

> I suspect that the conception of proper names, as we understand them, is not a very easy or early one. We now actually attach to names written and used in a certain way, a mental reservation that we are to look for no meaning in them. As regards the names of men and women this is quite a modern state of things. The surname still in some cases retains an intension of family and character, and is always of course more significant than the Christian name. But the law now admits of no purpose in names but that of distinction; and permits anyone to have any name which he makes it clear he is to be known by, and to change it at pleasure subject to the same condition. The history of Roman and I suppose still more of savage, names, proves that far more predicative significance attached to the actual name-word in early times than now. And the origin of English surnames illustrates the same truth.[27]

V

Criticism is many-sided. The first task of criticism is to identify the problem. In the case of Frege's division between objects and concepts, the problem is the traditional one, disguised somewhat by peculiarities of terminology, of explaining unity and difference—of subject and predicate-functions in the proposition. The second task of criticism is to show that a proposed solution to the problem is no solution at all. I argued that Frege's *division* of subject/predicate-functions into different 'functional entities' is an error because, in subordinating unity to difference, it could not then explain the combination of these functions in the one proposition or 'thought'. The third task of criticism is to suggest the lines along which a correct solution to the problem may be found. I suggested that the distinction

---

[27] Bosanquet, B., *Knowledge and Reality,* pp. 73-74.

of functions in the proposition is just that—a *distinction* of functions, not a 'division of entities'. The one term, being categorially complex, can have *either* subject or predicate function;[28] what function it does have in any particular proposition being determined by interests. The fourth task of criticism, one often overlooked, is that of giving some account of how the error could have occurred given the material and circumstances of the problem. My suggestion here was that Frege confused *the term* with *the terms having a certain function in the proposition,* such that if it has a subject-function, then it must be a 'subject-entity' (object) while if it has a predicate-function then it must be a 'predicate-entity' (concept). We could say, in general, that Frege's position here is one of 'vicious intellectualism'—the assumption that something has one and only one function or office, and that if we recognise universality, for example, then we have to recognise something 'whose business it is to be universal and nothing else'.[29] What emerges from this criticism is the view that Frege's division between objects and concepts, far from being a 'great philosophical achievement', is, philosophically, a backward step.

B. C. BIRCHALL.

UNIVERSITY OF NEW ENGLAND.

[28]This point is also recognised by Husserl: 'What is said about adjectivity, substantivity, etc., must not be understood as if we were concerned here with differences of linguistic form. Even though the designations of these core-forms are drawn from the mode of designation of linguistic forms, nothing more is meant by them *than difference in the manner of apprehension. At one time an object or an objective moment can become a theme as existing "for itself", and at another in the form of "in something"*, and by no means must these differences in the manner of apprehension always correspond also to a difference in the linguistic form of expression . . . ' *(Experience and Judgment,* pp. 210-11, my emphasis). It is interesting to note that neither Kneale nor Bochenski mentions Husserl in his respective 'history' of Logic. But then the absolute idealists, Hegel, Bradley, Bosanquet, who wrote prodigiously on logic, did not rate a mention either!

[29]Cf. Anderson, J., *Lectures on Alexander's Space, Time and Diety,* 1949, copy from D. M. Armstrong, (unpublished), pp. 38-39.

BIBLIOGRAPHY

Alexander, S. *Space, Time and Diety,* Vols. I & II, Dover, New York, 2nd ed. 1927.

Anderson, J. *Lectures on Alexander's Space, Time and Diety,* given at Sydney University in 1949, unpublished, copy from D. M. Armstrong.

Anderson, J. *Studies in Empirical Philosophy,* Angus and Robertson, Sydney, 1st ed. 1962.

Bochenski, I. M. *A History of Formal Logic,* trans. and ed. Ivo Thomas, Univ. of Notre Dame Press, 1961.

Bosanquet, B. *Knowledge and Reality,* Kraus Reprint Co., New York, 1968.

Bosanquet, B. *Logic or the Morphology of Knowledge,* Vols. I & II, Oxford University Press, London, imp. 1931.

Bradley, F. H. *The Principles of Logic,* Vols. I & II, Oxford University Press, London, rep. 1958.

Dummett, M. *Frege: Philosophy of Language,* Duckworth & Co., Ltd., 1st ed. 1975.

Geach, P. T. *Logic Matters,* Basil Blackwell, Oxford, 1st ed. 1972.

Geach, P. T. *Reference and Generality,* Cornell University Press, Ithaca, New York, 1st ed. 1962.

Geach, P. T. (ed.) *Translations from the Philosophical Writings of Gottlob Frege,* (co-editor, Max Black), Basil Blackwell, Oxford, 1952.

Grossmann, R. *Reflections on Frege's Philosophy,* Northwestern University Press, Evanston, 1st ed. 1969.

Hegel, G. W. F. *Logic: Part I of the Encyclopaedia of the Philosophical Sciences,* trans. W. Wallace, Oxford at the Clarendon Press, London, 3rd ed. 1975.

Hegel, G. W. F. *Science of Logic,* Vols. I & II, trans. Johnston and Struthers, George Allen & Unwin Ltd., London, 4th imp. 1966.

Hegel, G. W. F. *The Phenomenology of Mind,* trans. J. B. Baillie, George Allen & Unwin Ltd., London, 8th imp. 1971.

Husserl, E. *Experience and Judgment,* trans. J. S. Churchill & K, Ameriks, Routledge & Kegan Paul, London, 1973.

Jespersen, O. *The Philosophy of Grammar,* George Allen & Unwin Ltd., London, rep. 1935.

Joseph, H. W. B. *An Introduction to Logic,* Oxford at the Clarendon Press, London, 2nd ed. rep. 1950.

Klemke, E. D. (ed.) *Essays on Frege,* University of Illinois Press, Urbana, Chicago, 1968.

Kneale, W. & M. *The Development of Logic,* Oxford at the Clarendon Press, London, 1962.

Marshall, W. 'Frege's Theory of Functions and Objects', in *Essays on Frege,* ed. E. D. Klemke, University of Illinois Press, Urbana, Chicago, 1968.

THE PHENOMENON OF "THE LOOK"

The phenomenon of "the look" has been examined and analyzed in both philosophical and psychological literature. However, there has been no attempt made to indicate that the role of "the look" in, say, Jean-Paul Sartre's phenomenology of the experience of being fixed in the gaze of the other may, in some way, be related to major psychological studies of this phenomenon. Insofar as Sartre's phenomenological description of the encounter with "the other" *via* "the look" or *le regard* is referred to in psychological studies, it is often characterized as a description of a "pathological" response to being looked at or gazed at. This is somewhat curious insofar as a substantial number of psychological studies of reactions to gaze tend, for the most part, to substantiate or lend support to Sartre's descriptions of "the look" and its effects.

What we will be concerned with here is an examination of some of the major psychological studies of gaze in relation to the philosophical interpretation of the significance of "the look" in Sartre's thought. Psychological studies of the effects of being stared at or gazed at, as well as evidence uncovered in ethology pertaining to the effects of gaze, the phenomenon of the prolongation of tonic immobility in some animals and the apparent function of eye patterns in animals and insects will be considered.

We shall attempt to show that there is a hitherto unnoticed continuity extending from defensive eye patterns in insects and animals to responses to gaze in animals and typical responses of human beings to being the object of the stare or gaze of others. Our supplementary concerns include the following: to maintain that Sartre's description of typical responses to being looked at or stared at is not, by any means, an indication of a phenomenology of pathological responses and to show that Sartre's phenomenology, despite its merits, is a truncated phenomenological description of "the look" insofar as it excludes the apparent transformation of the significance of the gaze in encounters involving interest, attention, attraction, desire or sexual intentionality. There is a great deal of common observation and empirical evidence that the typical "conflict" nature of the gaze in human encounters is overcome or transformed in special circumstances or contexts in which reciprocal staring clearly indicates interest, attention, sexual attraction or fascination.

"The Look" and Tonic Immobility

In a variety of studies of tonic immobility in small animals, it has been found that such a state is prolonged by the mere presence of eyes. Tonic immobility is a cataleptic state that is typically induced in small animals by physical restraint. It is characterized by a waxy flexibility of the limbs, freezing in place and rapid eye fluttering. Presumably, this defensive behavior has the effect of exhibiting the absence of escape behavior. This state, in turn, reduces the amount of feedback stimuli present to the predatory animal. Distracted by other stimuli in the environment, the predatory animal allows the prey to escape. Under laboratory conditions, tonic states have been induced by the presence of a predatory animal or by the presence of stimuli representing a predator.

Experiments have been undertaken that indicate that the eyes play a central role as a stimulus representing a predatory animal. Research has shown that the mere presentation of taxidermist's animal eyes or even eye-like stimuli is sufficient to prolong states of tonic immobility. In chickens, lizards and other small animals it has been shown that the presence of eyes alone apparently represents the predator's attendance to its prey and that this attendance causes a fear reaction in the animals.[1]

Some recent experiments have indicated that states of physical immobility in chickens, lizards and blue crabs are prolonged by the presence of the experimenter, the presence of a stuffed Cooper's hawk or even only the presence of "detached glass eyes, suspended from wooden dowels." Eye-contact maintained by the experimenter prolonged the duration of tonic immobility in lizards *(Anolis carolinensis).* Even the presentation of detached eyes produced a similar, but smaller, effect. The results of this particular experiment with lizards suggested the postulation that the presence of eyes was not a sufficient condition for the occurrence of physical immobility itself. However, the presence of eyes seemed to increase the fear response and prolong the duration of tonic immobility once it had been elicited. An additional finding was that pupil size was a relevant factor in eye contact

---

[1] Hennig, C. W., "Effects of Simulated Predation on Tonic Immobility in *Anolis Carolinensis:* The Role of Eye Contact," *Bulletin of the Psychonomic Society,* 1977, Vol. 9 (4), pp. 239-42. Cf. Ratner, S. C., "Comparative Aspects of Hypnosis." In *Handbook of Clinical and Experimental Hypnosis,* New York, 1967.

with the lizard subjects. The larger the pupil size, the greater was the effect produced.[2] Because of the variety of species studied in relation to this phenomenon there is considerable across-species generality in these findings.

Eye-Spot Patterns

Although it has long been recognized that a number of insects, fish, and other animals display eye-spot patterns, the function of these patterns has been obscured until recently. Currently, it is assumed that the presence of such eye-spots supports the hypothesis that eyes are fear-producing stimuli for many species. Several varieties of the moth family *(Lepidoptera),* fish, birds, cobras, and peacocks display eye-shaped patterns. It is assumed that such patterns serve to ward off predators. These eye-spot patterns are said to have the effect of fixing the attention of both animals and man. It is sometimes assumed that such patterns serve either as warnings or as distraction signals.

Considering the phenomena of eye-spot patterns in coordination with experiments dealing with the prolongation of tonic immobility, it has been assumed that "eyes and eye-like stimuli participate in an important way in predator-prey relationships."[3] Presumably, then, eye-spot patterns or eye-like forms serve a defensive function by virtue of the simulation of a predator or because they function as warning signals or distractions. In most cases, these eye-like patterns protect the insect, fish, bird, or animal from attack by predators in their most vulnerable physical attitude. The eye-spot pattern on the cobra, for example, is displayed on the back of the cobra's body and is especially visible when it is in an attack position. Thus, the eye-spot patterns seem to protect the cobra from attacks from the rear.

Coinciding with the findings concerning the pupil-size of the eyes is the fact that the eye-pattern on the *Lepidoptera* displays very large pupils. Since the eye-like patterns are quite large in proportion to the size of the moth, it is reasonable to assume that the display of such patterns serves to simulate the presence of relatively large predators. Apparently, such various eye-like phenomena serve the function of threatening, warning, or distracting potential or actual predators. As previously noted, the presence of such eye-spots or eye-like patterns in

---

[2] Ibid., p. 241.
[3] Ibid.

a variety of creatures seems to lend independent support to the assumption that eye-contact is a central feature of threatening or conflict relationships between prey and predator.

Responses to Gaze in Primates and Man

In a variety of recent studies it has been shown that lower animals and primates typically respond to the gaze or stare of the experimenter with either attack or threat display behaviors. Conversely, one of the most frequently reported aspects of threat displays or "agonistic" responses is a steady, direct gaze at the object of aggression.[4] In general, a direct stare may be defined as a look or gaze that persists regardless of the behavior of the animal or human subject stared at. Although some attempts have been made to distinguish among staring, gazing, and looking, these terms are typically used synonymously in the theoretical and experimental literature.

An intense, fixed gaze is typical of aggressive behavior in chimpanzees and in a wide variety of monkeys and gorillas.[5] It has been found that gazing or staring is often a prelude to attack or a substitute for it in primates. Aggressive staring is common to dominant animals in an encounter or animal interaction. For the most part, aversive gazing is characteristic of subordinate animals. In studies of primate behavior it has been observed that "there is often a visual attention structure, in which attention is directed upward to more dominant animals."[6]

Submissive animals will often employ gaze aversion in an encounter with another animal in order, apparently, to reduce the likelihood of attack. Analogous dominance and submission patterns have been found in human subjects involved in experiments measuring responses to gazing or staring. In one interesting experiment it was shown that if the experimenter stared at a caged rhesus monkey,

---

[4] Ellsworth, P. C., J. M. Carlsmith, and A. Henson, "The Stare as a Stimulus to Flight in Human Subjects," *Journal of Personality and Social Psychology,* 1972, Vol. 21, No. 3, p. 302. Cf. Cook, Mark, "Gaze and Mutual Gaze in Social Encounters," *American Scientist,* 1977, VI (65), pp. 328-33. Cf. Exline, R. and B. T. Fehr, "Applications of Semiosis to the Study of Visual Interaction," in *Nonverbal Communication and Behavior,* eds. A. W. Sigman and S. Feldstein, Hillsdale, N.J., 1978.

[5] Ibid.

[6] Cook, M., "Gaze and Mutual Gaze in Social Encounters," *American Scientist,* 1977 (65), p. 332. Cf. R. V. Exline, "Visual Interaction: The Glances of Power and Preference," in *Nebraska Symposium on Motivation,* Lincoln, 1971.

the monkey reacted half of the time by launching an attack. If the experimenter averted his gaze, the monkey responded in such a way that the likelihood of an attack was reduced by half.[7] In general, it has been found that both primates and man exhibit signs of *physiological arousal* in situations in which they are stared at.

Experiments dealing with human responses to staring are a fairly recent phenomenon. When early observational studies of reactions to staring were carried out in the 1960s, there was virtually no other research in this area being conducted. Since 1965, the research on gaze has expanded so rapidly that it has led to the development of a new field of study in social psychology: nonverbal communication.[8] In general, it has been found that looking, gazing, and staring are the central nonverbal signals in human communication. In terms of importance, such activities overshadow other nonverbal cues such as facial expression, posture, proximity, and voice tone.

It has been hypothesized that eye gaze behavior or staring generates an "emotional arousal" in man. Experiments have been performed in which the Galvanic skin response was employed as a means of measuring emotional responses to being stared at. Since Galvanic skin responses are controlled by the sympathetic section of the autonomic nervous system, and since they have proven reliable in measuring the experience of, or anticipation of, mild stress, they are considered as effective indicators of the occurrence of an emotional response in subjects.

Experiments confirm that eye contact provokes emotional arousal as measured by Galvanic skin response activity. In addition, it has been shown that "prolonged eye contact can result in tension or even anxiety." In a particular experiment it was found that eye contact induced significantly greater amplitude and frequency of Galvanic skin responses than "unreciprocated gaze" did.[9] What is to be noted in this regard is that eye contact *per se* was shown to have produced a nonspecific "emotional arousal" or emotional response in the experimental subjects.

Although a variety of responses to fixed staring have been noted by psychologists, there are some experimental investigations that have indicated that staring or gazing is often a stimulus to flight in man. With the assistance of "confederates" who stared at motorists at an in-

[7] Exline, R. V., op. cit., pp. 163, 206.

[8] Cook, M., op. cit., p. 328.

[9] Nichols, K. A. and B. G. Champness, "Eye Gaze and the GSR," *Journal of Experimental Social Psychology,* 1971 (7), pp. 625-26.

tersection in a field experiment, observers found that the motorists who were stared at crossed the intersection at significantly faster rates than did those who were not stared at. The flight from the situation in which one was intently stared at was characterized as an "avoidance reaction." The primary effect induced by staring was found to be one that is common to primates. That is, that staring or gazing can act in the same way as a primate threat display.

Another interesting finding in this field experiment was that the duration of the stare was apparently irrelevant to the avoidance reaction. For, the increased speed of departure from the intersection occurred even when the duration of the staring was quite short.[10] There is little doubt that the gazing or staring of the "confederates" in this study was perceived as threatening. For, even before the rapid departure from the intersection, the motorists stared at displayed gaze aversion or other behavior that served to avoid the stare of the experimental assistants or "confederates."

Staring or gazing in itself seems to be a salient stimulus that arouses tension, produces emotional arousal, and induces avoidance responses. In some instances, reciprocal staring in an impersonal social encounter engendered an "emotion akin to panic" or stimulated intense "hostile arousal."[11] It has also been observed that positive dislike or hostility is often exhibited by means of staring. In the so-called "hate stare" there is a deliberate violation of the norm that Goffman characterizes as a "civil inattention" to strangers in public places.[12] Intense staring in children has often been observed to be a prelude to the onset of fighting.

It has been found that autistic children, as well as children suffering from schizophrenia, exhibit specific gaze avoidance behavior to such an extent that this phenomenon is sometimes used as a diagnostic cue. The speculation here is that such children are chronically "overaroused" and, therefore, tend to avoid contact with others. This is especially the case in regard to the significant stimulus of the gaze or the stare of another person.[13] Apart from pathological

[10] Ellsworth, P. C., J. M. Carlsmith, and A. Henson, op. cit., p. 310.

[11] Exline, R. V., and B. J. Fehr, "Applications of Semiosis to the Study of Visual Interaction," *Nonverbal Communication and Behavior,* p. 117. Reference is made to Norman Mailer's description of his staring duel with a member of the American Nazi Party. Mailer characterized the intense staring as producing a violent, hostile arousal that was "not unlike holding an electric wire in the hand." Norman Mailer, *Armies of the Night,* New York, 1968, pp. 160-63.

[12] Goffman, E., *Behavior in Public Places,* Glencoe, 1963.

[13] Cook, M., "Gaze and Mutual Gaze in Social Encounters," p. 231.

instances of gaze avoidance, it would seem that being stared at (particularly by strangers) is experienced as threatening or, at a minimum, as discomforting or disturbing.

The observed responses to, or reactions to, being stared at vary. In impersonal social encounters, however, typical responses include feelings of tension, emotional arousal, discomfort, anxiety, panic, or fear. In general, it would appear that being gazed at or stared at by a stranger in an impersonal social situation produces an arousal reaction that seems to be analogous to the responses of insects, birds, fish, and small animals to the presence of eyes (especially those with large pupils). It is not too much to say that there is an apparent continuum extending from the responses of primitive life-forms to the presence of eyes to human responses to being stared at or looked at by strangers. Expressed in another way, the human responses to being stared at may be construed as a replication of the prey-predator relationship in simpler life forms. In addition, displays of eye-patterns in various species as a defense mechanism seem to coincide with the experimental discoveries concerning behavioral responses to eye-contact or being stared at in primates and man.

Although we shall consider alternative responses to being stared at in man in our concluding remarks, it may be noted that there is considerable evidence that, under specific conditions and in particular circumstances, a common response to being stared at is an emotional arousal that is often described as a negative reaction, as the experience of discomfort, tension, fear, or panic.

"The Look" and Pathology

As previously indicated, it has been observed that autistic children, schizophrenic children, and, in some cases, adult schizophrenics tend to have unusual reactions to being gazed at by others. R. D. Laing has noted that negative responses to being stared at (or even imagining that one is being stared at) are enhanced in schizoid individuals and pronounced in psychotic patients.[14] It has been assumed that the subjective feeling of being looked at that is experienced by schizophrenic patients is a manifestation of "ideas of reference." This subjective experience of being stared at is said to be the result of "projection."[15] It has also been pointed out that occa-

[14]Cf. R. D. Laing, *The Divided Self,* New York, 1969.

[15]Siomopoulos, V., "Psychiatric Note on Sartre's Concept of the 'Look'." *Psychological Reports,* 1976 (38), p. 983.

sionally psychiatric patients "suffer from delusions about being looked at" and report that they feel as if they will be turned to stone or will suffer a similar fate by virtue of this.[16]

Because of the supposed relationship between Sartre's phenomenological description of "the look" or *le regard* and pathological experiences of being stared at, it has been argued that Sartre's description of this phenomenon and of an individual's response to it is a description that is appropriate to pathological phenomena or experiences. Sartre's comments on the probability that "the other" is looking at me when I hear footsteps behind me have been taken as indications that his conception of the look "draws upon psychopathological states."[17] The following passage from his novel, *The Reprieve,* is put forward as 'evidence' that Sartre is describing or relying upon pathological states in his phenomenology of the look.

> You must have experienced, in the subway, in the foyer of a theatre, or in a cafe, the sudden and irksome sense that you were being looked at from behind. You turn around, but the observer has buried his nose in a book; you can't discover who was looking at you. You turn back, but you are sure the unknown eyes are again upon you; there's a faint tingling all over your back, like a sudden twitch of all your tissues. Well, that is what I felt for the first time, on September 26, at three o'clock in the afternoon, in the hotel garden. No one was there . . . no one at all. But the look was there . . . since then, I have been continually under observation . . . what anguish to discover that look . . . from which I can't escape! But what a relief as well! I know at last that I am . . . I need no longer bear the responsibility of my turbid and disintegrating self: he who sees me causes me to be; I am as he sees me.[18]

What is curious about the citation of this passage is that while it does, in one sense, reflect the experience of being looked at, it also indicates that this surrender to the anonymous gaze of the unseen "other" on the part of the character Daniel signifies, for Sartre, his "bad faith." It signifies his attempt to become an inert "being-in-itself" without freedom. To construe oneself as completely objectified by the look of the other is precisely to renounce one's essential freedom or "transcendence" of factual determination. What Sartre is presenting in fictional form is a possible response to the universalization of "the look" on the part of an individual who wants to deny his freedom, his choice, his responsibility for becoming himself. This passage from *The Reprieve* is a classic description of an individual who lives in bad faith and is not based upon, or derived from, any

[16] Cook, M., op. cit., p. 329.

[17] Siomopoulos, V., op. cit., p. 984.

[18] Sartre, J. P., *The Reprieve,* New York, 1968, pp. 314-15.

pathological phenomena. There is certainly no justification for the exaggerated claim that "some basic existential concepts, at least in Sartre's philosophy, may . . . originate in common psychopathological experience."[19]

The question concerning the ostensible "pathological" account of responses to being stared at that some find in Sartre's phenomenology of the look leads to some curious reactions on the part of the psychological investigators. Some note with astonishment that "philosophical psycholgists" such as Merleau-Ponty attribute deep significance to the phenomenon of being stared at. They cite Merleau-Ponty's interpretations of *le regard* as if they were completely independent of Sartre's phenomenology (which, in fact, is their inspiration) and quote the claims that a person feels "stripped of existence" or "transformed into an object" as if they were esoteric or strange observations that are far removed from research on the effects of the look in psychological literature.[20] Ironically, as we have seen, there is considerable evidence in psychological studies of "gaze aversion" and the effects of gaze (including avoidance behavior) on individuals that indicates the generally negative responses to being stared at in *normal* individuals.

The descriptions of the responses to being looked at put forward by Sartre and, after him, Merleau-Ponty are consistent with the psychological observations of the experience of gaze as social "rule-breaking" or as a "threat display." For, staring is often construed by individuals subject to it as hostile or aggressive in impersonal social situations. Certainly, being gazed at is experienced quite often as vaguely threatening. In one study it was found that individuals stared at in a library showed signs of uneasiness and, in some cases, they abruptly left the library.[21] If we grant that Sartre's language is sometimes overly dramatic, his account is, nonetheless, not alien to some reported normal responses to being stared at. The charge that he and Merleau-Ponty are describing pathological reactions to being gazed at are quite unjustified.

The subjective experience of being an "object" for others when we are stared at in a manner that we construe as judgmental or critical is also confirmed in some psychological studies. It has been found that gaze aversion occurs when individuals seek to avoid high

[19] Siomopoulos, V., op. cit., p. 987.

[20] Argyle, Michael and Mark Cook, *Gaze and Mutual Gaze,* London, 1976, p. 85.

[21] Ibid., p. 92.

levels of arousal, when they are concealing something or feel guilty about something, or when they have low levels of self-esteem. In addition, so-called Machiavellian personalities tend to use gaze as a means of attaining control, dominance, or power over others.[22] It has also been suggested that manipulative, Machiavellian personality types, as well as psychopathic personalities, are able to resist gaze aversion and "stare down" critics, opponents, or authority figures. These exceptional cases serve to remind us that normal individuals typically respond to being stared at by feeling everything from uneasiness to panic.

The point we are making is that gaze aversion, avoidance responses, flight reactions, feelings of discomfort, anxiety, or fear are common normal responses to being stared at by others in impersonal social situations. In this regard, there is no reason to assume that Sartre's phenomenology of "the look" is solely applicable to pathological reactions. In point of fact, as we have seen, there is a continuum extending from primitive responses to "the look" in nonhuman subjects to the negative reactions to being gazed at in human subjects. Since Sartre's phenomenology of "the look" is often misrepresented by, or misunderstood by, psychiatrists or psychologists, and since it is an extensive analysis of this phenomenon, we shall briefly examine his phenomenological description of "the look."

Sartre's Phenomenology of "the Look"

The occasion for the introduction of a descriptive analysis of *le regard* or "the look" in Sartre's *Being and Nothingness* is the elucidation of that mode of being that is characterized as "being-for-others." There are forms of human behavior that suggest a reference to others. Specifically, the experiences of shame, pride and fear. However, the presentation of others to our consciousness presents something of a problem for a phenomenological description insofar as our most immediate awareness of others is as "objects" for our consciousness. Sartre offers an account of the encounter with other individuals that starts with a subjective sense of the presence of the "strange freedom" of another in order to bridge the gap between my consciousness of the other an as object and the other as a conscious subject. He maintains that the primitive character of this encounter between oneself and the other is as a reciprocal relationship that is ex-

[22] Ibid., pp. 145-46.

perienced as "conflict."[23]

Insofar as the other cannot be, from a phenomenological perspective, an object of "knowledge," Sartre searches for manifestations of the "Other-as-subject" that signify the presence of the other individual as a conscious subject who modifies my being and my world. Being looked at is a sign of the presence of the other as a conscious individual. Being in the face of the other in the world is a universal characteristic of our being, one that is indicated by our awareness of the "alienating reality" of the other as an anonymous reality.[24] This aspect of Sartre's thought is often overlooked in allusions to Sartre's phenomenology in the psychological literature. What he is maintaining is that we sense that we exist in relation to an other-in-general originally and that concrete encounters with particular others are instantiations of this generalized awareness of being for an anonymous other. Being in the world in the face of a host of others is a condition of our being in which we feel that we are actual or potential objects of the gaze of an anonymous other. The generalized experience of being for another is said to be the condition for the possibility of the experience of being an object for a specific other.

At any rate, "the look" is a signification of a direct encounter with another subjective individual. In *le regard,* Sartre avers, we feel objectified by others and experience ourselves as fixed in the gaze of the other individual. This objectification is experienced as the "negation" of our free consciousness or of our "transcendence" of the other. By seeking to elude this objectification of ourselves *via* the look, by negating ourselves as mere objective entities for the other, we testify to our "being-as-object" for another. In order to wrench ourselves away from this condition of being fixed as a determinate object in the gaze of the other, we must negate, in Sartre's Hegelian terms, the negation of our free self-consciousness on the part of the other person who objectifies us.[25]

Cutting through Sartre's elaborate and sophisticated description of the relation between oneself and others, we see that being fixed or objectified in the gaze of another indicates that one is in the presence of a subjective, conscious being. This encounter with the other entangles us in a negative "bond" with a conscious other. Expressed in terms that Sartre does not use, we may say that the experiential en-

---

[23]Sartre, Jean-Paul, *L'Être et le néant,* Paris, 1943, p. 431.

[24]Ibid., p. 341.

[25]Ibid., p. 348.

counter with others by means of "the look" is primarily experienced as negating and threatening. The experiential process is complex. By seeking to negate myself as an object for another, I testify to the experience of being objectified by a conscious other person. By asserting my nonobjective freedom, I transcend the state of being fixated as an object for the gaze of another. In addition, I seek to objectify the other person by fixing him in *my* gaze; but the other, as Sartre expresses it, transcends my transcendence. At the heart of the relationship between oneself and the other is a dialectical tension or conflict.

In the experience of shame or pride an individual attests to an awareness of the other individual as a consciousness that is judgmental, a consciousness that expresses itself through "the look." Shame and pride imply our relationship to others as objects for their awareness, their judgment, their approval or disapproval. When I look at others, Sartre claims, I measure my power. And when others look at me they measure their power.

What is particularly interesting in Sartre's phenomenology is that he construes the gaze as signifying that we are objects of evaluation and judgment for conscious subjects. This cannot simply be attributed to an ostensible "pathological" projection insofar as this experience of being the "object" of the stare of others, the sense that one is being evaluated or judged by others when they stare or gaze at one, is a rather common reaction of normal individuals. By simplifying Sartre's phenomenology of "the look" and applying his general theory of the central features of an encounter with others to psychological studies of responses to being stared at we find at least some corroboration of his assumption of the negative, conflicting nature of primordial relations between oneself and others.

Based upon the empirical data pertaining to eye contact, being stared at or gazed at, the analogies between human reactions to being stared at and the reactions of a variety of creatures to the presence of eyes or to being the object of the look of others are striking. And, in addition, they tend to support indirectly Sartre's original description of responses to "the look." Despite this, there are empirical findings that undermine the assumption that reactions to, or responses to, being stared at are invariably negative or are indications of a conflict relationship. Both informal observations and some psychological studies indicate that in certain contexts and under particular conditions, staring signifies attention, interest, mutual attraction, or erotic desire. In this regard, Sartre's phenomenology of "the look" is incomplete and truncated.

Symbolic Transformation of "the Look"

There are many social situations in which the gaze indicates attention, interest or fascination. The way in which a group of people focuses its attention on a performer, a speaker or a teacher under normal conditions is usually by means of "the look." In fascination and curiosity there is also a tendency to focus one's gaze upon the individuals, the events, situations or phenomena that stimulate such reactions. It is clear that the social context in which staring is manifested is an important factor in determining the meaning of staring at or looking at someone. In situations in which an individual is offering a presentation, performing, giving a speech or lecturing it would be unusual for the object of visual attention to interpret staring as hostile, aggressive, or menacing. The intentionality of the gaze varies in relation to the context and the ambience in which it is manifested. In addition, of course, the relationship between the individuals engaged in reciprocal gazing affects the interpretation of the meaning of being stared at. It may be the case that a kind of sublimation of a more primitive response to "the look" takes place and permissible eye contact is tacitly accepted. Or it may be that the context, circumstances, or social relations that prevail being about a symbolic transformation of the meaning of "the look."

That something like a symbolic transformation of the primordial signification of gazing may actually take place in certain contexts is supported by the two-factor theory of emotion that has been postulated in psychological theory.[26] We have already seen that being stared at elicits a measurable emotional or physiological arousal. This arousal state, according to the two-factor theory, is subject to various interpretations. Thus, an immediate response to being stared at that induces tension, discomfort, anxiety, or fear may be transformed by virtue of a reinterpretation of the initial emotional arousal. The cognitive interpretation of a subjective arousal state would, no doubt, be affected by contextual cues. The social context, then, would determine the nature of the interpretation of an initial arousal state. Both the context and the behavior of the individual who is staring may elicit contradictory and inhibiting factors that transform the more typical, negative responses to being the object of the gaze of others. When an individual is interesting to another, the eye contact involved in this situation may simply indicate fascination or interest. The

[26] Schacter, S. and J. E. Singer, "Cognitive, Social and Physiological Determinants of Emotional State," *Psychological Review,* 1962 (69), pp. 379-99.

social situation conditions the response to being the object of the gaze of another or of others.[27] The arousal reaction may be similar to the response to being looked at that elicits negative reactions, but the meaning of the emotional state is transformed.

The typical reciprocal staring or persistent eye contact in situations in which two individuals are emotionally or sexually attracted to one another indicates that the subjective meaning of the encounter is a highly relevant factor. Curiously enough, the prolongation of tonic immobility in small animals that was induced by eye contact and conditioned by the pupil size of the eyes finds its symbolically transformed simulacrum in erotically tinged eye contact. It has been found that an increase in pupil size is an indication of emotional arousal and attraction. Conversely, large pupils are perceived as more attractive than smaller pupils.[28] Here we have an apparent reversal of previously indicated responses. Prolonged eye contact, intense staring and large pupil size are, under certain conditions and in certain social contexts, experienced as signs of attraction, interest, or desire. A conscientious phenomenology of "the look" must accommodate these polarities of response to being the object of the gaze of another. It would appear that there is a cultural transformation of primitive reactions to "the look" that enables man to reinterpret its meaning in social contexts in which negative responses to being gazed at would be inhibited or inappropriate. In terms of the polarities discussed, it would seem that the intentionality of the look is interpreted in radically different ways. The apparent break with the continuity running through the negative reactions to being gazed upon may be accounted for in terms of the symbolic transformation of specific experiences by means of an infusion of cultural meaning. Perhaps the negative reactions to "the look" in man are residues of primitive, natural responses to eye contact or to being stared at. And perhaps the positive responses to being gazed at are the result of a kind of cultural transsubstantiation of primordial reactions.

Although we cannot pretend to have dealt with all of the relevant dimensions of the phenomenon of "the look," we have indicated a curious continuity in the responses to, or the effects produced by, eye contact or staring that can be traced from the lower organisms to man. One consequence of this discovery is that Sartre's

[27] Cook, M., "Gaze and Mutual Gaze in Social Encounters," p. 330. Cf. R. V. Exline and M. Cook, "Affective Relations and Mutual Glances in Dyads," in *Affect, Cognition and Personality,* London, 1966.

[28] Hess, E. H., "Attitude and Pupil Size," *Sci. Am.,* 212: 46-54.

phenomenological description of *le regard* is neither peculiar nor exclusively appropriate, as some psychologists believe, to pathological reactions to being the object of the look of others. On the other hand, we have shown that Sartre's phenomenology of the experience of being stared at is incomplete and, in terms of current empirical knowledge, ultimately inaccurate. Although a phenomenology need not be restricted by empirical findings nor, in its classic form, affected by empirical data at all, we believe that when the method of phenomenology is applied to phenomena that have been and are objects of study in the empirical sciences, it should not fly in the face of experimental data. If phenomenology is to be more than a kind of subjective, introspective report, it should, ideally, take into consideration currently available empirical information pertaining to the phenomenon it purports to describe. By doing so, it only enhances its validity and its persuasive power. In the case of the phenomenon of "the look," we have seen that a great deal of the empirical data seems to substantiate what has sometimes been characterized as an idiosyncratic phenomenology. That Sartre's unique description of "the look" is incomplete and in need of revision does not undermine the validity of its intuitive insights.

GEORGE J. STACK
AND
ROBERT W. PLANT.

STATE UNIVERSITY OF NEW YORK,
COLLEGE AT BROCKPORT.

THE ORIGINALITY OF HUME'S THEORY OF OBLIGATION

I

As I read him, David Hume contends that there is no such thing as *the* obligatory view, not to mention the moral or political points of view. That is to say, there are no principles of obligation *per se*. Here, the so-called open question argument, employed by G. E. Moore, has some relevance. One can always ask (in a form, of course, which is closer to Prichard and Ross than to Moore), "But *ought* one always to do this or that?" Now, I have never claimed that the open question argument is definitive. In fact, I doubt very much whether any argument or counter-argument is ever definitive. Long ago, William Frankena fought the open question argument to a draw, though he supposed that he did more. But he was mistaken. The open question, "But ought one (or I) to do this?" is, at best, of an inductive sort. Let me give one or two examples. One can always ask whether one ought to keep, or has an obligation to keep a certain promise. One can always ask whether one ought to pay his lawfully acquired debts. One can always ask whether he ought to remain loyal to his country, or that he would be wrong in committing an act of treason. Of course, one can indeed always reply, however plausibly, "Yes, certainly, he indeed ought to do so." My point is that, while the open question argument *proves* nothing, in the strict sense, it has a good deal of plausibility. Whenever one stops asking the open question, because he is tired of raising it for the time being, he can go on and on raising it, from case to case. Thus, as I see it, the open question argument has a great deal of inductive force.

My view is that in Hume's case, there really is, in an unstrict sense, something that amounts to a "proof," that the concept of obligation must always be open. Perhaps a better way of putting it would be to say that we can only have conceptions of obligation, and that there is no such thing as *the* concept of obligation.

Of course, there are many modes of obligation. There are moral obligations, political obligations, professional obligations, religious obligations, and so on. But none of them is definitive. One may say that there are necessary, or sufficient, conditions of any sort of obligation, or even of obligation itself. But there are *no* definitive, necessary and sufficient, conditions of obligation as such.

Let us now return, or rather proceed, to the question of moral obligation. Hume himself plainly distinguishes, in the *Treatise,* two senses of the term "moral." In one sense, he applies it to all "moral subjects" which includes practically everything save mathematics and empirical science. It includes morality in the sense understood by Moore and Frankena. But it also includes obligations which, as I have said, pertain to those normally ranged under politics, law, as well as religion. As I shall later argue, "moral obligation" in the wider sense, is in the end hardly more than a name for "obligation" itself. I will go further. For I am convinced that in the end the same may well be true of moral obligation. In the narrower sense, moral obligation contrasts fairly clearly with political obligation. But this is never absolutely clear or definitive, and here again one may make use of the open question argument. In the narrower sense, we intuitively understand that political obligations are obligations of allegiance (for example) to a nation-state. Moral obligations, in this sense, are those which survive when a state, or politically organized society of any sort, is in a state of civil war or revolution. But we must never forget that despite his conservatism, which was as great as that of Burke, to whom he is sometimes compared, he, unlike Burke, always insisted that revolutions may be justified, even though the first thing to be done, when a revolution is over, is to reestablish its rules of justice, which for him were largely concerned with property and property rights. The question that must now be asked is whether moral obligations, in this narrower sense, provide the basis for political obligations, and Hume's answer to this in the *Treatise* is unequivocably "No." Obligations of allegiance are not dependent upon, or necessarily justifiable, in terms of moral obligation. Perhaps they provide a reason, possibly even the reason, for establishing a politically organized society in the first place, though Hume, as we know, considered the whole ideal experiment of a state of nature as hogwash. However, once a state is established, political obligations, however weakly, become independent.

What, then, are the surviving moral obligations, once a state, or political system, has been constituted or reconstituted? Are they the obligations (and rights) of human beings to one another simply as such? One may think so, but if one did so, one would be wrong. There are many obligations which are not mutual, but merely reciprocal. Obligations are mutual when the rights and responsibilities of both parties are precisely the same. They are, for the most part, however, merely reciprocal. Let me give one or two examples. The rights and responsibilities of parents and their children are obviously different. So, too, are the rights and responsibilities of rulers and ordinary citizens. But they are not mutual.

Let us now turn to the question whether there can be uncategorized obligations simply as such. Hume's answer, as I read him, is undoubtedly "Yes." There are, for example, obligations between you and me, or, if you prefer, I and Thou. These are obligations between ourselves simply as individual persons and, of course, the concept of a person does apply to individual human beings, although not exclusively to them. There are also obligations (not necessarily attended by rights of any sort at all) on the part of human beings to others who have no obligations whatever. One or two examples makes this obvious. I may have an obligation to take care of my dog, although it would be nonsense to say that my dog has any obligation to me. He may like me, be fond of me, or do my bidding, but the idea of obligation never enters his mind. There are also many other circumstances in which men and women have obligations to other so-called human beings, who cannot be supposed to have any obligations whatever. An individual in a coma may have certain rights. He may have a right to life and to be kept alive. But surely he cannot be thought of as having any obligation whatever to his physician, his parents, or anyone else. A man on his deathbed may have the right to be eased of his pain, if he remains even minimally conscious. But he has no obligation. Examples of this sort are endless, and they need not be extended.

Whether they realize it or not, philosophers are after knowledge about meanings or forms of words. They are also after knowledge, therefore, of forms of life, whether they realize that or not. Man may not be the rational animal or the laughing animal, but he is certainly that talking and writing animal. This is his great and unique endowment, which distinguishes him from all other forms of life whatever. I would almost be prepared to say that it is definitive, though I abhor definitions, save for practical purposes. In his own time and in his own fashion, Hume was certainly a philosopher of language in the widest and richest sense. Here it is unnecessary to reaffirm this proposition. This whole paper is a demonstration of Hume's extraordinary acumen as an analytic or linguistic philosopher.

However, Hume did pursue wisdom, not only for himself, but for all members of "the party of humanity." No other philosopher, not even Socrates, loved wisdom more than he. He contributed to our common fund of wisdom in virtually every sphere, philosophical and nonphilosophical, if such a distinction has any meaning. I say this, precisely because all men do pursue wisdom in their own ways, however limited, and however misguided their various searches for it may be. Think of it: Hume contributed to our wisdom through his epistemological and metaphysical investigations, through his studies of ethics, politics, law, philosophy of art, and religion. He was also a distinguished economist, as Adam Smith testified. And economics or, as I still prefer to think of it, political economy (since there can be no economy independently of politics and government) is a foundational human subject.

Let me now say something, in Hume's behalf, about the fundamental question of religious obligation. Whether he regarded it as fundamental is no matter, though it may seem that he did not do so. Suppose that, as it were, we augment a you into a Thou. Suppose, in short, that we treat you not simply as a moral or political person, with the rights and responsibilities pertaining thereto, or suppose that we begin to see, no matter how dimly, that your moral or political being has a religious aspect of some sort. It does not matter which. You have become, and I am still speaking for Hume, to me, a Thou, a being whom I regard as holy. In our book, the religious life is not to be defined in terms of one's relationship to God, if God there be, but to virtually anything which one regards and treats as holy. I may find anything at all, the sea or the universe, if such there be, as holy. In one of his great sonnets, Wordsworth roars out, "Lo, the mighty being is awake, and doth with his eternal motion make a sound like thunder everlastingly!" Wordsworth has been called a pantheist. But pantheism is no less a form of religion than theism or polytheism. What, then, shall we say about the religious mood save that it invests its object with one's own sense of its holy being?

If this be so, it becomes difficult to understand religious obligation as a definitive *kind* of obligation. It is found everywhere, in every sort of form, and in every degree. In fact, it is probably one of the most common and indiscriminate of all forms of obligation. So now let me ask, for Hume, whether there is any way whatever of distinguishing religious obligations from obligations of any other sort. In short, what is not, in some respect, a religious obligation? Or, to put the same point in other terms, what obligation has no vestige of holiness? I think, again for Hume, that there is none. I fail to see, therefore, how it is possible to speak with any clarity or distinctness, of a unique form of obligation which we may call "religious." There are, of course, religious institutions, churches, synagogues, sects, and so on. But these are not necessarily holy, even when they profess to be so. Again, the open question. Is the Catholic church a holy institution? Catholics, when they are sincere, so regard it. So, also, in the case of the Jews, Moslems, and other "churches," creeds and religious practices. Still, we may seriously ask whether this or that church or creed is *really* holy.

I have said that any obligation whatever becomes religious when it is augmented. Let us now reverse the question. Is it possible for one's sense of the holy to diminish? The answer to this question seems obvious. One may diminish by stages any Thou back into a you, a you, in fact, to whom one feels or has no responsibilities whatever. Despite everything that we have said earlier, one is always faced by diminutions of the sense of holiness that are so great that in the end it disappears altogether. One falls into a coma, as will most people one day, then one's sense of the holiness of anything, including one's own person and life, simply disappears.

For Hume's contention is, then, that religious obligations and rights are not only indefinable but describable only in a variety of nonsynonymous terms.

II

Back, now, to Hume in earnest. My contention is that there is no such thing, in Hume's view, as *the* obligatory view, let alone the moral, or the political, points of view. If religious obligations are subject to the open question, so are moral obligations, political obligations, legal obligations, and the rest. There are, in short, obligations simply as such. And this concept of obligation, although describable, is indefinable, and it is hard to suppose that there is such a thing as *the* concept of obligation.

What are the consequences of this view? They are, in fact, virtually incalculable. For they imply, in effect, that the whole topic of obligation has been misconceived from start to finish. They imply, not only that there is no such thing as *the* religious point of view, *the* moral point of view, or, indeed, any such point of view. They also imply that the open question argument usually still has an important use in any domain of discourse or activity. They also imply that, in the case of language, we can raise the open question about the meaning of virtually any term whatever. For example, we can always ask about any definition of man. "But is he a man, as *that* definition conceives him?" Is man a rational animal? Yes, and no. Is man a laughing animal? Yes, but not always. Is God, or the term "God," definable? Well, many monotheists offer definitions of "God," but it is always possible to ask, "But is God almighty, omniscient, and all merciful?" The point no longer needs belaboring.

That we have obligations is undeniable, although a few philosophers, such as Paul Ziff, have argued that they can get along without them altogether. But even Ziff, so far as I know, confined himself only to promising. Nietzsche, in his talk about going beyond good and evil, seems to some to have had such a notion in mind. But both *The Genealogy of Morals* and *Beyond Good and Evil* go no further, he says so explicitly. So-called "noble" men do have obligations. For they have responsibilities to other noble men, and they have rights from other noble men. But everyone knows this. What needs emphasizing here is that no coherent theory of obligation as such has been offered.

Back to Hume. Some may think that I have been using Hume as a clotheshorse on which to hang my own antitheory of obligation. If we care to, we can describe obligations, whether *simpliciter* or with any qualifying adjective such as "religious" or "moral." But all such descriptions leave plenty of room for open-mindedness about them. And this is precisely what is true in Hume's case.

The fundamental concept, in Hume's philosophy, is that of *Sentiment.* Not only does he speak of moral sentiments and religious sentiments, in the first *Enquiry,* he actually holds not only that statements of fact are statements which express sentiments of approval and disapproval, but also that the same holds true of statements about matters of fact. Hume was one of the least sentimental of men in the present-day pejorative sense of that term, as his *Autobiography* shows. He was only speaking the truth when he claimed to be a member of the party of Humanity. Few of his friends would have described him as sentimental, although they would have described him accurately as a man of sentiment (in the 18th century sense of the term). Most of his sentiments were benevolent, and he well deserved to think of himself as a humanist, in the best sense of the term.

III

What does Hume mean by the term "sentiment," aside from speaking of it as a "calm passion"? The following description may be helpful here, although what I shall say about it is scarcely more than a redaction of his own statements about moral sentiments.

Let me put it this way. A sentiment is, so to say, a cognitive emotion or, alternatively, an emotional cognition. It is passional; it is active; it is also an action guide. But it is also cognitive. And the expression of a sentiment is, or may be, true or false, or, better, probable or improbable. Hume tells us this explicitly, in the *Treatise,* in pages 581-83.

Let me now take the liberty of quoting him, from time to time, in the following pages in order to demonstrate my claim.

First of all, let us get the terms "approval" and "approbation" out of the way. Many emotivists, and especially C. L. Stevenson, have explicitly construed "approval" and its cognates as merely emotive terms. Thus, as we know, his description of the meaning of a value judgment goes something like this. When I say that X is good, I am saying something which, as he puts it, goes like this. "I approve of X; (kindly) do so also." Stevenson never doubts that the term "approve" is itself an emotive term. But this is plainly false. When one says, "I approve of X," one is not simply expressing, or venting, one's emotion or feeling toward it. In Stevenson's view, approving and wanting, desiring, or taking an interest in something, differ in meaning in no significant way whatever. Nor does he think anything more needs to be said about his view. But if I should say, "I approve of Thomas Jefferson," my words express a *judgment.* Such a statement is tantamount to saying, "I *judge* that Thomas Jefferson was a good man." Stevenson's position simply will not do. A judgment is a statement, whatever its subject, and it asserts something which is confirmable or disconfirmable in one way or another. So nothing more needs to be said about the terms "approval," "approbation," and their cognates which occur so frequently on Hume's pages in the *Treatise* and in the *First,* not to mention the *Second Enquiry,* which I shall not pause to examine here.

Let us return to what Hume has to say on pages 581-83 of the *Treatise.* In that work, he explicitly holds that moral approbation is a principle of judgment. Its role is not merely to modify other passions but to *correct* them. Why so? Well, consider the following statement: "I do not feel the same lively pleasure from the virtues of a person, who lived in Greece two thousand years ago, that I feel from the virtues of a familiar friend . . ." (*Treatise,* page 581). Again: "Yet I do not esteem the one more than the other. Nor does my approval of the behaviour of the one differ, in principle, from that of the other" (*ibid.*). And again: "It would be impossible that we could ever converse together on any reasonable terms, were each of us to consider characters and persons, only as they appear to us from his peculiar point of view. In order, therefore, to prevent those continual *contractions,* and arrive at a more *stable* judgment of things, we fix on some *steady* and *general* points of view; and always in our thoughts place ourselves in them, whatever may be our present situation" (*Treatise,* pages 581-83).

Thus, as Hume tells us, our particular moral sentiments vary a good deal, according to our present situation or nearness or remoteness with respect to the individual whom we praise or blame as morally good or right or as morally bad or wrong.

The point may be extended without sweat. In regard to our judgments of beauty, whether in art or in nature, it is obvious that the same holds true. In fact, Hume explicitly tells us in "On the Standard of Taste," that what we now call aesthetic judgments are quite different from mere expressions of taste, which may well be mere expressions of emotion or feeling. He has an example which is worth recalling. As he says, in effect, I may prefer Ogalvie to Milton, but one does not on that account, unless one is mad, judge Ogalvie (whoever he was) to be a better, more admirable, poet than Milton. On the contrary, one judges the latter to be a greater poet than the former, whatever may be one's taste about the respective poems. Obviously, there is no disputing about tastes. But this is so only because taste, or expressions of taste, are largely noncognitive and nonjudgmental. But literary approbation is an entirely different matter. To announce one's literary approbation of a poem is to make a judgment, and a judgment, as we have seen, is cognitive. Here, we do well to remind ourselves of what Aristotle says about judgment. A judgment is, as Aristotle puts it, a statement that is "true for the most part." Literary, and indeed all aesthetic judgments although true for the most part, are clearly cognitive. But enough about Hume's account of these matters in the essay "On the Standard of Taste."

Our particular sentiments thus tend to vary according to our present situations. Nevertheless, we normally ignore them in our general statements, or judgments, and still apply the terms that express our liking or dislike, much as if we remained in one point of view (cf. *Treatise,* page 582). This happens, so he says, only through experience, which soon teaches us the same method of correcting our sentiments, or, rather, our language (cf. *ibid.*).

Such corrections would be unavailing, however, and hence

pointless, were the corrective method in question inert. For, it could then exert no influence upon our variable sentiments or the passions from which we derive them. As Hume argues in *Book II* of the *Treatise,* no passion can be modified save by another passion. Hence, if the attitudes expressed by the more general decisions to which he refers were wholly inactive, they could make no conceivable difference to our conduct, moral or otherwise.

At this state, Hume now goes well beyond anything he has said earlier about the subject. In so doing, he provides an extremely interesting basis for my own view concerning his general notions of rational in other domains. Thus, it is worth quoting his own words again. As he says, "Such corrections are common with regard to all the senses; and indeed 'twere impossible we could ever make use of language or communicate our sentiments to one another, did we not correct the momentary appearances of things, and overlook our present situation" (*ibid.*). This is a remarkable passage. But I will fix, here, on one word only. That word is "communicate." The point, surely, is that Hume does regard expressions of sentiments as forms of communication. And it is doubtful whether it makes much sense to speak of emotive discourse as a form of communication. Then, in order to make sure that despite all early appearances of contradiction, or, rather, conflict, shall now be removed, he goes on to say that no matter how rarely we are able to bring ourselves to it, and no matter how unreadily our uncalm passions follow our judgments, the rules of morality represent a form of *reason.* And he goes on to say that this usage will be readily understood "if we consider what we formerly said concerning that *reason* which is able to oppose our passion; and which we have found to be nothing but a general calm determination of the passions, founded on some distant view or reflexion" (*Treatise,* page 583). This is the crucial passage; it goes far toward proving the case that in Hume's view virtually *all* judgments, whether general or particular, whether of principle or not, are expressions of sentiments of approval or disapproval.

I may seem to have taken a long time getting to the point. Having made it, however, my opinion is that Hume's conception of all forms of judgment is largely inconsistent with that of any form of emotivism whatever. Hume is not an emotivist, despite all his hemming and hawing, and despite the common impressions to the contrary, his entire theory of obligation, on all levels, is strongly antiemotivist. Moreover, despite all contrary appearances, his position is not, in Moore's sense, naturalistic. He is *the* philosopher of "sentiment." Herein lies his genius. For this is the word that provides the key which unlocks the door to all that is most original and most interesting in Hume's philosophy.

IV

It is the business of all philosophy, I believe, to love and to pursue wisdom. And wisdom largely consists in the formation of sentiments in precisely the way Hume describes them and forms them. Of course, no one can be wise if he merely forms them. For there has rarely been a wise man capable of discourse. Imagine a lover of wisdom indifferent to some concern, for the means to his own survival and those he loves! Only saints, and few of us are saints, are indifferent to the world's goods. Hume was no saint and would have laughed had anyone called him one. Leslie Stephen called Mill "the saint of rationalism," but Stephen was a sentimentalist, and Mill would have been the last man to accept such a description of his work or his life. Thus, I am prepared to say that for Hume, sainthood is not a useful moral or religious category. Saints are religious neurotics. We are men! Our business is with life on this earth and with our conduct of life here.

Let us now conclude. The originality of Hume's theory of obligation is beyond question. It has taken us through an examination of the moral point of view, the political point of view, the religious point of view. It shows us, piece by piece, why such points of view, when taken as Frankena or Baier do in their writings, will not do. Indeed, it shows the so-called moral point of view that cannot be fully understood, even as an ideal philosophical experiment. That there are points of view, in any domain, cannot be doubted. But they are the points of view of individuals or communities. They evolve, or develop, historically. They differ widely from culture to culture and from civilization to civilization. There is no way of disputing this fact. Thus, there is no such thing as *the* obligatory view, and definitions of "obligation," as well as "moral" or "political" or "religious" "obligation," are illusory. This has been shown (not demonstrated) in the preceding pages. And, for the present, this is all that needs to be said on the subject.

HENRY DAVID AIKEN.

BRANDEIS UNIVERSITY.

PERSONS AND MORALITY

Although persons bear many descriptions, they are above all moral beings. This is the most basic, comprehensive, and philsophically revealing thing we can say about them. Their actions are subject to moral appraisal; and moral appraisals of their actions reflect on them as persons—how they, presumed to have adequate personal powers, perform or are disposed to perform as persons. Thus moral discourse has a unique logical connection with person-talk. The intellectual fortunes of the two stand or fall together. Moral skepticism and nihilism challenge the concept of a person, and, indeed, personhood itself, for the concept of a person is internal to and constitutive of persons.

Persons, according to moral talk, are beings who have a life of their own to live. There is no moral truth more universally accepted. Not to recognize this of a person is the highest insult. To treat one merely as a tool, an instrument, or a commodity is to treat him or her as a thing. To regard another as one's slave or pet is to deny his or her personhood. To exercise power over others by whatever means so that they cannot live their own lives is to injure, to cripple, or to hobble them as persons. To the extent one is in the power of another as an instrument of his or her will, one is not a moral agent but an extension of the other person. But to the extent one subjects oneself to the will of another or to the extent one has the power to liberate oneself, one must bear responsibility for one's condition and for what one does, for they are parts of one's own life.

Living a life is not simply existing biologically between birth and death; nor is it simply suffering or enduring a sequence of events. It is not even a succession of responses, pursuits, and lived episodes. It has a unity. Living a life, I submit, is a matter of setting and pursuing one's own goals, under the guidance of one's own experience, beliefs, and critical judgments, in such a way that there is a progression from one's lived past through one's lived present to one's anticipated future, a progression that is subject to rational appraisal and for which one is responsible. It has an intentional structure that embraces a life plan as an integral part of one's normative self-image and sense of identity.

One may not be able to talk clearly and accurately about the life one is living, but one is aware of it in many ways. One cannot live a life without direction, review, foresight, and criticism from a position of present- and self-transcendence. Some sense of one's overall life plan has to feature in one's response to a given event. Otherwise the response would be more or less arbitrary or hardly a *response* at all, only an effect of the given event. This is the plea sometimes made for a quick reaction, grounded in suddenly aroused emotion. The more thoughtful an act is the more it is thought to fit into one's life plan and thus the more it is taken to be one's own. Also one's life plan is revealed in what one considers as options for oneself, in one's choices, in one's sense of success or failure, in one's regrets and satisfactions, in one's morale or depression, in one's self-esteem or lack of it, in one's aspirations and expectations, and the like.

A person, we have said, is a being who has a life of his or her own to live. But what is it *to have* a life to live? It is, I suggest, a normative matter. A person is a being who by his or her nature ought to define and to live a life of his or her own. As the holder of an office has the responsibilities in terms of which the office is defined, a person has the responsibility to define and to live a life of his or her own. The emphasis here is on *responsibility*. It is not merely that people have an inclination to live by their wants and choices and to resist being yoked to the will of another; nor is it simply a fact that they develop patterns of behavior and make plans. People feel themselves to be under an imperative to define and to live their own lives; they feel that it is proper and fitting for them to do so; that it is improper or not fitting for them not to do so; they feel pride and self-esteem in doing so, and self-contempt in not doing so; they feel indignant at those who would not allow them to do so—that those who deny them the opportunity to define and to live their own lives violate their personhood. In like manner, we feel contempt for those who have the opportunity but do not define and live their own lives; and we feel indignation at those who prevent others from defining and living their own lives. If such feelings and judgments are not universal, they tend to appear with heightened consciousness and what we consider the advancement of humankind, unless weakened by philosophical skepticism about the normative dimension of the culture.

The point of these remarks is that a person's normative self-image as a human being, in its normal state, contains the imperative to define and to live one's own life. One's normative self-image as a person is peculiar, as previously remarked, in that it is not simply of and about oneself, but, indeed, constitutive of oneself. One could not be a fully functioning human being without the normative conception of oneself as a person. One's powers of self-criticism and self-direction would be impossible without it. An imperative grounded in one's status in this manner and operative through being known is just what we mean by a responsibility.

Granted that people have the responsibility to define and to live their own lives, does it matter what kind of life one lives so long as it is one's own? Are there any guidelines? Clearly some life plans lead to wrecked lives; some keep those who try to live them in trouble and make for frustrated and unfulfilled lives; some seem to be successfully lived but fail to make for happy lives or to win moral approval; and some seem to make for happy lives and to gain moral approval. These facts suggest that life plans are, in a sense, life-hypotheses to be tested in the living of them. We seem to learn something about how to live in the living of our own lives, in knowing others, and in studying biography. Playwrights and novelists define and test life-hypotheses in the development of characters in imaginative living; and, in doing so, they seem to instruct us about life plans and what it is to live them. All of this seems to indicate that there are constitutional principles, something to be responsible to and to get right, in defining and living a life; perhaps even that there is a kind of master plan, a skeletal plan, that anyone's life plan must embrace, if it is to make possible a well-lived, happy life that is worthy of moral approval. If there is such a master plan, it is not one that we generate by our choices; nor is it one that we bear responsibility for in the way in which we do for our specific life plans.

The central controversies of moral philosophy focus on whether there is a normative constitution or master plan for human life, and if so, what it is and what status it has. Those who believe, as I do, that human beings as such are dialectically committed to moral appraisal of their behavior in much the same way as they are to logical appraisals of their thought and who believe that moral judgments admit of objectivity and validity, believe that there is inherent in human beings a normative constitution or a master life plan that is caught up in our normative self-image as a person and presupposed by and reflected in our moral appraisals.

Even if we should accept the claim that the only condition one's life plan must meet is that it be authentically one's own, what would this amount to? Could a life plan be authentically one's own if it did not stand approved under one's own rational and moral criticism? I think not. Simple rational criticism reveals the formal requirements that one's life plan be coherent, comprehensive (take into account the whole of one's life), and possible for one under the circumstances of one's existence. Any life plan that does not meet these minimum conditions gives rise to frustration and failure in the living of it.

Furthermore, the responsibility of other persons to define and to live their own lives endows them with certain rights, the freedoms and conditions necessary for them to have an opportunity to define and to live their own lives. These rights of others impose normative restraints and requirements on one in defining and living one's own life. One whose life plan lacks respect for other persons is both logically and morally at fault. Such a life plan is inconsistent, for one cannot be a functioning person without a normative image of oneself as a being who has the responsibility, and thus the correlative rights, to define and to live his or her own life; and this entails the same for other persons. The moral fault lies in the fact that lack of respect for other persons calls into question one's willingness to accept and to execute one's responsibility to be a self-defining and self-directing agent. In other words, to define and to live one's own life in a way that does not respect the basic responsibility and rights of others does violence to oneself. Such a life cannot be authentically one's own.

But does being authentically one's own, and thus approved under one's own rational and moral criticism, require more of one's life plan than coherence, comprehensiveness, realism, and compatibility with the basic responsibility and rights of other persons? In other words, does the master plan provide some positive content, some generalized goal that every life plan should embody? Is there anything presupposed in moral discourse about the goal of life other than to live in a manner that is beyond reproach relative to the restraints indicated above?

The answer, I think, must be *yes.* Moral praise goes beyond being morally clean. Indeed, moral condemnation goes beyond being morally unclean. We blame people for failure to fulfill moral contraints and we praise them for doing things for which we would not fault them if they did not do them. There are acts of supererogation; there are noble deeds. Furthermore, we appraise people not only on the scale of moral excellence, but also in terms of moral greatness. Thus our moral appraisals indicate a positive content to our ideal or master life plan.

Moral philosophers have proposed several interpretations of the master life plan presupposed by moral appraisals. They divide, for the most part, into two broad categories: those that define the end of life in terms of virtue and those that define it in terms of maximization of values through action. Among those who emphasize the virtuous life, Plato talked about the proper organization and functioning of the several elements of the soul; Aristotle spoke of the activity of the soul in accordance with virtue; Stoics think of the good person as one who understands and accepts reality with tranquility; Christians see the good person as loving and caring; Kant thought of the good person as one with good will, a will determined by respect for the moral law. We may call the second group utilitarianians, those who think that moral appraisals indicate that the goal of life is to maximize values through the effects of action. The emphasis in the first group is on what a person ought to be and in the second on what one ought to do.

Clearly the two positions are intimately related. Being a certain kind of person involves being disposed to act in certain ways; and acting for (or judging one's actions in terms of) the maximization of values involves being a person of a certain kind. But there are important differences. The utilitarian conceives the self and defines the moral point of view so that there is a problem about why one should be moral. Those who emphasize virtue and define morality in terms of what one ought to be and how one ought to function as a person locate the moral point of view in the self in such a way that there cannot be a separation between the authentic point of view of the self and the moral point of view. The person who does not develop and accept the moral perspective is, according to this view, either undeveloped as a person or perverted and self-alienated.

Utilitarianism, I submit, is a theory of ethics from within a general philosophical perspective that cuts the foundations out from under the moral being approach. A theory of knowledge (such as most versions of modern empiricism) that makes possible, ontologically speaking, only factual structures and compels rejection of objective values and essences gives rise to views of the self and world that make some form of utilitarianism necessary. But from within a value realism that recognizes normative structures, along with existence and factuality, a sufficiently rich conception of selfhood becomes available and even compelling for the moral point of view to be anchored in one's identity as a person. Accordingly, moral appraisals will be understood as concerned with how well one is constituted and performing as a person. And so concern with being justified under moral criticism and meriting moral praise will be seen as concern with being fully oneself as a human being. On this view, happiness will be regarded, not as a life free from pain and full of pleasure, but as a perception of one's moral health, a sense of one's own well-being and well-functioning as a person.

A convincing case can be made for the latter position, I believe, for anyone with the logical space for it within his or her epistemological and metaphysical assumptions. Furthermore, the lack of logical space for such a view of the self and the moral enterprise puts a heavy burden on those beliefs that crowd them out, for some of the primary realities we know are thereby rendered problematic. Our epistemology must accommodate the kind of knowledge that is essential for us to be and to function as persons.

I conclude, then, that the goal of morality, and thus the universal goal of human life, is human development and the moral health of persons. By extension, this means social development and the moral health of institutions and society as well, for, as it can be easily shown, the development and moral health of persons require the development and moral health of society.

We have been talking about the goal of life presupposed in moral discourse, not the direct ends of action. In confronting a concrete problem, one would not ask, "What action in this situation would tend to perfect my being and support the human enterprise?" One would ask, however, "What should I do here and now? What does this situation require of me?" Some might say that the utilitarian comes in at this point with an answer, namely, "Of all the options, choose the one that will have the best consequences." But how do we evaluate the consequences? And why does the set of consequences judged best overall impose an overriding requirement on me? In most situations, this would seem to be a pale responsibility in comparison with others we bear to special individuals, including ourselves. In discovering what a given situation requires of a person, we must, I think, rely on what informed, morally virtuous persons would judge that the situation requires of him or her. There are no principles or rules to apply that can save us from judgment. Coherence of judgments on the part of informed, morally sensitive, wise persons is the only criterion of moral truth. This is not to deny that there is a body of moral wisdom (analytic moral truths and a set of more or less consensus moral judgments) about abstract cases, but in reality we face concrete situations. The abstract wisdom is helpful, but it is not conclusive.

By way of summary, then, moral discourse reveals that to be a person is to have an office, so to speak, an office constituted by the responsibility to define and to live a life of one's own under the guidance of one's own beliefs and judgments, along with the rights that are grounded in this responsibility. Living a life involves having a life plan that is caught up in one's normative self-image and sense of identity. Any life plan one develops should embrace and be consistent with a master life plan that is presupposed by one's own rational and moral appraisals, which have a universal intent and seek confirmation in the appraisals of others. In order for one's life-plan to stand justified under such criticism, and thus be authentically one's own, it must not only be coherent, comprehensive, realistic, and compatible with the self-defining and self-directing responsibility of other persons and their human rights, but such that in living it one perfects one's own being, maintains one's own moral health, and supports the life development and moral health of others and the development and moral health of a social order that furthers the human enterprise.

E. M. ADAMS.

THE UNIVERSITY OF NORTH CAROLINA
AT CHAPEL HILL.

AQUINAS ON GOD'S OMNIPRESENCE AND TIMELESSNESS[1]

The doctrine that God is omnipresent and the doctrine that God is eternal are two doctrines essential to the theology of St. Thomas Aquinas. They are essential to his theology in the sense that Aquinas resolutely maintains that the property of being omnipresent and the property of being eternal are two of the properties which God possesses necessarily, that being omnipresent and being eternal are included in the very essence of God. In other words, to be God is to be, among other things, both omnipresent and eternal. The latter doctrine, that God is eternal, can be understood in at least two different ways. It can be understood either as the claim that God's duration is temporally infinite or as the claim that God is timeless, that God is neither in time nor subject to literal temporal predications. The view that God is timeless is the one supported by St. Thomas and it is also the view most generally accepted by philosophers and theologians in the middle ages, most notably, by Boethius, Augustine, and Anselm.

But if God is indeed omnipresent then it would appear that he must have been in the United Nations Building *yesterday* as well as the day *before* yesterday. And if God was in the United Nations Building *both* yesterday *and* the day before, then it would appear that he is in time and that temporal predications do actually apply to him. So, it would appear that God is *not* a timeless being if he is omnipresent and that two doctrines crucial to the theology of Aquinas are logically incompatible.

At this point defenders of Aquinas are almost certain to object to the preceding argument by claiming that the contradiction it establishes is not a real contradiction when the argument is applied to Aquinas and that this apparent contradiction dissolves with a detailed understanding of his explication of the two doctrines in question. I will show that this line of defense does not work. By examining Aquinas's conception of eternity as timelessness and his conception of omnipresence, I will show that the doctrine of divine eternity and the doctrine of divine omnipresence as they are enunciated by Aquinas do indeed jointly entail a contradiction, that the preceding argument actually does apply to St. Thomas.

[1]This paper was written under a Faculty Research Fellowship for 1977 from the Research Foundation of the State University of New York.

The most detailed account of eternity provided by Aquinas occurs in the *Summa Theologiae,* part I, question 10. In article 4 of that question he makes it quite clear that on his view eternity is timeless and not simply endless temporal duration by claiming that there are manifest differences between time and eternity. One of the differences consists in the fact that eternity has neither a beginning nor an end while time has both a beginning and an end. But for Aquinas this difference is only an *accidental* difference for he also holds that even though time has both a beginning and an end it might have had no beginning and no end. So, while it is a necessary condition of eternity that it have neither a beginning nor an end that condition is not a sufficient condition of eternity. It is not a sufficient condition because even if it were true that time had no beginning and no end, time and eternity would still not be identical. For Aquinas there would still remain a difference between time and eternity and that difference is for him an *essential* one, not an *accidental* one. The essential difference that obtains between time and eternity is that eternity is *tota simul,*[2] an instantaneous or simultaneous whole, while time is not. So, on Aquinas's view eternity is essentially different from time and, hence, on his view eternity is atemporal or timeless and not simply endless temporal duration. Moreover, on this account eternity is essentially different from time and so is timeless by virtue of the fact that it is *tota simul.* But the notion of eternity as *tota simul* is not in itself altogether clear and so the idea that eternity is timeless is not altogether clear. Consequently, understanding St. Thomas's conception of God and eternity as timeless, and understanding the exact nature of the essential difference that is supposed to obtain between time and eternity, requires a clear understanding of his claim that eternity is *tota simul* while time is not.

In article 1 of question 10 Thomas defines time as nothing more than the numbering of motion or change according to before and after; that is, time is nothing but the numbering of successive beginnings and ends in a sequence of changes. Moreover, in both article 1 and article 4 he subscribes to the principle he attributes to Aristotle that time measures only those things beginning and ending in time. In the same passages he also contrasts time and eternity by pointing out that eternity is *tota simul* while, on the other hand, in time there is before and after, that is, there are beginnings and ends. So, it

---

[2] Aquinas follows Boethius by name in claiming that eternity is *tota simul.* The passage referred to by Aquinas occurs in Boethius's *The Consolation of Philosophy,* Book V, prose 6.

would seem that successiveness is the essential attribute of time for Aquinas; and it would seem that for him time is *not tota simul* by virtue of the fact that there are beginnings and ends (there is successiveness) *in* time while eternity *is tota simul* and, hence, timeless by virtue of the fact that there are no beginnings and ends (there is no successiveness) *in* eternity.

It would appear, then, that there is a second necessary condition of eternity. Not only is it a necessary condition of eternity that eternity *itself* have neither a beginning nor an end, but it is also a necessary condition of eternity that there be no before and after, no beginnings and ends, *in* eternity. Time could, though it in fact does not, satisfy the first of these two necessary conditions of eternity, but time does not and *cannot* satisfy the second one. Time *cannot* satisfy the second one because while the first one marks only an accidental difference between time and eternity, the second one marks *both* the essential difference between time and eternity *and* the essential characteristic of eternity by virtue of which it is *tota simul* or *timeless.* Indeed, it is a sufficient condition of time that it does *not* satisfy the second necessary condition of eternity. That there are beginnings and ends *in* time appears to be the single feature of time which alone distinguishes it essentially from eternity on Aquinas's view; and that there are no beginnings and ends *in* eternity appears to be the single feature of eternity which alone makes it *tota simul* or timeless on his view.[3] Nevertheless, having neither a beginning nor an end *and* being *tota simul* or timeless do *not* jointly entail that a measure is identical to eternity. Even though these two conditions are both necessary conditions of eternity they are not, on the other hand, jointly *sufficient.* For in article 5 of question 10 Aquinas claims that there is yet a third measure which can satisfy *both* of these necessary conditions of eternity, but still differ essentially from *both* eternity *and* time. According to this account the *aevum,* or as I shall call it, demeternity, is a measure which falls midway between time and eternity and both demeternity and the things in it have a beginning, but no end.

However, this feature does not distinguish demeternity as essentially different from either time or eternity because Aquinas holds that having a beginning but no end is only an accidental feature of

[3] It is important not to confuse the necessary conditions for being timeless with the necessary conditions for being eternal. On Aquinas's view a measure is essentially different from time and so is timeless if and only if it is *tota simul* and, as we shall see shortly, on his view a measure can be *tota simul* or timeless even if it has both a beginning and an end.

demeternity, not an essential one, and it marks only an accidental difference both between demeternity and time and between demeternity and eternity. For even if demeternity and the things in it always had existed and always will exist, or even if God should bring demeternity and the things in it to an end, demeternity would still be essentially different from *both* eternity *and* time. It would be essentially different from time and so be timeless, according to Aquinas, by virtue of the fact that demeternity, like eternity, is *tota simul* while time is not *tota simul* (and this would be true even if demeternity had *both* a beginning *and* an end). It would be essentially different from eternity on his view by virtue of the fact that it is possible for demeternity to be connected to or associated with *(conjungi)* before and after or beginnings and ends while before and after or beginnings and ends are not compatible *(neque compatitur)* with eternity; that it, it is not possible for eternity to be in any way connected to or associated with before and after or beginnings and ends. In short, time has beginnings and ends *in* it, demeternity has no beginnings and ends *in* it though it can be connected to or associated with them, and eternity has no beginnings and ends *in* it, neither can it in any way be connected to or associated with them. It turns out, then, that on Thomas's view the necessary *and* jointly sufficient conditions that a measure must satisfy in order to qualify as eternal are that the measure *itself* have neither a beginning nor an end, that there be no beginnings and ends *in* the measure, and that it be impossible for the measure to be in any way connected to or associated with beginnings and ends; and it turns out that on his view the necessary and sufficient condition that a measure must satisfy in order to qualify as *tota simul* or timeless is that there be no beginnings and ends *in* the measure. Moreover, the essential difference between time and eternity turns out to be that time has beginnings and ends *in* it while eternity, being *tota simul* or timeless, does not have beginnings and ends *in* it; the essential difference between time and demeternity turns out to be that time has beginnings and ends *in* it while demeternity, being *tota simul* or timeless, does not have beginnings and ends *in* it but is *only* connected to or associated with beginnings and ends; and the essential difference between eternity and demeternity, both being *tota simul* or timeless, turns out to be that demeternity can be connected to or associated with beginnings and ends while eternity cannot. By comparing them in this manner, then, Aquinas attempts to distinguish his three measures from one another and to characterize the difference between a temporal measure and a timeless measure.

In spite of the confidence with which Aquinas discusses these comparisons, though, it is not at all clear that they actually succeed in making any genuine distinction between the temporal and the timeless. This is unclear because Aquinas never really explains or makes clear what the difference is between actually possessing beginnings and ends (i.e., being temporal) and not possessing them but merely being connected to or associated with beginnings and ends (i.e., being timeless). What he does say about the subject occurs in article 5 of question 10. There he says that demeternity and the things in it have a beginning but *no end* and that time measures those things whose being consists in or is subject to change while demeternity, on the other hand, is the measure of those things whose being neither consists in nor is subject to change *though they are nevertheless connected to or associated with (adjunctam) some actual or potential change.* His examples of demeternal things are the celestial bodies and angels. According to his examples the celestial bodies have unchangeable being though along with this unchangeable being they also *have* changeableness of place. On this same account angels, too, have unchangeable being though along with this unchangeable being they also *have* changeableness of choice at the natural level and changeableness of thoughts, affections, and, in their own mode, place as well. As examples of temporal things Aquinas mentions all movements and even the very being itself of all things capable of having an end *(omnium corruptibilium).*

Presumably, then, Aquinas holds that the things measured by time have changeable being by virtue of the fact that the very being of each of these temporal things has a beginning and an end marking that changeability. According to this understanding time would have beginnings and ends *in* it because the very being itself of everything measured by time has both a beginning *and* an end. Conversely, he holds that the things measured by demeternity have unchangeable being by virtue of the fact that the very being of each of these demeternal things has no beginning *and* end that would mark any changeability in their being. According to this understanding demeternity would have no beginnings and ends *in* it because the very being itself of everything measured by demeternity does not have both a beginning *and* an end though demeternity is connected to or associated with beginnings and ends because the things measured by demeternity have beginnings and ends marked by changes that occur *to* them.

On this account, then, demeternity has no beginnings and ends *in* it and so is *tota simul* by virtue of the fact that the being of demeternal things neither consists in nor is subject to change, that is, has no beginning *and* end. But there are two difficulties with this account of the difference between actually possessing beginnings and ends and not possessing them but merely being connected to or associated with them. First, in article 5 of question 10 Aquinas resolutely maintains that God has it within his power to bring demeternity and the things in it to an end and that having no beginning *and* end is only an *accidental* feature of demeternity and demeternal things. It follows from this that the difference between having no beginnings and ends *in* it and having beginnings and ends *in* it is not an essential difference between demeternity and time. So, that difference does not distinguish demeternity and time as a timeless measure and a temporal measure because it is a necessary condition for a measure to be timeless that the measure be essentially different from time. Even though demeternity has no beginnings and ends *in* it, it is not by virtue of that fact timeless. In short, being *tota simul* or having no beginnings and ends *in* it does *not* characterize demeternity as timeless. Second, as we have just seen, Aquinas holds that while the *being* of demeternal things does not change, demeternal *things* do nevertheless undergo change because they change with respect to such dispositions as place, thoughts, affections and the like. He is also committed to the principle that time measures those things beginning and ending in time. But, then, since changes do occur to demeternal things and those changes are measured by time and occur in time because they begin and end in time, it would appear to follow that the things measured by demeternity are also measured by time and that time and demeternity are *not* mutually exclusive measures. Hence, it follows that demeternal things are temporal things, not atemporal or timeless things, and that demeternity is a measure of temporal things, not a measure of atemporal or timeless things. Indeed, Aquinas himself admits as much and supports this understanding of his account of time and demeternity when he says in his reply to objection 1 (article 5 of question 10) that demeternal things are measured by demeternity with respect to their natural being, but are measured by time with respect to their display of successiveness, that is, with respect to the successive beginnings and ends marked by the changes that occur to them.

It turns out that demeternity is not timeless and a measure of timeless things and that demeterntiy and time are not mutually exclusive measures. According to Aquinas's account of time and demeternity the difference between actually having beginnings and ends and not having them but merely being connected to or associated with them does not succeed in distinguishing a timeless measure from a temporal measure. Consequently, the difference between having beginnings and ends *in* it and having no beginnings and ends *in* it does not distinguish a temporal measure from a timeless measure nor does it distinguish two measures as mutually exclusive; and being *tota simul* or having no beginnings and ends *in* it does *not* characterize a measure as timeless and a measure of timeless things.

But the problems with Thomas's comparisons do not end here. There is one more difficulty though this one is not insurmountable and can be overcome by making a relatively minor revision. Recall that for Aquinas eternity does *not* differ in any significant way from time simply on the grounds that eternity has neither a beginning nor an end while time has both a beginning and an end. This difference is only an accidental one on Aquinas's view. Rather, eternity differs in a significant way from time on the grounds that eternity is *tota simul* because it has no before and after or beginnings and ends *in* it while time, on the other hand, is not *tota simul* because it does have before and after or beginnings and ends *in* it. This difference was supposed to be the essential difference between eternity and time and as such was supposed to characterize eternity as timeless and a measure of timeless things on Aquinas's view. However, it has now been shown that, by his own account of time and demeternity, having no beginnings and ends *in* it does not characterize a measure as timeless and a measure of timeless things.

So, in order to sustain his claim that there is an essential difference and not merely an accidental difference between time and eternity by virtue of which eternity is timeless, Aquinas cannot hold that the essential difference between the two consists only in the fact that time has beginnings and ends *in* it while eternity does not. He must say more about the difference between them if he is going to continue to hold that there is an essential difference which makes eternity timeless and, indeed, he does say more. In his comparison of time and demeternity in article 5 of question 10 Thomas says that, unlike demeternity, eternity is in no way even compatible *(neque compatitur)* with before and after or beginnings and ends. The reason he gives for this is that like the being of demeternal things the being of the things measured by eternity is unchangeable, but unlike the being of demeternal things the being of the things measured by eternity cannot even be connected to or associated with *(nec adjunctum)* changeableness and this follows from his view that unlike demeternal things the things measured by eternity do not undergo any changes of any kind. But, then, if the being of eternal things is unchangeable *and* eternal things have absolutely no beginnings and ends at all because they do not change in any respect whatsoever, it follows that eternal things are not measured by time because time measures only those things beginning and ending in time. So, on his own view, it would be easy for Aquinas to revise his account of the essential difference between time and eternity in such a way that eternity is a measure of things that are *not* also measured by time. He could hold that time and eternity differ essentially by virtue of the fact that the being of temporal things is changeable and temporal things change with respect to other dispositions as well while the being of eternal things is unchangeable and eternal things do *not* change with respect to any other dispositions at all. On this revised account time and eternity would differ essentially and eternity would be timeless and a measure of timeless things because the things measured by eternity would not also be measured by time. If Aquinas would not accept this revised account or one very much like it, then he has failed to characterize any essential difference between eternity and time and on his view eternity turns out to be nothing but endless temporal duration. It is reasonable to think that Aquinas would accept some revision of this kind since it is quite plain from question 10 that on his view eternity is timeless and a measure of timeless things and that things measured by eternity not only have unchangeable being but also do not undergo any other kind of changes whatsoever.

Moreover, it is equally plain from question 8 of the *Summa Theologiae* that on Aquinas's view God is omnipresent. In article 1 of question 8 Aquinas makes it unequivocally clear that on his own view God is in everything as an agent is present to a patient upon which it acts. His reason for claiming that God is in everything in this manner is that God is the causal agent of the existence of all created things and every such agent must be *connected to* or *associated with (conjungi)* every patient upon which it acts immediately and it must be in direct *contact with (contingere)* every patient through its own power. Aquinas justifies this reason by appealing to the more general principle which he attributes to Aristotle that both the mover and the moved, both the agent and the patient, must exist *simul,* that is, must exist together, and, hence, at the same *time.* So, Thomas is committed to holding that God and any given created thing exist at the same time and in direct contact with one another. He further claims that the existence of created things is the proper effect of God and that this effect in things is caused by God not only when created things first begin to exist, but also for *as long as* they continue to exist. Aquinas concludes from these claims that God is necessarily present to a created thing for as long a *time* as it exists and that not only is God in everything but he is in everything innermostly because existence is innermost and most fundamentally present in all things.

So, from his own account of divine omnipresence it is clear that Aquinas cannot subscribe to the doctrine that God is timeless. On his own view Aquinas is committed to holding that God undergoes changes which occur in time and so he is also committed to holding that God is measured by time. For on his own view God is in each temporal thing, God is in each temporal thing for as long a time as it exists, and God and any given temporal thing exist at the same time. But, then, since the existence of each temporal thing had a beginning and will also have an end, it follows that God's presence in each temporal thing had a beginning and will also have an end. Hence, God changes with respect to being in temporal things. Moreover, since the existence of each temporal thing begins and ends in time, God's presence in each temporal thing begins and ends in time and so the changes that occur to God with respect to being in temporal things are changes which occur to him in time. Consequently, God is measured by time on Aquinas's view of divine omnipresence because God's presence in temporal things begins and ends in time and Aquinas insists that time measures those things beginning and ending in time. It turns out, then, that on Aquinas's own view God is not timeless and, hence, not eternal, if he is omnipresent.

Furthermore, from his own account of divine omnipresence Aquinas is committed to holding that God is in the United Nations Building for as long a time as it exists and that God and the U.N. Building exist at the same time. But since the U.N. Building existed yesterday as well as the day before yesterday, it follows from Aquinas's view that God was in the U.N. Building both yesterday and the day before. So, because this argument holds for God's presence in all temporal things, it further follows that God is continuously measured by time as long as time exists. The result of all this is that the doctrine of divine eternity as timelessness and the doctrine of divine omnipresence as they are enunciated by Thomas do jointly entail a contradiction and the argument with which this discussion began actually does apply to St. Thomas.

RICHARD R. LA CROIX.
STATE UNIVERSITY COLLEGE AT BUFFALO.

SPEECHLESS BRUTES

Recent attempts to provide animals with languages comparable to those employed by human beings suffer from a number of confusions. (1) They move too quickly from the claim that the behavior is communicative to the independent claim that it is linguistic. (2) They move without warrant from the fact that a particular activity is language-like to the claim that it is linguistic. This confusion is apparently an extension of our natural tendency to anthropomorphize animal behavior. (3) They assume—wrongly, I argue—that because a certain activity is part of the linguistic repertoire of a language-user, any creature engaging in that activity is thereby using language.

Without wishing to claim that language has an essence, I argue that linguistic behavior differs interestingly from nonlinguistic behavior in the possession of certain central features which I suggest are, themselves, necessarily linguistic. If the communicative activities of animals could be shown to possess any of these features, it might be more plausible to regard those activities and their accompaniments as genuinely linguistic.

Do animals other than human beings ever behave in such a manner as to warrant the claim that they are using a language? I take this question to be one about the sorts of things that animals *do,* not one about causal connections of a certain sort holding between the inner states of animals and their behavior. Not everyone would agree. Some have argued that only behavior issuing from a particular sort of internal mechanism could count as linguistic behavior. Yet we know that human beings sometimes use language without knowing much at all about the sorts of mechanism that underlie this capacity. It comes close to begging the question, then, to claim that only actions produced in a certain way can be genuinely linguistic.

We know that animals can communicate with one another and with their human trainers. This, in itself, is hardly surprising, however. A dog accompanied by a particular pungent odor communicates to us the fact that it has accosted a skunk. Yet we are not tempted to suppose that, it smelling the way it does, the dog is using a language. The same dog scratching at the door communicates to us its desire to go out. Again, we are not inclined to view the scratching as a use of language. To the extent that we may be so inclined, we are assimilating language to communication. As the first example illustrates, however, instances of communication are not necessarily instances of the use of language. It seems, then, that to identify an activity as linguistic, we must do more than show that communication is brought about by it.

Those who feel that animals sometimes do employ or may be taught to employ languages occasionally claim that skeptics are simply chauvanistic about human beings. They regard those who doubt the linguistic abilities of animals as being motivated by the pre-Darwinian notion that human beings are special, somehow above other species. Yet the opposite seems closer to the truth. It is manifestly easy to feel that animals are, in many ways, just like little people. The success of stories and animated films in which animals are depicted as persons, our natural tendency to anthropomorphize the activities of our pets and the like incline, if anything, in a direction clearly favoring the proponent of animal languages. There is tremendous pretheoretical appeal in the notion that animals might be taught to speak and, once taught, might tell us what they had all along been thinking silently as they interacted with us (cf. John Collier's *His Monkey Wife*).

It is a simple matter, then, to see a good bit of the behavior of animals as human-like. Just because of this, it is crucial that we distinguish cases where it is possible to see it this way from those in which it *is* this way. Bennett[1] has suggested that we might distinguish linguistic behavior from behavior that is (merely) linguistic-looking by determining whether or not descriptions of the behavior necessarily mention rules which are followed or broken by the creature we are investigating. This seems to me to be on the right track. I should, however, like to suggest a slightly different sort of test.

Suppose we observe a creature engaged in behavior that is more or less obviously communicative—"requesting" its dinner by ringing a particular bell, say. There is a strong and quite natural inclination to describe this sort of bell ringing as the framing of a request. Those who are bothered by the fact that so simple an act has no syntax might want to insist that the animal's behavior consists of distinct bits ordered in a certain way. Very well, we may imagine its ringing a series of bells in a particular order.

If the animal we have trained has learned to ring bells in this way

[1]Jonathan Bennett, *Rationality* (London: Routledge and Kegan Paul, 1964), cf. esp. ch. 6.

when it wants its dinner, then its ringing communicates to us the fact that it wants its dinner. It communicates a variety of other facts as well: that it is hungry, that it is alive and mobile, that it has learned the knack of ringing bells. Do we want to say, without qualification, that in ringing bells in this way it is *telling* us that it wants its dinner, *requesting* its dinner? We do often say such things, of course, in describing the actions of our pets or of animals in a zoo. So why not here? Children often speak of their dolls as wanting tea or as asking to be taken for rides. These ways of speaking about pets and dolls are perfectly natural, no one is liable to be confused by them. It is pointless to insist that our dog might not really be telling us anything when it whines for its dinner. But it is not so pointless to ask whether or not its telling in this way is very like your telling me that you are hungry in uttering the sentence "I am hungry." We speak of fear of bears and fear of success. Both sorts of fear may be genuine. But we may be misled if we try to understand a person's fear of success as very like a fear of bears (only with a different "object").

It is not, of course, that fear of success is utterly unlike fear of bears. Nor is a dog's telling us that it is hungry or that it wants to go out completely unlike my telling you that I am hungry or want to go out. In both cases of telling, something is communicated, an observer acquires a belief as the result of something done by the observed. And in telling you what I do, this may be all I mean to do. We may thus be led to feel that the dog's behavior, since it may bring about the same end, is an instance of the same sort of behavior. And we may begin to feel more strongly that this is so if we train the dog to ring bells in a certain definite way when it wants a particular thing rather than simply whining, yelping, or scratching. We think: why else would it take the trouble to ring a series of bells if not to tell us what it wants?

Concentrating on animals trained in this way to express their wants may, however, turn our attention in the wrong direction. We have known all along that animals may be taught to replace natural responses with learned responses. Learning may also be used to increase a creature's repertoire of responses. Thus a dog that simply whined for food in the past may learn to whine in different ways or to ring different sequences of bells for different sorts of food. But why are we inclined to regard these learned reponses as more impressive than the natural responses that they replace? What is it about the learned whinings or bell-ringings that makes us want to regard them as genuine tellings? Suppose we train a dog to ring a sequence of five bells when it wants one sort of food and a different sequence when it wants a different sort of food or wants to go out. Where formerly it did one thing, whine, it now does five things. Is there anything else to it? I can't see that there is. I can't see that our teaching a creature to push sequences of buttons or to ring sequences of bells to obtain food or some other reward in any way elevates the behavior of the creature above the normal whinings and scratchings that it exhibits naturally.

By focusing on complex and impressive tasks that animals have been taught, theorists are, I believe, facing us in the wrong direction. They have established, perhaps, that animals can be trained to perform complex feats. But we have all, from time to time, been amazed by the tricks performed by animals in circuses. The issue isn't whether animals can be taught to engage in complex activities that resemble, at some level, the human use of language. The issue, rather, is whether or not there is more than simply a resemblance between what animals do when suitably trained and what human beings do when they employ a language. An actor may learn to imitate persons with complex emotional states. If the actor is good, we may find ourselves attributing such states to him when, in fact, he is only acting. If a companion fails to recognize that the actor is acting, it may be impossible to show him his mistake by pointing to anything the actor does while playing his part. To say that the actor's behavior merely resembles the behavior of a lover or a tyrant, say, is not necessarily to say anything about the behavior *per se,* but to say something about how it fits into the life of the actor. An actor who learns to portray love or fear is not someone who learns to love or fear oddly or defectively. Acted love or fear very often looks just like genuine love or fear.

It is surely, then, a mistake to suppose that we can settle the question of whether or not a particular creature's activities ought to be described on a particular occasion as using language simply by noticing what the creature does on those occasions. A creature's behavior may look linguistic (just as an actor may appear to be angry or in love), but whether or not it is linguistic is another matter. Further, given our natural tendency to anthropomorphize the activities of animals, there is a special danger of moving from the simple claim that a creature looks like it is using a language to the claim that it is using a language. Again, this is not because the genuine use of language is necessarily underlain by unobservable states of mind, but because central cases of language use involve complex doings and interactions that animals other than human beings, to date, seem not to have engaged in.

What of the claim that creatures have been taught to employ

primitive or rudimentary languages? If we are allowed enough latitude in characterizing what is to count as a language then, indeed, beasts have mastered simple languages. Yet there seems to be not much of interest here. If a creature is taught to move pawns in the proper way, is it illuminating to say that it has learned rudimentary chess? It may be pointed out that chess masters move pawns. But, of course, their moving of pawns fits into a complex setting which includes a great deal more. A master may learn about chess by first being taught to move pawns, but it doesn't follow that a creature who has learned to advance pawns has taken the first steps toward playing chess. First steps are first steps only when followed by later steps.

All of this suggests that there may be many cases in which there is no simple or obvious way to decide whether a creature's behavior should or should not count as linguistic. In such cases it may not be that we lack information about the creature but that the information we have is not of the right sort. In observing its activities we may not have missed anything, yet we may still be reluctant to say that those activities constitute a genuine use of language. If we notice that a companion advances pawns in the correct way on a chess board, we have not yet seen him play chess. We may want to say this later, and later we may be sure that his pawn-advancing was chess playing. But that will depend on what other sorts of things he can do.

There are, however, activities which can only be brought about through the use of language. If a creature could be taught to do any of these things, then, I believe, we could be certain that its activities were linguistic. Further, in the case of such a creature, other activities that were formerly borderline would begin to look genuinely linguistic. It appears, too, that in the case of such necessarily linguistic activities, as I shall call them, the gap between behavior that has the property of being linguistic and behavior that is merely linguistic-like is broken down. And it is this gap that seems to be the source of much of the debate over the linguistic capacities of animals.

As an example of an activity that is, in the sense desired, necessarily linguistic, we might consider the use of tensed expressions, the use, that is, of items the human counterparts of which denote states of affairs or events temporally remote. If a dog or a cat wants to be let out, it may scratch at the door; if it wants to be fed, it may become restless or whine in a certain way. We may, if we like, say that an animal doing these things is telling us something, provided we recognize that all we mean by this is that the animal's behaving in the way it does brings about in us a certain belief. A particular fact is communicated via our observation of a piece of behavior and our beliefs about certain causal connections holding between behavior of that sort and conditions that affect the animal. Suppose we train the animal to ring a series of bells instead of whining or scratching. I have argued already that nothing much of interest follows from the fact that the animal can master such tricks. The new behavior may look more like what human beings do when they ask for food or to have the door opened, but there is no very good reason to say more than this. Suppose, however, we train a dog somehow to ring a series of bells in a particular way when it wants to go out tomorrow or out at some other definite time in the future. Leaving aside difficulties about the capacity of animals to have tensed beliefs, it seems that in such cases we should be forced to describe the dog's behavior as linguistic: whatever else it is doing, the creature is, *inter alia,* referring to a temporally remote state of affairs. It no longer makes sense to ask whether or not the creature in question might only look like it is referring. We have no other way to describe what it is doing. The gap between merely looking linguistic and being linguistic is closed in such cases.

This is not to say that it would be an easy matter to teach an animal to employ tensed expressions or to determine when it had mastered such expressions. The latter point, especially, is fraught with complexities. We could not, for example, test for the mastery of expressions denoting future states of affairs simply by looking out for the occurrence of those states of affairs. A language-user may express a desire for something at some future time then, when the time arrives, fail to have, for whatever reason, the anticipated desire. In such cases we should say that the speaker had been mistaken about his projected desires, not that he hadn't mastered the semantics of tense. We would say this, at least, if a number of fairly obvious though informal conditions obtained: if he could account for the absence of the desire; if he could explain why he said what he said (which, in turn, would require the complementary use of expressions in the past tense); if he recognized objections to the disparity between his original statement and the actual state of affairs. The application of such informal tests, however, seems not to pose any special logical difficulties in the assessment of the activities of beasts, difficulties, that is, which differ markedly and in principle from those encountered in the successful teaching of ordinary nontensed expressions.

I am not, it should be emphasized, claiming that the possession of a tense system is a necessary condition for an activity's being linguistic. Very likely it is a sufficient condition, however. What I do want to suggest is that there are certain things that are, in some obvious sense, central to the family of activities that we regard as undeniably linguistic. Tensed expressions are only one example. It is not difficult to think of others: the use of expressions denoting spatially remote states of affairs ("There is a bone in the butcher shop a mile up the road"); the use of expressions that assert principles ("Bones are good"). Such things seem to be those that make linguistic behavior interesting, those that set it off so markedly from non linguistic activity. They are related in obvious ways to the oft-cited slogan that human language is not stimulus-bound. Surely one of the features that elevates linguistic behavior in our estimation is that the use of language enables us to relate ourselves to occurrences and items not in our immediate environment. The fact that language is a vehicle of communication, though undoubtedly of first importance, is not what sets it off from much else that human beings and nonhuman creatures do.

I have tried to argue that nothing much follows from the fact that beasts may be trained to behave in ways which resemble the behavior of human language-users even if the behavior is undeniably communicative. The conceptual gap between "behavior *b* looks linguistic" and "behavior *b* is linguistic" is all too often filled by our natural inclination to anthropomorphize rather than by sound argument. This inclination is abetted by the fact that the activities of human language-users incorporate those simpler sorts of activity creatures can be taught to engage in. It is fallacious to argue, however, that if a certain activity is a part of the repertoire of a language-user, any creature appearing to master that activity is thereby using a language. Moving pawns is a part of a game of chess for a chess player. It does not follow, however, that a creature that has simply learned to move pawns is playing chess, even that it is playing rudimentary chess.

Linguistic behavior is set apart from nonlinguistic behavior not in being communicative, but in enabling language-users to be communicative about states of affairs other than those discoverable in the immediate environment. Activities that enable us to do that are, I believe, necessarily linguistic. A creature whose behavioral repertoire, however sophisticated or articulated or language-like, includes no such activities is not, I believe, genuinely linguistic.

JOHN HEIL.

UNIVERSITY OF CALIFORNIA, BERKELEY.

HUME'S MISSING SHADE OF BLUE

It is a fundamental tenet of Hume's empiricism that any simple idea in someone's mind is an exact copy of some simple impression previously found in his mind. For convenience I'll call this the Copy Thesis. It is curious that Hume himself, however, proposed what seems a solid counterexample to this thesis — the case of the missing shade of blue. Suppose, he says, that someone has seen all the colors there are except for one particular shade of blue. We present him with a graduated series of all the shades of blue, say on cards, except that one shade is missing, the shade he has never seen. Hume suggests that such a person would be able, "from his own imagination, to supply this deficiency, and raise up to himself the idea of that particular shade, though it had never been conveyed by his senses."[1] We seem to have here, Hume admits, "a proof that the simple ideas are not always, in every instance, derived from the corresponding impressions." And indeed, unless it can be shown that this is not a true counterexample, Hume would be compelled to drop the universality of his claim that *all* simple ideas are exact copies of simple impressions, for the missing shade of blue that is imagined is not such a copy. Hume, however, is not bothered by this counterexample, not because it fails as a counterexample, but because it is "so singular, that it is scarcely worth our observing, and does not merit that for it alone we should alter our general maxim."

Does Hume want to water down what seems elsewhere in the *Enquiry* and the *Treatise* to be a claim about all ideas into a mere generalization about most ideas? Are we to understand the Copy Thesis merely as a very reliable rule of thumb? Such a watering down, I think, would do great harm to Hume's program of empiricism, much of which proceeds by assuming that *any* simple idea must be derived from a corresponding impression. Were Hume to present his Copy Thesis merely as a general and not a universal truth, he would not be entitled to make this assumption. In any instance where he had found a simple idea and wanted to press the search for the corresponding simple impression, a critic might always respond that here, as in

[1] *An Enquiry Concerning Human Understanding,* ed. Selby-Bigge (Oxford: Clarendon Press, 1975), II, pp. 20-21. Cf. *A Treatise of Human Nature,* ed. Selby-Bigge (Oxford: Clarendon Press, 1967), I, I, 1, pp. 5-6.

the shade of blue case, there just might be no corresponding impression.

In this essay I would like to do three things. First I want to show that the case Hume proposes is not nearly as singular as he thought—there are many similar phenomena. Secondly, I want to respond to a recent suggestion that such cases need not worry Hume because they are unverifiable. And thirdly, I want to suggest that Hume's empiricism can survive even if we are forced to reject the Copy Thesis.

I

Let us begin by examining some phenomena similar to the shade of blue case. In Hume's example we are supposed to present the person with "all the different shades of" blue (except one). But there is in fact no finite set of the shades of blue; between any two shades there will always be other shades. Now perhaps a person might be able to imagine a shade which is exactly half way between two given shades, even if he had never seen that shade. But he need not imagine just that shade in order to provide us with a counterexample to the Copy Thesis; *any* shade (which he has never seen) between those two shades will do.

Colors differ from one another in three "color dimensions": hue, saturation, and brightness (What Hume calls "shade" is a combination of saturation and brightness). It is estimated that a person with good color vision under ideal conditions can discriminate between about 7,500,000 colors when they are presented as surfaces reflecting light, and about 10,000,000 colors when presented as emitted light.[2] Now no one could just sit down and imagine anywhere near that number of colors. But if we assembled a graduated deck of 7 million color cards, removed every other card, and presented the abridged deck to a person with good color imagination, he might be able to imagine a color to go in each of those 3,500,000 gaps between the cards. Or if this would be too difficult a task, we might take our deck of 7 million cards and now throw away cards 2-10, 12-20, 22-30, etc., until we were left with a deck of 700,000 cards with much larger gaps between them. A person with good color imagination would then have little trouble imagining colors to fit between these cards; he would be able to imagine, that is, roughly 700,000 colors. Now if we

[2] Robert Burham et al., *Color: A Guide to Basic Facts and Concepts* (New York: John Wiley and Sons, 1963), p. 162.

can assume that he had previously seen even 600,000 of these colors, that would still leave over 100,000 new colors which he was imagining without ever having seen.

In addition to this "interpolation" with shades of one hue and mixtures of different hues, we are also capable of "extrapolation"—if someone is shown the lightest shade of blue he has ever seen, he will be able to imagine one or more shades just a bit lighter; and shown the darkest shade of blue he has ever seen he can imagine one or more shades just a bit darker. Similarly, we can imagine a redder red-orange than any red-orange we have seen, a bluer blue-green, etc.

This ability to interpolate and extrapolate with visual images, moreover, is not limited to colors. Presented with surfaces of differing visual roughness, we could imagine surfaces of intermediate degrees of roughness, though we have never seen surfaces with just those degrees of roughness we are imagining. The same is true with perceived size. Given two lines one of which runs across exactly half of our visual field, and the other slightly longer, we could imagine lines of intermediate length, even though no line we have ever seen took up exactly the expanse of our imagined lines. Indeed, for any visual image we can come up with in imagination, the chances are good that no visual impression has ever been of *exactly* that size.

A similar kind of interpolation and extrapolation occurs with sounds. We may have never heard the sound of a guitar string vibrating at 808 cycles per second. But if someone tunes a guitar appropriately and plays the familiar diatonic scale starting at a note of 404 cycles per second for do, and so on through re, mi all the way to ti, and then stops, we can imagine the next note, high do, at 808 cycles per second. Indeed, if we have a good ear for tunes, and someone starts off a familiar tune with notes at frequencies we've never heard before, he can stop after a few notes and we will be able to imagine the rest of the tune, even though none of the notes we are imagining (except those repeated from his part of the melody) are notes we have heard before.

Because our powers of discrimination are less fine with the senses of smell, taste and touch, than with the "higher senses" of sight and hearing, and because there is seldom any call to imagine what something smells like, tastes like, or feels like, most of us are not able to imagine as many odors, tastes and tactile feelings as we are sights and sounds. Even with the largest part of our brains devoted to vision and hearing, nonetheless, our memories are able to store several thousand odors. And insofar as these odors can be arranged along scales of intensity, we might well be able to imagine an odor intermediately pungent, say, between two given pungent smells, even though we have never smelled anything with just that degree of pungency.

What we call the tastes of things usually includes their odors to some extent, but leaving aside the odor component of taste, we can find four features for which we have taste buds: sweet, salty, bitter and sour. Because these features all admit of degrees, we can imagine some taste of an intermediate sweetness, saltiness, bitterness, or sourness between two given samples, even though we have never tasted anything with exactly that degree of that feature. We can also extrapolate, if we have good gustatory imagination, and imagine something just a little saltier or more sour than anything we have ever tasted.

Since the qualities we perceive tactually, like heat, cold and texture, can also be arranged along scales, a similar kind of interpolation and extrapolation in imagination also occurs with them. Once we see how many qualities there are which admit of degrees in this way, we can see that Hume's shade of blue case is not at all an isolated case, and so he is wrong to dismiss counterexamples to his Copy Thesis with the simple claim that "the exceptions are very rare."[3]

II

In Section III I will examine what is wrong with the Copy Thesis and how Hume's empiricism can be adjusted to account for phenomena like those we have been discussing. But before doing this, I want to answer a recent argument that Hume need not worry about the counterexamples we have presented. In an article entitled "Hume's Blue Patch and the Mind's Creativity," Bernard Rollin claims that "there was in fact no need for Hume to worry about this [blue patch] case on purely logical grounds."[4]

We must distinguish, Rollin says, between two different claims Hume is making in the missing shade of blue case. Hume is claiming (a) that on looking at the series of shades of blue the person will become conscious of a gap in the series, and (b) that he will form an idea of the missing shade, for which he has had no previous impression. Now (a) is clearly true, according to Rollin, for it can be verified by asking the person to point to where the gap is in the series. But this

[3] *Treatise*, I, I, 2, p. 7.

[4] *Journal of the History of Ideas*, 32 (1971), 121.

ability to notice the gap does not constitute a counterexample to Hume's Copy Thesis. A person can notice that the difference in color gradation between two samples is greater than the difference between other pairs of color samples, but this ability does not require him to form an idea for which he has had no previous impression. To challenge the Copy Thesis we would have to use (b). But (b) is of no use as a counterexample here, Rollin argues, because, unlike (a), it is unverifiable. "How can we determine whether the subject has an idea of b_j [the missing shade of blue] without being able to peek into his consciousness and actually inspect the idea?"[5] We cannot present the missing shade to him and ask him whether this is the shade he was thinking of, and we cannot ask him to pick out the shade he was thinking of from among several color samples. Nor can we give him paints to mix and ask him to mix the color he was thinking of. For by doing any of these things we would be allowing him to have an *impression* of the missing shade, and we are testing to see whether he had the idea *before* having the impression. "We would have no way of knowing whether he had the idea prior to our supplying of that impression, or whether we gave him the idea by giving him the impression."[6]

Similarly, Rollin argues, it would be impossible to verify the claim that someone has imagined a musical tone which he had not previously heard. If a person says that he can imagine a tone missing from a given tune, for example, it doesn't matter what he might do to prove his claim—he might always be cheating. Even if he proceeds to sing the missing note, he may be doing so not by attending to an aural image in his mind, but merely by applying to the notes he *has heard* some relational rule about the interval required to get to the missing note. We need not worry about this whole family of cases similar to the shade of blue case, in short, because for any claim and any evidence offered that a person had formed an idea without having had the corresponding impression, there would always be an alternative explanation. Claims like (b) are unverifiable and therefore do not count against Hume's Copy Thesis.

Rollin's argument here suffers from a kind of oversimplified understanding of the relationship between evidence, meaning, and truth, similar to that which beset early versions of the verifiability criterion of meaning. His operating principle seems to be that if a

[5] Ibid, 127.

[6] Ibid., original in italics.

claim cannot be verified, by which he means cannot be conclusively shown to be true, then it cannot be accorded any weight as a claim (or perhaps cannot be true? or even meaningful?). But this is surely too strong a principle. For *no* claim can be *conclusively* checked, if what is required is the ruling out of *any* conceivable alternative explanation for the evidence. If a person claims to have an idea, e.g., whether copied from an impression or not, then *no matter what he does* to show us that he has the idea—whether he talks, draws, etc.—it *might* always be the case that he exhibited the behavior in question without having had the idea he claims to have had. He *might* be lying and his behavior *might* be based on his cleverness in operating with existing clues, or simply on a lucky guess as to how somebody with that idea should act. It is even logically possible that at the moment we are testing him, his body is possessed by some demon who wants to mislead us into thinking that this person had this idea.

If the total ruling out of alternative explanations for evidence which Rollin requires in the shade of blue case were required universally, even empirical claims in the physics laboratory would have to be discounted. If someone claimed that he had a bar of iron in his hand, for example, then whatever evidence he offered us that this was iron, we could always respond that there were alternative explanations for what he offered as evidence. If he showed us the readings from tests with electrical currents through the bar, we could always respond that he may have switched bars before the test, or he may be using malfunctioning equipment. It is *always* possible, in short, that test results do not establish what they appear to establish.

But none of these logical possibilities shows that the state of affairs we are testing for—whether it is a bar's being iron or a person's having a certain idea—cannot occur, or that we cannot justifiably claim that the state of affairs obtains, once we have a certain amount of evidence. If an apparently sincere subject in Hume's shade of blue experiment were to tell us that he had imagined a shade of blue between two given shades, and then proceeded to offer us evidence by taking paints and mixing up the shade he was imagining, then we would be justified in saying that he has imagined that shade. And so we would be justified in saying that we had a counterexample to Hume's Copy Thesis. It is logically possible, of course, that the person is lying or that the evidence is faulty in some other way. But this danger exists whenever anyone accepts evidence for any empirical claim whatever.

There is another good reason why Hume would probably not accept Rollin's "helpful" argument here. Hume is rightly not concerned with how we would verify that the man had in fact imagined the shade of blue, for he is performing a thought experiment based on *his own* intuitions about *his own* ability to imagine a shade of blue he had not seen. His claim that the missing shade *could* be imagined is plausible as a counterexample to the Copy Thesis just because on reading it each of us can imagine himself as the *subject* in the experiment coming up with the image for which he had had no previous impression. And with ourselves, surely, Rollin's reservations about the possibility of the subject cheating simply do not apply.

III

We must take seriously, then, the counterexamples to the Copy Thesis discussed in Section I. These phenomena are important, I would suggest, because they reveal a feature of human imagination which Hume overlooked. In one sense his basic insight that "all ideas are derived from impressions"[7] is correct, but there is a freedom in human imagination which is not accounted for by the Copy Thesis.

When we are presented with a task like that of imagining the missing shade of blue, for example, we do not proceed by checking a storehouse of remembered shades of blue to see if the missing shade is there. Even if we are told that we *have* seen the missing color before, this is not how we proceed. Indeed, until we have formed the proper image, how would we even know what shade it was we were looking for? What we actually do—whether or not we have seen the color before—is to concentrate on the hue involved, say blue, and familiarize ourselves with the degree to which one shade is lighter than the next in the series presented. We might say that we derive a pattern or rule for the gradations, though, of course, we need not do anything at this conscious a level. Once we are familiar with the increment of gradation between the given shades, we can produce in our minds an image of the shade missing from the series.

Or if we are given the task of imagining a shade lighter than (or darker than) a given shade, the same holds true. Even if we are fully aware that we must have seen shades lighter than (or darker than) the given shade before, we do not proceed by *recalling* an appropriate shade. (Indeed, unless we are artists or paint technicians, most of the thousands of colors we see are forgotten immediately.) What we ac-

---

[7] *Treatise,* p. 19.

tually do here is concentrate on the hue involved and being familiar with the relation lighter than (or darker than), we produce in our minds an image of a color lighter than (or darker than) the given shade.

So too with imagining musical notes; when asked to imagine the note one octave higher than a given note, no one rummages through a store of ideas of notes he has heard, and tries to find the one that is exactly an octave higher than the given note. As with imagining colors, before we had imagined the note, how would we know what we were looking for? What we actually do—whether we have heard the note before or not—is a bit of "calculation" with the note given us. We know the general relation of notes to their octaves, what it sounds like for a vibrating guitar string to be shortened to half its length, or what it feels like in the throat, perhaps, to sing a note and then jump an octave. To imagine the octave of a note given us, we apply this experiential knowledge of the relation of notes to their octaves to the note in question.

When we learn a melody, we do not learn a specific group of notes, one at, say 300 cycles per second, the next at 260 cycles per second, etc. What we learn is a pattern, a set of relationships, that is not tied to any specific frequencies. Having learned a tune we can be presented with the first few notes in a different key, and we will still be able to imagine the rest of the tune, though perhaps in notes at frequencies we have never heard. In fact, it is conceivable that each time we imagine a tune in our heads, or sing it, we do so with at least slightly different notes.

Because there is this freedom in our imagination of colors, sounds, etc., we must give up Hume's Copy Thesis. But this does not mean giving up Hume's whole program of empiricism, for there is an important sense in which Hume was right that "all ideas are derived from impressions." To appreciate this point, we might turn from examining what the imagination can do to what it cannot do.

Though we can imagine shades of blue we have not seen, we would not be able to imagine any shades of blue at all unless we had seen the hue blue in several of its shades. We are not free, that is, to imagine a new hue, in the way that we are free to imagine new shades of some familiar hue. Similarly, though we can imagine mixtures of green and yellow we have never seen, we would not be able to imagine any such colors unless we had seen both these hues before, as well as how they affect each other when mixed in various proportions. A particular color we imagine may be new in that we have never perceived this hue, or combination of hues, with just this degree of saturation and brightness. But our imagining such a color will always depend on our previous impressions of the hues involved, and on our experience with mixtures of those hues and with different degrees of saturation and brightness.

In our auditory imagination the basic quality is timbre, the characteristic quality of a sound which makes the sound of a flute, for instance, different from the sound of a guitar. The other qualities of sound—pitch, duration, and intensity (loudness)—are to timbre what saturation and brightness are to hue. Just as we can imagine a familiar hue in a new shade, so we can imagine a familiar timbre at a pitch we have not heard, lasting for an interval that we have not heard that sound last, and at an intensity that we have not heard. And just as we cannot imagine a new hue, but at most a mixture of familiar hues, we cannot imagine a new timbre, but at most a mixture of familiar timbres. The person who has heard a flute and has heard a guitar may be able to imagine the sound of a flute and a guitar together, but the person who has not heard the sound of a flute cannot imagine that sound. When we imagine new sounds, what is new is not any *distinctive* sound quality (timbre), but only the *degree* of some familiar quality (pitch, duration, and intensity) common to all sounds.

With taste (considered apart from smell) the four features mentioned earlier—sweet, sour, salty, and bitter—are the basic qualities. Someone who has not experienced a sweet taste, for example, cannot imagine any degree of sweetness, but once we have experienced sweetness in several different degrees we are able to imagine degrees we have not experienced. The same is true with odors (though there are many more basic odors than basic tastes), and also with tactile qualities like heat and cold.

While Hume's case of the missing shade of blue and related phenomena make the Copy Thesis untenable, then, a careful investigation of these cases should turn up nothing threatening to Hume's empiricism as a whole. For what we imagine in these cases is not some new quality that we haven't experienced, but only a new degree of some quality like brightness, intensity, cold, etc., with which we are already familiar.[8]

JOHN MORREALL.

NORTHWESTERN UNIVERSITY.

[8]I am grateful to Larry Friedman for discussing many of the issues in this paper with me.

THE FUNCTION OF FICTION

Linguistic products such as novels and fairy tales are classified as 'fiction'. They *are* fictions. Their production and consumption are universal in all human societies. That fictions have an important function in cultural life is unquestionable. What then is the function of fiction? The question is not a linguistic one; rather it is a psychological one. We are not asking what kind of linguistic function the language in a fiction has, but rather what kinds of function *tout court* a fiction has as a linguistic product for the producer and for the reader as well. The answer, however, cannot be given without knowing the linguistic function of the language in a fiction, for the subject matter of our inquiry is after all linguistic products.

1

But what does the concept of 'fiction' mean in the first place? Fiction is contrasted often with fact. Fiction in this use refers to our imaginary or unreal objects such as a unicorn or a golden mountain. As we havm already indicated at the beginning, the concept of 'fiction' refers also to linguistic products such as *Madame Bovary* and *Alice in Wonderland*. Yet these works are by no means unreal imaginary objects. They are as real as trees, pencils, scientific books, and historical reports. They make a certain part of the furniture of the universe. Further, *Madame Bovary* can be read as a biography of a real woman, and conversely *The Confessions* of Rousseau can be enjoyed as a first person novel. It is clear then that what differentiates a fiction from a nonfiction is not some property or properties that we can physically identify. There is no internal evidence that warrants our calling the former 'fiction' and the latter 'nonfiction'. If *Madame Bovary* is a fiction, this is not because the book is fictitious, and if *The Confessions* is not a fiction, this is not because the book is not fictitious. It follows then that if there is any distinction between a fiction and a nonfiction, the distinguishing property must be something which, to use Danto's expression, "the eye cannot decry."[1] What then is this peculiar property of a fiction?

---

[1] Arthur Danto, "The Artworld" in *Aesthetics: a Critical Anthology*, edited by George Dickie and Richard Sclafani (New York, 1977), p. 29.

Talking about artistic identification, Danto quotes a Chinese Zen-Buddhist, Ch'ing Yuan:

> Before I had studied Zen for thirty years, I saw mountains as mountains and waters as waters. When I arrived at a more intimate knowledge, I came to the point where I saw that mountains are not mountains, and waters are not waters. But now that I have got the very substance I am at rest. For it is just that I see mountains once more as mountains, and waters once again as waters.[2]

The mountains and waters that the Buddhist saw at the end of his reflection *are* not in a way the same as the mountains and waters that he saw at the beginning of his reflection, although there is no physically identifiable difference at all between the two cases. The same mountains and the same waters are perceived from two different perspectives. They have two different meanings. This difference is thus not physical in kind. It makes sense then to talk about a nonphysical property or properties, whatever these properties might be. The property called 'fiction' is analogous to the property by which the mountains and waters the Buddhist saw at the end of his reflection are distinguished from the mountains and waters he saw at the beginning of his reflecton. How can we then characterize this kind of nonphysical property? What is that which distinguishes *Madame Bovary* as a fiction from *Madame Bovary* read as a nonfiction?

The property in question is conventional in nature. If one becomes president of the United States, he is not different from the physical point of view. Yet Reagan as president is not the same as Reagan as a mere male. What distinguishes the former from the latter is the nonphysical property endowed by the American political institution.[3] Analogously it is by convention that *Madame Bovary* is called 'fiction,' whereas the Bible is not. To say that *Madame Bovary* is a fiction is to say that the words and sentences in this linguistic product are governed by an additional convention to the conventions by which the words and sentences in *Madame Bovary* as well as in the Bible are governed.

It is a linguistic convention in a double sense. It is linguistic because it is a convention about language; it is also linguistic because

---

[2]*Ibid.*

[3]In essence the same idea is advanced by Maurice Mandelbaum in his paper, "Family Resemblance and Generalization Concerning the Art" in *American Quarterly*, vol. 2, no. 3 (1965), and by G. Dickie in his *Art and the Aesthetic: An Institutional Analysis* (Ithaca, 1974). The former talks about 'non-exhibited property' and the latter 'institutional property'. I call them 'conventional properties'.

it is a convention concerning a way in which a language in a linguistic product is used. The convention consists in stating that words and sentences in a linguistic product should not be taken as referring to any real things, events, facts, and situations, that is, to the real world. To call *Madame Bovary* and *Alice in Wonderland* 'fiction' is to indicate that the words and sentences in these linguistic products are not used to refer to the real world. If we immediately recognize *Alice in Wonderland* as a fiction, that is because the linguistic product indicates itself that what is talked about in it is not real. If *Madame Bovary* by itself cannot be immediately recognized as fiction, that is because the book by itself does not show that what is talked about in it is fictitious. Fiction is then a linguistic convention about reference. The convention says that the language in a fiction means what it means without its real referent. As Macdonald pointed out, "in fiction language is used to *create*."[4] It is in this sense that self-reference and semantic autonomy are the defining characteristics of the language in a fiction and in literature in general.

Given this definition of the function of the language in a fiction, what is said in a fiction cannot be either true or false. In regard to fiction, the very question of truth or falsity does not arise logically. This fact, in its turn, seems to entail that the language in a fiction does not have cognitive import. The function of a fiction is not to give or to increase information about the world. It would appear then that the production and consumption of fictions are frivolous, if not superfluous, activities. Must all serious activities be cognitive? Is truth the only thing which is important?

2

In recent years Goodman has argued for an outright and thorough cognitive theory of literature and art in general. According to him knowledge is not a copy of the world which would exist without language representing it. There is no world *tout court,* no knowledge *tout court*. The world is made by the act of knowing it, and knowledge is constructed by a conceptual system. Since there are various ways of devising a conceptual system, and since knowledge is relative to a conceptual system there are as many forms of knowledge and as many sorts of the world as conceptual systems. An artwork is one of many possible symbol-systems. The world artwork shows—bet-

[4] Margaret Macdonald, "The Language of Fiction" in *Philosophy Looks at the Arts*, edited by Joseph Margolis (Philadelphia, 1978), p. 432.

ter constructs—is one of many possible worlds. If science is one of the ways of worldmaking, so is art, and there are many other ways of worldmaking. Knowledge and truth are not the monopoly of science. Art does not need to compete with science in its capacity of worldmaking, of constructing truth. It is simply a different way of worldmaking. And truth is relative to the way of worldmaking. Poems and literary works in general are some of many forms of art-worldmaking.[5]

The view is very comforting for those philosophers, poets, painters, and musicians, and a lot of art lovers, who cannot stand the idea that art has no cognitive import, and the consequence that art is thereby trivial. Indeed the Goodmanian influence seems to be spreading. But such a fact does not validate his theory.

Goodman, just like anyone else, is free to decide that novels, poems, and artworks in general are symbol systems whose function is to denote the world in order to organize it. As a matter of fact, anything—for instance, a stone, a tree, and a desk—can be taken as a symbol, and a collection of them as a symbol system. But the question is not whether anything can be taken as symbol or not, but rather how different things are classified differently, and how they function differently. Our problem is to elucidate the reason or reasons for which certain linguistic products are classified as fiction in distinction from other linguistic products.

Granted that words and sentences are clearly symbols in the sense of signs, yet not all symbols are cognitive. Suppose the language in a novel or a poem is cognitive. Then what it says must be decided as in principle either true or false. And yet few of the claims which are supposed to be made in novels and poems can be proven to be either true or false. Of course Goodman would reply that truth is relative to a conceptual system. Truth in a novel needs not to be truth in another novel, because, insofar as they are two different novels, they are two different conceptual systems. But what could we do if two contradictory truth claims could be deduced from a single novel with equal cogency? How could we interpret the fact that often great novels are made of trivia? What would it mean if the reader of a novel did not care for the truth or truths in a novel? Truth or cognition is not the function of a novel, even though often we learn a lot of truths in reading novels.

---

[5]See Goodman, *Language of Art* (Indianapolis, 1976) and *Ways of Worldmaking* (Indianapolis, 1978).

More generally, so long as we agree that the defining characteristic of the language in a fiction is its nonreferential use, and that as a consequence to take a linguistic product as a fiction is to waive the very question of truth and falsity, it is logically self-contradictory to consider a fiction, if not literature in general, as a form of knowledge.

Weitz agrees on this point. Yet he insists that a literary work contains a lot of true statements and that this is an important factor in a work. Thus, Proust's *Remembrance* and Eliot's *Four Quartet* reveal respectively different profound truths. "Indeed, there is that added moment of greatness in *The Brothers Karamazov* or *Anna Karenina* precisely because Dostoevesky and Tolstoy in these novels see something which is true about our world that neither Eliot nor Proust nor many others ever do."[6] The argument is, however, besides the point. Obviously most novels contain a lot of apparently true statements, when they are considered as nonfictions. The question is, however, not whether they contain such sentences, but whether such sentences can be taken as statements at all, that is, whether the function of a novel and literature in general is to make statements in the first place. The answer is already in the very concept of fiction. Since the language in a novel does not refer to the real world, the sentences in that language cannot be statements. The point is not how to characterize the function of the language in *Madame Bovary* when it is taken as a biography, but to find out the function of the language in *The Confessions* when we take it as a novel.

Still it would seem very hard to think that fictions have nothing to do with truth. It is then understandable that many philosophers, poets, and critics tend to believe that literature expresses certain special truths which are different from scientific or philosophic truths. Literature reveals certain realities which cannot be revealed in scientific or philosophic discourses. In this view, scientific or philosophic description is doomed to distort reality because it abstracts from reality which in itself is necessarily concrete. For this reason, it is often claimed that poetic representation is more genuine and that poetic truth is more profound and subtle than scientific or philosophic truth. The language in a poem or a literary work in general does not refer to a chair or a tree, but to normally undifferentiated and overlooked aspects of a chair or a tree. Thus Ricoeur

---

[6] Morris Weitz, "Truth in Literature" in *Aesthetics*, edited by John Hospers (New York, 1969), p. 224.

writes:

> The reference here is not abolished, but divided. The effacement of the ostensive and descriptive reference liberates a power of reference to aspects of our being in the world that cannot be said in a direct descriptive way, but only alluded to, thanks to the referential values of metaphoric and, in general, symbolic expressions.[7]

Ricoeur calls this reference of poetic language 'split-reference'.

Such a referential function may be found in the language of a poem. Thus, a poem may be thought of as expressing a certain truth. But it is contradictory to say that the language in a novel has such a function, for *ex hypothesis,* the fact that it is a novel, rules out the referential function of the language in it to the very extent that it is a 'fiction'. For this reason it seems that the way language works in a novel is quite different from the way in which language functions in a poem, although we tend to think that the poem is a more sophisticated form of the novel, and thus to lump together a theory of the poem and a theory of the novel under the name of a theory of literature. A novel need not be concerned primarily with truth.

At this point we recall the famous Logical Positivist's distinction between cognitive language and emotive language. In this view every sentence and every discourse functions either as cognitively or emotively. A discourse is congitive if its truth or falsity can be in principle determined. Among all discourses which are supposed to talk about certain empirical facts, only scientific discourse is cognitive because only the truth or falsity of this discourse can be in principle determined. All other discourses are emotive. Metaphysical, ethical, religious, aesthetic, and literary discourses are emotive because the truth or falsity of these discourses cannot be in principle determined.

To say that a language is emotive is to say that its function is not to refer to any thing, not to describe it, and not to give any information about the world, but to induce emotion in the reader. Words and sentences in a literary work, in a fiction in particular, are to be seen as the expressions of the writer's feeling or emotion, which are intended to induce the same feeling and emotion in the reader. Thus they are like 'Ach' or 'Hurrah!'. They are not used to function as a semantical vehicle, but as symptoms of the writer's emotional state. A semantical vehicle has a meaning which is conventionally related to what it means, whereas a symptom is a effect which is causally connected to a physiological or psychological state of an individual. To read a novel is then not to understand its meaning but to respond to it. A novel is a

[7] Paul Ricoeur, *Interpretation Theory* (Fort Worth, Tex., 1976), p. 37.

series of 'Achs' and 'Hurrahs', to which the reader is supposed to be causally responding.

Such an implication of the emotive theory of fiction is hard to accept. In the first place it is false that a writer is in an emotional state when he produces his linguistic work, even if his intention is to express certain emotions he experienced. On the contrary, instead of being in an emotional state, he plans, thinks, and calculates. In the second place the reader does not respond or react to the words or sentences as physical objects, but understands their meanings. Language is not something primarily to react against, but meaning to be understood. To be sure, a novel may give rise emotion to the reader. But then anything and any kind of discourse can and does give rise emotion to the audience, to the observer, and to the reader. Contrary to the Logical Positivist's view, the function of language is not limited either to the description of things or to the expression of feeling. The distinction between cognitive language and emotive language is too simplistic. Since Austin, and even before him, since Wittgenstein, we know that the function of language is far more various and complex.

If the emotive function is not the primary and defining function of the language in a fiction, what kind of function does it have? I shall propose what I would call 'projective' theory.[8]

3

The language in a fiction is 'projective'. As we have seen, the language in a fiction does not have any real referent, but it is still about something. This something, however, is not real, but 'projected'.

What is projected is not real, but only conceived, not actual, but possible. Mountains are real, but golden mountains are only conceived; two-horn stags are acutal, but unicorns are only possible. Hence what is projected is not really a thing, but an idea or conception. Golden mountains and unicorns are not real things but ideas or conceptions. They are truly *created* stuff. It is not by accident that novels, literature in general, and artwork in general are said to be created. As Glickman has shown, what is created is not particulars but types, not concrete things but ideas or conceptions.[9] So-called creativity refers to the capacity of generating such types, that is, such ideas. The words and sentences in *Madame Bovary* as a novel refer to conceived persons, conceived events, conceived experience, conceived

---

[8]It is in the above book that I pick up this notion.

[9]See Jack Glickman, "Creativity in the Art" in *Philosophy Looks at the Arts*, pp. 145-46.

situations, and conceived story. To read *The Confessions* as a fiction is to take the words and sentences in the book as referring to conceived events, conceived human beings, and conceived situations.

But it is not really correct to say that words and sentences in a fiction *refer* to conceived things, conceived events, conceived persons, and conceived situations. In a fiction such conceived things do not exist prior to their conceptions. Words and sentences in a fiction do not refer to those conceived things which exist already prior to their referring acts. In a fiction the language which refers to something and the things which are referred to by that language are not separable the one from the other. The word 'unicorn' or the word 'golden mountain' in a fiction does not refer to the already existing conceived animal, that is, a unicorn, or the conceived mountain, that is, a golden mountain. They are by themselves a newly conceived unicorn or a newly conceived golden mountain. The conceived Madame Bovary does not exist before Flaubert writes the words, Madame Bovary. The conceived story of *Madame Bovary* does not exist before Flaubert produces the actual concrete linguistic product called *Madame Bovary*. In this sense, if there is a reference in a fiction, the reference is created. In a fiction, and perhaps in artwork in general, conception or idea is not separable from the actual, concrete, and particular product. Therefore, as Margolis pointed out, artwork exists necessarily as type-token.[10] Thus the language in a fiction is not about anything. It is about neither real things nor conceived things. It is by itself simply the conception of something, some event, some person, or some situation. More precisely, the language in a fiction is simply certain conceptions.

Not all conceived things and events are the subject matter of a fiction or literature in general. The idea of a golden mountain, the idea of a unicorn, and the idea of a green cow are not the projected things writers and readers of a novel or a fairy tale are interested in. What they are interested in are certain conceivable things, events and situations related to human life. If there are conceived things, conceived events in a fiction, they are relevant to the fiction insofar as they are connected with human life. In short, what a writer really tries to create in a fiction and what a reader tries to find out in a fiction is certain conceivable human life. Thus Ricoeur is correct when in talking about the nature of fiction, he says that "What we understand first in a discourse is not another person, but a 'project', that is,

---

[10]See Ricoeur, *Interpretation Theory*, p. 37.

the outline of a new way of being in the world."[11]

It is in the light of a projected world or worlds that the actual life can be better perceived, critically examined, and evaluated. It is in the light of various conceived lives that we can live at least imaginatively more and other lives than our own which are destined to be one, unique, and irrevocable. In the former capacity, a fiction enriches our life, because ot allows us to live different lives we can never live in reality, in the real world. For us, a fiction is then not really fictitious; it is inseparably related to our concrete and actual life, to our real world. It has unimaginable relevance to us. "The wonder-world of Alice is of course derived from and related to our world; were it not so we could not enter it. Alice's world leads us back to our world, too, and we see our world anew: . . . *Happily*, rather because the very movement between her wonderland and our no man's land can release our dreams, fulfill us, and help us to become much more than we merely are."[12] If in fact the world of a fiction is related to our real world and, at the same time, if the world of a fiction is fictitious to the very extent that it is merely a conceived idea, how can this relationship be accounted for? How are the two worlds related to each other?

The conceived world is by definition not real, but imaginary. But such a world cannot be conceived out of nothing, in a vacuum. A golden mountain and a unicorn do not exist, but if these conceived ideas are intelligible for us, it is because they are indirectly tied to our actual knowledge of the actual world. If we did not know actual mountain and actual gold, actual animal and actual horn in the real world, we could not understand the meanings of these ideas. It is on the basis of our actual knowledge of the real world that we can conceive even the most fantastic ideas, the most extravagant world. Without being related to the real world, no words and sentences, except syncategorematic words, can be intelligible and significant at all. If we are often excited in reading certain fictions, it is because we can indirectly relate the fictitious people, events, and experience to actual people, events, and experience.

A form of critical reflection of our real life, a fiction is an expression of our transcendence. A form of enrichment of life, a fiction fulfills our dream of transcending one life and its limits.

YNHUI PARK.

SIMMONS COLLEGE.

[11]See Joseph Margolis, "The Ontological Peculiarity of Works of Art" in *Philosophy Looks at the Arts*, pp. 213-22.

[12]Douglas N. Morgan, "Must Art Tell the Truth?" in *Aesthetics*, edited by Hospers, p. 237.

CONTEXT DEPENDENT KNOWLEDGE

It is possible to suggest, on Wittgensteinian grounds, that no general analysis of knowledge exists, since no general analysis could capture the richness and variety of contexts in which human beings recognize instances of human knowledge. The most durable general analysis of human knowledge is the justified true belief analysis, but a vast literature bristles with counterexamples to this proposal. What has perhaps not quite been noticed is that the analyses of knowledge developed by many philosophers have looked to mathematics and science for paradigm cases of human knowledge, while the counterexamples proliferate in domains associated with everyday life. There may be a clue to the avoidance of scepticism about knowledge in this distinction. Perhaps there is justified true belief that may be taken as knowledge in mathematics and in science, but this situation may be rare or nonexistent in everyday life. If an appropriate distinction of epistemological domains can be found, then the counterexamples may make us pessimistic about knowledge claims in everyday life, but the existence of the counterexamples doesn't rule out mathematical and scientific knowledge. That is the possibility I wish to explore in this paper.

Suppose someone advances a knowledge claim. Let *a* be the person and let the knowledge claim be abstracted to *Kap,* where *p* is the proposition said to be known. There are two well-travelled routes to rejecting such a claim. First, any reason to think that *p* is false is a reason to think *Kap* false. So much is unarguable. Second, any reason to think that *a*'s position is such that he doesn't have a sufficient epistemological justification for thinking *p* true (even though *p* may be true) is a reason to think *Kap* false. For an action oriented animal, action based on a false but revisable hypothesis is no doubt preferable to sceptical suspension of belief. This no doubt explains our willingness to place various eyewitness reports and authoritative assessments in our knowledge bank for practical purposes even though we do not know them to be true according to certain philosophical criteria. The same thing might be said about our acceptance of various scientific claims. Some philosophers have argued that we can pursue epistemological goals without ever accepting knowledge claims, by assigning probability structures to consistent sets of beliefs. The alternative may seem to be scepticism in the absence of a satisfactory general analysis of knowledge.

Scepticism about a knowledge claim can't be pressed without assuming something. For our purposes, agent *a* need not accept the position that he doesn't know that *p* simply because he cannot refute the claim that he might not be epistemologically completely justified in thinking that he knows that *p*. This is one form of scepticism's wedge. From the fact that an agent might always be wrong it does follow (by instantiation) that *a* might be wrong in any particular case. But this does not furnish a reason for thinking that *a* is wrong in this particular case. Consider an everyday example. Agent *a* claims to know that *p* because he remembers that *p*. But one might misremember in any particular case. The fact that *a* might be misremembering *p* is not therefore, by itself, a reason for thinking that he *is* misremembering *p*.[1] A reason for thinking that he *is* misremembering *p* must be context dependent. Perhaps *a* holds that something is true which is extremely unlikely if *p* is also true. Perhaps *b* remembers that $\sim p$ and is an equally credible witness. Then one may reasonably object to *a* that he might be misremembering, and perhaps does not know that *p*. This objection (by itself, and in the absence of a definite context) is perhaps relevant, and perhaps not. If it is the sort of objection that could be formulated to any remembered claim, then it seems a spurious doubt or objection and one of the kind that I shall call *metaphysical* hereafter.[2] On the other hand, if it is formulated because of *a*'s specific claim and in virtue of particular features of that claim that seem to conflict with certain facts, then it will be regarded hereafter as a *nonmetaphysical* doubt or objection.

We can analyze the notion of metaphysical doubt by gradually accumulating a list of stipulated metaphysical objections. Any general objection that one might be dreaming; that one might be

[1] One might argue that this requires another explicit assumption in any full analysis. So be it. It would seem however, that the assumption is required of any epistemology compatible with certain intuitions. Compare this example. The fact that Joe might be in Barcelona is not (in general) a reason for thinking that he is in Barcelona. He might be there in the sense that it is physically possible, but we don't have a reason for thinking that he is there without some further information about Joe's travel plans and his recent states of mind.

[2] A distinction between ***metaphysical*** **and** *nonmetaphysical* doubt appears in the writings of rationalists, for example, Descartes, and also of pragmatists, for example, Peirce. In this literature, nonmetaphysical doubt is usually called *real* doubt. No prejudice regarding metaphysics is here intended by the use of the term *metaphysical doubt*. The term is convenient because of the noted historical connections.

under hypnosis; that one might be insane or deluded; that one has misremembered what one takes to be clearly remembered; that someone has made an (unspecified) contrary claim; all of these are metaphysical objections provided that no particular evidence differentially supports them in a given case. This *list* of metaphysical objections will here be taken as illustrative for purposes of this paper; if the general character of the analysis to be proposed seems right to sustained scrutiny, this list can easily be revised as a result of more detailed discussion. The touchstone of a metaphysical objection is the ease with which it can be formulated to address new knowledge claims. Once we have mastered a metaphysical objection we can find a variant of it for perhaps all knowledge claims. There can also be metaphysical objections relativized to a class of knowledge claims. For example, all knowledge claims based on statistical sampling are subject to the objection that the sample may be biased. Unless there is a particular reason to expect bias in a particular sample, however, the objection that the sample *may* be biased is metaphysical. For the most part, we will be concerned with metaphysical objections not relativized to a class of knowledge claims. The Gettier counterexamples to justified belief analyses are not metaphysical objections as they have been characterized here. Metaphysical objections are general objections to human knowledge, if one takes them seriously, as many sceptics do. I don't have an argument that the sceptic *must* be wrong, but I think such generalized scepticism is difficult to maintain in the face of specific examples of human knowledge.

Let us consider two scientists who might be said to have come to know something as a result of their research. The first scientist counts some red blood cells in a grid on a slide and then claims to know that there are 17 cells in the grid. The second scientist examines a great deal of demographic evidence involving the contents of graves, the distribution of potsherds, etc., and then claims to know that a population migration occurred at some point in time between two Indian villages. Unless an analysis of knowledge can count such instances (with the facts filled in) as examples of human knowledge, it would seem to have hopelessly lost contact with the presumed object of analysis. Perhaps it will be obvious that the circumstances surrounding the first scientist's observations might be filled in at least in some cases of this kind of direct observation so that only metaphysical objections could be brought against the knowledge claim. The second case is different. The scientist in question cannot be sure that the system he is analyzing is closed in a relevant sense. A spaceship might have picked up the population of the first village and placed alien replicas into the second village for all that his evidence can show him. Nothing counts against this as a logical possibility. Is it a relevant objection to his knowledge claims that such an event might have happened? It is, to be sure, a logically possible nonmetaphysical objection to his knowledge claim, since it does not depend on a metaphysical objection, but is specific to this situation. Much of the interesting conflict between philosophical scepticism and everyday assumptions about knowledge seems to lie in just such cases. The philosopher considers all possible logical nonmetaphysical objections to knowledge claims, but the scientist is interested only in objections to his knowledge claim that seem scientifically relevant and plausible at the time that a scientific knowledge claim is advanced. Should one wish to find an analysis of knowledge accomodating scientific intuition, it is consequently clear that knowledge claims will have to be evaluated with respect to scientific plausibility at the point in time when the knowledge claim is advanced.

Suppose it is initially proposed that a knowledge claim is true if the claimant can meet all of the plausible objections that could be brought against the relevant knowledge claim when the claim is advanced. It is clear on this proposal that if p is found to be false, then Kap might have been a legitimate knowledge claim in the past, but can be no longer. We do not maintain "$Kap \supset p$" as a theorem of our analysis, and this would seem sufficient to rule out this analysis as far as many philosophers are concerned. If there is a general analysis of knowledge, perhaps there are some generalizations true of knowledge, and this would seem to be an obvious candidate to express one of them. But if there is no general analysis of knowledge, the desire to find theorems of this kind would be considerably diminished. I propose to see if we can do without it, at least in this untensed version.

There is some evidence from our use of language that the concept of knowledge embedded in ordinary language is highly context dependent and temporal. An example is the following:

> Kit Carson knew that since the edges of the tracks were sharp, the Indians could be overtaken within two hours.

It is clear from one point of view that Kit Carson could have known no such thing. Neither logic nor the laws of nature permit Kit to have known that the Indians could be caught. One can imagine many pitfalls—say that the Indians could cross a rope bridge and destroy it. Kit could have known that the Indians could be overtaken only if, great scout that he was, he could have ruled out such circumstances from his knowledge of the terrain and the local weather. A modern Kit Carson would confront a different set of circumstances. Modern Indians might have a rendezvous arranged with a helicopter or an airplane, hardly a problem for the original Kit Carson. Confronted with identical tracks, terrain, and weather, the modern Kit Carson might not be able to make any assertions about overtaking the Indians. The past tense of *know* seems often to be used where one might say that someone knew something that one could not know now due to the development of scientific and mathematical knowledge in the interval.

Further support for this claim can be gathered from the locution "I used to know." In contrast to "I thought I knew," this locution suggests not that one didn't know because one doesn't know now, but that one did know something which one doesn't know now due to some intervening development. "I used to know where Harry could be found on Saturday midnight" suggests that one knew but doesn't know now due to some change in the interval. Harry's habit patterns may have changed as a result of a new love affair, or whatever. Further, these points about tense are relevant to the development of science. It seems to me relevant to ask what chemists knew about valence in the nineteenth century, or what physicists knew about the atom at the turn of the century. The straightforward answer to such questions is to cite the evidence available to scientists at the time in question, and then to relate what they knew on the basis of this evidence, as opposed to what they merely believed or conjectured. Apart from the desire to accomodate a philosophical theory about knowledge, it seems obvious to me that something can be known at one point in time, and then become replaced by other knowledge, perhaps in conflict with it, at a later time. If this possibility is ruled out, scepticism threatens with a vengeance. Since we can't know now what is true (what will never be discovered false) among all the propositions scientists think true and accept, we couldn't say that they know anything unless we adopt an analysis of knowledge that works in fixed contexts.

Scepticism about knowledge is buttressed by the so-called Gettier counterexamples and the subsequent literature.[3] These counter-

[3]Edmund L. Gettier, "Is Justified True Belief Knowledge?" *Analysis* 23 (1962-1963), pp. 121-23). Gettier's original paper, along with important papers from the ensuing controversy, can be found in Michael D. Roth and Leon Galis, *Knowing* (Random House, 1970).

examples show that no justified true belief analysis of knowledge can work in every presumed case. In the counterexamples, the claim supposed known is taken as true, but the evidence the agent uses to support the claim is misleading, despite appearances to the contrary. In one type of case, the evidence can be assumed to be true even though it can be shown that the claim might be false given the evidence in such a fashion that the agent isn't in a position to establish the truth of his claim on the evidence. What the counterexamples can be taken to provide is a relevant nonmetaphysical objection to the knowldge claim such that the rational agent would withdraw his knowledge claim if he were to be confronted with the objection. Consider one well-known case in greater detail. Tom claims to know that someone in his office owns a Ford. Someone in his office does own a Ford, only it is not Smith (as Tom thinks), but Jones. Tom's justifying evidence is that he has seen Smith driving a Ford, has seen Smith's registration for the Ford, and so on. We assume that Tom's evidence is as strong as the analysis requires of justified belief. Now in fact Smith has just sold his Ford and bought a Chevrolet. Tom's claim is true (someone in his office owns a Ford), and he is justified in believing it, but it is not a knowledge claim. The reason is that the fact that Smith does not own a Ford is a relevant nonmetaphysical objection to Tom's knowledge claim. In accepting the counterexample, we suppose that we know what Tom does not, that Smith does not own a Ford. The full evidence would show conclusively that Smith does not own a Ford. If Tom, assumed here to be rational, were also to come to accept this, and not merely to be confronted with somebody's claim to this effect, he would presumably retract or revise his own knowledge claim. Tom's evidence is only accidentally related to the truth of his knowledge claim. We know it is accidentally related because we know a fact that constitutes a relevant and unanswerable objection to Tom's claim, since his claim is based on his view that Smith owns a Ford. Tom is not familiar with this objection, but the counterexample supposes that he could not dispose of it if it were to be brought to his attention.

This way of looking at the Gettier counterexamples suggests that someone might be said to know something if he or she can meet the objections that could be brought against the knowledge claim at the time when it is advanced. Considered abstractly, the space of possible objections to any given knowledge claim may seem unmanageable, and hence it may seem that knowledge as justified true belief about something can never be achieved. Do not the Gettier counterexamples force the view that a Gettier counterexample might be constructed for any piece of presumed knowledge? Now the facts might not be kind to Gettier counterexamples across the board. Perhaps people sometimes do know things and the facts won't allow a real world Gettier counterexample to be constructed. But is not a single Gettier counterexample a refutation of the general thesis that knowledge is justified true belief? It would seem so, and yet there might be cases where we could show that Gettier counterexamples couldn't be constructed, and wouldn't these cases admit the possibility of genuine knowledge? The Gettier counterexamples arise (and gain their plausibility) from features surrounding the everyday matters of fact that they deal with. We frequently know little about our co-workers and casual acquaintances, and may even know little about other members of our immediate family. No piling on of evidence would seem to rule out every possible counterexample to our leaps from evidence to presumed knowledge in these cases. Further, we may keep our opinions to ourselves, or those with counterexamples may not hear of our opinions, or may prefer that we remain ignorant of various facts. The situation appears to be quite different in science and mathematics. Here the objects of inquiry can be isolated and manipulated in every conceivable way, making legitimate counterexamples to the link between evidence and theory difficult to construct. Further, the practice of publishing claims and encouraging their refutation makes it fairly likely that possible counterexamples to knowledge claims will make an appearance.[4] Perhaps here, at least, the space of possible counterexamples is sometimes manageable, so that sometimes we may justifiably be said to know things.

In mathematical cases, the possibility that $\sim p$ is often a blanket relevant nonmetaphysical objection to a mathematical claim that p, partly because of the atemporality of mathematical propositions. Proving a contradiction from $\sim p$ is sufficient (classically) to prove p, and we may regard the production of such a contradiction as exhausting the logically possible nonmetaphysical mathematical objections to p. In other words, in many mathematical cases, the current objections to p may be equivalent to the logically possible objections to p. The more obvious problems with such a suggestion can be met.

[4]The role of criticism in scientific knowledge has been emphasized in Sir Karl Popper's philosophy of science. Jerome R. Ravetz, in *Scientific Knowledge and its Social Problems* (Oxford, 1971), especially in Part II, has made an extremely interesting analysis of the role of refereeing and journal citation in the creation of scientific knowledge.

For example, this might not seem to be so when new mathematical structures are discovered, to which previous knowledge claims are inadequate. Here a process of relativization allows the mathematician to keep his knowledge claims intact by relativizing them to the original structures. Claims about geometry were relativized to claims about Euclidean Geometry (but otherwise preserved) after the discovery of non-Euclidean Geometry. The account of mathematical knowledge offered to this point would require some revision for intuitionist approaches to mathematical knowledge. For our purposes, we need merely note that intuitionism is a way of trying to insure that all possible relevant nonmetaphysical objections to a claim are met by a constructive procedure that rules out these objections as the construction proceeds. Mathematical knowledge can then be regarded as constructive and cumulative.

Any full discussion of scientific knowledge would encounter many difficulties, particularly the fact that even elementary laws and theories are always disputed by some scientists. But the laws of classical mechanics, for example, are agreed to sufficiently to constitute an example of scientific knowledge. They are, of course, limited to certain systems because various relevant systems for which they are inaccurate were not known in the nineteenth century. At the same time, so many controlled experiments have ruled out alternative possibilities that these laws can be defended against any known objections, and *a fortiori* against the objections raised and discussed historically.

To know what scientific knowledge is in hand requires something other than a logical analysis. The state of science must be mastered, including current controversies and experimental results. Science has an institutional structure that makes public to a great extent the process of giving and meeting objections, and perhaps this process allows the space of possible objections to become precise enough to talk about the legitimacy of justified true belief analyses here. The journals encourage argument and rebuttal, and the process of criticism is pursued in meetings between scientists. If we argue that mathematical and scientific knowledge at any time is what can be defended against mathematically and scientifically plausible objections, although the analysis is not precise, it is not clear that Gettier counterexamples could be produced for specific cases, and the sceptical wedge driven into the subject matter.

In everyday matters of fact, the amorphous nature of possible objections to knowledge claims becomes unmistakable. People working in areas where there are rule of thumb generalizations know that they cannot control and explain and predict that which is subject to some deeper understanding than they know that they have. Nevertheless, books about plumbing, cooking, gardening, and so on, are written and consumed. At least in these areas, some knowledge clearly exists, and an analysis should allow for this fact. Controversies are settled partly by convention, partly by natural history and detail. Having seen something is generally better than having been told about it, and so forth. But in many of these cases, there is no analogue to the result of scientific and mathematical practice in deciding what constitutes sufficient evidence for the truth of some belief. The counterexamples are perhaps a sufficient warning that claims to knowledge in these areas should be circumspect and guarded. In retrospect it may seem that a lot of the emotional heat in the philosophical controversies about the nature of knowledge has been generated by attempting to extend analysis of mathematical and scientific knowledge to cases where it cannot fit.

ROBERT ACKERMANN.

UNIVERSITY OF MASSACHUSETTS
AT AMHERST.

DISCUSSION

THE LIMITATIONS OF SENSE EXPERIENCE

The Aristotelian position in general and that of the empiricists in particular is that there is nothing in the mind that is not first in the senses. To this some of the descendants of Comte have made the addendum that what is not sensibly verifiable has no part in philosophy.

To these general theses and particularly to the notion that sensibly verifiable questions are the only legitimate ones, I would oppose not a duality of human inquiries, but a trinity. The present thesis is that significant thinking investigates three distinct domains. If this be the case, efforts to close off all except one are misguided.

The domain perennially favored by tough-minded philosophers—and the descriptive phrase *tough-minded,* following James, is intended neither to disparage nor to praise—is the empirical one, sense experience being epistemologically at the apex of what we can know. It is by this orientation that metaphysics has within the last hundred years been eclipsed and *scientism*—again neither disparagement nor praise—has enjoyed an unprecedented esteem.

The first of the two domains thus crowded out of focus is that of logic and mathematics. To use the language of Plato, this realm is before the mind rather than before the senses. The 'circle' roughly drawn in the sand or on a modern blackboard is before the senses but of course is not a circle at all, but merely the sensible representation of one. The mind goes on to consider it as composed of a line (which, lacking breadth, would be imperceptible to the senses) equidistant from the center no matter how imperfect in this respect the representation before the eye may be. Euclid was undoubtedly aware of this distinction and whatever one may think of Plato's reality of forms, such a distinction affords a paradigm *par excellence* of that between the sensible world and that reality.

And whether we be inclined to accept or reject Plato's belief in the preeminence of that other, intelligible realm, it cannot be denied that the realm of mathematics constitutes a legitimate domain of inquiry. In mathematics we have, to put the matter in a few words, a domain which is at one time *not* sensible, but quite legitimate.

The reply from the time of Locke might well have been that

mathematics is an abstraction born out of sense experience. But during the last century and a half, light thrown by non-Euclidean geometries on the nature of mathematics has made such a rebuttal preposterous. It is undeniable that (1) the historical development of much of mathematics rests on the practical, i.e., empirical aspects thereof (men were computing for millenia prior to Peano and the practical surveying of Egyptian floodlands preceded even Euclid's work); and (2) mathematics has empirical applications at many turns. But the present consensus is that mathematics and logic are a domain quite apart from the empirical one. As Poincaré made clear at the beginning of this century, our 'real life' employment of Euclidean geometry (or that of any alternative) rests principally on the convenience it affords rather than on any inherent conformity to the physical universe (Conventionalism). Modern logic affords further illustration of this independence of concept from percept: the *interpretation* of a logic is by no means a criterion for judging its legitimacy—*n*-valued sentential logics have as proper a place in this domain as true-false varieties. So if in Locke's time it could be argued that the mathematician abstracts from empirical data, what is to be said post imaginary numbers, Cantor's transfinite numbers, and the like? As Russell pointed out with even greater profundity than wit, in mathematics we don't know what we are talking about (the interpretation of a mathematics is beside the point) nor even if what we are saying is true (what it corresponds to empirically may be unknown to us).

The acknowledged applicability of mathematics in science and technology appears to spring from the capacity of many mathematical systems to be 'mapped onto' the sensible world. This can be judged to occur when the primitive ideas of the mathematics have their counterparts in the sensible realm as, e.g., Euclid's points, lines and planes have their correspondents in the X on the surveyor's stake, the path traveled by light from the distant pole to his transit, and the plane swept by that line as the transit telescope is turned.*

Here, then, in mathematics and logic is a realm of inquiry which would be quite swept aside were we to heed literally the dictum that there is nothing in the mind that is not first in the senses. Were the doctrines of innate ideas and empiricism contradictories of each other, the falsity of one might well betoken the truth of the other.

*That arithmetic 'fits' the sensible world is attributable to the fact that its *materia prima* conceptually is discrete units. That the sensible world abounds with these accounts for the quasi-universality of arithmetic's applicability.

They stand as contraries, however, each of which can be false. That the mind is afforded notions at birth may be objectionable. So also is the limitations of the mind's activities to the material offered it by the senses.

Before broaching the third realm, as separate from mathematics as it is from the sensible, there is further light to be thrown on the two realms at hand by a consideration of the roles which axioms play in each. Despite what dictionaries may still declare, an axiom is not an axiom because it is self-evident. Quite the contrary, some of the axioms of non-Euclidean geometries and other branches of mathematics defy the intuition and would be classified as anything but self-evident. They are axioms, nonetheless, because—and this is the real hallmark of any axiom—they are assumed without proof and assumed for the purpose of proceeding to some theorems deducible from them.

Now it is characteristic of the axioms of mathematics or of logic that they can be selected *ad lib.* This is not to say that all axioms are equally productive of a suitable system. In the sentential logic, for instance, a nontautological axiom would result in a system, to be sure, but one which would be of interest to a very few logicians. But as long as an axiom is consistent with other axioms of a system, there is nothing to hinder any selection, however arbitrary. In this sense a mathematician or logician creates the properties of the domain he is investigating, decreeing in a godlike fashion what is *to be*.

The systematizing of the sensible realm—let it be called science—is afforded no such breadth of liberty. The scientist must finally and above all respect the data. If he ever ignores the data which run counter to his science, it is only provisionally. Ultimately, if he cannot square observation with theory he must square theory with observation. A mathematician's investigations may or may not prove applicable to the sensible world. The scientist's must. There is no point in his theory unless such a fit exists, his purpose being to match his theoretical description to the facts at hand.

Despite this demand, the stance it results in, and the resulting orientation, science adopts certain axioms of its own. By this is meant that certain propositions are adopted without proof and for the sake of building on the foundations they constitute. One such axiom is that nature is uniform. Without this postulate no science would be thinkable; the entire scientific enterprise would collapse. Nor is it less an axiom because our experience bears it out, for we 'bear it out' precisely by basing our science on it and then congratulating ourselves on our success. Any supposed *proof* of the uniformity of nature is an indication resting on the results of a systemizing which assumes it before it can take a single faltering step. There are other instances of scientific thinking that evince a dependence on what *we* put into the system rather than what observation contributes, and which for this reason can be said to share the flavor of axioms. The conservation of energy principle, for instance, was salvaged by declaring that energy can be in more than one form: kinetic or potential. The assumption that energy is unchanging in quantity has since been traded in for a more suitable assumption, viz., that mass-energy is unchanging. Part of this switch is attributable to the results of observation, to be sure, but this is only to say again that in science the axioms are not freely chosen as in mathematics, but must be chosen with an eye to the suitability of what is deduced from them.

It is in this inquiry into the sensible realm that the empiricist's dictum is most justified. In science there is much that is *in the mind;* but most of that content is there because it is compatible with what is *in the senses.* Despite this, or perhaps because of it, axioms characterize science as well as mathematics. For better or for worse, it assumes, it postulates.

The third realm of legitimate inquiry is philosophy itself. And if it appears that this is a defense of philosophy from its own onslaughts, the appearance may reveal more than it obscures. Those who have contended that to discard metaphysics out of hand is itself a position entailing a metaphysics will find comfort in what follows.

That what is not finally related to the empirical cannot be a suitable subject for philosophy may be a current idol of the theater. But the error in such idolatry is less of principle than of application. Let us examine what is meant by *empirical,* the better to judge what is to be discarded as bath water and what is to be kept as cleansed.

A tight meaning of *empirical* would restrict the word to what is before the senses, whether directly or indirectly. This tight meaning is appropriate, consummately so, to the scientific enterprise. Poets may talk of elves, classicists of mythical beasts, theologians of God; but elves, centaurs, and God are not scientific concepts. Neither directly nor indirectly can we secure any pointer-readings by their employment.

There is a looser meaning of *empirical* which also deserves consideration. Hamlet's experiences provided him with a point of view, a *weltanschauung,* which rested rather firmly on those experiences. His appeals to experience had little of the pointer-readings about them.

Such experience might well be dubbed existential rather than sensible, but certainly it was consequential. The loss of Ophelia's sanity infinitely outweighed, in Hamlet's world, the somersaults of the acting troop. The waves against the rocks below him were a part of Hamlet's empirical world, but a minimal and inconsequential part when compared to his contemplation of the rub of dreams after death. To assume, knowingly or unwittingly, that *empiricism* is to be equated with *sense-experience* is to simplify philosophizing, to be sure, but at the cost of the most significant portions of human experience.

For philosophy to be a handmaiden of science — a la Carnap et al — affords a clearheaded progam and a certain enviable cleanliness and singleness of purpose. It makes for unclutteredness, if only relatively. But what name shall we now award to those inquiries that respect the meaningfulness and significance of the 'human situation'? Whether we espouse or renounce the existentialist's jargon, what their jargon refers to will not go away.

To speak of good and evil or, if we flee those words, of desirable and undesirable, or prizeworthy and unesteemed, is to turn our attention to something which has no place in either the realm of mathematics of that of science. These themes, of the highest legitimacy, have their place only in a third realm.

It is unlikely that this last realm should be confused with that of mathematics, but failure to distinguish it from that of science has produced a great deal of bad thinking, as I shall next undertake to show.

For as *God* is not a scientific concept, neither is the methodology appropriate to science suitable for the third realm delineated. There are two words that serve to increase confusion on these matters. One is *truth* and the other is *reality*.

Consider the distinction between logical truth and empirical truth. Logical truth — *Either today is Tuesday or it is not Tuesday* — is empty of information but is (systematically considered, at least) spotlessly indisputable. Empirical truth — *Oswald assassinated Kennedy* — may be uncertain or debatable, but at least takes us off the 'blackboard' into the 'real world.' Right or wrong, it purports to give information, and if right then *true* information. It is in such contexts that the terms *true* and *false* seem most incontestably to fit. These are the contexts in which sensible verification is possible, at least in principle. Logical tautologies have no connection with the sensible realm and to qualify the word *truth* with the adjective *logical* yields only an inch where a mile is wanted. If there existed an entirely different word for analytical truths, the distinction between them and empirical truths would become as forthright as it is currently slighted and obscured. For the purposes of the present reflections, I propose to rename logical truth, calling it *trath.* The words *true* and *false* will thus be reserved for the sensible realm; sensibly verifiable statements will then be matters of truth (even when they are false). Mathematical and logical statements, devoid as they are of content, will be called matters of trath. We shall decline to say of them that they are true or false; they will be called correct (i.e., they follow from the axioms of the system in which they are made) or incorrect. Tautologies, contingencies, and self-contradictions will alike be matters of trath.

Briefly to exercise this distinction: That $2 + 2 = 4$ is a matter of trath; that two eggs and two eggs come to four eggs is a matter of truth. *P* represents a trathful assertion. *Today is Monday* is in the realm of truth. That the number of primes is infinite is a matter of trath. That *7* is a prime is trathful. Euclid's fifth postulate is a statement of trath. It is true that Kennedy was assassinated. The Pythagorean theorem is trath. That humans first appeared in Africa is (whether true or false) a matter of truth.

That one ought to treat his neighbor as he would be treated is neither of these. Not being the kind of statement that sensible observation will corroborate or disconfirm, it is not a matter of truth. Not being a part of an empty and arbitrary mathematical or logical inquiry, it is not a matter of trath. It appears almost self-evident that axioms underlie this third realm, witness the axiomatic quality of any "I ought to . . . " But such an axiom is entirely distinct from its counterparts in mathematics or science. An axiom in mathematics, as non-Euclidean geometries make plain, is a starting point chosen for systematic reasons without regard to sensible intuition; hence it can be said to be freely chosen at the whim of the investigator, as in *n*-valued sentential logics. An axiom in science is not freely chosen: its value is determined by its fertility, not in some empty system but in the world of three dimensions—in the realm the investigation of which always returns finally to sense-experience. The axioms embodying values—whether moral or esthetic, although as freely chosen as those of mathematics, are such as *matter profoundly in the life of the axiom-maker.* They also resemble those of science in that they are shaped by their fertility, but they differ in that they are not subject to pointer-reading verification. Such axioms, since they are characterized above all by the freedom with which we individually espouse them, I propose to call axioms of *troth.* The manner in which one plights his troth to another, committing himself to certain modes of behavior, appears to reflect perfectly the commitment a man makes to his values and the responsibility he freely assumes thereby.

The third realm embraces all prizings and in the respect just noted, they are all alike: the election is made as one's *choice* and it *determines behavior.* (So much are values determiners of behavior that where a man offers only lip-service to a value, we do not hesitate to say that his values are really not what he says they are.) This is a far-reaching realm. Not only is a preference for peaches over kumquats a part of it; so also is a preference for Plato over Aristotle or vice versa. Need we blush to acknowledge that each philosopher has his own bent, his preference, his predisposition, his predilection? This is only to say that each feels impelled to commit himself in an honest way. Commitments may change—one may divorce Aristotle and wed Plato—but the elements of election and responsibility for that election is present in each case.

To say, then, that philosophy's business concerns the abstractions of science is to make a trothful statement. To say that she should be the handmaiden of religion is to make another. To say that Spinoza was right, or Plotinus was, or Comte, is to speak trothfully, just as trothfully as when we say that we should or should not treat others as we would be treated. To 'take the cash and let the credit go' is to act trothfully, as is also to 'heed the rumble of a distant drum.'

It follows that arguments about reality reflect differing commitments. 'This world'-ly mindedness is a commitment. 'Other-world'-ly mindedness is a commitment. Logical positivism, existentialism, pragmatism: commitments all, each in this realm of troth. The 'reality' of God or His 'nonexistence' are matters of troth. I believe it is plain that such an acknowledgment does nothing either to ennoble or to deprecate such assertions. To say that they are matters neither of trath nor of truth is only to clarify their nature; it need not alter their standing. After all, the standing of prizings, expecially the more sweeping and life-determining ones, needs no defense.

To say that man first appeared in Africa is a truth-realm statement. To say that God made man is a troth-realm statement. The fear on the part of some Fundamentalists that one or the other must be wrong is misguided. It is a mistake, in my opinion, to suppose offhand that the true-false character of statements in the truth realm have a counterpart in the realm of troth. Recall that trath is characterized by tautology-or-contingency, by it-follows-or-it-does-not-follow rather than by true-false alternatives. It is one kind of a contradiction to assert both *p* and *non-p:* a trathful contradiction. To assert that today is Tuesday and it is also Friday is a truthful contradiction even though a trothful counterpart can be made. What of statements such as *there is a God* and *there is no God?* Were these truthful or trathful statements, they would be contradictory. To say that there may be no contradiction here at all is a bold conjecture even though this is frequently acknowledged tacitly whenever it is plead that "it all depends on how you feel about it." The concept of God being a matter of troth, may it not be that truth-logic and trath-logic are alike out of place? The disciples of the Buddha, on inquiring whether we survive death, were told in effect that the answer *Yes, you do* would be misleading and so would the answer *No, you don't.*

A last remark about the word *reality,* then. Certain realities—Aristotle's—have a true-false quality about them. *The reality of the mathematical realm* is a phrase the very debatability of which betokens how differently the idea of reality can be conceived; but its purported reality is by no conception that of the sense world, so that *true* and *false* are inappropriate words. They are equally inappropriate for the realm of troth, as is even the word *reality* if it be conceived only in the empirical or truth-sense. The *is* of *There is a God* (troth) is neither the *is* of *There is a town to the north* nor the *is* of *There is an infinite number of primes.*

The confusion of truth with troth lies sometimes on the very surface, quite visible; at other times it lies deep, obscured and therefore the more treacherous. If the distinctions here presented are legitimate, the wielding of either truth or troth as an iconoclast's hammer cannot be justified.

GERALD STANDLEY.

GAINESVILLE, FLORIDA.

DISCUSSION

SEEING OUR OWN FACES: A PARADIGM FOR INDIRECT REALISM

As the canonical 'causal theory' of perception, indirect (or 'representational') realism has failed to generate very much enthusiasm among contemporary epistemologists. Buttressing the Scottish common-sense polemic against the indirect realism of Descartes, Locke, and many others, criticisms by latter-day figures such as Prichard, Austin, and Chisholm have succeeded in making it reactionary to avow belief in the existence of mental or private objects of perception ('sensa') which—as the only '*directly* perceived' entities—manage to mediate our awareness of their causes, i.e., public objects and events. Additionally, does not Chisholm's 'adverbial' account of appearances do the requisite job while enjoying the advantage of ontological parsimony? Interestingly enough, however, there is much to suggest that neurophysiologists and psychologists of perception seem (on balance) rather more receptive to the notion of sensa than are philosophers. For example, John Eccles, a physiologist of no small eminence, is sympathetic to the view that sensa constitute the only objects of direct perception.[1] Also, in introducing a recent collection of articles on perception from *Scientific American,* Richard Held raises the question of the significance of 'illusions of the senses' for the 'relation between image and object'[2]—a question which suggests that indirect realism may constitute something more than an awkward stage on the way to epistemological maturity.

Additionally, it should be noted that the recent *philosophical* literature can boast a number of very good papers which have some supportive things to say about indirect realism.[3] While I find this to

[1] Cf. J. Eccles, *The Brain and the Unity of Conscious Experience* (Cambridge: Cambridge University Press, 1965), pp. 17-18. This passage is quoted in James W. Cornman, "On Direct Perception," *The Review of Metaphysics* (1972), p. 43. Cornman's article constitutes what I believe to be a first-rate and long overdue sorting out of the 'metaphysical' from the 'epistemological' implications of 'direct' and 'indirect' perception.

[2] *Image, Object, and Illusion* (San Francisco: W. H. Freeman and Co., 1974), p. 2.

[3] In addition to Cornman's article (op. cit.), cf. Andrew Ward, "Direct and Indirect Realism," *American Philosophical Quarterly* (1976), pp. 287-94.

be heartening, it seems to me that considerable work remains (and deserves) to be done if it is ever to become evident that indirect realism has been the victim of an undeservedly bad press. My specific purpose in *this* discussion, however, is to establish that what clearly is the dominant and venerated objection to indirect realism simply lacks the force which it has traditionally been taken to have. While this will not involve me in any attempt to argue for the *truth* of indirect realism, it seems clear that overcoming the objection in question constitutes a very important *prelude* to any resolution of whether indirect realism ought to be regarded as a true (or plausible) account of how we perceive and acquire perceptual knowledge of the 'external world.'

I

I suggest that the following constitutes a concise and reasonably rigorous formulation[4] of what is central to the doctrine of indirect realism:

> For an indirect realist if a physical object, *P*, should be perceived by someone, *S*, then *S*'s perceptual experience of *P* would consist of *S* experiencing some sensum or group of sensa which is different from *P*, is neither a constituent of *P*, nor has *P* as a constituent. Thus . . .
>
> All physical objects which are perceivable are indirectly perceivable.

It seems clear that the dominant objection to this epistemological doctrine can be rendered perspicuously as follows:

> If 'direct' perceptual experience is confined to entities which are nonidentical to physical objects/events, these latter thereby take on the status of inferential or *theoretical* entities, i.e., entities the existence and properties of which can at best be inferred rather than perceived. In short, the doctrine of indirect realism entails that it is causally impossible for physical objects/events ever to constitute *perceptual* objects. Hence, not only does indirect realism justify skepticism with regard to the 'external world,' but, since it purports to constitute an account of *perceptual* knowing (and thus *presupposes* that physical objects are not unperceivable), it is an utterly self-defeating or paradoxical doctrine.

This objection, of course, has long been the rallying point for *direct* realists throughout the course of their time-honored polemic against indirect realism.[5]

It seems clear, then, that for direct realists and other opponents

---

[4] I borrow here gratefully from Cornman, op. cit., pp. 49-50.

[5] As confirmed, for example, by Ward, op. cit., p. 287. Interestingly, though (I suggest) unfortunately, Ward himself appears to accept 'the inferential nature of indirect realism' (loc. cit.) as a matter of course.

of indirect realism, to perceive some x 'indirectly' is not really to *perceive* that x in any proper sense; rather, it is to perceive something nonidentical to it (which is neither a constituent of x nor has x as a constituent) from which the existence and properties of x can at best be *inferred*. This does not, of course, imply that there is a deliberate 'act of inference' from sensa to physical objects which is performed by percipients during the normal course of perceptual experience; rather, it is simply to charge that, according to indirect realism, the justification of physical object claims must inevitably employ premises which involve reference to the (direct) perception only of sensa.

II

For present purposes, let us dub this long-standing objection to indirect realism 'The Paradox of Indirect Perceptual Knowing' (in the sequel, however, I shall often use 'the paradox' as a convenient shorthand). Note that the crucial assumption which underlies 'the paradox' can be spelled out as follows:

> An object *O* can be known perceptually—as opposed to inferentially—only if there is no entity *O'*, nonidentical to *O* (and which is neither a constituent of *O* nor has *O* as a constituent), which must be perceived in order for *O* to be known. Hence, and necessarily, if *O* and *O'* are nonidentical (and *O'* is neither a constituent of *O* nor has *O* as a constituent), no experience of *O'* ever consists in an experience of *O*.

It seems to me that this assumption ought to be rejected—nothwithstanding that critics of indirect realism tend to view it as axiomatic—and, consequently, that the notion of Indirect Perceptual Knowing ought not be regarded as paradoxical. My argument in this regard is as follows:

1. That faces are invisible to their owners ought to be regarded as false.

2. Seeing one's own face constitutes a paradigm case of indirect perception.

Therefore, it ought to be regarded as false that there is something paradoxical inherent in the notion of Indirect Perceptual Knowing.

Taking it to be clear that my argument is valid in form, what needs to be established is its soundness, i.e., the truth of its premises. To begin with premise 1, it seems to me that there is very little to which one can appeal in order to derive anything like a knockdown drag-out *argument* for its truth. However, it seems clear that there are any number of true (or reasonable) propositions which cannot be shown to be true (or reasonable) in precisely that way. I suggest, however, that premise 1 receives some significant confirmation from cases such as the following: John is attending a stag party with friends and having a very enjoyable time. His friend Don (known to those present as a practical joker) asks John where he got that 'big smudge of lipstick' on his forehead. When everyone in the room laughs, John begins to wonder: *Do* I have a big smudge of lipstick on my forehead? Did my wife kiss me on the forehead before I left for the party? He then takes the predictable route to satisfying his curiosity—i.e., he dashes into the bathroom and looks into the mirror. Sure enough, there it is: a big smudge of lipstick on his forehead.

Now I suggest that it would be patently unacceptable to deny that John *saw* the smudge of lipstick on his forehead. If, upon reentering the living room, Don asked him: 'Well, John, did you see for yourself?', what would we think if John replied: 'Not really, Don, the best I could do was *infer* that there was a smudge of lipstick on my forehead from what I *was* able to perceive' (more on this latter point to follow). While I have very little sympathy for the view that ordinary thought, judgment, and language dictate the resolutions of matters epistemological, metaphysical, etc., it seems to me—as it did to G. E. Moore and does to many thinkers in his tradition—that our preanalytic convictions ought to be regarded as a significant test of the soundness of philosophical positions in the absence of some good reason for believing those convictions to be mistaken. Hence, pending some good reason for regarding it as mistaken to claim that persons can see their own faces, I conclude that it is eminently proper to maintain that faces are not invisible to their owners.

But exactly how, to anticipate our critic, does the foregoing tend to exonerate indirect realism from the time-honored charge of paradoxicality? That is, even if it *is* proper to maintain that faces are not invisible to their owners, precisely how does this call 'the paradox' into serious question? In short, what reason does it give us for believing that premise 2 of our argument is true? The answer, I suggest, is simple and straightforward. In order to see my own face, I must see something which is nonidentical to my face (and is neither a constituent of my face nor has my face as a constituent). For in order to see my own face, I must see an image of it in a reflecting medium,[6] and,

[6] For present purposes, I shall assume that persons do not see their faces when seeing *photographs* of their faces, i.e., that their visual experience in any such case is limited to a 'representation' of their faces. It is not at all clear to me, however, that this view is correct.

consequently, the visual perception which I have of my own face on any such occasion just *consists* in an experience of that image. Clearly, however, and regardless of the *sort* of image in question—whether it be an afterimage, reflective image, etc.—it is unimpeachable that

> Images of objects are nonidentical with the objects of which they are the images

constitutes a necessary truth. Consequently, seeing one's own face in a reflecting medium serves as a paradigm of Indirect Perceptual Knowing—in which case, of course, the notion of Indirect Perceptual Knowing can hardly be considered paradoxical.

Now it seems possible for a reflective image of one's own face to be so distorted that an experience of it would *not* consist in a veridical experience of one's own face (note that the reliability of any given reflecting medium is readily testable, i.e., we need just 'hold up' some ordinary object and gauge the accuracy of the reflection). While this is so, it is simply irrelevant to the point being driven, i.e., that in those cases (presumably the vast majority) wherein persons *do* have a veridical experience of their own faces when looking into a reflecting medium, such an experience must consist in their visual experience of something which is nonidentical to their own faces.

III

In all fairness, the critic of indirect realism might venture something very much like the following objection to the foregoing:

> It is not the case that seeing one's own face in a reflecting medium constitutes a paradigm of Indirect Perceptual Knowing. For it is not the case that one must see—when seeing one's own face—some entity which is nonidentical to one's own face. Rather, the mistake here has been to conflate what is (properly) 'adverbial' with what is (improperly) 'entitative,' i.e., to regard '*N* sees his face reflected (imaged)' as entailing 'The object of *N*'s direct perception is a reflection (image) of his own face.' However, there is no basis for believing that the latter proposition is entailed by the former. Hence, there is no good reason for believing that some entity which is nonidentical to one's own face is what is directly perceived when one sees one's own face in a reflecting medium.

While this anticipated rejoinder is indeed suggestive, it simply will not suffice as a satisfactory rebuttal of the argument that seeing one's own face in a reflecting medium constitutes a paradigm of Indirect Perceptual Knowing. For the relation between any object and its reflective image, i.e., a 'mirror image' relationship is

> . . . the relationship exhibited by two similar *but nonsuperimposable*

crystals or molecular structures.[7]

Since this is not a *contingent fact* about the relation between any object and its mirror image, but is rather what *constitutes* the relationship between any object and its mirror image, '*N* sees his face reflected (imaged)' *does* entail 'The object of *N*'s direct perception is a reflection (image) of his own face.' It seems to me that an alternative but no less decisive way of making the very same point is this: it is clear that reflective images are of a different 'ontological order' than the objects of which they are the images. For a reflective image of *x* depends for its existence at any given moment upon the existence (and proper positioning) of *x* at that moment, whereas it is obvious that the converse is not the case. Surely, however, it would be absurd to claim that entities of different ontological orders could be extensionally identical. Hence, it is false that I need not *(a fortiori* that I *do* not) see something which is nonidentical to my own face in order to see my own face. This being so, any visual experience which I have of my own face just consists in the 'direct perception' of a reflective image of my own face.

IV

To sum up: The dominant and time-honored critique of indirect realism has been that the notion of Indirect Perceptual Knowing is paradoxical. I think it has now been shown that 'the paradox' ought to be regarded as bogus, and, consequently, that it ought not be supposed that indirect realism fails *(if* it does) as a theory of perception because there is something conceptually awry about the view that physical objects/events are perceived 'indirectly.' On the contrary, since it ought not be held that faces are invisible to their owners, and since any visual perception of one's own face constitutes a paradigm of Indirect Perceptual Knowing, we have no good reason for regarding the putative paradox as genuine. This is not, of course, to suggest that the relation which obtains between objects and their reflective images is analogous *in every respect*[8] to that which (for the indirect

[7]Cf. *Webster's Third New International Dictionary* (Springfield, Mass: G & C Merriam Co., 1968), p. 1441 (my emphasis).

[8]It might, for example, be held that—unlike sensa—the *esse* of mirror images is not *percipi,* i.e., that mirror images are 'in the world' in a way in which mental or private entities such as sensa are not. While it is correct to regard mirror images as 'public' in contradistinction to the sensa of the indirect realist—no one (including

realist) obtains between sensa and physical objects/events. Rather, what I believe has been shown is that the relations in question are analogous in the very *crucial* respect which permits the conclusion that, unless and until it is shown that faces are invisible to their owners (or that it is proper to believe that that is so), the critics have precious little foundation for holding that indirect realism confers the status of inferential or theoretical entities upon physical objects/events, and, consequently, constitutes a self-defeating or paradoxical theory of perception.[9]

ROBERT OAKES.

UNIVERSITY OF MISSOURI-ROLLA.

myself) needs to *perceive* my mirror image in order for it to 'exist,' while it would clearly be the height of folly to speak of 'unperceived sensa'—such images have considerably more in common with sensa than the physical objects/events by virtue of not existing in physical space. Hence, they—along with certain other 'public' phenomena—might reasonably be regarded as 'objective' sensa (or sense-data). Indeed, Virgil Aldrich has called them just that: see his very interesting paper "Objective Sense-Data," *The Personalist* (1979), pp. 36-42.

[9] What has been argued herein lends additional support to the thesis which I attempted to establish in my previous article, "How to Rescue the Traditional Causal Theory of Perception," *Philosophy and Phenomenological Research* (1978), pp. 370-83.

DISCUSSION

EVOLUTIONARY EPISTEMOLOGY IS SELF-REFERENTIALLY INCONSISTENT

Evolutionary epistemology is self-referentially inconsistent. Stephen Toulmin, in his book, *Human Understanding,* Vol. I (Princeton: Princeton University Press, 1972) proposes a typical evolutionary epistemology. His theory claims to be relevant to actual science and provides an impartial rational standpoint for conceptual evaluation. He distinguishes conceptual choices in fact made from those demanded by the genuine needs of specific problem situations (pp. 480-488). He claims to justify this by reference to the substantive intellectual goals of the disciplines concerned. Fulfillment of these goals presumably justifies theory selection. Two theories within the same discipline can thus be impartially and rationally compared. The better theory more fully realizes the goals of the discipline. This applies to any intellectual discipline. So far Toulmin's justification of conceptual change appears analogous to an Aristotelian justification in terms of the final cause of the discipline concerned. There is a difference, however. Toulmin's own theory is evolutionary. His disciplinary goals continuously evolve. They are not invariant. Scientists will sometimes try to determine what general intellectual goals they should be aiming at (p. 236). The good scientist does this in light of a long-range vision. This vision includes what the science was, is, and should become in order to fulfill most completely its general ideas of scientific understanding (pp. 241, 289). These general ideals also continuously evolve. They are open-textured (pp. 495-500). This does not, says Toulmin, result in relativism. Our conceptions of these general disciplinary goals must adapt to a nature 'that goes beyond all human tastes, and all human power to alter' (p. 245). At any given point in time impartial rational comparisons would still be possible even if the general goals of a discipline themselves later evolve. Impartial rational considerations indicate the success men in fact achieved in the pursuit of the goals they set for themselves in their own time (p. 489).

Toulmin's evolutionary epistemology is self-referentially inconsistent. Toulmin's evolutionary theory itself evolves. Thus, it should someday evolve into a nonevolutionary theory. General ideals of scientific understanding will then no longer evolve. But Toulmin's theory claims that these general ideals continuously evolve. Thus, Toulmin's theory is self-referentially inconsistent and, therefore, untenable.

Toulmin denies that there are invariant metascientific truths. His denial is self-referentially inconsistent. The claim that there are no invariant metascientific truths is, if true, itself an invariant metascientific truth. Toulmin believes it is applicable universally to all sciences at all times. If it were true, we would therefore have it itself as an example of a standard whose truth and meaning stays the same no matter what different theories we may hold; thus *by its very statement,* it would be false. Hence, it *cannot* be true. Toulmin's view, and his philosophical attitude toward it, are therefore untenable.

Toulmin claims that "No judgment on Man's success in the rational organization of his experience is ever final or immune to reconsideration" (p. 501).

Is this claim itself immune to revision? If so then, by its very statement, it would be false. In this case it should, therefore, be abandoned. If not, then it can be revised, and hence can be false. Thus, by its very statement, there can exist a statement immune to revision. But Toulmin's position denies just this for one important sense of 'can'; namely when 'can' means 'sometimes'.

Toulmin might reply by saying that to reconsider a theory need not change its truth value. He might wish to reconsider theories in some way other than redistributing their truth values. This, however, is unclear without specification of new technical meaning for *reconsider.*

If Toulmin were proposing new metaconcepts to replace the present ones, then he should specify his new metaconcepts, defend them by showing what is wrong with the present metaconcepts, how the new metaconcepts avoid the difficulties, and in what ways they are more exact and fruitful. Toulmin attempts none of these tasks.

Epistemology is not itself "final or immune to reconsideration." Evolutionary epistemology is self-referentially inconsistent.

CARL R. KORDIG.

CHICAGO, ILLINOIS.

REVIEWS

Alexius Meinong: On Objects of Higher Order and Husserl's Phenomenology. MARIE-LUISE SCHUBERT KALSI. The Hague: Martinus Nijohff, 1978. Pp. 252.

This book contains Marie-Luise Schubert Kalsi's translations of three of Meinong's essays and his critical notes on Husserl's *Ideas,* as well as a lengthy (50 pp.) and informative introduction by Kalsi herself. It is a welcome addition to her previous translation of and introduction to Meinong's *On Emotional Presentation* (1972).

The three essays translated by Kalsi center on the theme of "objects of higher order," which include relations and wholes ("complexions"). The first two essays, "On the Psychology of Complexions and Relations" (1891) and "An Essay Concerning the Theory of Psychic Analysis" (1894) show Meinong still under the influence of psychologism. He confounds contents of acts with the objects of these acts, and this results in his confused definition of relations and complexions as contents. It is not until his third essay that Meinong recognized relations and complexions to be objects in their own right. This essay, "On Objects of Higher Order and Their Relationship to Internal Perception" (1899), is by far the most important of the three essays, and is one of the central works in phenomenological literature. In this essay Meinong undertakes a ground-breaking investigation into the nature of the ideal, imperceptible realm that would become a major theme of later phenomenological studies (e.g., by Husserl, Pfänder, Scheler, Hartmann, *et al.).* According to Meinong, the objects in this realm include relations and complexions, and they have their own distinctive mode of being, viz., subsistence. These ideal objects differ from real objects in that they are not perceived, but are cognized in an immediate fashion through a process of "founding." Comparing two objects and apprehending them as "different," and combining several objects and presenting them as "four," are examples of "founding." Meinong points out that these ideal objects are "unfinished," and become "finished" only through being attached to the objects upon which they are founded. For instance, the relation "difference" is unfinished by itself, and becomes finished through being presented as the difference between two objects.

Meinong observes that relations and complexions are not independent of one another; rather every relation belongs to a complexion, and every complexion includes a relation. A complexion consists of its component parts and of a relation among these parts. For example, the complexion of "a melody" consists of its component parts, the individual notes, and of the relation of these notes to each other that makes them comprise this melody and no other.

Along with the three essays on relations and complexions, there are a series of critical notes that Meinong made on Husserl's *Ideas*. These notes are not as illuminating as one might hope them to be. They are somewhat cursory, and the criticisms Meinong makes are frequently based on misunderstandings of Husserl's ideas. For example, Meinong argues that the epoche is superfluous in eidetic intuition, as eidetic intuition by its very nature is not an apprehension of real being. This argument is based on the assumption that the epoche brackets only real being (existence) and not ideal being (subsistence). But this is contrary to Husserl's statements. Husserl expressly includes ideal being in the epoche; he wishes to bracket the ideal being of essences as well as the real being of the world of the natural standpoint (cf. *Ideas,* secs. 29, 59-61). Thus if the epoche is properly understood, it is incorrect to say that it is superfluous in eidetic intuition.

One would expect Meinong to develop in these notes an incisive criticism of Husserl's idealism; in fact, few phenomenologists would be in a better position to develop such a critique. But Meinong does little more than remark that "it is better to say 'acts which apprehend being' " than " 'acts that posit being' " (p. 244).

It is primarily the translation of "On Objects of Higher Order and Their Relationship to Internal Perception" that makes the present book an important contribution to the (still) limited availability of Meinong's works in English. One hopes now that Meinong's two main books, *Über Annahmen* and *Über Möglichkeit und Wahrscheinlichkeit,* will be translated.

QUENTIN SMITH.

LOUISVILLE, KENTUCKY.

Semiotics and Linguistic Structure. R. M. MARTIN. Albany: State University of New York Press, 1978. Pp. xx, 321.

This book relies primarily on first-order functional calculus as an underlying basis for logic, semiotics, and linguistic structure. Written clearly but perhaps with an overabundance of formulas, it covers or touches on such topics as virtual classes, events, reference, Harris's linguistic views, generative semantics, prepositional relations, and temporal adverbs.

Events play a central role. In order to handle relations, for example, we consider some event which evidently relates an agent to a patient. Then to assert that the relation does relate the agent to the patient, we simply assert the event and assert that the agent is the agent of the event and that the patient is the patient of the event. This approach is in contrast to the logically more natural approach according to which any sentence that mentions two entities can be regarded as implicitly asserting that a relation holds from one to the other, or conversely, thus avoiding any choice as to which is agent and which is patient, a difficult or impossible choice for many common relations. Of course a relation seen in this logically more natural way is an abstraction from a proposition, and is avoided by Martin since he wishes to have nothing to do with anything so Platonic as either a (real) abstraction or a (real) proposition. His whole purpose is to develop an intellectual scheme which basically countenances (to use that weasel word of Quine's) only concrete entities such as events and physical objects. This prejudice of Martin for the concrete is on a par with the finitist dislike of the infinite and perhaps includes this dislike as a special case. It is not really so virtuous, however, to eschew the abstract and cleave to the empirical. The important thing is to avoid paradox and contradiction in our theorizing, and this can best be done by constructing demonstrably consistent systems that are adequate for whatever purposes are at hand. Of course concretists and finitists hope that their highly limited techniques will guarantee consistency and freedom from paradox, but this is only a hope, in contrast to an actual proof of freedom from contradiction. Also, science would be intolerably impoverished by elimination of all abstractions, as in relativity theory and quantum mechanics. Even the limitation of logic to first-order functional calculus, as apparently advocated by Martin, does away with self-referential arguments that are so important in philosophy, and destroys much of the usual Platonic foundation for mathematics, without offering any clear and viable substitute. Still, this book, as far as it goes, is to be considered well written and successful.

FREDERIC B. FITCH.
YALE UNIVERSITY.

Wilhelm Dilthey: Pioneer of the Human Studies. H. P. RICKMAN. Berkeley, Los Angeles, London: University of California Press, 1980. Pp. viii, 197.

Until recently Wilhelm Dilthey has been little studied in English-speaking countries. Furthermore, although he is recognized by some intellectual historians as their outstanding forerunner and as a refined judge of German philosophy, poetry, music, and historiography, Dilthey has been particularly unknown or underestimated as a philosopher in his own right.

It could not be otherwise as long as the model for philosophy was seen in G. E. Moore's or B. Russell's analytical method and the standard of philosophical prose was drawn from Wittgenstein's laconic formulations.

It was difficult, moreover, to take seriously a thinker whose attention comprehended so broad a range of culture and philosophy. One could see a historian in Dilthey, but recognizing a philosopher in him seemed problematic. Taken at face value, he did not reveal any distinctive philosophical personality: he united too many points of view to be reconciled at once and did not identify any philosophical friends or foes. So great was his erudition that he expressed himself on subjects as diverse as the history of the young Hegel, German baroque music, and English philosophy of history, not to mention French psychology and social thought. One can find, consequently, but few critics who would be able to estimate the value of Dilthey's views taken as an integrated whole. Of course, the famous erudition of the heir to the German tradition of the "Historical School" can seldom be found in today's universities. It is no surprise, then, that Dilthey's accomplishments have delayed his fame.

The rising interest in Dilthey's philosophy of the human sciences is a significant event. Although Diltheyan erudition is irrevocably gone, an approximation to his breadth of learning is particularly needed today in philosophy and the humanities. The recognition that a comprehensive humanistic education is a necessary preparation for philosophical inquiry would contribute towards the integration of the various humanistic disciplines. Once these disciplines have determined their roles in philosophy they could cooperate in a unified effort to search for an answer to the question: what is man?

In this situation, a new interest in Dilthey having arisen, Rickman's book can play a particularly useful role, for it provides us with a lively and popular introduction to more analytic reading on Dilthey. *Wilhelm Dilthey: Pioneer of the Human Studies* clarifies without oversimplifying and can be read with interest and advantage by a wide audience.

Rickman has not only supplied us with a popular introduction to Dilthey's work, he has managed to make a convincing case for the importance of this nineteenth century thinker for the contemporary situation in the humanities—a situation where an immense effort must be performed in order to integrate the various attempts to answer the philosophical questions concerning the nature of man. Contemporary knowledge about man as a cultural being is too vast and specialized to be mastered by a single mind, and so the collaboration of the different humanistic disciplines is becoming an imperative if we do not want to lose from our sight the continuity of man's consciousness in history. In the philosophical depiction of his nature man cannot avoid using these varied resources of humanistic knowledge—that is how philosophy and the humanities meet.

The main discovery of Dilthey's that Rickman recognizes is the complementary character of the various humanistic disciplines, each of them inquiring into a particular kind of "expressions of life" or "objectifications of mind."

Rickman's book, as it is popularly written, cannot, of course, be as analytical as a Diltheyan scholar would prefer. Taking for granted the rules of the popular style we cannot at the same time demand from Rickman a painstaking analysis of such Diltheyan notions as *expressions of life, understanding,* and *interpretation.* Nevertheless, Rickman is sometimes more general than he need be, and consequently the reader is often given insufficient guidance and the interpetation of key Diltheyan concepts. This is the case in Rickman's presentation of the Diltheyan theory of understanding and in his interpretation of relations among different humanistic disciplines: rather than presenting us with a clear account of Dilthey's notion of understanding, Rickman confines himself instead to assuring us that human life cannot do without this process and that understading cannot be reduced to any other cognitive procedure. As a matter of fact,

Diltheyan cognition "by insight"—understanding—is neither so mysterious nor so undetermined as we would assume on the basis of Rickman's book.

Pointing out the futility of any attempt at reducing understanding to a description of behavior, Rickman fails to notice that meaning of "Verstehen" which has fundamental significance in Dilthey's theory of cognition in the humanities. Having in mind this meaning, Dilthey was not concerned with the understanding of gestures, facial expressions, and behavior. Although he did not deny this kind of reciprocal understanding of men in everyday life, this kind of understanding was not his main concern. Dilthey's conception of the proper subject-matter of human studies focused his attention on the understanding of higher spiritual structures, which he saw in works of art, especially in those for which language was the means of expression. According to Dilthey, the understanding employed in everyday situations does not bring us closer to knowledge of man's nature, but rather leads to confusion. Rickman correctly suspects that belief in the transparency of language as used in everyday situations is naive. But this does not lead him to recognize that there is an unveiling as well as a concealing use of language. For Dilthey, true art is able to use language in a transparent way, one that does not lead us astray. In this way he came to the conviction that only through the "higher expressions of the spirit," through works of art, can human nature be displayed, brought to an unfalsified expression, and grasped in cognition. In great art no obstacle appears between the lived experience and its objectified form: artistic performance. It is in this context that we find Dilthey's most characteristic use of the concept of understanding, although he spoke about the understanding in everyday life as well. In order to distinguish between these two uses: the use of understanding in everyday communication and its use in the domain of higher culture, we should probably follow the suggestion of O. F. Bollnow and describe the first meaning as the practical knowledge required to manipulate men and tools, as opposed to the second meaning that applies to the authentic understanding of man and is grounded on works of art and philosophy.

However, understanding in the proper Diltheyan sense cannot be identified with the understanding of words—as Rickman claims. The object of understanding is made up of psychological structures, not linguistic ones. Moreover, directed towards psychical structures which lie behind the words, understanding never has as its subject matter single individual objects, but always part/whole relations.

That is why the question of understanding the wholes from the parts and the parts from the whole — known as the hermeneutical circle — is so decisive for the Diltheyan notion of understanding and its object.

Rickman finds the guiding principle of Dilthey's philosophy of human studies in the idea of unity. This idea, according to Rickman, governs the whole integration project of human disciplines as well as the pantheistic world outlook of Dilthey himself. The idea itself of integrating all the humanities is seen by Rickman as following from that Diltheyan feeling for unity that allowed the philosopher to recognize the same human mind in works of poetry and music as well as in philosophical treatises and legal documents. We cannot, however, agree with Rickman as far as the details of that Diltheyan awareness of unity are concerned.

Rickman maintains that Dilthey, at various periods of his attempt to create a unified and systematic whole to all human studies, ascribed the "unifying" role to different disciplines. We are told that the founding role was first performed by psychology, and later (from 1900) psychology was replaced by hermeneutics. One cannot agree with Rickman at this point for two reasons.

The less important reason is that Dilthey never considered hermeneutics to be a discipline (or a science) in the sense psychology was. He considered hermeneutics to be rather a tool that emphasizes and reveals the meaning and significance of the expressions of life; in other words, hermeneutics displays the inner meaning embodied in the external expressions of life. This process of deciphering or interpreting performed the role of a universal tool which could be employed in the subject matter of any human discipline.

These considerations lead naturally to the second, more important, reason why one cannot agree with Rickman's interpretation of Dilthey's search for unity in the humanities. The hermeneutical approach led Dilthey to a rejection of the very project of founding humanities on one chosen discipline and building all the humanities in this way "from below." The project of founding the humanities in psychology has been replaced by the hermeneutical approach, according to which all human disciplines are seen as supporting and complementing each other without being rooted in any unique foundation. According to that conception, the humanities do not make up an edificelike structure well founded from below, but rather a weblike system of reciprocal conditioning and interactions.

Rickman is particularly successful in fulfilling an important expectation of the intended reader of his book: to a greater degree than authors of more analytic studies, he satisfies the reader's curiosity concerning the philosopher's private life. None of these other studies on Dilthey go further in depicting his life then just enumerating the stages of his academic career and listing those works that had not been published during his lifetime. It hardly seemed that Dilthey had a private life at all; one imagined his life as filled with the work of producing over twenty volumes of surprising erudition. Potential biographers of Dilthey have been discouraged, perhaps, by H. Nohl's opinion that no one could claim he had known Dilthey. From one book to another this view of the "mysterious old man" has been repeated. Rickman ventures to reveal some of the mysteries of his life: we get accounts of the broken engagement, his later marital troubles, and the problems with his family that kept him from work. Although these facts, as Rickman describes them, do not seem to have influenced the world outlook expressed in the philosopher's work, they should be welcomed. Rickman has taken the first step on the way towards uncovering Dilthey's life.

One can hope that sometime in the future Dilthey, who was himself the author of a paradigmatic biography of Schleiermacher, would find a biographer for himself. The task of that biographer would be to find in the life of Dilthey the sources of those views that cannot be explained in a purely theoretical way. Rickman gives us a foretaste of how revealing Dilthey's biography could be if its author succeeds in relating the events of his life to those of his philosophical reflection and in deriving them both from one origin—the actual lived experience.

ELŻBIETA PACZKOWSKA-ŁAGOWSKA.
JAGELLONIAN UNIVERSITY, CRACOW.

RECENT PUBLICATIONS

Chirovsky, Nicholas L. and Mott, Vincent V., *Philosophical Foundations of Economic Doctrines.* Florham Park, N.J.: Florham Park Press, 1981. Pp. 204. $15.00, cloth; $5.95, paper.

Rollin, Bernard E., *Animal Rights and Human Morality.* Buffalo: Prometheus Books, 1981. Pp. xii, 182. $17.95, cloth; $9.95, paper.

Haller, Rudolf, *Sprache und Erkenntnis als Soziale Tatsache.* Vienna: Verlag Hölder-Pichler-Tempsky, 1981. Pp. 147.

Nute, Donald, *Essential Formal Semantics.* Totowa, N.J.: Rowman and Littlefield, 1981. Pp. xiv, 186. $18.95.

Routley, Richard, *Exploring Meinong's Jungle and Beyond: An Investigation on Noneism and the Theory of Items.* Canberra: The Australian National University, 1980. Pp. xix, 1035.

Relph, Edward, *Rational Landscapes and Humanistic Geography.* Totowa, N.J.: Barnes & Noble Books, 1981. Pp. xi, 231. $23.50.

Human Inquiry: A Sourcebook of New Paradigm Research. Edited by Peter Reason and John Rowan. Contributions by R. Harre, J. Heron, I. Mitroff, and others. New York: John Wiley & Sons, 1981. Pp. xxiv, 530. $61.25.

Leblanc, Hugues, *Existence, Truth, and Provability.* Albany: State University of New York Press, 1982. Pp. x, 466. $45.00, cloth; $19.00, paper.

Pitt, Joseph C., *Pictures, Images and Conceptual Change: An Analysis of Wilfrid Sellars' Philosophy of Science.* Synthese Library, Volume 151. Dordrecht/Boston/London: D. Reidel Publishing Company, 1981. Pp. x, 165. Dfl. 65.00, $34.00, cloth; Dfl. 35.00, $14.95, paper.

Rockmore, Tom; Gavin, William J.; Colbert, James, G., Jr.; and Blakeley, Thomas J., *Marxism and Alternatives: Towards the Conceptual Interaction Among Soviet Philosophy, Neo-Thomism, Pragmatism, and Phenomenology.* Sovietica, Volume 45. Dordrecht/Boston/London: D. Reidel Publishing Company, 1981. Pp. xiv, 311. Dfl. 115.00, $49.50.

Spiegelberg, Herbert, *The Context of the Phenomenological Movement.* Phaenomenologica, 80. The Hague/Boston/London: Martinus Nijhoff Publishers, 1981. Pp. xvi, 239.

Imagery. Edited by Ned Block. Contributions by: R. Brown, D. C. Dennett, J. A. Fodor, and others. Bradford Books. Cambridge: The MIT Press, 1981. Pp. viii, 261.

Property, Profits, and Economic Justice. Edited by Viginia Held. Contributions by: G. Alperovitz, L. Becker, M. Cohen, and others. Belmont, Calif.: Wadsworth Publishing Co., 1980. Pp. vi, 250.

The Mind's I: Fantasies and Reflections on Self and Soul. Edited and arranged by Douglas R. Hofstadter and Daniel C. Dennett. Contributions by: J. L. Borges, C. Cherniak, D. C. Dennett, and others. New York: Basic Books, Inc., 1981. Pp. x, 501. $15.50.

Philosophical Perspectives on Metaphor. Edited by Mark Johnson. Contributions by: M. C. Beardsley, T. Binkley, M. Black, and others. Minneapolis: University of Minnesota Press, 1981. Pp. xiv, 361. $29.50, cloth; $10.95, paper.

Philosophy: The Basic Issues. Edited by E. D. Klemke, A. David Kline, and Robert Holinger. Contributions by: R. Blatchford, W. K. Clifford, C. Darrow, and others. New York: St. Martin's Press, 1982. Pp. xiv, 666.

Conceptual Encounter: A Method for the Exploration of Human Experience. Edited by Joseph de Rivera. Contributions by: J. Funk, S. Goodman, T. Kreilkamp, and others. Washington, D.C.: University Press of America, 1981. Pp. xii, 369. $23.25, cloth; $13.25, paper.

Bowie, Norman, *Business Ethics.* Englewood Cliffs, N.J.: Prentice-Hall, Inc., 1982. Pp. xiv, 159.

Bubner, Rüdiger, *Modern German Philosophy.* Trans. by Eric Matthews. New York, Cambridge, London: Cambridge University Press, 1981. Pp. xii, 223. $34.50, cloth; $11.95, paper.

Cassirer, Ernst, *Kant's Life and Thought.* Trans. by James Haden. Introduction by Stephan Körner. New Haven and London: Yale University Press, 1981. Pp. xxvi, 429. $24.50.

Collier, Richard Bangs, *Pleneurethic: A World-Class Philosophy.* Smithtown, N.Y.: Exposition Press, 1981. Pp. vi, 352. $20.00.

Crump, Thomas, *The Phenomenon of Money.* Boston, London and Henley: Routledge & Kegan Paul, 1981. Pp. xiv, 366. $40.00.

Csikszentmihalyi, Mihaly and Eugene Rochberg-Halton, *The Meaning of Things: Domestic Symbols and the Self.* New York, Cambridge and London: Cambridge University Press, 1981. Pp. xiv, 304. $39.95, cloth; $13.95, paper.

Dufrenne, Mikel, *Esthétique et Philosophie.* Tome III. Paris: Éditions Klincksieck, 1981. Pp. 210.

Jeans, Sir James, *Physics and Philosophy.* New York: Dover Publications, Inc., 1981; first published in 1943. Pp. 222. $3.50, paper.

Levinas, Emmanuel, *Totality and Infinity: An Essay on Exteriority*. Trans. by Alphonso Lingis. Martinus Nijhoff Philosophy Texts Series. The Hague, Boston, London: Martinus Nijhoff Publishers, 1979. Pp. 307. Dfl. 58.00, $30.50.

Levinas, Emmanuel, *Otherwise than Being or Beyond Essence*. Trans. by Alphonso Lingis. Martinus Nijhoff Philosophy Texts Series. The Hague, Boston, London: Martinus Nijhoff Publishers, 1981. Pp. xlii, 200.

Madell, Geoffrey, *The Identity of the Self*. Edinburgh University Press, 1981. Pp. viii, 148. $17.00.

Martin, F. David. *Sculpture and Enlivened Space: Aesthetics and History*. Lexington: The University Press of Kentucky, 1981. Pp. x, 276. $24.00.

Mellor, D. H., *Real Time*. New York, Cambridge and London: Cambridge University Press, 1981. Pp. xii, 203. $29.95.

Moline, Jon, *Plato's Theory of Understanding*. Madison: The University of Wisconsin Press, 1981. Pp. xvi, 256. $22.00.

Moore, Brooke Noel, *The Philosophical Possibilities Beyond Death*. Springfield, Ill.: Charles C. Thomas, Publisher, 1981. Pp. x, 222. $22.75.

Neblett, William, *The Role of Feelings in Morals*. Washington, D.C.: University Press of America, 1981. Pp. viii, 106. $18.25, cloth; $8.25, paper.

Newton-Smith, W. H., *The Rationality of Science*. International Library of Philosophy. Boston, London and Henley: Routledge & Kegan Paul, 1981. Pp. xii, 294. $19.50, cloth; $11.50, paper.

Plott, John C., with James Michael Dolin. *Global History of Philosophy*. Vol. III. *The Patristic-Sutra Period*. Delhi, Varanasi, and Patna: Motilal Banarsidass, 1980. Pp. xiv, 604. Rs. 90.

Rescher, Nicholas, *Scepticism:* A Critical Reappraisal. Totowa, N.J.: Rowman and Littlefield, 1980. Pp. xii, 265. $30.00.

Schmidt, Alfred, *History and Structure: An Essay on Hegelian-Marxist and Structuralist Theories of History*. Trans. by Jeffrey Herf. Studies in Contemporary German Social Though Series. Cambridge: The MIT Press, 1981. Pp. xxvi, 146. $17.50.

Thompson, Jan E., *Being and Meaning: Paul Tillich's Theory of Meaning, Truth and Logic*. Edinburgh: Edinburgh University Press, 1981. Pp. xii, 244, $30.00.

Wittgenstein, Ludwig, *Tractatus Logico-Philosophicus*. Trans. by C. K. Ogden, with an Introduction by Bertrand Russell. Boston, London and Henley: Routledge & Kegan Paul, 1981. Pp. 207. $6.95, paper.

Barnes, Hazel E., *Sartre and Flaubert*. Chicago and London: The University of Chicago Press, 1981. Pp. x, 449. $25.00.

Carrier, Leonard S., *Experience and the Objects of Perception*. Washington, D.C.: University Press of America, 1981. Pp. vi, 182. $18.75, cloth; $9.50, paper.

Croce, Benedetto, *Poetry and Literature: An Introduction to Its Criticism and History*. Trans. with an Introduction and Notes by Giovanni Gullace. Carbondale and Edwardsville: Southern Illinois University Press, 1981. Pp. lxxiv, 210. $24.95.

Davies, Martin, *Meaning, Quantification, Necessity: Themes In Philosophical Logic*. International Library of Philosophy. Boston, London and Henley: Routledge & Kegan Paul, 1981. Pp. xii, 282. $32.00.

Donaldson, Thomas, *Corporations and Morality*. Englewood Cliffs, N.J.: Prentice-Hall, Inc., 1981. Pp. x, 214. $12.95, cloth; $8.95, paper.

Frongia, Guido, *Guida alla letteratura su Wittgenstein*. Urbino: Argalìa Editore, 1981. Pp. 342. Lire 8.500.

Hospers, John, *Understanding the Arts*. Englewood Cliffs, N.J.: Prentice-Hall, Inc., 1982. Pp. x, 431. $15.95, paper.

Macklin, Ruth, *Man, Mind, and Morality: The Ethics of Behavior Control*. Philosophy of Medicine Series. Englewood Cliffs, N.J.: Prentice-Hall, Inc., 1982. Pp. x, 130.

McCarthy, Thomas, *The Critical Theory of Jürgen Habermas*. Cambridge: The MIT Press, 1981; first printed in 1978. Pp. xviii, 484. $12.50, paper.

Mounce, H. O., *Wittgenstein's "Tractatus": An Introduction*. Chicago: The University of Chicago Press, 1981. Pp. vi, 136. $19.00, cloth; $7.95, paper.

Mueller, Ian, *Philosophy of Mathematics and Deductive Structure in Euclid's "Elements."* Cambridge: The MIT Press, 1981. Pp. xviii, 378. $37.50.

Munevar, Gonzalo, *Radical Knowledge: A Philosophical Inquiry into the Nature and Limits of Science*. Foreword by Paul K. Feyerabend. Indianapolis: Hackett Publishing Company, 1981. Pp. x, 125. $15.00, cloth; $6.25, paper.

Ricoeur, Paul, *Hermeneutics and the Human Sciences: Essays on Language, Action and Interpretation*. Edited and trans. with an Introduction by John B. Thompson. New York, Cambridge and London: Cambridge University Press, 1981. Pp. viii, 314. $34.50, cloth; $12.95, paper.

Sorgi, Guiseppe, *Per uno studio della partecipazione politica: Hobbes Locke, Tocqueville.* Lecce: Edizioni Milella, 1981. Pp. 174. Lire 9.000.

Sartre, Jean-Paul, *The Family Idiot: Gustave Flaubert, 1921-1857.* Vol. I. Trans. by Carol Cosman. Chicago and London: The University of Chicago Press, 1981. Pp. x, 627. $25.00.

Springborg, Patricia, *The Problem of Human Needs and the Critique of Civilization.* London: George Allen & Unwin, 1981. Pp. 293. $28.50.

Steele, Susan, with Adrian Akmajian, Richard Demers, and others. *An Encyclopedia of Aux: A Study in Cross-Linguistic Equivalence.* Cambridge: The MIT Press, 1981. Pp. x, 268. $15.00.

Tillich, Paul, *The System of the Sciences According to Objects and Methods.* Trans. with an Introduction by Paul Wiebe. Lewisburg: Bucknell University Press, 1981. Pp. 233. $22.50.

Thompson, John B., *Critical Hermeneutics: A Study in the Thought of Paul Ricouer and Jürgen Habermas.* New York, Cambridge and London: Cambridge University Press, 1981. Pp. x, 257. $35.00.

Wallace, John Bruce, *Genesis: Involvement: Generation.* Washington, D.C.: University Press of America, 1981. Pp. x, 139. $7.75, paper.

Klein, Peter D., *Certainty: A Refutation of Scepticism.* Minneapolis: University of Minnesota Press, 1981. Pp. ix, 242.

Matthews, Gareth B., *Philosophy and the Young Child.* Cambridge and London: Harvard University Press, 1980. Pp. 115. $10.00.

Theunissen, Michael, *Kritische Theorie der Gesellschaft.* Berlin: Walter de Gruyter & Co., 1981. Pp. 57. $4.90.

Theunissen, Michael, *Selbstverwirklichung und Allgemeinheit.* Berlin: Walter de Gruyter & Co., 1981. Pp. 55.

Bolzano, Bernard, *Gesamtausgabe. Philosophische Tagebücher, 1911-1817.* Stuttgart: Formmann-Holzboog, 1981. Pp. 246.

Infinity and Continuity in Ancient and Medieval Thought. Edited by Norman Kretzmann. Contributions by D. J. Furley, R. Sorabji, F. D. Miller, Jr., and others. Ithaca: Cornell University Press, 1982. Pp. 367. $27.50.

VOL. XLII JUNE 1982 NO. 4

PHILOSOPHY
AND
PHENOMENOLOGICAL RESEARCH

A Quarterly Journal

Published for the

INTERNATIONAL PHENOMENOLOGICAL SOCIETY

by

BROWN UNIVERSITY

CONTENTS

I. ARTICLES

Sociological Knowledge: Winch, Marxism, and *Verstehen* Revisited by KAI NIELSEN 465
Phenomenology of Memory from Husserl to Merleau-Ponty by DAVID FARRELL KRELL 492
Value Judgments by JOEL J. KUPPERMAN 506
Unspoken Connections in the Design Argument by JAMES DUERLINGER 519
Marx's Critique of Philosophical Language by DANIEL J. COOK 530
Some Ways of Going Wrong: On Mistakes in *On Certainty* by DEBORAH H. SOLES 555
Nonevidential Reasons for Belief: A Jamesian View by STEPHEN L. NATHANSON 572
Choice by ROBERT G. BURTON 581

II. DISCUSSIONS

A Memo on Method: Hilary Putnam by R. M. MARTIN . . 587
Semantical Rules and Misinterpretations: Reply to R. M. Martin by HILARY PUTNAM 604
What Is Husserl's First Philosophy? by JEFFNER ALLEN 610

III. REVIEWS

Paul Ricoeur's *Main Trends in Philosophy* by RODGER BELL HUNTER 621
D. M. Armstrong's *The Nature of Mind and Other Essays* by EARL CONEE 622
Alvin Plantinga's *Does God Have a Nature?* by WILLIAM E. MANN 625

IV. RECENT PUBLICATIONS 631

SOCIOLOGICAL KNOWLEDGE: WINCH, MARXISM, AND *VERSTEHEN* REVISITED

The appeal to *verstehen* is gaining a renewed currency in discussions of the foundations of the social sciences. This is not only true where one would expect it, that is, among ethnomethodologists and the Continental Tradition of hermeneutic phenomenology (Gadamer and Ricoeur), but it is also beginning to have its day in more analytic circles. Such tough-minded and rigorous theorists as Anthony Giddens and Hilary Putnam have both recently stressed the importance of such an appeal.[1]

Such an appeal is not now defended as an alternative source of evidence for sociological hypotheses. However much it may help us in coming to form or interpret hypotheses, it does not provide the materials for testing hypotheses. There we require empirical evidence.[2] (Indeed the very phrase 'empirical evidence' is probably pleonastic.) Rather the appeal to *verstehen* is an appeal to what must be presupposed to have an understanding of human interaction. Many have come to believe that *verstehen* is essential for gaining an understanding of the institutions of society, of how we relate and of how we can come to understand people in a culture very different from our own. In fine, a reflexive understanding of the way *verstehen* works is necessary for an understanding of how we make sense and indeed sometimes fail to make sense together.

Such talk nonetheless requires considerable elucidation and demythologization or at least a clear statement. Yet, on such crucial theoretical issues, the ethnomethodologists are elusive and, while the vast tomes of the hermeneutical phenomenologists contain much that is interesting and worthy of close study, there is not in the work of these Continental theorists any great penchant for exact statement. I believe that in trying to come to grips with what is fundamentally important about the appeal of *verstehen,* we should at first, at least,

---

[1] Anthony Giddens, *Studies in Social and Political Theory* (London: Hutchinson & Company, Ltd., 1977), pp. 165-78. See as well, his *New Rules of Sociological Method* (London: Hutchinson & Company, Ltd., 1976). Putnam's treatment of *verstehen* is in his *Meaning and the Moral Sciences* (London: Routledge & Kegan Paul, 1978), pp. 67-68, 73-75.

[2] Ernest Nagel, "On the Method of *Verstehen* as the Sole Method of Philosophy," *The Journal of Philosophy,* Vol. 50 (1953).

turn to some work of a generally Wittgensteinian inspiration. There, in the work of Charles Taylor and most extensively in the work of Peter Winch, we have the most forceful statements of such an approach.[3] In the last decade, Winch has been much discussed. Some of this discussion has been perceptive, but all too frequently he has just been rather patronizingly misunderstood and dismissed as a Wittgensteinian obscurantist.

Because of the importance of the appeal to *verstehen* and because of the perceptiveness and clarity with which he in effect elucidates the role of such a conception and makes plain its centrality, I want to return here to the work of Peter Winch. I shall attempt to state, clearly and sympathetically, a very central point of his that seems to me unassailable and then (a) to defend it from some understandable misunderstandings and (b) to try to show its force. In the course of doing this, I shall attempt to show that such a Wittgensteinian approach functions, not as a rival to, but as a complement of, a Marxian analysis of the foundations of social science. Their claims and interests are, of course, very different, but their claims do not cut against each other but importantly reinforce each other in such a way that they can quite naturally be combined into a more adequate picture of the nature of sociological knowledge and the rationale of the social sciences. That, at least, shall be the burden of my argument.

Winch, I should remark as a final preliminary, does not utilize the term *'verstehen'* or any English equivalents, but the concept, as we shall see, is central to his account, with its stress on the primacy of the participant's unreflective understanding for any subsequent more reflective and theoretically developed and systematized understanding of society. I shall proceed by first setting Winch's distinctive utilization of the concept of *verstehen* in the overall context of his theory, starting from his placement of tradition and rules and his distinctive utilization of a context dependent conception of rationality and an Wittgensteinian conception of forms of life.

---

[3]Charles Taylor, "Interpretation and the Sciences of Man," *The Review of Metaphysics*, Vol. XXV, No. 1 (September, 1971) and his "Neutrality in Political Science," *Philosophy, Politics and Society*, third series, edited by Peter Laslett and W. G. Runciman (Oxford: Blackwell, 1967). See also, my "Social Science and American Foreign Policy," *Philosophy, Morality and International Affairs*, edited by Virginia Held, *et. al.* (London: Oxford University Press, 1974). Peter Winch, *The Idea of a Social Science* (London: Routledge and Kegan Paul Ltd., 1958) and Peter Winch, *Ethics and Action*, (London: Routledge and Kegan Paul, Ltd., 1972).

II

Peter Winch has well stressed that a "human society cannot be adequately described without use being made of the notion of a developing tradition."[4] An indispensable object of social studies is behavior which is either directly or indirectly rule-governed, involving the witting or unwitting utilization of norms. This sets it apart from the object of study of the natural scientists. To understand society, it is necessary to know how various elements in our social life evolve, get ramified, and develop. We cannot, as Lucien Goldmann also stresses, gain an understanding of society without developing a historical consciousness.

Understanding a tradition involves the notion of rule-following and rule-following involves the conception of doing something correctly or incorrectly, getting something right or getting something wrong. For rule-following to be possible, a certain way of responding must be appropriate to the situation and a certain way of responding inappropriate. Norms, conceptions of rationality and reasonability, are built in to our very conception of action, for actions, unlike mere movements, are directly or indirectly rule-governed. They have a rationale—though sometimes only a crazy rationale—and they cannot be understood without understanding the distinctive norms of rationality, which are integral elements of human actions such that without them, they would not be actions. The "conception of human society in general cannot be grasped except in terms of the concept of rule-following" and that, in turn, requires an understanding of what, in various domains, constitutes a rational response or a reasonable way of doing things. So both rule-following and rationality are central elements in the study of society.[5]

Winch agrees with Michael Oakeshott in (a) rejecting a rationalistic conception of rationality "according to which standards of reasonable behaviour exist absolutely and are brought in, as it were, from outside to regulate our conduct" and (b) in stressing, and re-

---

[4] Peter Winch, "Social Science," *British Journal of Sociology*, Vol. VII (March, 1956), p. 33. This is a succinct, clearly-argued preliminary to his *The Idea of a Social Science*. Winch's central ideas are forcefully articulated in this early article. In his "Language, Belief and Relativism," *Contemporary British Philosophy*, fourth series, edited by H. D. Lewis (London: George Allen and Unwin, 1976), Winch defends himself against the charge that his account has paradoxical and unacceptable relativistic implications.

[5] Peter Winch, "Social Science," *British Journal of Sociology*, Vol. VII (March, 1956), p. 25.

garding as essential to elucidate, "the connection between the idea of reasonable conduct and the modes of social life."[6] Rationality, in short, is put on the agenda of social theory. There is no explaining or understanding actions or social intuitions without an appeal to it. Consider Lina Wertmuller's film, *Swept Away*. We see Gennarino, a proletarian and an Italian Communist, marooned on an island with Raffaella, a wealthy and indeed, bitchy, spoiled bourgeoise. Stripped of the trappings of civilization and culture, their class conflict becomes open and intense. Gennarino resorts to a raw machismo where he expresses his masculinity by beating and humilating a woman, and Raffaella is quickly transformed into a subservient female who loves being domineered and finds, for the first time in her life, full sexual pleasure under such conditions. How we regard and explain such behavior is not independent of our conceptions of what human nature and human rationality are like. Some might take this behavior to be showing what human masculinity and human feminity really are like, i.e., that women are passive and deep down wish to be dominated and that men are domineering—apes at heart needing very deeply to control and subdue females. I think, on the contrary, that such behavior shows very little about 'raw human nature'—once the restraints of civilization are taken away—but shows both Gennarino and Raffaella unconsciously role-playing, even on their island, and uttering the platitudes and acting out the fantasies of people from very distinct classes in a distinctive, late capitalist society. I am not trying to defend my reading here—much more background would be needed for that—but I simply wish to illustrate how an understanding and explaining of a stretch of human behavior will and indeed must be affected by the conceptions of rationality of the social theorist explaining or interpreting the behavior. There is no neutral ground on which the theorist can stand without his needing to make judgments about the rationality or irrationality of the behavior he studies.

Suppose I am asked to explain what Zande witchcraft practices or Jewish dietary practices really are all about or really signify. My explanation of them, indeed my understanding of them, will unavoidably and necessarily be deeply affected by what I myself consider to be rational or irrational behavior and beliefs. If I think the beliefs in question are irrational, it is appropriate for me to look for a causal explanation of what brings them about and to try to uncover

[6] *Ibid.*, pp. 21-22.

the psychological needs they satisfy. If, however, I believe they are rational, I will try to account for them quite differently. I will then try to show the evidence for the beliefs and the reasoning that went into them and the rationale of the action. I will not typically be interested in the causal conditions that brought about the belief or led to the action. What type of explanation or interpretation is appropriate for human action or for the way certain institutions or practices work depends on our assessments of their rationality. A Marxist sociologist or Freudian will give a rather different account of the life and times of Luther and Zwingli than will an orthodox Christian sociologist.

While stressing the necessity of utilizing conceptions of rationality in social description, interpretation, and explanation, Winch also stresses, following Oakeshott, the contextual, form-of-life-dependent nature of the canons of rationality. What they are, Winch contends, is not independent of certain determinate domains of discourse or modes of social life: religion, morality, law, natural science, Azande magical conceptions, and the like. We do not have a system of norms of rationality which exists independently of these modes of social life as norms whose criteria can be specified without reference to a given domain of discourse or which can be used to assess these different domains such that we could sensibly claim that law or science or even religion is irrational.

Oakeshott, Winch argues, in rightly rejecting rationalistic conceptions of rationality, too readily construes rational conduct merely as habitual conduct and "misconceives and underestimates the importance of *rule-following,* in human affairs."[7] A person's behavior may be rule-governed without his being aware of it or even without his or anyone else on occasion being able to formulate the rules or rule to be followed. There is a very considerable number of activities which "are based very largely on the unreflective acquisition of skills in practice" but which nonetheless can be and should be described as rule-following and which presuppose distinctive conceptions of rationality. They are not like conditioned reflexes; they are not like 'blind habits'; they are actions which have a *rationale* and the agents doing them characteristically understand the *point* of their acting in this way rather than in some other way.

Human actions are a principal constituent of social activity and social activity is activity such that the concepts used to describe such activity must be possessed by those engaged in these activities. *In that*

[7] *Ibid.*, p. 22.

way, they cannot do them without knowing what they are doing. To say that someone is engaging in the activity in question is to say of him that he is in possession of such concepts. As you cannot play bridge without being able to use words such as 'revoke' and 'trump' or their non-English equivalents, so "you cannot pay bills without understanding the use of arithmetical symbols . . . "[8] Social understanding involves a participant's understanding of norms of behavior and institutional practices which are prior to and independent of the social scientist's distinctive rules and practices.

Winch rejects a certain very common view of rationality and the social scientist's conception of his relation to his subject matter well exemplified in the work of Vilfredo Pareto. In effect, skipping over the vital distinction between that which is nonlogical and that which is illogical, Pareto distinguishes between *logical conduct,* which on his account defines rational behavior, and *nonlogical conduct,* "comprising all behaviour which in one way or another does not measure up to the specifications of logical conduct." Logical conduct "is conduct directed towards the achievement of a definite purpose, and making use of means the efficacy of which has been established by 'logico-experimental reasoning' (i.e., roughly, the methods of natural science) . . . "[9] For Pareto to be rational is to engage in logical conduct and to eschew nonlogical conduct. This is what Habermas and Goldmann would characterize as a plain and unadorned form of scientism. While Winch does not talk in that manner, he would surely agree. The criteria of natural scientific thinking, as Winch puts it, is treated by Pareto "as if they were something absolute and in a completely special position vis-à-vis the concepts used in other forms of social activity."[10] But concepts such as those utilized in ordinary social interaction and in artisitc, moral, political, and religious contexts, do not fit into the pattern of 'logico-experimental reasoning' and they cannot be made to so fit without an emasculating sea-change. Yet they are none the worse for that. Rather, these concepts, as well as the scientific concepts themselves, can only be understood in terms of the distinctive activities in the context in which they are applied; and these activities in turn "can only be understood in terms of concepts appropriate to them."[11] Moreover, given this scientistic

---

[8] *Ibid.,* p. 19.

[9] *Ibid.,* p. 20.

[10] *Ibid.,* p. 21.

[11] *Ibid.*

account of Pareto's, too much behavior, and too heterogeneous a collection of activities, is counted as *nonlogical* and thus as irrational. Dropping the application of such scientistic and specialized norms of rationality, such conduct could more appropriately be understood in terms of the diverse rationale of those activities and their related concepts. In general—though not, of course, in some particular circumstances—the employment of these norms seems straightforwardly appropriate in their distinctive contexts. The burden of proof is on someone with a position like Pareto's to establish that there must be something subjective and ideological about them.

A related central conception of Pareto's similarly distorts our understanding of social reality and the human sciences. Pareto attaches great importance to a distinction he draws between *residues* and *derivations*. *Residues* are certain constant or nearly constant elements in human societies which are, according to Pareto, explanatorily central. *Derivations*, by contrast, are not so constant and do not cut across diverse places and times. According to Pareto, they, like ideologies, are a kind of pseudotheoretical window dressing for the genuine reality involved, namely the residue. Derivations purport to explain why certain things were done or are being done. But in reality they are pseudoexplanations, making quite groundless rationalizations of the activity in question, so as to provide it with a rationale—a rationale which is in reality a rationalization for a pointless activity which is not performed for any reason at all but which in reality results from (is caused by) certain fundamental human sentiments. What the social scientist should do is to ignore the derivations, expressive of nonlogical conduct, for they are functioning as ideological rationalizations from the subjective standpoint of the agents who are involved in the social activity in question. What, according to Pareto, the social scientist should do to attain a genuinely scientific understanding of the social behavior he is studying is to uncover the *residues*. With such an 'uncovering' he will have come to have an understanding of the real nature and causes of the behavior he is studying.

Against the above conceptions, Winch in effect argues that such conceptions utilize a *scientistic* model of ratonality and reality, taking as real only what can be characterized in natural science terms and as rational only what can be understood in accordance with Pareto's conception of *logical conduct*. But this is an arbitrary and stultifying representation of reality, for it takes concepts at home in one kind of context and used for definite but limited purposes in those contexts (namely, those purposes which give point to activities such as physics, chemistry, biology, and the like), and insists on using them in contexts in which they are not at home and in which they have no application. Moreover, with Pareto's use—albeit unwittingly metaphorical—of the language of mechanics in describing social events, one sees, as Winch puts it, "a hankering after a purely phsyical description of social actions."[12] But that is an impossibility, for human actions are not merely bodily movements—though they are that as well—but are movements done deliberately and with at least some sort of rationale and done against a background of norms in accordance with which they can be done rightly or wrongly, correctly or incorrectly. Compare, on the one hand, slipping on a banana peel or breathing with, on the other, skating or doing one's sums. The latter pair, as different as they are, are rule-governed in the way the former are not and there is a correct way of doing them. Human action and the concept of societal behavior "cannot be grasped except in terms of the concept of rule-following and rule-governed behaviour . . . "[13]

If there is to be any social science at all, which actually gives us an understanding of social life, we must come to understand that, in the various domains of discourse and in the various things that humans do, there are distinctive forms of activity or forms of life, and it is in accordance with those forms, and with an understanding of their rationale (point), that human actions are understood and a society is understood. It is those forms of activity which are the underlying structural determinates of what it is reasonable, rational, or even intelligible to do. Without a participant's grasp or a participant-like grasp of how they work, there is no understanding of social life. (It is here, without using the traditional vocabulary, where the concept of *verstehen* is employed by Peter Winch.) And there are no form-of-life-independent canons of rationality in accordance with which we can assess these forms of life. Belief in such context-independent canons of rationality is a myth. It is not such general canons of rationality which determine which forms of life or what form of activity is rational or irrational, but it is the forms of life and the diverse forms of activity themselves which determine what is rational or irrational. There is no set of abstract general principles of rationality which will give us an Archimedian point in accordance

[12] *Ibid.*, p. 21.
[13] *Ibid.*, p. 25.

with which we can access the various practices and forms of life of the human animal.[14]

III

Winch's conception of social science appears at least to conflict sharply with a Marxian conception of what social science should be. This will come clearly to the fore if we examine G. A. Cohen's important essay "Karl Marx and the Withering Away of Social Science."[15] Marx, in speaking of the political economists and social observers of his day, remarks that they stay too close to the surface appearance of things and do not probe beyond appearances to the real forces that move society. The participant's knowledge that Winch stresses as essential for an understanding of society would surely appear at least to be of this nature. Winch seems at least to have forgotten Marx's dictum that "if there were no difference between essence and appearance, there would be no need for science."[16]

There are philosophers influenced by Winch who would respond, "Indeed in the social studies there is no need for 'a science' and indeed—certain parts of economics apart—no possibility of a science that goes beyond careful participant's observation or participant-like observation, description, and interpretation." However, Winch does not claim that himself. Moreover, given that we do not take this road and given that we do maintain this appearance/reality distinction, do we not have to go significantly beyond anything simply embedded in our participant's knowledge of society to do social science? (In this very question danger lurks for has it been established yet that there is some nonideological way of drawing this very distinction? It is very difficult here to distinguish just where, if at all, an ideological claim is

---

[14]Steven Lukes and Martin Hollis have argued powerfully against Winch and for such abstract principles in their articles in Bryon R. Wilson, editor, *Rationality* (Oxford: Blackwell, 1970). I have responded by arguing, essentially in defense of Winch, that even though there are certain abstract principles of rationality, they are not sufficiently determinate to provide us with an Archimedian point to make such assessments of forms of life or social practices. See my "Rationality and Relativism," *Philosophy of the Social Sciences,* Vol. 4 (December, 1974), my "Rationality and Universality," *The Monist,* Vol. 59, No. 3 (July, 1975) and my "The Embeddedness of Conceptual Relativism," *Dialogos,* Vol. XI, No. 29-30 (November, 1977).

[15]G. A. Cohen, "Karl Marx and the Withering Away of Social Science," *Philosophy and Public Affairs,* Vol. 1 (Winter, 1972), pp. 182-203.

[16]Quoted by G. A. Cohen, *op. cit.*, p. 182.

being made.)

Marx, as Cohen remarks, conceived his *Capital* "as an attempt to lay bare the reality underlying and controlling the appearance of capitalist relations of production."[17] His theories, as he was well aware, are abstruse, going well beyond a participant's knowledge. But this is unavoidably so for science, for, as Marx remarks, "science would be superfluous if the manifest form and the essence of things directly coincided."[18] Science, from the vantage point of everyday experience, is invariably paradoxical; but it is this everyday experience which catches only the delusive appearance of things.

Here we have something which manifestly and directly conflicts with the beliefs of Winch and other Wittgensteinian-oriented social theorists. Marx argues, we must not stick with the ordinary concepts of price and profit, perfectly familiar to every businessman, if our aim is to achieve an understanding of the nature of capitalism.

To understand what Marx is driving at, consider the following analogy. The sun seems to be moving across the sky but, since Galileo, science teaches us that experience here is mistaken: it is a mere appearance which science corrects. The same thing is true of air. We experience it as elemental while science reveals it being composed of distinct substances. Can similar things be said about society and human actions? Consider Marx's very central claim that only the expenditure of labor can create economic value in proportion to the amount of labor expended. From this claim, two counterintuitive, contracommonsensical implications follow which would not be held by the plain man in the society in which the economic concepts being talked about are extant. The propositions in question are (a) the workers fail to receive the whole value of what they produce and thus are not paid for all the labor they have performed, (b) profit flows from capital investment only if it is investment in labor power. These claims are counterintuitive. They are not beliefs any reasonable man would hold who only had a participant's grasp of the concepts involved. Unless there is some patent fraud or breakdown, is a worker not paid for every unit of time he contracts for and completes? How can it be that he is not paid for all his labor? That runs against what we can plainly observe, namely that he contracts to work so-and-so many hours at such-and-such a wage and that he in fact works so-and-so many hours at such-and-such a wage and that he indeed

[17] *Ibid.*, p. 183.

[18] *Ibid.*

receives that wage. But the theory of surplus value shows, if correct, that our common sense grasp of social reality here is mistaken. The reality the theory enables us to see is that the worker is only being compensated for part of his time; the unremunerated part is appropriated as profit. We must not, in doing science, save appearances here; it appears to be the case that the worker is rewarded for all his labor, the profit accruing to the capitalist appears to have a source other than in the worker's labor. The participant's way of viewing things, utilizing the notion of *verstehen,* makes this appear to be plainly and obviously the case. It is Marx's contention that operating from a commonsensical, but very ideological point of view, profit will appear to flow from the capitalist's thrift and cleverness in reinvesting his money or in the power of the machines he owns. The person caught up in the ideologies supporting bourgeois social relations will not draw the critical and crucial distinction, between *profit-creation* and *profit-allocation.*[19] The profit which is *created* depends altogether on the amount of capital invested in labor-power. The amount of profit that is returned to or comes back to an enterprise in a competitive economy is directly proportional to the *total* capital—investment in labor power, raw materials, machines, modernization, and the like—which is laid out for production. Labor-intensive industries have the highest rate of profit-creation, but a more equalizing flow of profit-appropriation goes out into the other industries. The capitalist is interested most directly in profit-allocation—on the volume of his return—so he will ignore or treat as inessential these facts about profit-creation. The appearances will answer to his interests and he will not plunge below the surface and come to understand how profit is created.

Pulling together this discussion, Cohen remarks:

> The notion that the worker's labor is fully rewarded or that every unit of capital invested by his employer participates in the creation of profit—these are not a result of misperceiving the shape of captialist arrangements. They record surface features of capitalist society. But anyone who thinks the fundamental lineants of that society are present on its surface and open to observation fails to apprehend its nature.[20]

However, Marx's distance from Winch and Wittgenstein may not be so great as it would at first appear. But, to bring out more fully what is involved in their very different stresses, we should first bring out other ways in which their picture of what social science should be

[19] *Ibid.,* p. 184.
[20] *Ibid.,* p. 185.

up to is very different indeed. Marx argues that there is a genuine distinction to be drawn between appearance and reality "when and only when the explanation of a state of affairs renders unacceptable the description that it is natural to give of it if one lacks the explanation."[21] Certain social theorists, who are also reformers or revolutionaries, have longed for and indeed sometimes thought to characterize and even establish "a social order which eliminates the gulf between essence and appearance in which things are as they appear to be."[22] It is hoped, and often expected, by some of these theorist-activists, that socialism, eventually establishing a classless society, will satisfy that desire. But the ideology, deeply embedded in the participant's view of things, obscures and mystifies our understanding of social reality, for, if we were correctly to understand what was happening to us, this would, in class-divided societies, have a destabilizing effect. If, to take an example, workers in capitalist societies were to come to learn that they were not paid for all their labor—that they were being exploited—and that there was nothing in their circumstances which necessitated that this should continue to be so, they would begin the move toward social revolution. If they were, that is, apprised of a correct social theory, they would become social revolutionaries.[23] The mirage generated by the wage form is a key element in capitalist ideology and an element that would—so it might be claimed—enter into the description of social reality of a Wittgensteinian social theorist such as Winch. So utilizing *verstehen* with an appeal to the centrality of a participant's understanding can lead to a confusion of an ideological picture of social reality with a scientific picture of that reality.

Given Marx's conception that science is only necessary when there is a gulf between appearance and reality—when things appear as they appear because reality is being misunderstood—and that they would not appear as they do if reality were in fact different than it is, we should readily come to recognize, as a corollary to that, that "science may study a social formation only if it is held together by mechanisms that disguise its basic anatomy."[24] Social science will have no role to play where the true content of social interaction and the correct nature of social conditions and social relations are not hid-

[21] *Ibid.*, p. 186.
[22] *Ibid.*, p. 187.
[23] *Ibid.*, p. 192.
[24] *Ibid.*, p. 193.

den. If the rationale and import of economic activity becomes publicly manifest to the vast majority of human beings, there is no longer the need—given the above assumptions—for a science of economics.[25] Where this is generally true of all social relations, social science becomes superfluous. Yet in all societies, there plainly seems to be a need for some further explanation and interpretation of social phenomena.[26] Even after the achievement of a unity of theory and practice in a rational world, there is, *contra* Marx, Cohen argues, still a need for a further understanding of society.[27] Marx wanted what might aptly be called, a *subversive* social science capable of revealing to us our major illusions about our condition. It would in addition be a tool in the overcoming of illusion, though he realized revolutionary activity was required as well. For while social science can have an emancipatory thrust, it is the activity of the working class and not social science which will liberate us. However Marx, Cohen argues, was mistaken in thinking that all scientific activity reveals a gulf between appearance and reality. Sometimes science "expands pre-scientific information without prejudicing it, and sometimes confirms it without expanding it. The claim that the work of socialist economics does not embarrass pre-theoretical belief simply does not entail that it is not science."[28] Science can teach us that water consists of two highly inflammable gases, but this does not subvert or cause us to reverse our belief that we can put out fires with water. There is no gulf here between appearance and reality. There are similar pretheoretical beliefs of a social sort such as the belief that Blacks in South Africa are paid less than Whites for the same work and the belief that most factory workers are paid by the hour. These beliefs are quite compatible with the highly ramified theoretical claim that labor power alone creates profit. What should be said is that while scientific explanation always uncovers a reality unrepresented in appearance, it only sometimes discredits appearances. When it does discredit appearances it is subversive, when it does not, it is neutral. In social science, as elsewhere, we can have both neutral and subversive science. Central social processes require theoretical explanation. That very attempt will very often lead to a subversive science, but it sometimes will lead to neutral science.

---

[25] *Ibid.*
[26] *Ibid.*, pp. 195-96.
[27] *Ibid.*, p. 197.
[28] *Ibid.*, pp. 200-201.

IV

Cohen's reading and slight revision of Marx seems to me to be persuasive. Our participant's knowledge is often not sufficient to give us a correct understanding of what is going on in our society and to stick with our ordinary understanding of things does often lead us into ideological mystification. We do not need to be committed to a Pareto-like conception of residues to recognize that both he and Marx had insight into the way our ordinary understanding of social processes is subject to ideological distortion. However, an acceptance of this seems to me perfectly compatible with what I take to be Winch's more basic, because more logically primitive, conception of what understanding society comes to. Winch, as we have seen, stresses that a participant's understanding or a participant-like understanding of the society in which he lives or the society he studies underlies all other understanding of that society and *(pace* Pareto) cannot be bypassed or dispensed with. But Winch also stresses that with it as 'a ground floor' the more technical and specialized understanding of the various social sciences can be in place and indeed, for certain purposes, quite essential.[29]

Implicitly probing the 'ground floor' metaphor, can it ever replace a participant's understanding? The correct answer, it seems to me, and the answer I believe that Winch would give, is that sometimes for some specific claims it should be replaced and indeed often is replaced, but that massively there can be no complete rejection or bypassing of such a participant's understanding and a turning to categories and conceptions which do not presuppose them so that we could start *de novo* without such a participant's understanding. We repair the leaky ship while afloat, sometimes utilizing quite drastic methods. But this analogy breaks down in one crucial respect. There is, in understanding society, nothing comparable to abandoning ship such that we could just abandon our participant's understanding—*verstehen*—altogether and come to understand what is going on without reference to it. In catching ideological distortions and mystifications—in recognizing appearances as mere appearances—we need to rely not only on our theoretical conceptions but also on a massive background of quite ordinary understanding without reference to which our iconoclastic interpretations, further-

---

[29] Peter Winch, *The Idea of a Social Science,* pp. 89-90. This passage is almost always overlooked in commentaries on Winch.

ing a subversive scientific understanding, could not even be intelligibly formulated let alone be understood and confirmed or disconfirmed.

To show the force of the above claims and arguments, we very much need to work with an example. There is a convenient one in Cohen's own text which will illustrate my point and is important in its own right. Cohen explicates Marx's argument that under feudalism, one has a *Gesellschaft masquerading* as a *Gemeinschaft.* (A *Gesellschaft* is a type of social relation in which relations between people are that of impersonal and contractual assocations grounded on mutual benefit [utility]. A *Gemeinschaft* is a type of social relationship between people which is that of a *community* in which, on analogy with kinship, the relations flow from personal status and involve nonutilitarian social bonds.)

Capitalist societies are plainly *Gesellschaft-type* societies. In capitalist relations, a man is a means to another man; people, in such impersonal associations, contract to make use of one another, as when we hire a cab, a lawyer, or a guide. In such a society, human relations are, broadly speaking, utilitarian relations. Feudal society, by contrast, was thought by its participants, and many others as well, to be a quite different type society. It was thought to be a genuine *Gemeinschaft* in which social relations were relationships of personal status. This Marx takes to be appearance, surface phenomena only; yet this ideology of *Gemeinschaft* in feudalism was a saving lie essential for the maintenance of that sort of social order. It is indeed true that the bond between lord and serf does not come from a freely-entered contract. It is conceived as a set of personal relations. The lord provides protection for his manorial dependents; he is, where it is necessary, committed to fight for them. Centrally his role is to protect them. In turn, the serf in filial homage labors for his lord. He sees it as his filial duty to provide for the household of his paternal protector. There is, according to the ideology, a mutual concern for the welfare of each other. There is not a purely disinterested concern *just* to gain protection or *just* to gain provision; there is instead the quasi-paternal, quasifamilial relation of fatherly protector and filial dependent. (Note the language of Russian novels of the nineteenth century where the last remnants of serfdom remained.) Men are not, according to the ideology of *Gemeinschaft,* merely the means to each others ends but are bound by noneconomic ties of loyalty and tradition in which the position of everyone, great and small, is respected by his fellows.

Marx argues that this *Gemeinschaft* is a sham. And here, as much as in a capitalist society, one in reality has a *Gesellschaft* rooted in economic need. Both feudalism and capitalism were in reality exploitative societies with a *surplus product* being extracted from the worker's labor power. The community was not the intimate one portrayed in the ideology—modeling the macrocosm on the microcosm of a colleague bringing back a catch of fish to another colleague while that colleague watches after the other colleague's dog. The ideology apart, the actual relation between lord and serf was utilitarian in basis, however much the parties to it might have been unaware of that fact. Given the state of the productive forces and the technology of the Middle Ages, the manorial scheme was the most efficient scheme for provisioning human beings. Serf and lord were in reality tied together by economic necessity. This, not tradition and loyalty, provided the actual rationale for such a society; *Gemeinschaft* was the saving lie to keep them together in a plainly exploitative situation. It required the myth of quasifamilial relations.

What I want now to show is that if we reflect on the above example, it will show clearly and forcefully the correctness of the Winchian claim concerning the primacy and the indispensability of a participant's understanding of society, i.e., of *verstehen.* It will help us see how such an understanding is presupposed by any scientific or for that matter any 'philosophical' understanding of society. To understand that there is sham in the above situation is to understand what it is a sham of and that requires the background of a participant's understanding of the social relations in question. But an acceptance of this thesis is perfectly compatible with also accepting the Marxian claim about the strategic importance of subversive social science. To even be able to either affirm or deny the claim that the *Gemeinschaft* of the Feudal period was a sham, we need, as I have just remarked, first to understand in a more primitive less problematic way what it was a sham of. To understand that claim about sham and about how it was a necessary ideological mystification, we must be able to understand plain statements such as the claim that in the feudal period the bond does not come from a freely-entered contract and that in turn requires an understanding of such concepts as lord, serf, and contract. To understand these is to come to have a participant's or a participant-like understanding of such concepts with their built-in conceptions of rationality and propriety. *Verstehen* is here essential. And one does not have any understanding of the concept of lord and serf at all unless one understands that they are supposed to stand, vis-à-vis, each other, in certain relations. To argue about whether the putative *Gemeinschaft-relations* are indeed genuine or a sham, presupposes a more primitive and less tendentious, but morally and socially speaking much less interesting, understanding of concepts such as loyalty, homage, filial duty, family, protection, supply, having one's own plot, being a serf, being a lord, labor, manor, fief, and the like. We need to have an understanding of them including, of course, a knowledge of their functioning in their distinctive contexts. Our understanding here must be like the most ground floor knowledge an ethnographer seeks to gain of the tribe he studies. For an ethnographer to understand what is going on in a tribe whose mores he is studying and trying to describe in an ethnographic monograph, he needs a participant-like understanding of that society. He must come to understand the rules, implicit and explicit, operative in that society and he must grasp how they are applied and come to understand the norms of rationality operative in that society. He must come to have something approximating an insider's understanding of those forms of life. We need this kind of understanding of our own society or another to have any understanding of it at all. And all social scientists, not just anthropologists, must presuppose this kind of ordinary understanding in any of their specialists's inquiries. They need, that is, the kind of ordinary understanding—or in the case of the anthropologist something approximating that—that a representative member of the tribe would come to have in being socialized in such a tribe. The having of such an understanding is presupposed in the more sophisticated understanding of social science. It can challenge a part of it—perhaps any part of it—but it must massively presuppose it in carrying out such a challenge.

There would be no being taken in by a sham or being mystified by the ideology of *Gemeinschaft* without this comparatively non-problematic participant's understanding. Only certain things can even count as appearances such that a more adequate understanding would subvert those appearances. For the pretense that the lord stood in a paternal relation to his serfs to even succeed, certain forms of address, distinctive behavior and attitudes would have actually to obtain. Without that there could not even be the appearances.

Social science, going beyond the everyday participant's understanding, can, and in many instances should, be a subversive science directed to exposing appearances and exhibiting the conditions that require ideological entanglement in those appearances. But, for this to be possible, there must be a background of understanding of society which is quite different. We need this everyday understanding to have any understanding at all and we will typically come to have, as well, a reasonable amount of tolerably neutral social science which explicates, interprets, and explains the pretheoretical beliefs of our everyday participant's understanding of society.[30] A specialized understanding of certain things in our society can replace bits of our understanding of society with a more adequate understanding. We can come, for example, to know that their lord protects them out of self-interest and not out of a quasifamilial loyalty rooted in tradition. A specialized understanding of a key element in a society can come in a way to replace or modify our everyday understanding. But for this to be possible, it must be the case that a very considerable amount of a society's self-understanding remains in place.

However, it is also important to see—and this is perhaps something that Winch and Wittgensteinians generally miss—that a crucial self-image that a society might have of itself might be mistaken. Our above example shows how this can be so. A typical medieval man with his participant's knowledge of his society would see it as a *Gemeinschaft,* as a genuine community. Seeing that society, as Marx sees it, as a sham community, undermines the key self-image of that society. It destroys its self-image of itself. But for that to be able to happen, it also must remain the case that many pretheoretical beliefs in the participant's conception of his views must remain in place. Still, we can see, with our above example, how a society's self-understanding still could be subverted, and indeed rightly subverted, breaking the chains of ideology.

V

There is a further difficulty to untangle. (Perhaps, since it is so difficult to state properly, it might be better viewed as a perplexity to dispel.) I can perhaps best begin to express what is involved by juxtaposing two quotations, one from Cohen and the other from Winch.

In attempting to give an elucidation of the unity of theory and practice, Cohen remarks:

> Theory aims at the production of thoughts which accord with reality. Practice aims at the production of realities which accord with thought. Therefore, common to theory and practice is an aspiration to establish

---

[30] I advisedly use the qualifier here, for I do not want to claim that any interesting stretches of this interpretive sociology are utterly neutral. For some of the rationale here, Charles Taylor's articles cited in footnote 3 and my own article cited there, are useful.

congruity between thought and reality.[31]

By theorizing or by action or by both, we attempt to "arrange a correspondence between thought and reality . . . "[32] Thought, in optimum conditions, can maintain a correspondence with reality.[33] Cohen treats, and seems at least to regard, these as tolerably unproblematic notions. He assumes, as something obvious, that we have some reasonable understanding of what we are talking about when we speak of correspondence here.[34] Feuerbach and Marx fought against the discord between thought and reality and sought to "destroy illusion and initiate a harmony between reality and thought."[35]

It is precisely such talk of the correspondence of thought to reality that Winch finds problematic and, in a pejorative sense of the term, 'metaphysical'. This is clear enough in his remarks about the social anthropologist, Evans-Pritchard. Winch contends that Evans-Pritchard is "wrong, and crucially wrong, in attempting to characterize the scientific in terms of that which is 'in accord with objective reality.' "[36] This talk, Winch argues, is intellectually mystifying metaphysical talk, for we do not have any general and extra-linguistic conception of reality such that we would know what it would mean to claim, or what it would be like for it to be true or false, that scientific notions correspond to such a reality while nonscientific notions do not. Evans-Pritchard's talk of the criteria, applied in scientific experimentation as constituting a true link between our scientific conceptions and an independent reality, reflect an unexplained metaphorical use of such phrases as 'true link' and 'independent reality'. We know what it means to say that there is a true link between the mercury poisoning of the fish and the dumping of a certain substance into the river, and we know what it means to say Harry's fancies about his having cancer correspond to no genuine reality; but when we say that religious ideas or Zande conceptions of witchcraft make no true link with an independent reality while scientific ones do, it is thoroughly unclear, Winch argues, what, if anything intelligible is being maintained.

---

[31] G. A. Cohen, *op. cit.*, p. 198.

[32] *Ibid.*, p. 198.

[33] *Ibid.*

[34] *Ibid.*, p. 186.

[35] *Ibid.*, p. 199.

[36] Peter Winch, "Understanding a Primitive Society," *Rationality*, edited by Bryan R. Wilson, p. 80. In this context, for such conceptions in a nutshell, see Ludwig Wittgenstein, *On Certainty*, pp. 79-81.

Winch's central reason for believing this to be so, shows itself in the following oft quoted Wittgensteinian claim—the claim I want to juxtapose to my previous extended quotation from Cohen. Winch remarks:

> Reality is not what gives language sense. What is real and what is unreal shows itself in the sense that language has. Further, both the distinction between the real and the unreal and the concept of agreement with reality themselves belong to our language.[37]

Indeed, Winch continues, we cannot conceive of a language without a conception of reality, as we can conceive of a language without a conception of wetness. But, be that as it may, we could not in fact "distinguish The real from the unreal without understanding the way the distinction operates in the language."[38] Evans-Pritchard, like Pareto, and like Cohen (at least apparently), is trying to operate with a conception of reality that is independent of language. That is to say, there is with such a putative conception of reality, something against which the use of terms and indeed a whole domain of discourse or even a whole language could be appraised. But that is not possible. We can only understand the appearance/reality distinction in the context of the diverse and contrasting uses they have in particular contexts, e.g., these flowers are real and those artificial, that affection is real and that just put on. But when we say that science corresponds with reality but religion does not, we do not, Winch claims, have any even tolerably clear sense of what we are saying.

But why should such allegedly problematical talk of the correspondence of thought and reality pass so easily the critical eyes of philosophers and anthropologists if it is really so problematic? Perhaps, as philosophers often do, we are manufacturing a problem. In the contexts and ways in which Evans-Pritchard and Cohen employ such locutions, I believe we do have something which is genuinely problematic. I think it so readily passes as unproblematic because of a misleading picture which frequently dominates us when we think of such matters. In such contexts, we usually call to mind ' "the-cat-is-on-the-mat"-if-and-only-if-the-cat-is-on-the-mat-model'; that is to say, we think we understand such talk because what comes to mind is something there before us such as what might be expressed

[37] *Ibid.*, p. 82.

[38] *Ibid.*, p. 82. See, as well, his response to Jarvie. Peter Winch "Comment," *Explanation in the Behavioural Sciences*, edited by Robert Borger and Frank Cioffi (London: Cambridge University Press, 1970), pp. 249-59.

by the sentence (to switch the example) 'The cup is on the desk' or 'The cup is white' when the cup is sitting on the desk there before us. And we think that by ostension—by just looking and seeing—we can see that 'cup' denotes something there before us, that 'desk' similarly denotes and that, while 'white' is something more complicated, we can, by various ostensive techniques, come to see what 'white' stands for.

Wittgenstein has brilliantly shown what is mistaken and over-simplified by even this picture. But, all the same, we feel somewhat confident in speaking of a correspondence between thought and reality here. But for the typical and interesting claims that come up in the social sciences, we seem, at least, to be quite at sea about what talk about correspondence or lack of correspondence and related notions would come to. We unreflectively employ that picture but when we reflect on it, we can see that it does not apply. We can very well come to believe, if we reflect, that we cannot make anything of the claim that there is an independent reality which gives such talk sense by showing how it corresponds to that 'independent reality'. We can, as I do, think Gellener's accusation of idealism here is just so much arm-waving and still remain thoroughly baffled by talk of correspondence here.

To see how the-cat-is-on-the-mat-model works badly in some contexts, we should return to Marx's central claim, discussed by Cohen, that only the expenditure of labor can create economic value and his corollary claims that (a) workers fail to receive the whole value of what they produce, (b) they are not paid for all the labor they perform, and (c) that profit flows from capitalist investment only if it is investment in labor-power. These claims are paradoxical and seem to be in conflict with what we observe. We see people being paid for all their labor. They freely contract to do such-and-such—usually to work so-and-so many hours at such-and-such at wage scale—and they typically get paid for that as they contracted. Sometimes there is cheating but that is not the typical situation. Yet the Marxian claim is that once the theory of surplus value is properly understood and we clearly draw the distinction between profit-allocation and profit-creation, the situation will be seen differently. Observations made while utilizing the plain participant's way of speaking and viewing the matter will be seen to be capturing appearances only.

Compare the following utterance-pairs.

A. 'The cup is on the desk.'
'The cup is white.'

B. 'Labor alone can create economic value.'
'Workers do not receive the whole value of what they produce.'

We know how to establish the truth or falsity of the statements in the A group, but about the B group, we are rather at sea. There is even a temptation to believe that they are somehow quasidefinitional or alternatively, that perhaps they are value judgments, where value judgments are somehow thought to contrast with factual judgments and perhaps to be problematic. As still another alternative, if the utterance-pair in B is construed as a pair of factual judgments, they, unlike the utterances in the A pair, do not appear to be judgments we know in any straightforward way how to confirm or deny. If we accept certain theories and a certain mode of conceptualization — a certain conceptual framework — it is rather obvious how we can confirm them or deny them and why the statement that workers get paid for each hour they work would not deny them. Yet, not all economists, let alone all observers of and in our economic life, would characterize the situation as they are characterized in those propositions and in the talk which would naturally surround them. But, on these other accounts, they are not readily confirmable. We do not know what it would be like to get a pretheoretical account here so that we could describe the data in such a way that we would have a neutral specification of the data. The reason we are interested in a neutral specification of the data is that only with such a specification would it be possible to be able to make evidential appeals which could actually function in such a way in Marxian and neo-Keynesian accounts, or for that matter, in any general, theoretically ramified account. We want to be able to break out of those systems and appeal to something independent and common to all of them or at least many of them which could be of use in testing them. However, it is not at all clear that we can do that. If we adopt one vocabulary and framework, we then can easily enough confirm or deny certain statements but if we adopt another vocabulary and conceptual framework, then it becomes easy enough to confirm or deny other statements — statements which on the first framework remain strangely perplexing and not clearly confirmable. We do not have — or so it would appear — any neutral vocabulary in accordance with which we, independently of the contending theories, could confirm or deny to any reasonable degree at all the rival accounts. We do not seem to have anything like sufficient relevant theory-independent data.

Cohen, in setting out Marx's account, quite deliberately relies "upon an unrefined distinction between observation and theory."[39] He allows, for the sake of the discussion, the "concept of theory-free observation report, which moreover, counts as an observation report no matter what its context of utterance is," to go unchallenged, while recognizing full well that it is challengeable.[40] What may very well be the case is that experience and the elements entering into a social description may always or at least almost always be shaped by a theoretical perspective.[41] A Freudian will quite happily in his observation reports speak of unconscious thoughts and unconscious wishes and a Marxist will speak of principal contradictions in society or of class struggle. People with different, rather less theoretically ramified perspectives, will not couch their social descriptions and observation reports in those terms at all. They will regard such talk as theoretical talk, utilizing what seems to them to be highly complex, inadequate and ideologically suspect, theoretical constructs. Such considerations also reveal that the theory/observation distinction is not a sharp one, will shift with the theoretical perspective of the observer and is in part at least relative to the context of inquiry.

Winch would not be happy with such talk about 'a theoretical perspective' but it seems to me that a recognition of the force of the above claims would reinforce his overall arguments about the way we draw distinctions about what is real and what is unreal and concerning how we are to take talk about social reality. For him social reality is not something which is given neatly in observation statements which succeed in referring to what is independently identifiable simply by observation. Rather there are distinct language-games and constitutive practices which, like what Cohen calls a theoretical perspective, shape our experience and set how it is we experience our world. What is real and what is unreal is determined by our language and its distinctive categorial shape. That is to say, the culturally distinctive categories of our participant's discourse function very much like a theoretical perspective in determining what it is we shall observe and how we shall comprehend what it is we observe. What is real and unreal shows itself in the sense language has; there is no reality there, graspable and intelligible, independently of language, which gives

[39] G. A. Cohen, *op. cit.*, p. 200.

[40] *Ibid.*

[41] I have argued, in a way I now feel ambivalent about, that there are some exceptions. See my "Social Science and American Foreign Policy," *Philosophy, Morality and International Affairs*, edited by Virginia Held, *et. al.*, pp. 286-319.

our language the sense it has. In that sense talk of correspondence is quite without sense.

We can and should, as Cohen does, speak of thought being in accordance with reality or failing to be in accord with reality; we can even speak of a correspondence of thought and reality, but we must, there, be very careful how this is to be understood. If it is a kind of general motto to cover many distinctive occurrences, such as the need to say that reports on alcoholism in the Northern Territories corresponds with the facts, that poverty is linked with lack of education, that our *petit bourgeois* class perspective distorts our understanding of the relation between workers and capitalists, then such talk is quite in order. But generally—that is considering whole activities and clusters of activity such as a religion, capitalism, science, art or morality—it is not clear that anything intelligible is being said in claiming that they (say even religion or capitalism) correspond to reality or fail to correspond to reality. I do not at all want to give to understand that nothing can or should be made of such talk. I only want to make it evident how problematic and epistemically suspect such talk is. Before such grandiose claims can be sensibly made a rather considerable amount of clarification and self-conscious reflection should be done.

VI

Finally, there is a further and rather different cluster of considerations which should be examined. The thrust of them will be to establish that working in accordance with an account such as Winch's does not preclude the utilization of more theoretical conceptions, including conceptions such as those stressed by Marxist social theorists. I shall also argue that the kinds of conception that Winch stresses as being essential for an understanding of social relations are also essential for an understanding of these more theoretical conceptions.

It has been thought (by MacIntyre among others) that there is no room on Winch's account of the social sciences for conceptions such as ideology and false consciousness and that this is a very grave defect.[42] I agree that it is a grave defect to exclude such conceptions and I further recognize that Winch does not utilize such conceptions,

---

[42] Alasdair MacIntyre, "The Idea of a Social Science," *Rationality,* edited by Bryan R. Wilson, p. 118. See also, Thomas McCarthy, "The Problem of Rationality in Social Anthropology," *Philosophy and Social Theory, Stony Brook Studies in Philosophy,* Vol. I (1974), pp. 1-36.

but I see no good reason why someone convinced by his general approach could not accommodate them in his account. Indeed, I think he should, for they are conceptions of considerable moment in social science and in the understanding of ourselves. However, it also should be recognized that we need participant's talk, the appeal to *verstehen,* to give sense to those notions. Or, at least, that is the point I shall argue. I shall further argue that in showing how a notion is ideological and how false consciousness obtains, one needs to appeal to conceptions which presuppose a participant's understanding of the discourse.

Consider a patent bit of ideology. Suppose we were told in 1975 that New York City's troubles are symptomatic—though in an extreme form—of the troubles in the advanced industrial societies. We have overexpanded our social services and the nonproductive sectors to such an extent that our productive system can no longer accommodate them. So now is the time, if we are to keep our system stable, for sober second thoughts and a little prudent belt-tightening. We must pull together and keep the social contract. To do this, sacrifices will be required of us all.

If either a worker or a capitalist accepts this argument as even a justifiable simplification, he is being taken in by an ideology, though a capitalist could, and indeed some do, give currency to such propaganda in a self-conscious effort to reinforce the capitalist order. But such a claim is patently a bit of capitalist apologetics which would hardly survive scrutiny on an impartial account of what is the case. But in not accepting it—in spotting it as a bit of ideology—concepts and modes of reasoning and criteria of rationality embedded in our participant's talk about our social relations and our society are naturally utilized and quite unavoidable.

It is also true that in reflecting about such a case, rational, informed people would apprise the situation rather differently than it is apprised in that bit of capitalist apologetic. They would see the situation as an attempt on the part of the capitalist class to effect, in what is most likely only a minor capitalist crisis, some redistribution of wealth in favor of the capitalist class. (I do not say this is the only thing it does, but generally it is a redistributive device aimed at stabilization of the system.) Welfare state gains for workers are being in part reversed to place more money in the private sector or at the disposal of that sector. This money will in turn be used by that sector to increase its power and wealth and enhance its control over society. It will provide more capital for expansion into certain favorably placed underdeveloped countries, some money for redistribution to those countries in order to pacify their masses, and it will provide capital for research into future possibilities of expansion and control. The Seven Sisters, for example, realize how oil and natural gas will not be with us forever and they need, in order to protect themselves, to develop new technologies so that they will continue to maintain their hegemony over energy and hence their positions of power and control in society. Current welfare provisions stand in the way of most effectively maximizing those policies; moreover, it is not from the capitalist point of view a wise policy to continue to develop unnecessarily the skills and rising expectations of those sectors of society who might in the future, with rising expectations and skills and an enhanced knowledge, prove a challenge to that order. Where cutbacks can be effected without too much conflict—as it seems possible to do now in North America—it is prudent planning on the part of the capitalist class to make them. It is a rational move on their part to get back some of the advantages won by the working class and to pacify, through some redistribution of wealth, a rising working class in underdeveloped countries.

The above characterization did, of course, use terms which are, to a degree, theoretical: which go beyond a thoroughly detheorized employment of participant's talk. Yet, many of these terms are passing into our common language or are citified cousins of terms long employed in our common language. But 'capitalist class', 'capitalist crisis', 'welfare state', 'private sector', 'ruling class', 'underdeveloped countries', 'maximizing,' 'rising expectations,' 'capitalist order,' 'working class' are all moderately theoretical. But none of them are very distant from our participant's language and they could hardly be understood without such a knowledge. Indeed, (a) because we understand such plain notions as being poor and as having to work for a living in uncertain conditions over which we have very little control and (b) because we know what it is like to hope for a better future, it is the case that we understand conceptions such as 'rising expectations' and 'working class'. But, more importantly still, for the above critique of capitalist ideology even to appear plausible, there needs to be a perfectly ordinary understanding of how working people are badly treated, an awareness of what an enhanced understanding of what is happening around them would be likely to have on their attitudes and expectations, an understanding of how wealth is linked with power and control, and finally an understanding of how it is plausible that the wealthy would feel concerned—because they perceive themselves as threatened—about how an informed but deprived group would feel and act. We need our ordinary participant's understanding of human motives and rationales to understand what is going on here.

I am not trying to argue for the adequacy of the above critique of a bit of capitalist apologetics, but to use it as a sample to make the point, by the use of that sample, that both the specimen bit of capitalist apologetics and its critique require the kind of participant's understanding that Winch stresses is essential as a base for an understanding of social issues. I have further been concerned (a) to show how Winch's account can accommodate ideological critique and conceptions such as that of false consciousness and (b) to show that these very notions themselves cannot be understood if we do not have a participant's knowledge of the ordinary unscheduled rules and norms governing our ordinary human interactions.

KAI NIELSEN.

UNIVERSITY OF CALGARY.

PHENOMENOLOGY OF MEMORY FROM HUSSERL TO MERLEAU-PONTY*

"Memory," says John Locke, "is as it were the Store-house of our *Ideas.*" He elaborates—and qualifies—as follows:

> For the narrow Mind of Man, not being capable of having many *Ideas* under View and Consideration at once, it was necessary to have a Repository, to lay up those *Ideas,* which at another time it might have use of. But our *Ideas* being nothing, but actual Perceptions in the Mind, which cease to be any thing, when there is no perception of them, this *laying up* of our *Ideas* in the Repository of the Memory, signifies no more but this, that the Mind has a Power, in many cases, to revive Perceptions, which it has once had, with this additional Perception annexed to them, that it has had them before. And in this Sense it is, that our *Ideas* are said to be in our Memories, when indeed, they are actually no where, but only there is an ability in the Mind, when it will, to revive them again; and as it were paint them anew on it self, though some with more, some with less difficulty; some more lively, and others more obscurely. *(Essay,* II, 10, §2.)

Memory is a storehouse whose stores are nothing stored nowhere. . . . Call it then a power to revive perceptions of "ideas" once perceived, along with the assurance that one has perceived them before; a power of the mind to paint its "ideas" afresh on itself, though with varying degrees of verisimilitude. Verisimilitude? To what should memories approximate? Whence the assurance that one has perceived this or that before? Apparently memory *is* a storehouse?

"Locke sank into a swoon," says Yeats, and neither he nor we have come round yet. Phenomenology of memory is "idling," is "in neutral gear," said Merleau-Ponty in 1955, because no one can decide whether memory is fundamentally "conservation" or "construction," storehouse or interior decorator, passivity or activity. Interest in phenomenology of memory is obviously alive and well today: mnemonic phenomena are being compared in various respects to those of perception, imagination, fancy, hallucination, and so on. But whether the fundamental ambiguity of memory is being taken seriously today, the mystery that in one way or another has confronted all researchers in memory from Aristotle and Augustine to Bergson and Proust, I am not altogether sure. Locke, even in a

*Aron Gurwitsch Memorial Lecture, read at the New School for Social Research on February 22, 1979.

swoon, describes that mystery well:

> In this secondary Perception, as I may so call it, or viewing again the *Ideas,* that are lodg'd *in* the *Memory, the Mind is oftentimes more than barely passive,* the appearance of those dormant Pictures, depending sometimes on the Will. The Mind very often sets it self on work in search of some hidden *Idea,* and turns, as it were, the Eye of the Soul upon it; though sometimes too they start up in our Minds of their own accord, and offer themselves to the Understanding; and very often are rouzed and tumbled out of their dark Cells, into open Day-light, by some turbulent and tempestuous Passion . . . (§7)

In the present paper I want to approach that mystery by considering Edmund Husserl's lectures and notes on internal time-consciousness and passive synthesis. Husserl's approach takes memory to be a source of *phenomenological evidence.* I also wish to refer briefly to Merleau-Ponty's "Monday course" of 1954-55 on the problem of passivity. Merleau-Ponty's approach takes memory to be a source of *ontological ambiguity.* Because of the vast amount of material I want to bring to bear, I will provide very little analysis of specific problems; instead, I will unleash a series of provisional conclusions I have come to in my own work, which I call *Erinnerungsversuch,* an "essay" in memory. I fear my paper may be provocative, without my really wanting it to be so. But you would gain nothing from a pedantic, and in any case incomplete, rehearsal of the contents of Husserl's and Merleau-Ponty's texts; I would rather incur your wrath than induce listlessness!

Husserl remained intrigued by the related problems of time-consciousness and memory throughout his career, especially between 1893 and 1926. (Much of his work on these issues, but by no means all of it, has been taken up into volumes X and XI of the Husserliana series, *Zur Phänomenologie des inneren Zeitbewußtseins,* edited by Rudolf Boehm, and *Analysen zur passiven Synthese,* edited by Margot Fleischer, both volumes published in 1966.)

The Göttinger Vorlesungen of 1904-05, particularly influential since their publication in 1928, hope to shed light on a number of interrelated problems—perception, sensation, fantasy, figurative imagination, and memory—all within the perspective delineated by the title of the lecture course: *Hauptstücke aus der Phänomenologie und Theorie der Erkenntnis.* Husserl's guiding perspective derives from the tradition of *Erkenntnistheorie;* the focus is epistemological.

In his introductory remarks to the lecture course Husserl stresses the importance and the interdependence of phenomenology of memory and time-consciousness. They are issues of extraordinary complexity, which the *Logical Investigations* left virtually undiscussed:

> Indeed, the entire sphere of remembrance *(Erinnerung)* and thereby the conglomerate of problems for a *phenomenology of the originary intuition of time* are silenced to death, as it were, in that work. The extraordinary difficulties that lie here—perhaps the greatest in all phenomenology—I was not able to master. Because I did not wish to commit myself ahead of time, I preferred to be completely silent. (Konvolut F I 9/4a-b, cited by Boehm, X, xvi.)

From 1904 onward Husserl broke the silence, but not in order to commit himself. For the complex of remembrance and time-consciousness grew ever more intricate and bewildering as his study of it proceeded. Volumes X and XI of the Husserliana bear the traces of that intricacy and bewilderment. I confess that Husserl's texts, as they lie before us today in edited compilations, remind me of nothing so much as they do the texts of Nietzsche. Nietzsche—who says such unkind things about the ladies, then winks an eye and concedes that all these are merely "his" truths. Nietzsche—who says, "Do I contradict myself? Terrific!" Nietzsche—who says, "Congratulations, my dear Germans, again you misunderstand me." Husserl displays none of the bravado, but at the end of five pages of labyrinthine exposition, diagrams of coordinate systems, distinctions, objections and responses to objections, he is most likely to write, "The question is, of course, whether any of this is true." Or: "I wonder whether it is all that simple?" Nothing is more entertaining than to watch an intelligent and earnest philosopher trying to "refute" Nietzsche: he gets so many tweaks on the nose and jolly hits from behind that he is left hurting and—if he really is intelligent—laughing at himself. With Husserl, sober and utterly nonviolent as he is, things can be just as dangerous. I may provide a bit of entertainment myself by attempting now a critique of the second division of the time-consciousness lectures, §§7-33.

My complaint is simply that Husserlian phenomenology poses its questions concerning internal time-consciousness in a way that distorts the phenomena of perception, imagination, and memory to which it means to provide access. At the beginning of his exposition (§§1-2) Husserl proposes to bracket all assumptions about or references to *objektive Zeit* and to describe time as it is "lived," that is, experienced immanently in consciousness. Yet his descriptions throughout reflect prejudices that stem from the very realm of objective chronometric time that ought to have been excluded. For Husserl, time consists of a series of now-points *(Jetzt-Punkte)* each equal to each. Every point on the line-segment of time designates a location *(eine Zeitstelle)* for the positioning of objects; each point represents a unit *(eine Einheit)* possessing a discrete identity and individuality that serve to fix the identity of the intuited or perceived object which occupies the point, "fills" it. The now-point is the source of objectivity; Husserl speaks of the *Quellpunkt* (§§ 10-11). Thus, time is not sheer flux but a *continuum* which may be represented geometrically (§10) and calculated algebraically (§18), so that time-consciousness may approximate to the ideals of conceptual clarity and mathematical apodicticity (§§ 16, 21, etc.). In §§ 30-33 Husserl reinstates the *objektive Zeit* which phenomenology should in principle have nothing to do with, in order to secure the explicit identity of objects *(Gegenstände)*. He even invokes what he calls *absolute Zeit,* concerning which he formulates "a few *a priori* laws." But the reinstatement of "objective" time and the move to "absolute" time merely thematize what has been done surreptitiously from the outset: consciousness of time is interpreted exclusively on the basis of the inherited notion of linear time as a sequence of discrete units; the flow of such units can in a sense be stopped and reversed, so that the contents of each unit can be scanned from the outside, as though time were a sprocketed filmstrip with a sequence of frames. Husserl employs two metaphors in addition to the grand metaphor of the flowing river, namely, those of the comet's tail *(Kometenschweif)* and the linked chain *(Kette)*. The latter metaphor prevails.

The covert logic behind such an interpretation of time emerges when we consider the problem of remembrance. The criterion that distinguishes primary from secondary remembrance, that is, fresh retention from reproductive recollection, is the criterion derived from the now-point of perceptual experience, namely, *clarity of presence*. Although the example (the tone) is aural, the model is visual. It is the model of an object receding into the distance and diminishing in clarity (§§ 9, 21). The issue for Husserl is whether reproductive consciousness is trustworthy, that is, whether the *Vergegenwärtigung* exercised in reproductive recollection, especially in the remote sphere, can restore to consciousness what the primal impressions of perception, in *Gegenwärtigung,* once granted. On the one hand (§13), Husserl ridicules the idea of trying to compare the memory-image constituted in the "now" with the original intentional content of the memory, which is "not-now," since memory is not a figurative consciousness *(Bildbewußtsein)* which could compare portraits with originals. On the other hand (§§17, 42), he distinguishes fresh retention from recollection by saying that while the former really presents its object, as does perception, where the object is self-given, recollection "merely" presentifies it *(Vergegenwärtigung),* "only" re-presents it *(Vorstellung),* as though recollection were indeed the attempt to portray or somehow approximate to an original. Nevertheless, Husserl's strategy throughout is to secure for secondary remembrance the self-evidence of retention which retention derives from perceptual impressions and which perception derives from the "one and unique" objective time (§32). His preoccupation with memory arises from the need to obtain clarity and secure evidence concerning the constitution of a perduring objectivity. Husserlian phenomenology therefore goes to mnemonic things themselves only insofar as they conform to an inherited ideal of clarity. It has no interest in memory unless memory taps that *Quelle* of evidence that phenomenology seeks. Thus in the *Nachtrag und Ergänzung* to §32, printed as Beilage IV, Husserl affirms that he can "verify" by means of remembrance that what he has earlier perceived is the same as what he subsequently recollects. "This takes place in the straightforward remembrance, 'I have perceived that,' and in the recollection of the second level, 'I have remembered that' " (X, 108). What is so difficult for neurophysiology that it seems impossible (namely, "recall") is so easy for phenomenology that it seems inevitable. "If the object has been given once, then it can be given as often as one likes . . ." (ibid.). Such adequacy of recollection derives, to repeat, from the pure *Objektivität* of punctuated, sprocketed time, the various successive points of which can be identified and linked to a specific objective content "again and again." Husserl writes:

> To the constitution of time belongs the possibility of identification. I can perform a remembrance-back (a recollection) again and again. I can always produce each fragment of time with its filling "again," and then in the sequence of reproductions that I now have I can catch hold of *(erfassen)* the same thing—the same duration with the same content, the same object. The object is a unity of consciousness that can be proven to be the same in repeated acts (thus, in temporal sequence), to be what is identical in the intention. What is identical is identifiable in as many acts of consciousness as one likes, and indeed is perceivable, repeatedly perceivable, in as many perceptions as one likes. I can "at any time" convince myself of the identical "it is" . . . I can deploy myself back at every position of the flux and produce the flux "once again" (X, 109).

The "as often as one likes" *(beliebig oft)* of reproduction is extremely important, since it designates for Husserl the realm of *freedom.* Here consciousness finds refuge from sheer passivity. Freedom grants the kind of irrefragable *presence* that the tradition has always found in immanence and which phenomenology requires for its "evidence." Thus there is always something going on behind the scenes in the phenomenological drama. In §18 Husserl discusses the recovery *(Wiederholung)* of a given succession of past time which otherwise would be irrecoverably lost. Concerning such recovery Husserl insists:

> I "*can*" do that, indeed, "as often as I like." The presentifying of an experience lies *a priori* in the realm of my "*freedom.*" (The "I can" is a practical "I can," and not a "mere representation") (X, 42).

It is ultimately the realm of freedom, the practical "I can," that enables Husserl to claim for recollection a kind of evidence which, while not totally adequate to the evidence of perception, does participate in apodicticity. It is the *beliebig oft* that points in the direction Husserl's work was to take—with the question of passive synthesis. For if *beliebig* were understood to mean "totally arbitrary," if freedom lost its grip on the given world, then all *would* be lost. Phenomenology would become, as Husserl warned, "a fairytale."

But before proceeding, let me introduce some additional critical remarks concerning (1) distortions of phenomena in Husserl's analyses of time-consciousness, (2) the notion of "now-points" within a *continuum,* (3) Husserl's attempt to distinguish *Gegenwärtigung* from *Vergegenwärtigung* while securing the evidence of the former for the latter (in the form of secondary remembrance or recollection), and finally (4) the notion of freedom.

1. I began with the complaint that Husserl's preconceptions regarding time distort phenomena. Let me refer to §14 and the example—Husserl's *sole* example, *nota bene!*—of the remembered melody. We remember a melody heard recently at a concert. We can, Husserl insists, "run through" the melody note for note, as though we were hearing it now. He adds the phrase *mutatis mutandis,* but does not pursue the differences, insisting that we can let a melody run its course note for note, interval for interval. In remembrance we "hear," as it were, each tone, the first tone first, the second tone second. "In each case there is always one tone (or tone phase) in the now-point" (X, 35). What such hearing which does not hear *is,* Husserl does not try to describe, neither in its many modes and varieties, nor in its parallels and contrasts to remembered sights, smells, tastes, and touches. Surely, it is possible to "hear" a melody in the way Husserl describes, granted certain preconditions. It is even plausible that we hear that way when the demand to perceive punctuatedly, cinematographically, as it were, has been issued. But for the

most part, unless I am trying to prove something phenomenologically, I remember melodies in an altogether different way. Let me offer one example.

I have recently heard the bass intone, "O Freunde, nicht diese Töne! Sondern, laßt uns angenehmere Anstimmen und freudenvollere." I now try to let the melody run its course interval for interval. By the time "angenehm-" comes my reproduction is a jumble; the sounds—they are not tones—elide somehow and their duration and even their sequence become unstable. Husserl insists that he *can* reconstitute the melody perfectly because he is in possession of a diagram of retentions and protentions secured to each of those notes in "angenehm-." Husserl has the sheet music. He speaks of an "originarily constituted recollection" that "takes shape in a continuum of primal data and retentions," a recollection that "constitutes (better, re-constitutes) at the same time an immanent or transcendent objectivity of duration . . . " (X, 36). Whatever my recollection of the "Ode to Joy" does, it does not do that. It does not reconstitute discrete perceptual impressions (§15), and there is nothing readily identifiable to which it might be declared "adequate" (§16). It has essentially nothing to do with the geometric model of a "continuum of gradations in the direction of an ideal limit" (X, 40) which would be the self-givenness of perception and which I would be "free" to scurry back to at any time. For the ideal limit *(Limes)* is not "out there" as a kind of distant but inspiring horizon; it obtrudes at every moment of Husserl's recollective project. Beethoven's melody drowns in a clangor of expectations and demands.

2. Husserl is not altogether unaware of the problematic character of those points he designates as *Jetzt-Punkte*. (Cf. §31 of the later lectures on passive synthesis, XI, 145-48.) One of the problems has to do with the mathematical notion of "continuum" as such. A continuum is defined as a set having the same number of points as all the real numbers in an interval. Real numbers are identified as the set of rational numbers (i.e., the positive and negative integers, including all fractions whose denominator is not zero) together with the irrational numbers (i.e., those not expressible as quotients of integers, those that manifest a nonrepeating decimal expansion into infinity, so that in the effort to locate them on the number-line—as Joyce says—"nought nowhere was never reached"). Hence, to call time a "continuum" of now-points is to dissolve all points into the utterly dimensionless geometric objects they have been for mathematicians at least since Leibniz. Hegel for this reason calls the point "the *nega-*

tion of space itself" *(Enz.,* §256). The problem for Husserl becomes one of trying to conceive of *Jetzt-Punkte* as fixed units that frame a content which can be "located" in time. In his notes "Toward the Dissolution of the Schema *Auffassungsinhalt-Auffassung*" (1907-09), notes whose "earth-shattering" importance Rudolf Boehm has intimated, following Merleau-Ponty (cf. Boehm, X, xxxv-xl), Husserl writes: "Here there are infinities contained within infinities, and an infinite number of times" (X, 328). Even before that, in the third division of the lectures themselves, Husserl writes:

> If we observe . . . the *constituting* phenomena, then we find a *flux,* and every phase of this flux is a *continuity of profiles.* But it is impossible in principle to expand any phase of this flux into a continuous succession, hence to think the flux in a transformed manner, such that the phase would be extended into an identity with itself. Quite to the contrary, we find, necessarily and in principle, a flux of perpetual "alteration," and such alteration has the absurd property of running along just as it runs, so that it can run neither "faster" nor "slower" than it does. Thus, every object that might undergo change is missing here; and inasmuch as in every process there is "something" that proceeds, here it is not a matter of process. There is nothing here to be altered, and therefore we cannot speak meaningfully of something that perdures. Hence, it is senseless to try to find something here, within a period of duration, which for once would not change (X, 74).

3. The problem of the "continuum" would not be worth discussing at length were it no more than a metaphor for Husserl. I believe it is more than that, as I believe that what we have in Husserl's lectures is not a *phenomenology of time-consciousness* so much as a *phenomenon of mathematical imagination.* The "tone," for example, which Husserl invokes during his analyses is neither a heard tone—it possesses duration and intensity but no timbre—nor even a remembered tone. It is a hypothetical tone, produced by neither catgut nor reed nor synthesizer, but posited in and by the mathematical imagination. Thus even when Husserl describes the apodictically evident self-givenness of aural perception, he is attuned to, he "hears," a thoroughly modalized imaginative entity. The *Urimpression* and *Urinhalt* of the tone lies not in *Gegenwärtigung* but in *Vergegenwärtigung.* To those same notes on "Dissolution" Husserl appends the remark, "Urempfindung ist etwas A b s t r a k t e s" (X, 326).

4. Finally, regarding the notion of freedom, I note that Husserl never subtends to the "I can" a phenomenologically based "I *cannot.*" He does concede that there are "stages of clarity" in remembrance, that there is "fogging," "fusion," "displacement," and sometimes

even a "painting over" of memory contents. But at each stage of his analysis the effort is to minimize the possibility of error and to maximize the efficacy of the "I can."

A purely theoretical reply is difficult. But my own *Erinnerungsversuch* convinces me that exercise of the "I can" rests upon an irreducible ambiguity: after diligent practice I can remember more than I would have believed possible; with even greater diligence, and after further practice, I can also *fail* to remember. The narrator of Poe's "Ligeia," trying to call to mind the quality in Ligeia's eyes, says, "There is no point, among the many incomprehensible anomalies of mind, more thrillingly exciting than the fact—never, I believe, noticed in the schools—that in our endeavors to recall to memory something long forgotten, we often find ourselves *upon the very verge* of remembrance, without being able, in the end, to remember." As for error, fogging, fusion, and so on, they are not so easily minimized. Nothing rests more secure in the realm of the practical "I can" than the ability to be apodictically certain and still to be wrong. No one stands behind me who can establish the identity of what I remember and what was. When Piaget's plucky school children fail to reproduce properly a task they have learned some months before, in other words, when their memories fail them, they often remain convinced that they have remembered the solution perfectly. Piaget concludes (*Mémoire et intelligence,* p. 468) that "there is no difference of intrinsic quality or of content between a false remembrance and a true one: a false *reconnaissance* gives the same impression of *déjà vu* (and of its belonging to me, the impression of *"moi-ité")* as an accurate recognition."

In the text of Husserl's 1925-26 lecture course, *Grundprobleme der Logik,* now constituting the first part of the *Analysen zur passiven Synthese,* the problem of memory and phenomenological evidence receives its most detailed exposition. Here I can say nothing about the wealth of analyses—e.g., those of Division Three on *Assoziation, Affektion,* and *Weckung*—which *remain* central for any phenomenology of memory. I want to make a critical insertion into the second division, which Husserl called *"Evidenz,"* at chapter 3, "The Problem of the Ultimate Validity of Experience." Specifically, I will turn to §25, "Recollections, the Source for an In-itself of Objects," the second part of which deals with "Recollections of a Sunken Conscious Past." I will also be referring to a remarkable text from 1922-23, "The Apodicticity of Recollection," now printed as Beilage VIII, and especially to its ninth section, "Recollections of the

Remote Past."

Such recollections of a "sunken" or "remote" past are crucial for Husserl's project. For while it seems indisputable that we can hold on to the immediate past of any given perceptual experience by means of fresh retentions, the freedom to recall the distant past is more problematic. Here the lines of retention attenuate; their connection with the present of consciousness becomes ever more fragile. Yet Husserl asserts that "to every recollection of this group also there corresponds a necessary idea, that of an incorrigible self *(undurchstreichbares Selbst)"* (XI, 114). The incorrigibility, i.e., "noncorrectability," rests on the supposition that doubt concerning the objectivity of a given recollection can result only from an interpenetration *(Durcheinanderschiebung)* or fusion *(Verschmelzung)* of similar contents. Such contents have an affinity for one another by virtue of the fundamental associative law of similarity; hence they may interpenetrate even though they belong to different "points" of the past. But it remains the case, Husserl avers, "that the content of each remembrance characterized as false is false only with respect to the unity of the whole conglomerate; it remains true with respect to its parts" (XI, 115). Of course, we might object that such *Durcheinanderschiebung* can wreak as much *Durcheinander* or confusion as anyone could perversely wish: instead of a man standing before a parrot in a cage, I recollect a jailbird confronted by a loquacious, greenclad jailer. Husserl explicitly denies that memory can play such tricks *in infinitum,* since all confusion is a confusion of "discrete elements," so that "there must be an end" to it. He ignores the possibility that imagination or simply conjecture may—indeed must—intervene in reproduction, so that the jailer's flashy green uniform becomes evidence for the fact that it must have been St. Patrick's Day at the local precinct. What is the "end" where all deception and illusion must dissolve? Answer: the "self-givenness" of each part of the recollection at a discrete point of time in the past. Such self-givenness constitutes, as we know, the source of objectivity. Consciousness is linked to that source by a "chain of *Selbstgegebenheiten* that are no longer subject to correction" (ibid.). Husserl grants that this chain is an "idea," that is to say, that it is an image of the "ideal limit" of "the most complete self-givenness." Yet with one eye on the ideal limit and the other busy examining recollections "down to their kidneys," as Husserl says, the phenomenologist can plunge through the fog "to the true self."

Nevertheless, the search for mnemonic evidence ends, not in the heaven of ideas and ideals, but in a *Teufelskreis,* a vicious circle. The *Quelle* of evidence is the *Selbstgebung* that occurs in perception, *Wahrnehmung*. Yet perception, as the very first page of the *Analysen* demonstrates, is always subject to the play of perspectival profiles or *Abschattungen*. The *Abschattungen* cohere thanks to the passive synthesis that occurs in and as the stream of time-consciousness. And now the analysis of the stream appeals to *Selbstgebung* in perception as the font of its objectivity! Not even the programmatic retreat to a sphere of immanence (cf. §24) can rescue phenomenology from the circle. At the place where Husserl affirms the apodicticity and indubitability of "immanently constituted Being, in its living present," he is constrained to add the following marginal note:

> I am not altogether satisfied with this. The objective realm constitutes itself from the outset as temporal, and the moment-like phase is an abstraction that we must first formulate. Thus the incorrigibility of the moment is not something primary *(nicht ein Erstes)*. (XI, 110 n. 1.)

But, lest my paper be swallowed up in critique—which is always one-sided, always abstract—let me suggest the point at which the analyses of passive synthesis remain a positive source, if not of evidence, at least of useful descriptions. It is the point where the phenomenologist confronts "the inarticulate empty horizon" (XI, 376) of the remote past, at the "zero-point" of affective force, where the first stirrings of *Weckung* begin. How we are to account for these stirrings Husserl is at a loss to say. Surely his own attempt to derive all affective force from a perceptual present that radiates similar hyletic data—one of the last residues of sensualism in Husserl's work—is woefully inadequate. But he does pose the problem of "awakening" in such a way that positive future research will have to return again to Division Three, "Association." Here I can only provide the hint that such research must, as I believe, invoke the *finite* power of *embodied revery,* a power that has nothing to do with "transcendental subjectivity" or what I have called the "mathematical imagination," a power that cannot be described in terms of Husserl's metaphysical heritage.[1]

In his *Phenomenology of Perception* Merleau-Ponty insists that "passive synthesis" is not a solution but "an index designating a problem" (P, 479). At the opening of his Monday course in 1954-55 on the

[1] Only after this paper had been written and presented did I become aware of similar formulations and conclusions in Jacques Derrida, *Speech and Phenomena,* tr. David B. Allison (Evanston: Northwestern University Press, 1973). See esp. chap. 5.

problem of passivity, he emphasizes the ambiguous character of the human subject: he is no mere link in a causal chain which the sciences tend to identify with cosmic order, nor is he the reflecting Subject who reduces all obstacles to his own constituting activity. Perceptual experience, according to Merleau-Ponty, displays "a genre of being with respect to which the subject is not sovereign, but without his being imprisoned in it" *(Resumés de Cours,* 66). The ambiguities of perception carry over to the realm of memory, which is "inspired by a past that apparently escapes it" (66-67). The most stubborn among these ambiguities is perhaps that of "conservation" *vs.* "construction." Memory seems to be the latter, for it traffics solely in "representations." Yet there would have to be another memory behind the constructive one that could attest to the value of its constructions; there would have to be an access to a past "freely given," radically untouched by the workings of voluntary memory.

Merleau-Ponty suggests that the only way to remain true to the ambiguities of memory, e.g., the immanence and the transcendence of the past, the activity and the passivity of remembrance, is "to refrain from posing the problem in terms of representation" (72). For not even the present is granted in and as a *Vorstellung;* it is rather "a certain unique position-of-index for *l'être-au-monde.*" And as the present is not a representation, it is not granted at a discrete now-point on the line-segment of time. "Time is not a line but a network of intentionalities" (P, 477). Our relations to the present, as to the past and future, must be attributed to "a postural schema that possesses and sketches out a series of temporal positions and possibilities" (72). As the term "postural schema" suggests, this series of temporal positions and possibilities is a feature of the lived body. In the *Phenomenology* Merleau-Ponty compares time itself to a gesture that "envelopes all the muscular contractions that are necessary to realize it" (P, 479). The lived body is the proper source of that "sedimentation" of time of which Husserl speaks. Recall the famous passage at the beginning of Proust's *Du Côté de chez Swann,* (cf. P, 211 n. 1), which invokes the memory of knees, ribs, and shoulders. When I use the word "revery" I am not thinking merely of—or in—my head.

Finally, if memory is neither conservation nor construction, neither storehouse nor interior decorator, then neither is it the contrary of forgetting. "True memory," according to Merleau-Ponty, is to be found at the intersection of remembrance and oblivion, "à l'instant ou revient le souvenir oublié *et gardé par l'oubli,*" at the instant when a memory returns—a memory forgotten *and preserved in* its forgottenness (72, my emphasis). Both remembering and forgetting are "modes of our oblique relationship to a past that is present to us only by virtue of the determinate emptiness it leaves in us" (ibid.).

How, now, at the end, am I to conceive of the movement of thought at play in all that has gone before? One way is to speak of it as a move from phenomenological evidence to ontological ambiguity. That would be a regression, of course, if evidence (i.e., clarity of presence in a present) were truly free of ambiguity and if the Being of time posed no genuine problem. For Husserl they never ceased being problems. Let me therefore risk a formulation of the "essential task" for phenomenology of memory today, as though there were only one!

Phenomenology of memory must extricate itself from the epistemological context, for two reasons. First, the horizon of expectations already constituted by our tradition for the epistemological context causes us to ignore the greater part of mnemonic experience and to distort the part we do take up. Second, the epistemological project itself rests on certain *metaphysical* presuppositions, certain convictions about the Being of the beings it encounters, presuppositions and convictions that are not directly accessible to it, so that the seed-bed of the epistemological context is in fact a self-generating and self-reinforcing naiveté. To extricate phenomenology of memory from epistemology is therefore not to promulgate mugwump phenomenology; the extrication is in service to phenomenology's self-understanding.

It is of course ironic that transcendental phenomenology should founder where we would most expect it to succeed. In pursuit of memories which are its own, self-consciousness appears to circumscribe a domain of perfect interiority. Here all estrangement seems to be reconciled; here the sphere is turned inside out without puncturing its surface. Sensation and perception, which in spite of all epoché still bear traces of the natural world that is to be constituted, surrender their place to sheer immanence. Memory ought to be the seat, the throne, of absolute subjectivity.

At the close of the *Phenomenology of Spirit,* Hegel describes the ultimate stage of the science of the experience of consciousness, *das absolute Wissen,* in two words. The first is *Er-Innerung,* the contemplation by spirit of all the images it has cast in the course of its life history, with the recognition that these images are its self, reflections of its profoundest interiority. But Hegel requires a second word, a word to name the unassimilable exteriority such a history or passage entails, to name the happenstance that if spirit *can go inside* then it must *be outside,* and that word, you recall, is *Schädelstätte,* Golgotha.

Husserl too experiences—if from afar—the Golgotha of consciousness in the form of *Wiedererinnerung:* without its lifeline to retention or fresh remembrance, and ultimately to the *self*-givenness of objects in a *self*-constituting though accessible world, memory is abstract and empty—lifeless. Yet when phenomenology pursues the lifeline it finds that self-givenness rests, not upon the momentary ingestion of discrete particles of that world, but upon a sustained presencing of beings in time; and so it finds itself moving in a circle, a circle neither of heaven nor hell but of world and earth. To abide in this circling, however, is not to found a new *ἐπιστήμη*. The future of phenomenology lies in *σκέψις*.

DAVID FARRELL KRELL.

UNIVERSITY OF MANNHEIM.

VALUE JUDGMENTS*

It makes sense to divide the problems of ethics into problems of right action and obligation (of what one ought or ought not to do), and problems of value (of what is good, worth attaining, or worth having). Such a division may be only provisional, in that it is possible to argue either that to know what is good is to know what right action is to aim at, or that the only things that are really good are qualities involved in right moral choice. On the other hand, it also is eminently arguable that there is more to value than can be disclosed by even the most thorough investigation of right action, and that there is more to right action than can be disclosed by even the most thorough investigation of values. And even if the division between problems of value and problems of right action and obligation is only provisional, it may be useful in giving us a sense of the ways in which problems of ethical philosophy can be approached from different angles.

Recent ethical philosophy has been preoccupied with right action and obligation, to the virtual exclusion of problems of value. Various consequentialist views, including utilitarianism, have purported to give us a general theory of right action; rival views include Alan Donagan's defense of common morality, and the competing accounts of what ought or ought not to be done in the cause of economic and social justice offered by such philosophers as Rawls and Nozick. In all of this literature there is very slight discussion of problems of value. Frequently claims are made about value, as part of an argument about right action. Some utilitarians assume, for example, that satisfaction and the absence of dissatisfaction are important values, or that the satisfaction of human preferences always has intrinsic value whatever the preferences are. Rawls' view of justice leans heavily on the largely unargued assumption that money and social and economic power are of very great importance in comparison to the values praised by "perfectionist" philosophers. It is symptomatic of the cursory nature of Rawls' discussion at this point that Aristotle and Nietzsche are lumped together in the "perfectionist" category without much attention to the differences between them.[1] It would be wrong

*This work was supported by a grant for independent study and research from the National Endowment for the Humanities.

[1]Cf. John Rawls, *A Theory of Justice* (Cambridge, Mass.: Harvard University

to say that utilitarians and Rawls have paid no attention at all to questions of value, but it would be wrong also to say that they have paid adequate attention. When one surveys the general journal literature, both the quantity and the quality of what there is justify J. N. Findlay's remark about systematic investigation of value that "hardly any Anglo-Saxon philosopher has anything to do with it . . . "[2]

What follows is a preliminary account of value theory. Much of this consists of ground-clearing. I shall begin by exposing mistakes about value judgments that might appear tempting, or that some group or other of philosophers has fallen into. Then I shall say something about the epistemology of value judgments: about how we do and should arrive at value judgments. This will lead to a conclusion about the prospects for value theory.

The three mistakes that must be exposed are as follows.

1. To think X valuable is the same as desiring X.
2. Anything that is the object of a desire that would survive cognitive psychotherapy must be good.
3. We can arrive at reliable interpersonal judgments of value by collating our considered preferences with those of other people, giving preferences weight proportionate to the strength of preference.

I

1. When one speaks of mistakes as tempting, it may be useful to say a little about who will be tempted. Someone who keeps in mind traditional possibilities of rejecting or overcoming desire will not be tempted to equate thinking X valuable with desiring X. Someone whose models of desiring and valuing are drawn from the workings of a consumer society will be so tempted. If someone desires a possession or an experience, say a new stereo set or a Caribbean vacation, there is a certain sense in saying that the value placed on what is desired is proportionate to the strength of the desire. It then may look easy to quantify value: the final determinant of the value of something is how much it is worth to you, or to someone else. But even if one does not quantify, it looks plausible to say that desiring something is the

Press, 1971), p. 325. Pp. 62 and 92 relate wanting "primary goods" such as money and social and economic power to rationality, leaving room for interesting questions as to the rationality of monks.

[2] J. N. Findlay, *The Systematic Unity of Value* (Lindley Lecture at the University of Kansas, 1968), p. 3.

specific psychological manifestation of thinking it valuable and that one cannot occur without the other so that for all practical purposes they are the same.

Something like this may have been in John Stuart Mill's mind when he claimed that it is desire that tells us what is desirable. I have argued elsewhere that Mill's other major claim about desire, that we desire only pleasure, is, interpreted sympathetically, both true and analytic.[3] But this is because of specific connotations of the verb "desire." These connotations make the word "desire" as a noun suitable for translations of what Buddha said the enlightened person no longer has. The enlightened Buddhist still has preferences, and may be said in some sense to have appetites; but desire, with its logical links both to pleasure and to vulnerability to suffering, will have been eliminated.

There is of course a broad and loose sense of the verb "desire" in which the logical connections to pleasure and suffering are cut. In this broad and loose sense, even a placid martyr, who takes no pleasure in the thought of martyrdom nor anticipates it in the actuality, and who would not suffer if martyrdom were denied, may be said to desire martyrdom. In this broad and loose sense, even a dour and zestless Aristotelian desires to pursue the contemplative life. It can be claimed that even the Buddha, who claimed to have lost all desires, must have had, while alive and praising enlightenment, desires in the broad and loose sense of the word. This leaves room for the claim that one cannot think X valuable without, in a sense, desiring X.

Even if this were conceded, though, thinking X valuable could not be equated with desiring X. This is because of the phenomenon of desires thought bad by the person who has them. We may desire to do things that we think are wicked, or to have experiences that we think of as unworthy. And there is no sense of the relevant words that is either broad enough or narrow enough so that it is not true, in that sense, that we sometimes desire things that we do not think valuable. So much is obvious, but if our focus is on models borrowed from the economics of a consumer society we may forget what is obvious.

In the paper already cited I argued that, even if Mill was right about the link between desire and pleasure, the very considerations that showed this also made it very implausible to regard desire as the source of evidence about what is desirable. Someone who wishes to

[3] "Do We Desire Only Pleasure?", *Philosophical Studies*, vol. 34 (1978).

take "desire" in a broad and loose sense may dispute this. But if "desires," in a broad and loose sense, are our evidence of what is valuable, then this has to be added. We commonly assume that some desires are misleading, that as indications of value they are akin to hallucinations. In short, we commonly assume that not all desires are epistemologically equal. This enormously complicates the task of anyone who believes that we can infer what is valuable from what people desire (in a broad and loose sense of "desire").

2. One possible response to this difficulty is to attempt to devise a test, itself value-free, to weed out desires that are to be disregarded. We might pause briefly to consider the general prospects of such an attempt. An unsophisticated person might believe that the primary indication that a desire should be disregarded was that it was for something in fact not valuable. This is hardly a value-free test. But then (to bring up an analogy) it is not clear that we can definitively apply criteria for hallucinations without first determining what is real or at least what are real causal relations. Our sense of what is real can be modified in the light of evidence, but evidence also can be judged partly in the light of our sense of what is real. If desires are supposed to tell us what is the case, that certain things really are valuable, then perhaps we cannot expect to hit on a value-free test which will tell us which desires are to be taken seriously and which are to be disregarded?

Richard Brandt has defined a desire or aversion as rational (in his second sense of "rational") if and only if it is what it would have been if the person who has it had undergone cognitive psychotherapy.[4] Now it is true, as Brandt says, that some desires or aversions are in a sense mistaken in that a rational person with his desires just as they are had sometimes better undertake psychological treatment to remove a certain desire. Brandt's example of the member of congress who can realize the outcomes he most wants if and only if he gives up drinking excessive alcohol is apt.[5] No one also should deny the usefulness of the process of confronting desires with relevant information in an "ideally vivid way," which is what cognitive psychotherapy is, and which Brandt calls a "value-free reflection."[6] But is it true that all desires which would survive cognitive psychotherapy are thereby to be given weight? And even if

[4]Richard Brandt, *A Theory of the Good and the Right* (Oxford: Clarendon Press, 1979), p. 11.

[5]Ibid., p. 111.

[6]Ibid., p. 112-13.

they are to be given some weight, are they to be given weight proportionate to that with which they are felt?

A somewhat flawed test case is provided by the desires had by the inhabitants of Aldous Huxley's Brave New World. The flaw in relation to Brandt's view is that, in the novel, much is made of the conditioning techniques that led to the these desires; and this suggests that many might be extinguished by cognitive psychotherapy. But we can certainly imagine a society like that of *Brave New World,* or like the Land of the Lotus Eaters in the *Odyssey,* in the quality of the desires and pleasures had by its members, which was not the result of overt conditioning techniques. There are surely individuals, in our present society, who have pretty much these desires and pleasures. There is no reason to believe that cognitive psychotherapy would in most cases extinguish these desires. Does this mean that the objects of these desires have value?

Brandt's claims for cognitive psychotherapy bring to mind the ancient question, "Is virtue knowledge?" John McDowell in a brilliant essay has presented a case for a positive answer.[7] The link between virtue and knowledge, he argues, is the proper sense of what is salient in a given situation. But this sense is itself hardly "value-free." And to link virtue to knowledge in this way is very different from linking it to information. No doubt many unworthy desires are inconsistent with the pattern of our lives and can be eliminated by vivid representation of this. But what can cognitive psychotherapy offer someone who has woven a modest and conventional preference for the lower pleasures into a viable whole? Will cognitive psychotherapy give such a person a sense that there are better ways of life? Could Aristotle have used cognitive psychotherapy to convince people of the value of the contemplative life? Can cognitive psychotherapy cure philistinism?

Brandt claims that "there is no sentence in which the word 'good' appears, at least in that core complex . . . which makes an identifiable point which cannot be made by a sentence containing 'rationally desired' . . . in which no 'value-word' is present."[8] But if "rationally desired" is to be explicated (as Brandt says) in terms of cognitive psychotherapy, and if it is true that cognitive psychotherapy is neutral between what Mill called the "higher" and "lower" pleasures, then this is to beg the question against Mill's higher rating of the "higher" pleasures. Furthermore it is to treat as closed what

---

[7]John McDowell, "Virtue and Reason," *Monist,* vol. 62 (1979).
[8]Op. cit., pp. 127-28.

really is an open question: is that which is the object of a desire that would survive cognitive psychotherapy in every case really good? My own judgment is that the answer to this last question is indeed "No," that some modest and conventional desires for worthless things would survive cognitive psychotherapy. But all that is necessary for my argument is that one see that the question is open. It is not the case that objects of desires that would survive cognitive psychotherapy must be good.

3. In discussion of conative attitudes there is always at least a covert comparative element. What we are inclined to try to get depends on the circumstances of what else is available. We may "desire" something, in the broad and loose sense, if the alternatives are very unattractive, that we might not otherwise "desire." The reader may recall Maurice Chevalier's remark that being 70 years old was not bad, considering the alternative. In the light of this, it makes sense to adopt the language of comparisons and to speak of preferring. To speak of "preferences" has the added advantage that "preference" can take the adjective "considered." Even if it is true that we can desire what we think to be worthless or undesirable, it might be held that it is not the case that we have considered preferences for what we think to be worthless or undesirable.

There still is the problem of someone's considered preference for what judicious onlookers might consider worthless. Discussion of this is complicated by the following consideration. Even if some people's preferences seem to us to be directed toward what is worthless, we may reasonably feel obligated not only not to interfere with their pursuit of these preferences, but even to promote conditions in which they are likely to get what they want. Part of the social virtue of respect for others is that we treat other people's goals (as long as they do not pass certain boundaries, such as the one involving harm to others) as if they are worth attaining. We may despise the music of Lawrence Welk but yet direct people to the store where Lawrence Welk records are being sold. Furthermore, it is at least arguable that in a democracy we should construct social policy in such a way that all considered preferences are treated with equal respect and are given weight proportionate to the strength of the preference. There is also room for a more qualified view here, if we think, for example, that the arts should be supported to an extent greater than the amount of present and likely future preferences would justify. But social policy is not the subject of this paper. What is important here is that we see that the problem of considered preferences for what judicious onlookers judge to be worthless has at least two dimensions. There is the question of whether a considered preference *ipso facto* has value. Then there is the separate question of whether we should treat the objects of other people's considered preferences (within the aforementioned boundaries) *ipso facto* as if they have value. Social and political liberalism can make us answer an unqualified or a qualified "Yes" to the second question without committing us on the first question. For that reason it is especially important to keep the two questions distinct.

Some preference utilitarians argue as follows. In determining what course of action to choose one should, of course, have some sense of what it is like to be any of the parties to be affected by one's action. But one cannot know what it is like to be them without, to the degree of one's knowledge, imaginatively sharing their preferences. Thus an ideally intelligent moral agent will give proportionate weight to everyone's considered preferences.

This is a thesis about how we should behave; and indeed it is possible to view it as a more limited thesis, about how we should behave in situations in which the interests of others are significantly involved. The question at hand, however, is not that of whether we should treat the considered preferences of others as having proportionate weight, but rather whether the objects of considered preferences *ipso facto* have value. Alongside a liberalism about social policy and moral choice, one may place a liberalism about values. This liberalism holds, first, that any object of a considered preference *ipso facto* has value, and secondly, that we can determine how much value something has by summing over the number of people who have a considered preference for it and the degrees of their preference. There are some problems in working out the details of this liberalism about values. Does one weigh the preferences of people who are now dead, and how does one weigh or estimate the preferences of people not yet born? We can sidestep these issues, however; my argument is that liberalism about values is fundamentally misconceived.

Let us for the sake of argument agree that sensitivity to others involves, to some degree, imaginatively sharing their preferences. Someone who despises Lawrence Welk can have a sense of what it is like to crave an evening of listening to Lawrence Welk, and to that extent in imagination feel a preference that the entertainment be provided; an adult can in imagination share the fear and distaste of a small child about to be innoculated. The inference may now look clear at this point.

To have a considered preference for something is to think it valuable.

An ideally sensitive moral agent shares in imagination others' preferences.

Therefore an ideally sensitive moral agent must to some extent have a considered preference for the objects of others' considered preferences.

Therefore an ideally sensitive moral agent must to some extent think valuable the objects of others' considered preferences.

However this is fallacious. Another person's considered preference which I share in imagination is not thereby my considered preference. It is open to me to judge that what another person has a considered preference for is really worthless. In imagination I can have a sense of what it is like to be a sadist, and in imagination can share the sadist's preferences; but this surely does not commit me to believing that the experiences for which some sadists have a considered preference are of some value. Once we see this, we see that there is no requirement inherent in sensitivity to others that we accept their considered preferences as reliable indicators of value. Nor is there any reason to believe that mistakes about value as it were average out, so that one person's mistake about value will be balanced by another person's mistake in an opposite direction. Thus there is no reason to believe that we can arrive at reliable interpersonal judgements of value by collating our considered preferences with those of other people. Collating a large number of items, some of them unreliable, will not produce a reliable result unless there is averaging out of mistakes.

The misconception shared by all three of the mistaken views of value that we have discussed is this. They all assume that there is no such thing as a sense of value, apart from wanting something (either immediately or after consideration or psychotherapy). But if there were no sense of value, why would one judge that something was worth attaining or having? And why would reflective people sometimes worry that their values were mistaken? As Edward Bond has pointed out, we reflectively want what we value, but the valuation is not identical to the reflective want; rather it explains and justifies it.[9]

One certainly cannot prove that we have a sense of value. But it

[9]E. J. Bond, "Desire, Action and the Good," *American Philosophical Quarterly*, vol. 16 (1979), p. 56.

is clear, as Bond and others have pointed out, that we commonly talk as if we do; and, in the light of this, attempts to equate valuing with desiring, or to equate goodness with being the object of considered preference, both are question-begging and go against the grain of ordinary discourse. Finally, if a consistent and reasonable epistemology of value should turn out to be possible, then why would we deny that we have a sense of value?

II

In discussing the epistemology of value judgments we first should prevent some harmful elaborations. One can speak, as we normally do in colloquial English, of a sense of value, without invoking the correspondence theory of truth and constructing a realm of non-natural qualities or some other ontology. Whatever merits the correspondence theory may have in relation to statements about the weather, there is no reason why someone who regards some ethical statements as correct need apply it to ethics.[10] Neither does talk of a sense of value commit one to a faculty psychology, which would include a special value sense; no more, that is, than should talk of a sense of uneasiness. A sense of value may lead one to make correct statements, but there is no reason we need to embroider this. It is legitimate to ask, "What makes the statements correct?"; but a proper reply can consist in pointing out the standards we apply and the procedures we follow in looking for correct answers.

Raymond Polin speaks of values as "inventing the unreal, by attributing a transcendence to it that grants it a form of exteriority."[11] But careful attention to the way in which we think and talk about values shows that what typically goes on is far different from invention, and does not justify Polin's "ontological unrealism." People often worry that their values, or the values of their children or friends, are mistaken and that what is thought to be of high value is indeed not so. Sometimes a person will drastically change values; and this typically is experienced not as a re-invention but as a realization, that what had been valued is inferior to something else.

The source of the great majority of value judgments is either authority (the word of others) or experience (the experience of what is being evaluated, or the experience of something judged to be

[10] Cf. my *Ethical Knowledge* (London: Geo. Allen & Unwin, 1970), especially Chapter 2.

[11] Raymond Polin, "Values and Truths," in Joseph J. Kockelmans, ed., *Contemporary European Ethics* (Garden City, N.Y.: Doubleday Anchor Books, 1972), p. 197.

similar). A third source which should be mentioned is thought-experiments, either one's own imagination of what it would be like to be or have something, or the thought experiments provided by novels, plays, and films. (The honesty and reliability of these last vary enormously, and it is an interesting question of aesthetics how much this is related to aesthetic merit.) Clearly the reliability of any authority is no greater than that of the authority's source of belief, and clearly also one can find out from experience that a thought-experiment was misleading or misleadingly presented. Thus the great majority of value judgments rest directly or indirectly on experience, or must be verified by experience. The simplest kind of case is this. A experiences being or having X, finds it of high (or low) value, and says, "X is of high (or low) value." Even such judgments, based on direct personal experience, are not normally, when people talk about values, treated as incorrigible. A may be someone of limited experience and may have little to compare X with. If A had tried X for longer, A might have judged differently. Furthermore, one might impugn A's general qualifications for making value judgments. Some prime examples of this occur in Aristotle's discussion of values. Many people still hold that some people are wise and others foolish in matters of values and that there are ways of identifying those who are wise and those who are foolish.

Because of this, we must bear in mind that there is no such thing as impersonal or "neutral" data about values. One always considers the source. Philosophers of science in recent years have tended to scout the idea of a "neutral given," arguing that theory permeates and flavors experience. But relative impersonality is possible in the sciences, among adherents to a given theoretical approach. Perhaps members of the same monastic order can comparably share a relative impersonality in reports of values, but in the general run of cases encountered in the larger world it is not to be expected.

We normally consider that someone of wisdom and wide experience who has experienced X in a sustained way is in a good position to be confident of a value judgment of X. That is the optimal case. Very commonly, however, people judge the value not only of what they have experienced, but also of things thought to be like what they have experienced. This can be less than optimal. If one experiences an X as being of high value, and judges that X's are of high value, and if it turns out that X's vary tremendously, one may not have been in such a good position to judge the value of X's.

In fact we do not expect that any two people will have exactly the same experiences, so that if talk about values is to have any use it must be at least somewhat general. The danger is that other people's experience may differ from ours significantly in ways that are masked by the broad labels we use to describe experience and that this may vitiate our generalizations. This is a danger that many writers have warned against. One thinks, for example, of Nietzsche's discussion of "The Three Evils" and his insistence on the difference in value between a "wholesome, healthy selfishness" and the contemptible "selfishness" of "anyone who picks up even the smallest advantages."[12] Camus, in the *Myth of Sisyphus,* in presenting models of lives of lucid experience, points out that subtle variations in style can mean significant variations in value. We all know the gulf between someone's way of life and even a clever imitation. Thus generalizations about values experienced by different persons must seem problematic.

This however should be taken as indicating the need for caution and recurrent scepticism, and not as indicating that we cannot arrive at useful generalizations about values experienced by different persons. First, we must realize that some aspects of human experience seem to be more closely shared than are others. The experience of not having enough to eat, or of being in constant physical pain, no doubt varies slightly from person to person and from culture to culture; but there is a great deal to suggest that there are more similarities than differences. The core of traditional morality, indeed, consists of prohibitions on inflicting experiences judged to be of great negative value; and these experiences do appear very generally to be of great negative value. Thus, if we are to worry about value generalizations, those which are connected with generalizations at the core of traditional morality appear to be most secure.

A second point is this. It is possible to recognize that a number of items, to which we would apply the same broad label, vary a great deal in character and value, and still to make useful value generalizations about them. Only the value generalizations must themselves be broad and imprecise. For example, G. E. Moore maintained that the experience of affection for a person worthy of it is of high value.[13] We know that conventions of love and affection vary from culture to culture, and that affection has different cultural roles and degrees of

[12] *Thus Spoke Zarathustra,* trans. Walter Kaufmann (New York: Viking-Penguin, 1966), p. 190.

[13] G. E. Moore, *Principia Ethica* (Cambridge: Cambridge University Press, 1929), pp. 203-5.

importance. So that what we call affection will not, in its various manifestations, fit any precise formula; neither will it always have exactly the same value. But this does not prevent us from seeing that Moore's claim is right, as a rough generalization, with modifications and adjustments perhaps to be made for specific cases. In much the same way, Aristotle's highly favorable evaluation of the contemplative life can be held to have a rough general correctness, even if anything that might be called a contemplative life in classical China or in modern America might differ significantly from what Aristotle had in mind. Other rough generalizations can be made about the value of personal autonomy, variety of experience, peace of mind, etc. That these have to be treated cautiously is no reason for not making them. Indeed, because human experiences do have their similarities and recurrent patterns, value generalizations can be useful guides to others as well perhaps as having some use in discussions of social policy.

Furthermore, it may be possible to arrive at some generalizations of a more fundamental nature. J. N. Findlay's claim that it is "inevitable that conscious life, if sufficiently enriched and prolonged, should develop aspirations towards . . . the 'impersonal' . . ." might be such a generalization.[14] The ascription of the highest values to relatively impersonal states of mind fits the teachings of some great religions. That the "loss of self" means somewhat different things in different traditions does not rob the generalization of all value, and the convergences provide support. Findlay himself builds an elaborate case for his thesis; although in the end one can be uncertain as to how much of the basis of the thesis should be viewed as logical or metaphysical, how much should be viewed as a generalization about what one is prepared to evaluate highly favorably, and as to how relevant empirical evidence might be.

Let me summarize the main results of this paper. We cannot regard value judgments as automatically validated by the existence of desires, even desires that have survived cognitive psychotherapy, or by the existence of considered preferences for what is valued. The ultimate basis or test of value judgments is experience. As in the case of other kinds of knowledge, we can distinguish cases in which someone is in a position to be confident of a value judgment from cases in which someone is not in such a position. The optimal case is one in

---

[14]J. N. Findlay, *Values and Intentions* (London: Geo. Allen & Unwin, 1961), p. 227.

which someone of wisdom and wide experience makes a value judgment of something of which he or she has had sustained experience. Even such a person, however, may not always be in a very good position to generalize about the value of what other people have or experience. Value generalizations seem most secure when they concern highly negative values, such as those of starvation or intense physical pain. It is possible to arrive at useful generalizations about positive values, but these must be rough generalizations, because of the ways in which experiences of a general type can vary among cultures and even among individuals.

What follows for value theory I think is this. The systematic study of values can be pursued usefully, but it must rest on a phenomenology of values: on a careful study of the ways in which values occur in different lives. A science of values, if by a science one means something precise as well as systematic, in which precise and definite laws are based on impersonally shared data, is utterly out of the question.

JOEL J. KUPPERMAN.

THE UNIVERSITY OF CONNECTICUT.

UNSPOKEN CONNECTIONS IN THE DESIGN ARGUMENT

In his celebrated essay entitled "Gods" John Wisdom explores what he calls the logic of belief in divine minds.[1] He finds with the help of a series of analogies that some of its reasonings are not so much deductions or inductions as techniques for drawing attention to similarities and differences between things to bring about a decision to extend the application of the concept of mind. Near the end of his essay Wisdom speaks of the possibility of an "unconscious reasoning" which may incline one to believe that a divine intelligence exists. He thinks that such reasoning, which, since not articulated, is a matter of making "unspoken connections" between things, may very well form part of the logic of belief in divine minds.[2] The final section of "Gods" is an attempt to reveal a number of these unspoken connections. Wisdom seems to think that his examination of "the actual processes to belief" in divine minds reveals it to have a logic aimed at freeing us from our anxieties and releasing "something good we have for each other."[3] This logic, however, can scarcely be said to lend any reasonableness to belief in any divine mind in the sense that it lends some sort of rational support to the belief that a divine intelligence exists.

But there are, I believe, certain unspoken connections, certain processes to belief in divine intelligence, the logical pattern of which seems to be implicit in, and to give greater strength to, that pattern which is called the design argument for the existence of a divine mind. I hope to be able to show that the design argument is a better piece of analogical reasoning if unspoken connections most likely made by the proponents of the argument are incorporated into its logical structure. The unspoken connections I wish to pursue here were first suggested to me by David Hume who in the last book of the

[1] In *Philosophy and Psycho-analysis* (Oxford, 1964), p. 151. By "logic" he means not only the traditional deductive and inductive patterns of reasoning employed to arrive at belief, but also patterns of reasoning employed to decide whether or not to extend the application of a concept. In this extended sense of "logic" Wisdom explores the logic of making decisions about whether or not to attribute intelligence or mind to something other than human beings and animals.

[2] Ibid., p. 162.

[3] Ibid., p. 163-68.

Dialogues Concerning Natural Religion has Philo say that he has only a verbal disagreement with Cleanthes about the degree of design exemplified in nature, and hence about the degree of intelligence required to explain it.[4] Hume does not develop the idea that the design argument somehow involves connecting or associating degrees of design in nature with degrees of intelligence; nor, to my knowledge, has it been developed since.

How, exactly, would such an association work itself into the logic of the design argument, and what sort of evidence could be used to support the association? In what follows I shall argue that the logic of the design argument can actually be strengthened if certain unspoken connections between degrees of design and degrees of intelligence are incorporated into its logical structure. As I shall reconstruct the argument, it will portray a progressive series of different sorts of analogues to the universe, just one of which is an artifact, and each sort of analogue portrayed in the series will reveal a correlation between a degree of design displayed in nature and a degree of intelligence held responsible for it, thus providing rational support for the conclusion that the universe is produced by a being whose intelligence is greater that human. I have chosen to focus my discussion on various formal reconstructions of the design argument in order to drive home the point that the connecting technique I believe to play a part in the argument actually strengthens its inductive form.

The design argument for the existence of a divine intelligence has received many formulations and elaborations in its long and checkered history.[5] Logical criticism of the argument has usually

[4] *Cp.* J. Duerlinger, "The Verbal Dispute in Hume's *Dialogues*" *(Archiv Für Geschichte Der Philosophie,* vol. 53, 1971), for an explication of this claim and one of the many interesting connections the *Dialogues* has with Wisdom's essay on "Gods."

[5] Whether there are many different design arguments or many different versions of the same argument is a function of how vaguely the argument is characterized. I shall be concerned with those arguments or versions of the same argument only insofar as they are interpreted by logicians as being, fundamentally, the sort of argument by analogy I have listed as (1) below. I might point out that recent formulations such as that of F. R. Tennant *(Philosophical Theology,* vol. 2, London, 1930) and that of K. Nelson as reported by M. Diamond *(Contemporary Philosophy and Religious Thought,* New York, 1974) are in effect attempts to overcome Darwinean objections to (1)(b) below rather than to present a formal reconstruction of the argument in the manner I shall attempt here. For the use of (1)(b) as the second premise *cp.* A. Plantinga *(God and Other Minds,* Ithaca, 1967, ch. 4), and N. Pike *(Hume: Dialogues Concerning Natural Religion,* Indianapolis, 1970, pp. 150-57). But *cp.* L. Pearl, "Hume's Criticism of the Argument from Design," *(Monist,* vol. 54, 1970) and T. McPherson *(The Argument From Design,* London, 1972).

been based on the supposition that it is at bottom a simple argument by analogy, which, informally expressed, is

(1)(a) This artifact displays a certain sort of adaptation of means to ends and is produced by an intelligent being.
(b) The universe displays the same sort of adaptation of means to ends.

(c) The universe is produced by an intelligent being.

The principle upon which (1)(c) is inferred from (1)(a) and (1)(b) is that if two things are known to share a property, then, in the absence of further information, it may be inferred that another property of the one will be shared by the other.[6]

If we let A be the property of apparent design, B be the property of being a product of intelligence, *a* be some arbitrarily selected artifact, and *b* be the universe, the following is the simplest formal representation of the design argument.

(2)(a) $Aa \,\&\, Ba$
(b) Ab

(c) Bb

However, a more perspicuous representation of the form of the design argument as it has been traditionally conceived might very well represent the fact that objects of two different classes are being compared, where one of these objects, the universe, is the only member of a class. Thus, we might more accurately represent the form of the argument as

(3)(a) $(\exists x)((x \in \alpha \,\&\, Ax) \,\&\, Bx)$
(b) $(x)(x \in \alpha \supset \sim x \in \beta)$
(c) $A(\iota x)(x \in \beta)$

(d) $B(\iota x)(x \in \beta)$

[6] I shall not be concerned in this paper with the justifiability of our intuitions concerning the relative inductive strengths of the inductive forms I shall have occasion to use. Neither shall I be concerned with the thorny problems surrounding the use of (1)(b) in the argument, except to point out that the sort of adaptation of means to ends which the argument requires is that which does not definitionally imply the existence of an intelligence which adapts the means to the ends. Finally, I shall not address my remarks to problems associated with the argument by analogy to other minds, or, for that matter, to the similarities and differences between this argument and the design argument. I shall assume that the design argument actually proceeds by the comparison of things other than oneself to one another. The manner in which anyone initially connects the ideas of apparent adaptation of means to ends and intelligence will be irrelevant to the claims I shall make.

where α is the class of artifacts and β is the class of universes. (3)(b) is required because we wish to rule out the possibility that the one and only member of β is also a member of α, and so ensure that distinct things are being compared. (3) may be rendered in English as

(4)(a) Some artifact has design and is a product of intelligence.
(b) No artifact is a universe.
(c) The universe has design.

(d) The universe is a product of intelligence.

If we put aside the traditional attacks upon the premises of (4), we must still face the fact that (4) is a rather weak form of inductive argument.

It might be thought that (4) can be strengthened by comparing the universe to all artifacts rather than to some, and that it has the form

(5)(a) $(x)((x \in \alpha \,\&\, Ax) \supset Bx)$
(b) $(x)(x \in \alpha \supset \sim x \in \beta)$
(c) $A(\iota x)(x \in \beta)$

(d) $B(\iota x)(x \in \beta)$

But (5), as it stands, does not give inductive support to any of its substitution instances, since the following argument, which shares its form with (5), has true premises and yet provides no evidence at all that its conclusion is true.

(6)(a) If anything is a bird and is reflecting about the design argument, it can fly.
(b) No bird is a man who taught Ancient Philosophy at the University of Iowa in 1981.
(c) The man who taught Ancient Philosophy at the University of Iowa in 1981 is reflecting about the design argument.

(d) The man who taught Ancient Philosophy at the University of Iowa in 1981 can fly.

Hence, since the form of (5) gives inductive strength to any of its substitution instances only if it gives inductive strength to all of its substitution instances, I conclude that, since (6) is a suitable substitution instance which has no inductive strength, (5) also has no inductive strength.[7]

[7] It might be objected to my charge that an inductive argument can still be valid if most of its substitution instances which have true premises also have true

Since (5) fails as a validating reconstruction because of the possible reference failure of (5)(a), suppose we simply supply the needed reference as follows

(7)(a) $(x)((x \in \alpha \,\&\, Ax) \supset \beta x)$
(b) $(x)(x \in \alpha \supset {\sim} x \in \beta)$
(c) $(\exists x)(x \in \alpha \,\&\, Ax)$
(d) $A(\iota x)(x \in \beta)$

(e) $B(\iota x)(x \in \beta)$

Although (7) is stronger than (3), it is not much stronger, since only one class of objects is still being compared to the universe.

Alvin Plantinga, at first sight, seems to remedy this weakness in his version of the design argument,[8] the form of which I believe is best portrayed as

(8)(a) $(x)((Ax$ & we know whether or not $Bx) \supset Bx)$
(b) $A(\iota x)(x \in \beta)$

(c) $B(\iota x)(x \in \beta)$

Where A is the property of having apparent design, B is the property of being a product of intelligence, and β is the class of universes, (8) can be rendered, informally, as

(9)(a) All things having design and of which we know whether or not they are products of intelligence are products of intelligence.
(b) The universe has design.

(c) The universe is a product of intelligence.

The class of artifacts as the class of comparison is dropped from the argument, and the background information that we do not know of anything which has design and is not a product of intelligence is

conclusions. On this view valid inductive argument forms are to be contrasted to valid deductive argument forms, all of whose substitution instances have true conclusions if their premises are true. Consequently, (6) does not at all show that (5) lacks inductive strength, since to do this I must show that most substitution instances of their form do not have true conclusions when they have true premises. In reply, I can only appeal to my intuition that (6) has no inductive force and the fact that (5) and (6) have the same form. It follows that (5) cannot be given any force by virtue of the form it shares with (6), however one interprets the inductive strength of (5). In any case, it seems pointless to apply the notion of an argument form to inductive inferences if it cannot be used in the same sort of way it is used in the process of evaluating deductive inferences, in particular, to determine the validity of all of its substitution instances.

[8] Op. cit., p. 100.

cleverly incorporated into the argument. However, in light of the criticism I have leveled against (6), it is clear that Plantinga's reformulation requires an existential premise, and should read as

(10)(a) $(x)((Ax \,\&\, \text{we know whether or not } Bx) \supset Bx)$
(b) $(\exists x)(As \,\&\, \text{we know whether or not } Bx)$
(c) $A(\iota x)(x \in \mathfrak{B})$
(d) $B(\iota x)(x \in \mathfrak{B})$

This argument form is intuitively stronger than (7), but its gain in inductive force is made at the expense of a loss in specificity. At first sight this loss seems harmless, for it is assumed that the only functional class of comparison is that of artifacts. But suppose that there are in fact many more classes of comparison which, although not articulated, could be (and perhaps unconsciously are) compared to the universe with respect to their apparent design and being products of intelligence. To be sure, these other classes of comparison can be subsumed under the class of things all of which display design, but the fact that a great number of different classes of things both exhibit apparent design and are products of intelligence could be used to give the design argument even greater logical strength if used in an inductive argument in conjunction with (10)(a) above. Thus, if there are members of different classes of things which, whenever they possess design, are products of intelligence, there is more formal evidence for the conclusion that the universe, since it has design, is a product of intelligence. What is needed to beef up (10) is to specify various classes of comparison whose members both possess the requisite design and are products of intelligence. Are there such things?

In at least one common sense of "product" it can be said that human actions are products of intelligence. But on what grounds would one say that human actions are products of intelligence in this sense? It seems clear that a proponent of the design argument ought to say that it is on the basis of the apparent adaptation of means to ends they display. For if the design of artifacts is the basis upon which it is decided that artifacts are produced by intelligence, the design of human actions (at least the human actions of others) would be the basis upon which it is decided that they are produced by intelligence.

The use of this new analogue, moreover, has an interesting side-effect. It suggests that the design thought to exist in the universe will no longer imply that the universe need be something constructed by intelligence. To be sure, the idea that the motions of the universe are like the actions of an intelligent being (or that the universe is like an intelligent being whose actions bear the mark of its intelligence) may in no way be a superior metaphysical idea to that of the workings of the universe being like the workings of a well-designed artifact, but if the design argument suggests both ideas indiscriminately, its central thrust can be seen to lie in the design thought to be caused in the universe rather than in the specific kind of causal relationship the universe has to its intelligent source. This is perhaps the only advantage, however, since the difficulties which plague the idea that both artifacts and the universe display design seem to be identical to the difficulties which attend the idea that both human actions and the universe display design.

If my suggestion is right, the form of the design argument can be portrayed by

(11)(a) $(x)((Ax \;\&\; \text{we know whether or not } Bx) \supset Bx)$
(b) $(x)((x \in \alpha \,\&\, Ax) \supset Bx)$
(c) $(x)((x \in \beta \,\&\, Ax) \supset Bx$
(d) $(x)(x \in \alpha \supset \sim x \in \beta)$
(e) $(x)((x \in \alpha \vee x \in \beta) \supset \sim x \in \gamma)$
(f) $(\exists x)(x \in \alpha \,\&\, Ax)$
(g) $(\exists x)(x \in \beta \,\&\, Ax)$
(h) $A(\iota x)(x \in \gamma)$

(i) $B(\iota x)(x \in \gamma)$

where α is the class of artifacts, β is the class of human actions, γ is the class of universes, A is the property of apparent design, and B is the property of being a product of intelligence. It is necessary to add (11)(d) to guarantee that two distinct classes of individuals are being compared to the universe in the argument, while (11)(f) and (11)(g) are required to take care of the trivialization problem discussed above.

Although (11) is stronger than (10), it is not much stronger. Can we find a great number of kinds of things which are both ordered in the relevant way and are products of intelligence? Wisdom himself calls attention to such things when he analyzes the problem of determining the reasonableness of belief in divine minds into three components. There are, he thinks, (i) the problem of whether or not any evidence can support belief in any sort of mind, (ii) the problem of determining the extent of the likenesses and differences between (a) the patterns in nature to which the teleologist call attention and (b) "the human and animal patterns" on the basis of which we say that there are human and animal minds, and (iii) the problem of deciding whether or not the likenesses and differences found to exist between these warrant the patterns in nature being called mind-patterns.[9] The second problem Wisdom mentions implies that he himself may think that belief in animal minds or (more exactly) animal intelligence is a factor in the logic of belief in divine intelligence. I want to suggest that it does play a significant part in that logic, although on the level of unspoken connections.

It is a fact that men for ages have attributed various degrees of intelligence to some animals. But on what basis has a given degree of intelligence been attributed to them? It is, surely, something about what these animals make and how they act which is responsible for the degree of intelligence attributed to them. That the proponents of the design argument would call this something a degree of design is quite probable, since they assume that design and intelligence are linked in such a way that we are justified in inferring that what has design is caused by intelligence. If this is the assumption upon which the argument is built, it would seem to hold *mutatis mutandis* for the cases in which a degree of intelligence is ascribed to certain animals; for ascriptions of a certain degree of intelligence to these animals, on this view, would be based on a similar degree of design attributed to their products or actions. Man has believed for ages not only that he is more intelligent than animals but also that some animals are more intelligent than others. The recent discovery that chimpanzees can be taught to use a sign language is surprising only insofar as the extent of their intelligence has not been realized. The relative abilities of animals to use tools, communicate with one another, and solve problems have been studied scientifically since the turn of the century, most such research being aimed at determining just how intelligent different species of animals are. If the proponents of the design argument are correct about how one determines whether any being (other than oneself) is intelligent, it would seem that even these researchers judge the degree of intelligence of animals on the basis of the degree of design displayed in their actions or products. In any case, it seems obvious that man in fact has a tendency to extend the application of the concept of mind on the basis of such similarities. It is such a tendency, a sort of cognitive undercurrent, which draws anything perceived to be like what humans do or make in a certain way into the stream of things intelligently designed, which accounts for extended uses of the concept. The tendency has been often studied, but the

[9]Op. cit., p. 151-52.

precise way in which it ties into the design argument has not to my knowledge been explored. What has not been appreciated is that the tendency operates according to a logic, a logic which leads one to the belief in an intelligence greater than human if he believes himself to have discerned greater than human design in the universe.[10]

For the sake of simplifying my discussion I shall assume that we may distinguish at least five degrees for any quality. These five degrees we can mark off with a special notation. Let "A^1," "A^2," "A^3," "A^4," and "A^5," for instance, represent an ascending sequence of degrees of apparent design. The notation we happen to use is to some extent a matter of convenience, and can be altered to reflect greater and lesser numbers of ascertainable differences of degrees of a quality. To simplify my notation, I shall assume that the design possessed by the members of a class of things are possessed by all members to the same degree. Let "Cxy" represent the relation of something causing something, and "I^1," "I^2," etc., represent an ascending sequence of degrees of intelligence. Then "$(x)(\exists y)((x \in \alpha \,\&A^1x) \supset (Cyx\&I^1y))$" will represent the statement that all artifacts which have a given degree of apparent design are caused by a certain degree of intelligence, and "$(\exists y)(Cy(\imath x)(x \in \gamma)\&I^1y)$" will represent the statement that the universe is caused by that same degree of intelligence. The resultant form for the design argument will be rather complicated, since so many analogues to the universe can now be cited. I shall limit my formalization to just two analogues so the reader can get some idea of its structure.

(12)(a) $(x)(\exists y)((Ax$ & we know whether or not $(Cyx\&Iy)) \supset (Cyx\&Iy))$

(b) $(x)(\exists y)((x \in \alpha \,\&A^1x) \supset (Cyx\&I^1y))$

---

[10] Whether or not the logic of which I speak can ultimately be assimilated to, or developed into, our existing body of knowledge of logic is a nice question. I shall try only to make a first stab at a symbolization for it as it underlies the design argument. I shall not attempt to devise conceptual tools precise enough to articulate how statements of the degree to which something possesses a quality enter into valid inferences. Nor shall I deal with the ontological presuppositions of this logic. A logic which explains inferences which trade on statements of the degree to which something possesses a given quality presupposes the existence of a quality which is possessed by different individuals to different degrees. In effect, it assumes the existence of not only determinate, but also determinable, qualitites. What I shall call two degrees of one and the same quality some philosophers would claim are in fact two distinct qualities because their instances are not exactly alike. The issues at stake in this challenge to the existence of determinable qualities are knotty and cannot be dealt with here.

(c) $(x)(\exists y)((x \in \beta \& A^2x) \supset (Cyx \& I^2y))$
(d) $(x)(x \in \alpha \supset \sim x \in \beta)$
(e) $(x((x \in \alpha \vee x \in \beta)) \supset \sim x \in y)$
(f) $(\exists x)(x \in \alpha \& A^1x)$
(g) $(\exists x)(x \in \beta \& A^2x)$
(h) $A^5(\iota x)(x \in \gamma)$

(i) $(\exists y)(Cy(\iota x)(x \in \gamma) \& I^5y)$

The design argument, so construed, will be an inference to the existence of something with a greater than human intelligence if we identify α as the class of animal actions or products and β as the class of human actions or products, and γ as the class of universes. That the design argument is an inference to the existence of such an intelligence has long been recognized, and this formulation makes this fact explicit. (12) is itself not nearly so strong as the form the design argument might take, since in proportion as the number of premises of like kind can be incorporated into the argument, and in proportion as symbolism is introduced and used to depict a larger range of correlated degrees of design and intelligence, the argument's strength can be increased. Needless to say, the degree of formal inductive support the design argument so construed might provide for its conclusion, if its premises are true, is remarkable. Anyone who believed all of these premises to be true would also believe himself to have a rather powerful argument.

To claim that something like (12) better represents the logic of the design argument than do the alternatives I have considered is not to say that any proponent of the argument actually presents the argument in that form or that he is aware that it can be put into that form. It is to say that something like (12) is a form of the argument which explains better than the alternatives both how its preferred conclusion is supported and what conceptual connections it has to beliefs about the various degrees of intelligence possessed by living creatures. My reconstruction reveals "unspoken connections" among beliefs in human, animal, and divine intelligence. The argument, I am suggesting, is partially grounded in two pervasive practices, that of attributing intelligence to a great number of different sorts of things which produce what the teleologist would call design, and that of attributing degrees of intelligence, proportional to the degrees of design thought to be possessed by a great number of different sorts of things, to what are taken to be the causes of these degrees of design. When the teleologist looks to his experiences of the world to find evidence for the existence of an intelligence greater than human, even if he is consciously aware only of an analogy between artifacts and the universe, his awareness of this analogy is not unaffected by his unconscious awareness of many others, the cumulative effect of which is the belief that greater degrees of design require greater degrees of intelligence as their causes.

I have worked the above unspoken connections into the formalization of the design argument because I share John Wisdom's belief that "... in order to settle in ourselves what weight we shall attach to someone's confidence or attitude we not only ask him for his reasons but also look for unconscious reasons both good and bad."[11] To be sure, my reconstruction of the design argument does not show it to be a good argument for the belief in a divine intelligence, but it does call attention to important features of its logic which one ought to include in the over-all assessment of its reasonableness, features which reveal its analogical structure to be rather formidable. I have attempted to portray this structure in the notation of symbolic logic, but whether or not I have been, or anyone else can be, successful in this enterprise, that structure most certainly exists and its role in the logic of belief in a divine intelligence cannot be ignored. In any case, I hope to have called the reader's attention to a previously unnoticed rational pattern in the garden in which we live and think.

JAMES DUERLINGER.

THE UNIVERSITY OF IOWA.

[11] Op. cit., p. 162.

MARX'S CRITIQUE OF PHILOSOPHICAL LANGUAGE*

Though Marx never systematically developed a theory of language, he often commented in his early pre-1848 writings on the role of language in traditional philosophies and ideologies. In this paper, I wish to examine Marx's critique of philosophical and ideological language. The first part is devoted to sketching the origins of Marx's ideas on language as influenced by the radical change in conceptions of language in Germany in the late 18th century and by Hegel's treatment of language and consciousness in his *Phenomenology of Spirit* in particular.

The second part of the paper analyzes the two basic strategies Marx used in his earliest critical writings to criticize the "languages" of philosophy and ideology. One is directly influenced by Feuerbach's own translation or demystification of the language of theology; the other, lesser known technique, by Hegel's dialectical treatment of language and alienation, particularly in his portrayal of Culture *(Bildung)* in the *Phenomenology*. The third part examines at length Marx's (and now Engels') comments in *The German Ideology* on the role and use of language in furthering the ideological purposes of the ruling class. Marx further refines and develops the two strategies he used earlier to attack philosophical and ideological language.

The final part of the paper will briefly extrapolate Marx's own position on the nature of the proper language for philosophy and the social sciences. In this context, it becomes clear that Marx would have rejected later "Marxist" efforts to categorize language as something strictly class-bound (i.e., part of the "superstructure") which passively mirrors an underlying material reality (or "substructure"). Consequently, Marx did not preach (or await) the development of a totally new language for philosophy, nor even a radical change ("break") in the nature of such a language with the advent of a Communist society. Indeed, such a "break" cannot be found between his own early "humanistic" writings and his later "scientific" ones.

---

*Earlier drafts of this paper were read at the colloquia of the Philosophy Departments of the Hebrew University and the University of Tel Aviv. I wish to thank the participants for their ideas and suggestions.

I

Until the mid-18th century, the prevailing conception of languge was that, if properly refined, it could and would reflect the rational core of reality. Since there is only one "reason"—one universal and necessary set of truths—one language could presumably completely express these truths. Descartes' notion of a *lingua universalis* and Liebniz' extended attempts at a universal logic—a *characteristica universalis*—were predicated on this view of the nature of truth and language. One natural language may be more *advanced* (or more *primitive* in the logical sense) than another, but all were on the same line of development towards (or away from) a certain set of truths which were universal and identical.

While there were exceptions to this view (for example, Giambattista Vico who died in 1744), most philosophers—rationalist and empiricist alike—saw the properly constituted language as a "true witness to the unity of reason."[1] People argued over and speculated on the exact nature of this language and how it expressed or reflected reality, but the underlying assumption was rarely questioned. In search of such an elusive goal, many were willing to jettison natural languages as inadequate. Liebniz, who more than any other philosopher of the modern period concerned himself with the problem of language, apparently rejected all natural languages in his search for a universal one, hoping to the end of his days to invent, if not discover (e.g., in the hexagrams of the *I Ching)*, the appropriate set of symbols which would be the "Open Sesame" to understanding as well as actually uncovering and deductively proving the one set of universal and necessary truths.

About the middle of the 18th century, some thinkers began to reject such a view of language taking, in Ernst Cassirer's words, "an increasing interest in the *individuality*, the spiritual specificity of . . . particular languages."[2] Great importance was increasingly attached to the role of natural languages in expressing the "genius" of a people *(Volk)*. Each national language, for example, was seen as having its own distinctive "spirit"—its own deep connection to the people who spoke it. In a word, whereas the "classic" view often celebrated what all languages had in common, the later one increasingly focussed on what they did not. It is hard to disentangle the causes of this view

[1] E. Cassirer, *The Philosophy of Symbolic Forms*, trans. R. Mannheim, 3 vols. (New Haven: Yale University Press, 1953), 1:129.

[2] Ibid., p. 139.

which reached its peak in the early 19th century with Fichte contending the "the borders of a nation . . . are determined by language."[3] The rise of nationalism certainly played a role in fostering this radical change in the conception of language. Such a view fitted in well with Romanticism, which saw language as an expression of emotion, feeling, spontaneity—even subjectivity. The dynamics of speech—spoken language—now were championed against a view which saw language chiefly as a theoretical (usually written) instrument in the pursuit of intellectual(ized) truth. In Cassirer's words, "The emphasis in the study of language shifted from logic to psychology and aesthetics."[4]

However, if there are many languages, it would seem to follow that there are many "truths," thus undermining "the unity of reason." In other words, how are the *particularistic* implications of this new view of language compatible with the premise of *universal* truth? The answer was found by rethinking the notion of "universal"—it was no longer

> conceived as a self-contained reality, as the abstract unity of a genus juxtapose to its individuals, but as a unity which exists only in a totality of specific individuals. This totality and the law, the inner relationship expressed in it: these have become the true universal.[5]

This change in the notion of "universal" led to abandoning the search for a basic original language. "The true universal 'essence' of language was no longer sought in abstraction from differentiation, but in the *totality* of differentiations."[6] This totality was eventually interpreted in an historical sense—i.e., the development of man's language, like the development of truth, was an historical process which integrated the individual stages into a universal whole. This more dynamic view saw each language not as a finished, cultural product or a particular national spinoff of an underlying universal tongue, but as an ongoing, self-creating *activity*. In the words of the most famous proponent of this view, Wilhelm von Humboldt, "language is not a work *(ergon)*, but an activity *(energeia)*."[7] To be sure, this activity was essentially theoretical and evinced in the ideal spirit of a collective folk group.

This new approach to language and its relationship to philosophical truth finds its most systematic expression in the writings

---

[3]K. Popper, *The Open Society and Its Enemies,* 2 vols., 5th rev. ed. (Routledge and Kegan Paul, 1966), 2:53.

[4]Cassirer, 1:141.

[5]Ibid., p. 155.

[6]Ibid.

[7]Ibid., p. 161.

of G. W. Hegel. His dialectical method was the perfect way to relate and integrate the historical parts to the absolute whole. Definite romantic and national elements are also interwoven into his ideas on language, as well as other themes characteristic of this 19th century approach.[8] Quite early in his career (1805), Hegel declared that it was his intention to "try to teach philosophy to speak German." He likened his endeavor to Luther and his translation of the Bible.[9] If philosophical thinking could be communicated in a natural, living language, then philosophy no longer would be the province of an elite group, using terminology, symbols or language that an ordinary man cannot understand.[10] Such a demystification would bring about critical changes in the consciousness of its readers. The intellectual liberation of a people can begin only when it learns to think in its own language, not an ancient or foreign one. This began for the Germans when they stopped praying and reading the Bible in Latin, and will be consummated when they learn to philosophize in German as well.[11]

Karl Marx adapted this notion that a people needs its own language to develop and raise its consciousness towards genuine liberation. But for him, the "people" to be liberated were not the Germans, but the proletariat. They had to develop their own language—initially by demystifying the distortions of the ruling

---

[8]For a detailed treatment of these themes in Hegel's earlier writings, see the author's *Language in the Philosophy of Hegel* (The Hague: Mouton, 1973), pp. 60-73.

[9]Such translations are "the greatest present that can be given to a people; for a people is barbarous and does not consider the excellent things it knows as its own property until it gets to know them in its own language." Walter Kaufmann, *Hegel: Reinterpretation, Texts and Commentary* (Garden City, N.Y.: Doubleday, 1965), p. 314. "Hegel to J. H. Voss," *Briefe von und an Hegel,* ed. J. Hoffmeister, 4 vols. (Hamburg: F. Meiner, 1952), 1:99-100.

[10]Hegel often stressed the need for breaking down the "partition between the language of philosophy and that of ordinary consciousness: we have to overcome the reluctance against thinking what we are familiar with." W. Wallace, *Prolegomena to the Study of Hegel's Philosophy and Especially of His Logic,* 2d ed. rev. (Oxford: Oxford University Press, 1894), p. 8; J. Hoffmeister, *Dokumente zu Hegels Entwicklung* (Stuttgart: Frommanns Verlag, 1936), p. 371.

[11]The appropriation of philosophy in one's own language was not something that Hegel saw as a pecularily German necessity. In response to an inquiry about teaching at a Dutch university, Hegel wrote that he would be willing to begin lecturing in Latin—as was then the custom in Holland—but he continued, "If you would permit me to depart from this practice, I would like eventually to lecture in the national language, for I truly believe that genuine appropriation of a science requires that one possess it in one's native language." *Briefe,* 1:299.

ideological languages of philosophy, politics, and religion—with a view to liberating not only themselves, or any national group, but all of mankind. Just as the language of a "people" as a nation is a product and index of its intellectual development—its "spirit" or "genius" for Herder or Hegel—so the language of the "people" as the ruling class is a product of its characteristic material development for Marx. Marx will talk occasionally of the "language of the bourgeoisie," but he uses the traditional expression "language of a people" even when it is quite clear that he is not talking of a nation, but a class.

Also, like Hegel, Marx allowed for no ultimate distinction between the technical language of philosophy and ordinary language. Attempts to create a terminology which pertains to its own exclusive intellectual domain reflects the increasing isolation—one might say "esotericization"—of philosophy. Theorizing must be done in a language whose terms and ideas are anchored in a given concrete reality, so that it can be understood by all, not just the intellectually or materially privileged. For this reason, Marx would have rejected, like Hegel, the notion that such a language could be a mathematical or artificial one as Leibniz hoped. It is clear that in his use of the word "language," Marx is not interested in developing a *new* language—natural or artificial—for the proletariat; rather its "new" language will be a "purified" version of the old ones (i.e., German, French, English, etc.).

Implicit throughout this period, therefore, was the assumption that each stage of man's development, each type of consciousness, each "determinate form of Spirit," if you will, has an appropriate or indicative language. Nowhere is this theme of the connection between consciousness and language more important or more explicit than in Hegel's *Phenomenology of Spirit*. The "languages" used at different stages in this work constitute a powerful, yet subtle instrument for understanding the experiences consciousness undergoes as well as the dialectical relationship between them. Hegel is dealing here with concrete, existential situations, as they are actually experienced by each type of consciousness, with all the emotion, irony, and poignancy such situations entail.[12] The most obvious example of this role of

[12] One recent commentator of the *Phenomenology* has in fact said of Hegel's language what many have usually ascribed first (and often exclusively!) to Marx. ". . . Hegel had to employ a new vocabulary. . . . Hegel turned in reaction [to the Cartesian model] . . . to the language of intense emotion. Thinking was now an activity charged with feeling. It reveals as such changes do, a revolutionary temper.

language—spoken language—is the universalizing power of talking in the very first chapter of the *Phenomenology:* "Sense-Certainty."[13] The idea that different ways of speaking reflect different social, political, and even epistemological situations is one that Hegel develops in detail in the *Phenomenology.* Each type of consciousness in effect has its own "language."

One section of this work in particular elaborates extensively on the "languages" used in the alienated society of "Culture." This large section, entitled "Self-Alienated Spirit: Culture" *("Der sich entfremdete Geist; Bildung"),*[14] is the first place where Hegel deals systematically with the phenomena of social alienation. Though most commentators on Marx's early writings stress the influence of other sections of the *Phenomenology,* in particular the dialectic of the Master and Servant, it is clear that Marx owes much to this section of the book,[15] as well as to the one following: "Spirit that is certain of itself: Morality" *("Der seiner selbst gewisse Geist. Die Moralität").*[16]

In the first section, initially, in Hegel's words, "alienaton takes

---

Hegel's indifference to the classical distinction between passion and reason emerges at once in his choice of words. A great part of the novelty of the *Phenomenology* is due to his use of the language of emotions to discuss the work of reason." J. Shklar, *Freedom and Independence: A Study of the Political Ideas of Hegel's Phenomenology of Mind* (Cambridge: Cambridge University Press, 1976), pp. 4-5.

[13] *Hegel's Phenomenology of Spirit,* trans. A. V. Miller (Oxford: Oxford University Press, 1977), pp. 58-66; G. W. F. Hegel, *Phänomenologie des Geistes,* ed. J. Hoffmeister (Hamburg: F. Meiner, 1948), pp. 79-89.

[14] *Phenomenology,* pp. 294-363; *Phänomenologie,* pp. 347-422.

[15] Among the few interpreters to acknowledge the importance of this section of the *Phenomenology* for Marx's (1844) *Economic and Philosophical Manuscripts* are the editors of *Writings of the Young Marx on Philosophy and Society* (Garden City, N.Y.: Doubleday, 1967), Loyd D. Easton and Kurt H. Guddat. In their introduction, they say, "Marx finds man alienated from himself both in the process of labor and in its product which belongs to 'other men.' In this respect, he particularly leans on Hegel's *Phenomenology of Spirit* (ch. VI, B, i) where wealth and state power are viewed as alienations overcome in the movement of experience towards absolute knowledge. Marx warmly endorses Hegel's great insight that man is the historical product of his own work in a process of alienation and its resolution." Ibid., p. 18.

Though Marx was quick to attack the mystification of Hegel's *Phenomenology* and to see it as "the most conservative philosophy," he nevertheless thought it embodied many insights into human relations. ". . . Hegel's *Phänomenologie,* in spite of its speculative original sin, gives in many instances the elements of a true description of human relations. . . ." *The Holy Family* in *Marx-Engels Collected Works,* 4 (New York: International Publishers, 1975), 193 (hereafter referred to as *"CW"); Die Heilige Familie* in *Marx-Engels Werke,* 2 (Berlin: Dietz, 1958), 205 (hereafter referred to as *"MEW").*

[16] *Phenomenology,* pp. 364-409; *Phänomenologie,* pp. 423-72.

place solely in language,"[17] that is, it is apparent only in the *language* used; consciousness itself is not yet aware of the gap between its language and social/political realities. Marx adopts and adapts this idea and shows what happens when social, political, and economic theory (viz., his notion of ideology) no longer squares with present material circumstances, though people continue to believe—and want others to believe—that such theories are still true. If this condition continues, man's ideas and languages (for Hegel, the alienated man in culture; for Marx, the philosopher and ideologist), becoming more and more detached or "ruptured" from reality, develop into a world of their own.[18] Marx, as we shall see, thinks such a condition true to the speculative philosophies of his day, as well as to other ideologies.

Throughout these sections of the *Phenomenology,* Hegel illustrates the many ways—the many "languages"—used to mislead people, to avoid committment, or to be hypocritical. For example, in the final section on Morality, Hegel examines the problem of language and moral action. Briefly, the problem is that for an action to have moral significance, and not to be done arbitrarily or selfishly, such actions must be recognized as grounded in the universal claim of *duty* (in the Kantian sense). This is possible only if the agent explicitly and publicly so states; in this way, the moral action will be understood and recognized as such by others. Language here becomes all important once more; Hegel calls it the actual form of Spirit *("das Dasein des Geistes").*[19] In fact, since the intention and the statement are what count, "what is valid . . . is not the *action* as an *existence,* but the conviction that it is a duty; and this is made actual in language."[20] Such a view of morality of course easily leads to hypocrisy *(Heuchelei);* the language of duty and conscience becomes only that.[21] "Duty" becomes a matter of words and expressions of fine

[17] *Phenomenology,* p. 308; *Phänomenologie,* p. 362.

[18] Hegel calls such language the "language of rupture"—*"die Sprache der Zerrissenheit"*—which, as *the* language of self-consciousness estranged from its cultural world, is "the authentic existent Spirit of this entire world of culture." *Phenomenology,* p. 316; *Phänomenologie,* p. 370. Other examples of the languages used in these sections are "the language of ethos-oriented Spirit" *("die Sprache der sittliche Geist")* and "the language of flattery" *("die Sprache der Schmeichelei").* Hegel uses the word "language" *("Sprache")* quite often throughout the *Phenomenology* to describe the different linguistic situations of consciousness; Marx uses it in the same way. See section IV below.

[19] *Phenomenology,* pp. 395, 405; *Phänomenologie,* p. 458, 468.

[20] *Phenomenology,* p. 396; *Phänomenologie,* p. 459.

[21] *Phenomenology,* p. 504; *Phänomenologie,* p. 468.

sentiments. Marx's attack on the hypocrisy of bourgeois morality and language as well as his lifelong sensitivity to the different ways language, written as well as spoken, develops its own dynamic and consequently can be used to distort reality and mislead people is clearly influenced by these sections of the *Phenomenology*.

From what we have seen of Hegel's conception and use of language, it is clear that he saw it, like Humboldt, as a dynamic, though theoretic, activity. In his Jena writings, Hegel explicitly talks of consciousness' nature being characterized by its sign-making activity and of language as the means for helping consciousness gain an awareness of its own identity by asserting itself in the face of other consciousnesses.[22] Marx also stresses the importance of language as an activity, but as a practical, not only theoretical, one.

II

In dealing with the ideological and philosophical language of his predecessors and contemporaries, Marx perfected two basic strategies. One could be called direct, inspired by Feuerbach's transformational method; the other, an indirect, dialectical one, which gained its inspiration from Hegel. Marx used both, together and separately, from the very first of his critical writings.

The first strategy, which I shall call the "translative" method, was an excellent means for realizing a key element in Marx's early philosophical program: viz., to make the language of philosophy accessible and understandable to all. The opening sections of his first critical work—his *Critique of Hegel's Doctrine of the State* (1843)—are devoted to an attack on Hegel for unnecessarily mystifying political theory, by positing an unseen Idea or Spirit as the underlying *explanans* for specific political processes and institutions. Rather, Marx showed, the subject (in both the general *and* grammatical senses) of one's analysis should be these matters themselves; they are the basis for a valid theoretical explanation of the origins and development of specific political and social institutions.

> The crux of the matter is that Hegel everywhere makes the Idea into the subject, while the genuine, real subject, such as 'political sentiment,' is turned into the predicate. The development, however, always takes place on the side of the predicate.[23]

---

[22] *Jenaer Systementwürfe I,* eds. K. Düsing and H. Kimmerle, in *G. W. F. Hegel: Gesammelte Werke,* 6 (Hamburg: F. Meiner, 1975), 286ff.

[23] *Karl Marx: Early Writings,* intro. Lucio Colletti; trans. R. Livingston and G. Benton (London: Penguin, 1975), p. 65 (hereafter referred to as "*EW*"); *Karl*

Throughout this *Critique,* Marx comments at length on many passages in Hegel's *Philosophy of Right* in order to demystify them, demonstrating great sensitivity to the language as well as to the logic of Hegel's system. His critique is based on Ludwig Feuerbach's "transformational" method, a method which Feuerbach used with great success in order to show that the predicates or attributes we usually ascribe to God are nothing but projections, "objectifications," or transformations of specific, concrete, very human predicates. Hence the actual subject of religion is not God, but man. As Feuerbach demystified religion by discovering the secret of its language, so Marx wanted to do the same for political theory.[24]

Feuerbach translated religious language to liberate man from his deepest illusions, but such a liberation was theoretical. For Marx, genuine emancipation was possible only if such theory itself becomes a practical force. In his words, "theory . . . becomes a material force once it has gripped the masses."[25] This can happen only when man sees himself—and not God or "Spirit"—as the active subject of religion and history: "for man, the root is man himself."[26] But to gain this insight, the language of theory had to be demystified and translated so that the "masses" could understand it.

As Marx's thought developed, he became more and more aware of the various ways in which the language of theory—philosophical, political, economic—was as mystified or distorted as the language of religion was so obviously to him and many of his contemporaries. Indeed, Marx admitted a few years later that his *own* philosophical language at this time misled his contemporaries. *They* thought he was still simply theorizing like Feuerbach, but *he* claims that his "theory" in these writings had material implications as well. On hindsight, Marx saw himself as already going beyond Feuerbach even though he continued to use his terminology because he was examin-

---

Marx: Frühe Schriften. Volume I, eds. H.-J. Lieber and P. Furth (Stuttgart: Cotta, 1962), p. 266 (hereafter referred to as *"FS").*

[24] In a letter from the same period, Marx says, "The reform of consciousness consists *entirely* in making the world aware of its own consciousness, in arousing it from its dream of itself, in *explaining* its own actions to it. Like Feuerbach's critique of religion, our whole aim can only be to translate religious and political problems into their self-conscious human form. Our program must be: the reform of consciousness not through dogmas but by analysing mystical consciousness obscure to itself, whether it appear in religious or political form. . . ." *EW,* p. 209; *FS,* pp. 449-50.

[25] *EW,* p. 251; *FS,* p. 497.

[26] *EW,* p. 251; *FS,* p. 497.

ing "actual material premises as such" and hence developing a critical attitude towards the earthly world—not just the heavenly one.[27]

Whether or not Marx at this point was indeed doing *more* than simply translating the mystifying language of religion or politics into ordinary language in order to "explain consciousness' own actions to it," he believed with Feuerbach that the very act of translation—of demystification of language—was a crucial one.[28] Such a step would enable people to understand their actual condition so as to eventually emancipate themselves from it. Indeed, even after Marx broke with Feuerbach, he continued to use his style of "translation"—often on the master himself![29]

The other strategy that Marx developed to make people aware of the distorted language of philosophy and political economy used an indirect, dialectical method. Feuerbach's transformational method,

---

[27]"Owing to the fact that Feuerbach showed the religious world as an illusion of the earthly world—a world which in his writing appears merely as a *phrase*—German theory too was confronted with the question which he left unanswered: how did it come about that people 'got' these illusions 'into their heads'? Even for the German theoreticians this question paved the way to the materialistic view of the world, a view which is *not without premises,* but which empirically observes the actual material premises as such and for that reason is, for the first time, *actually* a critical view of the world. This path was already indicated in the *Deutsche-Französische Jahrbücher*—in the *Einleitung zur Kritik der Hegelschen Rechtsphilosophie* and *Zur Judenfrage.* But since at that time this was done in philosophical phraseology, the traditionally occurring philosophical expressions such as 'human essence,' 'species,' etc., gave the German theoreticians the desired reason for misunderstanding the real trend of thought and believing that here again it was a question merely of giving a new turn to their worn-out theoretical garment. *The German Ideology* (hereafter referred to as *"GI"), CW:* 5, 236; *Die Deutsche Ideologie* (hereafter referred to as *"DI"), MEW* 3: 217-18.

[28]This is exactly how Feuerbach saw his project in his major work, *The Essence of Christianity.* In his Preface to the Second Edition, he says, "My work represents an *authentic translation* of the Christian religion from the oriental languages of images into straightforward, intelligible German. Indeed, my work does not wish to accomplish anything more than a faithfully, sense-oriented translation, or to put it non-metaphorically, an *empirical* or *historico-philosophical analysis* of the Christian religion designed to resolve its enigmas." *The Fiery Brook: Selected Writings of Ludwig Feuerbach,* trans. Zawar Hanfi (Garden City, N.Y.: Doubleday, 1972), pp. 251-52.

One writer describes the history of Left Hegelianism in the 1830's and 1840's as a "process in which Hegel's speculative and mystical categories were translated into the language of everyday experience and common sense." N. Lobkowicz, "Karl Marx and Max Stirner," in *Demythologizing Marxism* (The Hague: M. Nijhoff, 1969), p. 83.

[29]"Moses Hess and Marx began translating Feuerbach's still 'religious' anthropology into the language of socialism." Ibid., p. 84.

which Marx used to great effect, is often incorporated in this approach. Marx, however, thought it was not enough to simply *translate* one level of discourse into another in order to explain it (i.e., Feuerbach's basic rationale for his approach);[30] it might be more effective instead to actually *use* it. To appreciate the condition of alienated man, for example, it is not enough to explain it away: it must be experienced, suffered, so that it can be genuinely criticized and ultimately transcended in reality. One way this condition can be experienced as it *is,* is by pointing up the gap between the distorted, alienated language at hand and an undistorted, direct, human one. Quite early in his writings (1843), Marx uses this figure of two languages, as I shall call it, to great effect. The poignancy he evokes is apparent.

> The only comprehensible language we have is the language our possessions use together. We would not understand a human language and it would remain ineffectual. From the one side, such a language would be felt to be begging, imploring and hence *humiliating.* It could be used only with feelings of shame or debasement. From the other side, it would be received as *impertinence* or *insanity* and so rejected. We are so estranged from our human essence that the direct language of man strikes us as an *offense against the dignity of man,* whereas the estranged language of objective values appears as the justified, self-confident self-acknowledged dignity of man incarnate.[31]

Here Marx clearly correlates the language of possessions and property—that is, the language where we estrange or *objectify* ourselves in what we own—with the "estranged language of *objective* values." Man's relation to his values (in effect to his very nature as a man—his "dignity") is the same as to his property, and both are expressed in the same type of language. This estranged language is contrasted by Marx with some other "human," "direct" one.

---

[30] "For what Marx attempts with respect to political economy is, in effect, a reduction program—a translation from one discourse to another, from that which expresses to that which comprehends, from political economy to philosophical anthropology. The language of the economists is to be translated into the language of Feuerbach. To do so will be to *explain* political economy . . . Following Feuerbach, Marx's critical program supposes that the reduction of one discourse to another is tantamount to the reduction of one level of experience to another." A. Levine, "Alienation as Heteronomy," *Philosophical Forum,* 8 (2-4): 262.

I think this description is good as far as the Feuerbachian strategy is concerned, but to talk of the "reduction" of one experience to another without mentioning the dialectical and historical development essential to the process of arriving at, and understanding, the relationship between these two experiences is to ignore a further, yet essential step in Marx's program.

[31] *EW,* pp. 276-77; Ergänzungsband, Erster Teil, *MEW* (Berlin: Dietz, 1968), p. 461.

In the section of the *Phenomenology of Spirit* mentioned above, "Self-Alienated Spirit: Culture," Hegel gives several vivid examples where consciousness' language is not at one with, or genuinely descriptive of, its actual circumstances—resulting in pathetic situations, not unlike Marx's example above. What is important here is that, according to Hegel, only by first experiencing such extreme alienation in one's very language can consciousness begin to gain the necessary detachment or perspective to become truly aware of its situation. Indeed, the whole purpose of this stage of "Spirit" in the *Phenomenology* (and in Hegel's theory of "education of Spirit" *[Bildung]* in general) is for self-consciousness to gain such awareness of its alienation, so that it may now transcend it.[32]

Besides simply contrasting two different modes of discourse in order to genuinely comprehend man's present estranged condition, Marx himself will often use the contemporary mode in order to transcend it. In other words, not every distorted or mystified language should (or could) be reduced to a human language by simple translation in order to understand it. A greater awareness of contemporary man's condition as well as the solution to this condition can be gained if one can see how the latter can (and historically *does)* arise out of the former. Such an approach gives Marx an opportunity to make excellent use of Hegel's dialectical method in the *Phenomenology* where consciousness itself must experience and express its condition *in extremis* in order to overcome it. The literary and dramatic advantages of this dialectical approach are not lost on Marx either.

An excellent example of this technique is found in the now famous (1844) *Economic and Philosophic Manuscripts.* It is not mere coincidence that Marx used the dialectical method particularly in the sections on the origins and development of alienated labor, the most elaborate and detailed of his writings on the phenomenon of alienation. In all matters dialectical, the *form* of the exposition is essential to presenting its *content.* Marx begins his discussion of alienated labor by saying:

> We have started out from the premises of political economy. We have accepted its language and its laws. . . . From political economy itself, using its own words, we have shown that the worker sinks to the level of a commodity, and moreover the most wretched commodity of all.[33]

---

[32] For Hegel, this is ultimately possible only in some form of religion (viz., the realm of "Absolute Spirit"), while for (the later) Marx it is possible only by understanding one's material conditions and consciously controlling them.

[33] *EW,* p. 322; *FS,* p. 559.

Rather than translate the capitalistic language of the bourgeois economists, or even contrast it with a "more human" one, Marx here allows such language "to speak for itself." In this way, the contradictions expressed by such a language can be seen for themselves and the solution—viz., the *Aufhebung* of the institution of private property—can be understood as dialectically arising out of the extreme conditions created by its very existence. Such an approach requires, both substantively and stylistically, that the theories of the political economists under discussion "tell it like it is," rather than dress up their exposition in empty moralizing and false pretensions. Marx therefore welcomed those economic theorists who did not "humanize" or moralize their expositions of how capitalism functions. It was, Marx says, "A great advance by Ricardo, Mill, etc., on Smith and Say, to declare the *existence* of the human being—the greater or lesser productivity of the commodity—to be *indifferent* and even *harmful* [to production]."[34] By spinning out the logical implications of the development of capitalism, the picture will be sharpened and the full force of its estrangement from humanity will become apparent to all.

> Not only does political economy become increasingly *cynical* from Smith through Say to Ricardo, Mill, etc., . . . the latter also become more estranged—consciously estranged—from man than their predecessors. But this is *only* because their science develops more logically and more truly.[35]

Marx in his treatment of alienation follows the same road that such theorists did in treating the problems of political economy: let it "speak its own language" so that the situation is made clear. If such a "language" does not appear to have a meaningful relationship to the concerns of traditional morality, it is because "it is inherent in the very nature of estrangement that each sphere imposes upon me a different and contrary standard; one standard for morality, one for political economy, and so on."[36] Thus one cannot accuse such thinkers of being amoral in their theories, because, as Marx continues, "Ricardo allows political economy to speak its own language. If this language is not that of morality, it is not the fault of Ricardo."[37] Marx in effect adopted the same strategy in his *own* exposition as he approvingly attributed to Ricardo and others,[38] but of

[34] *EW*, p. 336; *FS*, p. 577.
[35] *EW*, p. 343; *FS*, p. 587.
[36] *EW*, p. 362; *FS*, p. 614.
[37] *EW*, p. 362-63; *FS*, p. 614.
[38] Ricardo's cynicism in particular was a constant source of satisfaction to Marx

course with a view to its being dialectically *aufgehoben.*

III

Marx continues his criticism of philosophical language in *The German Ideology,* a work written jointly with Engels,[39] but it is now grounded in a materialist conception of society and history. The problem of philosophical language becomes part of the problem of ideological language in general. Marx's conception of language in part explains and is in part explained by his notion of ideology. Nowhere else in the Marxist *corpus* is so much space devoted to explaining and exemplifying the concept of ideology. The same can be said for Marx's ideas on language: *The German Ideology* is the *only* work where he directly concerns himself with the problem of language and disusses it in a systematic context.

It is striking to note that in the first systematic description of the relationship between material premises and ideological effect, the figure of two languages reappears.

> The production of ideas, of conceptions, of consciousness, is at first directly interwoven with the material activity and the material intercourse of men—the language of real life. Conceiving, thinking, the mental intercourse of men at this stage still appear as the direct efflux of their material behavior. The same applies to mental production as expressed in the language of politics, laws, morality, religion, metaphysics, etc., of a people.[40]

Marx distinguishes between two kinds of languages—"the language of real life" and "the language of politics, laws, . . . etc." Earlier, Marx used this figure to highlight man's alienation from his human essence. At that time, Marx's terminology, if not his outlook, were still idealistic (in both senses of the word). Here, in *The German Ideology,* he no longer talks of "a human language" or "human essence," but of the "language of real life," or "ordinary language." More to the point, he fleshes out what he means by such a language.

---

for this reason. In *The Poverty of Philosophy,* he writes for example, "Doubtlessly Ricardo's language is as cynical as can be. To put the cost of manufacture of hats and the cost of the maintenance of men on the same plane is to turn men into hats. But do not make an outcry at the cynicism of it. The cynicism is in the facts and not in the words which express the facts." Cited in S. E. Hyman, *The Tangled Bank: Darwin, Marx, Frazer and Freud as Imaginative Writers* (New York: Atheneum, 1962), p. 95; *MEW* 4: 82-83.

[39]Since I am stressing certain striking continuities in Marx's *own* treatment of language in this section, I will continue to talk of him alone, though it is clear that Engels contributed much to this particular work.

[40]*GI,* p. 36; *DI,* p. 26.

This "language of real life" is both part of the material activity of man as well as being a "direct efflux" of it. As such it is itself a "practical, constitutive activity," which is inseparable from all such productive activity.[41] To stress the material existence of consciousness or mind, Marx says it "is from the outset afflicted with the curse of being 'burdened' with matter, which here makes its appearance in the form of agitated layers of air, sounds, in short, of language."[42] Man's speech both constitutes *and* expresses his intersubjective self—a self which grew with and out of basic social material needs.

> Language is as old as consciousness, language *is* practical, real consciousness that exists for other men as well, and only therefore does it exist for me; language, like consciousness, only arises out of the need, the necessity, of intercourse with other men.[43]

As any other productive activity, man's language has a history, an ordered development, with different activities conditioning as well as being historically conditioned by definite stages of man's actual existence. As such an activity, language is molded by the material practice of a society, but also is part of what constitutes that practice. For, in Marx's words, "men, developing their material production and their material intercourse, alter, along with this their actual world, also their thinking and the products of their thinking."[44] It is important to stress that at this point, man's language as a "practical, constitutive activity," included both the "passive" and "active"—the conditioned as well as the conditioning. Initially, no distinction between man's basic language—viz., the "language of real life" or "ordinary language" as Marx calls it—and any other ideological one existed. As Marx puts it in *Capital,* "the practical relations of everyday life between man and man, and man and nature, generally present themselves in a trasparent and rational form."[45] There was no ideological "veil" shrouding and mystifying the "process of material production," rendering it "opaque" to man's understanding.

It is hard to know whether Marx's discussion here is meant to be

---

[41] Raymond Williams, *Marxism and Literature* (Oxford: Oxford University Press, 1977), pp. 29ff. Williams' chapter on language in this book is the only serious, nondogmatic attempt to come up with a coherent and meaningful Marxist theory of language this writer has seen.

[42] *GI,* pp. 43-44; *DI,* p. 30.

[43] *GI,* p. 44; *DI,* p. 30.

[44] *GI,* p. 37; *DI,* p. 27.

[45] *Capital: Volume I,* intro. E. Mandel; trans. B. Fowkes (London: Penguin, 1976), p. 173: cited in H. Lefebvre, *The Sociology of Marx,* trans. N. Guterman (New York: Vintage, 1969), pp. 62-63.

historical or hypothetical (as Rousseau's "state of nature"). In any event, there existed and continues to exist at each stage of man's development a language and consciousness that is true to man's actual material circumstances, even if it is not consciously articulated. But along with this language and consciousness, there arose another false or illusory consciousness and language: in a word, an *ideology*. How did this happen? More specifically, how did the "language of politics, law, morality, religion, metaphysics, etc." develop? This language, which expresses the ideology (the "mental production" as Marx calls it) of a people is also somehow conditioned by man's "material behavior" and is apparently derived from the first language—"the language of real life."

Marx believes that this other consciousness and its language originated with the appearance of a "division of material and mental labor."

> From this moment onwards consciousness *can* really flatter itself that it is something other than consciousness of existing practice, that it *really* represents something without representing something real; from now on consciousness is in a position to emancipate itself from the world and to proceed to the formation of 'pure' theory, theology, philosophy, morality, etc.[46]

Language, as inseparable from consciousness, becomes the most important means for conveying the ideas which enable their creators to sanction their emancipation from materially productive activity.[47] Just as philosophy or theology becomes "independent of the workings of the actual world,"[48] so also its language which expresses this condition. Indeed this is, for Marx and Engels, "the secret of philosophical language."

> *Language* is the immediate actuality of thought. Just as philosophers have given thought an independent existence, so they had to make

[46] *GI*, p. 45; *DI*, p. 31.

[47] "So far as the development of ideologies is concerned, the most important division is that between physical and intellectual labor, between creative action (operations upon things with the aid of tools and machines) and action on human beings by means of non-material instruments, the primary and most important of which is language. *From this point forward, consciousness becomes capable of detachment from reality*, . . . " Lefebvre, 67.

[48] "We have shown that thoughts and ideas acquire an independent existence in consequence of the personal circumstances and relations of individuals acquiring independent existence. We have shown that exclusive, systematic occupation with these thoughts on the part of ideologists and philosophers, and hence the systematization of these thoughts, is a consequence of division of labor, and that, in particular, German philosophy is a consequence of German petty-bourgeois conditions." *GI*, pp. 446-47; *DI*, p. 432.

> language into an independent realm. This is the secret of philosophical language, in which thoughts in the form of words have their own content.[49]

Besides developing theories of religion, morality, and philosophy which reflect the division of labor and the resultant classes of a society, the creators of ideology form or reform the language of the society so as to perpetuate this distinction. Consequently, the very vocabulary of a society becomes permeated with the ruling ideology of the period, for, according to Marx and Engels, the language of each period expresses the ideas and values of the ruling class: "the class which is the ruling *material* force of society is at the same time its ruling *intellectual* force."[50] They go to great lengths throughout *The German Ideology* (and not just in the usually published Part I) to point out how language is ideologically infiltrated. The book is strewn with examples of this technique, usually done unconsciously or involuntarily by the intellectual arbiters of the day. There are several ways that this is done. Most frequently and obviously, man's history is denatured or dematerialized by philosophers and theologians so that instead of talking about the individual in a concrete material and historical context, Heglian terminology like "self-consciousness" or "spirit" is substituted, distorting and ultimately reversing the whole causal process.[51] However, to give the appearance of being concrete or "materialistic," such terms are often changed

> into a series of persons, who represent the 'concept' in history, into the 'thinkers,' the 'philosophers,' the ideologists, who again are understood as the manufacturers of history, as the 'council of guardians,' as the rulers. Thus the whole body of materialistic elements have been eliminated from history and now full rein can be given to the speculative steed.[52]

Marx and Engels are adept at spotting this type of speculative

[49] *GI,* p. 446; *DI,* p. 432.

[50] *GI,* p. 59; *DI,* p. 46.

[51] Marx and Engels inveigh against the substitution of such abstractions for "the real individual man" in the opening lines of *The Holy Family,* written just before *The German Ideology.* "Real humanism has no more dangerous enemy in Germany than *spiritualism* or *speculative idealism,* which substitutes *'self-consciousness'* or the *'spirit'* for the *real individual man. . . ." CW* 4: 7; *MEW* 2: 7.

[52] *The German Ideology* is replete with translations, or demystifications, of this speculative language. Brief phrases like "this should read," "this means," etc., abound, each following a characteristically opaque passage from Max Stirner, the philosopher being attacked throughout most of the book. The same strategy is often used in *The Holy Family* as well, where phrases like "speaking *exactly* and in the *prosaic sense*" or "in plain language" are often used to deflate the pretentions of the "critical" language of Bruno Bauer.

language and the world view it seeks to perpetuate. Marx here continues the same Feuerbachian strategy of translation or demystification he used earlier, but now it becomes anchored in his materialist view of society and history. This gives Marx a powerful tool for detecting and unmasking such ideological language(s).

To translate or demystify what Marx and Engels see as a discredited mode of discourse into one which more truly reflects the actual (material) world, one has to be able to discover and uncover the various techniques used to justify a particular conception of private property and the attendant division of classes. I will deal here with only one particular example, though a whole catalogue of what they call "logical tricks" in this regard could be detailed.[53]

The main way that language can be used to reflect the interests of one class over another involves the justification of a specific meaning of certain basic philosophical or political terms. For example, it is shown that such words can be etymologically interpreted only in one way, a way that of course reflects the bourgeois conception of personal identity and property. In a lengthy passage in the third part of *The German Ideology,* Marx and Engels attack a rather far-fetched defense of private property which equated one's own *(eigen)* characteristic traits or properties *(Eigenschaften)* as an individual with private property *(Eigentum),* thus concluding that one cannot abolish private property without at the same time also abolishing one's particular individuality *(Eigenheit)*—which, of course, is absurd. This type of wordplay is "theoretical nonsense" in their words, but being able to indulge in such an exercise is not simply a charming coincidence of words. There is something deeper to it. First, this type of argument would not have even dawned on anyone unless "the actual private property that the communists want to abolish had not been transformed into the abstract notion of 'property.' "[54] This is just another example of the dematerialization constantly practiced by philosophers. Once this is done, it then becomes "easy to discover a contradiction in communism, since *after* the abolition of *(actual)* property it is, of course, easy to discover all sorts of things in communism which can be included in the concept 'property.' "[55] But even more importantly, such a wordplay can be effected because key words in modern language, Marx and Engels claim, reflect the material conditions of society. The modern bourgeoisie have not only ap-

[53]*GI,* pp. 205-32, 272-92 *passim; DI,* pp. 186-214, 253-74.
[54]*GI,* p. 229; *DI,* pp. 210-11.
[55]*GI,* p. 230; *DI,* p. 211.

propriated the means of production, but with this the means of expression as well!

> For the bourgeois it is all the easier to prove on the basis of his language the identity of commercial and individual, or even universal, relations, as this language itself is a product of the bourgeoisie, and therefore both in actuality and in language the relations of buying and selling have been made the basis of all others. For example, *propriété*—property [Eigentum] and characteristic feature [Eigenschaft]; property—possession [Eigentum] and peculiarity [Eigentumlichkeit]; *'eigen'* ['one's own']—in the commercial and individual sense; *valeur,* value, *Wert;* commerce, *Verkehr;* échange, exchange, *Austausch,* etc. all of which are used both for commercial relations and for characteristic features and mutual relations of individuals as such. In other modern languages this is equally the case.[56]

Selecting an exclusive, or at least primary meaning for the key words of social, political, and economic discourse is an excellent way to "ideologize" everyday language so as to reflect the interests of a particular class. To do so with rather esoteric philosophical terms like "self-consciousness," "alienation," or "spirit" may not be particularly persuasive since such uses of these terms are more obvious to the reader—often in fact having their meaning explicitly stipulated by the writer—and, in any event, such language is usually the province of a restricted group of theoreticians. Words like "property," "individuality," or "freedom" and "justice," on the other hand, are used in all walks of life—in all "languages"—both written and spoken. The core of ideological discourse is not found in the use of narrow philosophical terms, but in "the language of real life." It is this language which can be surreptitiously, yet easily, fashioned or refashioned to reflect a specific ideology.[57]

---

[56] *GI,* p. 231; *DI,* pp. 212-13. Another variation on this theme is to use "synonyms" or "ambiguous expressions"—what we would call "homonyms"—to make unwarranted connections between radically different meanings of the same sounding words. "Synonymy serves . . . to transform empirical relations into speculative relations, by using in its speculative meaning a word that occurs both in practical life and in philosophical speculation, uttering a few phrases about this speculative meaning and then making out that he [Stirner] has thereby also criticized the actual relations which this word denotes as well. He does this with the word *speculation.* . . . He rages against *philosophical* speculation and thinks he has thereby also settled accounts with *commercial* speculation, about [which] he knows nothing. On the other hand, this synonymy enables him, a concealed petty bourgeois, to transform bourgeois relations, . . . into personal, individual relations, which one cannot attack without attacking the individuality, 'peculiarity' and 'uniqueness' of the individual." *GI,* p. 277; *DI,* pp. 257-58.

[57] As Lefebvre puts it, "The most completely elaborated ideological representations find their way into language, become a permanent part of it. They supply

Though their primary concern is with ideology in its broader scope, Marx and Engels offer directions on how to deal with the narrower problem of speculative language. Once again, this first entails demystifying philosophical language by "dissolving" such language into one reflective of the material realities of the day. As they put it, "The problem of descending from the world of thoughts to the actual world is turned into the problem of descending from language to life."[58] The answer to the problem of philosophical language is its "translation" into "ordinary language." Then the true origin of philosophy in the abstraction from and resultant distortion of human *praxis* will be revealed.

> The philosophers would only have to dissolve their language into ordinary language, from which it is abstracted, to recognize it as the distorted language of the actual world, and to realize that neither thoughts nor language in themselves form a realm of their own, that they are only *manifestations* of actual life.[59]

However, Marx and Engels do not expect philosophers or ideologists to so easily or willingly "dissolve their language," for to do so they would have to fathom their own "philosophical illusion"—that is "the nature and origin of its [philosophy's] apparent separation from life."[60] Therefore it is not enough to simply recommend the translation or dissolution of philosophical language. Once again, Marx appeals to the other indirect strategy he used earlier. Rather than try to persuade vainly the users of such language to change, all that can be done until there is a change in the material conditions of man's life, and hence in his consciousness, is to point out the progressive absurdity of the theoretical language of much contemporary philosophy and social science. Marx and Engels thus demonstrate throughout *The German Ideology* how such language has become more and more "unreal," i.e., unrelated to man's changing material conditions. As the language of philosophy becomes more and more distorted because what it purports to describe no longer fits the actual world, it develops an existence of its own.

Marx, like Hegel before him, sees this phenomenon as an indicator of man's increasing estrangement from his world: "Language

---

vocabularies, formulations, turns of thought which are also turns of phrase." Lefebvre, p. 72. It is eventually these "old vocabularies" and "traditional modes of expression" which "come to stand in the way of the new elements in society and new approaches to its problems." Ibid., p. 69.

[58] *GI,* p. 446; *DI,* p. 432.

[59] *GI,* p. 447; *DI,* p. 432-33.

[60] *GI,* p. 449; *DI,* p. 435.

. . . becomes a phrase as soon as it is given an independent existence."[61] In the *Phenomenology,* when language enters its own, "appears in its characteristic significance," in Hegel's words,[62] it leads to dissembling, hypocrisy, and empty moralizing. The same thing is, or will be, happening to the thinkers of Marx's day. As the contradiction between "the ruling class" and the "advanced productive forces" develops,

> the more do the old traditional ideas, . . . in which actual private interests, etc., etc., are expressed as universal interests, descend to the level of mere idealizing phrases, conscious illusion, deliberate hypocrisy. But the more their falsity is exposed by life, and the less meaning they have for consciousness itself, the more resolutely are they asserted, the more hypocritical, moral and holy becomes the language of this normal society.[63]

In extreme cases, according to Marx and Engels, this can lead to the "end of philosophy" and "the end of all language." They even call it "the death of language." Philosophers begin to take refuge in the ineffable or in attributing "mysterious superhuman" powers to a specific word as Christianity did to Christ, hence ruling out any meaningful language. The final connection between philosophical categories and reality is ruptured; language and thought have become totally estranged from "actual [human] relations."[64]

IV

What does Marx mean here by "ordinary language" or "the language of the actual world"? It is clear that terms like "the actual world," "real life," etc., refer to the material, productive activities of a society. These activities determine the relations between individuals of the society (political, legal, etc.) and the concepts embodying these relations. It is with such relational concepts that Marx is primarily concerned in his discussions on language. His examples are always of terms that are conceptual, abstract, and relational: "property," "individuality," "morality," etc. These are the words which form what I earlier called the "core of ideological discourse." The origins or development of other parts of speech or of language in general did not interest Marx in this regard. Expressed differently, Marx displayed no concern in subjecting the syntactic structures of

---

[61] *GI,* p. 447; *DI,* p. 433.
[62] *Phenomenology,* p. 308; *Phänomenologie,* p. 362.
[63] *GI,* p. 293; *DI,* p. 274.
[64] *GI,* p. 448-50; *DI,* p. 434-36.

language to an analysis to determine whether they were in some sense class-bound; he concentrated his energies on semantic questions: viz., *how* and more importantly *why* the meanings of key words changed, especially those expressing the relations between individuals and classes. Such words were the battlefield upon which the struggle to demystify language and hence uncover its true import must take place.

The problem of philosophical and ideological language for Marx is clearly restricted to questions of the origin, use, and meaning of the theoretical and conceptual words of ordinary language.[65] Marx was not interested in developing a *new* language for philosophy; he was concerned primarily with reforming and reworking certain "parts" of the old, natural languages in use at his time. For this reason, 20th century attempts—Marxist and non-Marxist alike—to isolate those structural elements of language which are not classbound or to distinguish a basic, nonideological language for Marx are misguided.[66]

Consequently, when Marx talks of the ideological or class-conditioned nature of language, he is referring primarily to certain theoretical terms of a language and not to its overall structure. It is

---

[65]Thus Marx uses the word "language" basically as Hegel did in the *Phenomenology of Spirit:* each language represents the way a different consciousness relates to its world. See footnote 18.

[66]For a recent, non-Marxist, attempt to isolate such a "basic language," see John Plamenatz, *Karl Marx's Philosophy of Man* (Oxford: Clarendon Press, 1975), pp. 211-19.

In this sense, Joseph Stalin was the "true Marxist," since he objected to earlier attempts (by N. Y. Marr and others) to see language strictly as part of the superstructure. Like Marx, he saw language as the product of a historical development. Stalin also stressed the active, conditioning aspect of language, rather than its purely "passive," "neutral" dimension. *Marxism and Linguistics* (New York: International Publishers, 1951). p. 10. Furthermore, both Marx and Stalin cite the close relationship between language and the material forces in a given society. On the other hand, Stalin continues to talk of language primarily as the product of a base, though to be sure, a whole series of bases throughout history. Ibid. Thus language remains part of the superstructure in this regard, though not necessarily grounded in any single or existing one.

Marx was primarily interested in the semantic differences of certain key words—words which constitute the "ideological core," to use my expression—of a language, though quantitatively they may constitute, in Stalin's words, "hardly . . . one percent of the entire language material." Ibid., p. 37. Marx did not address himself to syntactic or grammatical matters, and certainly never espoused the view that the structure of a language or its grammatical rules were in any sense class-bound. It is the latter position which Stalin is particularly interested in demolishing. Ibid.

this "part" of language which becomes "part" of ideology. The meanings of certain crucial words and terms in a society do reflect the interests of the ruling class, but even this is the result of a dynamic, constitutive process of which language itself is an active element.[67] The notion of language as passively "mirroring" the material bases of society (i.e., the modes and relations of production) is much too simplistic. Marx realized that human language is too rich to be pressed into a Procrustean bed, using the jargon of ideology and base, superstructure and substructure.[68] Once in a great while Marx does use the "mirror" image in talking of the language of philosophy or politics,[69] but this was a common figure of speech well before Marx's time.[70]

Finally, if the key terms (and ideas) in theoretical or philosophical language are abstract, then it is clear that a purely nominalist language (whatever that would be), such as Feuerbach suggested, is quite inappropriate. The danger that Marx inveighed against was not the conceptual or abstract nature of the terms of the language of philosophy or politics *per se,* but that such terms and the ideas they express—given their *general* nature—inevitably lend themselves to specific abuses and distortions, since such "universals" are easily detached from their basis in the relations of production. Marx summarizes these points concerning the problem of language in the following citation from *The German Ideology,* worth quoting at some length.

> The hitherto existing production relations of individuals are bound also to be expressed as political and legal relations. Within the division of labor, these relations are bound to acquire an independent existence over against the individuals. *All relations can be expressed in language only in the form of concepts.* That these *general ideas* and *concepts* are looked upon as mysterious forces is the necessary result of the fact that the real relations, of which they are the expression, have acquired independent existence. Besides this meaning in eveyday consciousness,

[67] ". . . Marx lists literature among 'acquired forces of production, material and spiritual, language, technical skills, etc., etc.' " S. S. Prawer, *Karl Marx and World Literature* (Oxford: Clarendon Press, 1976), p. 405; *MEW* 18: 620.

[68] Prawer says, for example, "that in his actual dealings with literature, Marx never makes mechanical and rigid use of the 'base-superstructure' model, and that it does not in fact figure at all prominently in his appreciations of existing literary works." Ibid., p. 412.

[69] Prawer cites only two examples from the Marxist corpus. Ibid.

[70] For example, Leibniz often speaks of language as a "true" or "clear" mirror of the understanding. "Languages," Leibniz claimed, "are the best mirrors of the human mind." *New Essays Concerning Human Understanding,* trans. A. Langley (New York: MacMillan, 1896), Bk. III, Chap. vii, Par. 6, p. 368.

> these *general ideas* are further elaborated and given a special significance by politicians and lawyers, who, as a result of the division of labor, are dependent on the cult of these concepts, and who see in them, and not in the relations of production, the true basis of all real property relations. (Emphasis mine.)[71]

For Marx, then, abstract, conceptual terms are and always will be central to theoretic discourse, even when such discourse is grounded in material *praxis*. Whatever the new language of philosophy—or scientific socialism, if you will—it would in this important regard strongly resemble the traditional vocabulary of speculative thought.[72] Marx's own career also bears this out. While many of his writings after *The German Ideology* (and for that matter before) were written in an earthy, polemical vein, he continued to theorize in abstract, conceptual terms in many others.

Some recent commentators have claimed that there was a radical change in the outlets and consequently in the language Marx used between his "earlier" and "later" periods. Oddly enough, the writers who usually point this out are among those who otherwise stress the continuity and coherence of his thought between these two periods. According to this view, Marx's earliest writings were *esoteric,* understandable only to those initiated into Hegelian philosophy and its aftermath, whereas his later ones were *exoteric,* virtually understandable to anyone who read them. As one of them puts it,

> When Marx became convinced that the test of philosophy was not in interpreting the world, but in changing it—not in theoretical discussion, but rather in political action—it followed that the language of discussion must go from philosophical language, which by its very nature is the language of the few, to a language equally accessible to all. This [is a] transition from philosophy to propaganda, from theoretical discussion to polemical and combative writing, . . .[73]

For theory to become a material political force, it must be "capable of gripping the masses," to use Marx's words, but Marx

[71] *GI,* p. 363; *DI,* p. 347. "Alle Verhältnisse können in der Sprache nur als Begriffe ausgedrückt werden . . . diese Allgemeinheiten und Begriffe . . ."

[72] In this regard, a recent commentator says: "Marx clearly anticipates an eventual language reform which would result in the elimination of the word 'justice' and similar abstractions from our vocabularies. His own writings, on the whole, exemplify the anticipated new language in this respect; that is, Marx seldom uses such words in contexts in which most past social and political theorists would have used them." W. L. McBride, *The Philosophy of Marx* (London: Hutchinson, 1977), p. 76. The context may be different, but 'justice' and other abstract conceptions like it nevertheless are still *used* by Marx. Furthermore, it is not clear how such words could be eliminated, or used in a strictly nonabstract fashion.

[73] *Karl Marx: Early Writings.* Hebrew Translation, Introduction and Notes by Shlomo Avineri, rev. ed. (Tel Aviv: Sifriyat Ha-Poalim, 1976), p. 29.

never claimed that this meant creating a totally new vocabulary, let alone a new language, for theory. Marx's primary concern was that theoretical language be grounded in the actual conditions of *praxis,* thus preventing its use as an ideological tool which would foster and perpetuate a distorted picture of such conditions. Such a program entails, to be sure, the disappearance of some of the arcane and incomprehensible terminology of philosophers and social scientists, but the abstract, conceptual nature of basic theoretical language would remain. Marx never faltered in his optimism that once the esoteric quality of language was unmasked, the "masses" could theorize and learn for themselves, understand their situation, and act on this understanding. Hence what must be done is to criticize and purify existing language, rather than abandon it for another nonconceptual or concrete one, whatever that may be.

DANIEL J. COOK.

BROOKLYN COLLEGE, CUNY.

SOME WAYS OF GOING WRONG: ON MISTAKES IN *ON CERTAINTY*

There is an old story about a nineteenth century lawmaker who introduced a bill to change the value of *pi* to 3. When asked for his reasons, he cited a Biblical passage in which the distance around a lake was given as three times the distance across it.

Clearly, the lawmaker was wrong. But did he make a mistake?

*****

Anyone familiar with *On Certainty* will have grasped Wittgenstein's thesis that legitimate doubt, doubt which is to be taken seriously, always has a reason; reasonable doubt must be reasoned doubt. Granting this, the bare logical possibility of error is not sufficient to induce scepticism, and a genuine possibility of error presupposes propositions immune to sceptical challenges. The privileged propositions are themselves not justified by other propositions, nor are they somehow self-justifying, nor are they known with certainty; rather their immunity derives from their intimate relationship with the ways in which we *act*. Thus does Wittgenstein reject scepticism and its rivals, foundationalism and common-sensism.

Occupying a central position in the attack on scepticism is Wittgenstein's understanding of error. Like Plato in the *Theaetetus,* Wittgenstein suggests that a grasp of the concept of error makes a significant contribution to any adequate understanding of the concepts of knowledge and belief and certainty; unlike Plato, Wittgenstein finds that there are philosophically interesting differences between sorts of error and different "ways of things going wrong" (see *On Certainty,* 72, 641, 659).[1] Wittgenstein wants to say that only some of these ways of things going wrong can provide grounds for reasonable doubt; others cannot. Unfortunately, Wittgenstein's remarks on error in *On Certainty* are neither as clear nor as sustained as one might wish: while he repeatedly asserts the existence of different types of errors

[1] Ludwig Wittgenstein, *On Certainty*, edited by G. E. M. Anscombe and G. H. von Wright, translated by Denis Paul and G. E. M. Anscombe, (New York and Evanston: J. and J. Harper, 1969). All references to this work are given by section number and are incorporated into the text.

and says " . . . what we call 'a mistake' plays a quite special part in our language games . . . " (196), thus apparently distinguishing mistakes from other false beliefs, the precise nature of the role of mistakes is only hinted at. In his typical fashion, Wittgenstein approaches this topic from various perspectives and varied interests; in only one way does he attempt to describe explicitly the distinguishing characteristics of mistakes (see 74), and his statement is far from transparent. We are left wondering exactly what a mistake is, what roles things we call mistakes have, what it is that mistakes are being distinguished from. The point is of more than academic interest. In the absence of any sustained analysis of mistakes and other false beliefs, Wittgenstein's remark at 155 "[i]n certain circumstances, a man cannot make a *mistake*. ('Can' is here used logically, and the proposition does not mean that a man cannot say anything false in those circumstances)" makes his rejection of epistemological scepticism sound like sleight of tongue.

I think that Wittgenstein does have a set of consistent views on mistakes and other sorts of errors which underlies many of the remarks he makes in *On Certainty,* although I hesitate to say that Wittgenstein had a fullblown position worked out on these topics. What follows here is a Wittgensteinian view of mistakes and other errors; it may also have been Wittgenstein's. At any rate, I suspect that he would not have disagreed with it.

*****

Near the beginning of *On Certainty,* after introducing the possibility that one might be wrong about one's own long-standing and familiar address, Wittgenstein says:

> 71. If my friend were to imagine one day that he had been living for a long time past in such and such a place, etc. etc. I should not call this a *mistake,* but rather a mental disturbance, perhaps a transient one.

Wittgenstein then tries to distinguish between mistakes, or treating something as a mistake, and mental disturbances, or treating something as a mental disturbance. The solution he offers is that a mistake, unlike a mental disturbance, has a ground as well as a cause, ". . . [i].e., roughly: when someone makes a mistake this can be fitted into what he knows aright" (74). To illustrate the distinction between mistakes and mental disturbances, he suggests:

> 75. Would this be correct: If I merely believed wrongly that there is a table in front of me, this might still be a mistake; but if I believe wrongly

> that I have seen this table, or one like it, every day for several days past, and have regularly used it, that isn't a mistake?

Much later in *On Certainty,* Wittgenstein reaffirms this characterization of mistakes, saying that mistakes are false beliefs " . . . for which, as it were, a place is prepared in the game" (647). Time and again Wittgenstein relies on this distinction between mistakes and mental disturbances, but the remarks cited above are the only ones in which he attempts to specify, in anything resembling general terms, what the distinction amounts to. What are we to make of it? What does Wittgenstein have in mind when he says that a mistake has a ground, that a mistake can be fitted into what someone knows aright? Exactly what sort of erroneous beliefs are these that he is describing?

A reasonable starting place might be to look at how we actually do talk about and ascribe mistakes. But this approach is initially hindered by the fact that ordinarily, our talk of mistakes does not place a premium on distinguishing precisely the type of error made: our choice of words indicating the occurrence of a mistake is usually geared more toward attributing responsibility or blame, or avoiding censure, or offering excuses, and less toward marking off any interesting differences in kinds of mistake made. For example, J. L. Austin suggests an examination of our "mistake talk" about our less than praiseworthy or successful doings in order to get clearer on the concept of an excuse; the idioms he offers for consideration are: 'by mistake,' 'owing to a mistake,' 'mistakenly,' 'it was a mistake to,' 'to make a mistake in or over or about,' and 'to be mistaken about.'[2] These expressions are all applied by Austin to physical actions, and presumably, they all reflect what Austin believes to be " . . . the basic use of 'mistake,' where we simply, and not necessarily accountably, take the wrong one."[3] But when we apply these idioms to our believings and judgings, we find that there is more than one way of "taking the wrong one." I believe, by mistake as it turns out, that Sam is at home; owing to a mistake in my bookkeeping, I write checks that bounce; I mistakenly believe that the coupon is still valid or that Sarah is at work; it is a mistake to believe that advertisement; I make a mistake over the price; I make a mistake in buying that automobile; I make a mistake about the date of the dinner party.

Looking more closely, there seem to be at least three main classes

---

[2]J. L. Austin, "A Plea for Excuses" reprinted in J. L. Austin, *Philosophical Papers,* second edition, edited by J. O. Urmson and G. W. Warnock, (London, Oxford, New York: Oxford University Press, 1970), p. 198.

[3]*Ibid.*, p. 200 n.

into which we group mistakes. First, there are straightforward "factual" mistakes *about* something: about the characteristics of something, about the conditions under which something occurred or the relationship that some object has to another thing, about the present significance or future importance of some thing or some occurrence.[4] Wittgenstein most frequently talks about this type of mistake in the contexts of hypotheses of physical science, astronomical fact (52), the location of common objects (134), and the location and date of historical events (6); he also seems to be willing to extend this classification to cover errors about certain linguistic facts, notably those involving the use of unusual or technically-based terms. By and large, the most commonplace examples of this sort of mistake are misdescriptions and misidentifications. I see a medium-sized white animal under a tree on yonder hill and think, "Oh, a lamb." The animal rises and begins to bark—it is a Bedlington terrier. I mistake my neighbor for his brother. I make a mistake about the Battle of Hastings, believing it to have occurred in 1099.

Second, there are what we can call "tactical" and "strategic" mistakes. These are errors of planning and decision-making, and mistakes in choices made. A typical occurrence of this sort is found in cases in which the means we choose fail to bring about the end or goal desired. "It was a bad choice," I say, "it was a mistake to select that option." While Wittgenstein does not directly concern himself with this type of mistake in *On Certainty,* he does countenance the possibility of such mistakes when he talks of incorrect choices of phrasing *(Philosophical Investigations,* p. 218), and in *On Certainty,* he does allude to right and wrong choices.

The third sort of mistake is "procedural" or what Austin calls an "executive" mistake:[5] in executing some procedure, I muff it. My muffing it may simply be a slip, brought on by some minor physiological breakdown or by inattentiveness, as when I misdial a telephone number, or I misspeak, or mistype a letter or symbol, or sometimes, misspell a common word. Alternatively, and more interestingly, executive errors may have a significant cognitive dimension, such as when I miscalculate, or mistranslate, or make a mistake in sorting, or classifying, or when I misuse a specific rule. These are all mistakes *in* doing something, in performing or following some pro-

[4]This last is described by Austin, *op. cit.*, p. 194, as a "failure to appreciate the situation." Austin's own taxonomy of mistakes in "A Plea for Excuses" is presented in terms of temporal stages of a performance.

[5]Austin, *op. cit.*, p. 193.

cedure. We might be inclined to subdivide these procedural mistakes further: into those which are correct *performances* of a procedure, but the rule or procedure is applied to the "wrong" subject matter; and those which are incorrect performances of the appropriate procedure and the subject matter is "right." For example, in following a recipe, I can perform the specified steps correctly and in the proper order, but use the wrong ingredients; I can also use the right ingredients but combine them improperly. A chef's nightmare comes to mind: when told to make bread dough and pie dough the baker's apprentice kneads the pie dough for ten minutes and gently stirs the bread dough. But this scenario notwithstanding, the putative distinction in the notion of a procedural mistake is chimerical. The apprentice's mistake when kneading the pie dough is either one of mis-taking the pie dough for the bread dough, in which case the error is of the first or "factual" sort; or possibly it is a mistake in the making of pie. Kneading the pie dough is not a mistake in the making of bread.

The point is important, because we might be tempted to think that all mistakes are ultimately some kind of procedural or executive mistake—that they are all "mistakes in applying a rule." But not every mistake which occurs in the context of a rule-governed activity is a mistake in using or following some rule. The expression "making a mistake in applying a rule" is unhelpfully vague, for one can describe a variety of different errors as "making a mistake in applying a rule." I have already characterized three different ways in which this can occur: the choice of that rule in those circumstances may be a mistake, that is, it is a mistake to apply *that* rule then; a mistake may be made about the nature of the material to which the rule is applied; the rule itself may be incorrectly followed. At 28, Wittgenstein emphasizes this, saying, [w]hat is 'making a mistake in applying it [a rule]'?—*This*. And what is pointed to here is something indeterminate." In other words, one can make a mistake in applying a rule in a host of different ways which are left undetermined, that is, unspecified, by the rule itself. But this does not mean that we cannot talk about these mistakes at all, or that any remarks we make about mistakes are infected with this vagueness. In actual practice, we juggle successfully with different types of mistakes, and with aberrations which exemplify complicated combinations of mistakes, and can isolate, identify, and correct mistakes. Here, it is important to keep in mind that there is no kind of mistake which is the more fundamental sort into which all the others dissolve. In more traditionally Wittgensteinian terms, we do not play one and only one game at a time; most of our practices and actions and especially our more sophisticated intellectual endeavors involve very complex beliefs and procedures which themselves incorporate and depend on other games and other beliefs. Depending on the particular context in which a mistake occurs, it may be characterized in different ways, relative to the system of beliefs and practices and interests surrounding its occurrence.

Wittgenstein believes that mistakes occur only against a background of community-wide shared principles and information. But this still sounds like a plausible characterization of any false belief, given that the shared principles and information provide the parameters for truth and falsehood for that community. So while Wittgenstein might agree that this background of information is necessary for the occurrence of mistakes, it is not sufficient. When Wittgenstein says that a mistake, unlike a mental disturbance, can be fitted into what someone knows aright, he is saying that the false belief—the mistake—is one whose occurrence presupposes that the individual making that mistake knows how to get that sort of thing right or how to do that sort of thing correctly. The individual making the mistake is recognized by others to be in a position to get it right. And this in turn implies that that person usually does get that sort of thing right, or does know how to proceed correctly. Consequently, others can attribute a *mistake* to the person, instead of saying that the individual "really didn't know what was going on, after all" or "was just guessing." Wittgenstein repeatedly makes the point that in learning ways to judge, in learning rules, we also learn what the relevant mistakes are (29, 66). A person also learns how to ascertain that no mistake has been made; one learns how to check. It has been suggested that what Wittgenstein means by saying that the mistake fits into what someone knows aright is that the error could have been avoided, for example, by the individual taking "precautions which would have shown him the falsity of what he believed . . . [even though] it might have been quite irrational or obsessional to take these precautions."[6] But surely Wittgenstein does not have anything like this in mind: the taking of irrational or obsessional precautions is something he attacks time and again; he never recommends that precautions of this irrational or obsessional nature be taken, for this would be playing right into the sceptic's hands. In ordinary circumstances, one does not check a calculation twenty times to ascer-

[6]Christopher Coope, "Wittgenstein's Theory of Knowledge," in *Understanding Wittgenstein,* edited by Godfrey Vesey (1974; rpt. Ithaca: Cornell University Press, Cornell Paperbacks, 1974), p. 253.

tain that one has not made a mistake; checking it once or having someone else check it is quite adequate (77). If one were to take irrational or obsessional precautions, this would be evidence that one really didn't know "what was going on," for one would not be functioning in the appropriate way. At most, Wittgenstein suggests, one should take "due precautions," and what constitutes due precaution may vary according to circumstances (34, 143).

What then of the apparent criterion that Wittgenstein begins with: that a mistake has a ground? The most obvious thing that Wittgenstein might mean is that a mistake has a reason, in the sense that one can give reasons for believing that false belief which is labeled a mistake.[7] Such a reading treats mistakes as strictly symmetrical with knowledge: knowledge is justified true belief, mistakes are justified false beliefs. This putative criterion is much stronger that "fitting a belief into what someone knows aright," and so it should be entertained with caution. I think ultimately it should be rejected. While one may be able to offer reasons for many mistakes, there are many mistakes lacking reasons or justification. What reason have I for mistakenly believing that there is a table in front of me? What reason do I have for mistakenly believing that 4928 + 3271 + 6855 = 13,944? What reason have I when I make a mistake about the traditional lands of the Iroquois? That I opened my eyes, that I added them up, that I recall that someone or other once told me, may explain how I *come* to believe these falsehoods, but none of these responses is justification for the belief. The fact that I usually get this sort of thing right may *excuse* me from checking in these particular cases, but it alone does not *justify* my belief. My belief may have no justification. However, the fact that I usually get this sort of thing right does underlie my *mistake*. Thus, it is misleading to read 'reason' or 'justification' for 'ground' in passage 74, especially since Wittgenstein clearly intends that fitting a mistake into what someone knows aright be an amplification of 'ground'.

Interestingly, there are two different, but intimate, relationships between mistakes and reasons, both of which derive from the fact that mistakes presuppose what is known aright. First, one can give reasons to show that a mistake has *not* been made in some particular case. Wittgenstein frequently points out that simply the assurance that there is no mistake is unpersuasive—it needs to be *shown* that there is

[7]This seems to be the standard reading. Coope, *ibid.*, relies on it, as does Thomas Morawetz in *Wittgenstein and Knowledge* (Amherst: University of Massachusetts Press, 1978), especially pp. 40-41.

no mistake (see, e.g., 15, 21). Thus, one can check to see if there has or has not been a mistake. Second, we can give reasons to defend a mistake-attribution; we can give reasons to show people that they are wrong, that they made a mistake. We show then that there is evidence that their belief is a mistaken belief. Of course, in order to do this, we must know what would count as evidence for a correct belief, just as we know what counts as evidence for an incorrect belief. The cause of the mistake doesn't matter; it may be inattention, sudden interruption, indigestion; what is important is that reasons can be given to show that a mistake has been made. The reasons given will be reasons acceptable to all parties. This means that genuine mistakes all have the potential of being corrected, since they can be checked. As I shall argue, it is the corrigibility of mistakes, in the sense which I have outlined, that distinguishes mistakes from other false beliefs about the case, bad decisions, and misfiring procedures which are not mistakes.

Locating a mistake within what a person knows aright, and within the background of information and practices shared by the community, is not simply a matter of locating empirical claims within the framework of empirical verification, or locating mathematical claims within the framework of the "a priori." Wittgenstein remarks at 79: "[t]hat I am a man and not a woman can be verified, but if I were to say I was a woman, and then to explain the error by saying I hadn't checked the statement, the explanation would not be accepted." To better understand this, as well as Wittgenstein's remark at 71 about the friend who doesn't know his own address, we should look at the three-fold distinction Wittgenstein draws between "methodological propositions," such as that the earth has existed for ages past, and that 12 x 12 = 144; empirical propositions held fast for judging, such as the principles of chemistry; and other empirical propositions which are subject to normal checking procedures and revision. Neither methodological propositions nor empirical propositions held fast as rules for judging are genuinely open to checking or verification, although in the latter case, such propositions may be verifiable in unusual circumstances, and in the former, the truth of such propositions is not logically necessary. Propositions in either of these classes do not require or receive justification or verification in the ordinary course of events, because these propositions provide the parameters of truth and falsehood. "The *truth* of certain empirical propositions belongs to our frame of reference" (83).[8] Throughout

[8] I.e., our conceptual scheme or frame of reference is such that its adoption

On Certainty Wittgenstein struggles with a variety of ways of formulating the distinction between methodological propositions and empirical propositions held fast for judging, and between empirical propositions held fast for judging and empirical claims subject to judgment. He returns many times to the view that "there is no sharp boundary between methodological propositions and propositions within a method" (318), and similarly that there is no sharp boundary between propositions of logic and empirical propositions, or between rules and empirical propositions (319). This does not mean that there is no difference, but that the boundary is hazy. The difficulty with which Wittgenstein is grappling is one which stems from the fact that our "frame of reference" is not a single unitary system which is fixed once and for all, with universally recognized foundations, fully articulated, and uniformly covering all circumstances. The labels "methodological proposition," "empirical proposition held fast for judging," and "empirical proposition subject to judgment" mark off different roles or functions a proposition has, against a background of other propositions and activities; it does not reflect anything interesting about the particular *content* of the proposition.[9] Of course, within a given frame of reference, or fragment of such, certain sorts of propositions about certain sorts of things will often belong to the same category or have similar roles. But there is no necessity about this. Propositions which philosophers have judged privileged, such as mathematical or logical propositions, are, according to Wittgenstein, no more privileged than the proposition that the earth has existed for a very long time. Wittgenstein does not want to say of any particular proposition that it always occupies the same place in our frame of reference, or that it must do so (232). Even methodological propositions can lose their privileged position in our frame of reference: he points out that "whether a proposition can turn out false after all depends on what I make count as determinants for that proposition" (5),[10] and after all, there is "another" arithmetic. If the world changed

---

dictates acceptance of certain propositions. These then are true. Wittgenstein is not saying that one checks to see if the propositions are true and then accepts the framework.

[9]Here, Wittgenstein is sharply disagreeing with both Moore and with any sceptic who believes that propositions should be examined in terms of content or method of verification.

[10]Here, Wittgenstein is overstating his view: he does not really believe that an individual can determine what counts as determinants for any proposition. The point is rather that there is nothing *necessary* about what so counts; but that this is something decided upon.

in certain ways, or if we took up new or different ways of judging or acting, propositions presently out of the path of inquiry might be questioned; propositions previously nonarticulated may be formulated and examined; propositions previously judged to be empirical might come to function as part of the "rock-hard riverbed" of our thought. Our science changes, and these alterations in turn affect our actions and judgments. After all, "[m]en have judged that a king can make rain; *we* say this contradicts all experience. Today they judge that aeroplanes and the radio, etc. are means for the closer contact of peoples and spread of culture" (132).

In ordinary sorts of circumstances, the proposition that one is a man and not a woman does not function as an empirical claim up for assessment. Rather, it tends to function as a rule for judging and as a rule for acting. But it functions this way only in normal circumstances—and what counts as normal circumstances will ultimately depend on our frame of reference. We can imagine suitably peculiar circumstances in which the "error" would be a legitimate mistake, and in which the pseudo-explanation would be accepted as a legitimate explanation, say in the case of brain transplants.

Genuine mistakes, of the sorts of which Wittgenstein speaks, are never about propositions functioning at that time either as methodological propositions or empirical propositions held fast as rules for judging. They can only involve propositions which are accessible to checking, verification, or assessment.[11] The sorts of things about which one can make a mistake are the sorts of cases in which doubt *can be* reasonable. But the possibility of reasonable doubt here does not allow the entry of a sceptical wedge. The fact that doubt can be reasonable does not make doubt generally reasonable, and the fact that one may sometimes be wrong about these matters has never been the only stone upon which the sceptic grinds his ax. The sceptical challenge is that what underlies particular beliefs, mistaken or not, may be wrong; the sceptic uses the possibility of a perceptual error, for example, to challenge the veracity of all perceptual claims. This is exactly what Wittgenstein is arguing against: he argues that the fact that I can make a mistake in this situation does not entail that I can or do make a mistake in all similar situations, but rather it entails that I do *not* make a mistake. Nor do I make a mistake about other aspects of this situation (50).

---

[11] Particular calculations are subject to checking and to mistake; mathematical propositions are not. The distinction is one which Wittgenstein draws (see 650).

Wittgenstein suggests that those propositions which I cannot *know* (that I am in pain, that I see a white patch) are propositions about which I cannot make a mistake (425), and the propositions I can know are propositions about which it is possible for me to make a mistake. That I have not made a mistake can be established objectively—as objectively certain. For the propositions which one knows, one can *show* that there is no mistake, that one cannot be (i.e., *is* not) making a mistake (648). A proposition which I cannot know is a proposition whose putative verification is no more trustworthy or compelling than the proposition itself, and so is a proposition which lacks an accepted manner for showing it is correct, that no mistake has been made. Thus, I can make a mistake about what is under yonder tree or what foreign language that group of tourists is speaking, but I cannot make a *mistake* about whether this is my hand, or whether I am speaking English. Moore's claims to know that he has two hands, that he has parents, and so on, are thus misguided; Moore may accept them as incontrovertible claims, but he doesn't *know* them. He cannot make a mistake about them, but this doesn't entail that they are true or objectively certain.

*****

Recall that Wittgenstein's initial distinction is not simply between mistakes and mental disturbances, but also between treating something as a mistake and treating something as a mental disturbance. This notion of treatment should be emphasized. Treating a false belief as a mistake involves explaining or understanding a person's relationship to the error by placing that error within a context of beliefs and activities which the individual grasps, and which any rational person accepts. Put another way, it is being able to point out the mistake, to locate it within a framework of mutually shared beliefs, without impugning the individual's cognitive abilities or the individual's linguistic abilities (see 32, 67, 70, 81, 196). Treating a false belief as a mistake is treating it as corrigible. Mistakes once noted can be corrected—the false belief can be "replaced" by a correct belief, without significant alteration being made to the surrounding conceptual system, because the correcting process is provided by the ordinary checking procedures available. Treating something as a mistake is treating it as a false belief whose falsehood is in principle equally accessible to everyone, and whose correction is equally accessible as well. I can discover and correct my mistakes in the same way I can discover and correct yours. I can check my belief; I can check yours.

Errors, false beliefs which are not "grounded" in the way I have described, which do not fit into what one knows aright, do not count as mistakes. These sorts of false beliefs Wittgenstein labels as "mental disturbances." This characterization might seem unduly harsh if not downright misleading, and one might be tempted to think that Wittgenstein himself disowns it, substituting for it a *new* distinction between mistakes and being mistaken.[12] But reading Wittgenstein this way is to make retrograde progress, for the putative distinction between mistakes and being mistaken would at best be a different, and unilluminating, way of repeating the point that there are mistakes and there are other sorts of false propositions, without saying anything at all about the nature of these other propositions. But Wittgenstein has a great deal to say about these other propositons, and most of it is phrased in terms of mental disturbances: for one, these propositions are such that in the ordinary course of events, they cannot be understood without impugning someone's cognitive or linguistic abilities. Thus he says that anyone who denies that this is a hand would be regarded as demented; a person who doesn't know his own address is suffering from a mental disturbance (71); a person who continually questions a calculation is usually judged crazy (217), and so on (see also 108, 157, 158, 220, 281, 324, etc.). Wittgenstein does not mean to suggest that a sane person could never question or deny such propositions, but that in ordinary circumstances, such questioning or denial is taken as evidence for cognitive or linguistic malfunctioning. In extraordinary circumstances the questioning might be appropriate, but in the usual course of events these sorts of things are not questioned, and anyone who does challenge them does so by implicitly overstepping the frame of reference which gives meaning to these propositions and which in turn takes its meaning from them.

Like Quine, Wittgenstein refuses to draw a sharp boundary between cases in which linguistic abilities are to be impugned, and those in which cognitive abilities are judged faulty; like Quine as well, he is quite willing to admit that we have fair facility in adjudicating these matters in practice (236, 237). Wittgenstein points out that "only the

---

[12]See for example, Morawetz, *op. cit.*, especially pp. 104-7. This interpretation may be facilitated by a certain looseness in the translation of Wittgenstein's use of 'sich irren'; 'sich irren' is rendered in English as 'to make a mistake', 'to be mistaken', and 'to be wrong'.

accustomed context" of a remark "allows what is meant to come through clearly" (237), and it is in virtue of the context of a remark, and what we know of the speaker, that we will understand a remark. Similarly, it is in virtue of these same factors that we will attribute a mistake or will instead attribute linguistic impairment or some kind of cognitive deficiency, deviance, or malfunction.

There is no way to specify simply in terms of content which beliefs are to be judged mental disturbances. As with mistakes, one can be wrong about factual matters, procedural matters, and strategic matters: one can be wrong about the age of mountains, how to do history, or how to act. We can, however, follow Wittgenstein in recognizing that there are many different ways in which an individual may exhibit cognitive deficiency or deviance by considering the function or role of the correct belief in the community's system of belief which corresponds to the false belief in question. Five sorts of cases stand out, although, not surprisingly, there are not sharp boundaries between these sorts of cases.

First, there are cases in which a person questions, or denies, something which absolutely cannot be questioned, given the normal uses of words. Doubt or denial of these propositions is quite literally incoherent, for the formulation of the doubt presupposes the truth of what is to be doubted. The person who wonders if we are dreaming all the time belongs in the category, as would a person who, while asking what color a companion is presently seeing, also questions whether the companion understands English or intends to be deceptive in responding, whether the questioner's own memory is faulty with respect to color words, etc. (see 345). Second, there are cases in which an individual questions or denies a proposition which functions as a methodological proposition, such as the person who believes that desks and the like fade into and out of existence. Third are those cases in which an individual questions or denies a portion or fragment of our framework of beliefs, who assents to different (wrong?) basic assumptions or to different (wrong?) ways of making inferences, and who works with a different (wrong?) system of evidence. Here we place Wittgenstein's examples of the person who challenges our conventions of historical or scientific evidence. Into this category also would go the legislator who wanted to change the value of *pi*. Such an individual is challenging empirical propositions held fast as rules for judging; from the standpoint of the ordinary functioning of our system of belief, these doubts and challenges are not rational but irrational. Fourth are the cases in which an individual treats normal circumstances as abnormal ones, and uses procedures which are not appropriate or are unnecessary. The person who checks a mathematical calculation twenty times, the person who checks the number of toes on each foot, exhibits this kind of deviance, which we might call unreasonable doubt.[13] Lastly, there are cases in which an individual denies or questions something which that person ordinarily trusts, as the result of momentary confusion or disorientation.

The point of calling these phenomena "mental disturbances" is to emphasize the fact that each of them requires cure, not correction (see 92, 558, 578, 609, 611, 612). Upon initially confronting a person who denies or challenges what we accept as exempt from doubt, we will certainly question this person in order to determine what is meant by the denial or challenge; we may even try (unsuccessfully) to reason with the individual; but finally we will attempt to retrain, persuade pragmatically, convert or teach the afflicted individual. Occasionally, we may simply tell the person that the belief is false, and provide the correct belief or procedure. Sometimes, we may even let the aberration pass, unremarked, if it has no significant consequences for the behavior of its holder (338).

Wittgenstein frequently intimates that the training and teaching of a child is an enterprise closely connected with the remediation of mental disturbances.[14] In both sorts of cases, we are providing the individual with a (new) world view, a new picture of things, new or different ways of proceeding. When a child is small, we simply show and tell the child various things—to sit in a chair, to bring the violets; we do not attempt to offer reasons in an attempt to argue that child into agreement. As the child accepts and assimilates these commonplace instructions and bits of information, it also acquires those ways of believing and acting which define the conceptual system shared by the community as a whole and gradually acquires facility in operating with the community's standards of evidence. When we are attempting "cures," we do not offer reasons to "disturbed" individuals in order to show them they are wrong; we do not offer to check the disputed

[13] The difference between irrational doubt and unreasonable doubt seems to be that the individual who is engaging in unreasonable doubt, while needing cure, is still recognizably a member of our intellectual community, by and large; the individual with irrational doubts may not be. In both cases, we, as representatives of the rational community, may attempt a cure.

[14] We might even go so far as to say that Wittgenstein is tempted to include at least some kinds of ignorance, notably systematic ignorance, as a sort of "mental disturbance." The ignorance of such an adult, as well as that of a child, is to be cured, not corrected by reason.

belief to see if it is right, for such persons are in the position of a child who has not yet acquired fully the community's standards. An individual suffering from a "mental disturbance" is not in a position to accept the reasons we offer, nor the checking we proffer. Similarly, if the affected person tries to offer data as evidence which is supposed to make the questioning, doubt, or denial reasonable (i.e., to show that there is a reason to question, doubt, or deny), and thereby to show that the belief in question really is up for assessment, there is never any reason for us, in ordinary circumstances, to accept as evidence what is offered as evidence. We may listen, but reason does not dictate that we accept what is said (see 611, 641).

The practice of curing presupposes a body of belief, knowledge, practice, and behavior. On the basis of what we, the rational community, know, accept, and do, we will treat differently different deviations from the norm. The norm itself, qua norm, is protected from any challenge, simply because it is a norm. This does not mean that norms cannot or do not change, but because these propositions provide us with principles of evidence, which in turn define what is rational for us, there can never be any conclusive evidence that forces us, on pain of irrationality, to give them up. Deviations from these principles and standards may be major or minor; what counts as major or minor will be determined by the way in which the deviation affects the behavior of the deviating individual in a variety of circumstances. Treatment will be determined by severity of deviation and by how commonplace or widespread the particular form of deviation is, and how many people in that community share that deviant belief (see 132, 211, 217, 303, 304). If the community as a whole shares a particular belief, then acceptance or adoption of that belief cannot be judged a "mental disturbance," nor is any individual holding that belief a candidate for cure in that community (see 624, 625, 628). Others outside of the community, however, can judge that those within are wrong (see 132, 286).

Thus one is in a position vis-à-vis one's own "mental disturbances" different from that vis-à-vis one's own mistakes. For one thing, one cannot relate to one's own "dementia" as one can to another's—one cannot cure oneself, although of course the disturbance may be cured spontaneously, or one may mimic the behavior of others. Nor can one check to make certain that one is not accepting or acting on a particular deviant belief. One can at best find out that one is behaving or believing in opposition to the behavior or belief of others in the society.

The beliefs which are embodied in a person's actions have their own subjective certainty which, while no criterion for objective certainty, reveals their basic role in that person's system of belief. We act on many beliefs which we, as individuals, cannot countenance even as candidates for falsehood. One's own name and address, anatomy, that one's head isn't stuffed with sawdust, are the kinds of examples Wittgenstein provides. Of these sorts of propositions typically one says "I cannot be wrong." What then of the remark "I can hardly be wrong about this"? Does it mean that the speaker is admitting that there is a possibility of error about some basic propositions, or that there is some subjective uncertainty present? Wittgenstein seems to suggest that this is the case at 673, when he remarks that it is very hard to distinguish between propositions about which one cannot be wrong and those about which one can hardly be wrong. But distinguishing cases in which I cannot be wrong from those in which I can hardly be wrong in terms of propositions about which these claims are made is misleading. As Wittgenstein himself remarks, "I cannot be wrong" is a claim "which relates essentially to *me,* not to the game in general" (637). While (rational) people just aren't wrong about these sorts of things most of the time, very occasionally, in very odd circumstances, they are. Consequently the claim "I can hardly be wrong about this" is better construed as a remark that relates to more than just me. When the remark is seriously and literally meant, and is not simply a way of deflecting a sceptical challenge by refusing to treat it seriously, it is a way of asserting that while people sometimes, albeit rarely, go wrong about this sort of thing, I am not, at this time. For if I were wrong, if I could be wrong, on this occasion, this admission would be, to myself, a countenancing of doubt cast on all my cognitive abilities. Thus, at 69: "I should like to say: 'If I am wrong about *this,* I have no guarantee that anything I say is true.' But others won't say that about me, nor will I say it about other people."

Putting this another way, our entire apparatus for judgment leaves no room for a person to seriously assert "I am now mentally (cognitively) disturbed"; one can only attribute cognitive disturbance to others or to oneself at some time in the past (645). This means that there is no room in our conceptual system for the formulation of a radical sceptical doubt. "I cannot seriously assert that I am now dreaming" (676), nor can I assert that I am now in the grip of a delusion, nor yet can I coherently and literally assert the possibility that I am now dreaming. For while there is room for the admission that the beliefs which now provide the stable core of our conceptual scheme may change, within that scheme there is no room for rational doubt of those beliefs.

*****

Wittgenstein's remarks on mistakes and mental disturbances cast an interesting light on certain passages in the *Philosophical Investigations.* A recurring theme there is the therapeutic nature of the philosophic enterprise. Genuine philosophy is there conceived as an attempt to cure peculiar ways of looking at the world and to remedy pathological forms of thought. It aims at substituting a correct way of seeing things, in all their particularity, for the highly simplified, overly generalized, perspectives offered by traditional philosophers. Traditional philosophical positions are wrong, but are rarely mistakes or the result of mistakes. Hence Wittgenstein cannot offer evidence and argument against them; he must build up and point out new ways of looking at things, in the hopes that he can train his audience to see and to think as he does.

DEBORAH H. SOLES.

WICHITA STATE UNIVERSITY.

NONEVIDENTIAL REASONS FOR BELIEF: A JAMESIAN VIEW

In his essay "The Will to Believe," William James responded to the claims of various nineteenth century champions of scientific method who advocated the employment of rigorous standards of evidence not only in research but in all contexts of life.[1] Perhaps the most emphatic statement of this view came in "The Ethics of Belief" by W. K. Clifford. Clifford argued that there is a moral duty to regulate one's beliefs by reference to the strictest standards of evidence. No one, he said, "can escape the universal duty of questioning all that we believe."[2] Moreover, he claimed,

> It is wrong always, everywhere, and for every one, to believe anything upon insufficient evidence.[3]

In opposition to Clifford, James rejected the view that a belief had to pass strict standards of evidence in order to be legitimate. He argued that it could be rational to accept a belief on the basis of nonevidential considerations, that preferences, desires, and interests could provide legitimate bases for belief.

Readers of James' essay may be surprised to find me claiming that James defends the rationality of believing without adequate evidence, for James is often portrayed as an irrationalist. I think that this interpretation is mistaken, but I shall begin my discussion by focusing on a part of his argument which tends to support it.

James identifies as his primary thesis the view that:

> Our passional nature not only lawfully may, but must, decide an option between propositions, whenever it is a genuine option that cannot by its nature be decided on intellectual grounds . . . (11)

Part of his defense involves the argument that our passions do in fact determine our beliefs, that beliefs are frequently not based on com-

---

[1]The essay appears in *The Will to Believe and Other Essays in Popular Philosophy* (New York: Dover Publications, 1956; original ed., 1897). Page references will be cited in the text.

For historical background to James' essay and the development of his thought, see Peter Kauber, "The Foundation of James's Ethics of Belief," *Ethics*, Vol. 84 (1974), pp. 151-66.

[2]"The Ethics of Belief," in *Lectures and Essays* (London: Macmillan and Co., 1879), Vol. II, p. 183.

[3]Quoted by James, p. 8.

pelling evidence. Even our belief that there is such a thing as truth and that we are capable of knowing it is, he says, "a passionate affirmation of desire." If challenged by a sceptic, we can find no satisfactory reply. It is a matter of "one volition against another," of one person being willing to make an assumption which another "does not care to make." (10)

In places, James seems to see the ethics of belief controversy itself as an instance of passional conflict. There are two propositions—"We must know the truth" and "We must avoid error"—and each is put forward as the "first and great commandments for would-be knowers." (17) Which rule one gives priority to is, he says, a matter of personal temperament. Clifford's commitment to the ethics of belief derives from his passional nature. As James writes:

> We must remember that these feelings of our duty about either truth or error are in any case only expressions of our passional life . . . he who says, "Better go without truth forever than believe a lie," merely shows his own preponderant horror of becoming a dupe. He may be critical of many of his desires and fears, but this fear he slavishly obeys. (18)

James concludes that he *personally* is more fearful of losing truth than of succumbing to error. He prefers the path of risk rather than the path of caution.

What James seems to be saying in these passages is that particular beliefs and epistemic strategies appeal to people for reasons which have to do with temperament, rather than reason. Ultimately, all our choices are nonrational—even the decision to be rational.

If this were James' view, then he would not be claiming that he is correct and Clifford incorrect in their stances regarding the ethics of belief. He would simply be expressing his own preference, for the rational evaluation of risky versus cautious methodologies would be out of the question. What I want to argue, however, is that James' basic strategy was to show that reason itself required that we reject the ethics of belief position.

In supporting my interpretation, I will begin by noting that James does not simply state his preference and stop there. He often asserts that his methodological choice is superior to that of Clifford. Thus, he writes:

> . . . Clifford's exhortation has to my ears a thoroughly fantastic sound . . . In a world where we are so certain to incur [errors] . . . a certain lightness of heart seems healthier than this excessive nervousness on their behalf. (19)

> . . . where faith in a fact can help create the fact, that would be an insane logic which should say that faith running ahead of scientific

> evidence is the "lowest kind of immorality" into which a thinking being can fall. (25)
>
> . . . a rule of thinking which would absolutely prevent me from acknowledging certain kinds of truth if those kinds of truth were really there, would be an irrational rule. (28)

James indicates in these passages that he considers Clifford's rationalism to be "unhealthy," "insane," "irrational." By implication, his own view is healthy, sane, and rational. It is better and more rational to allow violations of the usual rules which tie belief to evidence than it is to insist on universal adherence to them.

But how can this be? How could James possibly be correct? In answering these questions, we must recall that James sanctions the role of the passions in belief choice only when what is being considered is "a genuine option that cannot by its nature be decided on intellectual grounds." (There is one passage where James withdraws this qualification, and I will consider it later.) While his opponents urged a uniform and constant use of the standards of scientific inquiry, James was quite sensitive to the variety of circumstances in which we think and act. In areas which are purely theoretical and do not directly affect practice, strict objectivity and great caution are appropriate. As James said,

> Let us agree, however, that wherever there is no forced option, the dispassionately judicial intellect with no pet hypothesis, saving us, as it does, from dupery at any rate, ought to be our ideal. (21-22)

In our daily activities, however, we are concerned with acting to further our interests and goals, and in these contexts, the employment of scientific methods and standards may be foolish. We need to evaluate the consequences of employing particular methods or standards in a given context. If applying rational methods of evidence assessment yields undesirable results, then the application of those methods is itself irrational.

To bring out this point, James develops the notion of a genuine option. This is a choice between two or more *live* (i.e., attractive) hypotheses which is *momentous* (i.e., which will profoundly affect a person for good or ill) and which is *forced* (i.e., which cannot be avoided because even indecision would commit a person to one of the options). Moreover, as we have seen, James adds the proviso that the truth and falsity of the hypotheses are intellectually undecidable. (See pp. 2-4).

James is asking that we consider whether it would make sense to follow Clifford's maxim in the following kind of situation. A person S is confronted with a choice between two hypotheses, p and q, each of which has just as much evidential support as the other. Moreover, all of the available evidence has been surveyed, and there are no opportunities for gathering further evidence. If p is believed and acted on and if p is true, S will enjoy immeasurably great happiness. If q is believed and acted upon and if q is true, S's life will be unaffected. If he makes no choice between p and q, his life will be affected just as it would be by the rejection of p and the acceptance of q. What should S do?

Two things are clear here. First, it is rational for S to prefer that p be true because its truth and the adoption of practices based upon it would bring him great happiness. Second, it would be irrational for S to believe q because it is recommended neither by the evidence nor by any possible benefits of belief.

Clifford's maxim would, of course, lead one to suspend judgment, but given the possible benefits of belief, would suspension of judgment be rational? Would it be irrational to accept p, which is unsupported by the evidence but which would be advantageous to the believer?

James' answer is that adoption of the belief would be rational and that adherence to Clifford's maxim would be an overly restrictive and counter-productive form of "rule worship" (to borrow a phrase from J. J. C. Smart). Whether reason *requires* that one believe p in such a case may not be obvious, but it seems clear enough that reason would at least *allow* belief, that it would not be *irrational* to accept p. Belief in this case is simply the relevant means to a worthwhile goal. If we grant the desirability of the end, the effectiveness of the means, and the general principle that an act is rational if it is an effective means to a desirable end, then belief in this instance is rational.

If one is inclined to label the choice irrational, that reflects a tension within the concept of rationality itself. The rationality of *belief* adoption is usually assessed by examining the relation of the belief to evidence for its truth. The rationality of *actions* is usually assessed by reference to expectable results—the extent to which particular actions further the purposes of the agent better than others. James' pragmatic outlook led him to see belief choices as actions and, hence, to see that the criteria of rationality which apply to actions could apply to beliefs. Contrary to Clifford, who saw evidence for truth as the only reason for belief, James allows the good results of belief to count as a reason for belief as well. A person adopting a belief in the circumstances James describes could certainly give reasons for his belief of a recognized sort, though they would not be the kinds of reasons which count as evidence.

I conclude, then, that in describing cases of genuine options which are not resolvable by evidential considerations, James effectively shows that our preferences, desires, and interests can play a lawful role in determining belief choice. Viewed from the perspective of means/end rationality, this influence of the passional nature can be described as rational.

I shall presently try to show that James' reasoning supports an even more radical conclusion, but before doing so I would like to clarify his position and reply to a few possible objections.

First, it is important to see that James' position is completely general in its formulation and has no special connecton with issues of religious belief. Though James was concerned with religious beliefs in his essay, that was merely one application of his general principles.

Second, one might think that the force of James' argument depends on Clifford's position being too simplistic and that a more sophisticated version of the ethics of belief would not be open to James' attack. But as Brand Blanshard has noted, James' main point is that "evidence is not the only thing that justifies belief."[4] This key point must be denied by even the most sophisticated advocates of the ethics of belief.

Third, it has often been claimed that James incorrectly assumes that believing is an action and that we have a degree of control over what we believe which in fact we do not possess. Since we cannot voluntarily adopt and reject beliefs in the way in which we can switch a light on and off, all the talk of options, choices, and decisions is misleading. We simply do not have it in our power to do what James recommends.

While this objection raises a number of significant issues about belief, it seems to me to leave James' position untouched. First, James himself recognizes that there are usually severe limits to our control over what we believe. This is precisely what he wants to emphasize in his contrast between live and dead hypotheses, for dead hypotheses are those which a person cannot even seriously entertain, let alone adopt.

Second, neither Clifford nor anyone who is a rationalist can consistently deny that we have some degree of control over our beliefs. Rational ideals make sense only on the assumption that we can deliberate about what to believe, and this presupposes that we can at

[4] *Reason and Belief* (New Haven: Yale University Press, 1975), p. 419.

least exercise indirect control over our beliefs by trying to focus our minds on relevant evidence, consider the force of arguments, exclude the influence of irrelevant factors, etc. Beliefs may not be the kinds of things we can switch on and off, but we can take steps which are likely to affect what we believe.[5] To deny this would undermine not only James' position but that of Clifford and classical rationalism as well.

Finally, the issue does not really turn on questions about our actual belief-controlling abilities. We need only to be able to imagine such an ability to make James' point because the basic issue is a matter of principle. Rationality involves two separate criteria—one evidential and one practical, and we want to know which if either of them is the dominant one. We try to decide by raising the following question: to whatever extent we are able to exercise control over beliefs, would it ever be rational to adopt a belief on pragmatic grounds? This question can be raised and debated without assuming total belief control, just as we can debate whether it would be more valuable to write a great symphony or to cure a dread disease, without assuming that we actually possess the power to do either.

None of these objections, then, undermines James' position, and I agree with his remark toward the end of the essay: "I do not see how this logic can be escaped." (29) If the argument to this point is correct, however, an even more shocking conclusion follows from it. Though I have so far defended belief on nonevidential grounds only in situations involving genuine options which are intellectually undecidable, James' arguments provide a basis for deleting this restriction and thus for concluding that it is rational to accept *any* belief that promises significant benefits to the believer. James himself took this further step, affirming that:

> . . . we have the right to believe at our own risk any hypothesis that is live enough to tempt our will. (29)

In this form, James' account supports the adoption of beliefs on passional grounds which are, on evidential grounds, thought to be *false*. All that is required for justification is a significant enough advantage.

Consider the following rather bizarre case, which is suggested by James' reference to situations in which "faith in a fact can help create a fact." Imagine a person who is not a millionaire being offered a

---

[5]For an interesting discussion of this point, see H. H. Price, "Belief and Will," *Proceedings of the Aristotelian Society,* Supplementary Volume XXVIII (1954). For an opposing view, see R. Edgley, *Reason in Theory and Practice* (London: Hutchinson and Co., 1969), pp. 61-65, and Bernard Williams "Deciding to Believe," in *Problems of the Self* (Cambridge: Cambridge University Press, 1973), pp. 136-51.

million dollars if he can succeed in making himself believe that he *is* a millionaire. This would literally be a case in which believing something would *make* it true. Nonetheless, in one sense, the hypothesis is not even live because the person has conclusive evidence that it is false. Moreover, it is assuredly not a case where the intellect is powerless to resolve the matter. Nonetheless James' argument shows that it would be rational to accept the belief, for this would bring about both the truth of the belief and an extremely beneficial change in the financial status of the person to whom the offer is made.

If this offer were made to Clifford or other proponents of the ethics of belief, their personal commitment to ideals of evidential rationality might be so strong that they would turn it down. We might even admire them for the rejection, viewing it as an act of epistemic heroism. Nonetheless, if the offer were accepted, we could not reasonably criticize its acceptance as irrational. Assuming the desirability of the wealth offered, the effort required to accept the false belief would be rational to make, even if it required a visit to a hypnotist or some other master of mental modifications.

This case is admittedly outlandish, but it does show that the results of beliefs are capable of being reasons for believing. One *could* object that it is only in fanciful examples that things work this way and that in fact no good ever comes of false or unjustified beliefs. This claim, however, surely cannot be known to be true *a priori*. Indeed, experience suggests that it is false and that actual cases arise in which someone is better off with a false belief than without it. Moreover, if we can make this judgment about someone, it would follow that he would have reason to avoid evidence which tended to refute his belief.

This bring to me to the final criticisms I shall consider, for I can well imagine that one might want to charge that James and I are doing nothing less than issuing an open invitation to massive self-deception and total irrationalism.

It is important to notice that there are two objections here, one involving self-deception and one involving irrationalism. With regard to self-deception, there is some justice in the objection, for if what I have argued is correct, then self-deception may at times be rational. Even if one would not want to encourage its widespread use, there seems no denying that it can be beneficial in some cases, and where this is so, my argument does justify it.

To sanction self-deception, however, is not to sanction irrationalism. Indeed, the strength of James' position is that he sees that rationality is a broader notion than his opponents allow, for it includes practical criteria of evaluation as well as evidential criteria. The person who acts on James' view satisfies the criteria of practical rationality by adopting effective means toward the realization of a desirable end. He must also be rational in another way, however, for in order for his passional belief choice to be rational, he must possess *strong evidence* that the adoption of the belief in question will have the desired effect and that it will not lead to ill effects which outweigh the advantages of belief. With respect to predicting the actual effects of his belief choice, the Jamesian rationalist will have to be as attentive to evidence as the most rigorous Cliffordian rationalist.

This point provides a reply to the objection that one who follows James' principle will inevitably be forced to make drastic distortions of reality. This objection is based on the view that a person who adopts a belief unsupported by evidence either a) will have to deceive himself about many facts which bear on the matter in question and, hence, will be forced to hold more and more false beliefs, or b) will acquire more false beliefs because the willfully adopted belief will come to function as evidence in assessing new questions, thus generating a "snowball effect" in the amount of falsity entering his system of beliefs. In either case, the result must eventually be harmful.[6]

Certainly, a rational Jamesian will have to consider these possibilities, but they would only rule out willful belief adoption if it inevitably generated greater and greater distortions. I would agree that in practice, the opportunities for rationally adopting beliefs which are unsupported by evidence are very limited, and James himself saw this quite clearly. Although he argued that "*in abstracto*" one could believe anything at one's own risk, he went on to say,

> *In concreto,* the freedom to believe can only cover living options which the intellect of the individual cannot by itself resolve. (29)

In theory, the very radical principle "it is rational to believe whatever is useful" is true, but in practice this usually reduces to the restricted thesis containing the requirement that the belief be a genuine option whose truth is intellectually undecidable.

My aim in this paper has been twofold. I have tried to show a) that it is rational to allow nonevidential considerations to play a role in belief choice, and b) that James' often maligned defense of this

[6]The first version of this objection is set forth by Williams in "Deciding to Believe," p. 151. I owe the second to William DeAngelis.

position is a powerful and perceptive piece of philosophizing.[7] It is understandable that persons committed to truth find James' conclusions distasteful, for James shows the need for rethinking traditional ideals of rationality, and this is something which even the tough-minded may find difficult.

STEPHEN L. NATHANSON.

NORTHEASTERN UNIVERSITY.

[7]Jack Meiland has recently defended the relevance of nonevidential reasons for belief in "What Ought We to Believe? or The Ethics of Belief Revisited," *American Philosophical Quarterly*, Vol. 17 (1980), pp. 15-24. Meiland, however, does not take himself to be agreeing with James on these matters.

CHOICE

According to the first entry in Webster's New International Dictionary—second edition unabridged, an act of choice is "the voluntary act of selecting or separating from two or more things that which is preferred." Now it is clear to both the hard determinist and the libertarian that such an act could not occur in a deterministic universe; nothing would be voluntary and there would be no alternative(s) to the one inevitable course of events. The soft determinist contends that determinism is compatible with genuine choice. But how can the future be both closed (as required by determinism) and partially open (as required by genuine choice)? James' charge that soft determinism is a "quagmire of evasion" has yet to be answered. So if, as I will contend, this definition does describe the act of choice as we experience it, then the determinist must hold that our experience of choice is illusory. In a word, the determinist must deny that experienced choice is ever genuine choice. So as we examine the phenomenon of choice and consider its role in human action, we will also be making explicit the nature and extent of the determinist's denial.

Perhaps the most salient thing about the act of choosing is the fact that it is always the act of choosing something. A choice is always a choice of some object just as consciousness is always consciousness of some object. The sentence, "I choose," is elliptical. So I will adopt as paradigm the following formula: "I choose X." Clearly the act of choosing contains the three terms found in all other acts of consciousness—a subjective pole, the mode of consciousness, in this case *choosing,* and the object being chosen, *X*.

Before proceeding with the analysis I should make it clear that I will be using the formula "I choose X" and its modifications in an effort to illuminate the act of choice as we experience it. This is not an inquiry into the meaning of various linguistic forms as such. Nor is it an attempt to legislate concerning the legitimate uses of such formulae. Rather, it is an attempt to develop a paradigm adequate to capture certain essential features in our experience of choice.

When we compare past-, present-, and future-tense forms of the paradigm, we may make a rather surprising discovery. A sentence of the form "I chose X" is either true or false. But a sentence of the form

"I choose X" is neither true nor false. And a statement of the form "I will choose X," taken literally, is unintelligible. A sentence of the form "I chose X" is simply an assertion that a particular event, viz., my act of choosing X, has taken place. In similar fashion, the sentence, "Napoleon was defeated at Waterloo," simply asserts that another particular event, viz., Napoleon's defeat at Waterloo, has taken place. But a sentence of the form "I choose X" is neither true nor false in any straightforward sense. It does not assert or report that an action of a certain type has occurred; its utterance *is* an action of a certain type. It is what J. L. Austin has called a performative utterance; it is an action performed with words. Its utterance, in the appropriate context, is a sufficient condition for its being the case that an act of choosing has taken place, but it does not report that action; it *is* that action. If, in the appropriate context, a person says, "I choose X," and then subsequently says, "I was mistaken in choosing X," this does not mean that his initial utterance was false. The question of fallibility simply does not arise since the utterance is not a report, fallible or infallible. It is a type of action that may be good or bad, wise or unwise, appropriate or inappropriate, and the subsequent utterance merely serves to indicate the agent's acknowledgement that his choice was in some sense a bad one. If we do sometimes use the expression "I choose X" to report a choice that we have made, perhaps in the immediate past, it would surely be more accurate to say either "I chose X" or "I have just chosen X."

But in what sense is a sentence of the form "I will choose X" unintelligible? The answer is implicit in an argument showing the logical impossibility that a genuine choice be causally determined in advance. If it were logically possible for a choice to be causally determined in advance, it would be at least theoretically possible for a person to know what his choice was going to be before making it since there would be no theoretical reason why he should not discover this "fact" either on his own or from some other person. But would it make any sense to say, "I know that I will choose X, but I have not yet chosen X"? Taken literally, the sentence is unintelligible. If I know that I *will* choose X in the same sense in which I know that I have been sitting at this typewriter for the past hour, the choice of X is scarcely a matter for further deliberation. And so any claim to such foreknowledge is either a tacit admission that the choice has already been made or a rather strange way of saying that one never really had any choice with respect to X. But if a sentence of the form "I know that I will choose X, but I have not yet chosen X" is unintelligible to one who attempts to interpret it literally, then a sentence of the form "I will choose X" is equally unintelligible since it involves the same category-mistake, the same absurd combination of the grammar of knowing and the grammar of choosing. Of course, there is nothing unintelligible in the expression "I will choose something or other" said, not as a performative utterance, but simply as an assertion *that* I will make a choice. And, furthermore, the meaning of this utterance is not altered when it is prefixed by the phrase "I know that . . . " any more than the assertion "p," made under ordinary circumstances, is altered by the prefix of the phrase "It is true that . . . " The grammar of knowing vis-à-vis the future is oriented to that part of the future that has already been decided, to that part of the future that is included in all of the real possibilities. But the grammar of choosing is oriented to that part of the future that is as yet undecided. One cannot choose X if one believes that X is already either inevitable or impossible. One chooses not what *will* happen but what to make happen. As an illustration of this, a young man dying of incurable cancer cannot choose whether or not to suffer an untimely death although he might still be in a position to choose some form of suicide as the preferred way. And to anticipate the sort of case that might be pressed as a counterinstance, there is nothing unintelligible about a sentence of the form "I will vote for candidate *X* on election day" which seems to say, "I will choose X on election day." But the resemblance is only superficial; if I *will* vote for candidate X on election day, my choice has already been made, and all that remains to be done on election day is for that choice to be officially registered.

Consider once again the paradigm: "I choose X." If a choice is always a choice of some object, what sort of object can be chosen? The answer is implicit in what has just been said. If one chooses not what *will* happen, but what to *make* happen, then one's choice is always the choice of some action, and, furthermore, it is always the choice of an action that one believes to be neither inevitable nor impossible. It must be an action that one believes to be among the possible actions that are within one's power to effect. One cannot choose that something happen if one does not believe that it is within one's power at least to help make it happen. But is a choice always a choice of some action? Doesn't one sometimes choose possible things rather than possible actions? For example, one goes to a restaurant and orders roast beef rather than chicken or fish. Now there is no doubt that this is the way one would ordinarily describe such a commonplace act of choice. But does one really choose roast beef *simpliciter* or does one not in fact choose to eat roast beef? Or suppose that an art collector chooses a particular painting at an art auction. Does he choose painting X *simpliciter,* or does he not in fact choose to buy and display, or hoard, or make a gift of, or do something else with painting X? Reflection would seem to indicate that any sentence that appears to embody a counterinstance will turn out to be elliptical; the more accurate rendering makes explicit the fact that the object of choice is an action and not merely a thing. So we will have a less ambiguous paradigm if we replace the original formula "I choose X" with "I choose to do X."

But our paradigm must undergo further alteration if it is to make explicit the structure of the act of choosing. Reflection has shown that the object of choice is always some possible action, or at any rate, some action believed to be possible by the agent making the choice. A necessary condition for my choosing to do X is the implicit, if not explicit, belief that I *can* do X in several important senses of "can." In the first place, I must believe that I can do X in the sense that it is logically possible for X to be done by me. From this it follows, for example, that I cannot choose to construct a square circle. In the second place, I must believe that I can do X in the sense that the doing of X is a real possibility for me. It must be a real possibility in the strict sense, an *opportunity* given the present state of affairs and not merely contingent upon some possible state of affairs. And finally, I must believe that I can do X in the sense that it is within my power or ability to do X. It sometimes happens that I choose to do something only to discover that I cannot do it. But it would be absurd to suggest that I could choose to do X while believing myself to be unable to do X. In short, my belief that I can do X in all three of these senses is a necessary condition for my choosing to do X. But if X is viewed as a possible action in these three different senses by the chooser of X, it must not be forgotten that X is still taken to be only possible, not inevitable. One always believes that he chooses to do X rather than some other equally possible alternative(s) to X. In this sense, a choice is always a free choice, and therefore the phrase "free choice" is redundant. And so the paradigm should be augmented once more to make explicit the fact that a choice is always made in a context of alternatives; "I choose to do X" becomes "I choose to do X rather than Y."

Is the paradigm now in a satisfactory form? I think not. If I choose to do X rather than Y, there must be some reason for choosing to do X rather than Y. This is not to suggest that the reason must always be stated at the time of choosing. As a matter of fact, the reason might never be stated. But it is a necessary condition for the act of choice that a reason *could* be given for the choice. A final addition to the paradigm will make this structural feature explicit: "I choose to do X rather than Y because . . . "

But what does it mean to say that an act of choice always has a reason? To say that an act of choice always has a reason is to say that an act of choice is a deliberate act; when one chooses to do X rather than Y, one does so deliberately. This does not mean that every act of choice involves prior deliberation, that the various alterntives are always carefully weighed before one of them is selected. But to say that a choice is always made deliberately is to say that it is always made consciously and, as we commonly put it, "on purpose." Thus, as is the case with "free choice," phrases such as "deliberate choice," "conscious choice," and "purposive choice" are all redundant. Strictly speaking, there can be no unconscious choices; psychoanalysts who speak of unconscious choices must use "choice" in a highly unorthodox way if they are to avoid a contradiction in terms. A phrase borrowed from physics, viz., "the resultant of forces," would seem to provide a much more appropriate way to characterize what they have in mind. And the fact that a choice is inherently purposive is indicated by the way in which choosing is oriented to the future. When I choose one possible action in preference to its alternatives, I do so because I believe it to be the best way to attain some end even if that end includes nothing beyond the doing of the chosen action for its own sake. In other words, I choose to do X rather than Y because I believe that the doing of X will better serve my purposes than the doing of Y. But to explain the connection between the doing of X and the purpose(s) that it is judged best able to serve is to give the reason for choosing to do X rather than Y.

By way of conclusion, I will comment briefly on situations requiring "indifferent choice" or "choice without preference." In situations of this sort there is no reason for choosing X rather than Y. But in the absence of reasons, must Buridan's Ass starve? I would contend that situations of this sort involve choice in only a Pickwickian sense. They do require selection from two or more alternatives, but by hypothesis there are no grounds for preference. However, it does not follow that Buridan's Ass must starve. In fact, the obvious solution to the problem is supported by good reasons. In the absence of grounds for preference, it is reasonable to use a randomizing instrument of selection such as a coin toss. An even simpler randomizing device would be the adoption of a policy of always taking the first noticed among equally desirable alternatives. Thus when confronted with a tray of virtually identical sandwiches at a party, one chooses either to have or to forego a sandwich for whatever reason. But if one chooses to have a sandwich, one is not thereby doomed to go hungry. The selection without preference of some sandwich or other by random selection is a rational resolution of the problem.

ROBERT G. BURTON.

UNIVERSITY OF GEORGIA.

DISCUSSION
A MEMO ON METHOD: HILARY PUTNAM[1]

In reading the work of Hilary Putnam, we will do well always to bear in mind, as he would surely wish us to do, two major themes: his realism and the rejection of the notion that mathematics is an *a priori* science. Neither of these themes is essentially new, but even so we have to work hard to eke out the precise form they take in the Putnam corpus, as well as his reasons for holding them.

The clearest statement as to what Putnam's realism is is perhaps that given in the introduction (p. vii). "The statements of science are in my view," he writes, "either true or false (although it is often the case that we do not know which) and their truth or falsity does not consist in their being highly derived ways of describing regularities in human experience [or ways of worldmaking (?)].[2] Reality is not a part of the human mind; rather the human mind is a part—and a small part at that—of reality." The use of 'part' here, of course, is not that of a calculus of homogeneous individuals. Reality might be mental in some fashion with human minds "parts" of it. But if reality is not mental, then the very meaning of 'part' must be construed in such a way as to admit heterogeneous individuals—provided of course that human minds are genuinely mental. The exact handling of 'part of' in philosophical discourse is always a matter of some delicacy, but without such delicacy contexts containing the word tend to be rather uninformative. For Putnam, anyhow, realism is not to be identified with materialism, but has to do rather with "the existence of material objects in the customary sense" and also with "the objectivity of mathematical necessity and mathematical possibility (or equivalently about the existence of mathematical objects) and about entities which are neither material objects nor mathematical objects—in particular, fields and physical magnitudes." The view, according to this description, is thus a kind of mathematical and physicalistic *reism,* reminiscent somewhat of Kotarbinski.

Putnam's philosophy of mathematics is based on the idea that

[1] *Mathematics, Matter and Method, Philosophical Papers,* Vol. I (Cambridge: Cambridge University Press, 1975).

[2] See H. Putnam, "Reflections on Goodman's *Ways of Worldmaking,*" *The Journal of Philosophy* 76 (1979): 603-19.

"the differences between mathematics and empirical science have been vastly exaggerated" and that "in mathematics too there is an interplay of postulation, quasi-empirical testing, and conceptual revolution leading to the formation of contextually *a priori* paradigms." But still mathematics is "much more '*a priori*' than physics," he notes. The "principles of mathematics are [thus] relatively *a priori*." Hence both "Platonism — the view that mathematics is about objects of which we have *a priori* knowledge — and Nominalism — the view that mathematics is not about real objects, that most of it is just make believe" are thrown by the wayside.

There may well be point to some of these, and allied, contentions, if stated precisely. Putnam is willing, however, to assume that that hoary old term '*a priori*' has a sufficiently clear meaning at least to get us started, Sadly, however, this is not the case. The term as Putnam uses it is hopelessly vague and cries out for definition. Actually, however, it is the phrase 'more *a priori* than' that is the central notion around which his own view centers and upon which his criticisms of other views rests. Nowhere does Putnam tell us what this term means or how it behaves logically. Not one principle is ever enunciated, or even so much as hinted at, concerning it. To be sure, Putnam does say that "the concept of an *a priori* truth that I reject is historically best represented by Descartes' notion of a clear and distinct idea. . . . [Such ideas] were in a certain sense self-certifying truths. They bore their validity on their face. Not only could it never be rational to give up such a truth; it could never even be rational to doubt one." But surely now, this description is not up to sophisticated contemporary standards. Putnam resuscitates it as a straw man easily to be knocked down. A more contemporary opponent would have been a more worthy one.

Putnam is fond of speaking of "equivalent descriptions of the same states of affairs," in particular, of equivalent *systems* describing the same states of affairs. In view of these, "representation-independent" answers to questions such as 'Do mathematical objects exist over and above ordinary physical objects?' are not feasible. In fact, this very question is not a "good" one. Instead, according to Putnam, we should recognize that "the knowledge of mathematical truth [is] dependent upon experience" and that "the existence of mathematics is representation-relative." But these contentions do not quite accord with the basic realist contention, already noted, that the statements of science "are either true or false [independent presumably of their representation] . . . and [that] their truth or falsity does not consist in their being highly derived ways of describing regularities in human experience." But knowledge of mathematical truth is dependent upon experience, we are told, more particularly, upon regularities in mathematical experience, and can be expressed only within representation-relative formulations, each one of which is surely a "highly derived way of describing regularities." Putnam's contentions here at best are obscure and at worst come dangerously close to self-contradiction.

Platonism, in the way in which Putnam construes it, is said to be a "research program; not something fixed once and for all but something to be modified and improved by trial and error." Putnam could with equal justice say the same of Nominalism and of many other views in the philosophy and methodology of mathematics. But if Platonism is "about objects of which we have *a priori* knowledge," this contention is strictly meaningless pending some clarification of either the meaning or designatum of '*a priori*'. It would be difficult to devise a contemporary research program based on trial and error concerning Descartes' clear and distinct ideas, worthy, say of NSF support. Putnam's construal of Nominalism is also awry, if it is supposed to concern contemporary views. What serious contemporary nominalist contends that "mathematics is not about real objects" *and* that "most of it is just make believe?" Here also Putnam's view is a quixotic thrust against a windmill of his own creation.

But let us move on to the body of the book.

In "Truth and Necessity in Mathematics" the aim is not to offer a thesis contrary to the "received" one of Carnap *et al.*, "but rather to call attention to facts to which 'ontological' and 'linguistic' accounts do not do justice." In particular Putnam aims to determine "what distinguishes [i] statements which are true for mathematical reasons, or [ii] statements whose falsity is mathematically impossible (whether in the vocabulary of 'pure' mathematics, or not), or [iii] statements which are mathematically necessary, from other truths." It would have been helpful if Putnam had told us whether [i], [ii], and [iii] are to be taken as the same or not. If the same, then the title of the paper is redundant. If different, we should be told straightaway precisely how. Actually, they appear to be the same, pending some subtlety to the contrary about which we are not told.

The two views under discussion, then, are the alleged "ontological" and "linguistic" accounts of mathematics. It is the refutation of these that forms the bedrock of Putnam's view. Unfortunately, both refutations fail on a "reasonable" sense of the terms.

That the ontological account is inadequate, Putnam thinks, is shown by producing "mathematically true statements which quantify over only material objects, or over sensations, or over days of the week, or over whatever 'objects' you like," but not over any specifically abstract mathematical objects. Two examples are given. The first concerns some statements about a physically realized Turing machine T as couched in a language with some specific predicates to describe its states and to articulate specific instructions (stated declaratively). The machine is then completely characterized by a finite sequence of such instructions $I_1, \ldots, I_k$ stated in the given vocabulary, together of course with a predicate 'halts' in the context 'HT' to express that T halts. The statement,

(1) 'As long as I_1 and I_2 and . . . and I_k, then T does not halt'

is then said to be a mathematically true statement and quantifies only over physical objects (the ratchets, bars, scannings, letters, and so on, constituting T and its operations). Putnam takes it for granted the (1) is "mathematically true." But is it? It may be true in some well worked out theory of Turing machines, but it is not a statement to be found, say, in Hardy's *A Course of Pure Mathematics.* Putnam does not tell us what he means by 'mathematically true', so there is not much point in disputing the matter. *Ordinarily,* we would say that (1) is not a mathematical truth. If it were, all manner of other statements would become mathematically true also. Thus, let I_i express now that Hilary does not succeed in climbing mountain i $(1 \leqq i \leqq k)$, where in fact there are only k mountains to be climbed. Let 'T' express the success of Hilary's endeavors in this regard, so that 'T halts' means that Hilary succeeds in climbing all the mountains to be climbed. As thus reinterpreted (1) becomes a truth concerning the failure of our mountaineer's endeavors, even perhaps a logical truth concerning them, but surely not a mathematically true one.

Incidentally, it may be doubted that (1), as Putnam construes it, quantifies only over "material objects," as he contends. If the language of Turing machine were to be characerized in full logistic detail, it may well be that "event" or "state" variables (plus perhaps still other kinds) would be needed fundamentally, and whatever events or states are they are not just a species of material objects.

Putnam's second example concerns the inscriptional syntax of an elementary system *E.S.* for a fragment of arithmetic. The statement he produces, purporting to be mathematically true, likewise is a statement only of inscriptional syntax. Are statements of the latter mathematically true, even though a principle of mathematical induction appears among the axioms? No, surely not in any ordinary or "reasonable" sense of the term.

Putnam thinks that "what seems to characterize mathematics is a certain *style of reasoning;* but that style of reasoning is not essentially connected with an 'ontology'." What is this style? *Deductive* reasoning, perhaps, from well-specified axioms by means of well-specified rules of inference? If so, why not tell us so explicitly, and if not, why not tell us precisely why? On either side there are traditions of long standing.

Putnam's example concerning arithmetic can easily be puffed up to concern a set theory. He thinks his example substantiates the claim that "even if no one has yet succeeded in translating *all* of mathematics into 'nominalistic language', still there is no difficulty in expressing a *part* (and, indeed, a significant part) of mathematics in 'nominalistic language.' " There are two fundamental errors in this statement. First, to think of the vast totality *all* of mathematics is, on Putnam's view, tantamount presumably to all deductive reasoning. Actually if mathematics is a style of reasoning, all of mathematics consists of all deductive *reasonings,* in the plural. Have these ever been successfully translated into any formal language? Next, think of the totality of mathematics in the usual sense, including the theory of transfinite ordinals and cardinals, up to and beyond $\aleph_{\epsilon_0}$, $\aleph_{\epsilon_{\epsilon_0}}$, and so on. Has this ever been translated into any formal language? One would have to work hard to produce one. Secondly, one can give an inscriptional syntax for a set theory, by essentially the methods Putnam uses for his *E.S.* The true sentences of that syntax, like those he produces for *E.S.*, are "mathematically true" in his sense, but not in the usual sense. Actually 'translation' as Putnam uses it, is ambiguous. He does not give a "translation" of the formulae of *E.S.* into a nominalistic language. Rather he shows how a nominalistic or inscriptional *syntax* of *E.S.* is forthcoming. But this is not a "translation" in the usual sense. Can it be that Putnam is confusing here these two readings of that much overburdened word 'translation'?

Next we come to the alleged refutation of the "linguistic" approach to mathematics. But let us distinguish straightaway, unlike Putnam, whether we are talking about the "linguistics," that is, syntax, semantics, and perhaps pragmatics, of the full natural languge, or of some specifically formulated systems for the relevant mathematical purposes. The problem as to how these latter are related to the former needs of course careful discussion. Also we should distinguish clearly, again unlike Putnam, between *accepted* as mathematically true and mathematical truth *simpliciter*.

Putnam writes that "according to a currently fashionable view, to accept a statement as mathematically true is in some never-quite-clearly-explained way a matter of accepting a rule of language . . ." This view is ascribed to Carnap who is said to maintain that "mathematical statements are consequences of 'semantical rules'." Of course if suitable semantical rules are available, the relevant language is obviously an interpreted one. And if it is a language for mathematics, the semantical rules are such as to "interpret" the mathematical expressions occurring. Interpreted mathematical statements are not then logical consequences of the semantical rules alone, but only of them together with the specifically mathematical assumptions of the language. The Carnap view is thus said to consist of an "uninteresting tautology," in effect, that "*mathematics* = language plus *mathematics.*" A "crushing rejoinder" to this view, Putnam says, is that it denies that "there is any such thing as Discovery [with a capital 'D'] in mathematics" other than in a psychological sense. However, Putnam never-quite-clearly-explains what Discovery in his sense is. To be sure, he puts forward "the picture of the Mathematical Fact as Eternally True [with capitals, notice] independent of Human Nature and human mathematical activity" and comments that he does "not find this picture at all misleading" and in fact has never "been told just *how* or *why* it is supposed to be misleading." But surely now, any "*intelligent* reader," to use Putnam's own words, will be "irritated" at this contention, especially if no account is given of what Mathematical Facts are, regarded as Eternally True independent of Human Nature. No one has ever, in the entire history of the subject, given a satisfactory account of these, and Putnam does not even attempt to do so. It is not just that the view is never-quite-clearly-explained; it is not explained at all, but rather referred to with capitals as though this raises the view above all suspicion and prevents it from being "misleading."

Putnam contends that the linguistic account of mathematics ascribed to Carnap leads to the "silly suggestion" that "once a mathematical assertion has been accepted by me, I will not allow anything to *count* against this assertion." But this is a far cry from anything Carnap ever believed or wrote. The decision to accept a given mathematical formalism is in part a pragmatical matter, according to him, and subject to continual revision. Much can count against a given formalism and compelling reasons for not accepting one can be given. New formulations may emerge as a result of new knowledge, contributing to the advance of the subject. There is thus nothing in the linguistic view, when properly stated, that prevents our changing "our minds concerning the truth or falsity of mathematical assertions" or recognizing that there may be "different *degrees* of revisability to be discerned even in elementary number theory"—to say nothing of other more controversial areas of mathematics.

Putnam's penultimate paragraph must be read to be believed that it could have been seriously intended. The "Rule-of-Language" account is supposed by him never to allow revising a rule. He contends that "*any* statement can be regarded as a 'rule of language' " on this view. Such a contention fails to take into account the very nature of semantical rules, which interrelate word and object in very special ways. Only statements of a quite unique kind are recognized as semantical rules, contrary to Putnam's contention. This latter is so awry, in fact, as to lead us to think that one more straw man has been set up in order to be knocked down with one more quixotic argument.

The point of these remarks is not to defend the various views Putnam is attacking, but merely to record that his various arguments against them totally fail of their mark.

The second essay, "The Thesis that Mathematic is Logic," is one with which he tells us he now largely disagrees. It is enough here to disagree with what Putnam agrees to; we need not go on to voice disagreement with his disagreements or the reasons why.

The third essay, "Mathematics without Foundations," has been criticized at some length elsewhere[3] and need not be repeated here. It would be a pleasure to be able to report that account of these criticisms had been taken in the reprint of this paper in this volume. But such pleasure we must forego. Putnam's views are obviously not *semper reformanda* in the light of careful critical scrutiny.

In "What Is Mathematical Truth?" we meet with some astonishing contentions in the very first paragraph. On the one hand Putnam wishes to interpret mathematics realistically and that "*something* [independent of the human mind] answers to such mathematical notions as 'set' and 'function'." But we are not to think then "that reality is somehow bifurcated—that there is one reality of material things, and then, over and above it, a second reality of 'mathematical things'." Very well, let us not do so. But then, in the very next sentence, we are told that "a set of objects, for example, depends for its existence on those [material] objects; if they are

[3] See the author's "The Elimination of Intensions *Sui Generis*," sec. 6, in *Belief, Existence, and Meaning* (New York: New York University Press, 1969).

destroyed, then there is no longer such a set." Let us not worry about the null set Λ here, which of course "exists" in some set theories in the sense that '$(Ex)x = \Lambda$' holds in them. But of course the null set does not exist in the sense of *having members.* Putnam is clearly confusing these two senses of 'exists'. A set of objects, in some suitable formulation of set theory, can depend "for its existence on . . . [material] objects" only in the sense that '$(Ex)x \in \alpha$' holds, but not in the sense that '$(E\beta)\ \alpha = \beta$' does. This latter concerns existence in the sense of being a value of the variables of the formalism. These two senses must be carefully distinguished if any cogent contentions concerning the existence of sets are to be maintained.

Further, Putnam is speaking of a set theory in which only "material" objects are taken as the *Urelemente.* Suppose now α exists in the sense that $(Ex)x \in \alpha$. If the members of α are "destroyed" then "there is no longer such a set." So sets are supposed to come into existence somehow and pass away with their members! If this were the case, set theory would have to be an even more complicated theory than it is. A theory of the destruction of the *Urelemente* would have to be given in terms of which the sets of which they are members would no longer "exist" in some sense of this word never-quite-clearly-explained. A set theory incorporating a theory of the destruction of the *Urelemente,* and also presumably a theory of their coming into being, is not a set theory in the usual mathematical sense.

Parenthetically Putnam admits that "of course, we may say that the set exists 'tenselessly', but we may also say that the object exists 'tenselessly': this is just to say that in pure mathematics we can sometimes ignore the important difference betwen 'exists now' and 'did exist, exists now, will exist'." There are at least two bad blunders in this parenthetical remark. To say that sets may exist "tenselessly" and that objects also may is not at all to say that in pure mathematics we can *sometimes* ignore tense differences. In pure mathematics, in the usual classical sense, we *always* ignore tense differences. The moment tense differences are brought into account, we enter into an *applied* mathematics. Also if material objects are admitted only tenselessly, then one of their crucial physical aspects, their temporality, is left out of account and they are no longer really material in any but a Pickwickian sense.

Putnam goes on to say that "not only are the 'objects' of pure mathematics conditional upon material objects; they are, in a sense, merely abstract possibilities." The first part of this contention fails to allow for set theories in which *no Urelemente* whatsoever are admitted at all as well as for set theories in which the *Urelemente* are *not* taken as material objects. In the second part of this contention, it is suggested that the objects of pure mathematics are to be regarded as abstract possibilities. But we are then told that "studying how mathematical objects behave might better be described as studying what structures are abstractly possible." We are thus presumably to get at the merely abstract possibilities of pure mathematics by means of the study of possible abstract structures. We are not told what these latter are, but even so the coordinality of the set of all of them is surely immense. This set would include all *consistent* structures, of course, but only a handful of them would be of any genuine interest to a pure mathematician. Most of them, it is to be feared, would be rather boring. Now what has become of Mathematical Facts on this account, and of Eternal Mathematical Truths? And what about such mathematical notions as *sets* and *function,* which would find no place whatsoever in most of these structures?

Putnam wants to argue not only that reality is not bifurcated into "material" things plus a second domain of "mathematical" things, but also that "mathematical knowledge resembles *empirical* knowledge" in the sense that "the criteria of truth in mathematics just as much as in physics is success of our ideas in practice, and that mathematics is corrigible and not absolute." We must be sure then that we see precisely how the two kinds of objects, mathematical and material, are to be accommodated in a unified "reality" that is not bifurcated, and also precisely how there can be Eternal Mathematical Truths that are corrigible and not absolute. Also we must become clear as to what is meant by "success [in mathematics] of our ideas in practice" where mathematics is understood to be the study of possible abstract structures, these latter being concerned merely with objects that themselves are merely "abstract possibilities."

Now of course there is an important difference between mathematical *praxis* and the formulation of precise logico-mathematical systems for specific areas of mathematical theory. The latter, however, is to be presumed included in the former. The study of the latter, especially in the early twentieth century, has added a chapter in mathematical rigor, but by no means should be thought of as usurping the whole subject. Mathematical praxis comprises a great deal more than merely studying abstractly possible structures. An even approximately accurate description of mathematical praxis seems never to have been given. It is a pity Putnam does not attempt one as a basis for his contentions. In particular, he thinks, praxis needs more than proof; it needs the notion of *mathematical confirmation* and reliance on "quasi-empirical" methods that are "analogous to the methods of the physical sciences except that the singular statements which are 'generalized by induction', used to test 'theories', etc., are themselves the product of proof or calculation rather than being 'observation reports' in the usual sense." Thus mathematical statements can be " 'verified' by a quasi-empirical method" and "what has been 'verified' at a given time may later turn out to be false." But if it turns out to be false, then it was not really verified at an earlier time, but only thought or believed to be. Of course in praxis a mathematician may believe he has verified a statement and discover later that he has not. And he may make all manner of *Gedankenexperimente* before asserting the statement in the first place. Also he may think he has "proved" a statement only to discover later—or be told gleefully by a colleague—that he has not. Surely all such "quasi-empirical" procedures are a part of mathematical praxis. Has anyone in any seriousness ever denied this? It is a pity that Putnam does not develop in detail his point concerning the status in mathematics of singular statements as compared with the status of such statements in the physical sciences. Of course there are analogies as well as disanalogies, and it would be helpful to have them listed in full. Putnam comments he believes "that it would be of great value to attempt to systematize and study these [quasi-empirical] methods" but that "perhaps such an enterprise is premature in the present stage of our knowledge." But it would at least have been helpful to get the enterprise started.

Putnam makes much of the fact that in mathematical *praxis* "quasi-empirical methods are constantly used to discover truths or putative truths that one then tries to prove rigorously." His observations call attention to a point thoroughly familiar to mathematicians the world over. Even more can be said. The good mathematician is often one who can discover a theorem, preferably an important one, and state it correctly, leaving the matter of rigorous proof to others or to his disciples. Actually, in mathematical praxis, rigorous proof probably plays a much less important role than even Putnam tends to think.

We now come to a crucial point. Putnam wants his cake and wants to eat it too. He wants to be a mathematical realist and to espouse simultaneously a kind of modal-logical view of mathematics in which one is not committed to the existence of mathematical objects. How is this possible? Well, it isn't, and Putnam's contentions collapse, as we shall see.

A realist relative to a given theory or discourse holds, we are told, that "the sentences of that theory or discourse are true or false" and that "what makes them true or false is something *external*—that is to say, it is not (in general) our sense data, actual or potential, or the structure of our minds, or our language, etc. . . . The question of realism . . . is the question of the objectivity of mathematics and not the question of the existence of mathematical objects." By way of spelling out this view, Putnam takes the stand "that mathematics has *no* objects of its own. You can prove theorems about anything you want—rainy days, or marks on paper, or graphs, or lines, or spheres [or angels or Homeric gods or mental events(?)]—but the mathematician, on this view, makes no existence assertions at all. What he asserts is that certain *things* are *possible* and certain things are *impossible*—in a strong and uniquely mathematical sense of 'possible' and 'impossible'. In short, mathematics is essentially *modal* rather than existential. . . ." In some never-quite-clearly-explained way, we are apparently not ontically committed on this modal view to the existence of the objects over which quantification is admitted.

The first item to observe is that here mathematics is in effect identified with the study of logical systems, no matter what their ontology, so long as one proves theorems about its objects. But—to vary a point already made above—the logical theory of rainy days, and the like, is not a part of mathematics in the usual sense. Some delimitation of ontology is surely needed. Further, not *all* "possible" structures, even in Putnam's view, should be included, but only "interesting," untrivial ones, in a uniquely mathematical sense of 'interesting'. For Putnam's view to have cogency, he must characterize precisely the uniquely mathematical senses of 'possible' and 'interesting' needed, and this he fails to do.

A third point concerns the semantical truth concept, all definitions of which (in the usual, translational kind of a semantics) are such as to employ fundamentally an object-language ontology. One cannot make sense of truth without variables and quantifiers over the object-language entities. Thus, if Putnam is using 'true' in the usual semantical sense, he cannot use the word independent of its relatedness to an ontology. Thus he cannot even make the very claim that in a realist discourse the sentences are true or false. Further, *necessary* truths are surely true and hence form a subclass of the truths. Thus all talk of necessary truths, and therewith of possible ones, relative to a given discourse, also involves reference to its ontology. If one defines 'true' in terms of the notion of being true in all models or "possible worlds," to use the current jargon, the resulting truths are still true. A model- or modal-theoretic notion of 'necessary' is not definable, on the basis of the usual translational semantics, without having variables and quantifiers over the object-language ontology. The model-theorist may have no special interest in that ontology any more than in any other. It is to this point, perhaps, to which Putnam should have drawn attention. As it is, however, his basic contention that there is a clear and precise modal view of mathematics, independent of considerations concerning mathematical objects, cannot be maintained, and in fact is impossible, on a most obvious meaning of 'impossible'.

There is of course *non-translational* semantics, of which Putnam makes no mention.[4] In non-translational semantics no variables over the object-language entities are admitted. The interesting question arises as to how, on a non-translational basis, one could build up an "immaculate conception" of the modal notions.[5] Undoubtedly this could be done by suitable technical manoeuvres, especially if higher-order quantifiers are assumed available. On the basis of a non-translational modal theory, we would have the kind of theory in which we could say that the sentences of the given discourse are true or false without being committed in the usual sense to the existence of mathematical objects. But even so, there would be implicit commitment to them in another sense.

Of what, then, does the "objectivity" of mathematics consist? Here is a key question that is never so much as even discussed.

Putnam thinks it an advantage of his modal view that it shows us that "one does not have to 'buy' Platonistic epistemology to be a realist in the philosophy of mathematics" and that "one doesn't have to 'buy' Plantonistic ontology either." As already noted, however, this last contention is incorrect, and therewith the previous one also. The poor little word 'Platonism' is misused by Putnam in several never-clearly defined senses.

Strong claims are made for realism as Putnam views it. In fact, we are told that it "is the only philosophy that doesn't make the success of the science [of mathematics] a *miracle.*" The "success" of mathematics is then contrasted with that of theology, and it is con-

[4]See *Truth and Denotation* (Chicago: University of Chicago Press, 1958), chaps. 8, 9, and 13.

[5]Cf. Bryan Skyrms, "An Immaculate Conception of Modality," *The Journal of Philosophy* 75 (1978): 368-87.

tended tha the latter "was" in fact highly *inconsistent.* All theologies are lumped together here and we are not told of what their inconsistencies consist. We are told, however, that even if a theology were fixed up "so as to restore consistency, the consistency would be a trivial result—doubtless it would follow from the existence of some kind of finite model." But surely now Putnam's conception of what theology is is naive. A well worked out theology should be such as to include mathematics as a part, and hence the problem of its consistency includes the problem of the consistency of its parts. This is the case for the Whiteheadian theology, for example, and for post-Whiteheadian theologies of appropriate logical seriousness.

As goes the philosophy of mathematics, so goes that of the physical sciences. Putnam's views here have been well aired in the literature and in discussion by distinguished scholars such as Henry Margenau, Eugene Wigner, Adolf Grünbaum, and John Stachel *inter alia.* The most important item, for the purposes of the present discussion, is the espousal of a *non*-standard logic for quantum mechanics. Putnam's earliest statement of the purport of such a logic seems to be in the paper "Three-valued Logic." The argument there, however, again, fails to make its point. A three-valued logic, for Putnam, is presumably a formalism *interpreted* in terms of notions of 'true', 'false', and 'middle' available in the metalanguage. And there they may be presumed to be *defined* in terms of the predicate for being accepted. Let 'Acptd' be this predicate, so that 'Acptd *a*' expresses that *a* is accepted (timelessly, so to speak). One then defines

'Tr *a*' as 'Acptd *a*',
'Fls *a*' as 'Acptd ('∼'⌢*a*)',

and

'Mid *a*' as '(∼ Acptd *a* · ∼ Acptd ('∼'⌢*a*))'.

The '⌢' here is the usual symbol for concatenation.

Those definitions are already a departure from Putnam's informal ones. Curiously, and probably contrary to the intent, Putnam's definitions are couched in a *metametalanguage!* "To give these words ['true', 'false', and 'middle'] more content, we may suppose," he writes, " . . . that, as is usually the case, statements that are accepted as verified are called 'true', and statements that are rejected, that is, whose denials are accepted, are called 'false'." In a footnote he then explains that "more precisely: *S* is accepted if and only if '*S* is true' is accepted." The basic notion 'accepted' is thus a predicate in the metametalanguage in terms of which the metalinguistic 'accepted' is defined. This technical blunder is a very minor one and makes little difference to the general thrust of the argument.

Actually 'Acptd' as introduced above is a *pragmatical* notion in disguise and is no doubt best construed in terms of a relational predicate 'Acpt'. Let this be significant in contexts of the form '*p* Acpt a, t' expressing that person *p* accepts statement *a* (of the given object-language) at time *t*. Then 'Acptd *a*' above may be taken as short for '(E*p*) (E*t*)*p* Acpt *a*,*t*'.

That a pragmatics based on acceptance is of use in all manner of interesting and important ways is beyond question. However, the use Putnam makes of it is suspect. He thinks the employment of a three-valued logic based on it is similar to the employment of non-Euclidean geometries, which "were first regarded as absurd; later as mere mathematical games; and are today accepted as portions of fully interpreted physical hypotheses. *In exactly the same way* [italics added], 3-valued logic and other non-standard logic had first to be shown to exist as consistent formal structures; secondly, uses have been found for some of them . . . " But the way here is not *exactly* the same at all; it is not even the same. Putnam himself interprets his 3-valued logic in a standard, quasi-pragmatical, 2-valued metalanguage (metametalanguage). Non-Euclidean geometries do not have to be "interpreted" within such a pragmatical metalanguage, nor even within a metalanguage containing in any usual sense Euclidean geometry itself. Non-Euclidean geometries are not Euclidean geometry minus a *tertium non datur* and similar laws. They are rather altogether new theories resulting—to state the matter very roughly—from suitable changes in the Parallel Postulate. Once non-Euclidean geometries are on the market, their Euclidean forbears no longer enjoy privileged status. Not so in logic, on Putnam's own showing! His 3-valued logic is interpreted within a metalanguage (metametalanguage) of the usual 2-valued kind, and this is essential in order to give "more content" to 'true', 'false', and 'middle' within the 3-valued scheme and in order to give them their full "cash value." Putnam's contention concerning the development of 3-valued logic as compared with non-Euclidean geometry is thus wide of its mark. To be sure, there may be a minor historical analogy, but that this is the case is not the point under discussion.

Putnam rejects the argumennt that "even if one uses a 3-valued object language, one must use a 2-valued logic in the metalanguage," in effect the argument used above. But only hear his reasons! "In the light of the foregoing, this can hardly be regarded as a *necessary* state of affairs." It is surely necessary, however, for Putnam's interpretation. "3-valued logic corresponds to a certain way of speaking," he goes on, and adds that "there is no difficulty in speaking in that way about any particular subject matter. In particular, one may assign truth-values to molecular sentences in the way we have discussed, whether one is talking about rabbits or languages or metalanguages." Of course, one may speak in any way one wishes; the problem is how our speech is to be interpreted. And again, one may "assign" truth-values in any way one likes, the problem being to "interpret" them in some cognitively responsible way. Putnam suggests no way of doing either of these other than in terms of a 2-valued metalanguage.

Putnam thinks that he has now paved the way for his discussion "The Logic of Quantum Mechanics" (previously published under the title "Is Logic Empirical?" an essay to which he attaches much importance). In view of the various criticisms put forward above, however, the way is still a rocky one. He argues that in the logic needed for quantum mechanics, "the *only* [—italics added—] laws of classical logic that are given up . . . are distributive laws, e.g., $p \cdot (q \vee r) \equiv p \cdot q \vee p \cdot r$; *and every single anomaly vanishes once we give these up* [italics added]." But surely now, this cannot be the case. In the first place, the various laws governing '·', 'v', ' ≡ ', and also '~' and ' ⊃', *no matter how interpreted,* are so deeply intertwined that if the distributive laws were "given up," their logical consequence would have to be abandoned also. Thus the so-called quantum logic without distributive laws is a much more complicated one than Putnam states. Then there is the question of the *interpretation* of the logical constants as occurring in quantum logic. Here is a key anomaly that does not vanish. An interpretation for these *must* be provided at some point before we know what quantum logic is. Any acceptable interpretation would have to be given within a standard, 2-valued metalanguage.

According to some experts, e.g., Abner Shimony, the "anomalies" in quantum mechanics persist mainly, perhaps entirely, because more *physical* knowledge, theoretical and/or experimental, in the field is needed. If this is the case, Putnam's contention is quite premature and at best based only on our present incomplete knowledge of a very complex subject. Further, if Putnam's contention were correct, the difficult problem would remain of explaining in cogent terms *why* classical logic has been so overwhelmingly successful in characterizing inferences in mathematics, the sciences, philosophy, and in such humanistic areas in which it has been applied, and yet fails somehow in the one case of quantum mechanics. Such an explanation Putnam nowhere gives.

Putnam thinks that the logical connectives can be given suitable "operational definitions" in the manner suggested by the physicist David Finkelstein. This is in terms of the notion of a *test*. "Let us pretend that to every physical property *P* there corresponds a test *T* such that something has *P* just in case it 'passes' *T* (i.e., it *would* pass *T* if *T* were performed)." But of course the notion of being a *test* and of *passing* a test are not logical but *physical* notions. Any "operational" description of the logical connectives in terms of these notions becomes of course a physical description, not a semantical interpretation of the usual kind. If one construes the connectives physically, then of course the laws of "quantum logic" are physical laws, not logical ones. This trivial observation, however, supplies no grounds whatsoever for Putnam's positive answer to the question "Is logic empirical?" Again, no substantial argument is put forward.

To show this in more detail, let us reflect a little further upon how Putnam, following Finkelstein, construes the quantum-logical 'v', '·', and '~'. Presupposing some fuzzy talk about "propositions," "properties," and "correspondence" between a property *P* and a test T_p, one takes " '*P* v *Q*' (as applied to a system *S*) as meaning . . . '*S* passes every test which is passed by everything that passes T_p and passed by everything that passes T_q' . . . " with analogous explanations of '*P* · *Q*' and '-*P*'. The quantifier over tests here should be noted, as well as the presumably normal truth-functional 'and' in the explanans. The language in which there is talk of tests and of passing them employs the standard quantifiers and truth-functional logic. Putnam and Finkelstein do not speak of a special quantum logic of quantification, or the like. No, quantum logic for them has exclusively to do with the connectives. As we see, however, their quantum logic is not strictly a logic but rather a certain theory concerning tests and passing them.

Several of the papers in this book are concerned with special problems in the philosophy of science that were under dispute in the 1960's; these need not be commented on here.

The last paper is a reprint without change of Putnam's little book *Philosophy of Logic*. This too has been commented on at some length elsewhere.[6] The glaring inadequacies of its content have not

[6]See *Events, Reference, and Logical Form* (Washington, D.C.: Catholic University of America Press, 1979), chap. 15.

been put to rights here.

Most of the difficulties with Putnam's general methodology can be traced back to his lack of interest in exact statement and formalization. He rests content with formalization in mathematics, but is slow to espouse it when we step beyond. He writes philosophy in the intuitive style of the working scientist. Curiosly, however, the methodological situation of the philosopher, as compared with that of the scientist, is just the other way around. Formalization in mathematics is of course of the highest importance, but is not always needed. The mathematician has the technical skill, partly as a result of training and partly as a result of insight, to handle the quantifiers, for example, with unexceptional correctness. And he may do this perhaps never having heard of the theory of quantification as such. Rare indeed is the philosopher of whom this could be said. In philosophy, and also in methodology and the philosophy of science, a very self-conscious use of the quantifiers is needed at almost every turn. And with the quantifiers of course, a host of non-logical predicates, including "hidden" ones, follows along, the exact theory of which constitutes the given domain of inquiry. To keep on the right track in domains of inquiry that are not primarily scientific, the self-conscious use of logical techniques is almost indispensable, as is more and more coming to be recognized. Putnam writes for the most part as though no advances had been made in such techniques since 1940 or thereabouts, and it is this that constantly leads him astray on very fundamental issues. Of course one can be led astray by many other means also, and keeping on the right track, both methodologically and content-wise, is, as we all know, a next to impossible undertaking.

RICHARD M. MARTIN.

DISCUSSION
SEMANTICAL RULES AND MISINTERPRETATIONS: REPLY TO R. M. MARTIN

I.

Following Quine and (on this point) Wittgenstein, I take it that the notion of a "rule" cuts no philosophical ice when it comes to accounting for our understanding of our first language. It may have a use in talking about formalized languages; but then all the problems reappear when one takes a formalized language to be a *model* of a natural language or of unformalized scientific practice.[1] Professor Martin writes as if Quine and Wittgenstein had never written. He and I thus inhabit different philosophical worlds. It is not surprising that by his standards everything I say is wrong, unclear,[2] and unscholarly. Rather than trying to say it all again, I shall examine in detail Professor Martin's criticism of one of my articles ("Truth and Necessity in Mathematics"—here abbreviated TNM), and just indicate what the response would be in the case of one or two of the remaining articles.

In the first part of TNM I show that *part* of mathematics can actually be done in a nominalistic language. Hence reference to abstract entities is not a *necessary* property of mathematical statements. Professor Martin registers two objections: (1) The nominalistic statements I produce are "logically true," but there is no reason to call them "mathematics"; and (2) They do not have the same meaning as the sentences of ES and, thus, I was wrong to speak of them as "translations."

Speaking to (2) first: the assertion that my nominalistic statements which are mathematically true are "translations" of the

[1]See my "The Analytic and the Synthetic," in *Mind, Language, and Reality, Philosophical Papers,* vol. II (Cambridge: Cambridge University Press, 1975).

[2]Professor Martin's idea of what clarity requires is unusually demanding! I define an *a priori* truth as one it could never be *rational* to give up, or even to doubt. This, Professor Martin says, "is not up to sophisticated contemporary standards." (At the same time, it is a "straw man easily to be knocked down.") It is not clear whether it is the use of the notion of rational revisability or the use of the modal notion ("could") that puts me below "sophisticated contemporary standards."

theorems of ES occurs only in Professor Martin's imagination. I nowhere speak of them as "translations." My argument was that these sentences can be mathematically proved without using anything non-nominalistic (even the induction principle needed can be nominalistically stated), that they express what it is reasonable to regard as mathematical facts, and that the activity of proving them in the mathematical way described is a characteristically mathematic activity.

Professor Martin disagrees. He would rather refer to these truths as *logical* truths. But their *proof* requires *induction,* and however fuzzy the line between logic and mathematics, if one is going to insist on a line at all, then what needs induction for its proof would seem clearly to be on the "mathematics" side of the line.

The second part of TNM criticized Wittgensteinian views (I referred to them coyly as "a currently fashionable view"—TNM was written in 1963). Professor Martin was misled into thinking Carnap was my target, although I speak of "a late refinement" of the Carnap-Ayer view, which I briefly criticize.

Let me now quote Professor Martin:

> Putnam writes that "according to a currently fashionable view, to accept a statement as mathematically true is in some never-quite-clearly-explained way a matter of accepting a rule of language . . . " This view is ascribed to Carnap who is said to maintain that "mathematical statements are consequences of 'semantical rules'." Of course, if suitable semantical rules are available, the relevant language is obviously an interpreted one. And if it is a language for mathematics, the semantical rules are such as to "interpret" the mathematical expressions occurring. Interpreted mathematical statements are not then logical consequences of the semantical rules alone, but only of them together with the specifically mathematical assumptions of the language. The Carnap view is thus said to consist of an "uninteresting tautology," in effect, that "mathematics = language plus *mathematics.*" A "crushing rejoinder" to this view, Putnam says, is that is denies that "there is any such thing as Discovery in mathematics" other than in a purely psychological sense.

A glance at TNM will verify that what I referred to as a "crushing rejoinder" to the Carnap-Ayer position is that *consequence,* in Carnap's sense, is itself a *mathematical* notion. Thus the statement that "true mathematical statements are *consequences* of semantical rules" *does* reduce to the uninteresting tautology—uninteresting to an *epistemologist,* that is—that mathematics = language plus *mathematics.*

I did remark that the Carnap-Ayer position *goes along with* the denial that there is any such thing as discovery in mathematics, other than in a purely psychological sense. Carnap and Ayer redefine "information" so that mathematically equivalent propositions are *said* to give the same "information." What I say in TNM is that this is a Pickwickian sense of "information," and that when Carnap and Ayer said that the conclusion of a valid mathematical argument contains no new "information," they "only enunciated the uninteresting tautology that in a valid mathematical argument the conclusion is mathematically implied by the premises."

Note that my central point, that the use of the *mathematical* notions of *consequence, equivalence,* etc., makes the Carnap-Ayer theory epistemologically *empty*—has been totally misrepresented by Martin.

Professor Martin writes (in the paragraph just noted) as if *Carnap* distinguished between "semantical rules" and "mathematical assumptions of the language." This is part of Professor Martin's tendency to treat "semantical rule" as a philosophically noncontroversial, standardized notion. But Carnap in fact treated at least some of the mathematical assumptions of a language as semantical rules ("Meaning Postulates"). In "Semantics, Empiricism, and Ontology" Carnap treats the verification/refutation procedures (or the confirmation/infirmation procedures, in the case of empirical sentences) for the sentences of a language as part of what we specify when we specify the *interpretation* of the language. It is just this elastic quality of the notion of a "semantical rule" in the writings of those who wanted the notion to do epistemological work that I was referring to (of course, Quine pointed this out in "Truth by Convention" [1936] and "Two Dogmas of Empiricism" [1951]).

Professor Martin goes on to write that:

> However, Putnam never-quite-clearly-explains what Discovery in his sense is. To be sure, he puts forward "the picture of the Mathematical Fact as Eternally True [with capitals, notice] independent of Human Nature and human mathematical activity" and comments that he does "not find this picture at all misleading" and in fact has never "been told just *how* or *why* it is supposed to be misleading." But surely now, any "*intelligent* reader," to use Putnam's own words, will be "irritated" at this contention, especially if no account is given of what Mathematical Facts are, regarded as Eternally True independent of Human Nature. No one has ever, in the entire history of the subject, given a satisfactory account of these, and Putnam does not even attempt to do so. It is not just that the view is never-quite-clearly-explained; it is not explained at all, but rather referred to with capitals as though this raises the view above all suspicion and prevents it from being "misleading."

The capitals that irritate Professor Martin are there for a reason.

I was mocking *Wittgensteinian* ways of mocking mathematical realism.

If a mathematical fact (without capitals) is, e.g., the fact that a certain Turing Machine will halt if started in a certain state scanning a blank tape, then *isn't* this "independent of human nature"? Certainly it is *causally* independent of human nature! *Isn't* this "eternally true"? Certainly it's *tenselessly* true! What sort of "account" is it that we have never been given? A *philosophical* account. My suggestion was that the assumption that such an account is possible or needed is what we ought to reexamine.[3]

Professor Martin extends his criticism of TNM by complaining that:

> Putnam contends that the linguistic account of mathematics ascribed to Carnap leads to the "silly suggestion" that "once a mathematical assertion has been accepted by me, I will not allow anything to *count* against this assertion." But this is a far cry from anything Carnap ever believed or wrote. The decision to accept a given mathematical formalism is in part a pragmatical matter, according to him, and subject to continual revision.

There are three points I wish to make in response to this: (1) Professor Martin apparently does not allow rules to have the form 'S is to be held immune from revision'. But Wittgenstein's "rules of description" and Carnap's "Meaning Postulates" seem to have something like this very form. (2) Of course there is, on *any* "Rule of Language" account, a possibility of *revising rules. This* is what Carnap regarded as a "pragmatic matter." But then one is not talking about the same *assertion,* since the meaning of the sentences has been changed. (3) The distinction (which Martin ignores) between revising a *rule* and revising an *assertion* is crucial to the Rule of Language position. Once it is given up, one has accepted Quine's view that there is no clear sense in which mathematics is "analytic."

Finally, Professor Martin writes:

> Putnam's penultimate paragraph must be read to be believed that it could have been seriously intended. The "Rule-of-Language" account is supposed by him never to allow revising a rule. He contends that "*any* statement can be regarded as a 'rule of language' " on this view. Such a contention fails to take into account the very nature of semantical rules, which interrelate word and object in very special ways. Only statements of a quite unique kind are recognized as semantical rules, contrary to

---

[3]But now I think that one has to say more about the notion of *truth*—in and out of mathematics—than I thought we did in 1963. A more recent account of my view appears in "Analyticity and Apriority: Beyond Wittgenstein and Quine," *Midwest Studies in Philosophy,* 4.

Putnam's contention. This latter is so awry, in fact, as to lead us to think that one more straw man has been set up in order to be knocked down with one more quixotic argument.

What I argued is not that rules cannot be revised, on the Rule of Language account, but that the *distinction* between revising a rule and revising an assertion is hopelessly unclear in natural language. If I was brief on this point, it was because I cover it at length in "The Analytic and the Synthetic."

II.

Professor Martin's criticism of the modal-logical interpretation of mathematics depends on misinterpretation. (He ignores "Mathematics without Foundations," which gives a fuller explanation than "What is Mathematical Truth.") My proposal, briefly put, was to use a language with primitive modal operators to do the work of set theory. (Charles Parsons has since verified that this can be carried out.) It was not to quantify over possibilia, nor to refer to formal systems. The description that "the first item to observe is that here mathematics is in effect identified with the study of logical systems, no matter what their ontology, so long as one proves theorems about its objects" is (so far as I can understand it) wrong. I leave it to the interested reader to consult my papers and not Professor Martin's description of my view for details.

III.

On quantum mechanics: In the 3-valued logic approach, "true" is not *defined* as "accepted" (any more than in classical physics). In quantum logic: I *reject* Professor Martin's view that an "interpretation" for the logical connectives must be provided before we know what quantum logic is. This disagreement goes back to his view that a language is understood through "semantical rules" and my view that a language is understood by learning how to employ it.

IV.

I am glad to be able to agree with Professor Martin on *something*. I agree that there was a tension in these papers between my realism and my conceptualism. Subsequent writings[4] have indicated how I would attempt to work out this tension.

HILARY PUTNAM.

HARVARD UNIVERSITY.

[4]Especially "Realism and Reason," in my *Meaning and the Moral Sciences* (Routledge and Kegan Paul, 1978) and "Models and Reality," in the *Journal of Symbolic Logic,* vol. 45, no. 3 (Sept. 1980). See also my *Reason, Truth and History* (Cambridge, 1981) and *Realism and Reason; Philosophical Papers, vol. 3* (forthcoming, Cambridge, 1982).

DISCUSSION
WHAT IS HUSSERL'S FIRST PHILOSOPHY?

The first article on Edmund Husserl's *First Philosophy (1923/24)*, volume I, *Critical History of Ideas*, states,

> Husserl's phenomenology has entered a period of new activity . . . the critical history of ideas is to be recommended in that it refers one directly to the systematic fundamental problems of phenomenology. In the future, no one can treat the history of thought philosophically without entering into it.[1]

The summary of *First Philosophy*, volume I, compiled by Ludwig Landgrebe, makes brief reference to the necessity of a historical introduction to phenomenology as first philosophy *(FPI,* p. 298).[2]

To inquire into the sense and significance of such comments, we ask: What is Husserl's first philosophy? To arrive at an exegetic and analytic response to this question, we propose an examination of the following topics:

I. Phenomenology as First Philosophy
II. First Philosophy as a Critical History of Ideas
III. Critical Reflections on the "Necessity" of First Philosophy

Throughout the examination we suggest that the unique sense and significance of *First Philosophy*, volume I, lies entirely in the issue of *whether and how it accomplishes something which could not be accomplished otherwise.* While this criterion is difficult to determine, it is only from its quite rigorous standpoint that the specific characteristic of Husserl's first philosophy can come to light and that the introductory remarks, cited above, can be justified.[3]

---

[1]Dieter Henrich, "Uber die Grundlagen von Husserls Kritik der Philosophischen Tradition," *Philosophische Rundschau,* vol. VI (1958), pp. 1, 26.

[2]Husserl, *First Philosophy (1923/24),* Part I: *Critical History of Ideas,* trans. Jeffner Allen (The Hague: Martinus Nijhoff, forthcoming). References to this text will be abbreviated *FPI,* followed by the German pagination.

[3]Husserl's *First Philosophy,* volume I, is the edited and completed text of the course which Husserl gave under that title, winter semester 1923-1924, at the University of Freibourg-im-Breisgau. The original manuscript, written in Husserl's shorthand, as was his custom, was expanded either just prior to the beginning of the course, winter 1923, or slightly later, during the winter of that same year. The first lecture took place November 2, 1923, and the last lecture of *First Philosophy,* volume I, was given December 18, 1923. The first typed transcription was made, at Husserl's request, by his assistant, Ludwig Landgrebe, during the winter

I. Phenomenology as First Philosophy

The term "first philosophy" was introduced by Aristotle but fell into disuse when replaced, in the post-Aristotelian period, by "metaphysics," a word which came into use by chance. Husserl adopts the term "first philosophy," maintaining that its literal sense may serve as an indication of the theoretical purpose of the new discipline of phenomenology.

The literal sense of first philosophy seems, initially, to be self-evident. It is that philosophy which, among the various philosophies which comprise philosophy as a whole, is precisely *the* first. The ways in which such a discipline is "first" also seem to be clear enough:

1. First philosophy is "first" for intrinsic reasons. It is first in value and dignity. All other sciences, including metaphysics itself, presuppose it and, accordingly, are "second" philosophies. The primacy of the new discipline is not posited at random but, Husserl maintains, is based on an order which the sciences bear in themselves.
2. First philosophy is "first" because it is guided by the teleological idea of science. The sciences are created by purposeful activity; the truths of the sciences stand under guiding ideas. All sciences are subordinate to first philosophy, which is guided by the supreme teleological idea of science itself. The teleological idea indicates an all inclusive unity for the sciences, a unity which expands endlessly and strives forward in ever higher forms. This is Husserl's preferred way of explaining the primacy of phenomenology.
3. First philosophy is "first" as a scientific discipline of the beginning. In itself, first philosophy is the beginning of philosophy as such. It is a self-contained discipline, with its own problems

---

1923-1924. A second transcription (listed at the Husserl Archives under MT3/F34Ia) contains numerous corrections and notations made by Husserl, but none of them seems to be later than 1928. The text published by Rudolf Boehm is in accord with the original manuscript, taking into account the later corrections and notations. Part II of *First Philosophy (1923/1924)* is entitled *Theory of the Phenomenological Reduction* and forms volume VIII of the *Husserliana* series. Information concerning the composition of the text is given in the "Introduction" by Rudolf Boehm, *Erste Philosophie (1923/24)*, Erster Teil: *Kritische Ideengeschichte (Husserliana*, vol. VII), ed. Rudolf Boehm (The Hague: Martinus Nijhoff, 1956), pp. xi-xxxiv, and in the "Avant-propos du traducteur," by Arion L. Kelkel, in Husserl, *Philosophie Première (1923/1924)*, deuxième partie: *Théorie de la réduction phénoménologique*, trans. Arion L. Kelkel (Paris: Presses Universitaires de France, 1972), pp. vii-xlvi.

concerning the beginning of philosophy. All other sciences are preceded by phenomenology as first philosophy, which founds them with respect to their method and theory. The beginner of first philosophy does research into the origins of thought: beginners of second philosophies reproduce, in their own insightful thinking, the truths previously thought by first philosophers.

In sum, the ways in which the new discipline is "first" form variants on the same foundational theme: there is an intrinsic order to all philosophies, for all philosophies are guided by a teleological idea of philosophy itself. Yet, this foundation for the primacy of first philosophy is, in itself, not clear at all.

The task of first philosophy is to fulfill the idea of first philosophy and, in doing so, to lead us to be beginning philosophers. It encompasses a theory of rational life, a theory of theoretical, axiological, and practical reason. In that its task has not been fulfilled by any philosophical systems, past or present, "it is a matter of nothing less than a reform of philosophy as a whole and, included in that, a universal reform of all sciences as such" (*FPI,* p. 17). The theoretical purpose of the new discipline of phenomenology is radical, going to the roots of all philosophy. However, insofar as the purpose of first philosophy is indicated by its literal sense, which itself, rests on an unclear foundation, its task is not immediately self-evident.

Unclear notions of intrinsic order and teleology appear to obscure, at least initially, the theme of phenomenology as first philosophy. Nevertheless, it is, perhaps, by means of their clarification that first philosophy comes to accomplish something which could not be accomplished otherwise. We will begin such a clarification by situating Husserl's first philosophy in its proper context.

II. First Philosophy as a Critical History of Ideas

> . . . in these considerations it is a matter of nothing less than uncovering the unity of motivation going through the centuries and which, as developmental drive, has lived in all philosophy insofar as it wanted to become true philosophy, and in all philosophical method insofar as it wanted to become true method. *(FPI,* pp. 141, 142)

The "unity of motivation" may be understood as a system of experience.[4] The unified system is constituted by the interrelation be-

[4]Husserl, *Ideas: General Introduction to Pure Phenomenology,* trans. W. R. Boyce Gibson (New York: Macmillan, 1931), p. 134.

tween objects indicating and objects indicated in actual experience, in actual experience which refers beyond itself to possible experience, and in possible experience which points to new possible experiences, *ad. inf.* History, the history of ideas in general, and particular moments in the history of ideas may comprise such objects. The unity of motivation arises when "certain objects or states of affairs *of whose reality someone has actual knowledge* indicate to him the *reality of certain other objects or states of affairs,* in the sense that *his belief in the reality of the one is experienced* (though not at all evidently) *as motivating a belief or surmise in the reality of the other.*"[5] The contents of such systems of experience may concern things already known or wholly unknown and still undiscovered. The relation between these states of affairs is not arbitrary but, rather, is guided by the content which the object posited always already includes within itself. With respect to the form of the motivation running throughout history, Husserl writes,

> We call it furthermore a *formal regularity pertaining to a universal genesis,* which is such that past, present, and future, become unitarily constituted over and over again. . . . But, within this form, life goes on as a motivated course of particular constituted performances with a multiplicity of particular motivations and motivational systems, which, according to *universal laws of genesis,* produce a unity of *universal genesis of the ego.* The ego constitutes itself for itself in, so to speak, the unity of a 'history.'[6]

The formal regularity in the motivation running between objects indicating and objects indicated forms a descriptive unity which, though often covered by the sediment of prejudices and presuppositions, underlies our various researches. Indeed, Husserl claims, it forms an "essential type," or "essential configurations,"[7] which are present in history and which can be uncovered only insofar as we follow a strict methodological procedure. At this point there arises, to be sure, an essential question to which we will return: Is the unity of motivation, constituted by reflecting subjectivity, to be equated with the teleological idea which is said to guide first philosophy?

If, however, we proceed to an examination of the type of method appropriate for investigation of "the unity of motivation running throughout the centuries," we find ourselves confronted with the

---

[5]Husserl, *Logical Investigations,* trans. J. N. Findlay (London: Routledge & Kegan Paul, 1970), p. 270.

[6]Husserl, *Cartesian Meditations: An Introduction to Phenomenology,* trans. Dorion Cairns (The Hague: Martinus Nijhoff, 1960), p. 75.

[7]Husserl, *Ideas,* p. 135.

issue: How is the unity of motivation disclosed? and, related inseparably to that, What is the unity of motivation disclosed?

Here it is clear that the proper context of Husserl's *First Philosophy,* volume I, is neither that of an empiricism, for which history would be an accumulation of objective facts which occur in cause-effect sequence, nor that of an idealism, for which history would be the accomplishment of a world-spirit. The appropriate context for Husserl's first philosophy is, rather, that of "eidetic" history, the history of ideas and, even more significantly, the history of the exemplary moments, the crucial paradigmatic moments, which form turning points in the development of philosophical thought. Since it is an eidetic history, individual philosophers are presented insofar as their thought contributes to the essential typology of philosophical consciousness. Husserl's project is also that of a "critical" history, namely, one that endeavors to break through customary assumptions about the history of ideas in order to discover its fundamental problems and the relation between them, as seen from the perspective of the present-day philosopher. Husserl's eidetic and critical history claims to be an account of the meaning of so-called objective historical facts and a rendering, as is often insufficiently established by idealist accounts of history, of the foundations of history in individual subjects. Eidetic and critical history is accomplished by a specific methodological approach to history: the historical reduction.

The term "historical reduction" was introduced by Rudolf Boehm as a distinctive way into phenomenology, as having a subject matter and approach other than that of the generally acknowledged three ways to the transcendental phenomenological reduction: the Cartesian way, the path of intentional psychology, the critique of the positive sciences and ontology. It has been used subsequently by numerous philosophers to designate the particular procedure used by Husserl to investigate the meaning of history.[8] In the most general terms, the historical reduction involves (1) a setting aside of customary accounts of objective facts of history, (2) description, from the viewpoint of the present-day philosopher, of the idea-content of major turning points in history, and (3) reduction of the history of

---

[8]Rudolf Boehm, "La Phénoménologie de l'histoire," *Revue internationale de philosophie,* vol. LXXI (1965), pp. 55-73; David Carr, *Phenomenology and the Problem of History* (Evanston: Northwestern University Press, 1974), pp. 110-33; Arion L. Kelkel, "Avant-propos du traducteur," in Husserl, *Philosophie Première (1923-24)* deuxième partie: *Théorie de la réduction phénoménologique,* pp. xxiv.

ideas to the fundamental interconnections between its most significant moments, together with disclosure of the unity of motivation which "has lived in all philosophy insofar as it has wanted to become true philosophy. . . ." Accordingly, the historical reduction is a specific methodology developed to accomplish a specific task: the understanding of history from the point of view of a critical history of ideas. Description of the basic stages of the historical reduction will precede critical reflections on it.

If we turn to the initial step of the historical reduction we find that, by a retrospective glance *[Rückblick]* at the historical tradition, it is possible to disengage the meaning of history from its naive objective facticity. Such meaning, which is at first hidden from itself, becomes visible when we "place ourselves in the motivation of the beginning, in the historical motivation which determined the Socratic and Platonic reaction [to the scepticism of the Sophists] and thereby determined the development of the idea of a philosophy having a new sense, and of a methodology which was useful for it" *(FPI,* p. 32.) Thus, the sense of history is disengaged from historical fact when we place ourselves within the beginning, that is, when we look back at the past by reliving it, albeit from the necessary and inevitable standpoint of the present.

Yet, one may ask, why is the retrospective glance necessarily and inevitably rooted in the present? Why does Husserl propose an overcoming of the past as it has been viewed customarily (by the modern-day philosopher) by way of a reliving of the past (as it emerges in the present situatedness of the contemporary philosopher)? Any approach to history as an objective collection of facts would consider Husserl's proposal a violation of the historicity of history itself. Or, in other words, how are we to understand Husserl's statement, made with reference to Kant, that "to take over his [Kant's] system as it is or to improve its details, this is not what is necessary above all else, but rather, to understand the ultimate sense of his revolution—and to understand him better than he himself, the trailblazer, but not the perfecter, was capable of doing" (*FPI,* p. 286).[9] Here the parenthetic remarks speak for themselves, for they indicate the often unnoticed and yet inescapable positionality of any approach to history. There is no nonpositional point—a point which would, in principle, have to

[9]Husserl, "Kant and the Idea of Transcendental Philosophy," trans. Ted E. Klein and William E. Pohl, *Southwestern Journal of Philosophy,* vol. V (1974), p. 55. This article also forms a supplementary text to *First Philosophy,* Part I.

be outside history—from which to view history. To understand that every viewing of history is positional is to begin to see history critically and eidetically.

Suspension of the natural, objectivistic attitude toward history, and establishment of one's positionality as a viewer of history, enables the philosopher to undertake a description of the idea-content of those turning points central to the history of thought. Salient features of Husserl's account include the fact that (1) each of the turning points is comprised by a juncture of theoretical, axiological, and practical reason, i.e., by a transformation and renewal of the life of reason as a whole, and (2) each of the major paradigms evidences a fundamental shift in the "preliminary forms" of intentionality, perhaps the major concept of phenomenology in general and certainly the major concept of Husserl's work. More specifically, and with respect to those philosophers whom Husserl finds to stand out above all others:

1. Socrates is viewed as a reformer of ethical life, of a life of pure reason, that is, "a life in which man, in untiring self-reflection and radical justification, submits himself to a critique—an ultimately evaluative critique—of the goals of his life and then, of course, by means of this, to a critique of the ways he lives his life and the specific means he uses" (*FPI,* p. 9).
2. Plato is seen as extending the Socratic principle of radical justification, both as "creator of the problem of philosopy and the science of method, namely, the method of systematically actualizing the supreme teleological idea of 'philosophy,' which is inherent in the essence of cognition itself," and as founder of the doctrine of social reason, of a truly rational human community, a theme which determines "the essential character and destiny of the development of European culture" *(FPI,* pp. 13, 17). Moreover, with Plato, genuine cognition, genuine truth (valid in itself, determinant once and for all) and being in the true and genuine sense (as the identical substrate of truths which are determinant once and for all), become essential correlates *(FPI,* p. 13).
3. Aristotle is examined as giving the first sketch of the science of subjectivity, namely, as a psychology.
4. The Sophists are considered as those thinkers for whom the naive pregivenness of the world became problematic and, along with that, the world itself with respect to the fundamental possibility of there being knowledge of it and with

regard to the principal sense of its being in itself. With Protagoras and Gorgias, subjectivity first appears as that in which or through which all conceivable objects receive for a conscious subject their content and sense *(FPI,* p. 60).

5. Descartes is understood as having discovered that which throughout antiquity remained imperceptible, even though lack of it always made itself felt in some way: the absolutely necessary beginning of philosophy in the *ego cogito.* By establishing the ego as the Archimedean point upon which genuine philosophy may be founded, he gives rise to an entirely new turn in the history of philosophy *(FPI,* p. 62).
6. With Hume, Husserl finds the first attempt at a science of the pure givens of consciousness, an attempt at a pure egology, if only Hume had not posed the I as a pure fiction. In fact, Husserl writes that Hume's *Treatise* is the first sketch of a pure phenomenology, though in the form of a purely sensualistic and empirical phenomenology *(FPI,* p. 157).
7. In Kant's work, Husserl maintains, philosophy begins to move, albeit naively, within the framework of the phenomenological attitude. With Kant there is realized "a turn predelineated in the essential sense of philosophy itself in its development from the natural to the transcendental method of cognition, from the positive or dogmatic to the transcendental cognition and science of the world." Or, as Husserl writes, "at last, the philosophical revolution incipient in the historically emerging philosophy of the modern age became fact. With its appearance there was revealed to philosophy itself the methodological form essentially necessary to it as scientifically true philosophy, that is to say, the genuine teleological idea which all further developments must strive to realize in consciously purposeful activity" *(FPI,* pp. 285, 286).[10]

Description of the idea-content of the major turning points in the history of thought, by means of an *eidetic and critical* reflection on the history of philosophy, contains within itself a need for the third stage of the historical reduction: reduction of the history of ideas to the basic relationships between its most significant moments, together with disclosure of the unity of motivation which pervades it throughout its development. Indeed, the third stage of the reduction

[10] Ibid.

has, in part, already been accomplished: we have seen how such relationships and the unity of motivation are disclosed, but we have not determined what, precisely, is the unity of motivation that is disclosed. We have viewed its specific content with respect to particular moments in the history of philosophy. We have not established whether and how it is related to our earlier analysis of motivation, to the teleological idea of philosophy, to the idea of first philosophy. Accordingly, we must expand and deepen our descriptive approach to Husserl's historical reduction by a critical reflection on the unity of motivation which it both discloses and presupposes.

III. Critical Reflections on the "Necessity" of First Philosophy

To the extent that the unity of motivation is disclosed by the historical reduction, *First Philosophy*, volume I, may have a necessity of its own. In contrast, to the extent that the unity of motivation is presupposed by the historical reduction, *First Philosophy*, volume I, may in some way not be necessary at all. Or, as Husserl writes in *Ideas*, volume I,

> . . . the concept of motivation undergoes on essential grounds various changes, but the equivocations that arise therefrom are not dangerous, and even appear to be necessary, as soon as the phenomenological states of affairs are cleared up.[11]

We will examine this state of affairs by inquiring further into what is the unity of motivation and, at the same time, by continuing the third stage of the historical reduction. More precisely, we will consider the motivational unity (1) as a regulative principle for the unity of thinking and willing, as exhibited in the ideal of a rational humanity, and (2) with reference to the historical reduction and to Husserl's formulation of the Cartesian reduction.

In one sense, the unity running throughout history may be seen as a regulative principle determinant for the relation between thought and will, philosophy and human culture, the history of ideas and the history of deeds. It brings together the idea of philosophy as a universal science which provides the foundation for all knowledge and the philosopher's will to attain clarity concerning such a rigorously founded science. It unifies the autonomy which arises with the subject's self-understanding and self-criticism and the freedom which emerges with the subject's self-responsibility. Landgrebe writes,

[11] Husserl, *Ideas*, p. 134-35. Slight alterations have been made in the English translation.

> It [Husserl's historical-teleological establishing of phenomenology] is . . . a "regulative" principle determinative for man's activity and behavior . . . This teleology of history is discovered only when it is taken up by the will of the one who reflects and who thereby takes upon himself this datum which serves to establish his own existence . . . it (this teleology) is a task posed to the beginning philosopher by his own history and grasped in resolve. . . .[12]

As such, the unity of motivation is disclosed as a principle for the renewal of the life of reason, theoretical, axiological, and practical, that is, as a principle for the development of a rational humanity.

In another sense, the unity of motivation is somewhat ambiguous in meaning. From the perspective of the historical reduction, it forms the beginning of all philosophy and it founds phenomenology. In the historical reduction the naive and anonymous accomplishment of the unity becomes a theme in its own right. Its identity is seen as always already posited in its hidden beginnings and elaborated progressively in the historical process, i.e., as the supreme teleological idea which guides the history of ideas. Recovery of the unity of motivation is understood as leading to the necessity of a new absolute beginning of philosophy in transcendental subjectivity. From the standpoint of the Cartesian reduction, it is transcendental subjectivity which founds philosophy absolutely and, moreover, it is the *ego cogito* that constitutes the sense of history, lifting it out "above the play of philosophical systems" *(FPI,* p. 286).[13] According to Husserl's formulation of the Cartesian reduction, the unity of motivation pervading the history of ideas appears as a presupposition which must be founded anew, albeit in terms of the system of motivated experience, which we discussed in Section II. Of course, one might say that both forms of the reduction are necessary and complementary, each leading into phenomenology in it own way. The historical reduction simply shows us the teleological idea which philosophy, until phenomenology, was unable to realize fully, but which can be realized anew by the beginning philosopher who carries out the Cartesian reduction. However, one might also say that beginnings and absolute beginnings are different in kind, such that the historical reduction is unnecessary, for in that it does not offer absolutely grounded knowledge, it cannot genuinely found phenomenology.

In sum, the ways in which *First Philosophy,* volume I, is and is

[12] Ludwig Landgrebe, "Husserl's Departure from Cartesianism," in R. O. Elveton, *The Phenomenology of Husserl: Selected Critical Readings* (Chicago: Quadrangle Books), pp. 284, 285.

[13] Husserl, "Kant and the Idea of Transcendental Philosophy," p. 55.

not necessary, correspond to the equivocal meanings of the concept of motivation. First philosophy is necessary to the extent that it accomplishes what could not be accomplished otherwise, that is, insofar as it discloses, rather than presupposes, various meanings of the concept of motivation. For instance, first philosophy is indispensable in that it discloses the unity of motivation as a regulative principle leading to the ideal of a rational humanity. It is indispensable in that it delineates a way into the method and content of the philosophical tasks of the present age, bringing them to light in a way which is not done by any other approach to philosophy. As such, it marks the beginning of a period of new activity for Husserl's work, leading, eventually, to his concern with history and the teleology of reason in *The Crisis of European Sciences and Transcendental Phenomenology.* It also refers us to the fundamental problems of phenomenology, for in the tension between the several senses of the concept of motivation it clarifies and keeps open, in particular, an ongoing problematic concerning what it means to be "first," what is the relation between historicity and apodicticity, and what is the scope and significance of "presuppositionless" philosophy. Furthermore, *First Philosophy,* volume I, is necessary for anyone who wants to treat the history of thought philosophically, for it initiates and carries out an eidetic and critical, that is, a phenomenological, view of the history of ideas. Most significantly, *First Philosophy,* volume I, is necessary as *first* philosophy, as a science of the originary sources of philosophy, for it attempts to lead the truth of the unity of motivation to its deeper and deepest epistemological grounding. The unity of motivation, whose sense it elucidates, serves as both the primal institution and the final institution of first philosophy itself.

In response to the question "What is Husserl's first philosophy?" we propose that *First Philosophy,* volume I, presents the ongoing task of going to the roots of thought, of reflecting on and thereby constituting the unity of motivation pervading history and, at the same time, of carrying on such reflections within the givenness of the unity of motivation that is always already constituted. In that its aim is the reactivation of the older and oldest motives of thinking and the shaping of completely new ones (*FPI,* p. 287),[14] it proposes nothing less than an unending reform of all philosophy.

JEFFNER ALLEN.

DEPAUL UNIVERSITY.

[14] Ibid., p. 56.

REVIEWS

Main Trends in Philosophy. PAUL RICOEUR. New York and London: Holmes and Meier Publishers, Inc., 1979. Pp. xiii, 469.

It is difficult to comment both briefly and at all duly on a work such as the one we have here; a more than usually severe practice of exclusion seems unavoidable. Accordingly, I shall dwell chiefly on synthesis, on the conception and execution of this work, to the neglect largely of its exceptionally manifold contents as such.

The first thing to be said is that the present volume is a reprinting of Chapters 7 and 8 of a "far-reaching" Unesco study, *Main Trends of Research in the Social and Human Sciences,* Part 2, Mouton/Unesco, 1978 (Part 1, 1970). Next, we should point out that Paul Ricoeur, while in large part directly the author of the present volume, refers to himself therein as its "rapporteur." For this work is the product of a collective and, to a considerable degree, international effort.

Ricoeur thus applauds his three "associate rapporteurs," Daya Krishna, Alan Montefiore, and Theodor Ilich Oizerman, responsible for, respectively, Asian, analytical, and Soviet philosophy, not only as direct contributors to the work, but as coordinators of the contributions of numerous specialized authorities, some of whom themselves make direct contributions. Ricoeur himself, appropriately enough, handles Continental philosophy.

It is to Ricoeur's credit to have devised the deployment he has of these rich resources. The work is divided into six " 'fields' or 'loci' " —briefly, "Modes of thinking," "Natural reality," "Social reality," "Language," "Action," and "Humanism." Within each of the first five fields, attention is directed first to the "present state" of the "sciences and corresponding epistemologies" that bear on that field, and then to the "broad trends which share each given field of philosophical thought." This organization results in a definite textual vitality.

Not that this is an overtly polemical work; if anything, it displays more a concern to disclose potential affinities. Nevertheless, it offers good opportunities to compare the merits of differing approaches to the questions each field poses. One need not begin as a "partisan in philosophy" to note, for instance, the advantage that accrues to Soviet philosophy, particularly in comparison with much that originates in the English language, by virtue of the emphasis in the former on the "historico-social." More too than "poets in philosophy" may have brought home to them the significance of the superior awareness in Continental thought of "the surplus of signifier over signified," whatever the permutations that awareness has undergone. (Trends within trends are clearly indicated, both divisions and displacements. The extent of both within Soviet thought may surprise.)

The work would profit from an index. Extensive footnoting is however supported by a 75-page bibliography. But a regrettable oversight preserves the pagination of the original in cross-referential footnotes. These flaws aside, the publishers have acted commendably in making more readily available a work which, by reason of its consistent perspicuity, its topicality, range, and authority, deserves the wider audience it otherwise might not reach.

RODGER BELL HUNTER.

TORONTO.

The Nature of Mind and Other Essays, D. M. ARMSTRONG. Ithaca: Cornell University Press, 1981. Pp. xii, 175.

The book is a collection of ten previously published papers by Professor David Armstrong on topics in the philosophy of mind. Most of the essays elaborate and defend Armstrong's version of Materialism: Every mental process is identical to a physical process and every mental attribute is identical to a physical attribute. I shall give a brief indication of the contents of each essay, offering a few evaluative considerations along the way.

'The Nature of Mind' is an admirably accessible introduction for general audiences to Armstrong's positions on issues in the philosophy of mind.

'The Causal Theory of Mind' is also introductory and programmatic. Good use is made of the concept of a poison to illustrate what typifies causal analyses.

'Epistemological Foundations for a Materialist Theory of Mind' goes into more detail, providing a prima facie case for Materialism.

In the course of so doing, Armstrong makes a remarkably puzzling proposal. He considers what a Materialist could do if it were shown that the concept of a mental process entails that any such process is immaterial. He contends that instead of abjuring mental processes, the Materialist could "revise" the concept of a mental process, "dropping" the necessary condition of being immaterial. Armstrong is explicit that this is to be "mere revision," not replacement (p. 45). Yet aside from the metaphors of "dropping" and "detaching," nothing is said about how this sort of revision might be accomplished. There is a clear way to remove a necessary condition for the application of a *word:* The speakers of the language are induced to take up a new meaning for the word which lacks that condition. That is replacement; the archaic meaning continues to exist. And of course doing that to "mental process" would not change the necessary conditions for being a mental process. So that would not help the Materialist. I cannot think of any procedure that Armstrong might have had in mind which would.

In 'What is Consciousness?' Armstrong distinguishes three senses of "consciousness." He offers suggestions about how an individual's having "introspective consciousness," i.e., perceiving his own mental activities, might give rise to a theoretical postulation of a continuing self, and to the belief that introspective consciousness is required for there to be any mental state or event.

'Acting and Trying' begins with a plausible defense of the view that doing something intentionally implies trying or attempting to do it. A definition of 'A does P intentionally' is given and defended. One of the defining conditions involves a causal influence of a special sort of practical reasoning which is specified only in this obscure way:

> The pattern of practical reasoning shadows out a pattern of operation of causal factors in [the agent's] mind (p. 79).

The condition is designed to help in cases where the intended effect is achieved, but not in the intended way. We cannot determine how well it works until we know what is to count as "shadowing out." The essay concludes with an account of the concept of trying hard to do something.

'The Nature of Tradition' contains an illuminating analysis of the concept of a tradition.

'Color Realism and the Argument from Microscopes' is a defense of the existence of colors as qualities of external objects against this objection: A surface displays one uniform color to the unaided eye, yet it looks mostly transparent when seen through a microscope; so the assignment of a "real" color to the surface seems arbirtary.

In 'Immediate Perception' Armstrong contends that we cannot draw a distinction between inferred and uninferred objects of perception in the case of examples given by sentences of the form *A perceives O,* where 'O' is replaced only by terms for objects, e.g. 'the fox', not 'that'-clauses.

'Perception, Sense-data, and Causality' argues at length against sense-data, making central use of various causal considerations. Armstrong's reasoning here about causal contingency and corrigibility contains two serious mistakes. First, in considering the supposition that a sense-datum's having a quality normally causes perception of it as having the quality, Armstrong writes:

> Cause and effect are 'distinct existences'. It therefore must be possible for the cause to exist but not its customary effect or, indeed, any effect at all. It follows that the perceiver's perceiving or sensing of the sense-datum does not have to be *veridical* perception or sensing (pp. 138-39).

Armstrong seems to have overlooked the possibility that perceiving is always veridical, while sometimes the sense-datum's having a given quality causes a perception of another of its qualities, or causes no perception. The second error occurs while Armstrong is reasoning from the assumption that a perception and its sense-datum are '. . . logically capable of existing in independence of each other *as* sense-datum and perception' (pp. 145-46). He continues:

> If such distinct existence is assumed, then it seems that the logical corrigibility of the perception must be granted also. For it must be logically possible for the perception to exist while the sense-datum does not (p. 146).

The neglected alternative in this case is that a perception is always veridical with respect to its sense-datum, but it is not always a perception of the same one. These flaws spoil Armstrong's arguments against a causal role for sense-data in perception.

In the final essay, 'Naturalism, Materialism, and First Philosophy,' Armstrong argues for Naturalism: The only entities are those of "the spatio-temporal system." To show that we have no good reason to postulate other things, a dilemma is offered. Either an entity "acts upon" the system, or not. Against the former alternative Armstrong maintains:

> It seems to me that the development of the physical sciences very strongly suggests that Nature, the spatio-temporal system, is *a causally closed system*. We have rather good scientific reasons to believe that, whatever occurs in the system, if it has a cause at all, is caused solely by other events (processes, etc.) in the spatio-temporal system (p. 153).

Consider what occurs when someone acquires knowledge of a

mathematical fact. It certainly seems that the fact of twice ten's being twenty and the numbers involved contributed to my learning that twice ten is twenty. And Armstrong has no Naturalistic analyses of the truths of mathematics to replace the accounts that appeal to what he calls "transcendent" entities like numbers. If we grant that only spatio-temporal entities make *causal* contributions, then, lacking any Naturalistic account of mathematics, we should class the role of mathematical objects in mathematical knowledge as some noncausal sort of contribution, much as it is intuitively preferable to say that mathematical objects play a noncausal role in determining the mathematical facts themselves. Nonetheless, such contributions give us reason to accept the reality of the objects. Armstrong simply denies that we can have any reason other than causal involvement:

> If any entities outside the system are postulated, but have no effect on the system, there is no compelling reason to postulate them (p. 154).
>
> . . . if the anti-Naturalist fails to endow his transcendent possibilities, numbers, classes, etc. with any this-wordly powers, then they explain nothing (p. 156).

Such a principle does the main work when Armstrong develops the other horn of his dilemma for the anti-Naturalist. But unless "effect" is construed broadly enough to include contributions to truth and knowledge like those attributed to mathematical objects, this is an unsupported implausible doctrine. Contingent effects are not the only things that call for explanation. It is just as reasonable to try to understand necessary truths and cognitive contents. If accounting for those things requires entities beyond the resources of Naturalism, that gives us as good a reason to postulate other entities as any explanatory theory ever provides.

EARL CONEE.

UNIVERSITY OF ROCHESTER.

Does God Have a Nature? ALVIN PLANTINGA. The Aquinas Lecture, 1980. Milwaukee: Marquette University Press, 1980. Pp. 146.

Among the beliefs held by many theists are the following:

(A) God is a person.

(B) God is essentially omniscient, omnipotent, and all-good.

(C) Everything distinct from God is entirely dependent upon him.

(D) God is not dependent in any way upon anything distinct from himself.

Doctrines (C) and (D) are intended to capture the notions of God's sovereignty and aseity, respectively. It is the task of Alvin Plantinga's newest book to argue that the sovereignty-aseity intuitions reflected in (C) and (D) conflict with other intuitions which we have, that various attempts either to resolve or dissolve the conflict are unsatisfactory, that the other intuitions are stronger, and therefore that the sovereignty-aseity intuitions cannot be accepted as they stand. The other intuitions, stronger than (C) or (D), are:

(E) There are at least some abstract objects—properties, kinds, propositions, numbers, sets, states of affairs, possible worlds, or what have you—whose existence and nature are logically necessary.

(F) There are some logically necessary truths and some logically necessary falsehoods.

(G) No abstract object is a person.

Central to (C) and (D) is the notion of *control* (pp. 78-83): if God is genuinely sovereign and exists *a se,* then the way everthing is must be up to Him. But now suppose that (E) is true. Then the abstract objects which exist do not exist because of God's sufferance. Nothing he can do could prevent them from existing. Moreover, their natures are what they are quite independently of any shuffling or arranging God could have performed: it was never in his power to bring it about that the number 7 is even. Thus it appears that if (E) is true, (C) is not in general true. Similar remarks hold for the pair of doctrines (F) and (C).

The embarrassment to deity becomes more personal when we consider the combination of doctrines (B) and (D). For if (B) is true, then it would seem as if there are properties, such as *being omniscient,* which God has and which are essential to his being the being he is. Thus God depends on his omniscience for being what he is. *Being omniscient* is, if you will, a metaphysical part of God such that if that part were missing, whatever was left over would not be God. If so, then God does depend on some things—his essential attributes—which in turn do not depend on him, if (E) is true. Hence, there is a conditional answer to the question posed in the title of the book: if God does have a nature, then we must either reef or strike our sovereignty-aseity intuitions.

Plantinga examines and rejects three major responses to these problems, each of which denies that God has a nature.

Divine Simplicity. According the Aquinas' version of the doctrine of divine simplicity (DDS), the sovereignty intuition encapsulated in (C) entails that all abstract objects, especially the Platonic Ideas, depend on God, while the aseity intuition captured in (D) entails that God can have no composition or complexity of any kind. Plantinga mercifully chooses to dodge the former of Aquinas' doctrines, and to concentrate instead on the latter doctrine. God's omniscience is not related to God as attribute to substance, for that implies metaphysical complexity. Instead, God's being omniscient or the omniscience of God just *is* God, where the 'is' expresses a necessary identity. (B) can be preserved, then, consistent with (D), if it is interpreted this way:

(B') God is necessarily identical with his own omniscience, his own omnipotence, and his own perfect goodness.

And where there is no diversity, there can be no dependence. Thus according to the DDS, God *has* no nature; he *is* his own nature.

Clearly the DDS cries out for elucidation. How, for instance, are we to construe phrases like 'God's being omniscient' or 'the omniscience of God'? Plantinga suggests that they might be construed as referring to either properties (pp. 46-47, 57-60) or states of affairs (pp. 48-50). No matter which, the DDS is subject, Plantinga claims, to a devastating criticism. Since God is identical with the omniscience of God, it follows that God himself is either a property or a state of affairs.

> If God is a state of affairs, then he is a mere abstract object and not a person at all; he is then without knowledge or love or the power to act. But this is clearly inconsistent with the claims of Christian theism at the most basic level. (Pp. 52-53. The analogous criticism *vis-à-vis* properties appears on p. 47.)

So in an attempt to make propositions (B) and (D) compatible, the DDS runs afoul of (A) and (G). Theists believe that God is a person; reason dictates that no abstract object is a person; the DDS tells us that God is an abstract object. Since (A) and (G) have a much stronger claim on our intuitions than does (B'), the doctrine of divine simplicity must be rejected.

I am not convinced by the case Plantinga mounts against the DDS. The cogency of the case depends on interpreting phrases like 'the omniscience of God' as referring to abstract objects. It is not clear to me, however, that the phrases need be interpreted so. Suppose we think of 'the omniscience of God' as referring to an *instance* of the property of *being omniscient,* just as we might construe 'the redness of Rosie' as referring to a particular instance of *being red.* In that case, to say that God is the omniscience of God is to say that God is identical to a property instance rather than a property. And if property instances can be concrete, as I think they can, then the force of Plantinga's criticism of the DDS is dissipated. I cannot pursue the issue further here; I investigate it, along with other features of the DDS in a forthcoming paper, "Divine Simplicity."

Nominalism. Recognizing the tension between (C) and (D) on the one hand and (E) on the other, Plantinga's nominalist abandons (E), eschewing abstract objects altogether. God has no nature, then, on which he depends, because to have a nature is to have some essential properties, and since for the nominalist there are no properties whatsoever, there are no essential ones. Of course God is not alone in being bereft of a nature, for by the nominalist's lights, nothing has a nature.

The chief difficulty with nominalism, as a response to the problems raised by (A)-(G), is that it is at best a halfway house on the road out of the thicket. As Plantinga points out, God's sovereignty and aseity will still be compromised by (F). Even without abstract objects there can still be necessary truths, such as 'if all men are mortal then it is not the case that some men are not mortal', whose truth it is not within God's power to control. Moreover, even if there is no property of *being omniscient,* it is necessarily true that if God exists, then he is omniscient. Hence, that he is omniscient is not something which is up to him (p. 86).

Possibilism. The natural next step would be, then, to deny (F) *on grounds of (C) and (D),* a strategy whose most noted philosophical proponent was Descartes. Descartes did not shrink from possibilism, the doctrine that God could have tampered even with the necessary truths. But in what way could God have affected the necessary truths? With typical lucidity Plantinga distinguishes between *universal possibilism* and *limited possibilism,* and argues—correctly, I believe— that universal possibilism is the position most in tune with Descartes' thought (pp. 95-114). Universal possibilism is the thesis that God could have made *any* proposition true or false. Limited possibilism is the thesis that God could not have made just any proposition true, but that he could have made any proposition *possible.*

> According to universal possibilism,
> (1) Possibly p
> Is true for every proposition p; according to limited possibilism, on the other hand, (1) is false but
> (2) Possibly possibly p
> is true for every p. (Pp. 108-9, propositions renumbered.)

The textual evidence which Plantinga musters makes it clear

that Descartes wavers between the two positions and almost certainly was not even aware of their difference. I would like to speculate on how this could have happened. Limited possibilism will collapse into universal possibilism unless the correct modal logic for depicting logical necessity and possibility is weaker than S4, for in S4 and stronger systems (2) implies (1). Now suppose that we think of logical possibility as conceivability. We might then deny that what is conceivably conceivable is conceivable. That is, some state of affairs, S_1, might be such that in all worlds accessible by conception from the actual world, S_1 does not obtain; nevertheless, for some world, W_1, accessible to the actual world, there is a world, W_2, accessible to W_1 but not accessible to actual world, such that S_1 does obtain in W_2. In other words, we can conceive of the denizens of W_1 having different conceptual abilities from our own, such that for them S_1 is conceivable. On this view of possibility as conceivability, the world accessibility relation is not transitive, whereas in the "possible worlds" semantics for S4 and stronger systems, it is. Some of the texts from Descartes which Plantinga reproduces display a tendency to conflate logical possibility with conceivability, and that conflation may explain the vacillation between universal possibilism and limited possibilism.

Descartes' universal possibilism can be defended against some criticisms (pp. 115-26), but inasmuch as it flouts (F) in order to save (C), it must be rejected. (F) is a much more securely grounded intuition than (C) is; (F)'s claim on our rationality must be respected (p. 139).

Three theories which imply that God does not have a nature have been shown, Plantinga alleges, to be untenable. The sovereignty-aseity assumptions which support the theories must also be abandoned or limited in scope. Plantinga ends by suggesting that theists should not resist the conclusion that God has a nature. The impression left with the reader is that this conclusion is wholesome and homespun; a welcome relief to all those perfervid theories which would deny it. But here I leave you with a note of caution. The nature of a thing, as Plantinga conceives it, is not quite what you may have thought it was. A thing's nature is a property which it has essentially and which includes each property essential to it (p. 7). Now Plantinga has a very generous conception of what counts as a property. *Being self-identical, existing, being either a material object or an immaterial object, being the referent of the term 'God'* (pp. 22-23), *being such that none of our concepts applies* (p. 25), and *being such that one does not know one does not exist* (p. 140) are all offered as genuine properties. In *The Nature of Necessity* (Oxford, 1974), Plantinga allowed that the property of *Socrateity* or *being identical with Socrates* is an essence of Socrates (pp. 71-72). Now if we countenance such a latitude of properties, then it is easy to see that if God has a nature, his nature is a *haecceity*. That is, it is logically impossible that any other being have the same nature. We seem to have thus dismissed at a stroke the possibility of polytheism. Those who do not like to win their theological battles that easily may pause to wonder whether something has gone wrong here.

This is an important and stimulating contribution to philosophical theology. It is written with the characteristic Plantinga panache; without suggesting superannuation, I would say it is vintage Plantinga. I found the following major typographical errors. On pp. 87 and 91 we are told that there are unaccountably many truths and abstract objects. There may also be unaccountably many, but I trust that Plantinga meant to say that there are *uncountably* many. On p. 104 an important clause is missing from Descartes' letter to Mesland; it can be retrieved from pp. 100-101. Finally, Plantinga attributes to Raskolnikov the thesis that if God does not exist everthing is possible. Does he have in mind Ivan Karamazov?

WILLIAM E. MANN.

UNIVERSITY OF VERMONT.

Erratum

In paragraph two of Wolfgang Schwarz's review of Fritz Marti's *The Unconditional in Human Knowledge* (Vol. XLII, No. 2, Dec. 1981, p. 297), the expression "from theologically precise term" should be replaced by "from the logically precise term."

RECENT PUBLICATIONS

Pollock, Lansing, *The Freedom Principle.* Buffalo: Prometheus Books, 1982. Pp. 130. $14.95.

Burbidge, John, *On Hegel's Logic: Fragments of a Commentary.* Atlantic Highlands, N.J.: Humanities Press, 1982. Pp. 280. $17.50.

Williams, C. J. F., *What Is Existence?* New York: The Clarendon Press; Oxford University Press, 1982. Pp. xviii, 359. $29.50.

Adorno, Theodore W., *Prisms.* Cambridge, MA: The MIT Press, 1982. Pp. 272. $15.00.

Essays in Kant's Aesthetics. Edited by Ted Cohen and Paul Guyer. Chicago: University of Chicago Press, 1982. Pp. x, 323. $25.00.

Halliburton, David, *Poetic Thinking: An Approach to Heidegger.* Chicago: University of Chicago Press, 1982. Pp. xii, 235. $22.50.

Hare, R. M., *Moral Thinking: Its Levels, Method, and Point.* New York: The Clarendon Press; Oxford University Press, 1982. Pp. viii, 242. $19.95, cloth; $7.95, paper.

Howard, V. A., Artistry: *The Work of Artists.* Indianapolis: Hackett Publishing Company, 1982. Pp. 212. $12.50.

Kaelin, Eugene F., *The Unhappy Consciousness: The Poetic Plight of Samuel Beckett.* Analecta Husserliana 13. Dordrecht, Boston, London: D. Reidel Publishing Company, 1981. Pp. xxv, 325. Dfl. 110.00; $48.00.

Miller, David, *Philosophy and Ideology in Hume's Political Thought.* New York: The Clarendon Press; Oxford University Press, 1981. Pp. ix, 218. $23.00.

Journeys Through Philosophy: A Classical Introduction. Edited by Nicholas Capaldi, Eugene Kelly, and Luis E. Navia. Buffalo: Prometheus Books, 1982. Pp. 484. $14.95, paper.

Ford, Marcus Peter, *William James's Philosophy: A New Perspective.* Amherst: University of Massachusetts Press, 1982. Pp. 124. $13.50.

Penco, Carlo, *Matematica e Gioco Linguistico: Wittgenstein e la Filosofia della Matematica del '900.* Firenze: Felice le Monnier, 1981. Pp. xiii, 259. L. 27.000.

Taylor, Richard, *Freedom, Anarchy, and the Law: An Introduction to Political Philosophy.* Buffalo: Prometheus Books, 1982. Pp. xix, 144. $8.95.

Gadamer, Hans-Georg, *Reason in the Age of Science.* Translated by Frederick G. Lawrence. Cambridge, MA: The MIT Press, 1982. Pp. xxxiii, 179. $17.50.

Vico: Selected Writings. Edited and translated by Leon Pompa. New York: Cambridge University Press, 1982. Pp. xvii, 279. $34.50, cloth; $12.95, paper.

Spinoza, Baruch, *The Ethics and Selected Letters.* Indianapolis, Hackett Publishing Company, 1982. Pp. 262. $15.00, cloth; $4.95, paper.

Edel, Abraham, *Aristotle and His Philosophy.* Chapel Hill: University of North Carolina Press, 1982. Pp. xii, 479. $26.00, cloth; $12.00, paper.

Sagal, Paul T., *Mind, Man, and Machine: A Dialogue.* Indianapolis: Hackett Publishing Company, 1982. Pp. 39. $1.75.

Deetz, Stanley, *Phenomenology in Rhetoric and Communication.* Current Continental Research 003. Washington, D.C.: University Press of America, 1982. Pp. 233. $21.50, cloth; $10.75, paper.

Husserl: Shorter Works. Edited by Peter McCormic and Frederick A. Elliston. Notre Dame: University of Notre Dame Press, 1982. Pp. xix, 440. $30.00, cloth; $11.95, paper.

Ameriks, Karl, *Kant's Theory of Mind: An Analysis of the Paralogisms of Pure Reason.* New York: The Clarendon Press; Oxford University Press, 1982. Pp. ix, 314. $27.50.

Cambridge History of Later Medieval Philosophy: From the Rediscovery of Aristotle to the Disintegration of Scholasticism, 1100-1600. Edited by Norman Kretzmann, Anthony J. D. Kenny, and Jan Pinborg. Contributions by B. G. Dod, C. H. Lohn, S. Ebbesen, and others. New York: Cambridge University Press, 1982. Pp. viii, 1035. $74.50.

Benditt, Theodore M., *Rights.* Totowa, N.J.: Barnes & Noble Books, 1982. Pp. ix, 148. $22.50.

Hansot, Elisabeth, *Perfection and Progress: Two Modes of Utopian Thought.* Cambridge, Mass.: The MIT Press, 1982. Pp. 219. $6.95, paper.

Perspectives on the Philosophy of Wittgenstein. Edited by Irving Block. Contributions by G. E. M. Anscombe, K. Blackwell, M. Dummett, and others. Cambridge, Mass.: MIT Press, 1981. Pp. xi, 244. $22.50.

Contemporary Philosophy of Religion. Edited by Steven M. Cahn and David Shatz. Contributions by R. M. Adams, J. Cargile,

S. M. Cahn, and others. New York and Oxford: Oxtord University Press, 1982. Pp. x, 310. $8.95, paper.

Alienation: Problems of Meaning, Theory and Method. Edited by R. Felix Geyer and David Schweitzer. Contributions by O. Adams, P. Archibald, A. C. Cherns, and others. London, Boston, and Henley: Routledge & Kegan Paul, 1981. Pp. xv, 283. $28.00.

Communication, Philosophy and the Technological Age. Edited by Michael J. Hyde. Contributions by E. G. Ballard, M. J. Hyde, D. Ihde, and others. Alabama: University of Alabama Press, 1982. Pp. 135. $12.75.

Advances in Social Theory and Methodology: Toward an Integration of Micro and Macrosociologies. Edited by K. R. Knorr-Cetina and A. V. Cicourel. Contributions by P. Bourdieu, M. Callon, A. V. Cicourel, and others. Boston, London, and Henley: Routledge & Kegan Paul, 1981. Pp. xii, 355. $21.00, cloth; $11.95, paper.

The Left Academy: Marxist Scholarship on American Campuses. Edited by Bertell Ollman and Edward Vernoff. Contributions by D. Bramel, R. Friend, H. Gintis, and others. New York: McGraw-Hill Book Company, 1982. Pp. 292. $8.95, paper.

Battin, Margaret Pabst, *Ethical Issues in Suicide.* Englewood Cliffs, N.J.: Prentice-Hall, Inc., 1982. Pp. vi, 200.

Bubacz, Bruce, *St. Augustine's Theory of Knowledge: A Contemporary Analysis.* In Texts and Studies in Religion Series, Vol. XI. New York and Toronto: The Edwin Mellen Press, 1981. Pp. vi, 234.

Croteau, Jacques, *L'Homme: Sujet ou Objet? Prolégomènes philosophiques à une psychologie scientifico-humaniste.* Montréal: Bellarmin, 1981. Pp. 200. $15.00, paper.

Cua, A. S., *The Unity of Knowledge and Action: A Study in Wang Yang-Ming's Moral Psychology.* Honolulu: The University Press of Hawaii, 1982. Pp. xiv, 133. $12.95, paper.

Formaggio, Dino, *L'Art.* Translated by Denise Gouat Punzi. Paris: Klincksieck, 1981. Pp. 219.

Grube, Bruce F., *Death, Politics and the Hubris of Consciousness.* Washington, D.C.: University Press of America, 1982. Pp. x, 109.

Hochberg, Gary M., *Kant: Moral Legislation and Two Senses of 'Will'.* Washington, D.C.: University Press of America, 1982. Pp. x, 227. $20.75, cloth; $10.25, paper.

Körner, Stephan, *Kant.* New Haven and London: Yale University Press, 1982, reprint of 1955 edition. Pp. 230.

LaCroix, W. L., *Four Questions on Persons.* Washington, D.C.: University Press of America, 1982. Pp. viii, 205. $20.75, cloth; $10.50, paper.

Lowe, Donald M., *History of Bourgeois Perception.* Chicago: The University of Chicago Press, 1982. Pp. x, 206. $20.00, cloth.

Mason, David R., *Time and Providence: An Essay Based on an Analysis of the Concept of Time in Whitehead and Heidegger.* Washington, D.C.: University Press of America, 1982. Pp. viii, 455. $27.50, cloth; $16.50, paper.

Madison, Gary Brent, *The Phenomenology of C. Merleau-Ponty.* Foreword by Paul Ricoeur. Series in Continental Thought. Athens, Ohio: Ohio University Press, 1981. Pp. xxxii, 345. $26.95, cloth; $14.95, paper.

Needleman, Jacob, *Consciousness and Tradition.* New York: Crossroads, 1982. Pp. 173. $14.95.

Petrie, Hugh G., *The Dilemma of Enquiry and Learning.* Chicago and London: The University of Chicago Press, 1981. Pp. viii, 238. $20.00, paper.

Polin, Raymond, *Hobbes, Dieu et les hommes.* Philosophie d'aujourd 'hui Series. Paris: Presses Universitaires de France, 1981. Pp. 240.

Ross, Stephen David, *Learning & Discovery: The University and the Development of the Mind.* New York, London, Paris: Gordon and Breach Science Publishers, 1981. Pp. x, 138. $29.50.

Velasquez, Manuel G., *Business Ethics: Concepts and Cases.* Englewood Cliffs, N.J.: Prentice-Hall, Inc., 1982. Pp. xii, 355. $16.95, paper.

Waters, Anthony, *An Introduction to Deductive Argument Analysis.* Washington, D.C.: University Press of America, 1982. Pp. x, 275. $21.50, cloth; $11.00, paper.

Young-Bruehl, Elisabeth, *Hannah Arendt: For Love of the World.* Yale University Press, 1982. Pp. xxvi, 563. $25.00, cloth.